CLAIRVOYANCE
FOR
PSYCHIC
EMPOWERMENT

Joe H. Slate, Ph.D.

Joe H. Slate holds a Ph.D. from the University of Alabama, with post-doctoral studies at the University of California. Dr. Slate was appointed Professor Emeritus in 1992, after having served as Professor of Psychology, Head of the Division of Behavioral Sciences, and Director of Institutional Effectiveness at Athens State University in Alabama. He is an Honorary Professor at Montevallo University and former Adjunct Professor at Forest Institute of Professional Psychology. Dr. Slate is a licensed psychologist and member of the American Psychological Association. He is listed in the National Register of Health Service Psychologists.

As head of Athens State University Psychology Department and Director of Institutional Effectiveness, he established the University's parapsychology research laboratory and introduced experimental parapsychology, biofeedback, hypnosis, and self-hypnosis into the instructional and research programs. His research includes projects for the U.S. Army, the Parapsychology Foundation of New York, and numerous private sources. He is founder of the Parapsychology Research Institute and Foundation (PRIF), which has endowed a scholarship program in perpetuity at Athens State University.

His official research topics have included: rejuvenation, health and fitness, the human aura, psychotherapy, reincarnation, precognition, retro-cognition, telepathy, clairvoyance, psychokinesis, objectology, numerology, astral projection, sand reading, crystal gazing, dowsing, dreams, the wrinkled sheet, table tipping, discarnate interactions, psychic vampires, hypnosis, self-hypnosis, age regression, past-life regression, the afterlife, pre-existence, the peak experience, natural resources, learning, problem solving, and the subconscious, to list but a few.

He has founded the Joe H. Slate Scholarship for the Arts at Athens State University, and the Joe H. and Rachel Slate Scholarship at the University of Alabama. Each scholarship exists in perpetuity and is awarded annually to students who need financial assistance.

Dr. Slate has appeared on several radio and television shows, including *Strange Universe,* the *History Channel,* and *Sightings.*

Carl Llewellyn Weschcke

Carl Llewellyn Weschcke is Chairman of Llewellyn Worldwide, Ltd., one of the oldest and largest publishers of New Age, Metaphysical, Self-Help, and Spirituality books in the world. He has a Bachelor of Science degree in Business Administration (Babson), studied Law (LaSalle Extension University), advanced academic work toward a doctorate in Philosophy (University of Minnesota), has a certificate in clinical hypnosis, and honorary recognitions in divinity and magical philosophy.

He is a life-long student of a broad range of Metaphysical, Spiritual, and Psychological subjects, and variously studied with the Rosicrucian Order and the Society of the Inner Light. After corresponding with Gerald Gardner and several of his associates in the late 1950s and early 1960s, he became known for holding the "Weschcke Documents" including a carbon copy of Gardner's own Book of Shadows.

He is a former Wiccan High Priest and played a leading role in the rise of Wicca and Neo-Paganism during the 1960s and 1970s. Author Donald Michael Kraig has referred to him as "the Father of the New Age" because of his early and aggressive public sponsorship of new understanding of old occult subjects. In the fall of 1973 Weschcke helped organize the Council of American Witches and became its chairperson. Weschcke rightfully prides himself on having drafted "The Thirteen Principles of Belief" Statement, one of the cornerstones of modern Wicca. This document went on to be incorporated into the U.S. Army's handbook for chaplains.

While no longer active in the Craft, he retains ties to the Wiccan and Neo-Pagan communities through Llewellyn. He is 7th Past Grandmaster of Aurum Solis, an international magical order founded in Great Britain in 1897. He withdrew from the order in 1991, and is not actively affiliated with any group at the present time.

Still actively associated with Llewellyn, he is devoting more time to studies and practical research in parapsychology, quantum theory, Kabbalah, self-hypnosis, psychology, Tantra, Taoism, Tarot, Astrology, Shamanism, Wicca, Magick, and World Spirituality. He is also actively writing, and has co-authored seven books and several "quick" books and four audio products with Dr. Joe Slate and a new edition with commentary of *The Compete Magick Curriculum of the Secret Order G∴B∴G∴* originally authored by Louis Culling in 1969. He is currently planning several books based on Tantra and the Western Old Religion as *systems* of spiritual self-empowerment. He and Dr. Slate are planning several more co-authored projects.

To Write to the Authors

If you wish to contact the author or would like more information about this book, please write to the author in care of Llewellyn Worldwide, and we will forward your request. Both the author and publisher appreciate hearing from you and learning of your enjoyment of this book and how it has helped you. Llewellyn Worldwide cannot guarantee that every letter written to the author can be answered, but all will be forwarded. Please write to:

Llewellyn's New Worlds of Mind and Spirit

2143 Wooddale Drive, Woodbury, MN 55125-2989, U.S.A.

Please enclose a self-addressed, stamped envelope for reply, or $1.00 to cover costs.

If outside U.S.A., enclose international postal reply coupon.

FREE CATALOG FROM LLEWELLYN

For more than one hundred years Llewellyn has brought its readers knowledge in the fields of metaphysics and human potential. Learn about the newest books in spiritual guidance, natural healing, astrology, occult philosophy, and more. Enjoy book reviews, New Age articles, a calendar of events, plus current advertised products and services. To get your free copy of *Llewellyn's New Worlds*, send your name and address to:

Llewellyn's New Worlds of Mind and Spirit

2143 Wooddale Drive, Woodbury, MN 55125-2989, U.S.A.

CLAIRVOYANCE
FOR
PSYCHIC
EMPOWERMENT

THE ART & SCIENCE OF "CLEAR SEEING"
PAST THE ILLUSIONS OF SPACE & TIME
& SELF-DECEPTION

Includes

DEVELOPING PSYCHIC CLARITY & TRUE VISION

The Tattva Connection Meditation & Visualization Program
Microcosm to Macrocosm & Macrocosm to Microcosm

Based on the Ancient Tantra Tradition
An Eastern Gift to Western Psychic & Paranormal Science

25 Developmental Practices for Accurate Clairvoyance
Divination - Dream Interpretation - Invocation - Magick

CARL LLEWELLYN WESCHCKE
JOE H. SLATE, PH.D.

Llewellyn Publications
Woodbury, Minnesota

FIRST EDITION
First Printing, 2013

Cover art: Flames: iStockphoto.com/Pei Ling W
Cover design by Lisa Novak
Editing by Connie Hill
Interior illustrations on pages 181, 231, 238, 284, 298, 307 and 309 © Chris Down. All other art by the Llewellyn Art Department

Llewellyn Publications is a registered trademark of Llewellyn Worldwide Ltd.

Library of Congress Cataloging-in-Publication Data (Pending)
ISBN: 978-0-7387-3347-0

Llewellyn Worldwide Ltd. does not participate in, endorse, or have any authority or responsibility concerning private business transactions between our authors and the public.

All mail addressed to the author is forwarded but the publisher cannot, unless specifically instructed by the author, give out an address or phone number.

Any Internet references contained in this work are current at publication time, but the publisher cannot guarantee that a specific location will continue to be maintained. Please refer to the publisher's website for links to authors' websites and other sources.

Llewellyn Publications
A Division of Llewellyn Worldwide Ltd.
2143 Wooddale Drive
Woodbury, MN 55125-2989
www.llewellyn.com

Printed in the United States of America

Other Books by Joe H. Slate & Carl Llewellyn Weschcke

Astral Projection for Psychic Empowerment (Llewellyn 2012)

Doors to Past Lives & Lives Between Lives (Llewellyn 2011)

Llewellyn Complete Guide to Psychic Empowerment: Tools & Techniques (Llewellyn 2011)

Psychic Empowerment for Everyone (Llewellyn 2009)

Self-Empowerment & the Sub-Conscious Mind (Llewellyn 2010)

Self-Empowerment through Self Hypnosis (Llewellyn 2010)

Other Books by Joe H. Slate

Astral Projection & Psychic Empowerment (Llewellyn 1998)

Aura Energy for Better Health & Happiness (Motilal Banarsidass 2002)

Aura Energy for Health, Healing & Balance (Llewellyn 1999)

Beyond Reincarnation (Llewellyn 2005)

Connecting to the Power of Nature (Llewellyn 2009)

Energy Psiquica (Selector 1998)

Handbuch der Aura-Energie (Bauer 1999)

The Kirlian Connection (Athens State College 1985)

Los vampires psiquicos (Editoria Diana)

Mas Alla de la Reencarnacion (Llewellyn 2006)

Psychic Empowerment (Llewellyn 1995)

Psychic Empowerment for Health and Fitness (Llewellyn 1996)

Psychic Phenomena: New Principles, Techniques and Applications (McFarland 1988)

Psychic Vampires (Llewellyn 2002)

Rejuvenation (Llewellyn 2000)

Rejuvenezca (Aquilar 2004)

Self-Empowerment: Strategies for Success (Colonial Press 1991)

Other Books by Carl Llewellyn Weschcke

The Complete Magick Curriculum of the Secret Order G∴B∴G∴ (An expansion of the original book by Louis T. Culling as authorized by his daughter) (Llewellyn 2010)

E-Books by Joe H. Slate & Carl Llewellyn Weschcke

Self Hypnosis for Success in Life (Llewellyn 2012)

Forthcoming Books by Joe H. Slate & Carl Llewellyn Weschcke

Spirit Communication for Psychic Empowerment

Audio Products by Joe H. Slate & Carl Llewellyn Weschcke

Clairvoyance for Psychic Empowerment Meditation CD Companion
(Llewellyn 2013)

Self Empowerment Through Self Hypnosis Meditation CD Companion
(Llewellyn 2011)

*Vibratory Astral Projection: Meditation Companion to Facilitate
Clairvoyant Development* (Llewellyn 2013)

Foreign Language Editions of Books by Joe H. Slate
& Carl Llewellyn Weschcke

Astral Projection for Psychic Empowerment
English U.S. book club, French

Doors to Past Lives & Future Lives
English U.S. book club, French, Chinese Simplified, Hungarian, Czech, Spanish

Psychic Empowerment for Everyone
English (India), Bulgarian

The Llewellyn Complete Book of Psychic Empowerment
English U.S. book club, Japanese

ABOUT LLEWELLYN'S "PSYCHIC EMPOWERMENT" SERIES

We all, to some extent, suffer from the illusion of *powerlessness.* Many of us live from day to day feeling that "something important" is missing, or that we are a victim of circumstances that make happiness and success impossible. We may feel a sense of un-fulfillment.

From childhood on we experience situations beyond our control. We learn from our parents that "we just can't do anything about it." In schools we learn about powers beyond our own. Religions teach that there is a "greater power" but we find it to be of no help in our personal affairs. As adults we may find meaning in travel and adventure, through advanced studies, in marriage and family, in our jobs. But slowly things dim and we find that our employer is unable to meet all our needs, and our government is limited in providing all the things we ask of it. The "outer world" is only part of the story.

But, let's look at "personal power" from another angle, and refer to it as "success." We all want to be successful whether in social or athletic endeavors, education and training, employment and career, in marriage and parenting and having the home we desire, participating in our community, attaining financial security, enjoying health and long life, and—ultimately—in personal accomplishment and the feeling of personal worth and spiritual wholeness.

Success is really what life is all about. It's how we may be measured after we depart mortal life. Success happens from *inside out!* Real success is *what you <u>can</u> take with you.*

The secret to success is really no secret at all. Just ask any successful person. The "secret" is really a universal truth that belongs to each and every human being on the planet. That truth is: Success begins in the Mind; and the greatest barrier to success is that illusion of helplessness and powerlessness. It is the illusion that you have no choices in life.

The good news is that you possess the power—inside yourself now—to sweep illusions from your mind and begin using your mind for what it was intended: to lift human consciousness to a higher plane and make this planet a better place for yourself and your children.

How is this done?

That's where Llewellyn's Psychic Empowerment and Self-Empowerment books come in. Techniques and tools are available to activate your inner resources and create exciting new potentials in your life. Some techniques specifically involve psychic empowerment because your innate psychic powers must be developed into psychic skills and integrated into your Conscious Wholeness.

Psychic empowerment techniques and tools directly engage your innate but mostly undeveloped and ignored subconscious powers and bring them into the conscious mind. Whether a simple affirmation or a complex empowering procedure, each technique embodies a firm regard for the divine spark of greatness existing in everyone.

Your psychic faculties are standing behind an inner door consciousness. With their development, you *become more than you are.* With the techniques presented in this book, you can open the door to understanding and enjoy accomplishment, adventure, and success beyond your wildest dreams.

Success is your destiny. When you are self-empowered, you become the sole architect of your life. Why wait? Seize your power now.

CONTENTS
(Annotated)

The "New Age" is genuine and represents a historic leap forward in expanded consciousness that is both evolutionary and revolutionary and calls for a New Science of the Paranormal to meet challenges and opportunities this brings.

Why should you develop your Psychic Powers? Because you were born gifted with great potentials that can only be fulfilled as you grow and develop your own natural powers. Your Psychic Development is ultimately Self-Empowerment and the fulfillment of all your potential that is involved. And the time for this is NOW.

Is Clairvoyance Safe? Should Psychic Powers be Encouraged? Is Psychic Empowerment Desirable? Only you can answer these questions, and only for yourself. In this book we provide background information so you can answer these questions rationally. Some teachers and yoga masters discourage students from interest in psychic powers but in this Aquarian Age, Consciousness Expansion is no longer a choice—it is happening everywhere to everyone to some degree. Psychic Powers are not ends in themselves, but growth and development are. The goal of clairvoyance is the direct perception of hidden realities.

Contents include: The Hazards of "self-aggrandizement"; New Age Energies and Consciousness Expansion; The Responsible Student. The Goals of Clairvoyance; More than only a Physical Body; Trust, but verify! Scientific Verification of Clairvoyance and its Practical Benefits; Programs to activate, and to develop, Clairvoyance.

Define your terms! No meaningful discussion is possible, no knowledge can be shared, without understanding the terminology used. Human growth can even be measured in terms of the size and validity of our vocabulary. BUT, when it comes to Esoteric terms we have many challenges for the simple reason that astral, mental, and spiritual things cannot be measured or precisely defined in the way physical things and ideas can be. Indeed, Esotericism, like many subjects, requires the use of a subject-specific *nomenclature* in which "words" often define *systems* rather than *things,* and the same word may have different definitions and uses depending upon the subject, and even upon the way the subject is applied in one book vs. that of another. Thus: *the importance of the Glossary in a break-through book like this.*

Clairvoyance is not a specific psychic ability but rather is—along with astral projection—a *master system* and *faculty* that functions in the background of all forms of divination.

Contents include: The need to define the subject and its terminology; The necessity of Esoteric Nomenclature; Objective vs. Subjective; The immensity of the physical universe; The even greater immensity of the Cosmos; The non-physical aspects of psychic phenomena; A bit of esoteric history; The Physical and the non-physical were part of a single reality; Restoring the physical and super-physical to a single reality; Religions vs. Science. Spiritualism, Theosophy, and Quantum Physics. New Age, New Terms, New Reality; An "engine" for Expanding Consciousness; Accelerating Psychic Development. Different kinds of clairvoyance. Objectivity increases with Understanding. "Vibrations" and Focus. Charts showing Seven Levels of Reality and Seven Levels of Consciousness. The Astral World and Emotionality. The need for "proofs;" *The Kinds of Proofs;* The "Big Picture."

Chapter One—Clairvoyance in Everyday Life 19

It's more than coincidence that things happen together. Coincidental, and causal, "connections" are forms of *extended awareness* that is at the foundation of most clairvoyance that is happening more often because of the greater consciousness unfolding in all of humanity at this time. The critical state of our global civilization requires that individuals undertake a deliberate program of psychic development. Clairvoyance is one of the most important innate psychic powers whose development will enrich and empower everyday lives.

Psychic empowerment programs are being developed for application in everyday activities—in business & professional training, in creativity and communications work, in sales and customer service, and in areas still thought of as "paranormal" but rapidly become *normal.* People who demonstrate psychic powers are not more "spiritual" than other people. A "New Science of the Paranormal" is growing out of advanced humanistic research programs led by Dr. Joe Slate and the Parapsychology Research Institute & Foundation (PRIF) involving participants in real-life paranormal activities, leading to the development and application of paranormal skills in everyday life. This chapter includes a Basic Meditation Exercise that focuses on personal health.

Contents include: It happens all the time: Clairvoyance, ESP, Telepathy, Precognition, even Psychokinesis (PK), all can and do happen spontaneously; By not acknowledging it, you deny yourself the opportunity to develop this natural power into a practical skill; It takes Development: Paranormal skills are developed through training and practice just like other skills and talents. The New Science of the Paranormal; What is Clairvoyance? Right Brain/Left Brain. Western culture is primarily Left Brain dominant, while the coming global culture is Whole Brain centered; Right Brain activities can stimulate paranormal sensitivities; *Table of Basic Functions of the Two Brain Halves; Analytical Table of Clairvoyant & Divinatory Practices. Tables of Augmented Psychic Perception associated with Measurable Physical Phenomena. Tables of Common Types of Divination involving Extended Psychic Awareness;* Clairvoyance augmented with PK. Clairvoyance is "purpose driven;" *The "ne plus ultra" of psychic experience;* Animal Clairvoyance; Practical Applications; Inner Clairvoyance; The Empowerment of Self; Clairvoyance and the Spirit Realm; Your Responsibilities in the Physical Realm; Clairvoyance and Dreams; Special Insight Enhancement; Clairvoyant Strategies; Your Responsibilities in the Physical Realm; *Basic Meditation Exercise: Yellow Square for Your Physical Health. Induction Strategies;* Practice leads to Greater Development.

An Eastern Gift to Western Esotericism. What are these Tattvas? Five fundamental energy patterns, i.e. the *astral forms,* behind all physical manifestation. They are the "true nature of reality." Through understanding the tattvas we become empowered to consciously act rather than unconsciously react. Everything is connected—our individual minds, working through Universal Consciousness, are the interface connections that enable you to access and work with these fundamental patterns and forces. The tattvas are present in your body and mind, and throughout the Cosmos. We live in both an inner world matrix and an outer world matrix—and the two commonly get out of synch. Our work here is to restore harmony between the two so that clairvoyant vision is true and accurate, not distorted by accumulated psychic and emotional "garbage." We present a series of meditation exercises to accomplish this, following the lead of Tantra Yogis in India and the Magicians of the Hermetic Order of the Golden Dawn who taught that tattva meditation is the fastest method of developing and enhancing clairvoyance as well as increasing your power to manifest your goals and desires. Represented in geometric patterns, tattvas are called "yantras" and are the primary building blocks of all magical symbols, sigils, and talismans. We present the ancient practice of "tratak" through which these yantras (and other symbols) are internalized to stimulate psychic empowerment. Relaxation is the necessary precursor to effective meditation, and we present the powerful system of "tension & release" followed by detailed exercises for harmonizing each of the five tattvas.

All Knowledge begins with theory and is fulfilled through Practice. In the "real world," i.e. the physical world, knowledge starts with observation followed by questions leading to speculation, and testing against further observations. All science is constantly subjected to challenge, and it is in response to the challenge that science advances. Law is a series of rational "statements" bound together in a logical system embodied in a written constitution or unwritten established practice. Religion is generally founded in a "Book" of sacred writings strictly or loosely interpreted by its theological scholars. Religion having its origin in the non-physical dimension has no legitimate "authority" in the physical world. Real world knowledge is always responsive to external challenge; while neither Law nor Religion allows external challenge. In the case of Law, challenge is perceived as an illegal act to be resolved in court. In the case of Religion, challenge is met with excommunication, voluntary departure, or execution. Religion demands belief without challenge; science demands challenge before belief.

Contents include: Knowledge contrasts with Law & Religion; The Knowledge of Law; The Knowledge of Religion; The Tragedy of Theocracy; Real World Knowledge; When Challenges are not allowed; Trust, Test, and Verify—Again! When Questions are not allowed; Science, and Common sense; True Learning never ceases because the purpose of life is to learn and grow; Our Goal: Practical Application; Clairvoyance, in Theory, is researched in 165 forms of divination; Consciousness and Awareness; A True Reading; Scientific Astrology & Palmistry. The role of the "PK" Factor. Table of Divinatory Systems incorporating Physical Touch & Manipulation. The Field of Awareness; Consciousness is not physically dependent: Clairvoyance in Practice; Everything is connected; Extended Awareness & Focused Attention. Divine Clairvoyance. *Three Levels of Divination;* Clairvoyant Strategies.

The exercise that follows in Addenda Three, and the 24 others included in this book, are presented as chapter addenda to give emphasis to their special—near alchemical—function in literally awakening and purifying the five primal elements and their twenty combinations in your body and personal consciousness. Each of the 25 programs should be spaced a week apart and be preceded by the Tension & Release Procedure or other relaxation program. The goal of these procedures is freedom from ignorance and reactive thought & behavior, and from the external impositions of irrational and regressive belief systems of all kinds. We are entering a "New Age" of expanding awareness into higher consciousness requiring personal growth and psychic empowerment. This introduction is necessary because real tantra is more than its popular rendition as "Sexual Yoga" and "Orgasmic Bliss." Tantra is a very ancient tradition, the most radical form of spirituality and the ideal personal "religion" of the modern world that has had a profound influence on Western Occult Philosophy and practice, and on the development of today's Neo-Paganism. It is this Tantra that is the source of our knowledge of the tattvas. So fundamental are the tattvas that they can function through their symbolic representations of all life and form with near mathematical precision. We see this most clearly in the geometric forms with which they are identified but we must—at the same time—use mind and imagination to "populate" the *Memory Files* we automatically create under name & form in our subconscious mind with "correspondences" derived from our perceptions, just as we also do with the Kabbalistic structure of the Tree of Life.

Clairvoyance, induced or spontaneous, is always empowerment driven. Its purposes can range from simply expanding awareness of past-life and distant realities to instantly intervening in extreme emergency situations. Within that vast range, it can provide the insight and the skills required to meet the demands of the moment while generating an emerging body of knowledge that is essential to our long-term success, because we are "one with the universe." Clairvoyance is both an extrasensory phenomenon and a growth process that enlightens, attunes, and balances the mind, body, and spirit. With clairvoyance you learn where you are and where you want to go to accomplish your goals.

Contents include: Empowerment without Limits. Clairvoyance is always Empowerment Driven. New Knowledge, New Skills. Clairvoyance challenges Conventional Science. Integrative Clairvoyance. Action and Accomplishment Oriented. Clairvoyance Facilitates Growth, and Extrasensory Development. *Guidelines to Clairvoyant Growth & Integration.* Expands Awareness & Generates New Resources. The Open Curtain Program mobilizing Mental & Psychic Resources. Problem Solving Information. Past-Lives Relevance. Liberation from Past-Life "Baggage." Experience New Beginnings. Release from Past-Life Trauma. Finding Lost Objects. Locating Missing Animals. Clairvoyance in Criminal Cases. Interaction with the Spiritual Realm. Growth through Practice & Application. Integrative Streaming of Clairvoyant Power. Continuous Growth & Empowerment.

Addendum 3, The Tattvic Connection— Meditation & Visualization Program #1 Earth/Earth

Earth *(Prithivi)* is the foundation for all life. Tables help simplify in the same way illustrations add dimensions that would otherwise require thousands of words. Note things like color and shape whose meaning expand when we raise the exterior two-dimensional view to the interior three-dimensional view. Your life has meaning, and the more conscious effort you put into it the more all benefit. We start with the first Tattvic Meditation Exercise for the primal element of Earth. With each of these exercises, note the relationships between each of the primary tattvas, the five physical senses, the sense organs, the related chakras, and their locations. Make *intellectual sense* of these connections and experience the *feelings* involved. Keep that process active as we continue on with later tables and exercises. You are developing an entire new filing & storage system with which to experience the world more broadly and adding to your growing ability to clairvoyantly "see behind the scenes." Now you understand the vast gap between "reading about" and actual "studying." *Reading,* of course, can be very pleasurable and can also be a form of experience and adventure. *Study* can be these things as well, but the true benefit takes real work and self-discipline to continue a regular program involving scheduling, reading, review, thinking about, perhaps experiments, "field trips," and even inner debate to bring about realization of all that is involved.

Done correctly, such personal study efficiently and effectively condenses a lifetime of "discipleship" with a guru or teacher into the equivalent of several such lives. Becoming, and then realizing, that you are your own "Master" is what this New Age of Aquarian Man is about. It is a vast acceleration of growth and development accomplishing a new phase of human and "planetary" evolution. Tattva Overview Table #1 (Body). Element Overview Table #1 for Earth. The Earth—Seed of Earth drawing. Tattvic Meditation & Visualization Program #1 Earth—Seed of Earth. *Basic Meditation Exercise: Yellow Square for Your Physical Health.*

Our thoughts, emotions, drives, and perceptions, both sensory and extrasensory, are all interrelated and converge at all levels of consciousness to take us from where we are now to where and what we want to be. By interacting with these inner components of our being, we discover new meaning to our existence and our capacity to shape our own destiny. Clairvoyance is the key to expanding our awareness and uncovering new knowledge and new powers. To facilitate the greater understanding and application of clairvoyance we need a "New Science of the Paranormal," and many easy to use procedures and programs available for anyone to use.

Contents include: To Discover New Meanings to our Existence. The Power to Shape our own Destiny. Expanding Borders of Awareness. The Dynamics of Clairvoyance & other Psychic Powers. Questions and the New Science of the Paranormal. Objective Verification of Subjective Experience. A Universal, and Innate, Mental Faculty. Clairvoyance Awareness is <u>always</u> Relevant. To Become Empowered. Psychic Empowerment Accelerates Cognitive Functions. Personal Enrichment & Life Enhancement. Using Psychic Power Tools. Using Maps as Psychic Triggers to Locate Lost Objects. Using Blueprints to Trigger Psychic Perception. Sensory Functions as Channels for Extra-Sensory Perception. The Third Eye Project. Mental Imagery to Trigger Clairvoyance. Practice, Practice, Practice to Develop Psychic Skills. Purposeful Psychic Activity. Clairvoyance Among Animals. Precognitive Animal Experiences. The Ultimate Test: Does Clairvoyance improve Individual & Group Well-being?

Water *(Apas)*—you can't live without it. It is the only primal element to exist in three forms: solid (ice), liquid, and vapor (steam). It is the universal solvent, our bodies are made of earth and water, we cook with it, we manufacture with it, we compound it with earthy resources to make products for our benefit and comfort, all life depends on it. It symbolizes fluidity, adaptability, and feminine softness. Its energy is chemical and magnetic; it is dark (as in deep water). It is feminine, passive, restricting, and receptive. Like all the primal elements, water if fundamental to our being and to all existence. Like all the elements, water is never in perfect and equal balance with the others. Everything exists in combinations that are unique to each individual. By following the meditation & visualization program for each tattva & their compounding, we can not merely restore to the original state but bring about a natural adjustment more ideal to current circumstances. Everything changes, and we can bring about positive change to coincide with need. That's what all self-improvement is about, and the tattvas are the basic foundation upon which we restructure and remodel our new home—our ever-changing body and personal self.

Don't see lists and tables as "rules" but as seeds for thought and opportunities for your own experience. Lists are *external* observations and experiences of the outer world, but we want you to bring them inside, to internalize the resultant experience of what is represented in the symbols of the tattvas. As children we memorized lists and repeated them in rote fashion with little awareness of meaning. As adults we must interpret words and symbols to understand their meaning in any particular situation or application. That's the difference between "information" and "knowledge."

As your own guru, your success is measured by the gain in knowledge, not just in access to information. Remember that word, *Think*. There are many references to aid your knowledge of each element, but the most important are those that well up from your subconscious mind to meet your changing reality. Meditate often, think what your realizations mean, and write them down for later review. Tattva Overview Table #2 (Elemental). Element Overview Table #2 for Water. Water—Seed of Water Drawing. Tattvic Meditation & Visualization Program #2 Water—Seed of Water.

Chapter Five—Chakras & Clairvoyance

We've always been clairvoyant (It's mainly a matter of focus) When you read ancient history and myths, you have the history of human evolution before the split from the unitary inclusive Universal Consciousness into the Personal Conscious Mind and the Subconscious Mind. History is the struggle between men dominated by masculine emotions and those more clearly dominated by their rational mind. It is the astral world and the astral-emotional body working through the physical/etheric complex that are fundamental to paranormal phenomena and powers—especially clairvoyance.

Contents include: History as a Struggle. The Dominant Male Culture. Pioneers in Consciousness Exploration. Modern Transmitters. We are more than we thing, and need to become more than we are. Psychic Technology. Chakra "Switches." The Etheric Double. Chakras & the Chakra System. The Spinal Column is the Middle Pillar. Chart of Chakras, Nerve Plexi, & Body Parts. The Importance of Symbols & their Correspondences. Symbols function like Search Engine listings. Passive Sensitivity. Intentional Perception. Limitations of "Faith." Levels of Consciousness. The Seven Major Chakras—locations, functions, relationships, associated senses, psychic powers, symbols, mantras. Chart showing chakras positioned on the physical body. How to Manifest Chakra Power. Constructing your Astral Room. Visualizing Chakra Images. Diagram of Chakra Tattwa Yantras. Images, Names, Locations, Yantras, Colors, Elements, Audible & Silent Mantras, three dimensional images. Preliminary External Chakra Dharana. Pronouncing Sanskrit. Internal Chakra Dharana. Growth & Transformation is "Forever." "On the Path." Tantric Erotic Rose Meditation. The Re-emergence of Indian Tantra. Solar Plexus Charging. The Ajna Meditation. The Third Eye. Psychic Breathing Technique. Sahasrara Meditation. The Rose of Sahasrara.

Addendum 5, The Tattva Connection—
Meditation & Visualization Program #3
Fire/Fire

Fire is the primal element that enables change and transformation. Fire is the foundation of human culture and civilization. The "taming of fire" was the beginning of technology and the foundation of science. As a "gift of the gods" (as indeed it appeared in relation to lightening from heaven above), but the real gift came when Man himself first ignited fire intentionally through his own "applied science" logically resulting from his observation of sparks and heat from friction. Thus, *the human mind is the gods' gift to Man.* Nevertheless, that gift was held as a "secret technology," giving its holder personal power within the group, establishing him as priest and magician.

From that point forward, human progress would be marked by slow accumulation of knowledge and mastery of ways to use that knowledge, but only in modern times, as the monopolies over secret knowledge were challenged by new scientists and the spread of knowledge through books and education, do we have a universal opportunity for self-development and personal empowerment that was previously limited to the few at the top of the hierarchical ladder.

The most important knowledge is understanding the hidden, *inner,* nature of Man and Cosmos, of Microcosm and Macrocosm—*As Above, So Below*—to accomplish the Miracle of the One Thing through Mind. With Mind we apply knowledge so that we grow and increasingly **become more than we are.**

In Tantra, Earth is the Goddess and many Goddesses, and through Love and Worship of the Goddess we enter into the forms and energies that they embody and symbolize. Such love and worship is another name for a unique meditation of entering into "oneness" with the nature of her form. We call this "invocation." As the one Goddess, she is Shakti, companion of Shiva the Sky God. Feminine and Masculine, Yin and Yang, Negative and Positive, Magnetic and Electric—all that exists comes from their union—a union of equals in which opposites are always in constant blending. Tantra Overview Table #3 (Emotional). Element Overview Table #3 for Fire. Fire—Seed of Fire drawing. Meditation & Visualization Program #3 Fire—Seed of Fire.

Chapter Six—Visualization for Clairvoyance

A trained imagination is a key factor to more accurate clairvoyance. And it is your ability to effectively visualize that turns your imagination into a psychic power tool for higher levels of clairvoyance as well as turning vision into reality. In clairvoyance, physical sight as well as the other physical senses are stimulated and extended to give vision greater "life." Training the physical senses by learning to pay attention to details enhances the psychic senses.

Contents include: The Importance of Visualization for Clairvoyance, and just about everything else. Visualization empowers Mind, Body & Spirit. More than "Seeing Things in Your Mind." The Five Physical Senses. Table of The Twelve Ways of Sense & Interaction. WILL is the necessary factor. Taking the Next Step. Visualization and Attraction in the New Age. Nikola Tesla. The "Great Secret." Imagination vs. Visualization. Movement & Change vs. Fixed & Present-Moment Reality. Spontaneous Imagination vs. Intentional Visualization. Dreaming & Day Dreaming. Visualization & Present-Moment Reality. The Five Physical Senses & Present Now. The Twelve Ways of Perceiving. Training the Senses—Paying attention to details. Fried Chicken. The importance of Visualization in Clairvoyance. Programming for Self & Family.

Air *(Vayu)* We know what Air is, but we now must understand more of this primal elemental force. Unlike Earth and Water, Air can be compressed and its release can be controlled in various utilitarian functions from cleaning to powering movement. Air can be readily mixed with other gases, just as water can be blended with other liquids. Air however, unlike water (unless it is constantly stirred), can carry some solids without blending with them. The Tattvic Blue Circle symbolizes Elemental Air. Work with this tattwa is used to enhance the ability to visualize and discriminate between one thought and another. Meditation on circles activates the subconscious mind to bring about greater ability to recover desired memories and information, and to communicate with particular spiritual beings and magical powers.

Vayu is prana that forms the etheric body and the vital force in the physical body that produces cells and circulates blood and fluids throughout the entire body. The yogic practice of pranayama becomes more important to physical health as we age. Air is the element of communication, the power of perception, the ability to be inspired and to inspire others. Air is the element of evolution, of self-integration, and transformation to become all we can be. Air is consciousness, awareness, imagination, and power to turn visualization into reality. Air is mind, the ability to anticipate and plan our actions, to choose and discriminate, and to reach into the world of spirit. Air is the power of positive thinking that enables us to create a new image of self and to become more than we are. Tattva Overview Table #4 (Magickal). Element Overview Table #4 for Air. Drawing for Air—Seed of Air. Meditation & Visualization Program #4 for Air— Seed of Air: Vayu YAM.

The shaman is the early researcher and teacher about the "other world" and the roles of gods and people. Shamanism was and is a predecessor to religion. While the role of the shaman is as a continuing exploration of the Unconscious, religion is locked in history by its founding myths. Organized religion denies paranormal power to the "common people" and saw any appearance of clairvoyance as proof of diabolism. The tide was broken with the appearance of Spiritualism and the beginnings of science and broad public distribution of books and the spread of secular education.

Contents include: He who has the Power; Conscious & Subconscious, Split between; Shamanic "Techniques" to access the Subconscious; The Shaman as "Outsider;" "Technique of Ecstasy;" The word "Spirit;" Intermediary between the Worlds; Spirit Guides; Technology of the Sacred; Keeper of Myth & Tradition; The appearance of Religion; Calling Down the Power; Paranormal Powers denied to Common People; The Coming of Change; Swedenborg's Call to reform Christianity; The Church of the New Jerusalem; The Potential to see Spiritual Realities; The Coming of Spiritualism; Murder, they said; The Women's Movement; Parapsychology & Metaphysics; America & Freedom from religious repression; The New Age of Spirit; The Nature of Spiritual Communication; Activating the Spiritual Medium Within; Clairvoyance and Trance; The Role of the Medium; Developing Mediumship; Physical Mediumship; The Spirit Cabinet; Ectoplasm; Mental Mediumship; The Development Circle; Spirit Guides & Controls; Trance Mediumship; Three Phases of Communication; Working with Spirit; Your Journal; Women Activists; The Nature of Spirit Mediumship & Spirit Channeling; Self-Determination; Script for Interacting with Spirit Guides; Script for Developing your Mediumistic Potentials; Tools and Techniques; Table Tapping; The Séance; Ouija and Pendulum: Spirit Communication for just One or Two; Automatic Writing; Prophets as Channels of God—Why Only in the Distant Past?; The Emergence of Popular Metaphysics; Mesmerism, the Scientific Study of Hypnotism, and Modern Self-Hypnosis; The Age of Enlightenment is for Everyone! The "Key" to Successful Channeling; Where do Spirits Live? Access to "Other Words" is entirely through your own Consciousness; You have the Power but you don't have the Knowledge to skillfully use it; Clairvoyance & Empowerment; Illusion is present Reality; The Astral World where Spirits Live; Your Astral Room; Invoking your Guardian Angel; Opening the Third Eye; The Magical Way: the Lesser Ritual of the Pentagram; Clairvoyance & the Astral World.

Addendum #7, The Tattvic Connection— Meditation & Visualization Program #5

Ether! Also spelled *Aether* and called "Spirit" and "Space," Ether is the source of the other four primal elements, and also their culmination in which there is a continuous interchange among all five. It is symbolized by an "egg" through which one kind of life is transformed into another to appear as a new birth. Alternatively it is symbolized as an "8-spoked wheel" whose constant rotation is fundamental to all manifestation. Spirit is also the *transitional phase* between the physical/material level and the subtle planes, between this world and those beyond the physical. Spirit is the "interdimensional" *function* through which things and entities seem to appear and disappear with a change in their nature, one aspect of which is life-to-death and death-to-rebirth.

When a subject is referred to as a "transitional phase," we must shift our thinking process away from definitive and purely rational as applied in the familiar physical world to something we call *metaphysical.* Think "spiritual," as the "space" *between* physical beings and objects that energizes their substance and the force of their self-expression. Think in terms of something closer to the *Divine Source* of being. We relate to particular concepts called gods and goddesses, or angels and archangels, or to saints and other beings that express or represent specific forces of creation and continued manifestation.

When Akasha is used as a "doorway" for scrying, the clairvoyant scans for information in the Akashic Records (AKA the "collective unconscious") containing all memories of human experience, personal and universal. In a personal "reading" these memories bring clarity and perspective to the visions rising out of the psychic field, and can place them within a larger context of greater relevance. The Collective Unconscious also contains *potential* future "history" in *seed* form as what is most likely to happen under current circumstances, but not what will necessarily happen because changes made today will change what happens tomorrow. The challenge is to understand the many connections between the details making up present reality as well as those contributing to the potential future so you know what changes are possible.

Tattva Overview Table #5 (Chakras). Element Overview Table #5 Ether. Drawing for Ether—Seed of Ether. Meditation & Visualization Program #5 for Ether—Seed of Ether.

Chapter Eight—"Techno-Shamanism"

We need "personal" clairvoyance to involve *everyone* to meet the serious challenges of our times—from economic, social, and political—including threats of political and economic collapse, religious terrorism and of outright war—as well as those relating to climate change, extreme weather, and threats to water and other natural resources involved in food production to meet the accelerating demands of dramatic popular growth. Across the globe, in every phase of life, "leadership" is failing to meet the crises—through political stalemate, intelligence failures, and inability to communicate rational vision.

"Natural" clairvoyance requires development and supplementation through self-activated programs and the use of tools & techniques to extend both innate powers and trained skills. Among these can be a limited range of "techno-shamanic" consciousness altering aids.

Contents include: *What can we learn from history?—What do we* want *to learn from history?* Two axioms: the Victors always write (and re-write) history. Learn from mistakes. Change, Adaptation & Building the future. Modern World characterized by vast & accelerating technological development. "Esoteric" Technology, East & West. Self-Reliance, not External Authority. The Modern World in Perspectives of Past, Present & Future, and the role of Personal Clairvoyance: #1 the Population Revolution, #2 the Knowledge Revolution, #3 the Technology Revolution, #4 the Urban Revolution, #5 the Industrial Food Revolution, #6 the Natural Food Revolution, #7 the Climate & Weather Change Challenge, #8 the Economic & Political Challenge, #9 the Irrational Beliefs Challenge, #10 the Gender Independent Evolution, #11 the Home/Work Evolution, #12 the Global Solution. *Can War be avoided? The Induction of clairvoyance, and Techno-Shamanism's tools of sensory isolation and deprivation?* Spirituality cannot ignore worldly concerns. Anyone can become psychically empowered; anyone can live a "Spiritual Life." Controlled sensory input. Constant "sensory bombardment." Individual & group possession. Tradition vs. Techno-Shamanism. Sensory overload. Sensory denial. Floatation Tanks. Isolation Rooms. Restraint of movement: the Eskimo Shaman, the Shrink-Wrapped Prisoner. Tools & Techniques of Shamanic Witchcraft. Trance & Possession. Tools are not necessary but may be helpful and thus practical. The Witches Sack. The "Real" Witches Cradle. Movement. The "Self-Hug". Floating in an ocean of consciousness. ASCID: the Altered States of Consciousness Induction Device. Sensory deprivation and personal clairvoyance. The limitations of ordinary vision. Personal Clairvoyance. The 1960s Drug Culture. Seeing "Beyond the Normal." Limitations of research. Movement as sensory experience. Restraint of movement. Rise of the "Serpent Fire." Experience of "Ritual Death." Through Ritual & Symbol to Archetypal Truths. The Witches Cradle today. Sleepsacks. Meditation Masks. Precognitive experiences. Past, Present, & Future. ESP testing. Personal visions. Benefits of self-imitated sensory deprivation. "The journey into the wilderness." Psychic Empowerment as part of your Life Plan.

Nothing manifest exists in a pure state. Everything we objectively experience is combined with other elements in various forms channeling various energies. Even as we meditate with the primal tattvas to balance and purify our subtle bodies and energies, we acknowledge the fact of their compounding. We use this knowledge of compounding to better understand the world as it is and to improve our own experiences: in our well-being, in relationships, the world around us, and in deliberate strengthening of the bonding of elements and forces for strategic purposes.

The Goal of Clairvoyance is *clear & accurate seeing* and of better interpretation & understanding the information sought. Our reality, both objective & subjective, is complex and it is by deliberately invoking a controlled inner experience of that complexity that we develop and enlarge our psychic capacity.

How tattvic meditation is applied in forms of divination, magick, and the particular form of meditation involved in "worship" and invocation—of *Becoming One* with the Primal Element fully represented in the complex symbolism of a deity.

Deities—gods & goddesses, the many angels and other deific beings (aside from "religious" associations) are long established complexes of psychic forces expressing the nature of that deity, whether an agricultural goddess, a fertility goddess, a god of the hunt, one of prosperity, or one of universal love. The nature of each such deity is represented through various symbolisms involving name (and "mantra"), color, form, costume & ornaments. There is almost always a "mantra" associated with deity, whether formal prayers, chant, hymn, song, or repeated names and titles. Sometimes these will be called "Words of Power," but their identification with particularized Force is always defined.

The nature of worship itself has always been one of *exchange*: worship the goddess in her established ways, and receive her grace in the form of her specific psychic force. Rather than experiencing deity as external, through meditation and visualization we internalize the experience and unite with the "Force" represented by the deity. The operation of "worship" is little different than the operation of Magick: it is a set of specific formulae of compounded substances invoking particular forces to accomplish a determined goal. Likewise, in our visualization of a primal element we are invoking the primal force behind that element. Incorporating it, becoming one with it, we are awakening it and "perfecting" our inner nature by *consciously uniting with a specifically identified Force.*

Knowledge, application, and empowerment—they go hand in hand. Through clairvoyance, you can acquire new knowledge and discover more effective ways of using it to empower your life while contributing to the greater good. Locating lost persons or animals, viewing distant events as they occur, intervening in situations of urgency, and gathering important evidence related to crime, to list but a few of the possibilities, are all within the scope of clairvoyance. The clairvoyant viewing of important documents and events can provide an information base unavailable from any other source. It can monitor unfolding events without intervention while providing knowledge for effective intervention or involvement. 62 percent of criminal investigative respondents reported openness to clairvoyance in the criminal justice setting. Cases are reviewed that used techniques of Automatic Writing, Psychometry, Dowsing, Map Reading with a Pendulum, Wrinkled Sheet Technique, and Distant Viewing.

Contents include: Clairvoyance in viewing documents & events; Clairvoyance and Automatic Writing in criminal investigations; Clairvoyance applied in Manufacturing, Construction & Business; Clairvoyant Objectology; Psychometry & Clairsentience; Map Dowsing & Pendulums used in criminal investigations and surveillance strategies; The crumpled paper technique.

With the practice of compounding the Tattvas (Primal Elements) the role of the chakras becomes more important. In such applications as Healing, the location of the primal tattva presence may become a specific factor, as subtle energy centers are powerful factors in specific applications of divination, magick, and spiritual growth. With Divination, you ask a question and look for an answer; with Magick you look at the answer and decide to act upon to accomplish a particular goal; with Worship (Invocation) your goal becomes an inward quest for psychic empowerment and spiritual growth. Each of these could be the subject of one or more extensive studies but we are only concerned here with their relation to Clairvoyance. Traditionally, each of these applications involves the use of dedicated aids or tools often chosen either by the user's affinity and expertise with the particular device, or by the nature of the operation. Divination often makes use of crystal balls, divinizing rods, cards of various types, dice, yarrow stick, etc. Magick and Invocation both may use incenses, costumes, controlled gestures, chants, symbols, and more to raise specific energies and a particular state of consciousness, and then to give direction in the case of magick to the accomplishment of an external goal and in the case of invoking meditation to identification with a particular cosmic force usually identified with a particular deity.

The Practices of Divination and Magick: The essential actions for all of these operations are: To establish the goal; To chose the pertinent associations; To focus consciousness (meditation) with particular intent. Here we present a table guiding your meditation to invoke the Earth Energy & Consciousness and become identified with the cosmic principle, and then a second table to guide a simple magickal working (active meditation) to develop a talisman for success. We also discuss the concept of Goddess Energy in both Eastern (yoga) and Western (magickal) traditions.

Primary Locations on the Human Body of Chakras, Tattvas, and Endocrine Glands. Drawing of Earth—Seed of Earth. Divination Guide to Earth—Seed of Earth. Element Overview Chart #9 (Earth Application). Element Overview Table #10 (Magickal Working for Success).

Chapter Ten—Clairvoyance and Espionage in War & Peace 359

The "Cold War" may be over, but espionage is alive and well, and not limited to pure military objectives but with accessing industrial, technological, WEB & e-communications, space, cyberspace and particular scientific areas. And, yes, once again a growing interest in the paranormal sciences.

Rather than specifics, this chapter is intended to provide a background understanding of methods and techniques involving the paranormal to supplement other "regular" spy work and preparedness for destructive espionage. It is interesting to bear in mind that warfare, cold and hot, seems to result in rapid advances in science and technology that becomes very profitably deployed in consumer and industrial products. We may never know "government secrets" about "psychic discoveries behind closed doors," but the possibilities are exciting.

Contents include: Remote Viewing, Map Dowsing and Psychokinesis; Chinese reported to hack into American computers; Objectives of Espionage; Targets & Objectives; Not limited to Military Targets and "Enemy Combatants"; Butter as well as Guns—*everything's on the table, and everyone's in the game;* Biological, Mental, and Psychic (?) Manipulations; Perceptions and Realities of Wars Today; Single person's powerful weaponry changes the battlefield; Religious Idolatry vs. Rational Behavior; Fortress Strategy; Drug wars; "Black Budget;"Futuristic Weapons & Psychic Possibilities; Facts about psychic spies; commercial, technological & scientific targets; Assault on Intellectual Property; Greed as "Normal Human Behavior"; Normal is not necessarily Right; Individual Choice is fundamental to growth and freedom; Constitutional Rights, self-awareness and self-defense—*Don't be a victim!* Good Values mature from within; and not from authoritarian imposition from without; Know what to look for; Don't mix physical with non-physical; Distance clairvoyance, remote viewing: The Cold War of ideas & ideals; Lies, damned lies & everything else; The psychic arms race; psychic abilities lack specifics reliability; Weapons systems & mind power; "Voodoo Warfare;" the current situation; PK affect on electronics; astral projection or clairvoyance; remote viewing & astral projection; relaxation procedure; Eye Blink procedure; astral projection, clairvoyance & remote viewing programs; 3rd Eye; map dowsing; dowsing's practical applications; dowsing with a pendulum; hypnosis from far, far away; cold war paranoia; hypnosis & psychic powers; psychokinesis; mind over matter; PK in the Lab; induced PK; PK Bombardment Drill; PK & the Wellness Activation Program; The PK Rejuvenation Program.

Addendum 10, The Tattvic Connection—
Meditation & Visualization Programs #7–#10
Earth—And its Compounds 395

The Earth we are discussing is not familiar *physical* dirt and rock but its *astral* "matrix" composed of "emotional substance" from which all things material descend. Working with astral earth we are "behind the scenes" in clairvoyance, magick, and understanding. In real life, the Elements are compounded with one primary and others secondary.

Earth—Seed of Water: Timing is the Key to Success. Tattvic Earth is "Astral Earth," the precursor to manifest physical Earth. Earth is only "solid" in concept and "out of habit" because it has been manifest so long that our memories determine our perception. Through our clairvoyance we are looking "behind the scenes" to see things in the process of becoming and still affected by thought and emotion. The challenge here is in the compounding of one primary element with one secondary element, and then creating a single geometric yantra expressing the nature of this relationship.

Earth—Seed of Fire: Human Ambitions & Resource Potential; Earth—Seed of Air: Mind, & Matter; Earth—Seed of Ether: A Time of Transition—are described and each is activated through its own Tattvic Connection Meditation & Visualization Program along with unique compound yantras, tables and Divination Guides.

Chapter Eleven—Clairvoyance & Astral Projection

Parting of the Seas, or of the Ocean of Consciousness in which we have our being; Clairvoyance & astral projection are together the most dynamic & distinctive extension of human consciousness and the real foundation for all our knowledge, for all visionary art, poetry, music and or mythology—which is a metaphysical expression of history and cosmological science. With clairvoyance we are responding to "incoming" but with astral projection we are dealing with "outgoing." The mechanics of consciousness functions through many bodies and many levels. The New Science of the Paranormal is active, not passive, and global in approach combining East with West. It is at the leading edge of "particle metaphysics." Raising "vibrations," we expand our perceptions to new levels.

Contents include: Spiritual knowledge; increase in sensitivity; Incoming, or Outgoing; Many bodies & many levels; More than one type of Out-of-Body Experience; The right connections, ask the right question; "Active" sensitivity & seekers; Everything vibrates; Kundalini & the Chakras; "Up, up, and away!" Physical, etheric, astral, mental . . . a vehicle for the Soul; "Particle" metaphysics; expanding sensory capacities to perceive higher reality; projections of the astral body, of the etheric double, of the mental body. The Mental Thought Form as Vehicle. Vibrational Power

Addendum 11, The Tattvic Connection— Meditation & Visualization Programs #11–#15 Water—And its Compounds

Water, Water, everywhere—but not a drop to drink! You can't drink Astral Water to quench physical thirst, but you can imagine drinking fluids, and in your imagine *charge* wines and other physical fluids with emotional and mentally developed intentions. Water is a "fluid Solvent and Carrier" enabling the transfer of many substances from one place to another and enabling the application of the transferred substance's own characteristic to a different person, place, another substance, etc. Sometimes, the enabled *compound* has greater powers and different functions that either the carrier or the transferred substance as a result of Water's Solvent capability. All that is true of physical Water is even more so in the case of Astral Water and is further intensified in the compounding with its own element and the other primal elements.

The single geometric yantras expressing the nature of these relationships that characterize so much of our lives—Water—Seed of Water: Fluidity, Flexibility, & the Universal Solvent; Water—Seed of Earth: Initiation & Realization of Higher Potential; Water—Seed of Fire: Opposites Fire-Up Romance & Ambition; Water—Seed of Air: The Moon Rules the Motion of Water; Water—Seed of Ether: Feeling Guided by Intuition—are described and each is activated through its own Tattvic Connection Meditation & Visualization Program along with unique compound yantras, tables and Divination Guides.

Self-hypnosis with clairvoyance generates an unparalleled interactive state of personal empowerment. Self-hypnosis can generate clairvoyant awareness with the power to meet unexpected challenges and draw upon inner resources including those from past-lives. Together they open new doors to knowledge and new opportunities for growth.

Contents include: The Power of Together; Achieving your highest personal goals; Inner potentials of self-hypnosis & clairvoyance used together; the unification of power; the Blue Moon technique; the Unification of Power Self-Hypnosis Program; the Blue Sapphire; Past-life experiences; Applications in advancing technology; Self-hypnosis: the liberation of perception; expanding awareness; Self-Empowerment through psychic empowerment; protective shield; the Shield of Power Program; case histories: recovery of lost ring, extended sensory awareness & ESP, in criminal investigations, in science discoveries, in artistic creativity; Opening new doors to knowledge; new opportunities for growth.

Fire—the Element of Transformation and the Birth of Civilization; Astral Fire; the importance of applications; Fire—Seed of Fire: Human Control over Primal Power & Passion; Fire—Seed of Earth: The Human Powers to Initiate Transmutation & Cause Change; Fire—Seed of Water: Empowering of Natural & Human Resources; Fire—Seed of Air: A Powerful Combination, but Might does not Make Right! Take Care that Ambition isn't Blinding; Fire—Seed of Ether: Energized Enthusiasm, Empowered Intuition with Divination Guides.

Sleep provides the ideal mental and physical state for spontaneous clairvoyance that is conducive to increased awareness on a need-to-know basis. Clairvoyance during sleep is always purposeful and multi-functional—drawing upon conscious and subconscious resources, and identifying factors conducive to success. When these are acted upon, such success if almost always assured.

The sleep state can also organize our daytime experiences in ways that spontaneously activate our subconscious clairvoyance faculties during sleep. Pre-sleep strategies facilitate sleep clairvoyance directed to meet objectives.

Contents Include: Sleep & spontaneous clairvoyance, and the "need-to-know" factor; Principle of multiple causation, of multiple possibilities; clairvoyant perception during sleep is consistently purposeful and multi-functional; empowering possibilities in spontaneous sleep clairvoyance, with case histories; the interactive nature of clairvoyance; daytime residue and clairvoyant symbolism, with case histories; clairvoyance facilitators; Pre-sleep Guidance Program to facilitate clairvoyance; therapeutic power of clairvoyance during sleep; case history with a red rose; clairvoyant PK during sleep; future oriented clairvoyance.

Addendum 13, The Tattvic Connection— Meditation & Visualization Programs #21–#25

Astral Air, like all the other subtle forms of the elements, is both like and unlike the physical form. It is the astral energy forms that actually <u>condition</u> the physical manifestation, and so the more we understand their astral nature the more control we can gain over the physical. With each element we note their particular characteristics: with elemental water and fire we deal with emotional factors, while with elemental air we deal with mental factors. Air—Seed of Air: intuition, inspiration, discovery & invention; Air—Seed of Earth: turning inspiration into realization; Air—Seed of Water: stormy weather, or a lovely affair, OR plenty of mental excitement; Air—Seed of Fire: the power of inspiration; Air—Seed of Ether: planning for change with divination guides.

Chapter Fourteen—Clairvoyance in Business,

Part One: Clairvoyance is Purposeful and Empowerment Driven, by Joe H. Slate.

Clairvoyance is an etheric extension of sensory perception, consistently purposeful and empowerment driven. Spontaneous or induced, it is valued because of its capacity to unveil realities otherwise unavailable. By increasing our awareness of existing conditions, both present & future, clairvoyance empowers us to more effectively manage present realities and facilitate achievement of our personal goals. Pursuits related to all areas of our lives, including educational, business, work, and careers, are all enriched through clairvoyant insight and our readiness to apply it. *Through clairvoyance, we accelerate learning; and through learning, we increase our clairvoyant skills.*

Contents include: Clairvoyance unveils realities otherwise unavailable to us, and empowers us to effectively manage them and achieve personal goals. Clairvoyance bridges the gap between the known and the unknown. The Integrative Science of learning and success; The Fourfold Awareness of unseen realities and the relevance of clairvoyance to learning and success; clairvoyance in the real world; improved management programs; The Multiversal Power Program.

Part Two: Clairvoyance is part of Your Life, by Carl Llewellyn Weschcke

Clairvoyance can be an ever-present function in your daily life. Everyone has some clairvoyant ability, and that ability manifests in different ways, in varying degrees, and at different levels in the course of nearly all your activities—at home, at work, at play, at school. It's particularly prominent in the relationship between family members, between fellow students, workers, and associates, with team players, and any time you are "looking ahead," whether driving an automobile or spying on the enemy, or recognizing and solving a problem, inventing, innovating and being creative, and in sports activities where split-second decisions must be made with "that-moment" awareness of all the action around you. Clairvoyance is developed thorough (1) your recognition of it in your life and (2) its exercise with or without the particular aids we otherwise refer to as "tools and techniques." But it also benefits from study, development, exercise, and accumulating experience. And more so as you become aware of it as actually a real part of life—everyday in every way!

Fully explored are the factors of success pertinent in any business or organization activity, including the Group Mind and the Master Mind, the role of specific subject expertise, the challenges of specific management and financial expertise, the omnipresent need for ethics and self-responsibility,

Contents include: Clairvoyance is innate to everyone; extended awareness; where everything is above normal; tools of the trade; etheric extensions of sensory organs; Lower clairvoyance: gut feelings; middle clairvoyance; "feelings;" good or bad. Action is at the core of being alive; goals are <u>Beyond</u> "what is;" "Reaching beyond" is the nature of being Human! the method of achievement is called "Business;" Achievement is called "Success;" the source of personal empowerment; training for success; business science; the science of Futurology; the Group Mind; the Master Mind; give it a NAME and a Statement of Purpose; heart feelings; "Your Voice, Your Vote;" "Ask, and Ye shall Receive;" Talk and "Self-Talk" as technology; Higher clairvoyance: "Power Up!" the "Visionaries;" Great Answers to Great Problems.

Addendum 14, The Tattvic Connection— Meditation & Visualization Programs #26–#30 Ether—and its Compounds

Ether, Aether, Aethyr, Spirit, Space, and "Clear Sky:" Source & Resource, Start & Finish—and all these things and the source for the other four Primal Elements. As astral energies all these elements flow into one another and into Ether to become Universal Ether, and then flow out again as Ether, Air, Fire, Water, and Earth in a constant ascending and descending within the field of manifestation. From Spirit all things come; To Spirit all thing return. Spirit/Space exists in all things, and between all things. Things appear out of Space/Spirit and disappear back into Spirit/Space. But, "elemental" Spirit is not the same as "spirits of the departed or the Spirit of the "Spirit Body" or the "Spiritual Plane." Nor is it the "Holy Spirit" of Christian and other Trinities. But it is all these too. Astral Senses and Actions are extensions of physical senses and actions and are known as paranormal phenomena and functions.

Ether—Seed of Ether: Renewal, Rebirth & Time to Move Forward; Ether—Seed of Earth: The Past is Prologue to the Future; Ether—Seed of Water: The Higher Dimensions of Emotion; Ether—Seed of Fire: The Drive for Greatness; Ether—Seed of Air: The Power of the Word with Divination Guides.

Lab research is critical to understanding clairvoyance, but it is personal experience that provides compelling evidence of its relevance in daily life. Detailed case studies and cameo reports of personal experiences open a vast window into its diverse manifestations. Clairvoyance can become a critical key to successful problem solving and improved quality of life, facilitate better decisions, and generate insight in relationships and interactions. It is a particular factor—mostly unconscious—in the creative arts which can benefit from its conscious development.

Contents include: Clairvoyance at its best; Clairvoyant slips of the tongue; Therapeutic Clairvoyance; Creative Clairvoyance; Extreme Clairvoyance; Automatic Walking; Crime-related applications of automatic walking; Clairvoyant coming together in group practice; Automatic Biking; Animal Clairvoyance: fact or fiction; Insect Clairvoyance; a Master Dowser; the Three Critical Essentials to Successful Dowsing; Interdimensional Clairvoyance. Case examples are included in support of the conclusions.

The Life Force is almost universally recognized as feminine in myth, tradition, and cosmology. Not until the appearance of organized religion (organized and dominated by men) was the male given prominence. In the new world of modern science, gender is named "positive & negative" and given equal balance.

It takes two to Tango, and a Woman & Man together to make a baby—or does it? And, baby makes three? A woman's choice; "Virgin Birth" and parthenogenesis In myth and religion; And "Mom" is not always needed! The cosmological feminine force; the Great Mother as archetypal fact; Shakti, the Goddess of many names and forms. Clairvoyance and Woman's Intuition. The Wise Woman. The Great Goddess; clairvoyance & woman's intuition. The Tattvic Meditation & Visualization Program #31: The Feminine Force.

Only through research can the *science of clairvoyance* be advanced; but only through practice can the *art of clairvoyance* be mastered. When practiced on a regular basis, exercises in clairvoyance generate a multifunctional effect that is relevant to your total growth and development. Clairvoyant skills, once acquired through practice, will add power, meaning, and success to your daily life. Clairvoyance brings an expansion of consciousness that becomes global in application.

The human aura energy field envelops the physical body and manifests the forces that characterizes our existence as evolving souls. By interacting with the aura you can experience the fundamental nature of your existence—mentally, physically, and spiritually. You can activate your dormant mental & psychic faculties to bring forth empowering change in your life and the world.

Contents include: Developing Clairvoyance; commitment & practice; developmental guidelines; laboratory research in practical applications; a higher domain of power; inner domain readiness; the Human Aura: clairvoyant power at hand; Aura hand-viewing technique & interpretations; Aura self-embracement; objective aura viewing; Mind/Body interactive program; Pendulumology; clairvoyant sharing; crystal gazing; Spherical Screen technique with crystal ball; Re-education psychotherapy; frontals muscle relaxation; Clairvoyance from Beyond Exercise; interaction with the non-physical Realm.

Yes, we can shape and change the "Future" and make it happen but it requires knowledge and understanding of the surrounding circumstance in the present that are causal to the future, and vision of those "shadows cast from the future" that can still be modified. It can be done, but the scale is limited to one person at a time or the ability to mobilize sufficient numbers to focus on broader issues.

Can we shape, or actually change, the Future? (Yes) Know the Present, Plan the Future. Mind Magic. Enjoy! That's the Key. The Role of the Astral; the Power of the Imagination. *What is Magic?* Knowledge, Goal, Analysis, Program, Schedule. The Mirror Projection & Analysis Technique. Key Future Shaping Primal Elements. Program for Shaping the Future. Letting Go. Go with the Flow.

The meaning of modern (and ancient) esotericism: the Unity of all (the ultimate *unified field theory*), Nature as a Living Entity in which we participate, the "secret language" of symbols in Myth & Magick, self-directed personal and spiritual transformation. It is the science of psychic development and then psychic empowerment that results as inner revelations become the foundation for outward application and action. Today, we call it the New Science of the Paranormal and it includes a growing knowledge of human and non-human life streams, a growing ability to overcome limitations to human life, and a new understanding of feminine and masculine.

Contents include: Esotericism & New Age Occultism. What does "Esotericism" Mean? Theory of Correspondences. Theory of Nature as a Living Entity. Mediating Elements. Personal & Spiritual Transformation. Inner Sources. Sources for Esoteric Truths. The Source for Esoteric Power. Alone and Together, we ascend the Great Pyramid. The Western Tradition. More than the sum of its parts. Continuing Evolution— Personal & Cosmic. A Plan of Guiding Instructions. Gods in the Making. Human and non-human Life Streams. "Disturbances in the Cosmos." The Cosmic Shift and Clairvoyance. Not "Toys" but Tools & Aids. A Woman's Affair? Urgency for Clairvoyant Development.

The powerful yantras are used as astral doorways to enter into and tap into the resources of these inner dimensions, while at the same time healing emotional conflicts and restoring distorted energy flows in the physical & etheric bodies. There is a science to selecting an astral doorway but it also a personal art that is yours alone.

The Computer Monitor Screen to contain the image of a desired goal; powerful magical symbols don't have to be old; the immensity of the Astral World in which nothing is forgotten but remains in your sub conscious; emotional (Astral) substance; the Mind as instrument to perceive; Time: the 4th dimension; the interplay of astral with physical; maps, windows & doorways; selecting an astral doorway; Short list of Elemental Associations for the Five Primal Tattvas; Using the Astral Doorway as a Transformational Program; Where do we go from here? anywhere and everywhere: the Astral is infinite.

Even physical "Death" is not an Ending but a New Beginning as the Incarnating Spirit moves its focus to the astral level while the vacated physical body decays to become many new beginnings of life in other biological forms. The form changes, but *Growth*—in one way or another, in one dimension or another—is a constant. We can accelerate our growth, but we will never regress.

When you begin a new program—of any sort—in personal development, there will be consequences—even if you interrupt your efforts for a time. The "Great Work," once begun, continues in the background bringing you opportunities, contacts with helpful people and spirit entities, even seemingly chance encounters with books, articles, and happenings. It's as if the Universe is saying, *Welcome, "Pilgrim," welcome to the "Path."* The World of Action & Reaction is our field of dreams, our theatre of desire, our school of learning, our base for action. We are Consciousness, and we are also Agents of Consciousness. We are Co-Creators and (far, far from now)—*Gods in the Becoming*—manifesting Consciousness in increasing diverse forms throughout our World of Experience while at the same time focusing on our own developmental path.

Contents include: Everything has a beginning, but there are No Endings—only New Beginnings! The form changes but growth is constant; every action has consequences; in the Beginning: evolving consciousness; the world of action & experience; evolution: the Great Plan & the Great Work; what is Consciousness? The Tree of Life; can Consciousness know Itself? can Consciousness define itself? "I think, therefore I am!" and "I am that I am!" "I am, therefore I am!" Consciousness is divided: exoteric and esoteric; the great evolutionary plan; higher consciousness; most people are half-asleep; without INTENTIONAL FOCUS you are not fully awake; ordinary consciousness; spiritual approaches to consciousness; why the need to develop Higher Consciousness? the Next Step; the "Triumph of Will." The Crown Chakra; Kundalini Fire; A Crowning Meditation; Awakening the Crown Chakra Program. *All is Consciousness.*

Chapter Nineteen—Clairvoyance—for Psychic Empowerment & Self Empowerment

This book is not just ABOUT clairvoyance but the development and applications of clairvoyance FOR Psychic Empowerment. The "self" we seek to empower through life experiences and the specific development and exercise of abilities and skills is not the Higher Self, and not the Soul but that which we call the *persona*. Generally, the *persona* is thought of as the "mask" that we project to outwardly represent ourselves, and that too is correct, but we also mean that it is the self we want to be and that we are becoming, Becoming the best we can be, it is the essence of this self that endures and becomes part of the Higher Self and is refined into our Immortal Soul. "Empowerment" is a name for our life job; the accomplishment of learning and growth.

Clairvoyance, by itself, is an empty vision, a sound without meaning. But clairvoyance, when applied to a goal is not limited to a single vision of the single moment of time, but can expand to incorporate the *process* of Past into the Present and project into the Future. It becomes a vision filled with life, multiplied by surrounding details, and colored with meaning. Using *Visualization* as a process, vision can be projected into new reality. But this power, lacking specific knowledge, can be dangerous—so we need to learn, learn, learn, and never to stop learning.

The "promise" of clairvoyance is that it is the next step in human evolution. When we speak of "psychic empowerment," we are really talking about the culminating mastery of clairvoyance which involves the complete integration of all the lower levels of the Whole Person—the Astral, Mental, and Causal levels that use the Physical/Etheric Body as a temporary vehicle during incarnation. In developing our psychic powers (referring to any or all of those tools and techniques we call "psychic")—probably over several lifetimes of accelerating growth—we are completing construction of our "super consciousness," the third level of our triune persona.

Contents include: Clairvoyance FOR Psychic Empowerment. What is the "Psyche?" What is "Personality?" Clairvoyance & Astral Projection—separately and together; the weird astral world; the superstitions about "Higher" Worlds; knowledge builds on knowledge; it's all in the details; the Active Imagination & visualization; using our psychic power tools; Warning! Be wary of making "the Unreal the Real." Reach out and touch someone; Psychic Empowerment is both a process and a promise; evolution is inexorable, but empowerment is not! Humanity has to grow beyond itself. No, the Future is not pre-determined.

Chapter Twenty—The New Science of the PARANORMAL

(The intention of this chapter is to outline research areas and specific projects for volunteers, students, practitioners, and scientists to carry out for developmental study through the International Parapsychology Research Institute and Foundation (PRIF) and publications under the new category)

Parapsychology—at a "Dead End?" No, not exactly. But it's *stuck!* It's stuck in an outdated concept of a clockwork Newtonian physical universe while Paranormal Science has moved on to a consciousness-filled universe inclusive of Quantum Theory and non-physical realities as well as physical realities of matter and energy. In a way, parapsychology hasn't been much alive since it stopped dealing with dead people in the midst of 19th century Spiritualism and stopped being called "Psychical Research." Early 20th century parapsychology did serve to prove "there's something there" using statistical methods, but couldn't develop models that had a place for phenomena outside the closed environment of the laboratory and the closed thinking centered in a purely physical universe. Scientists, and others, preferred to say that anything outside of "normal" was nothing but superstitious nonsense and *dangerous thinking!*

Now such phenomenon is perceived and investigated within the "equation" of whatever psychic power or healing technique is being used. We no longer accept things by "faith" but look for logical consistency between theory and phenomena. The phenomena of the Divining Rod, for example, is consistent within the framework of geo-magnetic science and knowledge of the association between the vibratory rates of particular materials and that of the sample attached to the rod or the mental statement held in the diviner's mind.

We seek understanding and then practical application. Our horizons are far different today than previously, and our *New Science of the Paranormal* must be inclusive of the new sciences of Quantum Physics, Cellular Biology, Archetypal and Analytical Psychology, and new understandings of older practices like Lunar Agriculture, Magnetic Healing, Palmistry, Homeopathic, and other non-Allopathic Medicine practices, etc., and alternative views of the Universe through Astrology, the Kabbalah, Indian Tantra and Taoism, and such tools of insight as the Tarot, I Ching, Runes, and more.

We have an imperative need to broaden our horizons because it applies to everything we do—not just to our *New Science of the Paranormal*. We *are* in the New Age—one that is raising consciousness and expanding awareness in a new focused evolutionary drive that *commands participation in global citizenship*. But it is also through our practice of the New Science, through our development of Clairvoyance and other psychic powers that we grow into *more than we are* and attain the greater capacity and wholeness needed to meet these new challenges with personal responsibility.

Contents include: From the Dark Ages to Enlightenment and the Age of Reason; the American Revolution & the Bill of Rights; the reading revolution & universal education; the "real" New Age; "Knowledge Builds on Knowledge" in a constant process of review, renewal, and discovery—free of restraint, restriction, and isolation; the intellectual abuse and misuse of language; the origins of mythology & religion; "Truth," & fiction; religion vs. spirituality; "institutional science" vs. the scientific method; the denial of non-physical reality; "What the Mind Conceives to be Real, Becomes Real;" from higher to lower, and from lower to higher; the key to divination and the key to magick; the battle against religious domination of education and the threat of biblical theocracy; the birth of psychical research and parapsychology; magical illusions; recognized areas of paranormal research; new and broadened horizons of research; there is nothing "normal" about the paranormal; our multi-dimensional universe; accept no intellectual barriers: no *science* operates in isolation; the interconnected global society; the imperative need to develop clairvoyance; science & the psyche. Two approaches:

cosmic & personal; clairvoyance is the primary psychic skill; not "toys" but *tools* and aids. A call for personal & organizational research.

TABLE OF ILLUSTRATIONS

TABLES OF CHARTS, LISTS, FIGURES & TABLES

TABLE OF PROGRAMS & PROCEDURES

FOREWORD
A New Age & a New Science

Yes, those two words, "New Age," seem as hackneyed as a *NEW* anything. In modern product development, in promotion and merchandising of everything from electronics, entertainment, social services, education, drugs, and even politics, foreign policy, and even to religion. *New* is always presumed and presented as better, often bigger, and as the answer to all our needs and problems—until the next new, bigger, and better.

But "new" is not a bad word nor as meaningless and empty of promise as it may seem, even when the phrases using it are *out of fashion.* I use that expression deliberately because "fashion" does incorporate the very essence of phrase creation. It starts when we are very young and need *new* shoes for our growing feet, go to *new* schools to match our advancing years, meet *new* friends, discover *new* interests, plan a *new* career, perceive *new* ways of looking at things, and—of course—we always want to look our best and be seen as up-to-date with the *newest* fashions.

"New" also can mean a dramatic departure from the "old"—not just a transitory phenomena like a *new* look in fashions (that are often just revivals of an old look with a *new* twist) but *new* as in an <u>evolutionary leap forward</u>. That's the real meaning of the word "new" as applied in the two phrases titling the foreword to this book.

Clairvoyance is an old subject, always present in our psyche in the same way the five "normal" physical senses are. "Clear seeing" is a natural *subtle* extension of physical sight that happens unconsciously—but that also means that except in rare instances it remains a largely undiscovered and underdeveloped psychic power. Like any other normal and natural endowment it can be developed into a greater and more powerful skill. We see such developments as "normal" but exceptional—as in athletic skills of running and swimming faster and faster, of jumping higher and higher, hitting harder and harder, and so on. Each such achievement proves it can be done and opens the way for the next generation of athletes to surpass the previous.

But this "New Age" is more than improving our natural mental and psychic powers for it marks a historic transition and evolutionary leap in *consciousness* for everyone. Nevertheless, such an expansion of consciousness also requires development to take it to the *next step* in personal self-empowerment. It is such a historic fact that it has been identified in various ways as a zodiac age in Western astrology or a yuga in Hinduism, or another very long cyclic phase in cosmological science.

In referring to this as the "Age of Aquarius," astrology identifies certain characteristics that do apply but it fails to recognize the true nature of this development as a departure and step forward that not even the greater age perspective of Hinduism provides.

The *New Age* is new, and it is as revolutionary as it is evolutionary. Even though it applies to all life and being in our world, it requires individual and very personal effort not only to develop these personal powers of expanded consciousness but also in broadly dealing with the more universal and challenging repercussions of such a transition. It's the very fact of such an expansion of all kinds of power now at the command of an individual that calls for new ways to direct and control such powers.

A simple example—not one of psychic powers but of powerful weapons (and, in some ways it is a similar warning about expanded physic powers)—is the easy availability of cheap weapons of mass destruction giving a single terrorist the ability to bring down an airliner with hundreds of people on board, to sink a cruise ship with thousands on board, and even (as widely feared) to poison entire cities with radioactive materials and powerful poison gases.

There is "no turning back" to a simpler time when children were safe from molestation, when doors could be left unlocked, when women could safely walk a dark street, when the only guns were held by law enforcement officers, and when religions claiming the superiority of their faiths confined their rhetoric to the inside of their houses of worship. I mention these "dark" aspects of expanded consciousness because they are causally unrecognized. And when we don't know, when we don't understand or even believe the evidence before our eyes (like manifestations of global warming— also evidence of change), we don't have the means to solve a problem.

We stick with old ways when the call for new ways is evident from the broad changes in the global economy, the vast shifts and growth in populations, new diseases for which we have as yet no cure, the failure of politicians to meet real challenges, the collusions of special interests with regulators, and more than we want to list here.

The point is that we are in a New Age, and we need a New Science to begin to understand the opportunities for personal growth and empowerment at a higher level than present awareness and policies address.

This book is about Clairvoyance <u>for</u> psychic empowerment. It's about a higher level of "seeing and perceiving," and with that of also seeing and perceiving more broadly to address and resolve the challenging problems that accompany such a transition that we are now inescapably experiencing. With knowledge and understanding there is power and wisdom to transform liabilities into assets, challenges into solutions, and to meet problems before they become catastrophic. Knowledge <u>is</u> Power, but Power requires understanding to apply it peacefully and progressively.

Clairvoyance brings both Power and Knowledge, but it also calls for and can bring Understanding so that we can meet the challenges with ethical solutions beneficial to all.

Our New Science of the Paranormal will achieve the depth and breadth of knowledge of the expanding psychic consciousness and empowerment to lay the foundation for individual understanding and personal wisdom to enable the higher vision that is open to us NOW.

PREFACE

Should you become Clairvoyant?

Is Clairvoyance Safe?

Should Psychic Powers be Encouraged?

Is Psychic Empowerment Desirable?

There are many questions that really can only be answered for the reader by the reader. You, the reader, have to be the designated responsible person. You are the driver in charge of your life, and your destiny is your responsibility. No teacher, counselor, guide, guru, master, or angel should make decisions for you. In this book we will try to provide some background information to make it possible for your answers to be rational and sound in terms of your own needs and interests.

It is perfectly true that there have been, and probably still are, very valid Esoteric Schools and Yoga Masters that warn <u>serious</u> students of what is loosely referred to as "Spiritual Advancement" to avoid the *Siddhis,* or the Psychic Powers which are sometimes spontaneous accompaniments to expanding consciousness.

The Hazards of "self-aggrandizement"

Perhaps the most important reason for this is the self-aggrandizement that happens to many who experience these abilities, which may include not only clairvoyance but physical levitation, teleportation, materializations, and remote viewing—and, sometimes, seeming visitations from Advanced Beings. Most often these spontaneous developments occur when students are isolated in schools and *ashrams* separated from the exigencies of busy urban life. It is much more difficult for what we call "passive" or spontaneous development to occur with people with active family and work lives, or involved in full-time education.

Still, it happens and results in emotionally-based self-illusion that blocks further growth, and can lead others astray and dependent on this new, self-anointed, guru with such amazing powers.

There is, however, another important consideration that applies generally to clairvoyance and psychic empowerment: *Consciousness Expansion is happening as part of this "New Age."*

(Don't let that term, "New Age"—which has become overly commercialized and abused in order to merchandise everything from hair styles to *fashionably* torn jeans, from new music to new art, from meta-"fussy" books to dangerous psychological techniques led by self-anointed gurus, etc.—deter you from recognition of the Aquarian-like energies prevailing now and accelerating during the next two millenniums. *It's the real thing!*)

New Age Energies and Consciousness Expansion

These New Age energies and consciousness expansions are genuine, and your understanding of their Aquarian nature is important to both this discussion and your personal growth. Aquarius is the "water bearer" pouring forth new Knowledge for everyone's benefit, but the Aquarian Age is also that time when the student becomes the active acquirer of learning—in other words we now see the reason behind the explosion of Self-Study, Self-Help, and Self-Improvement opportunities so marked over the past half-century.

The Responsible Student

Good books are no longer just "about" subjects, or "how to" manuals, but the new books even go beyond "theory & practice" to fully develop the theoretical foundations of a subject, explain the whys and the benefits, often include case studies and examples, provide specific self-applied techniques for personal use, and sometimes even self-administered tests and questionnaires to affirm your understanding and knowledge.

It's not only such new books but the entire "responsible student" concept has carried over into self-study courses, on-line universities, down-loadable lessons, and has changed the style for author and conference lectures. Teachers are no longer reigning authority figures or unquestioned gurus but helpers taking their lead from students. As a result, more university classes provide for students to participate in research and experimentation on a co-equal basis with teachers for true "hands-on" study. In other words, everyone participates and everyone grows.

To back track a little: It certainly is not true that we don't believe there are "adepts" or advanced beings from higher, super-physical, levels of consciousness— "superhuman" in their development—who have given out at least partial *factual* information about the inner and greater realities of the Cosmos and the potential for our advanced development. It's almost self-evident. At the same time we believe that their work is "behind the scenes" and that it is real and effective. What we don't believe is that there is any contemporary direct communication between human and super-human beings—the point being that we have plenty of "esoteric" knowledge available and have every opportunity to grow and advance without supernatural intervention at this time—and that's what we are supposed to do.

Psychic Powers are not ends in themselves, but growth and development are. Active development of any innate power is an active growth in consciousness just as care and development of the physical body advances the Whole Person and Life itself. The resulting psychic skills are beneficial in the greater development of consciousness and in the related development of the means to increased direct perceptions of "hidden" realities so that we can make our own discoveries and learn to judge their quality and reality.

Every step in self-realization is a step in Realization of Self. That statement appears to be redundant but some careful thinking about it could be revealing.

The Goals of Clairvoyance

The goal of clairvoyance is the *direct perception of hidden realities.* The only thing "occult" about clairvoyance is exactly that the meaning of the word is "hidden" in the sense that something obscures *clear vision* (the definition of clairvoyance). Usually we mean a temporary obscuration, as when—during a solar eclipse—the Moon passes in front of the Sun and prevents our direct perception. In astronomy that is called "occultation." But, note this: while the solar eclipse hides the sun it also allows the perception of solar flares other solar phenomena and thus increasing our total knowledge about the sun and its relationship with Earth.

Clairvoyance isn't just about "secret" alternative knowledge, but is a means to expanded knowledge through expanded awareness. To understand this requires an understanding that you, every person, is more than you think you are and psychic development and empowerment is about *becoming more than you are.* It's about expanding your "objective consciousness."

However, there are some fundamental problems involved that become more apparent when you look at the "Big Picture" as will be shown in the Introduction and then fully explored and demonstrated in later chapters.

More than only a Physical Body

You probably wouldn't be reading this book if you thought a human being was no more than what is contained within the physical body, and that consciousness was just a function of the physical brain. You know that you are a mental and an emotional being as well as a physical one, and you either believe or hope that you are also a spiritual being. With a little thought, you may also perceive that you are also an energy being. We have given names to each of these "levels"—physical, etheric (or energy), astral (or emotional), mental, and causal (or soul). We also believe that the real you, which we call "the Monad," functions through all these levels.

Each of these levels has a specific nature and presents your whole being with particular perceptual opportunities and limitations. All awareness, clairvoyance included, functions at the energy, emotional and mental levels—and to some degree at the soul level—depending on the development of natural powers into trained skills.

Returning to the questions about the *safety* of clairvoyance and other psychic powers, it is the fact that while we function within a physical and etheric body (matter and energy), with perception of external reality mainly through five physical senses, we are primarily emotional beings and most psychic activity is emotionally based. Thus, we must recognize that clairvoyant perception is emotionally filtered.

Physical perception is objective while emotional perception is subjective. Both need to be "tested" against known facts. That's judgment, and is a mental act. Judgment is qualified by experience which recognizes that a factual basis "evolves" and can never provide absolute authority.

Some will argue that their psychic perception is "intuitive" and not limited or affected by their emotional hopes & fears, fantasies, or religious beliefs, but we would argue that intuition is super-human, and *we're not there yet!*

Trust, but verify!

Regardless: What you see is not necessarily what is. "Trust, but verify" was President Reagan's trademark principle. We would rather say "analyze and verify." Analyze your perception and verify it with known facts. When vision and facts are at variance, consider the reasons. Look at your *feelings* in relation to your vision and ask if they influence your perception.

We have to learn the art & practice of clairvoyance just as we do any other human skill, and there's a science to that. How's that for a mixed metaphor? It's just saying "Look at all sides before you leap from the frying pan into the fire." Clairvoyance is safe when balanced with our other faculties. Yes, we believe its development should be encouraged as a matter of growth and movement into wholeness. We believe psychic empowerment should be your goal because you should be an empowered person.

Yes, there will be many practical benefits to your developed clairvoyance as well—extending your inter-dimensional perceptions of reality means that you see more and are better able to judge the meaning and value of your inter-actions with the complex world in which you live. It gives you a greater foundation for the decisions you must make in life. You will gain deeper insights into your own physical and emotional reactions to both external events and internal issues.

The biggest benefit, however, comes with your personal realization that your clairvoyance is not a single function but one involving all levels of your consciousness, and—with judgment and experience—that the higher your level of focus the greater the depth and breadth and accuracy of your vision.

Scientific Verification of Clairvoyance and its Practical Benefits

Although clairvoyance is a complex, multifunctional phenomenon, it's receptiveness to scientific investigation has been repeatedly demonstrated in the controlled laboratory setting. Structured laboratory experiments in our labs at Athens State University along with simple instructional exercises in the classroom setting not only validated the existence of clairvoyance, they identified the variables associated with successful clairvoyance in daily life. They explored the relatedness of clairvoyance to various personal traits and the effects of practice in developing clairvoyant skills. They validated the many practical application of clairvoyance, including its usefulness in solving difficult problems, increasing creativity, improving relationships, promoting career success, accelerating academic achievement, and probing the subconscious, to list but a few. Aside from these, our studies also focused on the many unchartered areas of clairvoyance, including its global applications as well as its capacity to probe the distant reaches of the universe.

Clearly, controlled research has demonstrated the existence of clairvoyance as a powerful phenomenon with potential to increase awareness and acquire knowledge otherwise unavailable to us. That said, however, real life experience remains among the most impressive indicators of clairvoyance and its capacity to empower our lives. Consequently, we have included in these pages many personal accounts and case studies of clairvoyance as a purpose-driven phenomenon. The accounts range from everyday affairs involving decision making to extreme situations of danger in which clairvoyant insight prevented serious injury or even death.

Programs to activate, and to develop, Clairvoyance

We've also included in this book an array of programs designed to develop the clairvoyant potential existing in everyone. The programs range from simple techniques that activate clairvoyance in an instant to step-by-step programs that promote an empowering interaction with the clairvoyant faculty existing deep within the self. Through practice of these programs, you will experience a cumulative effect that unleashes new sources of power in your life while promoting the full development of your clairvoyant potential. Yes, in clairvoyance, practice does indeed make perfect.

Why learn Clairvoyance? Because it will enable you to become more than you are. Growing and Becoming is what life is about.

Joe H. Slate
Carl Llewellyn Weschcke

INTRODUCTION
Define Your Terms . . . BEFORE You Start Your Engines!
The need to define the Subject and its Terminology

Before discussing any subject, we should be sure that all parties to the conversation agree on what the subject of discussion actually is, and also agree on the basic terminology to be used. Specifically in the case of a non-fiction book—and, in this case, one dealing with your self-empowerment through psychic development—it is even more important because there is no later opportunity to say, "But, that's not what I meant."

Back in 1791, an undistinguished Scottish lawyer named James Boswell published his famous biography of the social and literary celebrity, Dr. Samuel Johnson (author of the brilliant *A Dictionary of the English Language,* 1755) whose wit and wisdom was famous throughout Europe. Johnson is important to us now for one proclamation: *"Define your terms, gentlemen, define your terms. It saves argument!"*

Even though the British "upper classes" of the 16th century apparently thought only men able to discuss and debate important ideas, we would normally be in total agreement with the need for universally accepted definitions, but there's a problem when working with super-physical phenomena and concepts. And that makes for some rather substantial problems related to our discussions of the super-physical world that we must understand before we can define "clairvoyance" in the context of this work.

The Necessity of Esoteric Nomenclature
It is important to state, right here and now, that the basic nomenclature in this Introduction is partly derived from the "esoteric" rather than familiar, scientific or mystical jargon. While Clairvoyance is often the subject of parapsychological study, which has largely adopted scientific language and has brought the subject into widespread respect and acceptance, our approach is more expansive and comprehensive than provided in physical science.

The subject of this book is not the esoteric cosmos, but some of our discussion and techniques require acceptance of those higher or inner levels of the super-physical that do have names meaningful to our study here. You can see them broadly outlined in Figures 1 and 2 accompanying this part of the book.

Objective vs. Subjective

When we deal only with strictly physical phenomena we can safely assume that things can be described in terms that are universally understood. We are able to analyze a physical object's chemical composition, measure its three physical dimensions, establish its weight, determine its electrical charge and other latent energy potentials, describe its colors against established criteria, determine reflected light capability, and other advanced "constants" that enable anyone to accurately understand what we mean and duplicate our experiments and procedures.

The Physical Universe (aka "Plane," to use one esoteric term) is the only one of the seven Levels making up Cosmic Reality within which we have our being where such specific definition is possible. That doesn't mean that the other six worlds of our immediate *metaphysical* environment are any less real nor any less important to us, but each has its own *substance* and *nature* that must be part of our discussion of super-physical phenomena and consciousness.

The Immensity of the Physical Universe

What is important right now is, first, to accept that the familiar *visible* physical universe is not only far larger in dimension than anything actually conceivable but that there is an immense *invisible* dimension of sub–atomic matter and energy that is the *foundation* of the visible universe. And, even more startling is the realization that at least certain aspects of this invisible dimension can be affected by human consciousness.

The Even Greater Immensity of the Cosmos

And second, in addition to the invisible dimension of the physical universe there are other, *super*-physical, levels of reality that are just as "real" as the physical but composed of different "substances" and operate under different "laws" of which we are generally unaware, even though we ourselves are composed of both physical and these other *subtle* substances.

Third, human consciousness exists at these non-physical levels but mostly, as yet in our present growth level, "unconsciously." Our goal is to become conscious and to function at these levels which have a unique, *controlling* relationship to the physical. It is at these super-physical levels that psychic phenomena occurs and where psychic powers function.

Many scientists, and some readers, have objections to such terms as *Etheric, Astral, Subtle, Super-physical, Spiritual,* etc., because their phenomena cannot be subjected to direct physical observation and analysis. Mostly anything "super-physical" is considered as *subjective* and thus beyond *objective* examination.

The Non-Physical Aspects of Psychic Phenomena

This also means that scientists and others will completely reject the existence of anything super-physical other than—possibly—a vague "Spiritual World" generally relegated to indefinable religious discussion if discussed at all. Likewise, most parapsychologists reject the non-physical concepts of psychic phenomenon—preferring to consider only physical factors.

Even for readers long familiar with psychic phenomena and esoteric concepts, the immensity of the journey ahead of us may be *truly mind boggling.* And yet, the promise is a journey that is glorious, a promise that every life has a far greater meaning than most have ever imagined, and the promise that the reality of *infinity* applies to your own human potential.

A Bit of Esoteric History

Long before modern times, Myth and Religion described universal reality without real separation between mundane or divine, objective and subjective, observable or beyond ordinary perception. Physical objects were "seen "and named and physically manipulated, while invisible forces were given the names and attributes of "gods." The gods were ceremonially worshiped by tribal rulers and priests, and their powers manipulated through prayers and rituals.

The physical and the non-physical were part of a single reality.

As we "fast forward," we arrive at the time of the Great Philosophers, both east and west, but it was in ancient Greece that the most transitional developments took place, starting the process that took our mental outlook nearly to the 14th century with the beginnings of the scientific revolution that separated the physical from the non-physical, which was then mostly relegated to a "Spiritual World" dominated by the Church and a few daring Occultists practicing their arts under great secrecy.

Throughout the "Scientific Age," it was only the *visible* physical world that was perceived as "objectively real," and hence anything invisible was not real at all!

Restoring the Physical and Super-physical to a single Reality

It was not until the late 19th century and early 20th that two new revolutionary movements began the process that has continued and accelerated in our current 21st century, and is once again restoring the physical and super-physical to a comprehensible single reality.

On the esoteric side we had the birth of modern spiritualism in 1848 with the rapping and other psychic phenomena surrounding the young Fox sisters in their Hydesville, New York home, later followed by the 1875 founding of the Theosophical Society in New York by the Russian Madame Helena Petrovna Blavatsky and the American lawyer and journalist Col. Henry Steel Olcott. Although the spiritualist movement can be traced to the earlier writings of Emanuel Swedenborg and the teachings of Franz Mesmer in the 18th century, it was only with the happenings in the 19th century that esoteric concepts became broadly widespread.

Religions vs. Science, Spiritualism, Theosophy & Quantum Physics

On the scientific side, it was the discovery of Cathode Rays by Michael Faraday in 1838 that revealed an invisible physical reality inaugurating the fundamental revolution we know today as Quantum Physics and leading to all the developments of modern technology ranging from radio and atomic bombs to computers, cell phones, DNA, and dramatic developments leading rapidly toward benefits in health, longevity, and cheap non-fossil energy that will result in vast reductions in costs in transportation, materials, and production.

What's this about <u>Starting Engines</u>?

While esoteric practices—such as yoga, meditation, the martial arts, and magical ritual—along with esoteric understandings of the comprehensive nature of reality— were long available in exclusive secret societies, it is only with the transition into the sudden *expansions* of conscious awareness that has been called "the New Age" that a new phase in human evolution has been initiated. "Infinity" is no longer limited to physical reality but now extended to your personal consciousness potentials.

New Age, New Terms, New Reality

In this New Age, new terms and broader understandings are inevitable. Yet there is always resistance to change and new ideas that challenge the status quo and institutions established to promulgate and defend old ways. "Special Interests" and vested positions too often seek to retain power and profit rather than to invest in the risk of new development and better ways.

Nevertheless, with the freshening energies of a New Age, resistance to change will be transformed and directed into more rapid deployments of capital and energy in education, research, and development. The new technologies and products of the last few decades will be rapidly surpassed creating new employment, new economies, and increased opportunities leading to peace initiatives everywhere.

An "Engine" for Expanding Consciousness

Each of us is an "engine" of expanding consciousness and for turning consciousness into objective awareness. Even unconsciousness contains knowledge and memories, and our subconsciousness does "feed" these memories and knowledge into the conscious mind in forms of subjective awareness that is not always useful to the everyday conscious mind that applies knowledge to our practical benefit.

But, our New Age is changing with energies and increasing vibrations *pushing* into our conscious minds and new techniques for "managing" the relation of conscious and subconscious minds, and opening the Superconscious mind. As individual "engines" we are all adding to this movement within Universal Consciousness and even to the most fundamental levels of Matter. Focused observation is actually accelerating evolution at all levels in accordance with the Great Plan.

What does this have to do with Clairvoyance and Psychic Empowerment, the subjects of this book?

Consciousness is universal, but is essentially divided into varying degrees and forms of "Un-awakened" and "Awakened" that are recognized under many names. With the particular energies of higher levels of consciousness accelerating over the coming decades, there will increased Knowledge of Reality and Life, accompanied by an acceleration of psychic development. While some of this is spontaneous, it is important that psychic powers become psychic skills through disciplined self-development.

While "training" in such development is always available, it is through personal efforts that the greatest advancement are made. And this is especially so with the energies of the zodiacal sign of Aquarius replacing those of Pisces. You don't need to be an astrologer to perceive the vast increase in organized access to knowledge available to self-study, and in the devotion to self-knowledge, self-understanding, self-responsibility, and self-reliance. It is the **Leitmotiv, or "guiding motivation"** of our age.

Do not mistake such "self" consciousness as selfish or self-centered in an adverse way. It is quite the opposite. As Consciousness expands, it is as comprehensive of the needs of others as it is respectful of their own self-dignity. We have reached the stage of a Global

Civilization which does not mean a loss of local and national cultures but instead provides for participation of the individual in the whole. *We are One, but we are also Many.*

With increased Self-awareness, there is *expanded* ability to <u>focus</u> attention at higher levels of consciousness giving access to the particular energies and capabilities that come with each.

Defining Clairvoyance

Clairvoyance simply means "clear seeing," the implication being the particular *psychic vision* involved (we'll get to that in a moment) reveals the hidden nature of an object, event, or person.

When we look at any object with our physical eyes we are limited to its three ordinary physical dimensions. We are not only unaware of the sub-atomic aspects functioning in the object, but many of us are not truly observant of the finer details of color, shape, odor, taste and feel and of **the *resident consciousness* fundamental to the object itself.** Yet, there *is* consciousness even in a brick, and more so in a blade of grass, a swimming fish, and on up the scale. And, where there is consciousness, there is *life. The universe is alive at all levels and in every dimension.*

On the physical level, we perceive with our physical senses. As we focus consciousness at higher levels, we don't perceive with "sense organs" but through awareness of the substance and changing vibrations emitted from the object of our attention. The higher we ascend in awareness, the greater our vision. At the astral level, we are aware of a fourth dimension, and at the mental level we perceive five dimensions.

And because there are many levels of reality and of consciousness, there are different levels of clairvoyance, each functioning in accordance with the laws and nature of that level. In the non-physical world, clairvoyance is not "objective" in the familiar sense, but neither is it "subjective." Rather it is a blending in, a merging, and identification with the object of our "clear sight" but without loss of our own self-awareness. In other words, this higher clairvoyance *is* objective but in another sense.

Think of it with this made-up example: The Ocean is like the sea of Universal Consciousness in which swim many fish. As a clairvoyant scuba-diver, you are interested in a very large fish that seems to be floating-in-place, asleep. You cautiously swim around the fish, even extending your hands to sense *vibrations* emanating from the sleeping fish. You project your conscious awareness to the fish while still, consciously, swimming around it. As you do so, the fish awakens and becomes aware of you, but without fear or reaction. You will sense the difference between the fish's sleeping-unconscious and the awakened-consciousness, and you may even feel a sense of camaraderie.

Note, in this example, that you retained your own conscious awareness and control, and self-identity, in order to continue your swimming, but you also extended awareness to merge—in some degree—with the fish. Like everyone, every being, everything, we are united in consciousness and can move between states of unconscious "awareness" and active conscious awareness.

What did you learn through this clairvoyant exercise? Maybe not much, but one thing, in particular, was evident: the large fish has consciousness, became aware of you, and made a decision that you were not an enemy or food. Two beings of different species objectively sharing consciousness is a kind of knowing in itself. Such sharing may also activate "ancient memories" in your subconsciousness where nothing has ever been forgotten including even our earliest evolutionary passages. It is also possible that you and the fish could directly share specific factual knowledge—like sights of a sunken pirate ship. *Who knows, until you ask.*

"Ask and ye shall receive." *(Ask, and it shall be given you; seek, and ye shall find; knock, and it shall be opened unto you. Matthew 7:7)* A specific question is like a *probe* that goes into a vast unknown and zeros in on its target. Ask too broad a question and you open yourself up to questionable answers influenced by fantasy and emotionality which is characteristic of the astral level. In other words, *Be careful what you ask for!* And learn to test the answers.

Different kinds, and levels, of Clairvoyance

Clairvoyance is not a single, specific, easily defined psychic ability because it operates in many different ways. It can simply be an expansion of etheric perception of *vibrations* at that "higher" physical level, often associated with various forms of divination and precognition. Then it is often one of many possible functions of the astral vehicle including remote viewing and out-of-body experience. It can also involve both mental and astral consciousness in relation to the interpretation of dreams, symbols, Tarot cards, Runes, and I Ching hexagrams.

Clairvoyance is also associated with reading or "viewing" the Akashic Records. Once again, however, we encounter levels of those "Records"—at the astral, mental, and the causal levels. Here, the importance of understanding the differences in substance and nature of each level is important. Remember that the alternative name for the Astral is "emotional" and that everything perceived and experienced at this level is qualified with emotionality. Just as "Love can be blind," so always is emotion—at least potentially—distorting.

Understanding leads to Objectivity

Each level reflects its own nature, even at the mental and causal levels. It is through understanding of these differences that a person can gain a more objective perception of the increased complexity and additional dimensions when functioning at these higher levels.

What, then, is our definition of clairvoyance? It is purely the ability to focus consciousness on the object at hand with full recognition of the nature of the different levels as indicated by the number of dimensions perceptible at that level.

Vibrations?

This word, "vibrations," (*vibes*) has taken on some of the worst "fuzziness" of *New Agey* vocabulary. It's been applied with ambiguity and without clarity to a vacuous sense of etheric level clairvoyance but with belief that it brings with it awareness of true character and veracity.

What it really refers to is the *motion* of physical atoms within all matter. It further recognizes that in our sharing of consciousness with all things, we can be aware of that motion. More importantly, however, the nature of matter and of consciousness changes as the *rate* of vibration changes. As we consciously raise our own vibrations we perceive the matter at different levels, or "planes."

"Motion" is, in another sense, the "Energy" fundamental—with Matter and Consciousness—to all existence, but it is not quite correct to say that "matter converts into energy." That, however, is not a necessary discussion in relation to Clairvoyance and Psychic Empowerment.

SEVEN PLANES & SEVEN BODIES

In a moment we will ask you to take an initial glance at the accompanying side-by-side tables titled respectively "Figure 1—Seven Levels of Reality" and "Figure 2—Seven Levels of Consciousness." Each has detailed footnotes for later reference.

Our use of the term "Levels" is self-evident and as practical as the term "Columns."

By way of introduction, we need to say that an increasing number of writers and readers in this subject area have come to prefer the terms "Worlds" and "Vehicles" rather than the older *Planes* and *Bodies* as better reflective of their real nature, and as practical terms for <u>active</u> development procedures.

However, we propose a kind of compromise.

We really don't use the word "plane" in reference to the "world" in which we live (unless we are geometricians), but we do normally think of our world as just the planet Earth (also called *Gaia)* whereas the Physical Level (or "Plane") really comprehends the entire *Physical Universe*. However, we can't really use concepts like "Astral Universe," Mental Universe," etc., with comparable understanding. Therefore, we will attempt to write in terms of the Physical Universe, and the Astral World, Mental World, on up to the Upper Manifestal World for what we collectively refer to as the *subtle worlds* to distinguish their nature from the solidity and density of physical substance. Again, the point is that we don't function in a plane but we do function in a world.

And the word "body" gets confusing when extended to the subtle nature of whatever it is that we occupy when experiencing worlds other than the physical. We can comfortably use the word "body" in reference to our actual, living, physical body with which we function in the physical universe, but the word "body" carries with it definitive boundaries that really don't similarly exist in the subtle worlds. We prefer the word *vehicle* as that which *carries* our consciousness when functioning in the subtle worlds beyond the physical.

The following is very important: **Even when using our subtle vehicles, we remain "anchored" to our physical body so long as it is alive by means of "cords" of Consciousness and of Life (the "Silver Cord").** It is "home" to the human being.

Before you turn to the two tables, we need to say something about the upper four levels vs. the lower three. In both figures you will note a solid black "belt" separating the "Human Kingdom" from the two higher Essential and Manifestal kingdoms. Referring to Figure 2 you will see that the three lower levels comprising the human kingdom actually are sub-divided into five bodies or vehicles which comprise a single unity for the Causal "Soul." It is this "First Self" (or Soul) that incarnates through the series of personalities born anew in the "Lower Self" of physical, etheric, astral, and mental vehicles for each human lifetime of awakening consciousness.

In an attempt to clarify: we have four "minds" incarnating in a series of mortal physical bodies under the rulership of an immortal Soul. From one perspective, these four minds correspond to the physical brain and chakra system, the subconscious, conscious, and superconscious minds. While the physical body is alive, these four minds operate as "yourself," and it is the series of such "selves" that you can re-experience as *past lives*, and that together make up parts of the evolving Soul that is the true Immortal Self.

Of course, it gets even more complicated and ever more interesting because each level is divided into seven sub-divisions, each having particular characteristics and each offering the whole person corresponding opportunities for expression, and growth.

At the same time it is important to learn that with every opportunity provided to the vehicles of consciousness operating at these levels and their sub-divisions, there is a corresponding limitation. This is particularly true of the Astral level, which by its nature is "emotional," and perceptions will be "colored" and even distorted by emotion (desire, hope, fantasy, fear) that you must mentally (and rationally) objectify.

The Need for "Proofs"

This is not the place to discuss this problem in detail, but we should mention the system of Proofs that you can lean to apply in connection with clairvoyant vision. These are:

The Kinds of Proofs

1. Logical Proof: Establish a series of non-conflicting facts, into which new facts must fit in.

2. Proof by Explanation: This is really a summary of logical proofs presented in sequence of one building on the preceding to demonstrate a logical conclusion.

3. Proof by Predication: A forecast is based on factual system which must then be followed by verifying events, or else be perceived as wrong.

4. Experimental Proof by "Magick:"—using physical/etheric material energies to bring about changes in denser physical matter.

5. Proof by Clairvoyance: <u>Objective Consciousness</u> at each level—physical, astral, mental, causal.

As you see, "Proof by Clairvoyance" is listed, but also note how it is qualified by "<u>Objective Consciousness</u> at each level—physical, astral, mental, causal." That's the goal, and it contrasts sharply with the common prescription for *passive "sensitivity"* commonly taught by many psychic schools.

Also note "Experimental Proof by 'Magick.'" This is as definitive as Proof by Prediction, and is essentially saying that if you truly understand the facts and know them as proven, the final proof of your clairvoyant ability is objectively testable. This is important. Your clairvoyance should be proven before you proceed to claim *insight* into such concerns as health, finances, relationships, or even world affairs.

It is also important to find ways to test the identity and "honesty" of any Angels, Spirits, Guides, or other Supernatural beings. "Faith" is not a valid approach to anything and has long been used in various forms of deception. "Faith," at best, is a *Belief System* and if valid it has to work successfully in real life circumstance.

Please also realize that such "logical thinking" as exemplified in such a system of proofs quickly becomes almost "instinctual" after you apply it consistently for a long enough period to establish habit.

The "Big Picture"

One final *caveat* before you study the accompanying figures: **It is through awareness of the "Big Picture" that the details gain meaning.** The fact is that Clairvoyance *can* be a function of the Astral Vehicle, the Mental Vehicle, and the Causal Self, but it also starts with expanded awareness at the higher Etheric level of the physical body. *But, the clairvoyance of the physical-etheric level is a function <u>only</u> of the physical brain—no more, no less.* Real psychic powers are a function of consciousness focused in the higher vehicles of the whole person you are. But, also, the higher includes the lower so development is incremental. The higher also controls the lower—which is how "magick" works.

The truth is that **you are more than you think you are, and it is your *responsibility* to become more than you are!**

It is your own growth and development that is the Great Game of Life, the fulfillment of the Great Plan that is the purpose of our being, and it is likewise the Greatest Adventure you can ever undertake for it leads not merely toward the infinity of the physical universe but more toward the infinity of consciousness wherein you become truly crowned with Glory.

There are no lesser words that can be used to inspire you to take this Great Journey that is opened before you with the information and the techniques of this book.

Bon Voyage
Carl Llewellyn Weschcke

FIGURE 1 - SEVEN LEVELS OF REALITY (Energy)

MATTER (Carrier of Consciousness) - MOTION=ENERGY (Perceived as "Vibration" and Acted upon through "Will") - CONSCIOUSNESS

Cosmos	Existence	Cosmic Involution	Solar Evolution	Names for the Levels of Reality, aka Planes (1) and Worlds (2)	Alternative Names	Hebrew Kabalah Names	WORLDS	Kingdoms	Sub-planes (Divisions)	Characteristics	Functions	Energies	Energies & Motions
		Vibrational Scales											
1	2	3	4	5	6	7	8	9	10	11	12	13	14
Cosmic Reality	Negative Existence	7 to 1	43 to 49	Sixth Cosmic Kingdom	Metaverse (1)	AIN		Cosmic Kingdoms	Father - Shiva	Omnipotene	CHAOS		Zero Point Energy
		14 to 8	36 to 42	Fifth Cosmic Kingdom		"Nothing"							Dynamis (2)
		21 to 15	29 to 35	Fourth Cosmic Kingdom	Singularity (1)	AIN SOPH			Son - Vishnu	Omniscience	Information		Gravity
		28 to 22	22 to 28	Third Cosmic Kingdom		"The Infinite"					(Instruction & Programming)		Electro-Magnetism
		35 to29	15 to 21	Second Cosmic Kingdom		AIN SOPH AUR			Mother - Brahma	Omnipresence			Weak Nuclear Force
		42 to 36	8 to 14	First Cosmic Kingdom		"Boundless Light"			(or Holy Ghost)				Strong Nuclear Force
		ZERO POINT FIELD		MATTER, MOTION, CONSCIOUSNESS							CREATION		
Super-physical "Subtle" Reality	Solar System	43:1	7:7	Upper Manifestal (2)	Upper Monadic (1)	Kether - 1	Atziluth - Archetypal World	Manifestal Kingdom				Manifestal Energy	
		43:2	7:6	Solar System "World"	Logoic (3)	"The Crown"							
		43:3	7:5		Adi (5)								
		43:4	7:4										
		43:5	7:3	Lower Manifestal (2)	Lower Monadic (1)	Chokmah - 2							
		43:6	7:2			"Lioght"							
		43:7	7:1	9 Dimensions									
		44:1	6:7	Submanifestal (2)	Divine (1)	Binah - 3						Submanifestal Energy	
		44:2	6:6	Interplanetary "World"	Monadic (3)	"Wisdom"							
		44:3	6:5		Anupadaka (5)								
		44:4	6:4							"Cosmic Fire"			
		44:5	6:3										
		44:6	6:2										
		44:7	6:1	8 Dimensions									
		45:1	5:7	Upper Superessential (2)	Upper Spiritual (1)	Daath	Briah - Creative World	Essential Kingdom				Superessential Energy	
		45:2	5:6	Planetary "World"	Atmic (4)	"Knowledge"							
		45:3	5:5		Atma (6)								
		45:4	5:4	Lower Superessential (2)	Lower Spiritual (1)	Chesed - 4							
		45:5	5:3			"Mercy"							
		45:6	5:2										
		45:7	5:1	7 Dimensions									
		46:1	4:7	Essential (2) "World"	Unity (1)	Geburah - 5						Essential Energy	
		46:2	4:6		Buddhic (3)	"Force"							
		46:3	4:5		Buddhi (5)								
		46:4	4:4										
		46:5	4:3		World of Love								
		46:6	4:2		& Bliss								
		46:7	4:1	6 Dimensions									
	Planetary Worlds	47:1	3:7	3:7 Greater Causal (1) World	3:5→3:7 Higher Heaven	Tiphareth - 4	Yetzirah - Formative World	Ideas		World of Ideas	Causal Akashic Records	Mental-Causal Energy	
		47:2	3:6	3:5→3:6 Lesser Causal (1)	World of Knowledge	"Beauty"							
		447:3	3:5	Causal Substance						Elemental Essence I			
		47:4	3:4	1:4 Mental World	Higher Mental (2)	Netzach - 3		& Human		World of	Mental Akashic Records		"Energy follows Thought"
		47:5	3:3		World of Thought	"Victory"				Fictions			
		47:6	3:2	Mental Substance	Lower Mental (2)								
		47:7	3:1	5 Dimensions	3:1→3:4 Lower Heaven					Elemental Essence 2			
		48:1	2:7	Astral (emotional) World	Emotional (1) (2)	Hod - 8		& Animals			Emotional Akashic Records	Astral (Emotional) Energy	Dark Energy
		48:2	2:6	2:1→2:6 Astral	2:4→2:6 Paradise	"Glory"				World of	The Astral Light,		
		48:3	2:5		Kama (5) Desire					Illusions	aka Astral Substance,		
		48:4	2:4								is used to create		
		48:5	2:3		World of Emotion						Thought Forms under		
		48:6	2:2	Astral Light, aka astral substance	& Reaction						direction of		
		48:7	2:1	4 Dimensions	2:1→2:3 "Purgatory"					Elemental Essence 3	Mind		
Physical Reality		49:1	1:7	Etheric aka Upper Physical	Sthula (5) "Dense"	Yesod - 9	Assiah - Material World	& Plant	Atomic	World of Etheric		Physical Energy	Dark Matter
		49:2	1:6	1:4→1:6 Upper Etheric		"The Foundation"			Sub-atomic	Energies			
		49:3	1:5		World of Life-force				Super-etheric				
		49:4	1:4	Etheric Substance					Etheric				
		49:5	1:3	1:1→1:3 Lower Physical Universe	World of Action	Malkuth - 10		Mineral	Gaseous				
		49:6	1:2	Physical Substance		"The Kingdom"			Liquid				
		49:7	1:1	3 Dimensions	1:1→1:3"Hell"				Solid				
		↓	↑	MATTER, MOTION, CONSCIOUSNESS	Chaos	Klipoth			Absolute Zero	Quantum Foam	LIGHT		MOTION=ENERGY
				Higgs Boson		"Antithesis of All"			Motionless Space	String	Waves or Particles		VIBRATIONS

FIGURE 2 - SEVEN LEVELS OF CONSCIOUSNESS

MATTER (The "Carrier" of Consciousness) - MOTION=ENERGY (Perceived as "Vibration" and Acted upon through "Will") - CONSCIOUSNESS

Vibrational Scales (Cosmic Involution)	Reality	Solar Evolution	Aura	Names for the Vehicles, aka Bodies or Envelopes (2)	Alternative Names	Hebrew Kabbalah Names	Some characteristics	Sub-divisions: Function	Actions	Consciousness	Chakras & Psychic Powers
1	2	3		4	5	6	7	8	9	10	11
7 to 1				Father	Shiva (5)	AIN					
14 to 8	Cosmic Consciousness					"Nothing"					
21 to 15				Son	Vihnu (5	AIN SOPH					
28 to 22						"The Infinite"					
35 to 29				Holy Spirit aka "Mother"	Brahma (5)	AIN SOPH AUR					
42 to 36						"Boundless Light"					
Zero Point				51 Dimensions							
43:1		7:7		Upper Manifestal (2)	Manifestal Selves (2)		7:7 Manifestal		The FATHER	TRUE SELF	
43:2		7:6		"Vehichle" of Spiritual	Monadic (4)		Atom		Universal I AM	Solar System	
43:3	Manifestal Consciousness	7:5		Manifestation	Logoic (4)		7:4 Manifestal			Consciousness	
43:4		7:4			Adi (5)		Molecule				
43:5		7:3		Lower Manifestal (2) - Lower						Spiritual Will	
43:6		7:2						THE THIRD SELF			
43:7		7:1		9 Dimensions				3rd Triad consists of			
44:1		6:7		6:7 Submanifestal (2)	Submanifestal Selves (2)		6:7 Submanifestal	43:4 etheric		Interplanetary	Omnipotence
44:2		6:6		"Vehide" of Spiritual	Divine Body (1)	YECHIDAH	Atom	manifestal molecule,		Consciousness	Divine Perception
44:3	Submanifestal Consciousness	6:5		Expression	Monadic (4)	The Divine Self		44:1 submanifestal			
44:4		6:4			Anupadaka (5)	From 7:3 down to		atom, and a 45:1			
44:5		6:3				5:4		superessenial atom			
44:6		6:2						in a 43:1-3			
44:7		6:1		8 Dimensions				manifestal			
45:1		5:7		5:7 Upper Superessential (2)	Sup[eressential Selves (2)		5:7 Superessential	involutional matter		Planetary	
45:2		5:6		Vehicle of Spiritual Will	Upper Spiritual (1)		Atom			Consciousness	
45:3	Superessential Consciousness	5:5			Atma (3)		SPIRIT				
45:4		5:4		Lower Superessential (2)			5:4 Superessential				
45:5		5:3					Molecule	THE SECOND SELF			
45:6		5:2						2nd Triad consists of		Collective	
45:7		5:1		7 Dimensions				45:4 etheric		Unconsciousness	
46:1		4:7		4:7 Essential (2)	Essential Selves (2)		4:7 Essential Atom	supperessential	The SON	World Consciousness	Omniscience
46:2		4:6		Vehide of Spiritual Intuition	Unity Body	CHIAH	The Percention of an	molecule, 46:1		Group Consciousness	Wisdom
46:3	Essential Consciousness	4:5			Buddhic Body (3)	THE HIGHER SELF	object is from within	essential atom, and		Spiritual consciousness,	Intuition
46:4		4:4			Buddhi (5)	From 5:4 down to		a 47:1 mental atom		understanding &	Universal Time
46:5		4:3			Intuitional Body	3:4		in I 45:1-3 causal		Judgment	Neshamah
46:6		4:2			Spiritual Soul			vehicle.			
46:7		4:1		6 Dimensions							Higher Unconscious
47:1		3:7		3:7 Greater Causal (I) Self	Causal (2)		3:7 Mental Atom		SOUL - incarnating	Knowledge of Reality and	Crown Chakra
47:2		3:6		3:5→3:6 Lesser Causal Vehicle	Upper Manas (5)		Conceptual Mind	Creates link between	by means of a series	Life	Precognition
47:3	Mental-Causal Consciousness	3:5		Causal Substance	Manas (5)		Objective Thinking	high & low selves	of lower selves	Unifying Awareness	Brow Chakra
47:4		3:4	Mental & Causal	3:4 Mental	Higher Mental (2)	NESHAMAH	3:4 Mental Molecule	1st Triad consists of	The Conscious Mind	3:4 Mental Intuition	Throat Chakra
47:5		3:3		3:1→3:4 Mental Vehicle	Lower Manas (5)	The Higher	Intellectual Mind	47:4 etheric mental	Systems Thinker	3:3 Perspeictve Thinking	Perception
47:6		3:2		Mental Substance	Lower Mental (2)	Unconsious	Subjective Thinking	molecule, 48:1	Creates Thought Forms	3:2 Principle Thinking	Telepathy & Clairvoyance
47:7		3:1		5 Dimensions	Egyptian KHU		Mental Aura	emotional atom, and	of mental & astral sub.	3:1 Deductive Thinking	Active psychic reception
48:1		2:7		2:7 Astral (emotional)	Emotional (2)		2:7 Emotional Atom		Sensation	Feeling	Heart Chakra
48:2		2:6	Etheric, Astral,	1:1→1:6 Astral Vehicle	Kama:Rupa (5)		and all Seven Chakras		Reaction	2:6 Positive Emotions	Omnipresence
48:3	Astral (Emotional) Consciousness	2:5		Vehicle of Desire	Spirit Body	RUACH	Devas (Angels)			2:5 Positive Emotions	Astral Substance is used
48:4		2:4	The Field of the HUMAN AURA		Dream Body	The Middle	Spirit Guides			3:4 Neutral Emotions	to create thought forms
48:5		2:3			Desire Body	Consciousness	Nature Spirits	The First Self	Directly relates to	3:3 Negative Emotions	
48:6		2:2		Astral Substance/Astral Light	The Animal Soul		Elementals		the subconscious	3:2 Negative Emotions	Out-of-Body Experience
48:7		2:1		4 Dimensions	Egyptian BA		Astral Aura		mind & memories	3:1 Negative Emotions	Passive psychic reception
49:1		1:7		1:7 Physical/Etheric	Etheric (2)	Nephesh	1:7 Physical Atom	Atomic	Receives & dis-	Subjective Awareness	All Seven Chakras and
49:2		1:6		1:4→1:6 Etheric Double	Energy Body	The Lower		Sub:atomic	tributes Prana via	The link between	three Currents
49:3	Physical Consciousness	1:5		1:4→1:6 I etheric template	Linga:Sharira (5)	Unconscious		Super:etheric	chakras & meridians	Inner & Outer	
49:4		1:4		forming the physical body	Egyptian KA		Etheric Aura	Etheric	for healh & healing	physical senses	Energy Healing
49:5		1:3		1:1→1:3 Physical Body	Physical (2)	Vehicle of Thought,	Acts, moves & senses	Gaseous	Acts. Moves & Senses in	5-7 Objective Consciousness	Base Chakra
49:6		1:2		Physical Substance	Sthula-Sharira (5)	Feeling, and	in the Physical	Liquid	the Physical Universe		
49:7		1:1		3 Dimensions	Action Body	Awareness	Universe	Solid		Autonomic System	Physical Brain
↓		↑								Deep Unconscious (?)	
										Unknown	

Notes for Figure 1—Seven Levels of Reality

"Names" for esoteric matters are a challenge as different writers have named things differently, and sometimes rather loosely naming two different things with the identical words.

While we have made a fundamental change by referring to "Levels" rather than the older, more familiar "Planes, "we have otherwise continued with those names that are more familiar for the three lower levels (or worlds) and those used by Henry Laurency (a modern esoteric) for the four upper ones. As a means to relate these names to other writings, we have included several alternatives in Column 6, with reference to their sources in the list below.

In addition, we have included two different numbering systems—"Involution" developed by Laurency and "Evolution" by Lee Bladon as a further method of bringing definition to a very complex matter. It may be more confusing than helpful at first, but as you work with the system we believe it will actually become more helpful and bring order out of chaos.

As explanation, the "Cosmic Involution" numbering scale in column 3 is *looking downward* from the beginning of creation to completion of "Reality." The "Solar Evolution" scale in column 4 is *looking upward* as "Consciousness" evolves through its various self-created forms and "selves."

It should be understood that, in reality, these Levels or Worlds are not spatial and do not exist as rigidly distinct layers above one another, nor around a central core. Rather, they are better thought of as "vibratory states" existing within a whole.

There is a distinct division marked by a "black belt" between the three lower levels and the four higher ones. It is the lower "Kingdoms" that provide the "field of operations" for humanity. It is highly unlikely that any of us (present readers and authors) will experience these higher levels or knowingly encounter any beings from them.

It must also be noted that the *nature* of the lower seven sub-planes—solid, liquid, gaseous, etheric, etc.—repeats in every level upward *according to the nature* of that level's own substance.

References for Names and Alternative Names:

1. Bladon, Lee. *The Science of Spirituality,* 2007, www.esotericscience.org

2. Laurency, Henry T. *The Knowledge of Reality,* 1979, Henry T. Laurency Publishing Foundation, www.laurency.com

3. Harris, Philip S. (Editor).*Theosophical Encyclopedia,* 2006, Theosophical Publishing House, Quezon City, Philippines.

4. Theosophy as included in Bladon (1) above.

5. Sanskrit as included in Bladon (1) above.

Notes for Figure 2, Seven Levels of Consciousness

Please refer to the notes for Figure 1 for explanation regarding the levels, sub-divisions, and numbering system. Since we are concerned primarily with the evolving consciousness it is the upward Solar Scale of numbering used in explaining details of relationships.

It is difficult to provide so much information in tabular form, yet it is a desirable presentation of the relationships between the various subtle vehicles (or "bodies") used by evolving consciousness and their functions that make up the total human person—both as presently active and as the potential for our awakening with growth and development. In reality, *very few people have any activity—as yet—above the Causal Soul* level. This separation is clearly indicated by a "black belt" between the third and fourth levels.

In other words, the reality is that a human person is really a unity of five vehicles/bodies—physical through causal—and those who have evolved to being active in higher vehicles are best thought of as "super-human" or simply as "evolved beings."

It should be understood that, in reality, the subtle vehicles are not spatial and do not exist rigidly separate from one another, not in layers above one another nor around a central core. It is also important to realize that there are no specific borders between vehicles but rather focused divisions of consciousness. Rather, they are better thought of as "vibratory states" existing within a whole. However, the image of the "higher" containing a "lower" is useful.

In particular, it should be noted that the boundaries between *Neshamah, Ruach,* and *Nephesh* in the Hebrew Kabbalah, column No. 6, overlap considerably and often function as a unity—the Personal Ego—over which our growth should lead to its domination by the Causal Body. (General source, but not a quote: Bladon, Lee: *The Science of Spirituality,* 2007, www.esotericscience.org.)

The Causal, Essential, and Lower Superessential vehicles function together as the unity, *Chiah,* that we can call the Higher Self, and sometimes the "Soul" although that term is also used in relation to the Causal Body alone.

There are physical inter-relationships between the physical/etheric body and the Chakras, particular physical organs and the physical brain:

Etheric Double 1:4 to 1:6 is linked to the Basal Brain (Reptilian Brain providing instinctive responses, including fear or anger, fight/flight, sexual arousal and the autonomic system).

Astral Vehicle 2:1 to 2:6 is linked to the Limbic System (Mammalian Brain for emotions, feelings, love, relationships).

Lower division of the Mental Vehicle 3:1 to 3:2 is linked to the brain's Left Hemisphere (intelligence, logical analysis & planning, memory, and concrete thinking).

Higher division of the Mental Vehicle 3:3 to 3:4 is linked to the brain's Right Hemisphere (creativity, ideas, imagination, concepts and abstract thinking).

(General source, but not a quote: Bladon, Lee: *The Science of Spirituality*, 2007, www.esotericscience.org.)

The Upper Superessential, Submanifestal, and Lower Manifestal Vehicles also function as the unity, *Yechidah*, also called the Divine Self or Spirit.

In terms of the Kabbalah's Sephiroth:

Tiphareth, Netzach, Hod, Yesod, and *Malkuth* form the "First Self" that incarnates into a physical body for which *Tiphareth* then is the "Soul" for most humans.

Daath, Chesed, Geburah, and *Tiphareth* form the "Second Self" for which *Daath* is Spirit, and the "Soul" for humans who have advanced to become "adepts" and "masters." (Please note these are <u>not</u> so-titled members of magical, esoteric or Masonic orders, but souls beyond the need to physically incarnate, but who may do so in service to the Great Plan.)

Kether, Chokmah, Briah, and *Daath* form the "Third Self" for which Kether us the Monad and "Soul" of those souls who function mainly in the Divine and Monadic worlds, but who may incarnate in service to the Great Plan.

(General source, but not a quote: Bladon, Lee: *The Science of Spirituality*, 2007, www.esotericscience.org.)

Also note the following:
1. Experience & Memories from previous incarnations flow from the Subconsciousness to the Causal Soul where they are abstracted & permanently retained.
2. There is constant interaction between the three lower bodies/vehicles (Physical/ Etheric, Emotional or Astral, & Mental) and the Lesser Causal Vehicle which abstracts Life Experiences into permanent Lessons retained by the Greater Causal SOUL.
3. The Human Being is a unity of the five vehicles (Physical, Etheric, Astral, Mental & Causal) evolving independently to be absorbed into the consciousness of the Monad.
4. The Lower Self, also called the "Persona," is the "First Triad" and consists of the 3:4 Mental Molecule, 2:7 Emotional Atom, and 1:7 Physical Atom.

5. The Higher Self is the "Second Triad," or Soul, and consists of the 5:4 Superessential Molecule, 4:7 Essential Atom, and 3:7 Mental Atom.

6. The Divine Self is the "Third Triad," or Spirit, and consists of the 7:4 Manifestal Molecule, 6:7 Submanifestal Atom, and 5:7 Superessential Atom.

7. The Self is the Monad and is embedded in the 7:7 Manifestal Atom.

Another important concept, which we decided not to incorporate into this Figure 2, is that of the sub-divisions making up the Subconsciousness: 1:1 to 1:6, 2:1 to 2:4, and 3:1 to 3:2, while the Superconsciousness is made up of sub-divisions 2:5 to 2:6, 3:3 to 3:4, and 3:5 to 3:7. The Conscious, Objective Mind, is present at 1:1 to 1:3—which may seem surprising until you realize all objective awareness has to be expressed at the material level.

Main Resources:

1. Bladon, Lee: *The Science of Spirituality,* 2007, www.esotericscience.org

2. Laurency, Henry T. : *The Knowledge of Reality,* 1979, Henry T. Laurency Publishing Foundation, www.laurency.com.

3. The nature of all seven bodies and their sub-divisions repeats in every one in relation to the nature of substance and consciousness.

4. Harris, Philip S. (Editor): *Theosophical Encyclopedia,* 2006, Theosophical Publishing House, Quezon City, Philippines.

5. Theosophy as included in Bladon (1) above.

6. Sanskrit as included in Bladon (1) above.

Other Sources:

Editor unknown: *A Working Glossary for the Use of Students of Theosophical Literature,* 1910, New York, John Lane Company.

CHAPTER ONE
Clairvoyance in Everyday Life

It happens all the time

Clairvoyance, ESP, Telepathy, Precognition, even Psychokinesis (PK), all can and do happen spontaneously when unrelated events happen sequentially. But, mostly we don't acknowledge it—calling it "just a coincidence," or something even less flattering.

You think of an old friend, and very soon after you receive a phone call or mail from your friend, or news about him or her. You live in one part of the country and a friend or associate lives in another; while traveling to a different location than either of you, casually think of that person and purely by chance bump into him or her while relaxing in a hotel bar. While reading a book or newspaper you have a sudden premonition of an event that does happen the following day. While looking for misplaced car keys, suddenly they are there where you know you had looked previously. You think of your spouse and wish he or she would bring home Chinese take-out dinner, and an hour later there it is.

Not a Coincidence

It's not a coincidence but a genuine case of spontaneous clairvoyance. By denying that simple fact and calling it something else, you deny yourself the opportunity to develop this natural power into a practical skill, and at the same time deny yourself the great opportunity to actually extend your field of awareness into non-physical "higher" dimensions.

Clairvoyance is an innate psychic power—*you were born with it!—And so were we all.* But in today's culture it's rarely recognized or developed. And clairvoyance is just one, but one of the most important, innate psychic powers whose development will enrich and empower everyday lives.

Or, to think of it another way, psychic powers are a manifestation of the greater consciousness unfolding in all humanity at this very critical—and particularly opportune—time. We are challenged to play an increasingly active role in social, economic, and political events in our community, and that community is becoming global. We cannot act intelligently without broader understanding of the external factors and increased awareness of the inner side that clairvoyance, in particular of these psychic powers, enables.

For convenience, some refer to this manifestation as the development of "higher consciousness," but that qualifier has misleading connotations suggesting the people who demonstrate psychic abilities are more "spiritual" and morally better than other people. Perhaps they are, but psychic abilities are not proof of that any more that superior math skills prove a person to be a greater spiritual being.

It takes Development

Many people are born with one or another wonderful talent, but even the best natural talent can become better with development, with training and practice. Even those of us who lack great birth talents can learn and develop chosen skills—perhaps not as great as those with a born head-start, but that all depends on effort and determination.

The need for development programs and procedures is even greater in the case of paranormal abilities because they have been generally placed outside of "normal" abilities and everyday expectations and instead seen in context with Religious beliefs, secret magickal orders, or the romance of wandering Gypsies, turbaned yogis, and recluses living in mountain caves or wandering in deserts.

Paranormal skills can be developed through training and practice just like other skills and talents. Born artists and musicians benefit from professional training, and it is a loss to both the individual and to "the Race"—to society and to the genetic pool that benefits future generations—when such native talents are neglected. But, beyond these "special needs," our everyday educational programs lack exposure not only to art and music but to the "arts" in general, to the sciences, to logic and the rules of thinking, and to the basics of law, economics, geography, technology, astronomy, politics, history, and to philosophy and comparative religion. These are all important to the contemporary demand from the increasing responsibilities of intelligent and informed citizenship in democratic societies and to basic abilities needed in any career choices. "Contemporary Public Education" is generally out of step with these needs.

There are "traditional" developmental methods for psychic empowerment and new programs resulting from the progressive research procedures at Athens State University and the cross application of established techniques of hypnosis and self-hypnosis, meditative procedures, and the Active Imagination method developed by Carl Jung. In addition, studies in non-deific religious and shamanic practices have suggested alternatives now being explored by holistic psychologists and individual practitioners.

Indeed, pioneering psychologists and "motivation" specialists have adapted various paranormal practices for modern business and professional training and management techniques—including Creative Visualization practices in marketing work and motivational seminars, Sensitivity Training in sales and customer service, the Group Mind in Executive Committees, Mental Telepathy and Creative Thought Forms in conference planning, and more.

Even the many activities now centered on the Internet have freed people to think <u>beyond "physical" barriers</u> and limitations in ways that unconsciously awaken paranormal abilities and functions.

The New Science of the Paranormal

"Paranormal" is a familiar word representing all psychic abilities and phenomena—from astral projection and aura reading to zoomantic divination and a lot in between. Because words like "abilities," "powers," and "skills" each have particular attributions when used with "psychic," where possible we will use the more neutral "paranormal" as either noun or adjective in our discussion. Thus, even "paranormal powers" carries less "baggage" (i.e. extra meanings) than "psychic powers," which call up images and associations from history, literature, religious writings, etc., that are often far from neutral!

We likewise prefer referring to "the Paranormal" than relating to "Parapsychology," which too often reduces the empowering paranormal to statistical abstractions that ignore emotion, intention, and even physiological factors relating to real world factors in their manifestation. Human beings are not just powerful and beautiful physical bodies with a magnificent brain but are complex, multi-dimensional beings, and—unfortunately—much of the old research in parapsychology labs did everything possible to isolate the physical from non-physical where the *paranormal* (by definition) happens.

The "New Science of the Paranormal" has grown out of the advanced and humanistic research programs led by Dr. Slate at Athens State University and furthered under the influence of the Parapsychology Research Institute & Foundation (PRIF). These programs have involved participants engaged in real-life paranormal activities rather than theoretical abstractions; activities that—even under true scientific controls—maintain human factors of feeling, thinking, and even normal physiological responses often suppressed in those older research programs dependent on "machine" measurements and interpretations.

Along with laboratory-based research programs, reports of paranormal experiences outside the lab were given equal respect and scientific analysis as those conducted within the labs. In other words, your common, everyday paranormal experiences are given recognition as "real" and not "just your imagination." As a result, practical technologies leading to paranormal experiences and the development of innate paranormal powers have been realized. Many of these technologies make use of self-hypnosis, thus enabling an individual to have full control of the development and application of the paranormal skills in everyday life.

What is Clairvoyance?

Clairvoyance is psychic phenomena traditionally defined as *the perception of tangible objects, current events, or existing conditions not present to the physical senses, but nevertheless having objective reality.* Unlike mental telepathy, in particular, clairvoyance functions independently of another mind, except in instances of collective clairvoyance during which the clairvoyant faculties of two or more persons are combined to more deeply perceive existing realities.

Although there is a long history of shamanic practices and religious rituals used to induce visions often associated with out-of-body experiences, clairvoyance is not specifically dependent upon such intense stimulation of sensory mechanisms, and—at the same time—is not seen as subject to the limitations of conventional sensory experience.

Right Brain/Left Brain

20th Century Science made many substantial advances in understanding the physiology of the human brain in relation to modes of *thinking* and *feeling*—the two fundamental characteristics of conscious activities. Of course, we must always work from the premise that the brain is not the source of consciousness but the instrument we use in the physical world to perceive and interact with material reality.

Without delving into the amazing complexity of the human brain, including the functions of each of the main structures, and the roles of pituitary and pineal glands to be discussed later, we recognize that there is a major "split" between the left and right hemispheres that is bridged by filament of tissue called the *corpus callosum* which allows the two halves to synthesize their functions so that we do utilize our Whole Brain in every moment we are alive.

But, each hemisphere involves major differences: physiologically, the left hemisphere relates to the right side of the body, and the right hemisphere to the left side. (From this point on, we are going to refer to these hemispheres as **Left Brain** and **Right Brain** because that terminology has become common and is directly applicable.) This may not seem important, but *right*-handedness relates to the Left Brain and this simple fact has enormous ramifications that simply should be kept in the background of your awareness as we continue the discussion.

The most important aspect of this 20th century discovery is that the Left and Right Brains "think" differently, and that the culture in which we live influences the way in which one or the other becomes dominant. And we now know that Western Culture is primarily Left Brain dominant as the result of our educational and cultural specializations that are both cause and effect.

The Coming, Whole Brain, Global Culture

Western Culture—which is rapidly becoming a Global Culture because of the pervasive roles of Mass Entertainment, International Communications networks, shared Technology, and World Economics—is Objectively based on Numbers, Facts, and Logic (mostly commonly expressed as *Common Sense*). Eastern Cultures, *until recently*, and what we tend to call "indigenous" and "third world" cultures, are subjectively based more on Metaphor, Symbol, and Feelings. And, more to the point in understanding historic differences as well as at least some of the contemporary world problems: Western culture has been and is centered on the "individual" person while Eastern culture has been centered more on communal and holistic "unity."

Why is this important to our study and practice of Clairvoyance? Part of what we've learned is that Right Brained people tend to more naturally psychic and to more easily develop their paranormal abilities. There is no value judgment in this recognition but it does provide opportunities for understanding a particular aspect of consciousness that we can adapt to in everyday awareness that itself can be developmental.

We must remember, however, that we really are *Whole Brained* people, and in consciously adapting to the characteristics of Right or Left brained functions, we are able to balance them with our dominant "other half." Such balance is—itself—a worthy and healthy goal that is part of our broadened everyday life, and would be a natural accomplishment of responsible contemporary education.

At the same time, if we want to increase our paranormal sensitivities we can deliberately adopt one or more Right Brain characteristic activities as described in the table on page 24. You could, for example, set out to learn Hebrew or even just to chant Hebrew phrases and mantras, read more fantasy literature, find ways to "enjoy the moment," and even practice doing things with your left hand. Note, of course, that some of the specific examples are just that, examples—there are other Right Brain languages than Hebrew, and other Left Brain languages than English.

Table of Basic Functions Characteristic of the Two Brain Halves
(Partially adapted from *The ESP Enigma* by Diane Powell, M.D., 2009, Walker & Co.)

LEFT BRAIN	RIGHT BRAIN
More often Right handed	More often Left handed
Cortex	Limbic System
Objective	Subjective
Logic-based	Feeling-based
Numbers	Symbols
Facts	Imagination
Serial or Linear Processing	Parallel Processing
Vertical Connections	Horizontal Connections
Reality	Fantasy
Literal Meanings	Metaphors
Speech	Perception
Language, Syntax, Semantics	Sounds, patterns, context
English	Hebrew
Reading Left to Right	Reading Right to Left
Physical Sciences & Math	Psychology & Philosophy
Looks to the Details	Looks for the Big Picture
Purpose-directed	Enjoying-the-moment
Strategies	Possibilities
Valuing the Individual	Valuing the Group
Dominant Neurotransmitters are Dopamine & Acetylcholine	Dominant Neurotransmitter is Norepinephrine
Running, Competitive Sports	Chanting, Dancing, Drumming
High Sound frequencies	Low Sound Frequencies
Daytime—any time	13:30 Local Sidereal Time

Every Day in Every Way

It is with a conscious and fundamental *Open-Mindedness* that we "invite" personal growth including paranormal development. As we've emphasized elsewhere, as human beings we are still "unfinished." Evolution did not come to a standstill when modern man replaced Neanderthal man 35,000 years ago.

Most people don't care to admit it, and religious institutions, and even some scientists, refuse to acknowledge even the possibility, but a thoughtful look at history and archaeology raises many questions and probable examples of evolutionary developments even in such short time-spans as a few hundred years, and more so in regular cycles of approximately 2,000 years.

Some astrologers suggest that we get a subtle evolutionary "kick in the pants" with every solar egress into a new zodiacal sign (the 2,000-year cycle), such as the one into the Aquarian Age that we are currently undergoing, and a more substantial one every 25,000 years or so on completion of the entire zodiacal cycle.

The concept of reincarnation likewise is evolutionary, as are the fundamental beliefs and practices of esoteric schools, training temples, "secret" orders, magickal lodges, and individual teachers.

Individual development, growth, and progress are matched with the progress of all mankind ("the Race"). Each person has a responsibility to serve all.

Clairvoyance is More!

Clairvoyance is far more than just the perception of realities not otherwise available to ordinary sensory awareness. It is one of the most significant of paranormal powers as can be easily demonstrated by its many "faces," some of which are listed in the following analytical table:

Analytical Tables of Clairvoyant & Divinatory Practices:
Direct Psychic Perception of an event, object, or person
(mostly contemporary) external to and hidden from the observer,
including:

Clairalience—*the smelling of odors without a physical source that provides some kind of insight.*

Clairaudience—*the hearing of sounds and voices without a present physical source that either provides information or messages.*

Claircognizance—*knowing without reference to a physical source, sometimes experienced as a "hunch."*

Clairgustance—*tasting without a physical source that provides a stimulus leading to some kind of insight.*

Clairsentience—*the acquisition of knowledge through the feeling and touching of an object or contact with an organic substance or part of a person or other creature.*

Clairvoyance—*"clear seeing," i.e. the perception of information without the use of physical senses and sometimes knowledge not limited to the physical dimension.*

ESP—*"ExtraSensory Perception"—basically an alternate expression for clairvoyance clearly indicating something "extra" to ordinary physical senses.*

Futurology—*predicting the future based on present conditions through ExtraSensory means.*

Precognition—*ExtraSensory perception of events that will occur in the future.*

Premonition—*warning of a future disaster through ExtraSensory means.*

Psychometry—*reading the history of an object, in particular its association with humans.*

Remote Viewing—*direct ExtraSensory perception of events at locations remote from the viewer.*

Retrocognition—*perceiving events that occurred in the past, often leading to a better understanding of present circumstances.*

Direct Psychic Perception by means of Altered States of Consciousness:

Dream Interpretation—*while often associated with the use of a "dream dictionary," it really involves methods of allowing the dream "to speak" to the dreamer.*

Oracles—*making contact with spirits or gods usually at a special location often associated with unusual environment conditions and a dedicated person in trance.*

Ouija—*while commonly used as entertainment, the proper use would be to enter into a trance and let the planchette spell out messages on the board printed with the alphabet and numbers.*

Prophecy—*revelation about the future, often ostensibly from a spiritual presence or deity.*

Shamanic techniques—*deliberate repression or excessive stimulation of the physical senses through various techniques of Ecstatic or Exhaustive Dancing, Fasting, Sleep Deprivation, Bondage, Isolation, Flagellation, Psychoactive Drugs, Drumming, Sexual or Physical Exhaustion, etc.*

Theomancy—*receiving messages or answers to questions through an oracle or direct contact with Deity.*

Direct Psychic Perception by means of Extended Consciousness:

Astral Projection—*intentional acquisition of information while Out-of-Body using the astral vehicle.*

Aura Reading—*perception and interpretation of the auric field usually involving some degree of etheric or even auric vision.*

Etheric Projection—*projection, or more communally, extension of part of the etheric vehicle (sometimes perceived as ectoplasm) to obtain information by touch or to move objects.*

Intuition—*a somewhat vague term for a non-verbal "feeling" message from the Higher Self.*

Mental Projection—*projection of the mental vehicle. (It should be clarified that all projections involve more than just the etheric, or just the astral, or just the mental vehicle but rather are inclusive, with each having one substance and level of consciousness that is predominant.)*

Indirect Psychic Perception through another person or entity:

Animal Communication—*most often a form of Mental Telepathy by which information is transmitted between the animal and a human generally by uncharacteristic behavior.*

Automatic Writing *(aka* **Autography** *and* **Psychography***)—unconscious written communication involving a spirit while the writer is in a trance.*

Mental Telepathy—*contact and exchange of information with another person.*

Projection of a Familiar—*this is a variation of etheric projection in which a Thought Form of an animal or person is created from etheric and astral substance under direction of the projector—either with a single duty "charge," or a longer-term duty charge. It is sometimes called "indirect psychic spying" in contrast to Remote Viewing.*

Sciomancy—*communication through a spirit guide who, generally, appears spontaneously.*

Spirit Communication—*contact with "spirits" of the deceased or other entities most often through a person acting as a "Medium" or "Channel" under the direction or "Control" of a Spirit Guide.*

Telesthesia—*indirect psychic awareness of a distant condition or happening involving a person related to the receiver.*

Augmented Psychic Perception by means of Divinatory Tools:

Dowsing (see also **Radiesthesia**)—*the use of a forked stick or bent steel clothes hanger or other metallic imitation of the forked stick in order to sense the presence of water or other resource or lost object. The instrument moves in the dowser's hands when he or she walks over the searched-for substance believed to radiate a perceptive energy.*

Handwriting Analysis—aka **Graphology** *and* **Graphoanalysis**—*measurement and interpretation of size, shape, spacing, impression, and other factors of handwriting, including most particularly signatures, the personal pronoun "I", and also doodles.*

Pendulum Work (Radiesthesia) aka **Divining, Dowsing, Water Witching**—*using a pendulum instead of a rod to determine the location of water or other resource, and also to respond to questions.*

Related techniques include:

Cleidomancy or **Clidomancy**: *using a key attached to a cord or string.*

Coscinomancy or **Cosquinomancy**: *using a sieve suspended from shears or tongs.*

Dactylomancy or **Dactlomancy**: *using a suspended ring.*

Rhabdomancy: *by using a stick or rod.*

Scrying—*seeing a vision while gazing into a transparent, translucent, or reflective object, inducing a mild trance. Such objects include:*

> <u>Crystal ball gazing</u>
>
> <u>Crystal gazing</u>
>
> <u>Fire Scrying</u>
>
> <u>Ink Scrying</u>
>
> <u>Mirror Scrying</u>
>
> <u>Smoke Scrying</u>
>
> <u>Water Scrying</u>
>
> <u>Wine Scrying</u>

Tea Leaf Reading—*interpreting the shapes, size and patterns of wet tea leaves either by inspiration or a special dictionary of symbols. Similar practices include:*

> <u>Coffee Ground Reading</u>
>
> <u>Egg Yolk Reading</u>
>
> <u>Strewn Rice Reading</u>
>
> <u>Wine Sediment Reading</u>

Augmented Psychic Perception by means of manually manipulated complex Symbolic Divination Systems with established rules and meanings:

<u>Cartomancy</u>—*using a deck or ordinary bridge or poker playing cards.*

<u>Geomancy</u>—*interpreting dots, lines and figures traced in sand, dirt or pebbles, or naturally occurring formations either intuitively or by standard meanings. It is a divinatory system prominently used by Golden Dawn magicians and with variants employed throughout Africa and parts of the Arabian Peninsula.*

<u>I Ching</u> aka <u>Yi King</u>—*the casting of sticks or coins to establish 64 Hexagrams each consisting of six solid or broken lines. The I Ching is the oldest and most universal system of Chinese divination originating at the very foundation of Taoism.*

<u>Oghams</u>, aka the <u>Celtic Tree Alphabet</u>—*a series of sticks marked with cuts to represent each letter of the Tree Alphabet, and then thrown and selected randomly for divinatory interpretation.*

<u>Runes</u>—*similar to, but older and more complex than Oghams and based on a very rich mythic system of Nordic/Teutonic mythology giving definition to each image. Runes are used both in divination and in magic (as charms and spells). Runes should be ranked with Tarot Cards for their symbolic interpretation and magical use.*

<u>Tarot Cards</u>—*a complex deck of 78 cards illustrated with symbols and images associated with the Hebrew and Greek Kabbalah. The Tarot is the most popular and important divinatory system in the Western world.*

Augmented Psychic Perception associated with Scientific Measurable Physical Phenomena:

<u>Astrology</u>—*the most scientific system for determining the value and meaning of "the moment" by measuring the celestial positions of the Sun, Moon, Planets, and sometimes of the fixed stars and asteroids and the appearance of comets in relation to exact "birth locations" on Earth. The resultant pattern is cast as a wheel, the horoscope, and interpreted through long established meaning based on thousands of years of observation and logical associations. The time and place of birth sets the "plan" and meaning for the life of a person, event, corporate or other legal entity, while changes to the celestial positions (transits) in relation to the birth horoscope will forecast coming events.*

<u>Cheiromancy</u>—see <u>Palmistry</u> (aka <u>Palm Reading</u>)

<u>Gematria</u>—*Each letter of the Hebrew alphabet has a numeric value representing a different creative force. When the numeric values of the letters in particular words, names and phrases are calculated it is assumed that words, names and phrases with the same*

numeric value have associated or equivalent meanings. Those values and meanings may be found in Kabalistic dictionaries and are employed in divination, prayer and magic.

Numerology (aka **Arithmancy**)—*a system of somewhat arbitrary assignment of numbers to the letters of the alphabet by which names and birthdates are given meaningful interpretation.*

Palmistry—*Like Astrology, Palmistry is more a scientific system of divination than it is psychic—nevertheless the psychic faculties always supplement the scientific reading. Palmistry is the science of the reading and interpretation of lines and shapes in the hand, often using detailed measurements of proportionate length, width, depth, and angles of the lines and apparent symbols. The system has been extended to include the proportionate length and width of the thumb and fingers, their flexibility, lines on the knuckles, and the shapes and lines in the fingernails (also called Onychomancy when treated separately from the palm).*

Pegomancy—see Palmistry

Common types of Divination involving extended psychic awareness

The following is just a selection of many divinatory systems, basically demonstrating the point that anything can be manipulated and "read" because the real meaning is found not in the object but in intentional human consciousness. In most cases, the "reading" is accompanied by a light state of trance. In some, but not all systems, there are established "dictionary" meanings. Further information may be found in the on-line *Llewellyn's Paranormal, Magical & Occult Encyclopedia.*

Types of Divination involving extended psychic awareness

Aeromancy—*interpreting atmospheric and related phenomena, such as perceived images in clouds, and also:*

Austromancy—*interpretation of winds.*

Ceraunoscopy and **Keraunomancy**—*interpretation of thunder & lightning.*

Chaomancy—*Sky Visions*

Meteromancy—*Shooting Stars*

Alectormancy, Alectromancy, Alectryomancy—*observing birds, usually a rooster, pick through scattered grains, and noting sequentially when the bird crows signifying a letter of the alphabet. If the rooster pecks at three grains and then crows it denotes the third letter: "c"*

Aleuromancy—*messages are written on paper and then inserted into units of dough that are then baked, such as Fortune Cookies that will be selected at random.*

Alomancy or **Halomancy**—*interpreting images drawn in spilled salt or dry sand.*

Alphitomancy, also called **"Cursed Bread"**—*if a person has indigestion after eating a loaf of barley bread, he or she will be judged guilty of a crime. A similar irrational tradition involved tying a Witch (always a woman in that historic period) and throwing her in water. If she drowned, she was presumed guilty; if she survived, it was sometimes said it was by supernatural force, so again it proved guilt.*

Amniomancy—*interpreting the caul (the part of the placenta remaining on the head) at a baby's birth.*

Anthropomancy, **Antinpomancy**, **Splanchomancy**—*interpreting the entrails of a human sacrifice.*

Apantomancy—*interpreting the chance encounter with an object, animal or person, such as a black cat crossing your path*

Arithmancy—*Divination using numbers, including:*

    Gematria—*interpreting Hebrew bible passages by assigned numeric values to letters of the Hebrew Alphabet*

    Numerology—*dates and words (often birthdates and names) are converted into numbers sequentially identified with the alphabet, and interpreted by a number dictionary.*

Aruspicy, **Extispicy**, **Haruspicy**—*interpreting the entrails of a sacrificed animal.*

Astragalamancy, **Astragalomancy**, **Astragyromancy**, **Cleromancy**—*interpreting dice casts by number associations.*

Axinomancy—*throwing an axe and observing the direction of the handle.*

Belomancy, **Bolomancy**—*shooting, tossing, or balancing an arrow, and interpreting what is observed.*

Bibliomancy or **Stichomancy**—*reading or interpreting randomly chosen passages in books, most often religious books. Also:*

    Rhapsodomancy—*Using a book of poetry.*

Botanomancy—*interpreting burning or burned leaves or branches.*

Brontoscopy—*interpreting the sound of thunder.*

Capnomancy—*interpreting rising smoke.*

Causimomancy—*observing changes in objects placed in a fire.*

Ceromancy and **Ceroscopy**—*interpreting shapes taken by melted wax poured into water.*

Cledomancy—*interpreting random events and statements.*

Crithomancy and **Critomancy**—*interpreting sacrificial cakes and breads.*

Cromniomancy—*interpreting the sprouting behavior of onions.*

Cybermancy—*divination through a computer.*

Cyclomancy—*interpreting the revolutions of a spinning bottle.*

Daphnomancy—*interpreting a burning laurel branch.*

Dendromancy—*divination by oak or mistletoe.*

Fractomancy—*interpreting the structure of fractal patterns.*

Geloscopy—*interpreting the sound or manner of laughter.*

Gyromancy—*walking or twirling around in a circle marked with letters until one is dizzy and stumbles or falls, thus spelling a prophetic message.*

Hepatoscopy, **Hepatomancy**—*interpreting the liver of a sacrificial animal.*

Hieromancy and **Hieroscopy**—*interpreting burnt offerings or ritually slaughtered animals.*

Hydromancy—*interpreting of water by color, ripples, and is ebb and flow, including:*

Hydatoscopy—*interpreting rainwater.*

Lecanomancy—*interpreting the sounds or the ripples as stones are dropped into water.*

Pegomancy—*interpretation of waters of sacred springs, wells, pools, or fountains.*

Ichthyomancy—*interpreting the behavior, or the entrails, or fish.*

Lampadomancy—*interpreting the flame of a candle, torch, or lamp.*

Libranomancy or **Livanomancy**—*by interpreting the smoke made by burning incense.*

Lithomancy—*divination with crystal or gems by their reflected light or their placement when cast.*

Lychnomancy—*interpreting the flames of three candles.*

Metoposcopy—*interpreting the lines and wrinkles of the forehead.*

Moleoscophy—*interpreting the moles of the body.*

Molybdomancy—*interpreting the hissing sounds as molten lead, or tin, when dropped into water.*

Oculomancy—*interpreting the eye, also*

Iridology—*interpreting the iris of the eye.*

Oenomancy or **Oinomancy**—*interpreting wine.*

Omphalomancy—*Interpreting the shape of the first born's navel, or the knots in the umbilical cord to determine the number of children that a mother will have in her lifetime.*

Onomancy—*the interpretation of names.*

Oomancy, Ooscopy, Ovomancy—*divination with eggs.*

Pedomancy—*by interpreting the impression made by a footprint.*

Phyllorhodomancy—*interpreting the sound made by slapping a rose petal against the hand.*

Physiognomy—*reading a person's character by interpreting the facial features.*

Podomancy—*by interpreting the lines and details of feet.*

Premonition—*A warning of a future event, typically an accident or disaster.*

Prophecy—*A vision or revelation of the future, typically provided by a deity.*

Psychomancy—*Soul Reading, perceiving a person's values and beliefs*

Pyromancy—*by watching fire*

Pyroscopy—*by burning paper*

Scapulimancy, Scapulomancy, Patulamancy—*interpreting the cracks in the burned shoulder bones of an animal*

Scatamancy—*interpreting excrement*

Schematomancy—*observing and interpreting the face.*

Selenomancy—*interpreting the appearance and phase of the moon.*

Sideromancy—*by placing straws on a hot iron and observing the resulting shapes.*

Spasmatomancy—*interpreting convulsions*

Spatalamancy—*interpreting skin, bone, or excrement:*

Spatilomancy—*interpreting animal excrement*

Spodomancy—*by interpreting ashes, cinders, or soot*

Stareomancy—*interpreting the classical elements of wind, water, earth, or fire.*

Sternomancy—*interpreting the marks or bumps on the solar plexus (breast to belly).*

Stolisomancy—*interpreting a person's style of dress*

Sycomancy—*by writing a question on a leaf and observing how quickly the leaf dries.*

Tephramancy—*by interpreting the ashes of burnt tree bark.*

Tiromancy—*by interpreting the holes in cheese.*

Transataumancy—*by accidentally seeing or hearing.*

Trochomancy—*by interpreting wheel ruts or tracks.*

Uromancy or **Urimancy**—*by interpreting the appearance of urine.*

<u>Urticariaomancy</u>—*by the location of an itch (e.g. your palms itch, you'll get money or your nose itches, someone is thinking about you).*

<u>Water Witching</u>—see Dowsing.

<u>Xenomancy</u>—*by interpreting meetings with strangers.*

<u>Xylomancy</u>—*by interpreting burning wood.*

<u>Zoomancy</u>—*interpreting the appearance and behavior of animals, including:*

> <u>Ailuromancy</u>—*interpreting the behavior of cats.*
>
> <u>Entomancy</u>—*interpreting the behavior of insects.*
>
> <u>Arachnomancy</u>—*interpreting the behavior of spiders.*
>
> <u>Myrmomancy</u>—*interpreting the behavior of ants.*
>
> <u>Skatharomancy</u>—*interpreting a beetle's tracks.*
>
> <u>Hippomancy</u>—*interpreting the behavior of horses.*
>
> <u>Myomancy</u>—*interpreting the behavior of mice and rats.*
>
> <u>Ophiomancy</u>—*interpreting the behavior of serpents.*
>
> <u>Ornithomancy</u>—*interpreting the behavior, flight, and song of birds.*
>
> <u>Theriomancy</u>—*interpreting the movements of groups of animals.*

<u>Zygomancy</u>—*Divination by using weights.*

Clairvoyance, sometimes augmented with PK

As we can readily perceive, nearly any object or action imaginable has been used in systems of divination in different cultures. Some are very rudimentary and others have grown into complex and sophisticated "technologies." In all of these, whether acknowledged or not, the clairvoyant faculty is at work, and is sometimes augmented with spontaneous "PK," or psychokinetic, actions.

Rudimentary or complex and sophisticated, the clairvoyant experience usually—unless specifically limited by the user—includes far more than a simple answer, often providing the attentive organization and practical application of both physical and supra-physical realities. For instance, the clairvoyant location of a missing animal can include detailed information regarding the animal's physical condition along with the most effective rescue approach. In the criminal justice setting, psychic clairvoyants have been known to provide crucial investigative information to include the location of missing weapons and physical descriptions of the perpetrators of crime along with the motives underlying the crime. At another level, clairvoyance can uncover important information relevant to a vast range of life circumstances and strivings, including personal relationships, health conditions, and career decisions.

The "ne plus ultra" of psychic experience

Clairvoyance is possibly the most intricate and advanced form of ESP, demonstrating the wondrous capacity of the human mind to expand its own field of awareness to encompass limitless realities. It is the *ne plus ultra* of psychic experience. It can bring the earth into panoramic view, and link us to the infinite expanse of the universe. As with the development of all our paranormal powers, clairvoyant enhancement enriches our vision of the cosmos to become a vivid and exciting playground for the psychic mind.

The underlying dynamics of clairvoyance are complex and not yet fully understood. They appear to be distinctly unlike those of either telepathy or precognition. In the absence of the influence of another mind, the sources of clairvoyant knowledge must lie within the self or as communicated by some external condition or energy source. The bulk of clairvoyant insight probably engages both sources, but we "see through a glass darkly" in our efforts to explain this remarkable and potentially empowering phenomenon.

Through spontaneous clairvoyance, you can acquire information available from no other source. In some instances, it can involve matters of life-and-death significance. For instance, a college instructor discovered through spontaneous clairvoyance the location of her young son who had wandered into the wilderness during a family camping trip. Following an exhaustive search as darkness fell, the instructor was guided by what seemed to be an unseen force to a bridge that crossed a rushing stream approximately a mile from the camp. As she approached the bridge, a detailed image of the child huddled under the bridge appeared before her. The child was promptly found unharmed, exactly as seen in the clairvoyant image.

Purpose Driven

Clairvoyance can also be deliberately initiated—but whether spontaneous or deliberately induced, *it is almost always purpose driven.* It can target a particular happening and provide critical information regarding surrounding circumstances. For instance, the parents of an Air Force pilot stationed in the Pacific were awakened in the night by a loud sound not unlike that of a jet plane exploding in mid-air. Sleepless for the remainder of the night, they experienced together the comforting presence of their son. Upon later being notified of their son's death in a collision with another Air Force jet over the Pacific, they again experienced his presence. The clairvoyant experience at the time of the crash seemed specifically designed to prepare them for the loss of their son.

Animal Clairvoyance

Even animals have been known to experience clairvoyance. In the above instance, the Air Force pilot's dog companion that was left behind in the care of his parents reacted with fright at the exploding sound, though none of the neighborhood residents reported hearing the noise. The dog remained restless throughout the night and the following day.

Like dogs, cat companions have also been known to experience clairvoyance, which can involve emergency situations. In a rather remarkable instance of apparent clairvoyant insight, a cat led a child's mother to an underground storm pit where the child and a playmate had become accidentally locked inside on a hot summer afternoon. The cat, a longtime family household pet called Sailor, first commanded the mother's attention by repeatedly clawing at a door leading to the outside. Once outside, he led her directly to the storm pit. The pit, with limited air circulation, could have posed serious danger for anyone trapped inside.

The deliberate induction of clairvoyance through specialized tools includes dowsing, crystal gazing, automatic writing, the pendulum, and the pyramid, and the many other tools and procedures mentioned previously. The fact that tangible objects are often instrumental in initiating clairvoyance suggests that it may not be altogether self-contained but may trigger multidimensional responses. Beyond simply providing the point of focus often considered critical to many psychic functions, some tangible objects seem to provide the conditions for mental interactions that extend beyond inner processes alone. The mind becomes engaged in a complex exchange which can generate profound psychic insight.

Practical Applications

In a remarkable example of dowsing as a clairvoyant technique, a skilled dowser used metal rods to identify the exact location of a mercury-contaminated stream flowing under a northern Alabama town. Upon discovering the noxious stream through dowsing, the 92-year-old dowser with a long history of successful dowsing used metal stakes driven into the ground and expertly tapped upon with a hammer to relocate the stream. Follow-on tests revealed the effectiveness of his procedures. The use of tools and techniques designed to induce clairvoyance is further discussed in a later chapter.

Specific clairvoyant data is often accessed through the deliberate use of related physical objects. Psychometry is the clairvoyant application of relevant objects to gain highly specific psychic information. A clairvoyant, for instance, located a teen runaway through information gained by holding the teen's bracelet. Psychometry also includes the clairvoyant use of non-personal but relevant aids to locate missing articles. For instance, a psychometry study group used a map of a shopping mall to locate a lost ring. A floor plan provided the framework required by another study group to locate a valuable antique brooch. The combined impressions of the group pinpointed the brooch's exact location: inside an old baby shoe stored in the bottom drawer of a bedroom chest.

Occasionally, the object spontaneously invokes the clairvoyant faculty, and then functions as the essential channel for the clairvoyant message. A mother, whose son was injured in a random, late night shooting in a distant city, awakened at the exact hour of the shooting to the sound of a trophy crashing to the floor in her son's vacant bedroom. She immediately sensed danger involving her son. In another instance, a student, distraught over the death of her grandmother, reported a dream in which her grandmother appeared with a yellow rose and the message, "This rose is especially for you. I send it with happiness and love." A few days later, she received a beautiful yellow rose from her grandmother's sister with the message, "This rose is especially for you. I send it with happiness and love." Although the dream experience could be interpreted as precognitive, the student saw it as a clear clairvoyant manifestation of her grandmother's successful transition, which was confirmed by the gift of the yellow rose.

Inner-clairvoyance

Whether spontaneous or deliberately activated, *clairvoyance is always purposeful and empowerment driven.* When focused outward, clairvoyance can reveal important physical realities not otherwise available to conscious awareness. When focused inward, clairvoyance can reveal important non-physical realities that are also hidden from conscious awareness. It can discover growth blockages and reveal ways of dissolving them. It can target subconscious conflicts and repressions and alleviate the anxiety generated by them. Inner-clairvoyance is, in fact, among the self's most powerful therapeutic techniques.

The Empowerment of Self

We now know that the best therapist, like the best psychic, exists within the developing self. Inner-clairvoyance is among that therapist's most effective tools. Major therapeutic breakthroughs are almost always inner-clairvoyantly driven.

Inner-clairvoyance can access the vast subconscious storehouse of past experience, including that of distant past-life origin. In that role, clairvoyance remains, by definition, the perception of distant realities not otherwise available to sensory awareness. Furthermore, it includes as with other forms of clairvoyance, the attentive organization and practical application of those realities. Given past-life enlightenment through inner-clairvoyance, you can awaken past-life memories and energize them with empowerment possibilities. Through inner-clairvoyance, past-life "baggage" becomes present-life growth resources.

Clairvoyance and the Spirit Realm

Complementing inner-clairvoyance as a source of personal insight and power are our clairvoyant interactions with the spirit realm. Rather than a distant, inaccessible dimension, the spirit realm is a present throughout non-physical reality that is not typically available to sensory awareness. It does, however, often manifest its presence through sensory channels. Examples include sensory perceptions of both sights and sounds that can announce a spirit presence. Often collectively perceived by two or more persons, sensory manifestations of spiritual realities offer convincing evidence of the existence of the afterlife realm. When we add to these the extra-sensory clairvoyant interactions, whether experienced inwardly or turned outward to embrace the spirit realm, our existence as endless souls is clearly confirmed.

At a deeply personal level, clairvoyant interactions with the spirit realm can provide important spiritual insight, including increased awareness of personal spirit guides and growth specialists. Through clairvoyance as a spiritual phenomenon, you can interact with them as sources of knowledge and power. They can provide guidance in clarifying your personal goals and promoting your success in achieving them. As a spiritual phenomenon, clairvoyance can become our best source of attunement and balance, both of which are critical to our spiritual growth and fulfillment.

Your Responsibilities in the Physical Realm

As with any clairvoyant experience, whether apparently sourced from the Spirit Realm or even perceived as coming from one's Higher Self, Guardian Angel, or some Inner Plane Adept, or Messenger of Deity, or as an interpretation of a symbol, it is important to engage with the Conscious Mind to bring the message into context of the physical world and your personal environment.

You have the ultimate responsibility for rational and practical application of all other-dimensional guidance in relation to physical plane matters. Be particularly wary of all guidance regarding money, property, relationships, etc., especially those that may benefit another person, religious organization, spiritual leader, or other while promising extraordinary benefits or "other-worldly" return on your investments. Remember the challenges of growing from childhood, through the hormonal teen years, into the early years of adult life, and then into the more mature years.

Understand that you are entering into expanded and unfamiliar areas of consciousness and awareness. It is somewhat similar to moving to a foreign culture where it sometimes is easy to misinterpret the language and culture. We have to grow into familiarity with these new worlds and "put away childish things" and accept the new responsibilities that go with vast new opportunities.

Clairvoyance and Dreams

Frequently, the dream experience provides the channel for clairvoyant knowledge. Clairvoyant insight, like precognitive awareness, often seems to reside in the subconscious. Dream mechanisms logically could promote a subconscious transfer of information to conscious awareness. Common among the dream's clairvoyant functions is the delivery of information concerning urgent situations. A building contractor's dream, for instance, identified a critical error in the design of a building under construction. In another instance, an attorney's dream identified the exact location of an important legal document which had been lost.

Unexplained synchronicity is sometimes observed in clairvoyant dreams, particularly among individuals who are closely associated or related. Two brothers, eighteen and twenty-one years of age, reported simultaneously dreaming of their parents' involvement in a serious train accident. Their dreams, according to their report, vividly detailed the accident at the exact time of the event.

The clairvoyant dream will often provide clues concerning its psychic significance. Among frequently reported clues are the immediate awakening of the sleeping subject upon conclusion of the dream, the vivid physical sensations accompanying the dream experience, and the convincing, often urgent nature of the dream. The clairvoyant dream can generate a strong motivational state to either act upon the dream or to investigate its psychic significance.

Serial Insight Enhancement

Clairvoyant dreams, like precognitive dreams, have been known to occur in a series that guides the dreamer, often symbolically, and monitors the dreamer's progress. This form of clairvoyant dreaming is usually characterized by a central theme and a succession of related events. Transitional life situations and personal crises tend to precipitate the serial clairvoyant dream. Its goal is empowerment through personal insight. Once recognized and understood, such dreams can provide important therapeutic support and guide the growth or recovery process. This was illustrated by a college student who was undergoing therapy to resolve the trauma of sexual abuse during childhood. His series of clairvoyant dreams provided a weathervane of his progress from social withdrawal to rewarding interpersonal relationships. The dreams further provided the essential support required for overcoming the painful trauma.

The serial clairvoyant dream is yet another manifestation of the skilled therapist existing within each of us. Our inner-therapist, like our inner-teacher, probes our world of experience with persistence and a singular purpose: the full empowerment of the self.

Clairvoyant Strategies

The clairvoyant faculty frequently engages our most advanced non-psychic faculties, including our creative imagery powers. These powers can translate clairvoyant impressions into images that depict meaningful realities. Not surprisingly then, exercises designed to develop clairvoyant skills are usually more effective when they emphasize activities that promote creative imagery, such as sculpting, drawing, painting, and other forms of creative work or play.

In later chapters we will provide special developmental programs and techniques, some relating to specific divinatory practices and others that are exercises involving etheric currents and specific chakras, particular mental and emotional engagements, patterns of physical actions, and more, but let's get started with recognition of some basic requirements.

Meditation exercises that focus on creative imagery seem particularly conducive to clairvoyant empowerment. You will find many of these in the coming chapters and addenda, and—no doubt—you will be inspired and motivated to develop your own modifications to benefit your own needs and goals. That's what growth and empowerment are all about. It's what becoming more than you are and thus becoming your own guru means.

It's the road to wholeness and identifying with your Higher Self.

Clairvoyance is our claim to oneness with the world in the here and now. Expanded awareness through clairvoyance empowers us with an unlimited width, breadth, and depth of knowledge, which reveals what we otherwise cannot see, as it enriches our lives with new ideas and creative solutions. Equally important as these profound revelations are the simple joys of the clairvoyant experience itself, such as that felt in the discovery of a lost possession or the sudden "Ah ha!" of clairvoyant insight.

Whatever the nature of its expression, clairvoyance is empowerment in highly practical form: It can provide the critical information we need to solve our most pressing problems and achieve our loftiest goals. Clairvoyance is so basic to the empowered life that, without it, we often grope in darkness, out of touch with critical sources of psychic enlightenment.

Perhaps the most important message of this chapter—as the chapter title announces —is that clairvoyance can and does become part of everyday life. As a psychic faculty, it is part of your fundamental nature and can become interactive with all your interests and activities. Clairvoyance can manifest simply as a "feeling," a "vision," in a dream, even as a compulsive certainty, or it may other times suggest that you look for a specific answer through one of the many tools and techniques mentioned. More information on these may be found in the recommended resource mentioned at the end of this chapter.

Let your expanding awareness speak to you without denial or repression. Don't deny your natural psychic faculties but learn to understand their nature and ways, and study their technology for accurate interpretation of their inner promptings. It would not be wrong to call them "God's gift to humanity," even as they are part of the ever-continuing evolutionary development of every person. Never be fearful of the paranormal as this growing awareness is natural to all of us, even as some misguided "teachers" attempt to convince you that all things psychic are "evil" and designed to lead you away from the "true path" that they will be willing to teach you. A loving God does not play tricks on you nor does the universe play games with you.

Recommended general resource for many of the clairvoyant tools and techniques mentioned:

Slate, J. H. & Weschcke, C. L. *The Llewellyn Complete Book of Psychic Empowerment: A Compendium of Tools & Techniques for Growth & Transformation,* 2011, Llewellyn.

Other Sources & Suggested Additional Reading:

Brennan, J. H. *Mindreach—How to Develop Your Personal PK Power to Move Objects with Your Mind,* 1985, Aquarian Press.

Katz, D. L. *Extraordinary Psychic—Proven Techniques to Master Your Natural Psychic Abilities,* 2008, Llewellyn.

Katz, D. L. *You Are Psychic: The Art of Clairvoyant Reading & Healing,* 2004, Llewellyn.

Ophiel. *The Art and Practice of Clairvoyance,* 1969, Llewellyn.

Powell, D. H., MD. *The ESP Enigma—The Scientific Case of Psychic Phenomena,* 2009, Walker.

PREPARING FOR PSYCHIC CLARITY

The Tattvic Connection—Meditation & Visualization Programs

Microcosm to Macrocosm & Macrocosm to Microcosm

By Carl Llewellyn Weschcke

Presented as addenda to seventeen chapters of

Clairvoyance for Psychic Empowerment

By Joe H. Slate, Ph.D. & Carl Llewellyn Weschcke

ADDENDUM #1 TO CHAPTER ONE

The Tattvic Connection

&

THE PRACTICE OF RELAXATION

THE TENSION & RELEASE PROCEDURE

An Eastern Gift to Western Esotericism

The Sri Yantra
The Most Important Meditational Power Symbol in Tantra & Hinduism

A half-century ago, a little-recognized American occultist named Ophiel told me that the greatest contribution from the eastern world to western esotericism was the Hindu Tantric practices involving the Tattvas. Later, I learned that work with the tattvas had been incorporated into the magical practices of the famous Hermetic Order of the Golden Dawn in the late 1800s, and then, in 1971, a brilliant Australian teacher, Dr. Jonn Mumford, taught me how to activate the tattvas in my own mind. And why!

What are these Tattvas?

They are the <u>five</u> fundamental elements—not four, not 92, and not the 110 physical elements you learned in school—that are the *Energy Patterns* <u>behind</u> the manifestation of all Matter composing the entire *Physical Universe*. At the same time it is vitally important not to think of these subtle elements as physical. They are the *astral form* upon which the physical elements become manifest. Also understand that they are not static but function continuously—like a wind that blows steady and constantly day and night forever—bringing both renewal and change. And, indeed, that is exactly what they do, constantly flowing in alternating waves whose timing can be accurately measured and whose individual nature can be used both in certain forms of divination and certain kinds of magick.

The word *tattva* is Sanskrit translated approximately as "true nature of reality," and our study of the tattvas brings understanding of the structure of the astral world and the hidden mechanics behind all physical manifestation and of the alchemical and magickal processes.

Another meaning of the word *tattva* is "energy," and you should remember from your physics classes the famous formula $E=mc^2$ that "Energy and Matter" are convertible. In one sense, then, the inner reality of physical matter is astral energy, and it is energy that powers all that acts, lives, and moves on the physical plane. It is through understanding the tattvas that we become *empowered* to consciously act rather than unconsciously react. Our knowledge empowers us with responsibility, and by acting responsibly we become intelligent actors in the cosmic drama we know as life.

(Not to add confusion to the discussion, but there are two additional tattvas and corresponding elements which we will lightly introduce later, making *seven* in all in relation to those levels of reality and consciousness in our immediate universe, while in another system there are 36 tattvas. There are still others for those higher levels only glimpsed by few very advanced beings.)

Just, for the moment, accept the possibility that what we call reality and what we call consciousness are far greater in extent and scale, and more magnificent than anything imagined or dreamed of. Let yourself believe that it's all grander and greater than religionists or scientists or mystics yet know. As Shakespeare has Hamlet promise:

> There are more things in heaven and earth,
>
> Horatio,
>
> Than are dreamt of in your philosophy.

Again, think about Einstein's famous equation $E=mc^2$ where "E" stands for Energy and "m" stands for Matter. It demonstrates that every *substance* is made up of these five (the more subtle energies have little if any impact at lower levels) elemental energies, but in addition it shows that there has to be a <u>pattern</u> to guide that conversion into particular forms that actually make up the physical world.

States of Matter States of Consciousness

Everything is connected. Our individual minds—working through Universal Consciousness—are the interface connection that enables you, with your mind, to access and work with these fundamental energies, patterns, and forces behind all material manifestation. We are destined and programmed to become active co-creators to bring about a better world while meeting the increasing critical challenges of Humanity's relationship with Nature. But, obviously, *it requires knowledge, understanding, and discipline for individual human minds to intelligently, and wisely, work with these higher forces.*

Otherwise, we are instruments of destruction and chaos.

The tattvas are present—beneath your conscious awareness—in your body and mind just as they are present throughout the Cosmos. In essence, we live in two worlds simultaneously—the <u>outer</u> world larger than just its material manifestation, and a true <u>inner</u> world of personal consciousness—each functioning as a "matrix" interfacing with *your world of body, mind, and spirit.*

We live both within an "outer world matrix" and with an "inner world matrix"—and the two worlds commonly get "out of sync" with one another at fundamental energy levels. This disharmony can start us on paths to ill-health, destructive habits, irrational decisions, and even social and civil conflict. But when you consciously *awaken* the "Tattva Connection" through meditation and visualization practices you can restore natural harmony between the inner and outer worlds, and opening the way to accelerating psychic, mental, and spiritual development.

Even more important, with the awakened "Tattva Connection" you will *accomplish the "Miracle of the One Thing"* described in the famous message recorded by Thrice Greatest Hermes on the mythic Emerald Tablet.

The Emerald Tablet

Truly, without Deceit, certainly and absolutely—

That which is Below corresponds to that which is Above, and that which is Above corresponds to that which is Below, in the accomplishment of the Miracle of One Thing. And just as all things have come from One, through the Mediation of One, so all things follow from this One Thing in the same way.

Its Father is the Sun. Its Mother is the Moon. The Wind has carried it in his Belly. Its Nourishment is the Earth. It is the Father of every completed Thing in the whole World. Its Strength is intact if it is turned towards the Earth. Separate the Earth by Fire: the fine from the gross, gently, and with great skill.

It rises from Earth to Heaven, and then it descends again to the Earth, and receives Power from Above and from Below. Thus you will have the Glory of the whole World. All Obscurity will be clear to you. This is the strong Power of all Power because it overcomes everything fine and penetrates everything solid.

In this way was the World created. From this there will be amazing Applications, because this is the Pattern. Therefore am I called Thrice Greatest Hermes, having the three parts of the Wisdom of the whole World.

Herein have I completely explained the Operation of the Sun.

Perhaps no other quotation so completely summarizes the fundamental principles of Esotericism as this ageless statement from which we derive the simple aphorism:

AS ABOVE, SO BELOW
As in the Macrocosm so it is in the Microcosm who is Mankind

There are many benefits that result from this program of harmonization, because once established you are able to influence many aspects of the immediate outer environment through the connection with the inner powers as directed by mind—but that's a subject for separate discussion.

The Astral Plane—Psychic & Emotional

Many people divide the human person into just two parts: Body and Soul, or Body and Spirit, and then think of anything "spiritual" as good and pure. We are far more complex than that, and western knowledge of the Spiritual World of subtle

bodies and planes was largely expurgated with the coming of the two major monotheistic religions whose organizations sought to deny knowledge of the superphysi-
cal to "common people" and so purged libraries of sacred writings, punished Pagans
and Gnostics for any contrary teachings, executed many non-believers who had other
ideas, and developed a rigid theology frozen to the time of its *politicalization*, leading
to imperialist competition between Christianity and Islam that continues to this day.

In the west, that "thought monopoly" was finally broken at great human cost with
the advance of science, the publication of books, the coming of democracy and free-
enterprise economics, and—most importantly—wide scale public, secular education.
The Islamic world has not yet been as lucky and world peace is increasingly threatened
by resurgent militancy directed rigid theocrats.

Modern Sources of Esoteric Knowledge

While some of the esoteric knowledge of the subtle bodies survived in ancient
Egyptian and Greek history and mythology, and can be traced in surviving Pagan
myth and lore, it is largely from India that we have gained detailed knowledge of the
complex reality of our spiritual nature originating in ancient times. Primary credit
must be given to British scholars for translating and publishing the historic sacred
writings of India and Tibet in English, then secondarily to the release of surviving
European magickal knowledge held by secret societies, and then to the sudden explosion of esoteric interest in the 19th century with the advent of Spiritualism and Theosophy. All the time, a great resource of western esoteric wisdom, the Jewish Kabbalah,
remained invisible because of their increasing segregation of the Jewish people from
mainstream society until the late 20th century.

Very complete and detailed knowledge of the non-physical dimensions is found in
the writings and practices of Tantra and Yoga in India and Tibet. Modern research has
led to actual understanding of certain practices that otherwise seemed purely symbolic and ceremonial. Yet, there are profound differences in ancient eastern and modern
western approaches to esoteric practices, and their science and psychology that we
explore elsewhere in this and other books.

The Astral Source of Psychic Powers & Phenomenon

The key point that must be mentioned here is the role of the astral dimension
as the primary source and location of psychic powers and phenomenon. The astral
level of consciousness is also the main component of our subconscious mind, and the
"vehicle" for the feeling and expression of our emotions.

Our subconsciousness, the astral body, remembers everything—including all our unconscious psychic perceptions and emotional reactions. Such unconscious and unresolved memories cloud and color your conscious psychic perceptions, and thus inhibit the "clear vision" that is the very essence of clairvoyance.

Becoming Clear & Accurate in Clairvoyant Perception

It is through the meditation and visualization program that we add to this and other chapters throughout the book that your clairvoyance will become clear and accurate at the astral and mental levels through the awakened "Tattva Connection" resulting in purification and harmonization between the inner and outer matrices. The Hermetic Order of the Golden Dawn taught that tattva meditation is the fastest method of developing and enhancing clairvoyance. It also increases your power to manifest your goals and desires.

The tattvas can be represented in drawn or printed images that are then called yantras. A yantra is defined by Dr. Mumford as "a tool for focusing the mind, encouraging conception, and invoking or evoking elemental forces." (All quotations in this addendum are taken from his 1997 book, *Magical Tattwas*, which is included with 25 Tattwa cards in a boxed set). Mumford also clearly described the function of the tattva yantras as "'information storage and retrieval devices' of amazing potency. They are the primary building blocks from which all magical symbols, sigils, talismans, ciphers and designs are composed." "The tattwa 'triggers' the psychic layers of our mind through the compressed power of its geometrical shape, the primal colors vibrating forth, and the implied numerical concepts in each shape."

> *Tattva or Tattwa—the same thing, but there seems to be a growing preference for the "v" spelling over the "w" in recent years. Actually, no "w" exists in Sanskrit so "tattva" is slightly more correct.

Through Mind, and by the *Miracle of the One Thing*, everything is connected and it is by means of these powerful (and universal) geometric symbols that your mind enters *into* the five elements and their permeations. The tattvas are not manifest in the physical world in their full purity,** but always in combinations. We refer to these combinations as one containing the "seed" either of itself or another tattva—thus there are 25 combinations of the basic five, as will be illustrated later.

> **As a point of clarification, nothing (that is: *no thing*), can manifest in the material universe in purity of form or substance. Even in advanced chemical processing, we can strive for substance purity, but there will always be some percentage of impurity, i.e. there is always some other element present even

in the most minute quantity. It is the fundamental nature of all things to combine.

The Eyes Have It

"Eyes are the Doorway to the Soul" is a poetic expression of a feeling felt between lovers. It does contain truth, and 2,500 years ago the Tantric Sāmkhya* masters employed the unique practice of Tratak to "burn" the image of the chosen tattva into your mind and thus awaken it in your consciousness.

> *Sāmkhya philosophy sees the universe as consisting of two realities: <u>Purusha</u> (consciousness) and <u>Prakriti</u> (material phenomena). Prakriti further divides into sensor and sensed realms while Purusha separates individual units of consciousness which fuse into the mind and body of the sensor. Tratak is one developmental practice to meld the external with the internal. See Glossary for more detail.

While this practice of tattva meditation and visualization can also be used in "mind magic" to shape future happenings, for chakra stimulation, in making of very powerful talismans, in physical and mental healing, in creative thinking and action planning and in other practical applications, our primary concern here is in the psychic development of clairvoyance and in achieving the clarity and accuracy of clairvoyant vision that makes this ability reliable and hence practical, in contrast to the more common experience of clients with "psychic readers."

There are three factors we will explore before undertaking the first meditation:

1. To preview the practice of tratak—the meditative system initiated by staring at an object (in this case, one of the colored tattvic yantras) *and then "seeing" the object in space before your brow chakra with closed eyes for <u>internalization</u>.*

2. To preview the actual practice and values of meditation and visualization.

3. To preview and illustrate each of the five "pure" tattvas, and then in their combinations with one another—a total of twenty-five.

The actual practice requires study of Tattva Overview Tables in the special addenda to later chapters relating each of the geometric shapes (the yantras) by their Names (eastern and western), Forms, Colors, and particular Attributes. (The preceding words are capitalized to impress their distinct importance upon the reader.)

And for the reader to either photocopy or re-draw the twenty-five images pre-sented in separate addenda throughout this book and then to color them as indicated, or obtain printed cards.*

> *There are always advantages to "doing it yourself" when it comes to obtain-ing such complementary developmental aids as described here. True—the "home-made" product may be far from perfect, but it will contain your energy and your desires in a near *alchemical process of psychological trans-formation*. We refer to this as "Craft Work," and it is a powerful stimulant to your inner growth. Many serious students will craft their own product for private use and obtain manufactured products for public use as in "read-ings" for others.

This set of twenty-five colored yantras will be a valuable aid to not only your clair-voyance development and practice, but their use will open many "astral doorways" for a systematic exploration of the psychic world in addition to their use in particular practices of divination and mind magic and other applications as mentioned previ-ously, and many others you will readily discover through experience and exploration.

THE TRATAK PROCEDURE

Probably with every self-improvement book you've ever read or course you've ever taken, along with meditation practices, programs of active imagination, Kabbalistic path-working, and various self development programs, you've been instructed to **VISUALIZE!**

A simple word: you know what it means and yet—unless you were born an art-ist—you probably realize that what you "see" when you visualize falls far short of what is really required. *True visualization* is more than what we commonly "see" when we imagine something. The visual images in dreams seem more vivid that these imagined ones, and yet they too usually fall short of the sharp clarity and steadiness of the pow-erful visual image that a sculptor—for one example—projects onto a block of stone and then chips away the stone to match the image.

Tratak is a special program that employs the natural physiology of eyesight to *internalize* a duplicate image of an external object so that it will float in the inner space in front of your brow chakra (between your eyes where the brow ridge starts)—most often with the eyes closed or open looking at a blank white wall or piece of white paper.

The "secret" is to stare fixedly at the center of a brightly lit object or image for as long as possible until your eyes actually feel that they are burning. (Hence Mumford's reference to "burning" the image into your mind) As you do so, the colors will start to "flash" around the edges and the image will almost float off the source of the graphic image, such as a tattva card.

Then, close your eyes and you will see an after image in *complementary* colors floating before your Third Eye (brow chakra). Initially, you may have better results by staring at a white space instead of closing your eyes, but—if so—use that as a starting point and do learn to see with both closed and opened eyes. Close your eyes, and then either focus on the blackness before your eyes or open them and focus on a white wall or piece of paper. You should see a vivid duplicate of the object or image in complementary colors.

In the case of the properly colored tattva yantras, the colors themselves gain depth, and appear in three-dimensional images. The psychic factor is enhanced by this and that is your goal.

True, three-dimensional Visualization is a fundamental key to the successful employment of your psychic, mental, and creative powers.

THE POWER OF THE SYMBOL

This is such an important concept that we were tempted to present it all in solid red capital letters to deeply impress it on the reader. But multi-color printing would require a higher price for the book, perhaps making it less available to the people we hope to help in their pursuit of spiritual growth.

A true symbol contains power because of its shape, form, color, and its traditional name which connects it to an established and constantly up-dating "system of correspondences" retrieved through the *information storage function* of the subconscious mind. Long established esoteric symbols are not mere artistic designs but are *archetypal* energy patterns found in Universal Consciousness recalled through your personal subconsciousness. As such they represent the collective wisdom available through meditation and forms of ritual (another form of active meditation) when performed correctly.

Just as their English name connotes, the tattvas—as *fundamental elements*—are the "primary building blocks" for the manifest universe (physical and much of the non-physical), and the ancient tattvic symbols, in turn, are the fundamental *esoteric* energy formulae from which (as quoted from Mumford previously) "all magical symbols, sigils, talismans, ciphers and designs are composed." These powerful formulae trigger "the psychic layers of our mind through the compressed power of its geometrical shape, the primal colors vibrating forth, and the implied numerical concepts in each shape."

We may, *unconsciously,* respond to many powerful symbols—meaning that they can, and often do, excite strong emotional reactions that lack the control of the conscious mind and may lead to (often manipulated with that intent by religious and political leaders) totally irrational, "out of (self-) control" behavior. We call this "crowd psychosis" because it often leads to riots, mass hysteria, to criminal anti-social acts, and even to war as ably described back in Charles Mackay's 1841 classic *Extraordinary Mass Delusion and the Madness of the Crowd.*

But when we *consciously* evoke the power of a particular *esoteric* symbol, it 'triggers' the psychic layers of our mind through its compressed power and brings forth the needed knowledge and energies to accomplish the set task. In this case, it is the awakening and purifying of the inner tattvic matrix to enable the clairvoyant to more clearly "see" and more accurately "read" and understand the external situation required by the task set forth. The clairvoyant may have to penetrate through a lot of "emotional garbage" attachments to see clearly—which is the goal of this fully developed psychic power.

MEDITATION

There are probably as many systems of meditation as there are teachers and authors writing about the subject. Wikipedia defines it simply as "any form of a family of practices in which practitioners train their minds or self-induce a mode of consciousness to realize some benefit." Yet, perhaps, the most concise definition of meditation is "one pointed focus on a single thought." In earlier times this kind of meditation was referred to simply as *concentration.*

Even for those systems that speak of a "blank mind," it really boils down to freeing your mind of all extraneous thoughts and sensory reactions.* You can then focus on "no thing" (which is not exactly the same as "nothing.")

> *The emphasis here is on *reactions.* Even in deep meditation, or in hypnosis, or in deep sleep, you can have a sensory awareness of something around you or even in your physical body without *reacting to it!* With training and experience—just as with dreams—you can then later recall the memory of that sense awareness and take care of it. The ability <u>not to react</u> is the foundation of such yogic or shamanic practices as walking on hot coals, licking a white hot steel bar, not bleeding from and immediately healing a knife cut. Sometimes such control is achieved with complete focus on something other than the happening—singing, chanting, listening, projecting awareness somewhere else, etc. Other times it is accomplished from the ability to focus "upward" on not reacting to a lower dimension. Start small and practice, practice, practice before going on to bigger things. Experience builds on experience, learning and modifying as you go.

Meditation is really a willed act of attention—*the act of the active, trained, disciplined conscious mind that should be the goal of all primary education.* And it results in an active self-directed mind able to make rational decisions in contrast to the uncontrolled emotionally possessed reaction to every passing thought and perception all too common in today's entertainment-dominated culture. To escape that, you must learn to self-direct attention, totally. The value of the self-directed mind is demonstrated in every kind of personal success story.

Many systems of meditation focus on aids such as particular mantras, dedicated prayers, prayer beads or rosaries, chanting or responsive repetitions, positions and gestures, etc., in relation to the teacher's "system of choice"—usually related to religious practice (Christian, Buddhist, Chinese, etc.) or particular proprietary programs based on traditional self-improvement systems (yoga, Tai Chi, any of the martial arts, ritual or shamanic dance, etc.),

While these many systems have training values, they can be limiting unless used developmentally within a larger dedicated *system* of transformation. In contrast, active meditation freed of such imposition will focus attention on an idea or subject in order to secure information or answer a question, or achieve a particular goal of state, or otherwise focus on single symbols (such as a tattva) or on a symbolic complex such as imagined movement ("path-working") on the Kabbalistic Tree of Life to accomplish particular goals. Included in this approach is meditation on such "primal" divinatory symbols as Runes, I Ching hexagrams, and even defined "signs" such as used in dream interpretation, tea leaf reading, handwriting analysis, palmistry, etc.

Focused meditation is one of the finest methods of study in such subjects as astrology and Tarot, and as adjuncts to such practices as dowsing, any type of academic and scientific research, forms of self-analysis and even medical diagnosis. It is perhaps the most "practical" as well as the most valuable mind techniques you can utilize. It contrasts with mere memorization and rote learning by its ability to call forth associated "correspondences" from the deep personal and the universal unconscious.

THE NECESSITY OF RELAXATION
THE PRACTICE OF "TENSION & RELEASE"

All practices of meditation and visualization call for relaxation of the physical body and a determined focus of the mental body. In between* the physical and etheric complex and the mental body is the emotional body, also called the "astral body."

*Don't perceive such spatially descriptive words such as *above, below, between, higher, inner, lower,* and *outer,* or other qualifiers like *brighter, darker, heavier,* and *lighter,* etc. as having the same *objective* meaning as they do when applied to objects in the physical universe. When used *subjectively* in esoteric and psychological applications their meanings are suggestive rather than absolute and measurable. Within esoteric applications, concepts like *planes, worlds, bodies, elements,* and *energies* are <u>not</u> physically and mathematically definitive. Astral, mental, and other <u>bodies</u> are coincidental with the physical and yet they have functional differences in terms of consciousness and life energies. The same is true of *astral, mental* and other <u>planes</u> or <u>worlds</u>. The differences are perceptive to clairvoyant vision and understood by the subconscious mind, but not generally to physical vision.

Emotions bring tension and stress to the physical body, and *repercuss* to the mental body. Emotional* energies are very powerful, and can be directed under Will and guided by Mind to beneficially affect physical manifestations as in healing, mind-magic and inspirational communication. More commonly, *emotions are reactive to physical, emotional and mental stimulus producing stress and tension at both the physical and mental levels that inhibit clarity of thought and vision in our psychic development.*

> *Emotion can be simply defined as "E-Motion"—*Energy in Motion*—because emotion is never static, and unless otherwise directed, feeds on itself. It can pull as a person "out of control," and itself infect other people's emotions.

Yes, in speaking of the subtle bodies and planes, "the higher always dominates the lower," but only as willed to do so, and then mind can make rational determinations for appropriate action at the physical and emotional levels.

STRESS KILLS! TENSION HURTS! RELAXATION HEALS!

Unmitigated and under-controlled, stress builds tensions throughout the physical body that induce destructive chemical, hormonal, nervous and electrical reactions right down to the cellular level that can bring on physical disease and shorten lifespan. Worse, tension builds on tension and can reactively induce dangerous emotional responses and irrational ideas that may totally alter and dominate the personality, leading to destructive personal and social behavior.

In our modern world we are constantly bombarded by stressing factors at both the physical and emotional levels, and even to some extent at the mental level with unexamined ideas. It is vital to both individual and communal health that stress be relieved regularly through relaxation programs. Likewise, relaxation is a necessary precursor to effective meditation programs.

While meditation is commonly presented as a method of relaxation and stress reduction, that is true mainly because most meditation programs do include relaxation steps. To give you a deeper understanding of the relaxation process, and thence of the real functions of meditation, we are presenting one of the most powerful relaxation techniques as a separate procedure which should then be first applied in the twenty-five meditation programs that will follow in other chapters.

NOTICE: The following *Empowerment Tension & Release Procedure* **is a Relaxation Program that only works** <u>if you actually do it!</u> **And we recommend to first-time users to repeat once daily for the first week, and then occasionally thereafter. After the initial experience, other relaxation procedures that are less demanding may be used so long as you find them effective.** *Remember: Stress from external sources induces Tension, and Tension induces further internal Stress in a dangerous repeating cycle.*

Stress and Tension are both detrimental to physical and emotional health and to the mental discipline and control necessary for success in all psychic self-development and psychological self-improvement programs.

Please exercise self-discipline and <u>schedule</u> **the "Work" of this and the Tattva Meditation Programs that follow in latter chapter addenda.** *Self-discipline and scheduling is your personal substitute for attending classes, and reporting to a teacher, guru, master, etc.* **"Do it yourself" has many advantages over outer-directed study, but merely reading about things is not as productive as doing it.**

THE EMPOWERMENT TENSION & RELEASE RELAXATION PROCEDURE

<u>Introduction</u>. This procedure is adapted from long established practices of Hatha Yoga, perhaps the most fundamental and efficient system of natural physical health maintenance there is. The purpose of this procedure is multifold:

A. It is experiential, giving you direct experience of Muscular Tension through its deliberate induction. At the same time you should consciously realize the connection with "nervous tension" and "emotional stress." At the muscular level, they are all the same.

B. With the intense experience of induced tension, you will learn to recognize the symptoms of tension, often overlooked because they are themselves symptomatic of most adult modern life. With knowledge you can begin to recognize the common sources of stress factors in your physical and social environment that induce tension. *With understanding, you can reduce tension producing reactions and you may choose to remove stress factors from your life.*

C. With the combined experience of induced tension followed by its deliberate release you will know and understand the function and benefit of tension-release procedures.

D. Through *progressive* tension and release of muscle groups from toe and foot to the top of skull, you will accomplish total relaxation and open the way to benefit from the Tattvic Connection Meditation & Visualization programs that follow.

E. Knowledge through actual experience gives you *somatic* understanding of what physical relaxation of the body really feels like so that it is always your objective and goal in any relaxation procedure, and—indeed—in your everyday life. Remember: *stress kills and tension brings harm and injury.*

F. Being now able to identify what relaxation is enables you to better relax the body, reducing stress, and removing tension at will even when you don't have the time and opportunity for the full procedure.

While we feel that tension & release is itself a foundational procedure, it can and should be augmented in numerous ways including breathing rhythms, visualizations, musical accompaniment, and more—but not all of these at once. Start *simple and add complexity* with mastery of the foundational procedures and understanding of the augmenting factors so that the foundational experience is always foremost.

Summary of Purpose & User Benefits.

Physical Relaxation is necessary for the free and unmitigated flow of Prana and other subtle energies throughout both physical and subtle bodies. Through the flow of these energies, controlled & directed purification of various physical and subtle body parts and energy channels can be accomplished, and then may be followed by specified stimulus of particular psychic centers to accomplish certain goals.

Step 1. Preliminaries.

Read through the procedure before beginning so that further reference is not needed.

Time & Space:

A period of approximately 30 to 40 minutes should be set aside for the active 16 steps of the procedure to be conducted in a comfortably warm, quiet, and safe setting free of interruptions.

You should repeat this entire procedure often, and particularly as needed—but not more than once daily. Like strenuous exercise, it can give you sore muscles if done too often in a single day. At the same time, we recommend that you do repeat it daily for the first week.

It is desirable to use this relaxation procedure or a more simplified procedure before a meditation program or magickal ritual for maximum value.

Note the following illustration specifically identifying areas of the body calling for intentional relaxation.

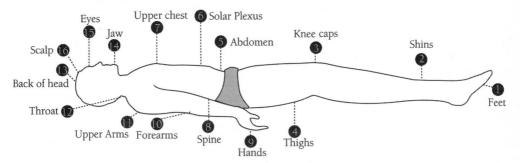

Classical Marmasthanani chart 1

Personal Preparations:

Remove shoes and keep clothing or covering minimal to minimize the effects of external stimuli.

Posture & Position:

Lie supine—or nearly so—on a recliner, the floor with a slight pillow for the head, or a bed with a relatively hard mattress. Stretch out in a straight horizontal position. Separate your feet about fifteen to twenty inches apart with toes and ankles relaxed to the outside. Place the arms alongside your body with the hands palms up (without straining to do so). Your shoulders should be flat and the small of your back relaxed. Feel yourself relaxed so that most of your body touches the surface on which you lie. If needed for comfort, place minimal padding under the knees, neck, and shoulders.

Special Lighting and/or Other Requirements:

While a darkened room is not required, freedom from both sound and visual distractions is advisable. Likewise avoid cooking and other odors if possible. If necessary make use of a sleep mask and soundless earphones or ear plugs.

Breathing:

It is always desirable to establish a rhythmic flow of your breath, mostly balanced between inhalation and exhalation. It is likely, however, that as you start this procedure, you will inhale as you tense the muscles, and then exhale with their release, but once you have gone through the procedure, you will more naturally exhale with the contraction (tension inducing) of the muscles, and then inhale with the release. You may inhale and exhale more naturally as you rest between each of the steps. With experience, you will find it easy to establish a natural rhythm inclusive of tension and release. That should become your choice rather than the intervals suggested in the steps below. In other words, follow instructions, and then adapt to what works best for you.

Vocalization:

Vocalizing, either silently stated or voiced aloud, the affirmations and the identification of muscle groups increases the effectiveness of the procedure. With each step 5 through 23, it is helpful to vocalize the words describing the particular muscles within the group.

Step 2. Goal Statement.

As mentioned in the Introduction to this section, your goal is two-fold:
1. To become fully familiar with the feelings associated with muscular tension and learn to totally relax the physical body.
2. To enable the healing and purifying flow of subtle energies throughout the physical and subtle bodies complex.

Step 3. Affirmations.

I am becoming free of all stress and tension.
I feel fully relaxed and naturally energized.
I feel clean and purified.

These affirmations may be spoken as goals at the beginning, and then as confirmations at the ending of the procedure.

Step 4. Mental Imagery.

Visualization:

Visualization, like vocalization, increases the effectiveness of the procedure. Let it happen naturally as you move through the procedure, and combine imagery with feeling. When you vocalize, for example, *I feel fully relaxed and naturally energized*, let an image form of your fully relaxed body and actually do feel relaxed, and at the same time, energized.

Spontaneous Imagery:

Let any spontaneous imagery, feelings, and vocalizations naturally and spontaneously happen. You might, for example, say "tense and tight" during the first part, and then sigh "ahhhh" during the second. *Do not, however, say or feel anything negative—like "That hurts."*

Keep the imagery natural and spontaneous, without planning and contrivance. Just let it happen, and it will. And expect it to change as you repeat this procedure again and again.

The following procedure is the core that should be followed exactly, but the images and feelings should be spontaneous. Don't worry about them, and don't force them. For each of the sixteen groups that are recognized in Steps 5 through 23, visualize and sense the individual parts and the group as a whole. Experience them for what they are to the body as a whole as well as what they do individually.

Get to know your body consciously and with appreciation.

Step 5. Feet, Toes, and Ankles.

Tense both left and right simultaneously, curling the toes upward for about 30 seconds and then downward for an equal amount of time. Note feelings both on bottoms and tops of feet and toes, and front and bank of ankles. Feel the tension in feet and ankles for the full 60 seconds, and then suddenly and completely relax. Letting go of all tension, feel total relaxation for about a minute.

We're spending more time on your feet than on other muscle groups because your feet are your contact with the Earth—and they "exhale" negativity to the earth and "inhale" positivity. Your feet are the polar opposite of your hands and the crown of your head, and energies circulate up and down between the two poles, and throughout the body.

Step 6. Shins and Calf muscles.

Tense both left and right simultaneously and hold for about 30 seconds. Because of the tendency of the calf muscles to cramp you should be cautious about extending this period to as long as 60 seconds, but no longer. Our goal is not endurance but experience. Feel the tension front and back, and then let go, and feel the relaxation. When you feel you really know the experience of this relaxation, you can move on—but wait at least ten seconds.

Step 7. Knee Joints and Muscles.

The knees are joints, but very special joints with a front and a back, and they are surrounded with muscles. Tense them both simultaneously for about 30 seconds, pressing the hollows behind each knee against the surface you are lying on. Feel the sensations, and be aware of just how important the knees are to all you are. Then, let go and relax. Feel relaxation peacefully and with gratitude for ten or even thirty seconds.

Step 8. Thighs.

The thighs are pillars of strength and the action limbs for the body's movements. Tense them both simultaneously, and hold for a minimum of 30 seconds. Feel the hard muscles both front and back and visualize yourself *striding* with vigor through all the paths of life. Release, and feel the satisfaction as if of a hard day's work well done.

Step 9. Abdomen, Groin, and Buttocks.

Tense both abdomen and buttocks simultaneously—pulling the abdomen inward, the groin upward, and squeezing the buttocks forward toward the abdomen. Hold for a comfortable period—30 seconds is recommended—and then release, letting go of all tension. This is a transition point, often blocking the flow of energies. When you truly let go and relax, feel the freely flowing energies upward and downward.

Step 10. Solar Plexus.

Pull the navel back toward your spine, hold briefly, and let go. *Tense and release.* For some people, the solar plexus holds a lot of nervous energy—hence the phrase "a nervous stomach." For these people, finding release of these tensions can be an enormous relief.

Step 11. Upper Chest.

Deliberately inhale and expand your rib cage to fill the lungs to capacity. Hold, and then let go and release the tension. We tend to "hold our breath" in particular moments (panic, pain, excitement, etc.) and this sometimes becomes a semi-permanent retention of energy—a continuous *tension*—that we need to release. Feel a deep sense of relief that is actually pleasurable with the cycle of release. Practice a pattern of comfortable full inhalation and exhalation to establish a natural and healthy rhythm and consciously re-assert that rhythm whenever you feel "out of sync" with the world around you. *Breath is life.*

Step 12. Spine.

The spine runs from the tail bone up to the neck just behind the jaw area. Pull the small of the spine back against the surface you are lying on. Hold and release as you push the rest of the spine back. In other words, it takes a double motion to flatten the entire spine in your moment of tension. And then release. You will feel tension moving out of the spine, liberating energy and bringing pleasant feelings. *Enjoy!*

The spine is your "Tree of Life" supporting all your physical and etheric being. It is magical and spiritual at the same time it is physical reality.

Step 13. Hands, Wrists and Fingers.

Curl your thumbs into the palms of your hands, and then your fingers. Squeeze them all together, feeling the tension right into your fingertips, and then release. Make your hands and wrists go limp and feel the relaxation spread into your body. Your hands are one of the three primal interfaces with the world (feet, hands, mouth) where you have conscious interaction. Your hands not only grasp and point, but act like antennae to transmit and receive between you, other people, and the world through the palms and fingertips. Tension inhibits that flow; release and relaxation encourages it. The fingers give direction.

Step 14. Forearms and Elbows.

From wrists to elbows, press both forearms down against the surface to create tension. Feel the tension, hold it, and then release and feel real relaxation.

Step 15. Upper Arms and Shoulders.

From elbows to shoulder joints, flatten down against the surface to create tension, especially in the shoulder area. Feel the tension, hold, and then release to experience relaxation.

Step 19. Neck and Throat.

Press the back of the head against the surface and pull your chin back. Feel tension, hold and then release. Feel the relaxation. Supporting the head is actually more demanding, and expressive, than you may realize. We thrust the head forward in aggression, pull it back in defense and retreat, turn right and left, move up and down as we relate to the outside world. Tension inhibits and relaxation releases energy.

Step 20. Back of Head.

Push the back of the head down against the surface for a few seconds to create tension, hold, and then release into relaxation.

Step 21. Jaws, Mouth, Lips and Tongue.

Tense the area from the tip of the chin back to the hinge joints (you can feel them with your fingers as you open and close your mouth). Press your lips together, push your tongue up strongly against the roof of the mouth where you can feel a point of sensation, feel the accumulating tension, hold, and then release. Feel the pleasure of relaxation.

Step 22. Eyes, Cheeks, and Forehead.

Sight is the most important of our senses, and the eyes are its vehicle. Squeeze your eyelids together and feel your cheeks and forehead all together tense, hold, and release. Feel refreshed vision as your eye muscles relax.

Step 23. Top of Scull and Scalp.

Try to feel the weight of the brain inside your skull while relaxing the scalp. At first, it will seem difficult to separate the two, but try and it will happen and you will feel the complete relaxation of your body from toes to the top of your head. From your toes and feet to the crown of your head, tension and releases has opened blocked energy passages and prepared the way for the Tattvic Connection to bring healing and clarity.

Step 24. Completion & Self-Realization.

We are more than the physical body, but we live in the body and it is the living foundation of our incarnate experience. We incarnate more and more deliberately with intention as we grow in the wholeness of our being—*becoming more than we are.* But modern life is stressful and the resultant tension inhibits our full living and growth opportunities.

To benefit from programs intended to accelerate psychic development and spiritual growth we must reduce the inhibiting tension and clear the physical and subtle bodies of psychic and emotional "pollution." We start with this procedure of Tension and Release Relaxation, and move on to the Tattva Connection Meditation & Visualization Programs added to chapters 2 through 20 that follow.

Step 25. Return to Normality.

It is always desirable to fully return to normality following any procedure, be it of relaxation, meditation, ritual, or intense period of work whether physical or mental, with a deliberate act of standing, stretching, flexing head and shoulders, hands and wrists, perhaps some deep breathing, and a bite to eat.

Step 26. Review, Record & Analyze.

Review the experience, and mentally summarize it. Record it in your journal. After a day or two, read what you've written and analyze it for any special values you note.

The Next Step!

By laying your own foundation of physical and emotional health, and mental and spiritual strength through such programs as these, you are actually participating in a purely voluntary and undirected worldwide movement building *New Worlds of Mind & Spirit*, and turning the age-old Dream into Reality. It's your world, it's our world, but it's not *their* World! It's not the world of powerful institutions controlled by bureaucracies serving ambition-driven leaders using sophisticated techniques of manipulation. It is your world, in which you are your own teacher with access to many sources of knowledge and to the esoteric techniques for your own development and transformation for which you—alone—are responsible as intended from the Beginning.

Sources & Suggested Additional Reading:

Mumford, Jonn. *A Chakra & Kundalini Workbook—Psycho-Spiritual Techniques for Health, Rejuvenation, Psychic Powers & Spiritual Realization*, 1997, Llewellyn.

Mumford, Jonn. *Magical Tattwas—A Complete System for Self Development*, 1997, Llewellyn.

Ophiel. *The Art and Practice of Astral Projection*. 1961, Peach.

CHAPTER TWO
Clairvoyance in Theory & Practice
*All Knowledge Begins with Theory
and is fulfilled through Practice*

All knowledge—even when we call it "science"—is a theory that begins with a theory and never stops being a theory. Even "statements of fact" are interpretations based on massive evidence that could be overturned with new discoveries, just as a person legally convicted guilty of murder could be proven innocent by new DNA or other evidence.

It happens!

The Knowledge of Law

"Knowledge" contrasts with Law and Religion, which are just what they are said to be. In the case of Law, whether statutory or traditional (the "common law") we have a series of statements bound together by some kind of logic embodied either in a written constitution (founding document) or unwritten in established practice. Laws can be changed by court decision based on some form of applied logic), or by legislative action or executive decree, both of which can be challenged and denied in "the court" itself founded (in most Western nations) on the Constitution or even older tradition.

The Law differs from ordinary theoretical knowledge because it is essentially based on a one-time statement of theory of how a free people can live together with dignity in the pursuit of happiness. That one-time statement of theory is the Constitution forming the law of the land.

The Knowledge of Religion

In the case of Religion—almost exclusively monotheistic Christian, Jewish or Islamic —the primary foundation is a "Book" of sacred writings attributed directly and indirectly to the single God as recorded, or reported, by prophets. The sacred writings were historically subjected to interpretation and then codification to form that religion's final and rigid theology, generally subject to very limited modification by the religion's leadership. In the modern world, some nations are founded as theocracies based on a religious leader's interpretation of the basic theology which then forms the law of that land.

The Tragedy of Theocracy

In a theocracy, all worldly knowledge, even "science," is dominated by the particular theology and dedicated to the purposes of the religious leadership. Thus you have real world conflict as historical exampled by the Catholic Church's Inquisition responsible for the execution of common wise women daring to heal with herbal remedies rather than by prayer, and the 17th century scientists like Galileo condemned as a heretic for teaching that the Earth rotated around the Sun rather than the Sun circling the Earth as claimed by the Church. Another 17th century scientist, Giordano Bruno, was burned at the stake for teaching that the universe contained other planets than Earth,

Religion, having its origin in the non-physical dimensions, has no legitimate "authority" in the physical world other than given to it by its adherents. Such "believers" may accept moral teachings but those cannot justifiably be *forced* on non-believers. Still, certain religions seek world domination to do just that.

Real World Knowledge

Real World (i.e. the physical dimension) Knowledge always starts with observation followed by questions which lead to speculation (or, to be absolutely honest, "guessing").

What makes it rain? Why does the wind blow? Who makes the grass grow green? Where does the Sun go at night? How does water get into wells? Where do babies come from? Where did Grandpa go when he "died?" Why do wolves howl at the Moon? Who built the Great Pyramid?

All these questions and many more seem childlike to our adult "ears," but that's how it begins. The first answers lead to more observations and they lead to more questions until at some point there is a generally accepted explanation which can be "tested" against further observations of similar phenomenon until such time arrives that we *perceive* a connection between cause and effect. With this understanding of cause and effect, we have a "theory" which is further tested by not only more observations but by experiments which <u>challenge</u> the theoretical assumption, even when designed to confirm it.

When Challenges are not allowed

Neither Law nor Religion allows challenges to their basic authority, although in real life there are always challenges. In the case of Law, a challenge is perceived as an illegal act that may lead to a new court decision or a new piece of legislation, and sometimes to an executive act—all of which may change the Law in a single and very particular application. But, it takes an act of Congress and confirmation by the People to in any way change the Constitution.

In the case of Religion, a challenge may be met with excommunication or voluntary departure from the religious body, or it may be met with execution for the sacrilege of disbelief or failure to obey a supreme leader's commandments. In other words there is the assumption that—even though the "words of the one God" were recorded and then interpreted by human hands—once *codified:* they cannot be altered or even re-interpreted and certainly not questioned even if there is historical evidence challenging the story about the origination of the sacred writing as recorded in "the Book."

Trust, Test, and Verify—Again!

Real World Knowledge is founded on challenges that are based on logic and rational examination of observation, experimentation (testing), and resulting evidence. To paraphrase President Ronald Reagan, we "Trust, but then we Test to Verify," and—as may be necessary—we move to repeat that action, again and again.

When Questions are not allowed

Most Real World Knowledge is reliable unless it has become in some manner "enthroned" as correct without further question. When this happens, we essentially have a "conflict of interest" as when one group of scientists issued a statement that "Belief in Paranormal Phenomena is unscientific," and then asserted that all statements to the contrary are "pseudoscience."

This is little different from the Church's demand that Galileo renounce his scientific finding that the earth rotates around the sun because it was inconsistent with Catholic theology. Or than the refusal of many doctors to wash their hands prior to delivering babies until Dr. Ignaz Semmelweise in 1847 demonstrated that "cleanliness is next to Godliness" for it saved lives.

The scientific method requires that experiment and observation takes precedence over belief in determining the nature of reality, but real life experience readily calls past proclamations into question. That's where we are today: real life experience and contemporary research substantiate clairvoyance (and other paranormal phenomenon) in theory and practice.

Science, and Common Sense

Most "Everyday Knowledge" is often called "Common Sense" because it is both logical and traditional. It mostly is communicated in the explanations and instructions given to children by parents and elders followed by age-related levels of education in traditional schools. That may be followed by higher levels of general or specialized vocational education, or beyond to professional (degree) advanced education.

And "advanced" education is not limited to institutional learning but is extended by experience and independent study often questioning basic assumptions in terms of new "evidence."

True Learning never ceases because the purpose of life is to learn and grow

An *accepted* science is the systematically organized body of knowledge about a particular subject. A *theoretical* science is that same body of knowledge continually subjected to systematic observation and experiment. Both *accepted* and *theoretical* sciences are theories. All science is constantly subjected to challenge, and it is in response to the challenge that science advances. Any claim that "everything is known" is *prima facie* absurd, but such proclamations have been made many times and are still observed in certain subject areas where the academic hierarchy cannot be threatened by outsiders or "newbies," no matter how qualified.

Technology is the practical and generally beneficial application of scientific knowledge to the general and special needs of people, and is itself a system of continual testing and verification through the "market place."

Our Goal: Practical Applications

Today, our goal is to demonstrate and establish the practical benefits to be found in the applications of clairvoyance and other "para-normal" skills to real life situations. (We placed the word between quotation marks and separated "para" from "normal" with a hyphen because we don't believe such practices to not be "normal.")

CLAIRVOYANCE IN THEORY

Our Definition

In Chapter One we defined Clairvoyance as "*the perception of tangible objects, current events, or existing conditions not evident to the physical senses, but nevertheless having objective reality.*" We also pointed out that "Clairvoyance is far more than just the perception of realities not otherwise available to ordinary sensory awareness."

In theory and practice, clairvoyance is commonly experienced in five ways.

How Clairvoyance is Commonly Experienced

1. As ExtraSensory Perception (ESP) of things beyond ordinary physical sensation,

2. As forms of Illumination and Intuition,

3. As spontaneous awareness of apparently "supernatural" entities,

4. As knowledge or information gained through communication with those "super-natural entities" whether spontaneous or deliberately "invoked," and

5. As knowledge or information gained by means of *divination,* which is the best known and most popular form of clairvoyance.

Some would state that experiences 1 and 3 above are the same thing, but we believe that the occurrence of spontaneity is an important distinction.

Then we went on to list a sampling of 165 of the most familiar forms of divination all involving some degree of clairvoyance to take the practice from mere physical manipulation or measurement of objects into extended fields of awareness where psychic dimensions of consciousness are activated.

Consciousness and Awareness

We want to further remind the reader that the "power" is not in the divinatory tool or technique but begins in the consciousness (conscious mind and subconsciousness) of the diviner and extends into the Universal Consciousness and includes even the very nascent and subtle consciousness embedded in the tool itself. In the case of the more sophisticated divinatory tools and *systems,* such as the Tarot or the Runes, that consciousness extends to the symbols, their complex interactions and "correspondences," and to further calls to the organizing structure and *heritage* of the system.

However, it is important to note that the specific symbols involved cannot simply be interpreted by means of the "dictionaries" commonly provided in commercial products. The dictionary meanings are *doorways* into the cumulative experience of past diviners and, hence, good starting points for a divinatory reading, but a *true* reading has to be "live" and multidimensional for which even the most extensive text or computer reading is not a substitute.

A *True* Reading*

A "true reading" often begins with the *outward* dictionary descriptions of words and symbols but must also turn *inward* to both evoke the accumulating experience of the reader stored in the conscious mind and invoke the extended knowledge stored in the subconscious mind and further called forth from the greater unconscious, also known as *"the Collective Unconscious."*

> *The use of the word "true" in this instance does not define that reading as TRUE—to be accepted without question—but refers to the process itself as independent of external authority and reaching, instead, into "higher"

dimensions for a specific and unique reading intended only for the "client" and the exact question asked by the client.

Scientific Astrology & Palmistry

Other divinatory systems are—on the surface at least—less "psychic" and more "scientific." The most important of these are Astrology and Palmistry, which both involve observations of very specific physical patterns and measurements of particular Signs and Symbols, and actual *tangible* objects: the palm, and the planets. The planets, as positioned in the Zodiac, are represented in the *Horoscope* (the map of these positions at the "birth moment and place" of the person or entity involved). Despite the scientifically detailed physical observations of the objects and the mathematical calculations of their relationships to one another and to the birth person or event, both astrology and palmistry have their foundation in a long heritage of recorded observation and experience upon which their "dictionaries" of interpretations are based.

In the case of Astrology (and also the Tarot) there has been an extensive and very rich psychological exploration of the horoscopic factors and Tarot symbols in relation to the living "archetypes" of the human psyche both in ancient times, East and West, and by the modern followers of the brilliant Dr. Carl G. Jung. Both astrology and the Tarot relate to a complete symbolic structure in which every factor has a place and logical relationships to others and to the structure itself.

Working with either of these system, clairvoyance comes into natural play—in part because of the "call" of the symbols themselves to the subconscious, and then further as the symbols connect to the whole structure. In the case of the Tarot, that structure is the Kabbalistic Tree of Life* and in the case of astrology it is the Zodiac. (Unfortunately, the depth of meanings behind the Zodiac, and behind astrology, have become abused by the popularity of what we call "Sun Sign Astrology" which has little other than a superficial entertainment value.)

> *There are many divinatory decks called "Tarot" that are not based on the Tree of Life and that should instead be referenced as "Oracles" and specifically delineated by the cosmological symbol system that is the source of their meaning. Some of these systems are Runes, the I Ching, particular Mythologies, etc. Unfortunately, some decks are little more than "pretty pictures."

With "real" astrology, *Scientific Astrology*, it is another matter altogether and natural clairvoyance is awakened and becomes part of the interpretation—leading to a "True" reading.

The role of the "PK" Factor

In addition, Clairvoyance is sometimes augmented with spontaneous "PK," or psychokinetic, actions causing movements of the divinatory tools and objects that go beyond their manipulation by the diviner.

This is more often the case with those systems incorporating physical touch and manipulation of the related tools as in:

Divinatory Systems incorporating Physical Touch & Manipulation

Automatic Writing—*unconscious written communication involving a spirit while the writer is in a trance.*

Cartomancy—*using a deck or ordinary bridge or poker playing cards.*

Dowsing—*the use of a forked stick or bent steel clothes hanger or other metallic imitation of the forked stick in order to sense the presence of water or other resource or lost object.*

Geomancy—*interpreting dots, lines and figures traced in sand, dirt or pebbles, or naturally occurring formations either intuitively or by standard meanings.*

I Ching *aka* **Yi King**—*the casting of sticks or coins to establish 64 Hexagrams each consisting of six solid or broken lines.*

Oghams—*a series of sticks marked with cuts to represent each letter of the Tree Alphabet, and then thrown and selected randomly for divinatory interpretation.*

Pendulum Work—*using a pendulum over a map to determine the location of water or other resource, and also to respond to questions.*

Runes—*similar to, but older and more complex than Oghams and based on a very rich mythic system of Nordic/Teutonic mythology giving definition to each image.*

Tarot Cards—*a complex deck of 78 cards illustrated with symbols and images associated with the Hebrew and Greek Kabbalah. The Tarot is the most popular and important divinatory system in the Western world.*

Tea Leaf Reading—*interpreting the shapes, size and patterns of wet tea leaves. Also of coffee grounds.*

There are many "minor" systems involving observation of natural events or movements, but they all essentially prove the point that any "thing" can be adopted for use in PK divination.

The basic principle is to select the thing, establish the intent to use it, set up a rule regarding the movements, ask the question, allow yourself to slide into a light trance, and *let it happen!* It's this last element that is important and often ignored or misunderstood. You have to "let go" for anything to happen.

For any of these systems, we follow that same formula, including allowing the experience of a light trance. Clairvoyance is a *subjective* experience but also—necessarily—one that is "purpose driven." The more important the question ("the purpose of the divination") the greater the energy that must be projected into the "higher realms"—whether we think in terms of the subconscious mind, or the spirit world, or the astral plane, or another—in order to find or construct the appropriate answer.

The Field of Awareness

In this regard, clairvoyance opens up a "field of awareness" that surrounds the physical object, person, or event so that resulting information tends to be organic and holistic rather than singular. For example, in the search for a missing person, the clairvoyant "sensitive" may pick up not only the missing person's location, but his or her situation, health conditions, factors around his or her disappearance, and—if a crime—the motivations of the perpetrators.

This example makes the point that Clairvoyance is almost always *purpose-driven*, and it seems that it is the "purpose" itself that provides the force that calls up the surrounding circumstances.

It must be noted, however, that Clairvoyance is not always associated with a physical object or tool. Or, rather, that the tool involved may only be for the function of identification in relation to the purpose of "the reading." A photograph of a missing person, sometimes just a name and address and possibly a birth date, or a letter or other object belonging to the person, and sometimes the presence or even a phone call from a relative will suffice to make the necessary connection.

In cases of "remote viewing" which will be discussed later, the geographic coordinates have proven sufficient for the purpose of gaining information which may include visions of buildings or property.

Consciousness is not physically dependent

Not all Clairvoyance is as physically functional as those described above. While seeing the aura of another person, animal, or object—or even your own aura—does involve the direct presence of the person involved, other clairvoyance moves further beyond the physical plane into the etheric, astral, mental and spiritual dimensions. Famous clairvoyants like Charles Leadbeater and Rudolph Steiner have seen visions of long-past historical places, of historic persons and the enactment of past events. They, and others, have seen the "invisible" side of religious sacraments and magical ceremonies, the most intimate inner details of sexual relations, the inner side of birth and death, have provided amazing insight into sub-atomic matter and energy only recently confirmed by high-energy atom smashers and further confirmed by today's quantum physicists involving aspects of PK.

Clairvoyance is about Consciousness, and consciousness is everywhere and in everything. But our "awareness" of particular areas of consciousness is limited by focus and intention. Yogi Berra said, "If I hadn't believed it, I wouldn't have seen it." A natural corollary to this would seem to be: "If you haven't seen it, you won't believe it." Thankfully, Yogi's statement is true, but the corollary is only partly accurate.

There are many ways we *learn* to see new things. We hear from others that have seen them. We study those reports and slowly open our consciousness to the possibilities of these new things. Even more exciting is the realization that we foresee the possibility of new things by building a logical structure based on our present vision and knowledge. Using Mind, Logic, and Imagination we prepare the way for becoming aware of something new. And then, we "Test and Verify" our perception of the new thing.

Mostly this happens unconsciously as we read, talk, and think about subjects of interest. Just as the future is built on the past, so our awareness builds on the past as we look to the future. Life is not static—we learn and grow until we die, and then we do it again. Awareness is always expanding so that what was hidden beneath the horizon becomes visible to us as we raise our consciousness to higher levels.

CLAIRVOYANCE IN PRACTICE

Looking back to our definition of clairvoyance in Chapter One as "*the perception of tangible objects, current events, or existing conditions not present to the physical senses, but nevertheless having objective reality,*" we have to discuss the role of "perception."

We think of perception in terms of our physical senses, because we function in and through physical bodies and perceive the *outer* world mainly through our organs of sensation: eyes, ears, nose, tongue, and our means of touching and feeling. What we sense, however, must be interpreted by means of consciousness expressed through the awareness that has been developed through parental guidance, education, and mostly through experience. All of this is filtered through the physical brain.

But, we know that Consciousness is not a function of the brain, nor physically limited to it in any way. ExtraSensory Perception is perception not limited by the physical senses. The "bridge" between Consciousness and Perception is *Awareness*. We perceive things specifically, but our awareness extends beyond the thing itself, whether it's physical or non-physical. Around the "thing," there is a field of energy that is not defined by its simple borders but may fluctuate as the thing itself is subjected to contacts with other energy fields.

Everything is Connected

No-thing (nothing) is isolated from other things. Every-thing (everything) is connected variously to other things. Just as *no man is an island,** so nothing is an island by itself.

> *"All mankind is of one author, and is one volume; when one man dies, one chapter is not torn out of the book, but translated into a better language; and every chapter must be so translated . . . As therefore the bell that rings to a sermon, calls not upon the preacher only, but upon the congregation to come: so this bell calls us all: but how much more me, who am brought so near the door by this sickness. . . . No man is an island, entire of itself . . . any man's death diminishes me, because I am involved in mankind; and therefore never send to know for whom the bell tolls; it tolls for thee." John Donne (1572–1631).

In addition to your own connections to everything and everyone, you have the capacity to directly focus your attention narrowly to one thing and its immediate field, or more broadly to the one thing's other connections as defined by you. Just as you can physically focus your eyesight exactly on an object, or let your vision expand to the surroundings of the object, so can you focus or extend your clairvoyant vision. Or, more broadly yet, you can extend your awareness to include non-physical visual, auditory, olfactory, and other perceptive variations.

Extended Awareness & Focused Attention

Clairvoyance is essentially a function of extended awareness and focused attention. Without focus, your psychically open and extended awareness could result in a kind of total sensory bombardment, like being in the middle of a rock concert with multiple flashing lights and massive discordant music while under the influence of hallucinatory drugs. You could be permanently damaged by such over-stimulation.

Thankfully, except for such sensory overload and the overload of the hallucinogen induced experience, your opened awareness can be more of a mystical experience of the oneness of all life and being that Richard Bucke (1837-1902) called "Cosmic Consciousness."

Developed clairvoyance is a controlled combination of extended awareness and focused attention on a specific thing and specified connections so that your resulting knowledge is meaningful and practical. It takes you beyond the *free-for-all* electronic dimensions of the World Wide Web into the defined and *narrowly-specific* but multi-dimensional "**Cosmos Wide Web.** "

Divine Clairvoyance

Well, no—not *Divine* in the sense of Godly or of Divine Origin as in the Latin *divinare* "to be inspired by a god"—but "to divine" in the sense of *divinus* "to gain insight" which is the concept behind practices of divination using traditional tools and techniques. In Chapter One we listed 165 forms of divination that provide a means of connecting one object to another, or—in the more sophisticated systems—to a carefully organized selection of other connections defined in a logical structure—such as Astrology or the Tarot.

Yes, there is a "higher" form of divination that can be described as "inspired by a god."

THREE LEVELS OF DIVINATION

In all, we can consider three "levels" of divination:

1. The use of a simple tool or technique to "gain insight" through a connection to an object. Dowsing and the use of a Pendulum are examples of an "active" and simple divination. The Crystal Ball and Tea Leaf Reading are examples of a more "passive" type of divination.

2. The use of a complex set of tools and techniques involving a connection with and through an organized structure of interrelated symbols may be found in Astrology and the Tarot.

3. The use of more complex techniques leading to inspiration relate to controlled energizing of particular chakras.

All three of these will be treated in subsequent chapters. Nevertheless, we want to emphasize that no matter which form of clairvoyance practice is used, the principle is the same: *Developed clairvoyance is a controlled combination of extended awareness and focused attention on a specific thing and specified connections so that your resulting knowledge is meaningful and practical.*

Even though clairvoyance functions through an altered state of consciousness, it must be integrated into our conscious mind in order to bring about its own fulfillment. We live in a world of physical reality, and whatever we learn through clairvoyance must be implemented by the conscious mind. We must remember that no matter how psychic or "spiritual" we may be, we integrate everything through our conscious mind and carry our actions out through our physical body operating in the physical world.

At the same time, through developing our psychic skills we are expanding our consciousness into higher realms and becoming more "whole." Clairvoyance extends our awareness so that we draw upon the energies and unique functions of our higher bodies, etheric, astral, mental, and causal. While each is bound by its own "laws"—just as our physical body is—through our conscious mind we can involve those other powers into whatever level of operations we choose.

Clairvoyant Strategies

The clairvoyant faculty frequently engages our most advanced non-psychic faculties, including our creative imagery powers. These powers can translate clairvoyant impressions into images that depict meaningful realities. Not surprisingly then, exercises designed to develop clairvoyant skills are usually more effective when they emphasize activities that promote creative imagery, such as sculpting, drawing, painting, and other forms of creative work or play.

Meditation exercises that focus on creative imagery seem particularly conducive to clairvoyant empowerment. The third eye, a chakra thought to be connected to the pituitary gland and associated with clairvoyance, appears particularly responsive to meditation strategies that engage the mind's imagery powers. The following exercise was specifically designed to develop that faculty.

Certain strategies for inducing the precognitive dream can be readily adapted to accommodate clairvoyant dreaming. The finger spread procedure can be applied to delay sleep while clairvoyant autosuggestions are presented. Affirmations such as those that follow are usually sufficient to promote clairvoyant dreaming.

My clairvoyant powers will be activated as I sleep.

My inner psychic powers will generate the insight I need as I sleep.

These general affirmations can be supplemented with specific statements to access solutions and detailed clairvoyant information.

Clairvoyance, like other forms of ESP, improves with practice. Practice in meditation designed to enhance the mind's creative capacities is particularly valuable, because it builds the basic skills underlying not only clairvoyance, but many other psychic faculties as well. Our surroundings also provide practice opportunities for developing clairvoyant skills. Effective activities involve familiar materials and everyday situations. Excellent practice exercises include guessing the time before checking, pulling a book from a shelf and guessing its total number of pages, and guessing the amount of change in your pocket or purse. With practice, these simple activities can strengthen clairvoyant skills and the capacity to initiate clairvoyance at will.

SUMMARY

Clairvoyance is our claim to oneness with the world in the here and now. Expanded awareness through clairvoyance empowers us with an unlimited width, breadth, and depth of knowledge, which reveals what we otherwise cannot see, as it enriches our lives with new ideas and creative solutions. Equally important as these profound revelations are the simple joys of the clairvoyant experience itself, such as that felt in the discovery of a lost possession or the sudden "Ah ha!" of clairvoyant insight.

Whatever the nature of its expression, clairvoyance is empowerment in highly practical form: It can provide the critical information we need to solve our most pressing problems and achieve our loftiest goals. Clairvoyance is so basic to the empowered life that, without it, we often grope in darkness, out of touch with critical sources of psychic enlightenment.

Sources & Suggested Additional Reading:

Besant, A. & Leadbeater, C. W. *Occult Chemistry—Investigations by Clairvoyant Magnification into the Structure of the Atoms of the Periodic Table and of Some Compounds,* 1951, Theosophical—available in reprints.

Bucke, R. M. *Cosmic Consciousness—A Study in the Evolution of the Human Mind,* 2007, Book Jungle—reprint of the classic.

Dale, C. *Everyday Clairvoyant: Extraordinary Answers to Finding Love, Destiny and Balance in Your Life,* 2010, Llewellyn.

Dow, C. *Tea Leaf Reading for Beginners: Your Fortune in a Tea Cup,* 2011, Llewellyn.

Greer, J. M. *Earth Divination, Earth Magic: A Practical Guide to Geomancy,* 1999, Llewellyn.

Katz, D. L. *Extraordinary Psychic: Proven Techniques to Master Your Natural Psychic Abilities, 2008,* Llewellyn.

Katz, D. L. *You Are Psychic: The Art of Clairvoyant Reading & Healing,* 2004, Llewellyn.

Leadbeater, C. W. *The Hidden Side of Things,* 1913, Theosophical—available in reprints.

Leadbeater, C. W. *The Inner Life*, 1912, Rajput—available in reprints.

Steiner, R. *Supersensible Influences in the History of Mankind,*1956, Rudolf Steiner Publishing.

Steiner, R. *Universe, Earth and Man,* 1955, Rudolf Steiner Publishing.

ADDENDUM #2 TO CHAPTER TWO
Microcosm to Macrocosm & Macrocosm to Microcosm
INTRODUCTION TO THE
TATTVIC CONNECTION PROCEDURES

The exercise that follows in Addenda Three, and the twenty-four others included in this book are presented as chapter addenda to give emphasis to their special—near *alchemical*—function in literally *awakening and purifying* the five primal elements and their twenty combinations in your body and personal consciousness. I recommend that each of the 25 programs be spaced a week apart, and each meditation should be preceded by the Empowerment Tension & Release Procedure or other relaxation program.

In that regard, I encourage the use of the Empowerment Tension & Release procedure several times before using a less time-consuming one, and I encourage the occasional use of the Empowerment procedure whenever you recognize the strong presence of Stress and Tension in your person. Remember, not only is stress a "killer," but it reduces the strength and accuracy of your psychic powers, and inhibits the free flow of the essential psychic energies for growth and transformation.

To Awaken!
"To awaken" is to be transformed. We awaken from the unconsciousness of nightly sleep to the consciousness of our daily life. But in the fairy tale myth of *Sleeping Beauty*, awakened from *poisoned* sleep by the kiss of her heroic Prince Charming, we have a deeper meaning: It takes both courage and positive action for humanity to awaken from its normal passive consciousness—*an actual sleep state*—into active higher consciousness and true self awareness. True self awareness becomes possible when we can focus attention on the primal elements within, awakening them to their purity, and assembling them into a new self, free of emotional reaction and sensual "bondage" to external events.

The goal of these procedures is freedom from ignorance and reactive thought and behavior, and from the external impositions of irrational and repressive belief systems of all kinds denying self-responsibility and the opportunity to achieve self-empowerment so generally characteristic of the passing Piscean Age.

We are entering into a "New Age" of expanding awareness into higher conscious-ness requiring personal growth and psychic development, but "changing times" always bring social unrest and reactive extremism that challenge psychic, psychological, and spiritual progress (and social and human progress as well) . We must each act with courage and boldness in our personal growth but without reaction to those who cling to the past systems of organizational and militaristic empowerment.

Why purify?

This book is a program to develop the psychic power of Clairvoyance and make it into a reliable and accurate psychic skill. The problem, however, is that clairvoyance (and other psychic powers) primarily function at the astral level of consciousness, and the astral level (both the astral body and the astral plane) is composed of astral "sub-stance"—identified esoterically as *emotional substance and consciousness.*

We are more than just a physical body with a computer-like physical brain: we are composite persons of physical/etheric, astral, mental/causal, and "spiritual" bodies each composed of particular substance known by the same term, with each operating according to the particular "laws" of those worlds. At the same time, these bodies and worlds are not really separate but do function in separate forms as directed under will from the Higher Mental level also known as the Causal World, and Causal Body.

It's from that causal level that the physical body is *formed,* along with the entire personal composite we know as "personality" and sometimes refer to as "Body and Soul" or as "Body, Mind, and Spirit." Neither terminology is particularly correct as reference back to the *Tables for Seven Levels of Reality* and *Seven Levels of Conscious-ness* will show.

We will discuss these further in another book, but our only concern here is to explain why we need to purify the primal elements in mind and body. As described in the addendum to Chapter 1, we are generally "emotionally reactive" to every passing thought and perception in our event- and entertainment-dominated culture. We too commonly lack the disciplined conscious mind to filter out what really amounts to a kind of "emotional pollution" that colors our perceptions. As a result, clairvoyant vision may be distorted by unrecognized emotional unconscious psychic attachments. *We change that by the Tattvic Meditation programs that follow.*

The Passage from Piscean to Aquarian "Man"

First of all, I must apologize for the seemingly *sexist* reference to "Man," but the last hundred years has brought a dramatic change to our gender perceptions. While sexual awareness and identity have brought new awakening to the universal and non-gender capabilities of women and a resulting gender-free empowerment in their roles in political, economic, professional, and social life, it has also brought important recognition of gender differences in matters of physical health, sexuality, emotional and body self-expression, and even in matters of perception.

As anyone in Western culture knows, this century of change has also led to and has been enabled by a century of revolution in the attainment of "women's rights" alongside the attainment of civil rights and liberties and a vast expansion of what such "progress" has meant in human development and advancement.

As a person himself nearly a century old who has witnessed and actively participated in this revolution, I see the word MAN as an all-encompassing spiritual symbol and an inclusive definition of Man-Woman that is beyond gender differences without loss of the meaning, power, and importance of sexual differences that extend to more than reproductive functions.

Why is this short preface necessary?

Because our next subject is an introduction to the system behind the science and practice of the Tattvas, the very ancient and once very secret and still vastly misunderstood Indian tradition of TANTRA.

Sure, many people think they know all about Tantra and believe it's a very *New Agey* "sexual yoga" in which a man holds back his ejaculation so that his woman partner can enjoy multiple orgasms through a variety of exotic positions, all while she's being worshipped as a goddess. *Who can resist that?*

More than "Sexual Yoga" and "Orgasmic Bliss"

Tantra is much more than "sexual yoga" and is *New Agey* in spirit only. The reality is that it is very *old age*, and its teachings are ageless. Some of the early writings go back to 700 BC, and scholars debate these and much earlier dates—usually meaning that the origins of the tradition go back long before any preserved writings and any thought that writings were important to a primarily oral tradition reaching back at least to 7,000 B.C. and perhaps much earlier. There are several very important points made about the tradition*:

> *Note: These remarks apply to the *ancient esoteric* "pure" tradition before modification and adaptation into modern "orthodox" religious practices identified as Buddhist Tantra, Tibetan Tantra, Hindu Tantra, etc., and adding requirements of guru guidance, priest-led rituals, multiple deities, initiatory practices, and more but all seeking authoritarian domination and regulation of private practices. We speak here only of the pre-Piscean Age esoteric personal practices. We further suggest similarities if not unities with

what has sometimes been called "the Old Religion" in the West, dating far before what is euphemistically called "the Pre-Christian Era."

A Basic Outline of Tantra as a Tradition

1. Tantra is not a "religion" per se, but is a consistent system of cosmic understanding and an equally consistent system of self-improvement developmental techniques and spiritual *practices*. Tantra has been adapted into three related systems of:

    a. Ritual and Deity Worship with Priestly functions and Theological Instruction;

    b. Graded Yogic Practices and Disciplines under the guidance of a Guru with initiatory ceremonies marking the grades;

    c. Self-Directed Psychological and Psychic Practices consistent with an organized body of esoteric knowledge proclaimed to be a universally true and accurate understanding of manifest and unmanifest "reality."

2. Generally, Tantric practices were oriented toward the "married householder" rather than the monastic or solitary person withdrawing from the world. In today's world, "married householders" might be better interpreted as adult men and women in established relationships actively involved in responsible employment and citizenship.

3. Tantra sees the world as *real* and not illusion—in contrast to other yogic and Buddhist traditions that, in essence, proclaim "that life is a mistake." Rather, we are born into the material world to grow and develop the whole person we are intended to be—not to turn away from it or "abandon ship."

4. Tantric practices are intended to bring about an inner realization that "Nothing exists that is not Divine," and their goal is freedom from ignorance and thus freedom from the suffering that many religions proclaim "to be our lot" and that "we are born in pain and suffering and should welcome the embrace of church and "the release of death."

5. Tantra is "world embracing" rather than "world denying," and sees the whole of reality as the <u>self</u>-expression of a single Creator Consciousness in which there is no division of spiritual versus mundane. As a psychological convenience this "Creator Consciousness" is termed *Divine* but without the overtones of worship.

6. Tantra is the source of esoteric knowledge of the complex nature of cosmic reality (not just the physical universe) inclusive of our physical and subtle bodies and the energetic system of chakras, nadis, tattvas, mantras, yantras, breath-

regulation, kundalini, and more that are developmentally important to the fulfillment of our Divine purpose.

7. Tantric principles should be incorporated into every aspect of daily life as a continuing spiritual growth practice. We live in a holistic universe and need to live holistically with awareness of the spiritual as part of our reality.

8. Tantric sexual practices, perceived as the union of male and female and the re-union of god and goddess, Shiva and Shakti, are a means into an intense and expanded (ecstatic) state of awareness, freed of mind-created material boundaries to reaffirm our identity with pure consciousness—as it was in the Beginning.

9. Tantra teaches that each person is a union of universal energy that is Divinity itself, and that everything we need for that realization is within us now.

10. In summary, Tantra is a complete system of esoteric knowledge and practice that in its ancient purity is a personal resource for every person seeking understanding and development.

Among scholars, Tantra is generally seen as the culmination of all Indian thought, the most radical form of spirituality, and the ideal <u>personal</u> "religion" of the modern world that has had a profound influence on Western Occult Philosophy and practice, and on the development of today's Neo-Paganism. It is this Tantra that is the source of our knowledge of the tattvas.

One scholar sums it up:

"Tantra is a holistic approach to the study of the universe from the point of view of the individual: the study of the macrocosm through the study of the microcosm. It draws on all the sciences . . . to provide a practical means of realizing the highest ideals of philosophy in daily life. Instead of separating and categorizing the different areas of human knowledge, Tantra draws them together like beads on one string. The beautiful rosary thus formed is a unique instrument for enhancing the physical, mental, and spiritual life of man and woman."

Through the study of the universe, we gain understanding of the laws of Nature, Tantra seeks to us that knowledge to promote the evolution of individual consciousness.

"The aim of Tantra, then, is to expand awareness in all states of consciousness, whether waking state, dream state, or deep sleep. To accomplish this, we need a kind of 'deprogramming' and 'reprogramming' of our human computer. . . . Tantra provides the methodology and the tools to identify the various factors

that influence our thoughts and feelings and to transcend the obstacles to our
evolution arising from ignorance . . ."

Johari, Harish: Tools for Tantra, 1986, Destiny Books

A Brief History of the Tattvas

**"The Universe came out of the Tattvas; it goes on by the instrumentality of
the Tattvas; it disappears into the Tattvas; by the Tattvas is known the nature
of the Universe."**

(Source of quote unknown)

*To do anything well requires some understanding of the system and philosophy
behind the programs, procedures & practices. Even common words and seemingly
familiar terminology take on different meanings depending on the system within
which they are used—which is why we include subject specific glossaries in each
book.*

Metaphorically, it is said that the Cosmos comes into being at the out-breath
of God and will culminate and disappear at the in-breath. Breath—in its different
energizing forms—is the force behind all manifestation, and its modifications are
the source of all diversity, all motion, and all meaning. The tattvas are those primary
modifications. In Western esotericism they are called the five fundamental elements
functioning on the astral plane behind material manifestation.

It is the "movement" of the tattvas that is experienced as *vibration* and perceived
through our five physical senses and ethereally by clairvoyance. In addition to their
fundamental presence throughout the entire physical world—including the physical/
etheric body—the tattvas flow as waves and sub-waves of Pranic energies of varying
time lengths throughout day and night. They are always present and active.

So fundamental are the tattvas that they can function through their symbolic representations of all life and form with near mathematical precision. We see this most
clearly in the geometric forms with which they are identified but we must—at the
same time—use mind and imagination to "populate" the *Memory Files* we automatically create under name and form in our subconscious mind with "correspondences"
derived from our perceptions just as we also do with the Kabbalistic structure of the
Tree of Life.

There's nothing difficult about this analytical exercise that only you can do with
either and preferably both these systems that bring you into what I refer to as "coincidental awareness" between the inner and outer worlds within and through which

you live and function. It's mostly a matter of awareness, but the greater the conscious effort you put into it, the greater the benefits that will permeate your being and life. The additional "Tattva Connection Procedures" presented here in these special chapter addenda bring the vital intellectual awareness down to the emotional and physical/etheric levels fundamental to health, well-being, and clarity of perception free of emotional and psychic baggage.

One particular note: It is Akasha (Spirit, Ether) from which the four other tattvas continually devolve and return—thus it serves as the library containing the sum of past history and the "womb" containing the seeds of future history. Astral Akasha functions as a clairvoyant doorway to the *Akashic Records* holding personal memories and collective knowledge. As our goal is to bring about clarity and accuracy to all psychic perceptions, understanding what is involved is the *Aquarian Age process* in which you become your own teacher, your own guru, discovering your own "Master" within.

Before going on to discuss the Primal Elements I want to emphasize something that needs to be deeply impressed in the reader's mind—that these *tattvic* elements are NOT physical but are instead astral and serve as a kind of matrix or structural model for the *elemental forces* to manifest in the forms we experience. At the same time, I must clearly emphasize that none of these tattvas manifest singly but always compounded with one element usually predominant. As example only, we could say that Prithivi manifests as half Earth and the other half made up of Ether, Air, Fire, and Water in varying percentages. Just to further illustrate. The compound might be 50 percent Earth, 25 percent Water, 10 percent Fire, 8 percent Ether, and 7 percent Air. Each of the lesser elements modifies the dominant element. Generally, however, it is sufficient for most of our purposes to recognize the two most predominant. In other words, continuing with the example, we would describe the compound as "Earth—Seed of Water" in contrast to describing the pure element as "Earth—Seed of Earth." We have to understand the dominant element before we look at the compounds.

We are studying, and absorbing into ourselves, something so fundamental and important that we need to proceed one step at a time.

Sources & Suggested Additional Reading:

Evola, J. *The Yoga of Power—Tantra, Shakti, and the Secret Way,* 1968, Edizioni Mediterranee; 1992 Inner Traditions International.

Johari, Harish. *Tools for Tantra,* 1986, Destiny Books.

CHAPTER THREE
Induced versus Spontaneous Clairvoyance
Empowerment without Limits

Clairvoyance is always Empowerment Driven

Clairvoyance, whether deliberately induced or spontaneous, is always empowerment driven. As a universal human trait, its purposes can range from simply expanding awareness of distant realities to instantly intervening in extreme emergency situations. Within that vast range, it can provide the insight required to meet the demands of the moment while generating an emerging body of knowledge that is essential to our long-term success.

New Knowledge, New Skills

As a mental faculty poised to empower our lives, clairvoyance beckons your interaction and invites you to use it at any moment. Whether discovering new meaning to your existence, finding the love of your life, or developing your inner potentials, clairvoyance provides a multifunctional key to success. It not only generates new knowledge, it unleashes the skills required to effectively use it. Equipped with that combination of knowledge and power through clairvoyance, you become empowered to achieve even your most difficult goals.

Clairvoyance challenges Conventional Science

In its capacity to increase both knowledge and power, clairvoyance challenges the status quo of conventional science and sets forth a new standard for success called *Empowerment Without Limits*. Once the self-perceived constrictions for awareness are dismantled, clairvoyance along with telepathy and precognition become liberated to function freely. As a result, the knowledge and power of even the most distant reaches of the universe become receptive to our probes and interactions. We become, finally, *at one with the universe.*

Integrative Clairvoyance

Clairvoyance is collective and interactive in nature. Through a combination of spontaneous and induced clairvoyance, you can generate a holistic effect that exercises your capacity to reach beyond the conventional constrictions of perceiving, feeling, and thinking. The result is a state of *integrative clairvoyance* in which clairvoyance, rather than simply expanding awareness, becomes a major force that brings together other relevant mental faculties and focuses them on important life goals.

As an integrative phenomenon, clairvoyance is both self-empowering and altruistically oriented. Integrative clairvoyance is not about competition, exploitation, and financial gain but rather about advancing personal growth while promoting the common good. It is not about who can gain the most power, but rather how to find ways of cooperating and working together. Collective in nature, integrative clairvoyance can bring together the myriad of forces that influence our growth and organize them into an integrated whole. In the hierarchy of personal growth, integrative clairvoyance functions at the highest level of personal development.

Action and Accomplishment Oriented

Integrative clairvoyance is both action and accomplishment oriented. It recognizes our growth potentials and our capacity to exceed all self-imposed limits that slow our progress. It embraces our affirmed goals as realities awaiting realization rather than just imagined possibilities. It can scan our past, including our past-life experiences, to uncover relevant resources and integrate them into our present strivings. It can uncover unseen opportunities, and activate the dormant mental faculties related to them. The result is a spontaneously integrated state of mind, body, and spirit that empowers us to overcome all barriers to success. Within that integrated, empowered framework, all the essentials related to our success are activated to work together in perfect harmony.

Clairvoyance Facilitates Growth, and Extrasensory Development

The guidelines that follow were designed in our labs to establish a holistic, integrated foundation upon which clairvoyant skills can be acquired and applied. Rather than a structured, step-by-step strategy, the guidelines are flexible and applicable to a wide range of life situations and personal needs. Of central importance to the guidelines is the recognition of clairvoyance as both an extrasensory phenomenon and growth process. Our studies consistently showed that through these guidelines, you can facilitate an integrated state that enlightens, attunes, and balances the mind, body, and spirit. In that integrated state, you can rapidly develop the skills required to access totally new sources of knowledge and power. Here are the guidelines:

Guidelines to Clairvoyant Growth & Integration

- **Embrace clairvoyance as an *essential part of your being.*** Clairvoyance is not only an important growth resource; it is a crucial, interactive component of your being. It is that "knowing part" of the *essential self* that reaches beyond the confines of sensory perception to engage totally new sources of enlightenment, energy, and power. Whether induced and spontaneous, clairvoyance not only accesses new knowledge, it integrates it into the self structure. The result is an empowered state of increased enlightenment that accelerates growth, promotes adjustment, and ensures success. Beyond these, clairvoyance can attune the self and connect you to the most advanced sources of power. Even the far reaches of the universe are not beyond the scope of clairvoyance as an integrative part of the essential self.

- **Generate a state of oneness within.** The integrative power of clairvoyance can bring the complexities of life together by generating a state of *empowered oneness within*. Once embraced, clairvoyance organizes the multiple functions of the mind and body into a synergized state of oneness. In that holistic state, each mental and physical function contributes to the other to generate an optimal state of self-empowerment.

- **Gain knowledge, and with it, power.** We've heard it before, "Knowledge is power." Through clairvoyance, you can gain knowledge and power otherwise unavailable to you. Power to make better decisions, solve complex problems, and generate new ideas becomes readily available through the integrative nature of clairvoyance. Given the power of clairvoyant knowledge, otherwise unattainable goals become reasonable possibilities.

- **Stay connected to nature.** Walking along a forest trail, viewing the night sky, observing the delicate beauty of flowers, scanning a magnificent mountain range, and noting the amazing diversity of animal life from earth's lowliest of creatures to the most regal can inspire, energize, and empower. It's during our interactions with nature that we often glimpse distant realities, including the spirit realm. The result is the highest form of integrative clairvoyance in which we become not only enlightened but balanced and attuned, both within ourselves and beyond. Simply viewing your natural surroundings from a distance and noting their splendor and unique beauty can be a breakthrough experience that inspires, comforts, and empowers. Your interactions with nature can banish conflict, dissolve fragmentation, alleviate stress, and promote continuity in your life, all of which are critical to the integration of clairvoyant power into your life. Fortunately, nature in all its beauty and power is available to you right now, even when viewed from the confines of your room. *Connect to nature and enjoy!*

• **Embrace your altruistic side.** Could acts of kindness toward persons, animals, and even the environment promote clairvoyance and its integrative effects? There's an emerging body of evidence that strongly suggests that possibility. Our studies over the years repeatedly showed that altruistic acts increased feelings of personal worth, built self-confidence, and among college students, improved academic performance. Our studies also found that retirees beyond age 65 who embraced their altruistic side and participated in worthy causes were both healthier and happier. On a variety of laboratory ESP tests, including clairvoyance, college students and retirees alike who rated high on altruism tended to perform better (and apparently enjoyed the tasks more) than a control group with average or below average ratings on altruism. *Could altruism be the new holy grail of integrative clairvoyance?* Conceivably, nothing is more personally empowering than daily acts of kindness.

• **Know where you are now and where you want to go.** Set personal goals and commit yourself to achieving them. Develop your clairvoyant skills, and let clairvoyance and its integrative power become contributors to your goal-related efforts. Incorporate clairvoyant insight and guidance into your goal strivings. Recognize the timing and accuracy of both spontaneous and induced clairvoyance. Your success in your career and personal life alike may rest in your willingness to integrate clairvoyance into your goal-related strivings. The integrative power of clairvoyance can become the critical component that securely melds your framework for success.

• **Keep your brain active.** Learn something new each day. Become cognitively and socially engaged. Our studies found that higher scores on laboratory tests of clairvoyance as well as precognition were directly related to active learning and positive social interactions. Our studies also found that staying physically active promotes healthful cognitive functions, including clairvoyance. Among wide-ranging age groups, exercising daily enhanced not only clairvoyance but memory and problem solving as well.

• **Overcome disempowering thoughts and emotions.** Eliminate negativity. Negative thoughts inhibit clairvoyance and its integrative effects. Remind yourself that you are a person of dignity and worth. Keep a positive view of your life—past, present, and future. Recognize your past accomplishment (or absence of them) as valuable learning experiences. Stay optimistic. Don't hesitate to challenge the status quo by exploring new possibilities. Keep in mind that the best is yet to come, and remind yourself that you can make it happen! There is no substitute for positive expectations. The simple assertion, *I am destined for greatness,* is the most powerful affirmation known. That assertion alone can generate an expectancy effect that cannot fail. It opens the door for integrative clairvoyance in its most powerful form.

• **Develop your imagery skills.** Imagery and concentration skills are critical to clairvoyance, which often unfolds in imagery form. Practice using maps, globes, pictures, and other articles can facilitate imagery and the development of a comprehensive world view with you at the center of it. Our studies found that practice exercises consisting simply of viewing a tangible aid such as a map or picture, and then with eyes closed forming a detailed mental image of it can promote the development of clairvoyant skills. Additional studies found that similar practice exercises can facilitate out-of-body travel to designated locations. Through such exercises, a cognitive map that includes not only destinations but the space between them can unleash cognitive awareness that is without limits. It's important to note that *space imagery* consisting of images of space among distant locations is equally as important as *destination imagery.* They together can form a cognitive map in which clairvoyance occurs. Given a *world (or universe) view* through practice using space and location imagery, you can develop your ability to deliberately target distant locations and clairvoyantly view them in minute detail.

• **Keep in mind: Complexity seeks simplicity.** Believe it or not, the simplest of techniques is often the most effective. For instance, our studies found that simply chewing gum promotes healthy cognitive functions, including clairvoyance. In a controlled study of college student volunteers, chewing gum immediately prior to the experimental exercise dramatically increased accuracy in clairvoyantly identifying cards that had been randomly drawn from a deck of ESP (Zener) cards. Temporarily chewing gum also resulted in a marked improvement in precognitive exercises along with a reduction in stress levels. Our lab studies of the human aura system found that temporarily chewing gum expanded and balanced the aura as measured by electrophotography. Breaks in the aura tended to close as the aura assumed greater brightness and symmetry. Aside from these effects, there is scientific evidence that chewing gum improves memory and accelerates the delivery of oxygen to the brain (L. Wilkinson, A. Scholey, and K. Wesnes, 2002. Chewing gum selectively improves aspects of memory in healthy volunteers, Appetite, 38:235–236).

- **Exercise.** The evidence is clear: Physical exercise facilitates healthful cognitive functions, including clairvoyance. Our studies of college students at Athens State University showed that students who exercised regularly typically performed better on tests of clairvoyance. Students who exercised for at least four hours per week performed significantly higher than controls on clairvoyance exercises requiring the identification of rare coins concealed in manila envelopes. As a footnote, experiments with animals have likewise shown that exercise improves certain mental functions (K. Nichol et al., 2009. Exercise improves cognition and hippocampal plasticity in APOE e4 mice. Alzheimer's and Dementia, 5:287:294).

- **Don't rush it.** Whether spontaneous or induced, clairvoyance can occur slowly or at lightning-fast speed. It can involve events than range from routine daily affairs to matters of life-and-death significance. It can provide enrichment, offer protection, generate insight, and build feelings of personal worth. Don't sabotage the experience. Allow it to unfold, embrace it, and when needed, act upon it.

- **Enjoy!** We typically perform better on tasks we enjoy. Finding pleasure in clairvoyance, whether spontaneous or induced, amplifies your clairvoyance potentials and increases the relevance of the clairvoyant experience. Persons with advanced psychic abilities typically report pleasure in exercising their clairvoyant skills, particularly when they contribute to the good of others.

Expands Awareness & Generates New Resources

There now exists a mountain of evidence that clairvoyance as an integrative phenomenon not only expands conscious awareness, it mobilizes the powers related to the demands and goals of the moment. Dormant resources, including but not limited to those of past-life origin, are assembled and activated as needed. Aside from that, clairvoyance can generate totally new resources through its synergistic and integrative effects. It can generate a holistic state that exceeds the combined powers of its parts. Even more importantly, it can connect us to the spiritual nature of our being by generating a mental, physical, and spiritual state of oneness within. In that empowered, attuned state, we have direct access to the limitless resources of other planes and dimension.

The Open Curtain Program

Mobilizing Mental & Psychic Resources

The Open Curtain Program was developed in our labs as a self-administered procedure designed to open the mind's clairvoyant curtain and reveal important realities—past, present, and future—that are otherwise unavailable to us. The program not only accesses new information but equally as important, it mobilizes the mental resources related to it. The goal of the approach is thus twofold: gaining new knowledge and with it, power. Although designed specifically to promote clairvoyance, the program has demonstrated equal effectiveness when adapted for other goals, including precognition as well as astral travel. Here's the 8-step program which usually requires approximately thirty minutes.

The Open Curtain Program should not be used while driving, operating machinery, or engaging in any other task requiring attention and concentration.

Step 1. Formulate your clairvoyant goals which can range from general to highly specific. Your goals can target information related to highly specific situations and needs, or they can focus simply on spontaneously experiencing the empowering effects of this program.

Step 2. Having formulated your goals, find a quiet, comfortable place, settle back, and with your eyes closed, focus you attention inward. Slow your breathing and give yourself permission to become increasingly relaxed. Affirm in your own words, either silently or audibly, the emerging flow of relaxation throughout your body.

Step 3. Visualize a vast theater stage with a closed curtain of any color. Focus your full attention on the curtain, to include its folds and shades of color. Note the sense of peace and tranquility that accompanies your imagery of the stage with its curtain of color.

Step 4. Visualize the curtain slowly opening to reveal a clear scene upon the stage. Take plenty of time for the curtain to totally open and for the scene to fully unfold.

Step 5. Once the curtain is fully opened, focus your full attention on the scene. Note the specific features of the scene, to include the presence of persons, animals, objects, actions, and the natural world. As you continue to focus your full attention on the unfolding scene, you will sense its relevance to stated goals and your present life situation.

Step 6. Affirm in your own words the significance of the experience, to include the emergence of new information and its relevance. Note the empowering effects of the experience, including the mobilization of your inner powers.

Step 7. As the curtain slowly closes, again affirm in your own words the empowering relevance of the experience.

Step 8. Open your eyes and take plenty of time to reflect on the experience. It is
often at this stage that additional clairvoyant information will unfold.

Problem Solving Information

In its capacity to access new knowledge and activate the mental powers related
to it, the Open Curtain Program has shown a wide-range of applications. It is especially effective in accessing information of problem-solving relevance. It can provide
important insight related to career decisions, relationships, and financial investments.
It's relevance to career planning was illustrated by an undergraduate college student
who was ambivalent regarding which graduate school to attend. During her application of the approach, a clear image of a certain school appeared with the name of the
university appearing in bold block letters over the entrance to the central administration building. She applied to the school and was promptly accepted.

In another instance of the program's relevance to decision making, a business
major who had been accepted for positions by two equally appealing firms used the
approach in an effort to decide which position to accept. In Step 5 of the procedure,
an image of the preferred firm clearly appeared. She accepted the position and later
asserted, "It was the best decision of my life." As it turned out, the rejected firm, a retail
business, later closed due to financial failure.

Past-Lives Relevance

The Open Curtain Technique has been highly effective in uncovering past-life
experiences of present-life relevance. Unlike past-life regression through hypnosis, the
self-administered program requires no formally induced trance state and often spontaneously targets past-life realities of important current-life relevance. Upon retriev-
ing a particular past-life experience, the Open Curtain Program effectively mobilizes
the resources required to integrate it and bring forth empowering change. Present-life
phobias, obsessions, and compulsions as well as conflicts, anxieties, and depression of
past-life origin are all receptive to this technique. In our studies that compared the use
of the Open Curtain Program and hypnosis in extinguishing phobias, the Open Curtain approach typically demonstrated a much higher degree of effectiveness, particularly
among individuals who showed low susceptibility or resistance to hypnosis. Long after
their resistance to hypnosis had been extinguished, many of our subjects retained their

preference for the Open Curtain approach. By their report, they felt more in command of the experience and their capacity to focus it on personal needs.

Liberation from Past-Life "Baggage"

In a remarkable example of the use of the Open Curtain Program in extinguishing phobias, a pre-law student who participated in our development of the approach experienced in Step 5 a detailed view of a past-life situation that instantly extinguished his life-long fear of cutting instruments, including knives and saws. With the curtain fully open, he saw a clear picture of himself as a soldier lying on a makeshift hospital bed in what appeared to be a Civil War setting. As the scene unfolded, he viewed his injured left arm being amputated by a surgeon, first by cutting through the flesh around the bone above the elbow and then by sawing through the exposed bone. As the curtain slowly closed in Step 7 of the procedure, he experienced his fear of knives and saws slowly fading and finally vanishing altogether. By his report, "The Open Curtain Technique provided not only the knowledge but also the power required to fully liberate me from the baggage of a life-long fear."

Experience New Beginnings

Among the most important therapeutic applications of this procedure is its capacity to alleviate depression and build feelings of worth and wellbeing. That function was dramatically illustrated by a social worker whose marriage had recently ended in a bitter divorce. As the curtain slowly opened during the procedure, she viewed a magnificent sunrise that bathed the sky with a golden glow. She stretched forth her hands as she viewed the scene and, by her report, felt a healing warmth that permeated her full body. In her own words, "The experience changed my life. With the parting of the curtain, for the first time I realized that the divorce, rather than a dark ending, signaled a bright new beginning filled with happiness and success."

Release from Past-Life Trauma

Our studies found that unexplained physical symptoms along with the anxieties associated with them are also receptive to the Open Curtain Program. That application is especially effective when the symptoms are related to past-life experiences. For instance, in Step 5 of the procedure, an engineer who had experienced for many years a persistent band of numbness around his right ankle viewed himself in a past-life prison setting bound with a right leg iron and restraint chain. By his own report, the numbness in his ankle suddenly vanished as he viewed the prison scene. For him, the Open Curtain Program not only explained the pain, it permanently extinguished it—a clear example of the power of past-life enlightenment.

Finding Lost Objects

This Open Curtain Program has been highly effective when used to discover missing articles, including jewelry. A college student who lost her engagement ring used the procedure to discover its exact location. In Step 5, the front entrance to her apartment emerged in striking detail. As she viewed the scene, the ring situated to the left of the entrance and half hidden in the grass commanded her attention. She later searched the site and found the ring situated exactly as depicted in the procedure.

Locating Missing Animals

Aside from tangible objects, missing animals have also been located through the application of this program. A high school student whose dog companion went missing during a forest hike used the procedure to successfully locate the dog. Having stated her goal in Step 1, she saw in Step 5 a forest cabin with the dog on a leash near the front entrance. She organized a search effort and with the assistance of a forest ranger located the cabin and successfully rescued the dog—located, as expected, near the cabin's front entrance.

Clairvoyance in Criminal Cases

The Open Curtain Program has shown unusual promise when applied as a criminal investigative strategy. Among the examples is the location of missing persons as well as the discovery of important crime-related evidence. With a clear formulation of goals in Step 1 of the program followed by the emergence of the crime scene in Step 5, the exact location of missing weapons and evidence is often revealed. In one celebrated case, Step 5 revealed the location in a remote wooded area of a bandanna that belonged to the perpetrator of a rape. The discovery led directly to his arrest and later conviction.

Interaction with the Spiritual Realm

Possibly the most advanced manifestation of the integrative nature of clairvoyance is its capacity to connect us to the spirit realm. Through the Open Curtain Program, we can pull back the curtain to that realm and directly interact with it. We can discover its most advanced planes and dimensions of knowledge and power. We can experience the spiritual origin of our existence as well as the abundance of spiritual resources available to us at any moment. We can interact with benevolent personal spirit guides and growth facilitators that often emerge during this stage of the procedure. By their own testimony, persons who experience the spirit realm during this procedure remain strongly connected to it long after the closing of the curtain.

Growth through Practice & Application

Practice is essential to the development of your clairvoyant skills. Whether applied to achieve such specific objective as interacting with the spirit realm or simply discovering missing objects, making quality decisions, solving pressing problems, the Open Curtain Program with repeated practice will effectively exercise your clairvoyant abilities and empower you to reach a totally new level of enlightenment and personal empowerment.

Integrative Streaming of Clairvoyant Power

Clairvoyance, whether induced or spontaneous, is an integrative phenomenon that not only expands the conventional boundaries of human experience; it unleashes an integrative effect with holistic empowering potential. The result is a continuous *integrative streaming of clairvoyant power* with unlimited possibilities. Although we are only now beginning to comprehend the complex dynamics of the integrative nature of clairvoyance, the evidence is clear: clairvoyance—both spontaneous and induced— can now become an on-going reality in your life.

Continuous Growth & Empowerment

You can at last generate an integrative state of enlightenment and wholeness that is continuously empowering. You can now assume full command of the forces that affect your growth, and as a result you can increase the overall the quality of your life. You can meet the complex challenges of life, overcome all blockages to your growth, and generate totally new opportunities for your personal fulfillment. All of these you can do for yourself through the integrative streaming of clairvoyant power.

Meditation exercises that focus on creative imagery seem particularly conducive to clairvoyant empowerment.

ADDENDUM #3 TO CHAPTER THREE
Microcosm to Macrocosm & Macrocosm to Microcosm

The Tattvic Connection—
Meditation & Visualization Program #1: Earth/Earth

Prithivi: Earth—Seed of Earth

The Miracle of the One Thing—*Through Mind*

Earth! We live on it, we stand on it, we walk on it, we share it with other living beings, we can dig down into it, we mine it for energy and mineral resources, we can use it to grow things and build things, our bodies are composed of it and water, it is the foundation for all we do and the mother to all life, it is our symbol and our reality for solidity, and masculine support. Its energy is mechanical and attracting, it is dark and light (night and day, underground and above ground).

Remember: Everything is connected and it is by means of powerful symbols and disciplined practice that your mind enters into the five elements. The following Tattva Overview Table #1 is just a very basic overview of the first five tattvas from a single perspective, the body. Other simple Overview Tables will follow in later addenda. Greater detail will be provided when we consider each tattva separately in preparation for each mediation exercise.

The main purpose of this series of Overview Tables is to emphasize that the tattwas—as with the chakras, our several subtle bodies and energy systems—are <u>not</u> separate things but are with us all the time as parts of the Whole Person we are. The astral body is really not separate even though it can function in a manner that is subjectively separate. Nor is your soul truly separate from the wholeness but is generally not *actively "connected" while* you are physically incarnate. Everything is connected, but the degree of conscious functioning is reflective of your knowledge and understanding, and upon the degree of *focused* conscious awareness.

All the many systems of self-development—psychic, yogic, spiritual, and even much of what appears limited to the physical body and material concerns—work to extend and expand your conscious awareness and wholeness.

TATTVA OVERVIEW TABLE #1 (Body)

Tattva Name	Element Name	Finger Name	Physical Sense	Sense Organ	Action Organ	Action Form
Prithivi	Earth	Thumb	Smell	Nose	Foot	Locomotion
Apas	Water	Fore	Taste	Tongue	Genitals	Procreation
Tejas	Fire	Middle	Sight	Eyes	Anus	Evacuation
Vayu	Air	Ring	Touch	Skin	Hand	Grasping
Akasha	Ether	Little	Hearing	Ears	Mouth	Speak, Sing, Chant

Don't let the appearance of these tables seem threatening. They exist to simplify in the same way a pertinent illustration adds dimensions that otherwise require thousands of words. They function to summate knowledge at a particular stage of study that you later consummate through actual practice. There are things to note: Color and Shape have meanings, and those meanings expand as we take the exterior two-dimensional view and raise it to the interior three-dimensional view. Both are "real" but with "evolutionary" differences whose active perception brings change and growth.

For now, just familiarize yourself with these simple characteristics of all five of the primary tattvas. Over the next four chapter addenda we will provide additional Tattva Overview Tables to continue developing your background awareness of how the five primal tattvas themselves constantly combine, modify, and recombine throughout not only all life but all material and subtle existence. Remember, nothing exists in isolation and existence itself is like a vast community of individuals whose individuality is supported through the community itself supported by those individuals. Individuals continue their evolution, as does Humanity, as does the material universe, and as does the Cosmos as a whole.

Growth is universal; our personal development is the fulcrum upon which that growth is leveraged for all, and is the axel about which the wheel turns. You are important and your life has meaning, and the more conscious effort you put into it the more will we all benefit.

Starting in this chapter addendum we will be doing a basic meditation exercise for each of the primary tattvas, and then for the compounded tattvas in which the one primary tattva is joined by a secondary tattva for the more complex ways we all experience life and relate to our psychic opportunities.

TATTVA OVERVIEW TABLE #1 (Continued)

Effect of Action	Body Areal	Body Function	Sexual Identity	Chakra Name	Chakra Location
Lasting	Anal	Construction	Active & Feminine	Muladhara	Base of Spine
Transitory	Genital	Sexuality	Receptive & Feminine	Svadhis-thana	Below Navel
Arousing	Solar Plexus	Digestion	Active & Masculine	Manipura	Above Navel
Reductive	Lungs	Resperation	Projective & Masculine	Anahata	Over Heart
Uniting	Neck & Throat	Vocalization	Universal	Vishuddha	Throat

You can easily memorize the tattva names, the associated senses and sense organs, their primary actions and function, and the associated chakra names and relative locations, but this only initiates the process of awakening the inner tattvas that will be addressed in each of the "Tattvic Connection" Meditation Exercises given in this book.

Notice, in particular, the relationships between each of the primary tattvas, the five physical senses, the sense organs, the related chakras, and their locations. Try to make *intellectual sense* of these connections while at the same time try to experience the *feelings* involved. Keep that process active as we continue on with later tables and exercises. You are developing an entire new filing and storage system with which to experience the world more broadly, adding to your growing ability to clairvoyantly "see behind the scenes."

Now you understand the vast gap between "reading about" and actual "studying." *Reading*, of course, can be very pleasurable and can also be a form of experience and adventure. *Study* can be these things as well, but the true benefit takes real work and self-discipline in a regular program involving scheduling, reading, review, thinking about, perhaps experiments and "field trips," and even inner debate to bring about realization of all that is involved.

Done correctly, such personal study efficiently and effectively condenses a lifetime of "discipleship" with a guru or teacher into an equivalence of several such lives. Becoming, and then realizing, that you are your own "Master" is a demonstration of what this New Age of Aquarian Man is about. It is a vast acceleration of growth and development accomplishing a new phase of human and "planetary" evolution.

Now, let us start the next phase of our tattva reprogramming of the adult person.

As always, when you see that particular word, *Think,* do that! And write down your own observations to make them both conscious and alive in your subconscious. You are *solidifying* your understanding.

THINK ELEMENTAL EARTH

First, however, we ask that you think about EARTH, the primal element, and what it is to each and all of us, to the natural world we live *in* and the planet we live on, and to the Cosmos within which we have our being. Elemental Earth (Prithivi) is a fundamental building block of the material universe we live in and of the body into which you incarnate and live this life. Earth is "Mother Earth," separate from but also forever paired with "Father Sky" and together they are our mythical and actual parents.

Mother Earth is always with us, just as our real mothers are in life and even progressively after physical death, while Father Sky is more objective and physically distant—although always loving and supportive.

Earth is everything solid, supportive, and sensory. We see, smell, feel, taste, and hear with physical organs. We survive by eating foods grown on earth, and what we consume is transformed and returned to earth in the physiological process of life and then of death. We stand upon, move upon, work upon, sleep upon, and live upon earth. We join with earth in love and reproduce our species as we journey on earth. We grow and become more than we are on earth from birth to death. Earth is both beginning and ending in a cosmic drama—the culmination of an *involutionary* process and the beginning of the *evolutionary* process.

Earth is incarnate manifestation, our birth place for growth and "becoming more than we are." Earth connects us to reality through routines and rituals. It is the element of practicality and necessity, of abundance and prosperity. Earth connects us with our source through rituals and ceremonies that awaken memories of who we are in reality and in potential. Earth connects us to traditions and establishes the foundations upon which we build our edifices while reminding us that we must follow rules of nature and keep our feet on the ground.

Earth is the teacher who requires that we take responsibility for our own actions and for our own security. It calls upon us to achieve our dreams and to nurture those of others. It is our connection to home and family and to the planet and cosmos. Earth is the provider of riches and rewards for the job well done.

In this first meditation exercise, think in particular of Elemental Earth's role in your personal physical health and security. And then extend that to your immediate family and then to the broader community in which you live—including the natural organic foundations of life—even if you live in a city of concrete, steel, electronics, and impersonal hustle and bustle. You stand, move, and live on this Earth that is more than a planet and more than a home to us. It is within your body and soul and you live in its body and soul. All is connected, and we are one with the All. Find PURE EARTH within, and without. In the following exercise, which you can and should practice again and again, you will experience Earth *consciously even if you are not yet aware of the depth of this experience.*

Subjectively, we (man and woman) experience our sexuality as feminine, active, restricting, and receptive. How does that concept manifest in how we relate our inner self to the outer world?

The following table offers a great deal of detail. Much of it may seem to have little pertinence now, but as you proceed with both the development of clairvoyance and then its practice, you may well have reason to refer back to it. The value is in getting used to seeing the many "correspondences"—things connected to things by their common element. The more you see such connectedness, the more will this become an intuitive experience and the multiple applications will be instinctual.

And, yes, the note that says "Correspondences for you to complete" is intentional. You can find many lists of correspondences: astrological, psychological, magickal, Kabbalistic, yogic, etc., and based variously on relationships to the planets, symbols, deifies of various religious and mythic pantheons, the sephiroth, the chakras, "occult anatomy," subtle energies, and many more. That's the point: the list can be endless, but what will really count are the selections you can make based on your own intuitions and your growing experience.

Many people have correctly called such lists of correspondences a "filing system" of information pertinent to your own self-development. You don't need to file everything—like some giant "Library of Congress"—but what you do recognize are those connections that become part of your own subconscious and conscious functioning.

> Note: The following Elemental Overview Table #1 for Earth is exactly what the title says—an "overview" intended to give you a fundamental awareness of the Elemental Qualities and Characteristics. You may notice some seeming conflicts but these represent particular sources and intended usage from Meditational and Magickal perspectives. An excellent source book for all this is David Hulse's "The Eastern Mysteries" which can be supplemented by the same author's "The Western Mysteries."

ELEMENT OVERVIEW TABLE # 1
ELEMENT OF EARTH—SEED OF EARTH:
Solidity, Foundation

Tattva Name: Prithivi	Tattva Form: square	Tattva Color: Yellow
Tattva/Primary Sheath: *Annamaya* (food sheath), physical*	Tattvic Animal: Black Elephant with seven trunks	Tattvic Taste: Sweet
Yantra Color: Purple or Violet	Yantra Form: Cube	Cosmic Plane: *Bhu* (Physical/Etheric)
Chakra Name: *Muladhara* (root support)**	Chakra Common Name: Root, or Base, Chakra	Chakra Bija Mantra: LAM
Chakra Body Location: base of spine—perineum or cervix	Chakra Body Space: Toes to Knees	Chakra Body Zone: Pelvic Plexus
Chakra Color: fiery red	Chakra Function of astral & etheric center: creativity; seat of consciousness & Kundalini	Chakra Goal: Awaken Kundalini and vivify each center
Chakra Petals (spokes): 4	Chakra God *(Shiva)* Energy: *Bhairava, Brahma*	Chakra Goddess *(Shakti)* Energy: *Dakini*
Chakra Meditation: mastery of speech and learning, resistance to disease, joy and happiness	Chakra Power: connects with Earth to draw up basic energies	Chakra Verbal Expression: I have

Chakra Problem: blockage low vitality, obesity, arthritis, knee problems, sciatica, depression, illusions of self-importance, arrogance
Chakra Symbol: 4 red petals inscribed vam, śam, ṣam, sam around a white circle with a yellow square with a red inverted triangle (yoni: female astral symbol) in which is an upright white linga (male astral symbol) with a red 3½ times coiled sleeping serpent, head up, connected to Psychic Knot of Susumna Brahma which must be unraveled for Kundalini to rise. Symbol should include white elephant with 7 trunks as a vehicle, and the Sanskrit word *LAM*

Chakra Vital Air: *Apana Vayu*	Chakra Yogini: *Shakini*	Chakra/Physical Gland: adrenals

Chakra/Program: Control of physical elements of body & earth currents, leading towards, material success, athletic prowess, strength, health & longevity
Chakra/Siddhi Powers: (when developed) Knowledge of Kundalini & power to awaken Her, resistance to disease, magickal speech
Indian Gods: *Indra* rides a white elephant, has 4 arms, and carries the 4-headed, 4-armed, solar child *Brahma* in his lap. In the Earth Square is apex-down Triangle in which is *Siva* in the form of a golden *linga* around which is the goddess *Kundalini* in her serpent form, sleeping and coiled 3½ times.

Indian Goddesses: Beautiful *Dakini* (pure intelligence) with red eyes and 4 arms, shining like a million suns. Also *Kamala, Sakini,* and *Kundalini.*		
Element Name: Earth	Elemental State: Solid	Elemental Action: Support
Elemental Function: Survival & Evolution	Elemental Motion: Horizontal	Elemental Nature: Initiative, Start up
Elemental Power: To create a new Reality	Elemental Quality: Dry, Cohesive	Elemental Strength: Focus, determination
Energy: Mechanical	Manifests through: Congealment	Quantum Force: Gravity
Emotional Characteristic: solidarity	Emotional Desires: basic comfort & survival needs	Emotional Drive: survival, security, collecting, saving
Emotional Family Role: Daughter	Emotional Nature: Passive, stable	Emotional/Psychological Level: Deep Unconscious
Emotional Reaction: Depression	Emotional/Sensory Block: Uncontrolled Emotion	Emotional Weakness: Pride, Greed
Emotional/Sexual Identity: Feminine, Active, Receptive	Emotional Strength: Instinct, care	
Mind Action: *Ahamkara* (Ego)	Mind Function: Human knowledge, Memory	Mind State: Waking intelligence
Physical/Action Organ: Feet	Physical/Action Form: Locomotion	Physical/Action Effect: Lasting
Physical/Astral Sense: Smell	Physical/Astral Sense Organ: Nose	Physical Body Function: construction, moving, sexuality
Physical Energy Correlations between physical/etheric & astral bodies—Fingers of Hand: Thumb		
Psychic Powers: levitation, pain control, psychometry	Psychic/Astral Work: Eyes closed, concentrate on tip of nose to awaken Kundalini. Chant *OM.*	
Alchemical Metal: Lead	Alchemical Planet: Saturn	Alchemical Quality: Cold, Dry, Feminine
Alchemical Symbolic Season: Autumn	Alchemical Symbolic Time of Day: Noon	Astrological Lunar Phase: Dark Moon
Astrological Types: Virgo, Taurus, Capricorn	Astrological Qualities: hard-working, disciplined, persevering, patience	Astrological Ruling Planet: Saturn, Mercury
Astrological Planetary Expression: Mercury—communication, business, mathematics, practical matters		
Egyptian Divinities: Geb, Nephthys	Greek God Form: Zeus, Dionysus,	Greek Goddess: Gaia, Demeter, Hestia, Rhea
Hebrew God Name: Agla	Runes: Berkano, Fehu, Jera, Mannaz, Othala, Wunjo	
Magical Angel: Phorlakh;	Magical Animals: owl, bear, boar, bull, stag	Magical Archangel: Uriel;

Magical/Mythical Beings: giants, goblins, satyrs, trolls	Magical Colors: Brown, Black, Green	Magical Day: Friday
Magical Direction: North	Magical Elemental King: Ghob	Magical/Elemental Spirits: Gnomes
Magical Energy: Feminine	Magical Enochian Watch-tower: Northern	Magical God Name: Adonai Ha-Aretz
Magical Herbs: mugwort, sage, oleander	Magical Incense: Storax, Cedar; Patchouli Oil	Magical Kerub: bull
Magical Metals: Lead	Magical Musical Note: C; musical note: Do	Magical Places: cave, forest, gardens, wilds
Magical Planet: Venus	Magical Plants: Hawthorn, ash, patchouli, Indian grass	Magical Ruler: Kerub
Magical Power: to be silent, make dreams real	Magical State: Physical Perception	Magical Season: Winter

Magical Rulership: agriculture, animals, antiques, buildings, business, conservation, construction, death/rebirth, ecology, fertility, food, grounding, health foods, investments, jobs, material things, money, museums, nature, old age, progress, promotions, prosperity, stock markets, structural foundations
Magical Stones: bloodstone emerald, fire agate, hematite, jade, jasper, jet, lodestone, peridot, ruby, sepentine, smoky quartz, tiger's eye, tourmaline

Magical Symbols: Pentacle	Magical Time of Day: Midnight	Magical Time of Life: Elder Years
Magical Tool: crystal, pentacle, staff,	Magical Work: alchemy, geomancy, talisman	
Tarot Court: Page, Princess	Tarot Suit: Coins, Pentacles	Tarot Trumps: Emperor, World
Tree of Life Path: 32nd	Tree of Life Sphere: Malkuth	Tree of Life Soul Level: Nephesch

*The physical body and the etheric body largely function together but also need to be studied separately. It is also called the *food sheath*
**Note that there is a direct (subtle) connection between Muladhara Chakra and Ajna Chakra & also Sahasrara Chakra.
Note: The various magical correspondences are only minimal selections. More complete information can be found in the resources listed at the end of the book.
For serious study, you should add to this list, & other lists you may be building. Correspondences build your inter-relationships between Inner & Outer, Subconscious & Conscious, Cosmic & Personal. All magical systems inter-relate and add to your personal memory/ library.

Earth—Seed of Earth

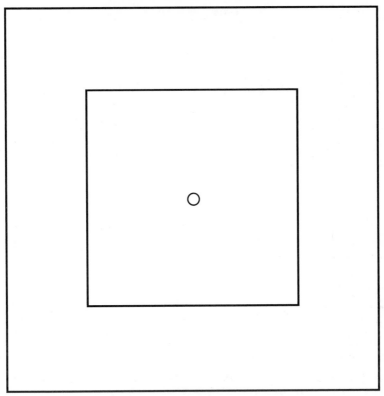

Color the tiny inner bindu circle white,
the inner square bright yellow,
and the outer square bright purple

Earth—Seed of Earth: Prithivi *LAM*

NOTICE: The following series of *Tattvic Connection Meditation Exercises* are a Developmental Program that only works <u>if you actually do them!</u> And we recommend to first-time users to space them a week apart, and then occasionally repeat thereafter.

Please exercise self-discipline and <u>schedule</u> the "Work" of these Tattva Meditation Programs that follow in later chapter addenda. Self-discipline and scheduling is your personal substitute for attending classes, and reporting to a teacher, guru, master, etc. "Do it yourself" has many advantages, but merely reading about things is not as productive as doing it.

TATTVIC CONNECTION MEDITATION PROGRAM #1:
Earth/Earth
Earth—Seed of Earth

Introduction. The Purpose & Function of this Procedure.

This procedure is adapted from many personal experiences of practices first under the guidance of Dr. Jonn Mumford* in the 1970s during the Gnosticon Events sponsored by Llewellyn, and then from those described in his 1994 book, *A Chakra & Kundalini Workbook*, and his 1997 book, *Magical Tattwas,* each written over summer visits to our home during long discussions about the subject.

> *Dr. Jonn Mumford (Swami Anandakapila Saraswati) is a direct disciple of the late Dr. Swami Gitananda Giri (South India) and Swami Satyananda Saraswati (1923–2009), who initiated him into the Sannyasa Order of Saraswati in 1973 in Monghyr, Bihar State, India.

I prepared this exercise and the others that follow specifically for the purpose of balancing and harmonizing the inner Tattvic Matrix of Body and "Soul" with the universal Cosmic Matrix. The result is a purification of the inner matrix so that clairvoyant visions will not be distorted by what I refer to as "accumulated emotional garbage."

It's not that emotions are bad—*far from it!*—but they are often distorted and charged with negative energies from external sources. Recall possible feelings of pain and hatred when you heard about incidents of child abuse, brutality toward women, criminal actions motivated by corporate or political greed, or led by gangs. Such feelings, while specific at the time, are like garbage in a pond polluting the whole water supply. Over time, most atrophy or are minimized under the influence of positive energies—*but nothing is ever forgotten in our subconsciousness.*

As you expand your psychic work and grow in consciousness, you don't want these memories to distort your growing abilities. These meditation exercises can be made very specific and individual by relating them to any of the correspondences and characteristics noted in the Overview Tables. In other words, you adapt them to fit *your current* needs. You are empowered, but—remember—with power comes responsibility. Through the responsible exercise of personal power you grow in all levels of your Self, your Soul.

You can repeat this entire procedure often, but not more than once daily. And I suggest that you allow a week between each of the exercises. In addition, in later adaptations for specific empowerment, do so carefully and in balance with others—not just one.

Summary of Purpose & User Benefits.

Just as Physical Relaxation is necessary for the free and unmitigated flow of Prana and other subtle energies, so is the controlled & directed purification of various physical & subtle body parts and energy channels. With this meditation we purify, balance, and harmonize the most primal elemental force in our body and soul: the earth tattva. As this is completed, along with other elemental meditations, you will be better equipped to follow on with specific stimulus of particular psychic centers to accomplish your projected goals.

Step 1. Preliminaries.

Always precede the *Tattvic Connection & Meditation Exercises* with complete physical relaxation.

This exercise is nearly identical with those that follow, except the specific references to the Tattva/Element involved, which are bold-faced for ease of identification.

Read through the procedure before beginning so that further reference is not needed.

Time & Space: Allow a period of approximately 30 minutes for the actual 16 step procedure to be conducted in a comfortably warm, quiet, and safe setting free of interruptions. While a darkened room is not required, freedom from both sound and visual distractions is advisable.

Personal Preparations: Remove shoes and keep clothing or covering minimal to minimize the effects of external stimuli.

Posture & Position: It is not necessary to lie flat for this procedure, but a relaxed posture in a recliner is helpful.

Special Lighting: You should arrange a small desk or reading light next to your chair that you can comfortably reach to turn on and off as required, and focus as directed.

Breathing: It is always desirable to establish a deep but natural, rhythmic flow of your breath, mostly balanced between inhalation and exhalation unless otherwise directed for specific functions.

Vocalization: Vocalize, either silently stated or voiced aloud, your affirmations, the name of the tattva, and then the sounding of the mantra in Step 9.

With each step 5 through 13, it is helpful to vocalize the words describing any particular feelings or even visions you experience.

Vibration: This is very important. In Step 9 you should chant or hum the Sanskrit name of the tattva, and then the tattvic mantra as instructed. You want to draw these words out and feel the *vibration*. Vibration means to lightly *warble* the words at the back of your throat, and as you do, you may want to raise or lower the "musical note" until it feels right. Do the same with the volume of sound but you don't want to wake the neighbors! You want to feel the words *vibrate* throughout your skull, and then in the location of the corresponding chakra. With experience you will be able to move the vibration to designated places inside your body, and then—in advanced work—intentionally into external objects.

The yantra, the name, and the mantra are your means to connect the inner tattva with the external tattva for purification and balance.

Step 2. Goal Statement.
Your goal is three-fold:
- To become fully familiar with the feelings associated with the **Earth** Element. You've read about it, you've seen the listed characteristics and correspondences, you've thought about it, but now we want you to *feel* the **Earth** in you, under you, around you, and *through* your entire inner being. To become aware of Elemental **Earth** as the *foundation* of the outer material universe.
- To identify inner **Earth** with outer **Earth**, and feel yourself purified and balanced through the *harmonizing of inner with outer.* You want the inner and outer to become One.
- *To address particular concerns:* As an example, we have suggested two areas—**physical health and strength**, and **material security**. You must determine the goals yourself and then *affirm* them simply and concisely in as few words as possible. Write them down, fix them in your mind, but do not consider them as the primary function of the exercise, which is the balancing and purification of personal elemental earth. (Note: particular concerns must relate to the Element being addressed—see the Overview Table.)

Step 3. Affirmations.
These affirmations may be spoken as goals at the beginning, and then as confirmations at the ending of the procedure. In addition to these, add the affirmation you wrote as one of your goals.

> *I feel **Earth** everywhere within me.*
> *I feel **Earth** everywhere around me.*
> *I feel purified and in harmony with all that is **Solid & Hard** everywhere.*

Step 4. Mental Imagery.
Imagery, like vocalization, can increase the effectiveness of the procedure. *Visualization:* Visualizing the tattvas as described is essential.

Spontaneous Imagery: Other images may appear at the end of the procedure, and that's alright *unless you have negative feelings about them—in which case you should willfully "banish" them.* (If you wish, you can simply visualize a box, imagine all those negative feeling going into the box, close the box tightly, and imagine burying it in the earth and pouring cement over it. Then smooth clean dirt over the cement, seed it with grass, and know that those negativities are gone forever.)

Recording: Other images that may appear spontaneously at the end of the procedure should be noted,0 along with any particular feelings or ideas, and then record them in your journal for later analysis.

Analysis: Always let a day or two pass before reading and analyzing your journal entries.

Step 5. Preparation.

Preparing the Yantra Card.

It is recommended that you photocopy the illustration on page 107, preferably on heavier paper or card stock, or draw it yourself in exactly the same sizes using a ruler and black pen. If you can manage it, using a drawing compass or a template, draw a tiny ⅛" inch diameter circle in the exact center. Leave the inside of the circle white. This inner circle or point aids your steady focus. It is not essential, but it is helpful. For the **Earth** Card, make the outer square 4" x 4" and the inner square 2¼" x 2¼", and the little circle in the exact center should be ⅛" in diameter and have a heavy black border around it, but not quite as thick as those around the two squares.

Coloring the Yantra Card.

It will be beneficial for you to color the image as follows: (a) Leave the tiny circle white; (b) color the smaller square bright **yellow**, and the surrounding larger square bright **purple**. Each square and the tiny inner circle are bordered with bold black lines.

Cutting the Yantra Card.

If you have reproduced the image on the heavy card stock as recommended, now measure off either one or two inches (your choice) on each side and cut away the surplus so you have a square 6" x 6" or 8" x 8" *card* with the colored image in the center.

This preparation will be repeated for 24 additional images during which you will have constructed a set of 25 Tattva Cards that can be used again and again in the clairvoyance process discussed in this book, and in many other functions to be discussed later.

Position & Lighting.

Holding the tattvic yantra card, recline in a comfortable chair in a quiet room where you will not be disturbed for a minimum of 30 minutes. Prior to doing so, arrange lighting focused on the card that you can turn the light on and off.

Note the preferred direction for placing the chair indicated in Step 9 (a and b).

Breathing & Relaxation.

Become fully relaxed, combining slowed rhythmic breathing, and progressive tension & release of muscles from your toes to you brow and scalp if you have not already followed the Empowerment Tension and Release Procedure described in the Addendum to Chapter 1 or other effective relaxation technique.

Step 6. Pranic Breathing Pattern.

With eyes closed, engage in a pattern of rhythmic breathing involving equally spaced —*without any stress*—in-breaths, holding, out-breaths, holding, and repeating throughout the process.

Step 7. White Light Circulation.

Then, with each in-breath visualize white light flowing into the body, while holding the breath visualize the light circulating throughout the body, while breathing out see the light being excreted knowing that it is carrying out impurities, and while holding the out breath realize that you have energized and cleansed the inner energy body.

Step 8. Psychic Shield.

While continuing the breathing pattern and the flowing light, turn your imagination outward and visualize an absolutely clear field around you, one that is as transparent as the clearest glass. Know that this shield protects you from external influences while containing the benefits of your tattvic meditation program.

Step 9a. Yantra Card Focus.

If you have constructed the tattva yantra card as described, turn on the light and focus it on the card held or positioned comfortably about a foot to a foot and a half in front of you.

If possible, arrange your chair to face the tattvic direction: **North.** Otherwise— think and feel **North.**

Vibrate the name of tattva: *Prithivi.* Repeat three times.

Chant or hum the tattva element mantra *LAM* (pronounced *LA-UUM*). Vibrate the mantra as instructed in Step 1, preliminaries. Repeat three times. Later, you can do more, but always in groups of three. And feel the mantra vibrate in the **Pelvis,** the location of **Muladhara** chakra.

Focus on the small white circle* at the center of the image, and stare at it for as long as you can without blinking. When you can't continue the "burning" feeling any longer, turn off the light, close your eyes and focus your inner sight on the space in front of your brow chakra (between your eyebrows and on the ridge you can feel just above your nose), and see the Yellow Square floating in the space before you and vibrating within the Blue Square. Then you will soon see the tattva image change into the complementary yantra colors.

Again vibrate the name to the tattva and chant or hum the mantra three times.

Absorb this image! **As you repeat the exercise, often, you will reach a point when you will be able to recall this image at will.**

> *The small white circle is called a "Bindu," and focus on it is comprehensive of the entire tattvic image and all its energies. There is a small spot on the back of your head that likewise serves as a comprehensive psychic center used in certain meditational exercises. A Bindu is also the name of a single drop of semen, the focal point of a new life. And "bindu" is likewise the single point from which all creation began "in the union of divine forces, Male and Female, God and Goddess, Siva and Shakti in all their names and images—i.e., the "Big Bang."

> Bindu is a point of leverage where force applied becomes force multiplied and directed to accomplish your particular goal. Now is the time to *vocalize* the mantra for the **Earth** element, **LAM.**

Step 9b. Yantra Visualization.

Alternatively, if you haven't made a **Prithivi** tattva card, immediately in front of you, visualize a large **purple** square, inside of which is a **yellow** square approximately half the size of the blue. See the **yellow** square gently vibrating within the **purple** square. The colors will reverse to their complementary yantra colors of **purple** and **yellow.**

Step 10. Experiencing Elemental Earth.

Feel yourself becoming totally *absorbed** in the tattvic **Yellow** Square while retaining awareness of the surrounding tattvic **Purple** Square. As the tattvic **Yellow** changes to the complementary yantra **Purple** feel *your* **Earthy** nature harmonize with the

Cosmic **Earth** Tattva, and feel all impurities in your **Earth** Tattva—all emotional garbage and unconscious psychic attachments—dissipate.

> *Becoming absorbed.* Enter into the **Earth** square and become one with it and feel surrounded by it. Moving outward from the bindu point to the outer edge of the large square become the **Earth** element in your body and feel it become harmonized and purified as it is balanced with the Cosmic **Earth.**

*In particular: feel the **Earthy** nature of your physical body become free of adverse thoughts and feelings. Feel your body becoming ideally healthy, strong, and energized. See your body in perfect **health**, free of any excess weight, free of pain and disfigurement, free of illness, and fully energized.*

Step 11. Knowing Elemental Earth.

Allow yourself to receive any information or messages from you're experiencing of **Elemental Earth.** *In particular: receive information involving your **physical health & strength**, and **material security**.* Receive the information without any emotional reaction.

Step 12. Dissipation of Images.

Slowly dissipate the squares, return to the clear field around you, continuing the breathing pattern of Step 6 above.

Step 13. Letting Go of Evoked Feelings.

Let go of all the particular feelings evoked by the imagery, slowly change your breathing to its natural rhythm and feel the physical relaxation achieved in Step 1 above.

Step 14. Completion & Self-Realization.

Feel yourself fully relaxed and fully self-contained. Feel yourself to be healthy, energized, cleansed, & refreshed. Know yourself to be strong and secure. These feeling should be part of your self-realization at the end of each of the Tattvic Meditation Exercises regardless of the Element involved. Your healthy body is the foundation of all your life and work.

Step 15. Return to Normality.

Open your eyes and return to the physical world knowing all is well. Stand up and move about. Have some refreshment and engage in some normal activity.

Step 16. Review, Record & Analyze.

Record in a journal all messages and feelings received in Step 11 above. At this point, merely record—do not analyze. After a few days, read what you've recorded and then write down an analysis of what you believe the messages mean for you at this time. Realize that when you repeat the exercise at another time, the messages are likely to change to meet new circumstances in your life.

Conclusion: This exercise has demonstrated the particular usefulness of clairvoyance focused on the single area of **physical health or material security** in Steps 10 and 11. At the same time the relaxation program and light circulation procedure provided healing benefits.

However, the entire 16-step Meditation is a basic program that is modified by changes in the tattvic element and then particular modifications in Steps 10 and 11, following this example which was also given earlier in Chapter One as an introduction:

Adapt the following by changing the color and shape of the Tattwa.

Basic Meditation Exercise:
Yellow Square for Your Physical Health

Preparation. Recline in a comfortable chair in a quiet room in which you will not be disturbed for a minimum of 30 minutes.

Step 1 Become fully relaxed, combining slowed rhythmic breathing, and progressive tension and release of muscles from your toes to you brow and scalp.

Step 2 With eyes closed; engage in a pattern of rhythmic breathing involving equally spaced—_without any stress_—in-breaths, holding, out-breaths, holding, and repeating

Step 3 Then, with each in-breath visualize white light flowing into the body, while holding the breath visualize the light circulating throughout the body, while breathing out see the light being excreted, and while holding the out breath realize that you have energized and cleansed the inner energy body.

Step 4 While continuing the breathing pattern and the flowing light, turn your imagination outward and visualize an absolutely clear field around you, one that is as transparent as the clearest glass.

Step 5 Immediately in front of you, visualize a large purple square, inside of which is a yellow square approximately half the size of the purple. See the yellow square gently vibrate within the blue square.

Step 6 Feel yourself becoming absorbed in the yellow square while retaining awareness of the surrounding blue square.

Step 7 Allow yourself to receive any information or messages involving your physical health. Receive the information without any emotional reaction.

Step 8 Slowly dissipate the squares, return to the clear field around you, continuing the breathing pattern of Step 4 above.

Step 9 Let go of all imagery, and just feel the physical relaxation achieved in Step 1 above.

Step 10 Feel yourself fully relaxed and fully self-contained. Healthy, Energized, Cleansed, and Refreshed.

Conclusion. Open your eyes, return to the physical world knowing all is well. Get up and move about. Have some refreshment and engage in some normal activity.

Specified Clairvoyance by Intent

This exercise has demonstrated particular usefulness of clairvoyance focused on the single area of physical health in Step 7. At the same time the relaxation and light circular provide healing benefits.

However, the entire 10-step program is a basic exercise for relaxation and light circulation that can be adapted by changes in Steps 5 through 8 to general meditation or other specific meditation by changes in the dominant symbol used in Step 7.

Sources & Suggested Additional Reading:

Hulse, D. *The Eastern Mysteries*, first published as *The Key to It All, Book One*, 1993, Llewellyn.

Hulse, D. *The Western Mysteries*, first published as *The Key to It All, Book Two*, 1994, Llewellyn.

Prasad, R. *Nature's Finer Forces*, 1915, Theosophical Publishing Society, London.

Swami Satyasangananda. *Tattwa Shuddhi—The Tantric Practice of Inner Purification*, 1984, Bihar School or Yoga and Yoga Publications Trust, Bihar, India.

CHAPTER FOUR
Clairvoyance in the Lab
To Discover New Meanings to our Existence

The Power to Shape our own Destiny

Our thoughts, emotions, drives, and perceptions, both sensory and extrasensory, are all interrelated. They converge at all levels of consciousness to take us from where we are at the present moment to where we want to be. By interacting with these inner components of our being, we discover new meaning to our existence and our capacity to shape our own destiny. In a word, we become *empowered!* Nothing in fact is beyond your reach when *you assume command of the powers within yourself.*

Expanding Borders of Awareness

Among the most important of those inner powers is clairvoyance. Unlike purely physical sensory perception, clairvoyant perception functions independently of fixed thresholds. By expanding our borders of awareness through clairvoyance, we discover new sources of both knowledge and power otherwise unavailable to us. It is quite possible that clairvoyance is the most intricate and advanced mental ability known, the *ne plus ultra* of human potential and experience.

The Dynamics of Clairvoyance &
Other Psychic Powers—Questions:

Determining the complex dynamics underlying clairvoyance, like many human behaviors, remains a difficult challenge. Questions linger concerning the genetic, environmental, developmental, and spiritual nature of the phenomenon. More specifically:

Is clairvoyance a learned behavior or does it occur effortlessly and full-blown?

Can practice in clairvoyance promote the development of this skill?

What are the similarities and differences between clairvoyance and other forms of ESP?

Does one's gender influence the development of this skill?

Are personality factors such as introversion, extroversion, altruism, and self-confidence related to clairvoyance?

Are differences in clairvoyant abilities influenced by one's career pursuits?

Is clairvoyance related to other mental functions, such as creativity, intellectual level, memory span, and intuitive thinking?

What is the role of motivation in the development of clairvoyance?

Once acquired, are clairvoyant skills transferrable in ways that promote the development of other psychic skills, such as precognition, telepathy, and psychokinesis (PK)?

What are the environmental factors that influence the development of clairvoyance?

Do cultural factors, global conditions, and future events affect the manifestation of clairvoyance?

Do animals, like human beings, experience clairvoyance?

Questions and the New Science of the Paranormal

These are only a few of the many questions that invite both speculation and future research. As new discoveries, and theoretical speculations, arise from new work in quantum physics and more study and research in what is becoming known as the "New Science of the Paranormal," we will see answers to these questions and the asking of many more questions. Science is an endless quest for understanding, and for knowledge enabling new programs and applications both for practical benefit and growth opportunities.

Objective Verification of Subjective Experience

Much of the early research conducted by the Parapsychology Research Institute and Foundation (PRIF), which was established at Athens State University in 1970, focused on the nature of clairvoyance and possible explanations of the phenomenon. A major goal of that research was to promote a reasonable balance between subjective experience in real life and objective verification in the controlled lab setting. Underlying that effort was the concept that enlightenment and empowerment are interrelated—you can't have one without the other.

A Universal, and Innate, Mental Faculty

Early on, PRIF found that clairvoyance, like other forms of ESP, is a universal mental faculty that exists to some degree in everyone. It is also a widely recognized phenomenon, though it may not always be labeled as "clairvoyant." In a landmark PRIF survey study of 483 college students, only 12 respondents concluded that the human mind has no capacities beyond those presently recognized by conventional science. Regarding clairvoyance, 181 respondents reported highly detailed personal experiences of clairvoyance, including knowing for no apparent reason about situations or events occurring elsewhere. They viewed clairvoyance as a valuable source of expanded awareness and enlightenment unavailable from any other source.

Clairvoyant Awareness is <u>always</u> Relevant

Early studies by PRIF also found that, while clairvoyant awareness is sometimes subtle and even disguised as in the clairvoyant dream, it is always relevant. It can be spontaneous and thus effortless, or it can be deliberately induced using certain acquired skills. It can range from impressions related to routine daily affairs to detailed awareness of dangerous, life-threatening situations. It can provide solutions and enrichment in the career setting, and it can enrich personal relationships. At another level, it can facilitate learning and promote development of our potentials for success and happiness. Given the insights made possible through clairvoyance, we can overcome barriers to personal growth and find solutions to our most pressing problems.

To Become Empowered

Simply put, *becoming clairvoyant* means *becoming empowered.*

Although our lab research in clairvoyance attempted to control the intervention of extraneous variables, including other forms of ESP, they can inadvertently enter the experimental situation even when stringent controls are in place. For instance, an individual subject in a group situation who experiences clairvoyant insight could conceivably transfer that information telepathically to other participants. Balancing that possibility, however, is the possibility that inaccurate information could be telepathically transferred as well. Although such extraneous variables as spontaneous telepathy as well as pre-cognition could have intervened in our group studies, the post-experiment interviews with successful subjects typically showed a high degree of confidence that their success was due to clairvoyance, not telepathy or pre-cognition.

Psychic Empowerment Accelerates Cognitive Functions

Throughout our research in clairvoyance, it became increasingly evident that development of the clairvoyance potential does not occur in a vacuum. Aside from improving performance in clairvoyance, clairvoyant development seems to *additionally* create a strong transfer of learning effect that accelerates development of other ESP skills, including both telepathy and precognition. Equally as important, our studies consistently showed an even wider generalization effect that included improvements in a variety of other cognitive functions, including problem-solving, memory, and comprehension as measured by appropriate pre-and post-tests.

Personal Enrichment & Life Enhancement

Aside from these effects, post-study interviews with our subjects revealed a host of personal enrichment effects, including greater self-confidence, more effective stress management, and improved social interactions. These enrichment effects add further support to our thesis that programs of psychic development are life enhancing and developmental of the "Whole Person" that we are all intended to become.

Given the extensive generalization and transfer effects of developing our clairvoyant abilities, we have further evidence that clairvoyance is indeed the *ne plus ultra* of human potential and experience.

Using Psychic Power Tools

Although clairvoyance appears to originate within one's own psyche, the process is often facilitated through the application of various external tangibles, such as the crystal ball, the pendulum, dowsing rods, and a variety of personal items as in psychometry. Aside from these, maps are sometimes used to activate clairvoyance, particularly in locating missing persons, animals, objects, and in some instances underground conditions and natural resources. In the criminal justice setting, maps have proved invaluable when applied as clairvoyant tools in locating missing persons and gathering forensic evidence. In the military, maps have been used clairvoyantly to locate unknown enemy installations and weapons' facilities.

In a striking instance of the use of maps in clairvoyance, a college student who as a child discovered a gold coin on the farm where he grew up decided to search the area as the possible location of additional coins. Using a map of the large farm still owned by his parents, he rested his writing pen upon the map and with his eyes closed, allowed the pen to automatically move about until it came to rest. He then calculated the exact location of the point on the map which, as it turned out, was an old abandoned home place. The exact site was then confirmed by the student through a pendulum held over the map followed by on-site dowsing.

By his admission, "I searched the site indicated by the pen, and found a treasure trove of buried gold coins." He speculated that the pen and map together became the antennae for his subconscious mind where the original location of the coin was clearly registered, a concept that begs the question: *What other treasures of information exist in the subconscious mind where they patiently await our discovery through clairvoyance?*

Using Maps as Psychic Triggers to Locate Lost Objects

At a highly practical level, one of the most common clairvoyant applications of maps is that of locating lost or misplaced objects. That application was illustrated by a group of 32 parapsychology students at Athens State University who participated in a class project designed to locate a diamond ring believed to have been lost on a mountainous nature trail. Each student was provided a detailed map of the trail and instructed to independently mark the expected location of the ring by relying upon their clairvoyant impressions. The maps were then compared, and the frequencies of the various locations were tallied. A certain rest area overlooking a river received the highest rank. An enlarged map of the rest area was then prepared and presented to each student with instructions to clairvoyantly pinpoint the exact location of the ring. As before, the frequencies of choices were counted, and the highest rank went to a certain park bench at the border of the area. A field trip was then organized and the rest area was searched by the group. The ring was found under the bench exactly as indicated by the group. As a footnote, none of the students participating in this exercise had previously walked the trail or visited the rest area.

This exercise, which became known as the "Lost Ring Project," suggested at least two interesting possibilities related to the use of appropriate tangible objects as clairvoyance empowerment tools:

The Lost Ring Project

1. Tangible objects can be used to activate the clairvoyant faculty and stimulate it to generate totally new levels of clairvoyant awareness, and

2. Clairvoyant awareness can exist in subconscious form that can be accessed and brought to conscious awareness, also through the use of appropriate tangible objects. Many of these have a long tradition of usage, while others—spontaneously chosen—affirm that while "the power" comes from within, it may be extended and even *magnified* by the tangible object.

Taken together, these possibilities reflect the complex dynamics of clairvoyance as a faculty with enormous growth and empowerment potential.

Using Blueprints to Trigger Psychic Perception

As with maps, blueprints can also be used as effective clairvoyant facilitators. They have proved particularly effective in identifying defects in architectural structures, such as buildings, dams, and monuments. In one celebrated case, a skilled clairvoyant consultant to a major Alabama construction firm identified upon viewing the blueprints of a parking tower under construction an architectural error that, if gone uncorrected, could have resulted in the collapse of the tower and tragic loss of life. The error, she noted, stood out on the blueprint as an "ominous discoloration" similar to a water stain. The discoloration, however, was visible only to the clairvoyant.

In our lab, several studies were designed to research blueprints as possible clairvoyant facilitators in locating defects or weaknesses in rocket components used by the US Army Missile Research and Development Program. The findings of our clairvoyant research were then investigated by other military contractors using advanced nondestructive testing technology. The results included an overall accuracy rate that was greater for clairvoyance than for advanced technology. When clairvoyance and technology were combined, the overall accuracy rate dramatically improved. When technology embraces clairvoyance or vice versa, the best of both is magnified. Together, they can provide an advanced tangible medium to access important knowledge that could remain otherwise unavailable to us.

Sensory Functions as Channels for ExtraSensory Perception

There's a mountain of evidence that sensory functions can be channels for extra-sensory perception, including clairvoyance. Among the familiar examples are derma-optic perception or the capacity of the mind to directly receive information, typically through the hands or fingers (also known as "Clairsentience"), and *psychometry* which uses tangible objects, typically of a personal nature, to active psychic functions. In our studies at Athens State University, the application of touch to activate clairvoyance included the use of such items as jewelry, photographs, and articles of clothing. The objectives ranged from investigating crimes to locating missing persons. In one unusual application of group psychometry, a student enrolled in a parapsychology seminar at the university circulated among students the collar to her missing dog companion named Bo. No other details were provided. Upon touching the collar, the students independently made notes of their impressions. They then shared their findings and put together the following details:

The dog, a black and white male of mixed breed, is situated approximately seven miles northwest of the student's residence in a secure rural setting called Summerview. The location includes a sandstone farmhouse, a gray and white barn, a silo, and a winding stream.

Although it was unclear exactly how the dog ended up at that location, the information proved accurate in every detail. The dog was found and safely retrieved.

The Third Eye Project & Developmental Procedure
Mental Imagery to Trigger Clairvoyance

Research in the controlled lab setting has repeatedly validated the relevance of mental imagery to successful clairvoyance. Clairvoyant impressions often emerge spontaneously in imagery form, at times in vibrant color and motion. Because clairvoyance and imagery appear to be interrelated, the development of imagery skills is almost always accompanied by accelerated development of clairvoyance. That relationship was dramatically illustrated by the "Third Eye Project" designed in our labs at Athens State University to promote the development of both imagery and clairvoyance. The centerpiece of the project was a seven-step exercise which can be used by individual as well as groups. Here's the procedure.

Step-by-Step Developmental Exercise & Procedure.

1. Take a few moments to view a picture, scene, or object, paying particular attention to details including color, shape, design, and so forth.

2. Close your eyes and recreate the view. Focus again on details as you note any feelings or impressions related to the view.

3. Open your eyes and again view the picture, scene, or object. Note any details that were incorrect or omitted.

4. Repeat the above 3-step exercise.

5. With your eyes closed, allow new images to spontaneously appear—clouds, mountains, buildings, animals, persons, events, and so forth. Note especially any feelings or emotions that accompanying these images.

6. As your eyes remain closed, allow yourself to flow with the image as new images emerge. Pay special attention to the potential clairvoyant significance of the images.

7. Record the experience in your clairvoyant journal and research the possible clairvoyant significance of the experience.

Our research subjects who practiced this exercise routinely experienced a marked acceleration in the development of their clairvoyant skills, both in the laboratory and in their daily lives.

Practice, Practice, Practice to Develop Psychic Skills

Our probes into the nature of clairvoyance consistently showed not only the existence of clairvoyance, but the developmental nature of the phenomenon as well. We now know that, with appropriate practice and experience, we can not only develop our clairvoyant skills but deliberately target them on designated goals as well. In our lab studies of the effect of practice, experimental subjects consistently improved their performance on such practice exercises as "down-thru-the-deck technique" (a procedure in which cards are called down through a shuffled pack before any are checked or removed). This simple exercise using either standard playing or ESP cards included careful record keeping with progress charts maintained for each individual. When these exercise were supplemented with such routine daily activities as guessing the hour before checking the time or guessing who's calling before answering the phone, clairvoyance in the controlled lab setting markedly improved,

Even greater improvements in clairvoyance were noted in our lab when the practice exercises included such meaningful tasks as locating concealed objects such as photographs, coins, and articles of jewelry. Among our controlled practice exercises was an experiment in which 20 subjects (10 males and 10 females) participated in a series of trials requiring the location of a fraternity pin randomly concealed in a small box among nine other identical but empty boxes. On a series of ten trials, the group progressively improved its average accuracy rate from a near-chance level to an average accuracy rate significantly above chance, but with wide individual differences in performance. They then appeared to transfer their acquired clairvoyant skills to other controlled tasks, such as identifying the number of pages in a book randomly selected from a library shelf. That so-called *positive transfer of practice* was strikingly illustrated by a psychology major who accurately identified on a single trial the exact number of pages in a dictionary. Immediately after she removed the unfamiliar dictionary from among other books on a shelf, the number 816 flashed boldly in her mind. By her account, "It was a maxed-out moment."

In a classroom exercise designed to investigate the effect of practice in developing clairvoyance skills, a group of 38 students (20 females and 18 males) enrolled in Experimental Parapsychology at Athens State University was given the task of identifying cards randomly removed from a shuffled deck of ESP cards and placed top side down on a desk at the front of the class. Throughout the series of 12 trials, the average performance of the class progressively improved with each trial. No significant gender differences were noted in the performance of the group.

Purposeful Psychic Activity

In another classroom exercise with the same group, the clairvoyance performance of students improved even more rapidly when the practice exercise was perceived by students as highly similar to a real-life situation, a condition called "mundane reality". For instance, in an exercise requiring students to locate a concealed key in one of five identical small boxes, the performance of students was much higher for locating a key to a dormitory room than for locating an ignition key supposedly for a space ship. Again, no significant gender differences were noted in the performance of the group.

When taken together, the clairvoyant studies conducted in our lab and classroom settings alike offered convincing evidence that practice in a variety of relevant exercises improves performance. Practice may not "make perfect," but it clearly does improve performance not only in the specific skill being practiced but in other related skills as well, thanks to the *positive transfer of practice effect.*

Animal Clairvoyance

Do animals, like humans, experience clairvoyance? Although controlling the possible intervention of extraneous variables is challenging in laboratory research in clairvoyance, there is considerable evidence that animals do possess clairvoyant abilities. Among the studies of animal clairvoyance conducted at Athens State University was a project designed to allow entrapped mice to choose a pathway from among three narrow mazes, one of which led to escape. On the first trial, six of the eight mice chose the escape maze. On the second trial, seven of the mice chose the escape maze. In a replication of that experiment using another population of mice, five of the eight mice chose on the first trial the escape maze. On a second trial, the remaining three mice chose the escape route.

Clairvoyant Animal Experiences

Outside the lab situation, reports of animal clairvoyance abound, especially among pet companions. Examples include apparent clairvoyant awareness of impending danger, especially involving children. A lab technician assisting in our studies of animal clairvoyance reported an instance in which her dog companion of several years blocked the path of her daughter, age six, who was about to cross a suspended bridge in a recreational park area. Later inspection of the bridge by a park official showed the bridge was near collapsing due to a damaged support cable. In another instance of clairvoyance among animal companions, an elementary school teacher reported an instance in which her blue and gold macaw screamed in panic when her front door bell rang, a reaction highly uncharacteristic of the bird. Deciding not to answer the door, the teacher soon received a call from her daughter that a neighboring floral shop had been robbed and the armed bandit was believed to be in her neighborhood.

Clairvoyance among animals, it seems, can involve the highest of altruistic concerns, including the care and protection of others.

The Ultimate Test: Does Clairvoyance improve individual & Group Well-being?

The ultimate test of the value of a given human ability is whether it promotes the well-being of the individual and others alike. Based on our lab studies, clairvoyance is a vehicle for growth that meets that critical test. That perhaps is the most important finding of controlled lab research in clairvoyance.

Sources & Suggested Additional Reading:

Diedrich, M. *What Animals Tell Me,* 2005, Llewellyn.

ADDENDUM #4 TO CHAPTER FOUR
Microcosm to Macrocosm & Macrocosm to Microcosm

The Tattvic Connection—
Meditation & Visualization Program #2: Water/Water

Apas: Water—Seed of Water

Water! We can't live without it, we drink it, wash with it, swim in it, sail about on it, fish in it, it exists as a solid (ice), as a liquid, and as a vapor (steam), it is the universal solvent, it cools us and warms us, our bodies are made of earth and water, we cook with it, we manufacture with it, we compound it with earthy resources to make drugs and other products for our benefit and comfort, all life depends on it, it enables us to produce food and fuel, it flows and falls, and it symbolizes fluidity, adaptability, and feminine softness. Its energy is chemical and magnetic; it is dark (like in deep water). It is feminine, passive, restricting, and receptive.

We start with our second Tattva Overview Table to continue the subtle process of building background "coincidental awareness" between the inner and outer worlds within and through which you live and function. This also serves as foundation for the more intense effort that goes into the Tattva Connection Meditation & Visualization Programs that—in a sense—reprocess your whole *adult* body *and* personality complex from the inner, *subtle,* levels.

We never stop growing, not even after death of the physical body, but in each life there are the two major phases: childhood and adulthood. The "age" dividing line between the two phases is a legal fiction (nevertheless, real enough when you apply for a driver's license or when you move on to "voting age") that is often set at ages 18, or 21, or 28 (the approximate timing of your first "Saturn Return" which astrologically marks adulthood).

TATTVA OVERVIEW TABLE #2 (Elemental)

Tattva Name	Element Name	Element State	Element Quality	Element Motion	Energy Action
Prithivi	Earth	Solid	Dry & Cohesive	Horizontal	Foundation Support
Apas	Water	Liquid	Cold & Contracting	Downward	Feeling, Adapting
Tejas[1]	Fire	Plasma	Hot, Dry, Expansive	Upward	Transforms, Projects
Vayu	Air	Gaseous	Hot, Wet, Moving	Outward[2]	Surrounds
Akasha	Ether	Spirit or Space	Space	Outward[3]	Unlimited Potential
1 Tejas is also commonly called *Agni*					
2 Outward motions limited to up, down, forward, backward, right, left.					
3 Outward motion in all directions.					

The point is not to see lists and tables as "rules" (unless that is what they are called) but as seeds for thought and opportunities for your own experience. Lists are *external* observations and experiences of the outer world, but we want you to bring them inside, to internalize the resultant experience of what is represented in the symbols of the tattvas.

As children we memorized lists and repeated them in rote fashion with little awareness of meaning. As adults we know that we must interpret words and symbols to understand their meaning in any particular situation of application. That's the difference between "information" and "knowledge."

As your own guru, your success is measured by the gain in knowledge, not just in access to information.

Now we move on to the second part of this addendum: to think and experience Elemental Water through the program of tratak, visualization and active meditation.

But, first, prepare yourself by reviewing the first table in this addendum, and then the following "think" exercise.

THINK ELEMENTAL WATER

Physical water dissolves Earth, hence it dissolves most solids and conforms to shapes, enabling it to cleanse away dirt and pollution and to absorb many gases as well. In addition *elemental water easily absorbs emotions and energies, especially when deliberately charged through magical ritual or religious blessing.* This applies to "Holy Water"

TATTVA OVERVIEW TABLE #2 (Elemental) (continued)

Energy Type	Manifest Through	Element Function	Element Power	Element Strength	Element Nature
Mechanical	Congealment	Survival, Evolution	Dream to reality	Start-up, Focus	Initiative
Chemical	Precipitation	Reproduction	Relationships	Fantasy, Feeling	Cool, Flowing
Thermal	Incandescence	Cycles of Life	Self-Expression	Fantasy	Hot, Climbing
Electrical	Gaseous Vapors	Bouncy	Command of Details	To Connect	Erratic
Nuclear	Space	Stellar Insight	Innovation	Change, Transition	To transform, Mixed

and to "Blessed Wine" where particular energies are visualized and felt to enter the liquid with a dedicated purpose.

Water is wet, fluid, and necessary for life. All liquid nourishment is ultimately water. All food crops require water by natural means or irrigation, while a huge portion of our food actually comes from water in the form of fish and sea weed.

The human body is composed of solids and water, but all the fluids of the body—blood, semen, vaginal secretions, breast milk, lymph, tears, gastric juices, saliva, etc., are also water-based, and many functions of the body from ingestion to elimination require the correct presence of water. Water is associated with Svadhisthana chakra and with sexuality for reproduction and pleasure.

We know of the relation between the ocean tides and the Moon, but we should also know that the same lunar cycle affects water in all its locations and functions—even within the body.

The Moon is our symbol for the Water Element, and meditation on the Moon increases our ability to feel, and to be sensitive to the moods and needs of others. Its crescent form reminds us of its constant reforming in its five phases of Full Moon, Three-Quarter Moon, Half Moon, Quarter Moon and Dark Moon—each with particular effects on all biological and emotional life. Water teaches to measure, and not to go over the brim—whether in fluids or emotions. Water is the element of receptivity, making us aware of the flow of needs, feelings, fears, and needs. As Earth is our foundation and security, Water is necessary for our survival and teaches us when to "go with the flow" and to live harmoniously.

Water reaches into the depths of the subconscious and connects collective unconscious and the planetary consciousness. It is the element of the womb and the ocean of life, and the feeling path to truth and acceptance. It is the element of imagination, dreams and fantasies often the source of creativity.

Water is the dreamer who yearns for love and adventure; it is the psychic element leading to divination and astral travel. It is feminine and receptive, yet it is daring and loves excitement. In every woman there is a 16-year-old girl yearning for love, laughter, and dancing in the joy of life.

Like all the primal elements, water is fundamental to our being and to all existence. Like all the elements, water is never in perfect and equal balance with the others. Everything exists in combinations that are unique to each individual—yet their representations can change and take us from a state of health and well-being to one of illness and even pathology. By following the program meditations and visualizations for each tattva and their compounding, we can not merely restore to the original state but bring about a natural adjustment more ideal to current circumstances. Everything changes, and we can bring about positive change to coincide with need.

That's what all self-improvement is about, and the tattvas are the basic foundation upon which we restructure and remodel our new home—our ever changing body.

Remember that word we started with, *Think*. There are many references to aid your knowledge of each element, but the most important are those that will well up from your subconscious mind to meet your reality. Meditate often, think what your realizations mean, and write them down for later review.

Now, we begin our active procedure. Review the following overview table, and then follow the Step-by-Step procedure.

> Note: The following Elemental Overview Table #2 for Water is exactly what the title says—an "overview" intended to give you a fundamental awareness of the Elemental Qualities and Characteristics. You may notice some seeming conflicts but these represent particular sources and intended usage from Meditational and Magickal perspectives. An excellent source book for all this is David Hulse's "The Eastern Mysteries" which can be supplemented by the same author's "The Western Mysteries."

ELEMENT OVERVIEW TABLE #2 : Water
ELEMENT OF WATER—SEED OF WATER: Diplomacy

Tattva Name: *Apas*	Tattva Form: Crescent or downward triangle	Tattvic Color: Silver, or White
Tattva/Primary Sheath: *Pranamaya* (energy body, breath)*	Tattvic Animal: Crocodile	Tattvic Taste: Astringent
Yantra Color: Black, or Purple	Yantra Form: "Melon Slice"	Cosmic Plane: *bhuvar* (lower astral)
Chakra Name: *Svadhisthana* (one's own space)	Chakra Common Name: Sex Chakra***	Chakra Bija Mantra: VAM
Chakra Body Location: between genitals & navel	Chakra Body Space: knees to navel	Chakra Body Zone: sacral & coccygeal plexuses
Chakra Color: Orange	Chakra—function of astral etheric center: vitalizes physical & astral body, memory of astral travels	Chakra (spokes) Petals: 6
Chakra Goal: control over muladhara chakra	Chakra God (*Shiva*) Energy: *Vishnu, Varuna*	Chakra Goddess (*Shakti*) Energy: *Rakini, Varuni*
Chakra Meditation: destroys egoism, lechery, and promotes eloquence and inspired discussion.	Chakra Powers: understanding the Unconscious, intuitional Knowledge	Chakra verbal expression: I feel
Chakra Problem: impotence, frigidity, bladder & kidney problems, stiff back		
Chakra Symbol: 6 orange-red petals inscribed with mantras bam, bham, mam, yam, ram, & lam surrounding a lotus flower within which is a silver crescent moon above a crocodile symbolizing the reptilian brain carrying the phantom of unconscious life. Here, also, may be represented Brahma, the creator, and his Shaki, Saraswati, the wisdom goddess. And the Sanskrit word *VAM*.		
Chakra Vital Air: *Prana Vayu*	Chakra Yogini: *Kakini*	Chakra/Physical Gland: gonads
Chakra/Program: Mastery of sex energy, sex magick, or positive (not repressive) sublimation.		
Chakra Siddhi Powers: (when developed) Knowledge of astral entities, healing of diseases, domination of other people, devotion		
Indian God: 4-armed Blue Vishnu, seated on a crocodile, is clothed in yellow wearing a lustrous jewel on his heart.		
Indian goddesses: Blue colored Rakini (sexuality), drunk on ambrosia, holding a spear, axe, damaru-drum, and a lotus. Also Shakini		
Element Name: Water	Element State: Liquid, Fluid	Elemental Action: Feeling, Adapting
Element Function: Reproduction	Elemental Motion: Downward	Elemental Nature: Cool, Flowing

Elemental Power: Cooperation, relationships	Elemental Quality: Cold, Contracting	Element Strength: Feeling, relationships, fantasy
Energy Type: Chemical	Manifests through: Precipitation	Quantum Force: Electromagnetism
Emotional Characteristic: Flexibility, peace	Emotional Desires: Meeting, procreation, family	Emotional Drive: Pleasure, sex, fantasies
Emotional Family Role: Mother	Emotional Nature: Romantic, intimacy, coolness	Emotional/Psychological Level:
Emotional Reaction: Hatred, illusion	Emotional/Sensory Block: Intellectual discrimination	
Emotional/Sexual Identity: Feminine, passive, receptive	Emotional Strength: Will	Emotional Weakness: Indecision, attachment
Mind Action: *Manas* (Emotion)	Mind Function: Intellect, Reason, Analysis, Logic	Mind State: dreaming, sensate mind**
Physical/Action Organ: Womb, Genitals, digestion	Physical/Action Form: Procreation, Nutrition	Physical/Action Effect: Transitory
Physical/Astral Sense: Taste	Physical/Astral Sense Organ: Tongue	Physical Body Functions: All fluids, generative center
Physical Energy Correlations between physical/etheric & astral bodies—Fingers of Hand: Fore Finger		
Psychic Powers: blood control, clairvoyance	Psychic/Astral Work: withdraw tip of tongue to the soft palate, concentrate on it, and contract muscles.	
Alchemical Metal: Brass, Iron	Alchemical Planet: Pluto	Alchemical Quality: ?
Alchemical Symbolic Season: Winter	Alchemical Symbolic Time of Day: Sunrise	Astrological Lunar Phase: First Quarter
Astrological Types: Cancer, Scorpio, Pisces	Astrological Qualities: Imaginative, sharp intelligence, diplomatic, sensitive	
Astrological Ruling Planet: Pluto	Astrological Planetary Expression: Pre-conscious memories, alien life, dark mysteries.	
Egyptian Divinities: Isis, Set	Greek God Form: Poseidon, Pan	Greek goddesses: Diana
Hebrew God Name: Eheieh	Runes: Dagaz, Ehwaz, Gebo, Hagalaz, Isa, Laguz, Pethro, Uruz	
Magical Angel: Taliahad	Magical Animals: dolphins, fish, sea-life, whales	Magical Archangel: Gabriel
Magical/Mythical beings: sea monsters, merpeople	Magical Colors: aqua, gray, green, silver	Magical Day: Monday
Magical Direction: West	Magical Elemental King: Nichsa	Magical/Elemental Spirits: Undines

Magical Energy: ?	Magical Enochian Watch-tower: Western	Magical God Name: EL, Elohim Tzabaoth
Magical Herbs: apple, hibiscus, lilac, thyme, rose	Magical Incense: Damiana, Gardenia; Jasmine Oil	Magical Kerub: Eagle
Magical Metals: Tin, Silver, Copper	Magical Musical Note: D; Musical Scale: Re	Magical Places: beeches, lakes, marshes, oceans
Magical Planet: Moon	Magical Plants: willow, alder, aloe, yarrow, lotus	
Magical Power: To dare, Talismans		Magical Ruler: Tharsis
Magical Rulerships: affection, ancestors, astral travel, beauty, childbirth, children, contract negotiation, emotions, family, fishing, friendship, healing, home,		
hospitals, love, medicine, nursing, partnerships, recuperation, scuba & other diving, receptivity, restoration, spirituality, swimming pool, unions, water professions		
Magical Season: Autumn	Magical States: psychic energy & psychic perception	
Magical stones: amethyst, beryl, carnelian, chalcedony, citrine, coral, geodes, holey stones, moonstone, mother of pearl, pearl, quartz, sapphire		
Magical Symbols: Cup, Inverse Triangle	Magical Time of Day: Sunset	Magical Time of Life: Young Adult, reproductive years
Magickal Tool: cauldron, chalice, cup, sickle	Magical Work: dreams, psychic divination, spells	
Tarot Court: Queen	Tarot Suit: Cups	Tarot Trumps: Moon, Death, Lovers
Tree of Life Path: 23rd–5 to 8	Tree of Life Sphere: Yesod	Tree of Life Soul Level: Neshamah-Higher Unconscious

*The Etheric Double (with Lower Astral) is the subtle energy bridge between the physical & astral bodies. At the same time, it should be noted that these divisions are not absolute like layers of a cake but loosely merge and interface. Thus, for convenience, we refer to this as a "Lower" Astral Plane.

**The sensate mind is also called the *emotional principle* which operates primarily through the physical & astral senses.

***However, it should noted that sexual energy itself originates with *Muladhara* Chakra.

Note: The various magical correspondences are only minimal selections. More complete information can be found in the resources listed at the end of the book. For serious study, you should add to this list, & other lists you may be building. Correspondences build your inter-relationships between Inner & Outer, Subconscious & Conscious, Cosmic & Personal. All magical systems inter-relate and add to your personal memory/library.

Water—Seed of Water

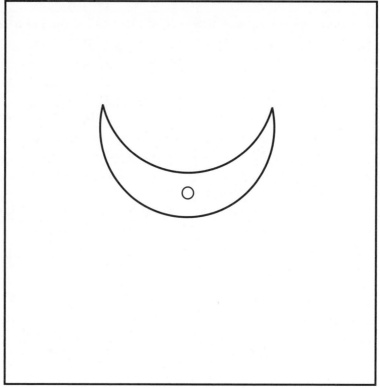

Color the tiny inner bindu circle white,
the inner crescent bright metallic silver,
and the outer square black

Water—Seed of Water: Apas *VAM*

The Tattvic Connection Meditation
& Visualization Program #2: Water/Water
Apas: Water—Seed of Water

Step 1. Preliminaries.

Always start with Physical Relaxation.

Read through the procedure before beginning so that further reference is not needed. Most of it is identical with the other *Tattva Connection Meditation & Visualization Programs* except for specific references to the specific Tattva Element, placed in boldface for ease of recognition.

Time & Space: Allow approximately 30 minutes for the actual 16 step procedure to be conducted in a comfortably warm, quiet, and safe setting free of interruptions.

While a darkened room is not required, freedom from both sound and visual distractions is advisable.

Personal Preparations: Remove shoes and keep clothing or covering minimal to reduce the effects of external stimuli.

Posture & Position: It's best to use a recliner or comfortable chair in which you can fully relax.

Special Lighting: Arrange a small desk or reading light next to your chair that you can easily reach to focus and turn on and off as directed.

Breathing: Establish a deep and natural, rhythmic flow of your breath, mostly balanced between inhalation and exhalation.

Vocalization : Vocalize silently or voiced quietly aloud your affirmations, and the name of the tattva and then the sounding of the mantra in Step 9.

With each step 5 through 13, vocalize the words describing any particular feelings or even visions you experience.

Vibration: In Step 9 chant or hum the Sanskrit name of the tattva, and then the tattvic mantra, drawing these words out and feeling the *vibration.* Vibration means to lightly *warble* the words at the back of your throat, raise or lower the "musical note" and the volume of your voice until it feels right. Feel the words *vibrate* throughout your skull, and then in the body location of the corresponding chakra. With experience you will be able to move the vibration to designated places inside your body, and then—in advanced work—intentionally into external objects.

Voicing the yantra, the name, and the mantra are your means to connect the inner tattva with the external tattva for purification and balance.

Step 2. Goal Statement.
Your goal is three-fold:
- To become fully familiar with the feelings associated with the **Water** Element. You've read about it, you've studied the characteristics and correspondences, and now you need to *feel* the **Water** in you, under you, around you, and *through* your entire inner being. Become aware of Elemental **Water** as the ***fluid** foundation* of the outer material universe.
- To identify inner Elemental **Water** with outer Elemental **Water**, and feel yourself purified and balanced through the *harmonizing of inner with outer and the resultant purification of the inner Tattvic Element.*

- *To address particular concerns:* As an example, we have suggested three areas—1) your **ability to make positive choices in relationships, 2) to control your tendencies to fantasize regarding other people's feelings & needs,** and 3) to **become more decisive in your work world.** You must determine the goals yourself and then *affirm* them simply and concisely in as few words as possible. Write them down, fix them in your mind, but do not consider them as the primary function of the exercise, which is the balancing and purification of personal elemental water. (Note: particular concerns must relate to the Element being addressed—see the Overview Table.)

Step 3. Affirmations.

These affirmations may be spoken as goals at the beginning, and then as confirmations at the ending of the procedure. In addition to these, add the affirmation you wrote as one of your goals.

*I feel Elemental **Water** everywhere within me.*

*I feel Elemental **Water** everywhere around me.*

*I feel purified and in harmony with all that is **Fluid & Flexible** everywhere.*

Step 4. Mental Imagery.

Imagery, like vocalization, increases the effectiveness of the procedure.

Visualization: Tratak & Visualization of the tattvas as described is essential.

Spontaneous Imagery: Other images may appear at the end of the procedure—and that is alright *unless you have negative feelings about them—in which case you should willfully "banish" them.* (If you wish, simply visualize a box, imagine those negative feeling going into the box, close the box tightly, and imagine filling that box with heavy weights, and throwing it into the deepest ocean where it sinks into mud at the bottom beyond all recovery, and know that those negativities are gone forever.)

Recording: Other images that may appear spontaneously at the end of the procedure should be noted along with any particular feelings or ideas, and then recorded in your journal for later analysis.

Analysis: Always let a day or two pass before reading and analyzing your journal entries.

Step 5. Preparation.

Preparing the Yantra Card.

It is recommended that you photocopy the illustration on page 134, preferably on heavier paper or card stock, or draw it yourself in exactly the same sizes using a ruler and black pen. Using a drawing compass or a template, draw a small ⅛" inch diameter circle in the exact center. Leave the inside of the circle white. This inner circle provide a point for your steady focus. Make the outer square 4" x 4" and the inner Crescent (horns up) should be about 2¾" wide and centered, and the little circle in the exact center should be ⅛" in diameter and have a heavy black border around it but not quite as thick as those around the Crescent and outer Square.

Coloring the Yantra Card.

It will be beneficial to you to color the image as follows: (a) Leave the tiny circle white; (b) color the **Lunar Crescent Silver (or White),** and the surrounding larger square **Black**. Each square and the tiny inner circle are bordered with bold black lines.

Cutting the Yantra Card.

If you have reproduced the image on the heavy card stock as recommended, measure off either one or two inches (your choice) on each side and cut away the surplus so you have a square 6" x 6" or 8" x 8" *card* with the colored image in the center.

This preparation will be repeated for all the additional images during which you will have constructed a set of 25 Tattva Cards that can be used again and again in the clairvoyance process discussed in this book, and in many other functions to be discussed later.

Position & Lighting.

Locate a quiet room where you will not be disturbed for approximately 30 minutes. Position your chair in the preferred direction indicated in Step 9 (a and b).

Arrange your light as previously instructed so that it can be focused on the tattvic yantra card held at a comfortable distance and position, recline or sit back in your chair. *Breathing & Relaxation.*

Become fully relaxed, combining slowed rhythmic breathing, and progressive tension and release of muscles from your toes to you brow and scalp if you have not already followed the Empowerment Tension & Release Procedure described in the Addendum to Chapter 1.

Step 6. Pranic Breathing Pattern.

With eyes closed; engage in a pattern of rhythmic breathing involving equally spaced—*without any stress*—in-breaths, holding, out-breaths, holding, and repeating throughout the process.

Step 7. White Light Circulation.

With each in-breath visualize White Light flowing into your body; while holding the breath visualize the light quickly circulating throughout the body; while breathing out see the light quickly being excreted carrying out impurities; and while momentarily holding the out breath *know* that you have energized and cleansed the inner energy body as well as the outer physical body.

Step 8. Psychic Shield.

Returning to a normal breathing pattern, continue visualizing the energizing white light flowing in and around your body, turn your imagination outward and visualize an absolutely clear field surrounding you in an egg shape reaching just beyond the distance measured by your outstretched arms. This field is as transparent as the clearest glass. Know that the outer surface of this field is a psychic shield protecting you from external influences while containing the tattvic meditation program. You can form this shield at any time you feel the need for protection against psychic influences, emotional energies directed against you, and to protect you from your own unwanted responses to advertising and sales pitches, political or religious proselytizing, and unethical and sham charitable requests.

Step 9a. Yantra Card Focus.

Your chair should be facing the tattvic direction: **West.** Otherwise—think and feel *West.*

If you have constructed the tattva yantra card as described, turn on the light and focus it on the card held or positioned comfortably about a foot to a foot and a half in front of you.

Vibrate the name of tattva: *Apas.* Repeat three times.

Chant or hum the tattva element mantra **VAM** (pronounced **VA-UUM**). Vibrate the mantra as instructed in Step 1, preliminaries. Repeat three times. Later, you can do more but always in groups of three. And feel the mantra vibrate in the location of **Svadhisthana** chakra, just **Below the Navel.**

Focus on the small white circle (the *Bindu** point) at the center of the image, and stare at it for as long as you can without blinking. When you can't continue the "burning" feeling any longer, turn off the light, close your eyes and focus your inner sight on the space in front of your brow chakra (between your eye brows and the ridge just above your nose), and see the **Silver Crescent** floating in the space before you and vibrating within the outer **Black** square. And, then, you will soon see the tattva image change into the opposite complementary yantra colors.

*The Bindu is more than a geometric center and focus point: it is the center in which the union of God and Goddess takes place, and hence the origin for all that is contained within the large Square representing the boundaries of the forces within. The Bindu is center from which all things manifest.

Again vibrate the name of the tattva and chant or hum the mantra three times.

Absorb this image! As you repeat the exercise, often, you will reach a point when you will be able to recall this image at will.

Step 9b. Yantra Visualization.

Alternatively, if you haven't made an **Apas** tattva card, immediately in front of you, visualize a large **Black Square**, inside of which is a **Silver Crescent** approximately half the size of the **Black Square**. See the **smaller Silver Crescent** gently vibrating within the **Black Square**. The colors will reverse to their complementary yantra colors.

Step 10. Experiencing Elemental **Water.**

Feel yourself enter into and becoming totally *absorbed* in the **Silver Crescent—** *become One with it*—while retaining awareness of the surrounding **Black** square. Become Elemental **Water** and feel *your* **Watery** nature harmonize with the Cosmic **Water** Tattva, and feel all impurities in your **Water** Tattva—all emotional garbage and unconscious psychic attachments—dissipate.

*In particular: feel the **Watery** nature of your physical body become free of adverse thoughts and feelings. Feel your **body becoming ideally healthy, strong, and energized.** See your Etheric and Astral bodies in clear and bright colors. See **your body as perfectly healthy, feel your whole being energized and clear of emotional pain and illness, and charged with Love.***

Step 11. Knowing Elemental **Water.**

Allow yourself to receive any information or messages from your experiencing of Elemental **Water**. *In particular: receive information involving your **Emotional & Psychic** health, strength, and security.* Receive the information without any emotional reaction.

Step 12. Dissipation of Images.

Slowly dissipate the **Crescent** and the surrounding **Square**, return to the clear field around you, continuing the breathing pattern of Step 6 above.

Step 13. Letting Go of Evoked Feelings.

Let go of all the particular feelings evoking by imagery, slowly change your breathing to its natural rhythm and feel the physical relaxation achieved in Step 1 above.

Step 14. Completion & Self-Realization.

Feel yourself fully relaxed and fully self-contained. Feel yourself to be healthy, energized, cleansed, & refreshed. Know yourself to be strong & secure.

Step 15. Return to Normality.

Open your eyes, return to the physical world knowing all is well. Stand up and move about. Have some refreshment and engage in some normal activity.

Step 16. Review, Record & Analyze.

Record in a journal all messages and feelings received in Step 11 above. At this point, merely record—do not analyze. After a few days, read what you've recorded and then write down an analysis of what you believe the messages mean for you at this time. Realize that when you repeat the exercise at another time, the messages are likely to change to meet new circumstances in your life.

Conclusion: This exercise has demonstrated the particular usefulness of clairvoyance focused on the single area of **Emotional** health, strength and security in Steps 10 and 11 At the same time the relaxation program and light circulation procedure provide emotional health and healing benefits.

However, the entire 16-step Meditation is a basic program that is modified by changes in the tattvic element and then particular modifications in Steps 10 and 11. Details about using elemental and other symbols were described in Addendum 3, page 104.

Suggested Reading:

Frawley, D. *Tantric Yoga and The Wisdom Goddesses*, 1994, Passage Press.

Wolfe, A. *Elemental Power: Celtic Faerie Craft & Druidic Magic*, 2002, Llewellyn.

CHAPTER FIVE
Chakras & Clairvoyance

We've always been clairvoyant
(It's mainly a matter of focus)

If you read the sacred literature of ancient India and China,* you will discover an amazing history of very ancient** humanity *seeing* and *understanding* the origins of the Universe, of Life, and of Consciousness. And, then, as you read the great myths of these very old cultures you'll realize that you have before you the early history of human evolution and of the historic split in human consciousness from a unitary inclusive Universal Consciousness (now, sometimes, called the Collective Unconscious) into the personal Conscious Mind and the personal Subconscious Mind.

> *The early sacred literature of the West, including the Middle East, was largely lost and destroyed during religious wars and persecutions related to the coming of monotheism. We have only fragments in the form of the Kabbalah, Gnostic writings, ancient mythologies, and remnants of the magical traditions of ancient civilizations of Egypt, Africa, and Mesoamerica, and then of the "lost" continents of Lemuria and Atlantis.

> **The "age" of humanity is constantly being pushed further back—far earlier than the Biblical interpretations of a few thousand years, back hundreds of thousands, and even millions of years; Even the ages of the "ancient civilizations "of Sumer, Egypt, Mesopotamia, and others lesser known, are increasingly found to be older than previously believed. We are learning that we older than previously believed, and finally understanding that our evolution was not just a past event but continues in the real world of expanding personal consciousness.

History as a Struggle

History is written as a struggle between *men* (gender specific) dominated by *Masculine* emotions emanating from the subconscious and other men dominated *more* by the developing conscious (rational) mind. The history of learning is that of the conscious mind struggling not merely to understand but to discover meaning and to bring meaning into their daily lives.

Women, in early human history, did not face the same split in consciousness because the *Feminine* Principle was directly involved with Life itself, and women did not experience the struggle between feelings and rational thought that men did. Life was too short, and the demands of woman-hood dominated their lives.

The Dominant Masculine Culture

The constant struggle for physical survival intensified as climates changed and populations soared, bringing tribal conflicts over food supply and territory. This struggle for survival necessitated the exterior focus for most men and thus a dominant masculine culture prevailed in most prehistoric communities.*

*The dominant masculine culture (especially as interpreted in the monotheistic religions) primarily saw the role of women through a man's eyes. She was the bearer of his children, she maintained his household, she prepared his food that he had killed and grown, she met his sexual "needs," she entertained his guests, and she served his god by his rules. Even in relatively modern times, she was seen as less than a man (derived from a single rib of a sleeping man) and thus capable only of menial jobs. From a similar perspective, the psychiatrist, Sigmund Freud, saw women as suffering from "penis envy."

The reality is that women and men are different, yet equal. Today we recognize their "equality" with men, but we still fail to understand, and respect, the differences between men and women beyond the physical. At all levels (etheric, astral, mental, spiritual) the differences are as substantial as they are in the physical body. In addition, between each level there is an alteration of positive and negative nature identified as masculine and feminine. The physical level is masculine, the astral (emotional) level is feminine, the mental is masculine and the spiritual is feminine.

These differences are expressed variously in all we are and in all we do—not just in personal relationships. And these differences function in the processing of the chakras, and in the nature of psychic development.

This will open "new territory" for the new science of the paranormal to explore in coming years.

Pioneers in Consciousness Exploration

Still, there were a few men, some as shaman (see previous chapter) but others simply honored as "holy men" living in isolation, who maintained their interior focus through which the subconscious mind became more organized and directly and specifically accessible to the conscious mind. And through their explorations of the personal subconscious they opened access to the Universal Consciousness, or Collective Unconscious, in which all history and all knowledge is present.

This was clairvoyance—their "clear seeing" that allowed them to see deeply into the ultimate consciousness behind all life and physical manifestation. Here were the visions that ultimately led to their poetic expression in the Hindu Vedas and the Upanishads, the Buddhist Sutras, the Pyramid Texts of ancient Egypt, the I Ching, and other sacred literatures. Here, too, was the knowledge and personal insights that led to such "technologies of the sacred" as Yoga, Tantra, the Tao, Magick, and—most importantly for our discussion—the "Occult Anatomy" of Man's inner organization of subtle energies and centers (chakras).

Modern Transmitters

Some of these writings and teachings have been translated for us—not just into modern language but into modern philosophical systems that we know as Occultism, and better as *Esotericism.* The writings of those 19th and 20th century "transmitters"— among them Blavatsky, Besant, Bailey, Fortune, Leadbeater, Sinnett, Steiner, and more recently Laurency—together present not just views of the "inner world" of humans but of the far past pre-history of the evolving universe, of evolving life on this planet, on evolving humanity, and of the continuing evolution of spiritual life in non-physical dimensions.

We are more than we think,
and need to become more than we are.

Today, these esoteric writings are joined by advancing sciences of sub-atomic quantum physics, sub-cellular life-sciences, inner dimensions of consciousness, and new understanding of the once *hidden side* of the physical and non-physical realities making up the totality of the human person, and the totality of the cosmos "we" all not only share but are intrinsic to the whole.

In addition, there are many thousands of "New Age"* practitioners, teachers, and students of esoteric growth and transformative technologies constantly contributing to a growing body of knowledge that is becoming more and more widely available through books, courses and online information.

> *We find it practical to continue using this phrase as descriptive of the present "explosive" expansion of alternative healing, mind-body medicine, psychic practices, growth practices, yoga, etc., alongside of new interests and renewed studies in Kabbalah, magick, Paganism & Wicca, Gnosticism, Hinduism, and more. While "metaphysics" is an alternative used more and more often in the

book trade, it doesn't carry the same connotation of "newness" that is fundamental to the real changes and expansions of awareness and consciousness that have been on-going and accelerating since the mid-nineteenth century.

Psychic Technology

Consciousness continues its evolution, and while the personal consciousness is still divided into conscious mind and subconscious mind, it is joined by the developing superconscious mind that brings both together with conscious and focused access to deeper levels of Universal Consciousness.

We think of "*technology*" as purely modern and primarily physical, but these older cultures have been using the "beyond-physical" *psychic* technology of clairvoyance to explore Cosmology and Occult Anatomy and develop "Inner" technologies for thousands of years. There are very powerful transformative and evolutionary programs and specific applications for this once secret knowledge now readily accessible for your personal developmental work.

Chakra "Switches"

Our interest in this chapter is specific: three of the seven major chakras *can* function as "switches" to the development and use of clairvoyance in particular applications. To understand how these switches can function, we do have to review the seven major chakras and their role with the whole person complex.

First, however, it is important to iterate what should be obvious to everyone today: The human body is a very complex biological system of muscle, bone, chemical, neurotransmitters, nerves, energies, cells and sub-cellular parts. But, *what holds all this together in a functional unity from conception to maturity?*

(We will avoid discussing the effect of aging in this book, but will be doing so in another book very soon.)

The Etheric Double

Beyond the limits of the purely physical body is the Etheric Double. We call it a "double" because it is essentially an exact twin to the healthy physical body in every detail and serves as its controlling "matrix" throughout the individual's physical lifetime. It's a "body" of subtle material and energy that completes an organic unity with the physical body, and when uninhibited by environmental and karmic factors, keeps the physical body in healthy repair.

But, the etheric double is more than a twin to the physical body because it has a unique system of "psychic" centers and energy channels called, respectively, *chakras* and *meridians.* Of course this physical/etheric composite if far more complex that can described in a few words in this single chapter, but our interest is very much centered on the chakras and the role they do and that they can play in our psychic development and action.

Chakras & the Chakra System

Chakras are centers of activity for the reception, assimilation and transmission of life energies.

Because of the inherent tendency to focus on physical correlates to anything psychic, we must clearly state: ***Chakras are not <u>physically</u> real!*** Nevertheless, *they are very real in the composite, whole-person sense.*

It also has to be stated that the chakras are not really singular although we write about them one-by-one out of the need to describe them individually.

To repeat: **there are no physical chakras.** Yes, there are physical body correlates that can be used to *define* the chakras in physical terms—in particular by the endocrine glands and nerve ganglia with which they are associated—but that can become both misleading and limiting. Like all things, chakras function within systems and no understanding is possible without relating the parts to the functioning whole.

Chakras function not only systemically with each other but with associated areas in the physical and astral bodies. Also, the chakras are located on the *surface* of the etheric double, and there are corresponding chakras located *within* the astral body projecting energies to the etheric chakras.

The Spinal Column is the Middle Pillar

Even the most casual look at the following chart showing locations of the Chakras, major nerve plexi, and related body parts illustrates the complexity of the body and the central importance of the spine from its base up and through the brain.

Esoterically, the Spinal Column is the Central Pillar of your living psychic temple, and corresponds with the "Middle Pillar" of the Kabbalistic Tree of Life—itself being the primary symbol integrating esoteric studies and practices in the Western Tradition, and the means to synthesizing Eastern and Western spiritual practices in a common union.

Chart of The Chakras, the Nerve Plexi, & Body Parts

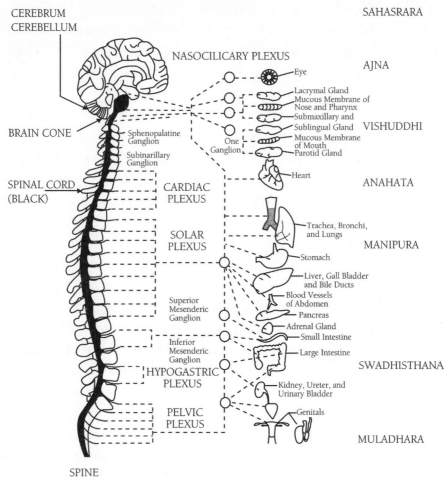

CEREBRUM
CEREBELLUM

SAHASRARA

NASOCILICARY PLEXUS

AJNA

Eye

Lacrymal Gland
Mucous Membrane of
Nose and Pharynx
Submaxillary and
Sublingual Gland

VISHUDDHI

BRAIN CONE

Sphenopalatine
Ganglion

Subinarillary
Ganglion

One
Ganglion

Mucous Membrane
of Mouth
Parotid Gland

SPINAL CORD
(BLACK)

CARDIAC
PLEXUS

Heart

ANAHATA

SOLAR
PLEXUS

Trachea, Bronchi,
and Lungs

MANIPURA

Stomach

Liver, Gall Bladder
and Bile Ducts
Blood Vessels
of Abdomen
Pancreas
Adrenal Gland
Small Intestine

Superior
Mesenderic
Ganglion

Inferior
Mesenderic
Ganglion

Large Intestine

SWADHISTHANA

HYPOGASTRIC
PLEXUS

Kidney, Ureter, and
Urinary Bladder

PELVIC
PLEXUS

Genitals

MULADHARA

SPINE

The Importance of Symbols & their Correspondences

Just as there are obvious connections between the chakra system, the spinal/brain system, the major body parts and their systemic functions in relation to the whole body, and hence to the whole person, the same "connectedness" exists in everything and everywhere.

Because we exist in individual physical bodies, mostly living independently from other people and other entities, and because we are legally identified as individuals by all the various "ruling powers" of politics, business, science, education, governments and their mediating bureaucrats, professionals, and other functionaries, we tend to lose sight and value of our connectedness. We look around us and see an environment dominated by separate houses, privately owned cars, and other personal possessions; we look above us and see separate stars, planets, the sun and moon, and airplanes and birds in flight; we look beneath us and see separate fish swimming, separate moles and worms working in the earth, we find minerals to extract, and so on—and all of this is valued in terms of individual interests and mostly valued only for their contribution to "the Economy" with little concern for community environment and welfare or global health.

*We tend to forget that everything is forever bound and connected together
from our common origin at the "Beginning."*

As the world has expanded and diversified, some connections between "things" have become weaker, marked by their observable differences—yet things that are naturally associated together, marked by their similarities, have stronger inter-connections (called "correspondences) than those having less. And those connected historically never lose that even as that connectedness weakens with age and over-burdened by newer but similar things.

Many things are *causally* related to Natural Forces, which then function as "rulers" of those groups. In the past, those forces and their rulerships were personalized as Gods, Goddesses, and their ministering agents, and these were identified by names and images. In the course of time, as populations expanded beyond tribal and cultural limitations, Symbols have come to replace those deities while connecting more universally—beyond culture—to these forces and their rulerships of related things. Symbols now provide the means to invoke the forces and to *divine (seek)* answers *to* specific questions through "correspondences" with things related by rulership.

Symbols function like Search Engine listings

As a result, symbols can function like a search engine listing. More specific addresses connect to smaller and more specialized groups, while a master address connects to the rulership. And symbols themselves become part of the system of correspondences. By means of symbols related by a system of organized correspondences on the Kabbalistic Tree of Life, we have a means—similar to mathematics—of relating parts (correctly) to the whole.

With the etheric chakras we relate the specific natural energies and psychic forces of each systemically to corresponding physical, etheric, and astral energies and forces, *symbolically* to their correspondences in the outer world. By "awakening" a specific chakra through visualization and meditation, we mobilize its psychic powers to *divine* the answers to our specific questions. Each chakra taps into a particular level of astral consciousness that relates to a corresponding level in the "thing" being divined. Thus we have a system of clairvoyance based on "Intentional Perception."

The more narrow our focus, the deeper the answer.

The Whole Person

As mentioned elsewhere, in addition to the physical/etheric composite, the entire spirit manifested "whole-person" is made up of the astral, mental and causal bodies. The chakras repeat in some manner through all the bodies, including the physical where they relate to the nerve complexes mainly located from the bottom to the top of the spinal column culminating with the brain. It is with the etheric chakras that we are most concerned, but it must be remembered that each etheric chakra is a *channel* between the physical nerve plexi and the astral chakras.

It is the astral world and the astral-emotional body working through the physical/ etheric complex that are fundamental to paranormal phenomena and powers—especially clairvoyance.

Passive Sensitivity

To understand the relation of innate psychic powers to developed psychic skills we have to distinguish between passive sensitivity and intentional perception.

The training going into the development of these two different approaches is only partly different: in case of passive *sensitivity* we are essentially "opening" to etheric and astral images and energies; in the case of intentional *perception* we learn to focus on perceiving *specified astral images* while sensing energy systems.

Intentional Perception

In both cases, "sensitivity" is important, and so is at least some degree of specification as to what or who we seek to "see." But the actual training for intentional perception starts with "visualization"—the formation of unambiguous specific images (often of symbols functioning as *keys* to particular information) in the imagination.

Even though the "directive" for any kind of training and development comes from the mind, "the *theater*" for the faculty of imagination is primarily an astral function. Every image you see—even though it may be entirely generated with physical sight— has an astral replica in the imagination.

An Illustrative Story of Intentional Perception

Now, turn the situation "upside down" when you don't have a physical sight of the person or thing present. (We are skipping over the use of photographs and pictures for the moment) Let's just invent a story: You are the President of the United States, and you are clairvoyant! You want to "see" what the President of China is up to at the moment. He, however, is in Beijing and you are in Washington. There is no power by which you could instantly "transport" his physical body into the Oval Room of the

White House, and doing so would not satisfy your *covert* desire to know what the Chinese President is thinking about while you are both preparing for a "closed door" summit conference.

As a clairvoyant, you visualize a clear image of the Chinese President in your imagination and that becomes your key to reaching across space and time to intentionally perceive and sense what you need to know about his activities and motives.

Let's just continue for a moment with our story-telling. As the current President, you are deeply interested in the previous presidents, and in this specific instance you would like to know how President Franklin Roosevelt would have "felt" about it. Obviously, Franklin Roosevelt is dead, but the White House has many portraits and memorabilia of all the Presidents. You easily form a "picture" of "FDR" in your imagination, and it opens a channel for you to sense his feelings in response to the question you ask.

What have we done?

The astral world is not limited by the dimensions of time and space as is the physical world. Thus it is "above" them that your visualized images create "channels" through the astral correspondences that tap into the Universal Consciousness where past and present exist simultaneously. You "see" and "feel" the response to your questions. It is a very challenging concept because we are anchored in the physical body and the physical world, and are taught through experience and instruction to see and function as if there are no other dimensions, no other realities, no Greater Cosmos, no Spirit, no Soul.

The Limitations of "Faith"

Yes, you may be asked to give "lip service" to a belief in the soul, a belief in something called "heaven" and beings called "spirits" and "angels"—but your church requires you to accept such belief as a matter of "faith" not to be tested in any way by ordinary people. Just *Believe!,* and support your church, follow its dictates, and you will surely go to heaven. But, of course, the churches of every religion give you the same instruction—to believe and have faith in their *particular* version of "truth."

"Faith" is powerful, but a faith based on one's demonstrated accomplishments is more powerful yet, and is proven again and again in the continuing exercise of your personal powers. It is by such application and testing that you learn, grow, and develop actual skills with practical benefit in your life.

Now, a fundamental point: *Nothing* of yourself (no astral substance or energy) was projected to present-day China or past Washington. *Everything happens in your Mind* (but really in your imagination under the direction of mind). The more accurate your visualization, the more inclusive of details, and the more specific your quest, the more correct will be your clairvoyant vision.

Levels of Consciousness

The astral body, like the astral world, has many "levels" delineated by the particular energies and range of consciousness you are able to deploy in your work. Let us presume your image of the Chinese President (to continue with our fictional example) is accurate and your quest for information is specific, but the nature of your vision is contingent on the level of consciousness and energy you are able to use.

Each chakra switches on particular range of consciousness and energy which may limit or even distort the information you are able to perceive about the target of your quest, i.e., the Chinese President.

We start by building a basic familiarity with the name, nature and functionality of each of the seven major chakras in relation to the manifestation of their particular energies in the physical body, their manifestation of psychic powers, and the ways each relates to the others and to the system as a whole.

Even though we can't describe every aspect of the individual chakra's relationship to the complete composite that is the whole physical/etheric, astral, and mental/causal complex whole-person, it is important to always keep that in the background as we continue our study.

The Seven Major Chakras*

Note: the descriptions that follow are largely adapted from the brilliant work of Dr. Jonn Mumford in his "A Chakra & Kundalini Workbook." Other major sources are Anodea Judith's "Wheels of Life," and personal correspondence with Cyndi Dale and her "Complete Book of Chakra Healing," "Kundalini," and "The Subtle Body." The adaptations are a blending of source materials and this co-author's personal observations and intuition.

See end of chapter for additional sources.

Muladhara

*1: **Muladhara*** (also called the *Basal* or *Root* Chakra) is located at the base of the spine between the anus and the perineum (about half-way between the anus and sex organs), and physically manifests through the pelvic plexus, the gonads (testicles and ovaries), and the muscle that controls male ejaculation. It relates to the basic instincts of security and survival, and basic human potentiality. Physically it rules our sexuality, emotionally our sensuality, mentally our stability, and spiritually our sense of security. It relates to the sense of smell. The element is Earth.

Its associated psychic powers are pain control, psychometry, dowsing, and telekinesis. Opening of Muladhara gives power over all the earth elements and metals, and the physical body. With the opening of Muladhara, pain control becomes a reality as demonstrated by walking on hot coals, lying on a bed of nails, insertion of pins through the tongue, etc.

It is the seat of the red bindu,* (also called "the female drop"), and Kundalini, both a goddess and a force symbolized by a serpent coiled three times about a black lingam. (Likewise, the genetic code lies coiled in the sperm and the ovum.) From this chakra three channels—*Ida, Pingala,* and *Sushumna*—emerge, separate, and spiral upward.

> *A bindu is a point of interface between physical and etheric that serves as a "seed" for meditation that, in this chakra, focuses on activating Kundalini.

Muladhara chakra is symbolized as a red square with 4 red spokes (sometimes called petals), and represented geometrically in a yellow square. The audible seed mantra is *LuNG,* followed by silent mental echo of *LuM.* (Pronunciation of these Sanskrit names will be explained later.)

Svadhisthana

2: Svadhisthana (also called the *Sacral* Chakra) is located in the sacrum over the spleen and below the navel, and physically manifests through the pancreas, kidneys, and the hypogastric plexus. Like Muladhara, it relates to the gonads, the production of sex hormones, and the female reproductive cycle. It relates to relationships, basic emotional needs, and sensual pleasure. Physically it rules our reproduction, emotionally our joy, mentally our creativity, and spiritually our enthusiasm. It relates to the sense of taste. The element is Water.

The associated psychic powers are empathy and psychic diagnosis. Svadhisthana is the fluid control point for the entire body system, including blood flow. Vaso-constriction and vaso-dilation of the arterioles are controllable at will. Stigmata, the percolation of blood through the skin, can also be demonstrated.

It is symbolized by a crescent moon within a white lotus with six orange spokes, and represented geometrically in a silver crescent. The audible seed mantra is *VuNG* followed by mental echo of *VuM*.

Manipura

3: *Manipura* (also called the *Solar Plexus* Chakra) is located in the lumbar area above the navel, and physically manifests through the adrenals, and the solar plexus. It relates to the conversion of food into energy, the expression of personal power, the formation of personal opinions, and the transformation of simple into complex emotional expression. Physically it rules our digestion, emotionally our expansiveness, mentally our personal power, and spiritually growth. It relates to the sense of sight. The element is Fire.

The associated psychic powers are clairsentience, empathy, premonitions & prophetic dreaming. This is the center of the salamander (fire-walker) whose inner life is sustained by the primal heat element. The fire-walkers of North India walking across beds of glowing embers and the Pacific islanders walking upon white-hot stones employ the Manipura chakra.

Other so-called "fire-eaters" unknowingly use Manipura chakra together with Anahata chakra to perform their feats, including dipping the hands into boiling water, boiling oil, molten lead, and molten steel.

Manipura is symbolized by a yellow inverse triangle within a lotus with ten spokes, and represented geometrically in a red inverse triangle. The audible seed mantra is *RuNG* followed by mental echo of *RuM*. Like Muladhara, it contains a feminine energy.

Simultaneous mastery of earth, water, and fire with subsequent immunity to pain and searing of flesh by heat is accomplished through manipulating the forces inherent in the first three chakras and culminating in Manipura, the Solar Plexus chakra.

Anahata

4: Anahata (also called the *Heart* Chakra) is located in the upper thoracic area over the heart, and physically manifests through the cardiac plexus and the thymus gland at the "heart" of the immune system and the site of T-cell maturation. It relates to compassion, tenderness, unconditional love, and personal well-being.

Physically it rules circulation, emotionally our unconditioned love both for others and for self, mentally our passions, and spiritually our devotion. It relates to the sense of touch. The element is Air. The associated psychic power is hands-on-healing.

It carries consciousness to the next life.

It is symbolized by a *yantra* consisting of a hexagram of two interlaced triangles representing the union of female and male, within a lotus with twelve green spokes, and represented geometrically in a blue hexagram. This yantra—more than a symbol of man and woman united—is a powerful meditation device for uniting lower with higher, feminine with masculine, inferior with superior, lesser with greater, microcosm with macrocosm, and human with the Divine. It is the heart of Man and the heart of the Divine manifest in Man. The audible seed mantra is *YuNG* followed by mental echo of *YuM.*

It is the Smile that lights up for everyone.

Vishuddha

5: *Vishuddha* (also called the *Throat* Chakra) is located in the cervical (neck) area, and physically manifests through the thyroid and parathyroid glands, the pharyngeal plexus and the vocal cords. The thyroid hormones are responsible for growth and maturation. Physically it rules our communications, emotionally our independence, mentally our fluent thought, and spiritually our sense of security. It relates to the sense of hearing.

The associated psychic powers are channeling, clairaudience, and telepathy. It plays a role in Dream Yoga and Lucid Dreaming.

It is symbolized by a silver crescent within a lotus with sixteen blue spokes, and represented geometrically by a black upright oval. The audible seed mantra is *HuNG* followed by mental echo of *HuM*.

Ajna

6: *Ajna* (also called the *Brow* Chakra, the *Eye of Horus,* the *Third Eye*) is located between the eyes but above the brow line, and physically manifests through the naso-ciliary plexus and the pituitary gland. It relates to the balancing of our higher and lower selves and inner guidance. Physically it rules our visual consciousness, emotionally our intuitive clarity. It relates to our sense of awareness.

It is the terminal point where the two nadis, *Ida* and *Pingala,* merge with the central channel, *Sushumna.* With its activation, the perception of duality ceases. *Sushumna*—along with *Ida* and *Pingala*—rises up from the *Muladhara* chakra to curve over the Crown of the head and then down to terminate in *Ajna,* while *Ida* and *Pingala* continue down to the two nostrils.

The associated psychic powers are clairvoyance, telepathy, telekinesis, precognition, remote viewing, and aura reading.

It is symbolized by an indigo-colored lotus with two spokes, and represented graphically in a white-winged globe. Actually, each petal or wing itself consists of 48 spokes for a total of 96. One wing is rose colored and the other is yellow. The two petals or wings represent the Sun and the Moon, mind and body, *Ida* and *Pingala.* The seed mantra is *AuM.* The element is *Manas,* "mind-stuff" the energy of consciousness.

Sahasrara

*7: **Sahasrara*** (also called the *Thousand Petaled Lotus* and the *Crown* Chakra) is located at and then just above the crown of the head. It manifests through the pineal gland, which produces melatonin—the hormone regulating sleep. Physically, it relates to the basis of consciousness—physically with meditation, emotionally with "beingness," mentally with universal consciousness. The female Kundalini *Shakti* energy rises from Muladhara to the crown to unite with the male *Shiva* energy to produce *Samadhi*. It relates to our sense of the Divine Connection.

The associated psychic powers are astral projection and prophecy.

It is symbolized by a violet lotus with one thousand multi-colored spokes (actually 12 in the center and then 960 around the center for a total of 972), and represented graphically by an image of a red rose. There is no seed mantra. The element is Thought.

RELATIVE POSITIONS OF MAJOR CHAKRAS ON THE PHYSICAL BODY

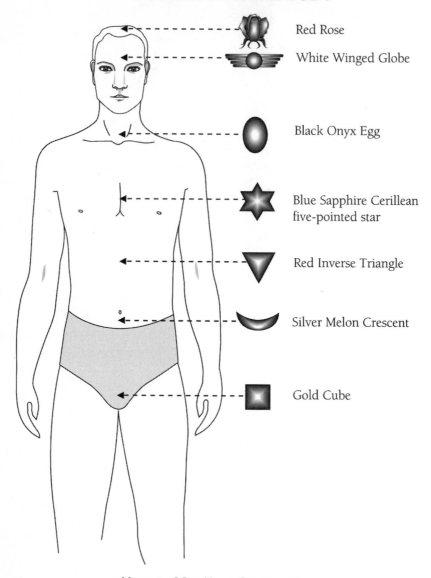

Red Rose

White Winged Globe

Black Onyx Egg

Blue Sapphire Cerillean five-pointed star

Red Inverse Triangle

Silver Melon Crescent

Gold Cube

How to Manifest Chakra Power

We've taken the first step by building some familiarity with the individual chakras and, to a lesser extent, the "system" of their relationships to each other, to the physical body and world, and the astral levels of consciousness and the associated psychic powers.

There are hundreds of esoteric technologies involving Chakra Power, but at their simplest they involve Concentration, Visualization, and Focus of Feeling/Awareness.

While there are many variations involving posture and movement, particular symbols and deity images, sounding or chanting of particular names and "words of power," gestures and positions of the hands and arms, these are all embellishments on the fundamental fact that concentration is the primary (and a safe and natural method) way to awaken the chakras as centers and sources of psychic powers.

Your Astral Room

Preliminary to all else is the Astral Room as described in the previous chapter. It really involves little more that selecting a space that is isolated, quiet, and designated to be undisturbed, in which you can use your imagination to create a temporary astral duplicate that visually defines your work area as an area of focused energies and a protected (psychic) perimeter. Intention is all it takes.

Within your Work Room, you need a reclining chair or lounge on which you can physically relax.

Visualizing the Chakra Images

The next step involves 1) concentrating attention on the 2) visualized chakra image, with focused feeling/awareness 3) in the appropriate body area, 4) mantra sounding, 5) conversion of the two-dimensional chakra images into three dimensional images. All of this is a step-by-step process leading up to the final step involving Concentration, Visualization and Focus of Feeling/Awareness in relation to the chakra's location.

In the following paragraphs we build a background of knowledge through specific exercises of memory and visualization.

The Chakra Images, Names, & Locations

See the diagram of Chakra Tattwa Yantras on the following page: a Square, a Crescent with its horns pointing upward, an inverse Triangle, a Hexagram of two interlaced triangles, and an upright Oval. These relate to the five lower chakras.

Relate these to their location along the spine:

1. *Muladhara*—Square—Base of Spine over Gonads
2. *Svadhisthana*—Upright Horizontal Crescent—Below the Naval over Adrenals
3. *Manipura*—Inverse Triangle—Solar Plexus above Naval over Pancreas
4. *Anahata*—Hexagram of two Interlaced Triangles—Heart area over Thymus
5. *Vishuddha*—Upright Oval—Throat over Thyroid

SIMPLE CHAKRA TATTVA YANTRAS

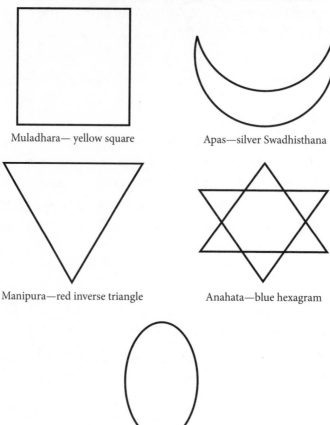

Muladhara— yellow square

Apas—silver Swadhisthana

Manipura—red inverse triangle

Anahata—blue hexagram

Vishuddha—black upright oval

Start Simple

These five simple geometric images are all you need to start. Simply focus on each image and remember their names. Next, close your eyes and visualize each while saying its name aloud.

Take as many small steps as needed to have full confidence in your ability.

The Chakra Names, Colors, & Elements

Once you can visualize these images, remember and speak their names, and feel them in your body, take the next step and see each in these colors and memorize their elemental rulership.

1. *Muladhara*—Yellow—Earth

2. *Svadhisthana*—Silver—Water

3. *Manipura*—Red—Fire

4. *Anahata*—Blue—Air

5. *Vishuddha*—Black—*Akasha* (Spirit)

A Warning!

Resist, at this time, drawing the images on cardboard and turning them into cards. The time will come for that, but if you do it too soon you will lose the value of visualization training.

At a future time, you should do that and use the cards for divination and as talismans—but *not yet!* And those are subjects to be treated in other books.

The Chakra Names & Audible Seed Mantras with their Bija Mantras

The next step is to pronounce the mantra while visualizing the colored image as follows:

1. *Muladhara—LuNG—(LuM)*

2. *Svadhisthana—VuNG—(VuM)*

3. *Manipura—RuNG—(RuM)*

4. *Anahata—YuNG—(Yum)*

5. *Vishuddha—HuNG—(HuM)*

The Chakra Names, Audible Seed & Bija Mantras, and Body Spaces

Then repeat and *visualize and feel* the images in their body space.

1. *Muladhara—LuNG—(LuM)*—Base of Spine

2. *Svadhisthana—VuNG—(VuM)*—Between pubic bone and navel

3. *Manipura—RuNG—(RuM)*—Between navel and sternum

4. *Anahata—YuNG—(Yum)*—Between nipples

5. *Vishuddha—HuNG—(HuM)*—Adam's apple

The Chakra Names & their Three-dimensional Images

Now we're ready for some more difficult but extremely important visualization work that hopefully will affirm the value of our step-by step work so far. Each of our two-dimensional images must now be seen in three dimensions, and—as you do this—feel these psychological attributes as you feel the image in its place.

1. *Muladhara*—Yellow Square becomes a golden cube—Solidarity, Cohesiveness, and Integration

2. *Svadhisthana*—Silver crescent becomes a silver melon slice—Flexibility, Equanimity, and Diplomacy

3. *Manipura*—Red triangle becomes a ruby red tetrahedron (an upside-down, three-sided pyramid)—Power, Passion, Energy, and Motivation

4. *Anahata*—Blue hexagram becomes a six-sided blue star carved out of blue sapphire—Compassion, Tolerance, and Understanding

5. *Vishuddha*—Black oval becomes a black marble egg—Communication, Empathy, and Freedom

Technique for Preliminary Six-Day External Chakra Dharana

Sit in a meditative posture or in a chair in a dimly lit room and visualize it as your astral room.

Day One

1. Close your eyes and visualize before you the yellow square Tattwa of *Muladhara* chakra. Contemplate the yellow square and audibly intone the chakra mantra "*LuNG*," with emphasis on the nasal-palatal "NG." (The sound vibrates the sphenoid bone, with the sphenoid sinus acting as a sound chamber, and the pituitary gland receives stimulation.) Continually pull the consciousness back into focus so awareness rotates around the square yellow field and the mantra "*LuNG*." Continue for five minutes to occupy your mind completely with the yellow square and the Bija mantra.

Day Two

2. Repeat the process the next day but switch to the silver crescent Tattwa for *Svadhisthana* chakra and the chakra mantra *VuNG*.

Day Three

3. Red triangle Tattwa of *Manipura* and chakra mantra "*RuNG*."

Day Four

4. Blue hexagram Tattwa of *Anahata* and chakra mantra "*YuNG*."

Day Five

5. Black oval Tattwa of *Vishuddha* and chakra mantra "*HuNG*."

Day Six

6. Start over and repeat the process two times for a total of fifteen days. More, if you feel it necessary, and again any time you wish.

Special Considerations with External Chakra Dharana

Three rotations of the five Tattwa images take fifteen days; this is suggested as the minimum before progressing to the advanced Internal Chakra Dharana.

The object is to quiet the consciousness by becoming more and more imbued with the geometrical shape seen, entranced with the color related to the form, and entrained by the Bija mantra reverberations.

This same process is used by performing "Tratak" (staring) on the same images drawn and colored on cards. We will explore this at a later stage but consider this visual training fundamental.

Pronunciation of Sanskrit Mantras

Note about pronunciation: The word *Sanskrit* means "perfectly formed," and it is believed that the language was scientifically structured 2500 years ago. Each of the thirty-three consonants is grouped according to the parts of speech used in vocalizing its spoken vibration. An additional tip about the Bija mantra for *Manipura ("RuNG")* is worth noting: Although the Sanskrit "r" is normally not trilled, the psychic effect may be enhanced by trilling somewhat as in Russian. "R" in Sanskrit is designated as a cerebral, along with five other consonants. A cerebral sound is one which is produced by the tip of the tongue flapping its underside against the roof of the mouth. The result is that a vibration is sent through the skull bones affecting the frontal lobes of the cerebral cortex. If you place one hand on the top of your forehead and strongly trill the "r," you will feel the frontal bone momentarily shake with the sound. This effect is physiologically and psychically effective if you can accomplish it. Unfortunately, some people cannot trill, and if that is the case, just get as close to it as you can.

Example Pronunciations for Each Mantra:

LuNG—Audible chant as in English "lung."

LuM—Silent Mental repetition as in English "lumbar."

VuNG—Audible chant as in English "vulcan."

VuM—Silent Mental repetition as in English "come."

RuNG—Audible chant as in English "rung."

RuM—Silent Mental repetition as in English "rummage."

YuNG—Audible chant as in English "young."

YuM—Silent Mental repetition as in English "yummy"

HuNG—Audible chant as in English "Hungarian."

HuM—Silent Mental repetition as in English "humming."

PRELIMINARY PREPARATION
FOR INTERNAL CHAKRA DHARANA

This is the most challenging procedure in the entire book, and it offers the opportunity to point out that you will encounter many effective procedures for the development and effective deployment of the clairvoyance skill throughout this book and many other books.

No one shoe fits every foot; no one healing procedure is effective equally for everyone; one man's food is another's poison, and so on. We believe that every procedure we offer in this book is effective, but having a variety to choose from is like shopping from a catalog and finding those that have the greatest appeal, and ultimate value, to you.

Growth & Transformation is "Forever"

They are all valuable, and we hope you will experiment and test them all, not only to gain what each offers but to then be able to select one or more that will be used regularly in your daily practice.

Psychic Development is a "forever" growth and transforming process, and you may constantly return to this book to work with another procedure and find additional and alternative benefits.

"On the Path"

One final point: Through this and other books, you are the empowered master and teacher. The more personal responsibility you take in your development work, the more help you will receive through both internal guidance and external helps.

When the student is ready, the teacher will appear—and may come in a dream at night or a book that falls off a shelf in front of your hands, or as a voice heard during meditation or a remark from a fellow student "on the Path," or a paragraph you read before that now speaks to you as it did not before.

Internal Chakra Dharana—with cards

We mentioned earlier that many readers would be inclined to draw the five geometric figures on cards, along with the names and other material for easy reference. If you did that, put them aside for now and do the same thing with five new cards but change the colors to those indicated below, which are the "complimentary" colors:

Internal Chakra Images in Complementary (Yantra) Colors

1. *Manipura*—a blue square with a small white bindu (dot) in the center.

2. *Svadhisthana*—a black crescent with a small white bindu in the center.

3. *Manipura*—a green triangle with a small white bindu in the center.

4. *Anahata*—a red hexagram with a small white bindu in the center.

5. *Vishuddha*—a white upright oval with a small open circle bindu in the center.

INTERNAL CHAKRA DHARANA YANTRAS

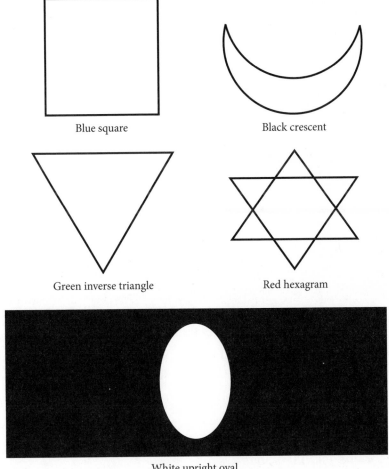

Blue square

Black crescent

Green inverse triangle

Red hexagram

White upright oval

The developmental concept for Internal Chakra Dharana is that by staring fixedly (Tratak) on the complimentary color Tattwa yantra we fatigue the specific color cone receptors at the back of the eyeballs. When the eyes are then closed, we will have an *inner* experience of the correct color. For example, the complimentary color of the yellow Muladhara square is blue. Tratak on the blue square for a minute or two, and then when you close your eyes the complimentary color of yellow will manifest as an afterimage that appears to *float* before your eyes.

Yellow, or course, is the correct color of *Muladhara* chakra.

The purpose of this exercise is to enable you to actually see the yellow square vividly *floating* in front of your eyes. Another way of putting it is to say that we're making the imaged chakra even more real. *Can you see the yellow square as vividly without tratak?* That's for you to find out. With practice, yes—it should be possible.

What are we doing? One way or another, we want you to be able to visualize vividly and clearly. In the case of the chakras, the better your visualization, the more effective will be your work with them as "triggers" to specified levels of clairvoyance.

TECHNIQUE FOR INTERNAL CHAKRA DHARANA—with cards

Sit in a meditative posture or in a chair, with a desk lamp available to illuminate the Tattwa yantra card.

Place the blue square complimentary color Tattwa yantra of *Muladhara* before you with the desk lamp fully illuminating it.

Gaze fixedly, without blinking, at the white bindu in the center. Continue gazing (it may take one or two minutes) until a rim aura of light starts to appear around the edges of the square and the blue color starts to pale. While watching, focus the inner self upon the silent repetition of the Bija mantra "*LuM*."

When the rim aura is well manifested, simultaneously switch the light off and close your eyes. Continue the silent repetition of the Bija mantra *"LuM"* while gently looking *through* your forehead and closed eyelids. With relaxation, a yellow square will gradually emerge, *floating* in the dark space in front of you. Watch the yellow square, constantly adjusting the focus of your attention, in order to perceive the afterimage as long as possible.

Three-dimensional Conversion

When the afterimage has totally faded, proceed to the final step by imagining you have moved the Tattwa symbol down into its appropriate space in your body. In this particular case (for *Muladhara*), visualize the yellow square as level with the base of your spine and occupying the pelvic floor.

Now turn the two-dimensional square into a three-dimensional solid gold cube.

Your unconscious mind will determine the size, and this image is uniquely yours. Continue concentrating on this for at least ten minutes. Be patient with fluctuations and simply recreate the cube each time it fades, distorts, or changes. Throughout this portion of the technique you still will be repeating the Bija mantra *"LuM"* to yourself.

Special Considerations with Internal Chakra Dharana

All of the geometrical yantras, when internalized, should be formed in three dimensions. You will imagine this by changing your perspective, with the following guidelines:

Converting Chakra Tattva Color & Form to Yantra Color & Form

1. *Muladhara*—Yellow square converts to golden cube. Bija mantra—*LuM*.

2. *Svadhisthana*—Silver crescent converts to silver melon slice. Bija mantra—*VuM*.

3. *Manipura*—Red triangle converts to ruby red tetrahedron (an upside-down, three-sided pyramid). Bija mantra—*RuM*.

4. *Anahata*—Blue hexagram converts into six-sided blue star carved out of blue sapphire. Bija mantra—*YuM*.

5. *Vishuddha*—Black oval converts into a black marble egg. Bija mantra—*HuM*.

Remember that the appropriate Bija Mantra with the "M" ending is used at all stages of Internal Chakra Dharana.

The technique of Chakra Dharana should be practiced for ten minutes or more each day. Begin with *Muladhara* chakra the first day, *Svadhisthana* chakra the second day, and so on, doing each chakra in turn until you return to *Muladhara* and start the cycle over again.

Internal Dharana within the Body

After the first two or three weeks, you may dispense with External Dharana in the form of concentration upon a Tattwa diagram and may proceed with just Internal Dharana upon the chakra symbols within the body.

With practice, a sensation of physical stimulation will be produced by mentally moving the Tattwa symbol down into its proper position along the spine and concentrating upon the area.

Visualization Guide to Chakra Body Space

1. The yellow square of *Muladhara* should be visualized as at the base of the spine.

2. The silver crescent of *Svadhisthana* is two inches below the navel.

3. The red triangle of *Manipura* is about three inches above the navel, level with the pit of the stomach.

4. The blue hexagram of *Anahata* should be visualized as level with the heart.

5. The black egg of *Vishuddha* chakra is level with the Adam's apple.

With the accomplishment of these three-dimensional visualizations and actually feeling them in their correct body locations, you have mastered a technique not only of value for our use of the chakras in psychic development but in employing chakra power in any physical/etheric, astral, and mental/causal application as you will continually discover. The creation of these Tattwa afterimages accelerates contact with unconscious archetypes.

TANTRIC EROTIC ROSE MEDITATION

The following meditation is a unique Tantric program to stimulate all the chakras from below to above, while also raising the psycho-sexual energy. It differs from most other programs by recognizing the specific differences between masculine and feminine energies.

Male visualization: Perform Tratak on the above rose drawing, close your eyes, and see it float before you as a *red* rose. Use it in the exercise as described.

Female visualization: Perform Tratak on the above rose drawing, close your eyes, and see it float before you as a *white* rose. Use it in the exercise as described.

It may be performed by couples or individuals and may be likened to a psychic acupuncture with an imagined rose bud. When done with attention, this can be very sensual and will also relieve tension in any stressed body area.

Male: Visualize a **red** rose bud on a stem. Female: Visualize a **white** rose bud on a stem.

Now *imagine* using the rose to psychically penetrate each of the secret, intimate parts of your body and then rotating the rose half a dozen times clockwise and half a dozen times counterclockwise.

Erotic Rose Stimulation Order and Location for Men

1. *Muladhara*—anus, urethra from head of penis inward.

2. *Svadhisthana*—halfway between pubic bone and navel.

3. *Manipura*—navel.

4. *Anahata*—breastbone, in line with the nipples.

5. *Vishuddha*—below Adam's apple

6. *Ajna*—between eyebrows.

7. *Sahasrara*—top of skull.

Erotic Rose Stimulation Order and Location for Women

1—*Muladhara*—anus, vulva, vagina (deep), clitoris.

2—*Svadhisthana*—halfway between pubic bone and navel.

3—*Manipura*—navel.

4—*Anahata*—breastbone, in line with the nipples.

5—*Vishuddha*—below Adam's apple.

6—*Ajna*—between eyebrows.

7—*Sahasrara*—top of skull.

Note: Women and men may also wish to psychically penetrate each breast through the nipple.

Feel the velvet bud sensually and slowly penetrate, while simultaneously imagining it merging deep into recesses and melting through skin and bone. Savor the rotations and sense the slow psychic withdrawal, allowing erotic shivers to go through you as you get ready for the next penetration point.

The Re-emergence of Indian Tantra

It is unfortunate that the British colonialism in India resulted in many teachers, Eastern and Western, repressing the use of sexual energies in spiritual practices. It is not only unfortunate, but a denial of our wholeness of being. Thankfully, both the re-emergence of Indian Tantra and the emergence of sane sexuality in modern culture have replaced such repression with liberation.

Much of modern occultism and Western Magick is based on Tantric principles that—contrary to popular belief—are far more than liberal sexual practices. While history is never complete, there are many sources that consider Tantra the foundation of Yoga and all Eastern spirituality, and with migration, of Tibetan and Chinese practices.

Whether historically accurate or not, it is important to include our fundamental energies among our esoteric resources.

Now, we are ready for the use of chakra power as specific triggers to corresponding astral levels of consciousness.

FIRST LEVEL: SOLAR PLEXUS CHARGING

Muladhara, Svadhisthana, and *Manipura* chakras are interconnected in an intricate web of fibers (Nadis) such that they function both synchronistically and synergistically, and culminate in the Solar Plexus—bringing together the psychic powers of all three in association with their elemental rulerships of Earth, Water, and Fire.

The Technique for Solar Plexus Charging

1. Lie supine, with your head north and feet south, in a semi-dark room, with your legs folded at knees and crossed as in a typical yoga posture and your hands clasped over the solar plexus.*

2. On a slow, even inhalation, visualize warm, golden pranic energy flowing in through your head and down the body into your thighs and lower abdominal region, where it is prevented from escaping by your crossed feet and is therefore stored.

3. On a slow, even exhalation, bring the accumulated prana up and around the solar plexus in a series of clockwise circles centered over the navel with twelve o'clock at the chest and six o'clock at the groin.

4. Make as many circles as possible while exhaling, concentrating upon feeling an internal heat developing with each visualization of energy sweeping around the solar plexus.

Continue the exercise for a minimum of thirty minutes. Upon completion you will experience considerable inner psychic heat.

> *Yoga physiology maintains that the hands and feet are terminals through which the body throws off psychic energy in the form of prana. The crossing of the feet and interlocking of the hands short-circuit the escape of prana and results in an additional source of energy for solar plexus charging.

SOLAR PLEXUS CHARGING ROTATION DIAGRAM

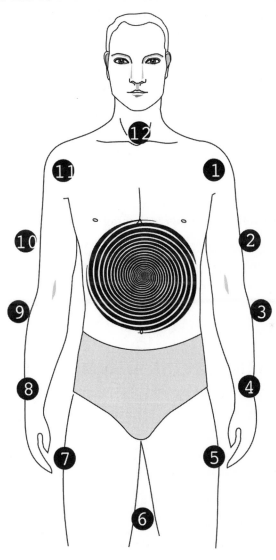

A supplemental exercise specifically intended to disrupt the "worry cycle" common to so many *urbanites* is to break each of the two phases into an inspiration-expiration cycle by themselves:

Breathing Pattern to Disrupt the Worry Cycle

(a). On inspiration, draw golden solar energy through the top of your skull to your solar plexus. The solar plexus is located under the diaphragm, above the navel, and just below the tip of the breast bone.

(b). On expiration, push golden energy down through the remainder of your trunk, through your legs, and out the soles of your feet.

(c). On the following inspiration, draw blue (or silver) moon energy up through the soles of your feet to the solar plexus region.

(d). On the subsequent exhalation, draw the blue-silver energy up through your chest, neck, and out through the top of your skull.

Continue the above sequence as long as desired.

The Solar Plexus, combining the natures of *Muladhara, Svadhisthna,* and *Manipura* chakras, is sometimes called the "abdominal brain."

The combination of the associated psychic powers of these three chakras in Solar Plexus Charging is a powerful stimulus to all creative work related to the elements of Earth, Water, and Fire. This includes most business and craft work, art and design, technological development, etc. Note, however, that the element of Air is not included and belongs with *Anahata,* the Heart Chakra.

LEVEL TWO: THE AJNA MEDITATION
"The Royal Road to the Unconscious"

As the culmination of meditations upon the prior chakras in sequence we next focus upon *Ajna* chakra.

Opening *Ajna* is called the "Royal road to the Unconscious." The element associated with *Ajna* is Manas, or "mind-stuff," the very energy of consciousness.

Ajna, the Brow chakra, is known as the Third Eye for two basic reasons:"

1—It is "the" clairvoyant trigger.

2—One of the best methods for opening it is by visualizing it as vertical 'third eye' located between your physical eyes and slightly above the eye-line.

As the Third Eye, it is the most universal clairvoyant psycho-sensory organ. Mentally focus on your desired vision (the solution to a question, the goal of your quest, the object of your desire) while retaining awareness of related symbols and pertinent correspondences.

It sounds more complex than it is, but it does involve more homework than simply wishing to see the equivalent of a free video.

Yes, as you will discover in this book there are many instances of spontaneous clairvoyance—but they rarely provide the answers to the questions you want to ask. Intentional Perception is the culmination of a study of the background facts about the target of your intended perception at which point you follow the procedure you have learned to open the Third Eye or otherwise activate this level of clairvoyance.

All your developmental work is cumulative. The visualization work with each of the lower chakras, the Solar Plexus Charging, the additional visualization work with Anahata and Vishuddha, and the work you will do here with Ajna are part of a process that only you can manage.

This meditation is divided into two stages:

1. Internal Chakra Dharana utilizing Tratak

2. Alternating Chakra Breathing

The more traditional yantra shows the triangle, apex down (as also found in the Chakra mandalas of *Muladhara* and *Manipura*), and the unconscious symbol of OM embossed upon a gold disc.

Traditional Ajna Yantra

Note in the above sketch outline of the traditional *Ajna* symbol that the two petals (to become the wings in our alternative symbol) have the Sanskrit letters upon them of *Ha* and *K'sha*, representing the Sun and Moon, mind and body, Ida and Pingala, all coming together at *Ajna* (at the root of the nose).

The Ajna Chakra "Third Eye" Technique

The alternative yantra symbol we use in this exercise to symbolize Ajna is a black winged globe, a visualized image by which we can "fly" anywhere, beyond limitations of space and time. When we perform tratak on the black winged globe, the complementary image of a white winged globe will float in space before our closed eyes. It is this that we merge with. The Bija mantra is *OM*.

NEW AJNA TATTVA CHAKRA YANTRA FOR INTERNAL DHARANA

Internal Chakra Dharana

1. Place yourself comfortably in either a sitting meditation pose or on a chair; in either case, have the control of a bright desk lamp within reach.

2. Place the *Ajna* Internal Chakra Tattwa Yantra at eye level or upon your lap.

3. Stare without blinking (Tratak) at the white Bindu or spot in the center of the black winged globe. After one or two minutes a white rim aura will appear around the black margins and the black itself probably will turn whitish or pale.

4. As you are performing Tratak, silently recite the Bija mantra *OM*, aligning it with the natural inspiration (Oh) through the forehead, and the natural expiration (Mmmmm)—the "Oh" flows into the *Ajna* with the inspiration, and "Mmmm" flows out through the *Ajna* point with the expiration. (See the illustration on the facing page.)

5. When the rim aura is well manifested, switch the light off and close your eyes. Continue the silent repetition of the Bija *OM*, as in Step 3, while gently looking through your forehead and closed eyes. With relaxation a white winged globe will gradually emerge, floating in the dark space in front of you. Watch the winged globe, constantly adjusting the focus of your attention, in order to perceive the afterimage as long as possible.

6. When the afterimage has totally faded, recreate it with your imagination and hold it between your two physical eyes while continuing with the Bija mantra meditation. This can be continued for up to twenty minutes.

After one or two weeks, you should be able to dispense with tratak on external *Ajna* Tattwa and visualize the white winged globe behind the forehead while focusing on the Bija mantra *OM* synchronized with the breath.

The creation of these Tattwa afterimages employed in this chapter accelerates contact with unconscious archetypes, opening channels between subconscious and conscious minds and tapping the resources of the Universal Consciousness.

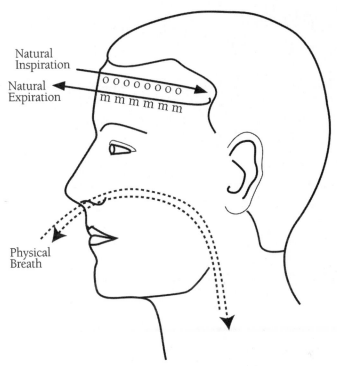

Natural Inspiration

Natural Expiration

o o o o o o o o
m m m m m m

Physical Breath

Ajna Bija Mantra & Breath Guide

Advantages of Internal Ajna Chakra Dharana

The External Tratak procedure establishes a conditioning procedure, which amounts to a ready-to-use "de-stressing" technique. Almost anywhere, anytime, the eyes may be closed, and an altered state of consciousness rapidly induced through focusing attention on the white winged globe yantra while sounding the Bija mantra *OM* with the uninhibited, spontaneous breath rhythm: in, "o;" out, "m."

This Altered State of Consciousness (ASC) is marked by physical signs accompanying each level:

Physical Signs of ASC levels in Ajna Dharana

1. Relaxed wakefulness: Subjective contentment with warming of hands and feet, slowing of respiration, and lowering of blood pressure.

2. Dreaming: REM (rapid eye movement) and sudden flaccidity of the neck muscles, producing head nodding, with subjective images, dream scenarios, and psyche-delic color patterns.

3. Deep dreamless sleep: Often accompanied by snoring. ***It is possible to retain consciousness in this state—Yoga refers to it as "Turiya."***

Some believe *Ajna* to be a literal "Third Eye" which will produce clairvoyance when opened. Meditating upon this point may produce psychic effects in two stages:

1. To spontaneously see the Third Eye, possibly appearing as an eye, blue pearl, or an intense point of light.

2. To actually see *through* the Third Eye.

This psychic sense, also called *intuition* or the *sixth sense,* is in reality our "inner tutor," resulting from a uniting of the right and left hemispheres of the brain. The right hemisphere (feminine, receptive) processes information and flashes the conclusion across to the left hemisphere (masculine, logical) producing an altered state of consciousness, sometimes experienced as a sudden "Eureka!" realization.

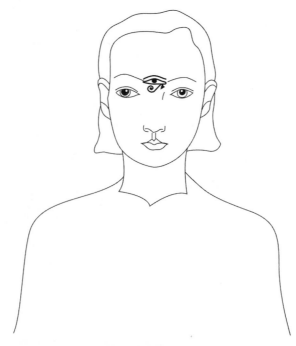

THE THIRD EYE

An interesting experiment that sometimes results in a genuine psychic develop-ment is to do Tratak on another person's eyes from a distance of about twelve inches. A Third Eye will appear between the other two so long as your partner doesn't look away. As psychic sensitivity increases, the partner should begin to feel the presence of the Third Eye and should try to "see" through it.

AJNA CHAKRA PSYCHIC BREATHING TECHNIQUE
Guide to Psychic Breathing for Ajna Development

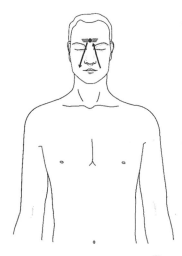

Breathe in the right nostral to Ajna, from Anja out the left nostril.

Breathe in the left nostral to Ajna, from Anja out the right nostril.

Breathing out of only one nostril stimulates activity in the brain hemisphere on the opposite side.

The left hemisphere represents Pingala, Shiva, the Sun, rational, and verbal processes; while the right hemisphere is the polar opposite, relating to Ida, Shakti, the Moon, intuitive, and non-verbal processes.

For this exercise, we visualize the white winged globe, while also visualizing the flow of breath and counting silently backwards from 10 to 1.

We occupy the left hemisphere by silently counting backward, in synchronicity with our breathing cycle, from 10 to 1. (Since we tend to count forward automatically, by counting backward the "gears" of the left brain hemisphere become more "engaged." The right brain is occupied by visualizing a stream of white light going into Ajna in synchronicity with the breath. Both hemispheres are occupied by the vision of the white winged globe over the Ajna region.

Simultaneous concentration upon an image, sound, and sensation achieves integration of both cerebral hemispheres, thus occupying the brain holistically.

The brain is the unique vehicle through which consciousness manifests on the physical plane. This exercise is effective for synchronizing the hemispheres, smoothing out the brain wave patterns, and allowing the parasympathetic branch of the autonomic nervous system to quickly gain ascendancy. As we singularly alter our brain state we experience "supra-consciousness."

Vertical Breathing for Ajna Development Procedure

With our vision of the winged globe in place, become aware of the natural breath flowing in and out of your nostrils. As the inhalation takes place, visualize energy (white, blue, or gold) flowing up your right nostril to the Third Eye where you feel the sensation of the visualized globe. As you exhale, imagine the colored energy flowing from the *Ajna* point down and out your left nostril. Then reverse so the incoming breath flows up the left nostril to the image, and on the subsequent exhalation, from *Ajna* out the right nostril. Silently count "Ten." You have now completed one round. Repeat the procedure, and on completion of the round mentally say "Nine," and so on until you reach "One," at which point you start again with "Ten."

1. Prepare yourself in a sitting meditation posture, on a chair or the floor.

2. Visual and feel the image on the Ajna spot.

3. While feeling the pressure of the image just behind the Ajna spot, become also aware of your breath flowing through the nostrils.

4. Begin to exclusively focus on breath movement in the right nostril, then exclusively out the left nostril, tracking the movement of air with a psychic imagined color leading up to Ajna on inspiration and down from Ajna on exhalation. Count down one round each time you return to Ajna. Count from ten to one and repeat.

Simultaneously, you imagine the colored breath reaching and receding from Ajna, you sense the presence of the winged globe at Ajna, and you count the rounds down and repeat for the duration of the technique.

10. In the right nostril to Ajna, from Ajna out the left nostril. In the left nostril to Ajna, from Ajna out the right nostril. Say "Ten."

9. In the right nostril to Ajna, from Ajna out the left nostril. In the left nostril to Ajna, from Ajna out the right nostril. Say "Nine."

8. In the right nostril to Ajna, from Ajna out the left nostril. In the left nostril to Ajna, from Ajna out the right nostril. Say "Eight."

7. In the right nostril to Ajna, from Ajna out the left nostril. In the left nostril to Ajna, from Ajna out the right nostril. Say "Seven."

6. In the right nostril to Ajna, from Ajna out the left nostril. In the left nostril to Ajna, from Ajna out the right nostril. Say "Six."

5. In the right nostril to Ajna, from Ajna out the left nostril. In the left nostril to Ajna, from Ajna out the right nostril. Say "Five."

4. In the right nostril to Ajna, from Ajna out the left nostril. In the left nostril to Ajna, from Ajna out the right nostril. Say "Four."

3. In the right nostril to Ajna, from Ajna out the left nostril. In the left nostril to Ajna, from Ajna out the right nostril. Say "Three."

2. In the right nostril to Ajna, from Ajna out the left nostril. In the left nostril to Ajna, from Ajna out the right nostril. Say "Two."

1. In the right nostril to Ajna, from Ajna out the left nostril. In the left nostril to Ajna, from Ajna out the right nostril. Say "One."

Repeat.

This countdown is done for the duration of the meditation (twenty to thirty minutes). If you lose count, that's just a sign of dropping into dreaming or dreamless sleep. When you do lose count and become aware of coming out of the state you are in, simply pick anywhere you thought you left off, or start at the beginning. The counting is a device intended to "cut out" the left brain.

THIRD LEVEL: SAHASRARA MEDITATION

The Yoga tradition says that when kundalini rises and unites with Sahasrara there is an actual shock to the nervous system that awakens the pineal gland from its dormant state and we finds ourselves possessed of *siddhis*, or psychic powers. These psychic powers are those natural to everyone but that are mostly dormant psycho-*sensory* faculties within us that have been lost through disuse and even denial.

For just one example, Dr. Jonn Mumford says that Australian aboriginals are still capable of tracking, by smell, just as a dog does. They can sense also water in desert areas and otherwise demonstrate their acute sensitivity to the environment that is lacking in "modern people. The aboriginal's psychic powers, like their counterparts in animal instincts, have remained active through need.

The very sparse population of the aboriginals spread over a huge desert area in central Australia with few opportunities for the conflict over food territories otherwise common to early humanity. As a result, the split into conscious and subconscious was not a necessary survival step. Similar areas were in Siberia, at the very southern tip of South America, and among the nomads of the Arabian Desert. However, these original peoples came into conflict with the expanding empires of czarist Russia and the Ottoman Empire, then of commercially motivated Western powers centuries earlier than the British occupation of Australia.

As the colonial powers, particularly the British, expanded into India, Africa, and the Middle East, their military and commercial interests were accompanied both by the Christian missionaries seeking to "save" native populations and academics seeking to understand their cultural and religious practices. Much of our esoteric knowledge resulted from British scholarship encountering native traditions of Tantra, Yoga, and Mystical and Shamanic practices.

Always, it is the transformation of subconscious psychic powers into conscious psychic skills that is the goal of what we refer to as Psychic Empowerment, and then of Self Empowerment.

The Alchemical Rose

The Rose is a symbol of both the Heart and the Crown chakras. In a sense, at least, it is the elevation of the Rose from *Anahata* to *Sahasrara* that represents the final "transfiguration" or completion of the integration of consciousness into wholeness. In our program, however, we have already worked through the six lower chakras and now we are at the crowning culmination of our journey. It must be noted, however, that the process is inclusive of the lower chakras. *The higher always includes (controls) the lower.*

The Rose of Sahasrara

Sahasrara's traditional symbol is a violet lotus with "one thousand multi-colored spokes," but there are actually 12 in the center and then 960 around the center for a total of 972). In our program it is alternatively represented by an image of a red rose. There is no seed mantra. The element is "Thought."

The stated goal is that the female Kundalini *Shakti* energy will rise from Muladhara to the crown to unite with the male *Shiva* energy to produce *Samadhi*, connecting you to the Divine, Universal Consciousness. The psychic powers of astral projection and prophecy are less a goal than a byproduct of the "Cosmic Consciousness" that accompanies the full unfolding of this Rose of *Sahasrara*.

We are completing our journey, and the last mile, like the last step, is always the easiest and most simple—like driving the car into your own driveway and parking in your own garage. You are home!

Look at the drawing of a rose and perform tratak by staring at the bindu point at its center. Close your eyes and visualize this rose in red.

Using your mastery of visualization move the image of just above your head, and then slowly bring it downward to occupy your skull. Feel it within your brain, feel its velvety surface, feel its redness, and feel it as a symbol of universal consciousness.

Sahasrara Rose for Tratak

Know that you are united with the source of all there is, and realize that your connection gives you the means to clairvoyantly see the answers to your carefully defined questions.

This "final" exercise is by no means limited to high-level clairvoyance, nor to the specified psychic powers of Astral Projection and Prophecy. You can, and should personalize it as a regular meditation practice, *bringing you back home.*

One way to develop further is suggested in the following diagram showing a glowing ball of light, or a glowing rose, cupped in your skull. Think about, and visualize, if it appeals to you, the respective forces of *Ida* and *Pingala* flowing downward to unite in *Muladhara,* and then flowing upward through *Sushumna* to flow upward into *Sahasrara* .

Think of *Ida* on the left as the feminine and receptive Moon force and as the Pillar of Mercy on the Tree of Life. Think of *Pingala* as the masculine and projective Sun force, and as the Pillar of Severity on the Tree of Life. Think of *Sushumna* as union of the white Moon and the golden Sun in the Middle Pillar on the Tree of Life. You can visualize it as a magical rod vibrating with energies, beginning as a white glow at the base of your spine and becoming a bright golden glow at your crown.

Flow of Ida & Pingala

Ida and Pingala flow downward to join the base, then flow upward through Sushumna to form a glowing ball of light cupped in the skull.

There can be no final conclusion to this chapter simply because it has been a journey on an open road that goes on forever. Each chapter in this book is exactly that: another chapter in a great book of life, another perspective that adds to our Great Work, another station on the Express Train of Transformation and Empowerment.

No one way is perfect and no one has the best or final answer. The next chapters add further perspective and real life cases which—next to our own individual experiences—are the best learning tools.

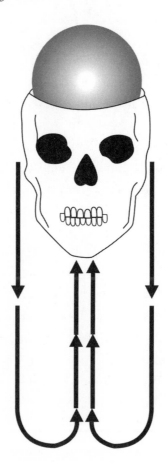

Sources & Suggested Additional Reading:

Bruyere, R. L. _Wheels of Light—A Study of the Chakras,_ 1989, Bon Productions.

Dale, C. _The Complete Book of Chakra Healing: Activate the Transformative Power of Your Energy Centers,_ 1996 & 2009, Llewellyn.

Dale, C. *Kundalini: Divine Energy, Divine Life,* 2011, Llewellyn.

Dale, C. *The Subtle Body—An Encyclopedia of Your Energetic Anatomy,* 2009, Sounds True.

Judith, A. *Wheels of Life: A User's Guide to the Chakra System,* 1987, Llewellyn.

Mumford, Jonn. *A Chakra & Kundalini Workbook: Psycho-Spiritual Techniques for Health, Rejuvenation, Psychic Powers & Spiritual Realization,* 1997, Llewellyn.

Slate, J. H., & Weschcke, C. W. *The Llewellyn Complete Book of Psychic Empowerment: A Complete Compendium of Tools & Techniques for Growth & Transformation,* 2011, Llewellyn. Chapter Four on the Chakra System.

ADDENDUM #5 TO CHAPTER FIVE
Microcosm to Macrocosm & Macrocosm to Microcosm

The Tattva Connection—
Meditation & Visualization Program #3: Fire/Fire

Tejas: Fire—Seed of Fire

Fire! It's the element that enables change and transformation, it enables us to live in cold places and to move where we want, it enables us to travel "to the stars" and beneath the seas, it makes our food safer to eat, it transforms ore into metal and fuel into heat and movement, it scorches solids, boils and evaporates liquids, blasts gases, and transmutes one thing into another, it is the foundation for technology and magic, it symbolizes passion, ambition, creativity, upward movement and masculine action. Its energy is thermal and incandescent (light). It is masculine, active, liberating, and projective.

The Element of Fire is recognized by many as the foundation of human culture, and—indeed—of civilization itself. Many proclaim that the "taming of fire" was the beginning of technology and the first foundation stone for science. The first historic experiences of fire were probably of those ignited by lightening, and then of some accidental coincidence of sparks from striking two pieces of flint together.

It took *thought* for the next development of igniting fire by the friction of rapidly moving wood against wood in a small accumulation of tinder. New evidence (*Atlantis Rising,* July-August 2012) reported by the University of Toronto and Israel's Hebrew University shows the presence of wood ash associated with stone tools and animal bones geologically dated to one million years ago. Tools, controlled fire, hunting are all associated with early civilization.

Fire was claimed as a "gift of the gods" (as indeed it must have appeared in relation to lightening from heaven above), but the real gift came when Man himself first ignited fire intentionally through his own "applied science" logically resulting from his observation of sparks and heat from friction. Thus, *the human mind is the gods' gift to Man.*

Nevertheless, that gift of the gods to *create* Fire was no doubt held as a "secret technology" giving its holder personal power within the group and probably established him as a priest and magician.

From that point forward, human progress would be marked by slow accumulation of knowledge and mastery of ways to use that knowledge. Such mastery established a hereditary hierarchy of leaders and followers eventually evolving into a caste system of warriors and priests, and with growing wealth and power there would be political chiefs and masters of the treasury.

Only in modern times, as the monopolies over secret knowledge were challenged by new scientists and the spread of knowledge through books and education, do we have a universal opportunity for self-development and personal empowerment that was previously limited to the few at the top of the hierarchical ladder.

The most important knowledge is that regarding the inner understanding of the hidden, *inner,* nature of Man and Cosmos, of Microcosm and Macrocosm, with which comes the ability to "bring Fire down from Heaven"—*As Above, So Below*—to accomplish the Miracle of the One Thing through Mind. With Mind we apply knowledge so that we grow and increasingly **become more than we are.**

Common sense tells us the importance of physical energies to *outer* life—without it modern civilization would descend into chaos and ignite wars for increasingly limited natural resources for an ever more burdensome population. Yet, even more important are our *inner* energies that heal the body and fuel our growing psychic and mental capacity to uncover and develop those infinitely greater resources of Mind & Spirit to liberate us from the tyranny imposed by the narrow vision of the material reality that is only a single pulse in the spectrum of cosmic reality.

Now we turn to our third Tattva Overview in our continuing exploration of the "True Nature of Reality" coming through our understanding of the tattvas, the primal elements behind all manifestation. And again I want to make the point not to think in terms of "layers" in which Elemental Earth would be perceived as lesser and separate from the four other elements. Earth is the foundation upon which the entire pyramid of life and consciousness rests.

In Tantra, Earth is the Goddess and many Goddesses, and through our Love and Worship of Goddess and Goddesses we enter into the forms and energies that they embody and symbolize. But such love is not carnal and such worship is not groveling before an empty statute but another name for a unique meditation of entering into "oneness" with the nature of her form. As the one Goddess, she is Shakti, companion of Shiva the Sky God. Feminine and Masculine, Yin and Yang, Negative and Positive, Magnetic and Electric—all that exists comes from their union—a union of equals in which opposites are always in constant blending.

Fire is energy, both controllable and uncontrolled—like emotion. Every Tattva is represented in emotions and in energies, but Fire and Water symbolize our experience of emotion and the benefits of our mastery over our emotions.

TATTVA OVERVIEW TABLE #3: (Emotional)

Tattva Name	Element Name	Emotional Character	Emotional Drive	Emotional Nature	Emotional Reaction	Emotional Strength	Emotional Weakness	Sexual Identity	Sensory Block
Prithivi	Earth	Solidarity	Security	Passive	Depression	Care, Instinct	Greed, Pride	Feminine (active) Receptive	Uncontrolled Emotion
Apas	Water	Flexibility	Sensual Pleasure	Intimacy, Romantic	Hatred, Illusion	Will	Attachment, Indecisive	Feminine (passive) Receptive	Intellectual Discrimination
Tejas	Fire	Passion, Extravert	Success, Power	Desire Enthusiasm	Lust, Anger	Ambition, Creativity	Over-extension	Masculine (active) Projective	Too many ideas
Vayu	Air	Compassion	To Move, Act, Love	Self-control, Balance	Envious Boastful	Unselfish Worker	Empty-headed	Feminine (active) Projective	Habits from Past Lives
Akasha	Ether	Commun-ication	Creativity Solitude	Future "memories"	Fascination	Trans-formation	Feeling lost	Uniting matter with Spirit	Visible form

These Overview Tables function to provide a general background to our overall developmental program—yet the details are very specific and can provide the foundations for many psychic, magical and other operations.

THINK ELEMENTAL FIRE

Tejas is associated with the element of Fire in Western Tradition. It is represented by a red equilateral triangle. The Fire of Tejas is also the interior fire of Kundalini which can be sequentially unfolded (awakened) through various yogic exercises or other meditation programs. But it may also be awakened naturally and spontaneously in the normal course personal growth and psychic empowerment.

The Fire Tattva is the fundamental life energy in the physical body and the base of our personal power, psychologically as well as physically. It is this tattva that processes food into prana manifesting

But Fire is also emotional fire: passion in love, passion for work, passion in self-expression, passionate desires, passion in living, and passions for life itself. Fire is also a special kind of energy that wants power and demands success. It can manifest in psychic healing and in the psychic power to control the body's reaction to heat and of Fire Walking. And Fire is also mental fire of reasoning and creativity.

Fire is the element of strength that gives courage and the power to protect the home and the weak, it drives ambition and motivates a life of high purpose. Fire is the drive to discover truth, the power of ideas, and the fire of devotion to ideals. Fire cleanses away the deadwood and transforms that which was into what will be. It is the spirit of revolution as it gives birth and rebirth to the best that we can be.

Fire is the element of lust and passion, the power in sex magick, the power to transform the mundane into the sublime that drives self-transformation and the self-perfection of body and soul. Fire doesn't accept the ordinary but in its place manifests the extraordinary. Fire is the celebration of life and the inspiration to become more than we are that turns us into gods intended from the Beginning.

Look at the following Elemental Table and let those various factors find answers as you are progressing through the Meditation Exercise that follows.

> Note: The following Elemental Overview Table #3 for Fire is exactly what the title says—an "overview" intended to give you a fundamental awareness of the Elemental Qualities and Characteristics. You may notice some seeming conflicts but these represent particular sources and intended usage from Meditational and Magickal perspectives. An excellent source book for all this is David Hulse's "The Eastern Mysteries" which can be supplemented by the same author's "The Western Mysteries."

ELEMENT OVERVIEW TABLE #3: Fire
ELEMENT OF FIRE—SEED OF FIRE: *Resolve*

Tattva Name: *Tejas*	Tattva Form: upward triangle	Tattvic Color: Red
Tattva/Primary Sheath: *manomaya*, mental body*	Tattvic Animal: Ram	Tattvic Taste: Pungent
Yantra Color: Green	Yantra Form: Pyramid, Tetrahedron	Cosmic Plane: *svaha*, higher astral plane
Chakra Name: *Manipura* (gem city)	Chakra Common Name: Navel Chakra	Chakra Bija Mantra: *RAM*
Chakra Body Location: Solar plexus, over the navel	Chakra Body Space: Navel to Heart	Chakra Body Zone: Solar Plexus
Chakra Color: Yellow	Chakra Petals: 10	Chakra verbal expression: I can
Chakra Goal: developing will power, evolving higher life	Chakra God (Shiva) *Energy*: *Agni, Rudra, Vishnu*	Chakra Goddess *(Shakti)* Energy: *Tara, Lakini, Svaha*
Chakra Meditation: gives the power to create and destroy, and grants the blessings of Saraswati.		
Chakra—function of astral & etheric centers: feelings, sensitivity; feelings of astral influence		
Chakra Power: finding hidden treasures, no fear of fire, freedom from disease		
Chakra Problem: diabetes, indigestion, ulcers, hypoglycemia		
Chakra Symbol: 10 dark blue petals inscribed with mantras dam, dham, nam, tam,tham, dam, dham, nam, pan, and pham around red downward triangle with a ram as vehicle to carry Vishnu and his shakti, Lakini. Chant *RAM*		
Chakra Vital Air: *Udana Vayu*	Chakra Yogini: *Lakini*	Chakra/Physical Gland: Pancreas
Chakra Siddhi Powers: (when developed) healing of diseases, domination of other people, devotion		
Chakra Program: union of prana & Apana in upward movement		
Indian God: Agni is seated on a ram with vermillion-red Rudra on his lap, smeared with white funeral ashes, and dispelling fear and granting boons.		
Indian Goddesses: Dark-complexioned Lakini (Authority) is dressed in yellow and has been drinking ambrosia. She holds the thunderbolt weapon.		
Element Name: Fire	Elemental State: Plasma	Elemental Action: transforms, projects
Elemental Function: cyclical	Elemental Motion: Upward	Elemental Nature: Hot, Climbing
Elemental Power: self-expression, fantasy	Elemental Quality: Hot, Dry, Expansive	Elemental Strength: feeling, relationships
Energy Type: Thermal	Manifests through: Incandescence	Quantum Force: weak nuclear force
Emotional Characteristic: extrovert, passion	Emotional Desires: to achieve, fame, power, wealth	Emotional Drive: Authority, power, success

Emotional Family Role: Father	Emotional Nature: enthusiasm, warmth, desire	Emotional/Psychological Level: Conscious Mind
Emotional Reaction: Anger, Lust	Emotional/Sensory Block: Ideas	
Emotional/Sexual Identity: Masculine, Active, Projective	Emotional Strength: ambition, creativity	Emotional Weakness: over-extension, self-blame
Mind Action: *Buddhi* (Reason, Discrimination)	Mind Function: Discipline, Will, Endurance	Mind State: Dreamless
Physical/Action Organ: Anus	Physical/Action Form: Elimination	Physical/Action Effect: Arousing
Physical/Astral Sense: Sight	Physical/Astral Sense Organ: Eyes	Physical Body Functions: appetite, digestion
Physical Energy Correlation between physical/etheric & astral bodies—Fingers of Hand: Middle Finger		
Psychic Powers: heat control, fire-walking	Psychic/Astral Work: *tratak* meditational exercises, vegetarian diet, yogic *Vajroli* abdominal contractions	
Alchemical Metal: Tin	Alchemical Planet: Sun	Alchemical Quality: ?
Alchemical Symbolic Season: Spring	Alchemical Symbolic Time of Day: Sunset	Astrological Lunar Phase: Half Moon
Astrological Types: Aries, Leo, Sagittarius	Astrological Planetary Expression: ?	Astrological Ruling Planet: Mars
Astrological Qualities: Leadership, tireless energy, unification, flamboyance, determination		
Egyptian Divinities: Horus	Greek God Form: Apollo, Helios	Greek goddesses: Athena
Hebrew God Name: Adonai	Runes: Ingwaz, Kenaz, Naudhiz, Sowilo, Thurisaz	
Magical Angel: Aral	Magical Animals: fox, horse, lion, lizard, snake	Magical Archangel: Michael
Magical/Mythical Beings: Phoenix, dragon, hawk	Magical Colors: crimson, orange, red, scarlet	Magical Day: Tuesday
Magical Direction: South	Magical Elemental King: Djin	Magical Elemental Spirits: Salamanders
Magical Energy: passion, will	Magical Enochian Watchtower: Southern	Magical God Name: YHhvh Tzabaoth
Magical Herbs: cinnamon, dragon's blood, garlic	Magical Incenses: olibanum; cinnamon, marigold	Magical Kerub: Lion
Magical Metals: brass, gold, iron, steel	Magical Musical Note: E; Musical Scale: Mi	Magical Places: deserts, dry plains, volcanoes
Magical Planet: Sun, Mars	Magical Plants: Red Poppy, nettle	Magical Power: Evocation, Sex Magick
Magical Power: Evocation, Sex Magick	Magical Ruler: Seraph	
Magical Rulerships: action, anger, athletics, banishing, competitions, conflicts, contests, courts, desire, dowsing, energy, gambling, good health, law, military, passion, police, private detectives, protection, purification, sheriffs, success, sex, Strength, terrorism, treasure hunting, war, will, work		

Magical Season: Summer	Magical States: Rational Resolution of problems	
Magical Stones: amber, apache tear, agates, calcite, diamond, fire opal, flint, garnet, malachite, obsidian, ruby, tiger's eye, sunstone, topaz, yellow citrine, zircon		
Magical Symbols:	Magical Time of Day: Noon	Magical Time of Life: Youth
Magickal Tool: Wand, Lamp	Magical Work: love spells	
Tarot Court: Knight, Lord	Tarot Suit: Wands	Tarot Trumps: Judgment, Tower
Tree of Life Path: 31st–8 to 10	Tree of Life Sphere: Netzach & Hod	Tree of Life Soul Level: Chiah-Higher Self
*The Astral Body is the Emotional Body, related to the Water Element, and called the Mind Sheath (not to be confused with the Mental Body)		
Note: The various magical correspondences are only minimal selections. More complete information can be found in the resources listed at the end of the book. For serious study, you should add to this list, & other lists you may be building. Correspondences build your inter-relationships between Inner & Outer, Subconscious & Conscious, Cosmic & Personal. All magical systems inter-relate and add to your personal memory/library.		

Fire—Seed of Fire

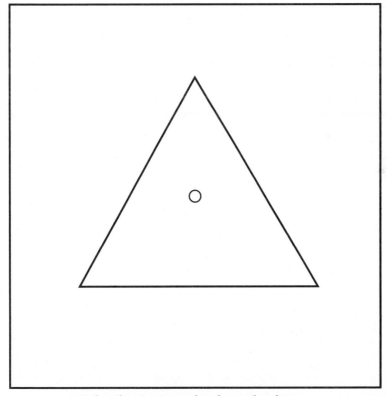

Color the tiny inner bindu circle white,
the inner triangle bright red,
and the outer square bright green

Fire—Seed of Fire: Tejas *RAM*

TATTVIC CONNECTION MEDITATION & VISUALIZATION PROGRAM #3: Fire/Fire
Tejas: Fire—Seed of Fire

Introduction. The Purpose & Function of this Procedure.

This procedure is intended to bring Tejas, the Fire Element, into an awakened state of psychic awareness. It is a procedure directed by your conscious mind, but the main operation occurs in both the subconscious mind and the body's autonomic system. It does not bring about dramatic changes, but it allows this element to be brought into balance with its cosmic equivalent.

Throughout life we create changes in the complex of physical and subtle bodies that combine in our vehicle of manifestation and experience in this life time. Some changes represent positive growth and others are negative and even destructive. These negativities, unrelieved, can live on and adversely affect not only your current lifetime but continue on into future lives. That is rare, but it has been given a name: Karma.

This exercise and those that follow are specifically intended for balancing and harmonizing the inner Tattvic Matrix of Body and "Soul" with the universal Cosmic Matrix. The result is a purification of the inner matrix so that clairvoyant visions will not be distorted by "accumulated psychic and garbage." And it can correct negative karma.

You can repeat this entire procedure often, but not more than once daily. And I suggest that you allow a week between each of exercise.

Summary of Purpose & User Benefits.

Just as Physical Relaxation is necessary for the free and unmitigated flow of Prana and other subtle energies, so is the controlled and directed purification of various physical and subtle body parts and energy channels. With this meditation we purify, balance, and harmonized the particular emotional & psychic elemental forces in our body and soul related to the Fire tattva. As this is completed, along with other elemental meditations, you will be better equipped to follow on with specific stimulus of particular psychic centers to accomplish your projected goals.

Step 1. Preliminaries.

Always start with Physical Relaxation.

Read through the procedure before beginning so that further reference is not needed. Most of it's identical with the other Tattvic Connection Meditation & Visualization Programs except for specific references to the Tattvic Element involved, which are in boldface for ease of recognition.

Time & Space: Allow approximately 30 minutes for the full procedure to be conducted in a comfortably warm, quiet, and safe setting free of interruptions. While a darkened room is not required, freedom from both sound and visual distractions is advisable.

Personal Preparations: Remove shoes and keep clothing or covering minimal to reduce the effects of external stimuli.

Posture & Position: It is to sit for this procedure, but a relaxed posture in a recliner is helpful.

Special Lighting: Arrange a small desk or reading light next to your chair that you can turn it on and off as required, and focus as directed.

Breathing: Establish a deep but natural, rhythmic flow of your breath, mostly balanced between inhalation and exhalation.

Vocalization : Vocalize, either silently or quietly spoken your affirmations, and the name of the tattva and then sound the mantra in Step 9.

With each step 5 through 13, it is helpful to vocalize the words describing any particular feelings or even visions you experience.

Vibration: In Step 9 you should chant or hum the Sanskrit name of the tattva, and then the tattvic mantra as instructed. Draw these words out and feel the vibration as a slight "warble" of the words at the back of your throat. As you do so, you can raise or lower the "musical note" until it feels right. You want to feel the words vibrate throughout your skull, and then in the location of the corresponding chakra. With experience you will be able to move the vibration to designated places inside your body, and then—in advanced work—intentionally into external objects. You can likewise adjust the volume of your voice, but don't shout.

The yantra, the name, and the mantra are your means to connect the inner tattva with the external tattva for purification and balance.

Step 2. Goal Statement.

Your goal is three-fold:

To become fully familiar with the feelings associated with the Fire Element. You've read about it, you've seen the characteristics and correspondences, but now we want you to feel the Fire in you, under you, around you, and through your entire inner being, and also to become aware of Elemental Fire as the fiery foundation of the outer material universe.

To identify inner Elemental Fire with outer Elemental Fire, and feel yourself purified and balanced through the harmonizing of inner with outer and the resultant purification of the inner Tattvic Element.

To address particular concerns: As an example, we have suggested two areas—your natural passion and creativity to fulfill your drive for Success, and to control any tendencies of over-extension and self-blame for things actually beyond your control. You must determine the goals yourself and then affirm them simply and concisely in as few words as possible. Write them down, fix them in your mind, but do not consider them as the primary function of the exercise which is the balancing and purification of personal elemental fire. (Note: particular concerns must relate to the Element being addressed—see the Overview Table.)

Step 3. Affirmations.

These affirmations may be spoken as goals at the beginning, and then as confirmations at the ending of the procedure. In addition to these, add the affirmation you wrote as one of your goals.

I feel Elemental **Fire** everywhere within me.

I feel Elemental **Fire** everywhere around me.

I feel purified and in harmony with all that is **Hot & Expansive** everywhere.

Step 4. Mental Imagery.

Imagery, like vocalization, can increase the effectiveness of the procedure.

Visualization: Perform Tratak and Visualize the tattva as described.

Spontaneous Imagery: Other images may appear at the end of the procedure—and that is alright unless you have negative feelings about them—in which case you should willfully "banish" them. (If you wish, visualize wood box with a lid that locks in place. Imagine those negative feelings going into the box, close and lock the lid so they can never escape. Now imagine throwing the locked box into a huge fiery volcano, and know that those negativities are gone forever.)

Recording: Other images that may appear spontaneously at the end of the procedure should be noted along with any particular feelings or ideas, and then recorded in your journal for later analysis.

Analysis: Always let a day or two pass before reading and analyzing your journal entries.

Step 5. Preparation.

Preparing the Yantra Card.

It is recommended that you photocopy the illustration on page 191, preferably on heavier paper or card stock, or draw it yourself in exactly the same size using a ruler and black pen. Using a drawing compass or a template, draw a tiny ⅛" inch diameter circle in the exact center. Leave the inside of the circle white. This inner circle provides a focal point for your Tratak exercise. Make the outer square 4" x 4" and the inner equilateral Triangle (apex up) should be about 2½" wide at the base and centered, and the little circle in the exact center should be ⅛" in diameter and have a heavy black border around it but not quite as thick as those around the Triangle and the outer square.

Coloring the Yantra Card.

It will be beneficial to you to color the image as follows: (a) Leave the tiny Bindu circle **White**; (b) color the **Upright Triangle Brigh**t Red, and the surrounding larger square **Bright Green**. Each square and the tiny inner circle are bordered with bold black lines.

Cutting the Yantra Card.

If you have reproduced the image on the heavy card stock as recommended, now measure off either one or two inches (your choice) on each side and cut away the surplus so you have a square 6" x 6" or 8" x 8" card with the colored image in the center.

Repeat this preparation for all 25 images to produce a set of 25 Tattva Cards that can be used again and again in the clairvoyance process and in many other functions to be discussed later.

Position & Lighting.

Holding the tattvic yantra card, sit or recline comfortably in your chair in a quiet room where you will not be disturbed for a minimum of 30 minutes. Prior to doing so, arrange lighting that you can comfortably turn on and off, and that can be focused on the card.

Note the preferred direction for placing the chair indicated in Step 9 (a & b).

Breathing & Relaxation.

Become fully relaxed, combining slowed rhythmic breathing, and progressive tension & release of muscles from your toes to your brow and scalp if you have not

already followed the Empowerment Tension & Release Procedure described in the Addendum to Chapter 1.

Step 6. Pranic Breathing Pattern.

With eyes closed, breathe rhythmically in equally spaced, without any stress, in-breaths, holding, out-breaths, holding, and repeating throughout the process.

Step 7. White Light Circulation.

With each in-breath visualize White Light flowing into the body; while holding the breath visualize the light quickly circulating throughout the body; while breathing out see the light quickly being excreted carrying out impurities; while momentarily holding the out breath know that you have energized and cleansed the inner energy body.

Step 8. Psychic Shield.

Returning to a normal breathing pattern, continue visualizing the energizing White Light flowing in and around your body; turn your imagination outward and visualize an absolutely clear field surrounding you in an egg shape reaching just beyond the distance measured by your outstretched arms. This field is as transparent as the clearest glass. Know that this shield protects you from external influences while containing the tattvic meditation program.

Step 9a. Yantra Card Focus.

If you have constructed the tattva yantra card as described, turn on the light and focus it on the card held or positioned comfortably about a foot to a foot and a half in front of you.

If possible, arrange your chair to face the tattvic direction: **South**. Otherwise—think and feel *South*.

Vibrate the name of tattva: *Tejas*. Repeat three times.

Chant or hum the tattva element mantra *RAM* (pronounced *RA-UUM*). Vibrate the mantra as instructed in Step 1, preliminaries. Repeat three times. Later, you can do more but always in groups of three. And feel the mantra vibrate in the location of *Manipura* chakra just Over the Navel.

Focus on the small white circle at the center of the image, and stare at it for as long as you can without blinking. When you can't continue the "burning" feeling any longer, turn off the light, close your eyes and focus your inner sight on the space in front of your brow chakra (between your eye brows and on the ridge just above your nose), and see the **Bright Red Upright Triangle** floating in the space before you and vibrating within the outer **Bright Green Square**. And, then, you will soon see the tattva image change into the complementary yantra colors of **Green** and **Red**.

Again vibrate the name to the tattva and chant or hum the mantra three times.

Absorb this image! As you repeat the exercise, often, you will reach a point when you will be able to recall this image at will.

Step 9b. Yantra Visualization.

Alternatively, if you haven't made a *Tejas* tattva card, immediately in front of you, visualize a large **Green Square**, inside of which is a **Red Triangle** approximately half the size of the **Green S**quare. See the **Red Triangle** gently vibrating within the **Green Square**. The colors will reverse to their complementary yantra colors.

Step 10. Experiencing Elemental Fire.

Feel yourself enter into and becoming totally absorbed in the **Bright Red Triangle**—becoming one with it—while retaining awareness of the surrounding **Bright Green Square.** Become **Elemental Fire** and feel your **fiery** nature harmonize with the **Cosmic Fire** Tattva, and feel all impurities in your **Fire** Tattva—all emotional garbage and unconscious psychic attachments—dissipate.

In particular: feel the **Fiery** nature of your physical body become free of adverse thoughts and feelings. Feel your body becoming ideally healthy, strong, and energized. See your Astral body in clear and bright colors. See your body as perfectly healthy, feel your whole being energized and clear of emotional pain and illness, and charged with Passion for Living, Loving, and Achieving.

Step 11. Knowing Elemental Fire.

Allow yourself to receive any information or messages from you're experiencing of Elemental Fire. In particular: receive information involving your Mental & Psychic health, strength, and security. Receive the information without any emotional reaction.

Step 12. Dissipation of Images.

Slowly dissipate the **Triangle** and the surrounding **Square,** return to the clear field around you, continuing the breathing pattern of Step 6 above.

Step 13. Letting Go of Evoked Feelings.

Let go of all the particular feelings evoked by the imagery, slowly change your breathing to its natural rhythm and feel the physical relaxation achieved in Step 1 above.

Step 14. Completion & Self-Realization.

Feel yourself fully relaxed and fully self-contained. Feel yourself to be healthy, energized, cleansed, and refreshed. Know yourself to be strong and& secure.

Step 15. Return to Normality.

Open your eyes, return to the physical world knowing all is well. Stand up and move about. Have some refreshment and engage in some normal activity.

Step 16. Review, Record & Analyze.

Record in a journal all messages and feelings received in Step 11 above. At this point, merely record—do not analyze. After a few days, read what you've recorded and then write down an analysis of what you believe the messages mean for you at this time. Realize that when you repeat the exercise at another time, the messages are likely to change to meet new circumstances in your life.

Conclusion: This exercise has demonstrated the particular usefulness of clairvoyance focused on the single areas of Passion and Creativity, Ambition and Success, and to control your tendencies of over-extension and self-blame in Steps 10 and 11. At the same time the relaxation program and light circulation procedure provide physical health and healing benefits.

However, the entire 16-step Meditation is a basic program that is modified by changes in the tattvic element and then particular modifications in Steps 10 and 11, can be further modified with the use of other symbols as you make further studies.

Source & Suggested Additional Reading:

Frawley, D. *Inner Tantric Yoga—Working with the Universal Shakti: Secrets of Mantras, Deities and Meditation*, 2008, Lotus Press.

CHAPTER SIX
Visualization for Clairvoyance

The Importance of Visualization for Clairvoyance,
And Just About Everything Else!

Visualization empowers Mind, Body & Spirit
Simply speaking, Visualization is the Trained Imagination

We start with the recognition that *to imagine is to create.* The imagination (image-plus-action) is our faculty that puts an image into action. Visualization is the recognition that to act upon an image is to turn it into reality.

An image may be a picture or representation of something remembered, seen currently, or dreamed of, but it may also be a picture created in the imagination as a representation of something not yet existent.

No matter its source, the image in the imagination was visualized—created wholly out of "mind stuff" which can become the seed or matrix or core of energy that becomes converted into matter to enter the world of reality through the visualization process. To enable that process to happen, the visualized image attracts energy and matter that becomes the thing visualized through any of a variety of processes.

More than "Seeing Things in Your Mind"

Visualization is more than "seeing things in your mind" even though it does work through *Visual Imagery.* Properly trained, Visualization brings together all the developed Psychic Senses (more about this later) to focus on a specific object, goal, program, and/or process, and then adds emotion (energy-in-motion) to attract the necessary substance to move towards manifestation and intellectual understanding.

Visualization is powerful, and it is for that reason that the visualized image must be specific in detail so that you actually get "what you wished for" and not something that may be surprising in unfortunate ways.

Starting with the Five Physical Senses

In order to forms images we start with knowledge of the physical world gained through the physical senses.

The Sensual Means of Physical Interaction

Think for a moment about what the physical senses do for us:

They are the means by which we perceive the world about us, including in and around the body;

The means by which we receive communications from the world around us, including mind and body;

The means by which we qualify and quantify food and other things for body and mind;

The means by which we are cognizant to pleasure and danger in the world around us; and

The means by which we interact with our loved ones.

And the imagination works with all of these and provides guidance to our primary interactions:

Speech and communication,

Movement and transportation,

Work and personal achievement,

Expressing emotions of joy, love, or anger,

Engaging in sexual love, sleeping and dreaming.

All of these physical involvements are duplicated at a higher level as we train and transform the imagination into visualization, and the physical senses and interactions into psychic senses and interactions. It is by such transformation that we become intentionally active in both the outer and inner worlds of body, mind, and spirit. It is thus that we become capable of Becoming More than We Are, and to Become—*potentially*—Whole!

The Twelve Ways of Sense & Interaction

Each of the five *outer* physical senses corresponds with five *inner* psychic senses, and the two ways we "see with the Mind"—Imagination and Visualization—make up the twelve ways of sense interaction between our objective and subjective worlds. Perceiving Inner and Outer, we encounter the Whole of Man Visible and Invisible, of Man and the Universe, and of Man as he is and of Man as he will be.

Each of our physical senses and our physical means of interaction, along with the Imagination, is duplicated and transformed at the "psychic" level.

Twelve Ways of Sense & Interaction

Physical Level Senses	Psychic Level Senses
Smelling	Clairalience, Clairolfaction
Tasting	Clairgustance
Touching	Clairsentience
Hearing	Clairaudience
Seeing	Clairvoyance
Imagination	*Visualization*
Physical Level Interactions	Psychic Level Interactions
Movement	Psychokinesis
Speaking	Telepathy
Sleep, Dreaming	Dreaming True
Sexual Loving	Sex Magick
Anger, Fear	Aura Shielding

And the 13th way is *WILL*—the Necessary Factor

Note: While there are corresponding "psychic" terms for physical level senses that are "established" with recognized meanings, the same is not completely the case for interactions. Is the Psychic Level interaction for Sexual Loving exactly and only that which is practiced as Sex Magick? *Probably not.* And the physical acts involved with Anger and Fear probably should be self-analyzed—or, if extreme—they may call for professional counseling.

Another factor to note is that the senses are basically "one-way streets" with sense perceptions being delivered to the sense perceiver. But Interactions involve degrees of action and response between the main actor and an object (in the case of Psychokinesis) or person or event, but also note that the psychic level of interaction to movement may be more extensive than suggested.

WILL is the necessary factor

Our focus is really not on the psychic level at this point, but—as you will shortly discover—on training at the physical level to truly perceive and understand the importance of accuracy in our perceptions of the minutest details. It is this that trains the psychic level as well as success at the physical level. We'll explain that shortly.

In the previous chart listing the twelve ways of sense and& interaction, you should note the additional 13th listing of **WILL** expressed in all upper case letters. It is this unique human power of WILL that makes *change* and *choice* possible. It is only as you

WILL to develop your psychic powers into psychic skills that true Psychic Development, and Self-Development, happens.

It's easy to read books about psychic development, about the marvels of clairvoyance and other psychic abilities, and about the techniques and methods for development, but *learning-about* and *understanding-about* is just the first step.

Taking the Next Step

You have to take the NEXT STEP which involves Willed Determination to undertake a training program of practice for development.

More about training the Twelve Ways of Perceiving will come later in this chapter.

Visualization and Attraction in the New Age

There has been a lot of talk and writing about Visualization over the last several decades. There is "Creative Visualization" employed to manifest things of our desire: Money, Career, Houses, Cars, etc. And there is "Attraction" where visualization is employed for mostly the same purposes but with an emphasis on attracting Love and Success into your life.

Visualization used in conjunction with your imagination is an important technique. Your ability to effectively visualize turns your imagination into a **psychic power tool** for use in psychic work, active meditation, astral travel, remote viewing, the development of clairvoyance, activating archetypal powers, the assumption of god forms, entering mythic worlds, Qabalistic path working, symbol "doorways" to access specific areas of the astral world, as well as in all forms of magical application, and much more. In each of these applications, visualization is a process of moving psychic energies along particular symbolic pathways. This includes techniques previously discussed involving the Chakra System and used to actually stimulate neural pathways in the physical body and brain.

Sometimes visualizations of persons, living or deceased, is used in making communications more accurate and more powerful. The visualization of a Spirit Entity or a God-Form can be employed in Evocation or Invocation (there is a difference) and in "conversation" with such beings to access Knowledge or specific Powers.

Effective visualization is the key to empowering your imagination to "make real the unreal."

Nikola Tesla

There is one famous example of the practical application of visualization from recent history. The mechanical and electrical genius, Nikola Tesla (1856–1943), inventor of the alternating current necessary for the long distance transmission of electric power, induction motors, and much more, did his research and development entirely in his imagination.

"Before I put a sketch on paper, the whole idea is worked out mentally. In my mind I change the construction, make improvements, and even operate the device. Without ever having drawn a sketch I can give the measurements of all parts to workmen, and when completed all these parts will fit, just as certainly as though I had made the actual drawings. It is immaterial to me whether I run my machine in my mind or test it in my shop. The inventions I have conceived in this way have always worked. In thirty years there has not been a single exception. My first electric motor, the vacuum wireless light, my turbine engine, and many other devices have all been developed in exactly this way."

Note Tesla's attention to and mastery of the "details" of the image: there is no wavering of the images, no indefinite edges or unwanted movement. The visualized image could be described as "mental" rather than "emotional," which is the distinction between the Mental Body and the Astral Body.

Similarly, realistic sculptors state that they are able to project a three-dimensional mental image onto a block of marble, and then chip away the marble to conform to the image; realistic artists say much the same thing—they see their image as if projected onto the canvas, and paint the picture as if the image was printed on the canvas; illustrators have the same ability—projecting an image onto paper and then sketching the picture by following the image.

The "Great Secret"

What they claim to do is to make the imagined image as "real" as REAL. That's their "great secret," that and reaching down into the Sub-Conscious and through it to the Universal Consciousness to actually *energize* the image by your *conscious intent* to bring about the specific change in existing reality to that of your intended reality.

The "energy" is there, but the more energy you actually are able to *charge* your image with through ritual and meditative practices, the better. In addition, you can draw upon your personal energy called variously "the Power," Kundalini, Chi, Prana, and many other traditional names.

Imagination vs. Visualization

Imagination and Visualization are two sides of the same coin, but definitely not the same thing! And the differences are very important.

In both cases we see things in our "mind," and both can be called "visual imagery." But, with rare exception, what you see in your Imagination is less vivid, less precise, and less "fixed" than what you see with a trained Visualization ability.

Movement & Change vs. Fixed & Present-Moment Reality

The quality of an image being "fixed" is one of the two most important distinctions between Imagination and Visualization. The other is "present-moment reality." Both these qualities are part of effective Visualization and are absent in Imagination.

The ability to visualize in "fixed" detail is extremely important to clairvoyance, and particularly to "higher" clairvoyance. Images perceived clairvoyantly should be definitive; otherwise we lack confidence in their accuracy and meaning.

By "fixed" detail we are contrasting an image seen with the trained visualization faculty with the common experience of an imagined image where the detail lacks clarity and will likely change and move about.

Go back to previous chapter addenda where we performed *Tratak* on the colored *Tattwa* elemental images. Even though the image eventually faded from the screen behind your closed eyes, it was sharp and did not move about or rapidly become something else.

Even more important, *it was not a "verbal" image.* You were not listening to a voice in your head describing or guiding your vision.

Spontaneous Imagination vs. Intentional Visualization

Imagination is a constant process—our imagination is active at all times and is mostly spontaneous, while Visualization is a time and event determined process—and a dedicated and mostly intentional process.

Imagination is the first step and Visualization is the second step in turning our image-making faculty into a reality-making power.

Dreaming & Day Dreaming

Dreaming, and "Day Dreaming" both are actions of the imagination, but the energy is passive and the "Will" is not involved. Your Sleep Dream images are often symbolic and may or may not be representative of real people or events. Day Dreams usually represent real people and events as you may wish (or fear) them to be. But you know they are not in your present-moment reality.

We read a novel and see the characters and their situations in our imagination. They are moving and acting as described in the book, and sometimes—additionally—as we wish they would do. We see a movie or an episode on television and then dream about it in our sleep—sometimes if a horror movie it may turn into a night mare. If awakened, you know they are not in your present-moment reality.

Perhaps we are employed as a fashion designer, and use our imagination to develop new designs and then alter the images as we plan the practical aspects of their production. The creative imagination is very important in design work in every field, and then in adapting the designs to their application and their reproduction. You know these designs are not in your present-moment reality.

Perhaps we are single and meet an attractive new person of interest. We may find ourselves imagining making love with this person—experiencing not only imagery but physical feeling as the "day dream" takes shape. Even though you have real physical feelings, you know that the imagined lover is not in your present-moment reality.

Instead, perhaps we are active in politics or evangelical religion and see ourselves leading a "crusade" involving a lot of physical movement and emotional reactions, a lot of singing, chanting, swaying, dancing, and spontaneity, etc. Your intention is to motivate your audience to change, and—often—to "go forth and conquer." *You're* planning and action may be in the present, but you know that the events hoped for are not in your present-moment reality.

What is the characteristic of imagination in the examples considered here? Flexibility, movement, and change. *And the lack of present-moment reality.*

Visualization & Present-Moment Reality

When we are employing Creative Visualization to gain something desired, *we establish present-moment reality.* We bring the perception of the object or situation desired into present-moment reality as if we possess it NOW, in present-moment reality.

In every act of Visualization, we use our visual power to see the object, person, or situation as if existing in present-moment reality, and use our other psychic-level senses as appropriate to further confirm that present-moment perception.

That perception of present-moment reality contrasts sharply with working toward future-moment reality that is the essence of the Creative Imagination.

But note also that "Visualization" involves all five of the psychic senses appropriate to the situation, plus the conscious and intentional use of the imagination. In other words, visualization is the higher agency of the imagination just as clairvoyance is the higher agency of physical sight, and clairaudience is the higher agency of physical hearing, etc.

All five of our physical senses, plus imagination, are involved in every act of physical level perception even though the emphasis may be on just one sense. When reading a book—aside from awareness of the environment in which we are reading—we hear the sound of the page turning, smell (however minutely) the paper and binding, feel the texture of the paper, and even taste the minute particles thrown off into the air or more specifically if we are one of those who wets a finger to get a "grip" on the page to turn it.

And just as all five of the physical senses are involved in our reading of that book (or any act of physical perception), so are all five of our psychic senses plus the faculty of visualization.

Even though it is all in a "process of becoming," we do act and perceive as a *Whole Person.* We act through and with all *twelve* ways of perception (explained further below).

The Five Physical Senses & Present Now

In the above discussion, we've used the same terms as we would if describing the physical sense of sight—seeing with our actual physical eyesight.

This is important: even though we are describing a process involving an image behind closed eyes, not only is the terminology the same but the process relates to and builds on physical sight—even in the case of a person blind from birth!

Clairvoyant "clear seeing," otherwise described as "psychic sight," does (generally) involve a <u>psychic</u> stimulation of the <u>physical</u> sight mechanism from behind the eye to the neurons in the brain. The same thing is true for the other psychic senses—for hearing, feeling, smelling, tasting. Even dreaming of things seen, heard, felt, tasted, smelled causes neurological activity from the physical sensory organs and into the related areas of the brain.

While being born blind and deaf and otherwise sensorially impaired *may* be limiting in the development of the equivalent psychic senses, it does not prevent their development and in some cases the psychic senses may instead be exceptional. As in all things, there is a correlation between input and output: the very struggle to work with limited physical senses may strengthen the development of the psychic senses.

The Twelve Ways of Perceiving

Each of the five *outer* physical senses corresponds with five *inner* psychic senses, again like two sides of the same coin we encountered with the two ways we "see with the Mind"—Imagination and Visualization. Perceiving Inner and Outer, we encounter the Whole of Man Visible and Invisible, of Man and the Universe, and of Man as he is and of Man as he will be.

Just as Imagination must be trained to become Visualization, so should the physical senses be trained to become more effective psychic senses.

Even for the person suffering from the physical disability of hearing or seeing, the technique is basically the same but relies on the imagination to provide the basis for the training.

Training the Senses

The steps we take to train the physical senses improve the corresponding psychic senses. What we need to is, first of all, to realize the need for training, and what that training involves is nothing more—*but also nothing less!*—than **"paying attention to details."**

Other than sight, testing the senses is going to be rather subjective, and the challenge is all yours! Be inventive. The following are presented only as examples illustrating the method of *paying attention to the details* to make that a normal process for you. Think of the importance of details as if you were on the witness stand in a murder trial. It's your valid remembrance of details that may save an innocent person's life or condemn a criminal to life in prison or execution.

Think of a familiar odor, and write down a description of it from memory. Then go the source of the odor and smell it, and again write down a description. Compare them and write down a score. Repeat several times. Determine that you are going to be "observant" of odors, and repeat the test with a different odor. Keep up the effort until you feel confident that you have improved both your physical and psychic sense of smell to the point where you can "memorize" the different smells, and can duplicate them in your mind.

Repeat the process with taste. Taste is a bit more objective than smell, and the descriptive vocabulary is much richer. Don't get carried away with exotic verbiage, but do go beyond the basics of salt, sugar, etc., and pick something relatively complex in which you must distinguish and describe several flavors. For example, you might first taste something as standard as tomato soup. Taste it, analyze it, describe it, write down the details, memorize, and duplicate it in your mind, and then move on to vegetable soup and try to break down the flavors into the various ingredients. When you can describe them, try to compare the tomato flavor in the vegetable soup with that of the tomato soup, and duplicate them in your mind.

The next test is more important, that of feeling and the sensation of touching or being touched. What is the feeling experienced with different materials: leather, felt, velvet, rubber, silk, cotton, etc. Then go on to the experience of these in heavy and light touches, wet and dry. Start with simple thing, like the touch of silk against your face: analyze it, describe it, compare it with other fabrics, write down the details, memorize, and then duplicate the feeling in your mind.

With the sense of hearing, try to pick relatively simple and familiar sounds, and stay away from the complexities of song and music and don't get carried away into poetic or exotic descriptions. Take something simple like the sound of a person walking across your kitchen floor and analyze the loudness, the number of steps per minute, the sense of vibrations through the floor to your own feet, and the differences made by rubber or leather soles, the clicks of hi-heels or the softness of stocking feet, and so on.

Analyze, describe, compare, write down the details, memorize, and then try to duplicate the sound in your mind. Don't embellish on it—just duplicate.

Now on to sight, the most important sense of all. Again, start with something plain and simple, but make it something important to you: perhaps a favorite footstool. Analyze it, describe it, compare, write down the details, memorize, and duplicate it in your mind.

Fried Chicken

Finally, find something that will combine as many senses as possible. Perhaps your spouse cooked dinner tonight. Just for illustrative purposes, we're going to suggest you are a man in the kitchen with your wife and that she is frying chicken. She is home from work at a fashion boutique, and she is still wearing hi-heels so there is the sound of her walking on the floor. There is the smell and the sound of frying chicken, she wants you to taste the basting mixture she is using and you hold her hand as she gives it to you, and there is the sight of all that is going on. It's all familiar to you, so excuse yourself and go into another room, close your eyes, and duplicate the smell, taste, sound, touch and sight of that familiar but special moment.

You used all five of your physical senses in the kitchen, and then—with your eyes closed in another room—you duplicated it all in your mind employing all five of your psychic senses.

Think about this, and pretend that you are actually traveling in another part of the country after talking to your wife on the phone and learning that she is just home from the shop, frying chicken for dinner. You can imagine it all in detail. Yet, another time, on another trip, you wonder what is happening back home, and you get a quick vision of a somewhat similar scene. You phone home, and find that your vision was exactly correct.

You have moved from an actual physical experience to an imagined one and on to a clairvoyant vision of one.

Regardless of some of the improbabilities of the example (you are perhaps a bit tired of fried chicken right now!), we hope to have demonstrated the importance of enriching the physical senses with detail in our training for visualization and clairvoyance.

The Importance of Visualization in Clairvoyance

We hope we have both demonstrated the importance of Visualization to the accuracy of clairvoyance visions, and provided you with a simple, self-activated training program that will make attention to the details perceived in each of the senses an automatic life-long process.

"Paying attention to the details" is a very serious responsibility that is a key to success in almost any endeavor. It is, unfortunately, an *overlooked* detail in the educational process. It is assumed that when you study any subject that you are paying attention to the details. Test scores easily demonstrate that is largely not the case.

Programming for Self & Family

But, not all is lost! You are fully capable of training yourself to observe these details as we've described in this chapter. What's more, you can make paying attention to the details a fun daily game for the entire family. Young children will love doing it—competing against each other, competing against their own parents and other "elders."

Sources & Suggested Additional Reading:

Denning, M., & Phillips, O. *Practical Guide to Creative Visualization: Manifest Your Desires,* 2001, Llewellyn.

Ophiel. *The Art & Practice of Creative Visualization,* 2001, Weiser.

Slate, J. H. & Weschcke, C. L. *The Llewellyn Complete Book of Psychic Empowerment: A Compendium of Tools & Techniques for Growth & Transformation,* 2011, Llewellyn.

Webster, R. *Creative Visualization for Beginners,* 2006, Llewellyn.

Wiehl, A. *Creative Visualization,* 1958, Llewellyn.

ADDENDUM #6 TO CHAPTER SIX
Microcosm to Macrocosm & Macrocosm to Microcosm

The Tattvic Connection—
Meditation & Visualization Program #4: Air/Air

Vayu: Air—Seed of Air

Air! We all know what air is—we breathe it, we walk through it, we fly through it, it surrounds us and adapts to us, it buoys us up, it expands things, it supports combustion, it is movement—from calmness to hurricane force, from steady wind to whirlwind tornadoes, it is electrical (light and lightning), it provides us life-sustaining oxygen that we can't live without. Air is hard to get hold of and to see and examine as we can Earth and Water, and even Fire is localized. Air is the Earth's atmosphere, but is only vaguely localized to the planet as a whole—becoming thinner at higher altitudes.

Unlike Earth and Water, Air can be compressed and its release can be controlled in various utilitarian functions from cleaning to powering movement. Air can be readily mixed with other gases, just as water can be blended with other liquids. Air however, unlike water (unless it is constantly stirred), can carry some solids without blending with them.

THINK ELEMENTAL AIR

The above paragraphs are objective and cosmic. Here, in this paragraph, we need to be subjective and personal. We say of Air that it is feminine, active, liberating, and projective. How do we relate those concepts to our inner life and its outer expression? Air is within and without at all times—we breathe it in and breathe it out and it is everywhere at once outside our bodies. We share it completely with all life on this planet, except for some few forms living in sulfur vents in very deep ocean locations.

The Tattvic Blue Circle symbolizes Elemental Air. Work with this tattwa is used to enhance the ability to visualize and discriminate between one thought and another. Meditation on circles activates the subconscious mind to bring about greater ability to recover desired memories and information, and to communicate with particular spiritual beings and magical powers.

Vayu is prana that forms the etheric body and the vital force in the physical body that produces cells and circulates blood and fluids throughout the entire body and its organs to keep them active and healthy. The yogic practice of pranayama becomes more important to physical health as we age.

Air is the element of communication, the power of perception, the ability to be inspired and to inspire others. Air is the element of evolution and of self-integration and transformation to become all we can be. Air is consciousness, awareness, imagination, and power to turn visualization into reality. Air is mind, the ability to anticipate and plan our actions, to choose and discriminate, and to reach into the world of spirit. Air brings the inspiration of humor, the ability to laugh, to master illusions, and to experience and express joy. Air is the power of positive thinking that enables us to create a new image of self and to become more than we are.

Sometimes an element becomes easier to grasp when we relate to it astrologically through the associated sun signs, here of Gemini, Libra, and Aquarius—described as having the qualities of adaptability, harmony, and balance. While each has its own characteristics, they share in the recognition of humanity and intelligence. They are imaginative and compassionate, often literary and artistic, and good speakers.

And they are often interested in magickal and religious practices. The following Tattva Overview Table is intended to give you an inkling of some of the factors involved with a Magickal perspective.

Some readers will object to discussing the subject of *Magick* in direct relation to the study and development of Clairvoyance as being outside the scientific domain of parapsychology. Parapsychology generally approaches the various psychic powers, or skills, as lacking any potential for development. It's an approach that more or less says, "You either have it or don't, and either way we'll measure it statistically and try to subject it to *laboratory standards* which we expect will disprove it." And if it is not totally disproved they conclude it is too rare to have any practical application.

Some relatively famous names will precede one step further and introduce *stage "magic"* (also known as prestidigitation) to <u>prove</u> that anything "paranormal" is an illusion or deliberate fakery. In other words, they use *fakery to prove fakery.*

Dr. Slate and I have approached the subject from a contrary *positive* rather than *negative* point of view in which his scientific research work has demonstrated the validity of both paranormal phenomena and psychic powers, and studied methods for their development and their practical application.

My own approach has been to question why some clairvoyance is often vague and sometimes reflective of personal bias, and then to apply established methods to correct the problems. That is what we do with *the Tattva Connection Meditation & Visualization Programs* contained in these chapter addenda. The point is to recognize

TATTVA OVERVIEW TABLE #4: Magickal

Tattva Name	Element Name	Kabbalah Sephiroth	Elemental Direction	Magick God Name	Magick Archangel	Magick Angel	Magick Stone	Magick Tool	Magical Incense	Magical Color	Magical Plant
Prithivi	Earth	Malkuth	North	Adonai Ha-Aretz	Auriel	Porlakh	Ruby	Pentacle	Cedar	Brown	Patchouli
Apas	Water	Hod	West	Elohim Tzabaoth	Gabriel	Talihad	Coral	Chalice	Damiana	Aqua	Aloe
Tejas	Fire	Netzach	South	Yhhvh Tzabaoth	Michael	Aral	Fire Opal	Wand	Cinnamon	Red	Nettle
Vayu	Air	Yesod	East	Shaddai El Chai	Raphael	Chassan	Emerald	Sword	Lavender	Blue	Acacia
Akasha	Ether	Tiphareth	Center	AHIH	Metatron		Turquoise	Voice	Frankincense	All	Almond

the problem, understand its causes, and apply a proven technique to remedy the cause and to improve the vision.

As the following note says, the table is only an overview and like any overview of this sort, it is incomplete and may contain some seeming conflicts with other sources you may have encountered or will encounter in future studies. We are not dealing with *material science* where concepts can be specific and terminology definitive. In *esoteric science* we are dealing with worlds that are more subtle and where the developing consciousness of the viewer is ever-changing in its perspective and clarity of vision. It's somewhat comparable to the expanding and changing vision of the person climbing a very tall mountain, with the added complication of the effects of the rarified atmosphere (with lowered oxygen content) and extreme cold temperatures affecting the climber's consciousness.

In esoteric terms, the higher you go (in consciousness) the more you will see. That simple statement begs for further clarification. In the physical world, we see <u>three</u> dimensions, in the astral we see <u>four</u>, in the mental we see <u>five</u>, and *so on!* Additional dimensions bring changing perspectives, and altered states of consciousness reveal realities previously hidden. As higher levels of consciousness are integrated in the Whole Person you are becoming, new understanding of the whole cosmos brings new clarity to what we knew before.

> Note: The following Elemental Overview Table #4 for Air is exactly what the title says—an "overview" intended to give you a fundamental awareness of the Elemental Qualities and Characteristics. You may notice some seeming conflicts but these represent particular sources and intended usage from Meditational and Magickal perspectives. An excellent source book for all this is David Hulse's "The Eastern Mysteries" which can be supplemented by the same author's "The Western Mysteries."

ELEMENT OVERVIEW TABLE #4: Air
ELEMENT OF AIR—SEED OF AIR: Nurture

Tattva Name: *Vayu*	Tattva Form: Hexagram, Circle	Tattvic Color: Sky Blue
Tattva/Primary Sheath: Vijnanamaya (Mental Body)	Tattva Animal: Antelope	Tattvic Taste: Acid
Yantra Color: Orange, or Red	Yantra Form: Globe, Hexagram	Cosmic Plane: *maha,* lower mental
Chakra Name: *Anahata* (unstruct sound)	Chakra Common Name: Heart Chakra	Chakra Bija Mantra: YAM
Chakra Body Location: over the heart	Chakra body Space: Heart to Mid-eyebrows	Chakra Body Zone: Cardiac Plexus, Chest

Chakra Color: Green	Chakra Function of astral & etheric centers: understand astral vibrations, sense control, inspired speech	
Chakra Goal: Releasing knots of Susumnas Vishnu	Chakra God *(Shiva)* Energy: Maheshvara, Isvara	Chakra Goddess *(Shakti)* Energy: Kali, Kakini
Chakra Meditation: ability of intense concentration, brings wisdom, control of the senses & passions.		Chakra verbal expression: I love
Chakra Petals (spokes): 12	Chakra Power: your wishes will be fulfilled, compassion, awareness of others' feelings, mastery of speech	Chakra Problem: asthma, high blood pressure, cardiac disease, lung problems
Chakra Symbol: 12 red petals inscribed with mantras kam, kham, gam, gham, nam, cam, cham, jam, jham, nam, tam, and tham, surrounds yellow upright *(Shiva)* triangle interlaced with downward *(Shakti)* triangle containing an upright *linga* (astral male symbol) called *bana,* inside an inverse *yoni* triangle to release the second block to rising Kundalini. Shiva as Rudra and Shakti as Kali ride a black antelope. Chant *YAM.*		
Chakra Vital Air: Pran*a Vayu*	Chakra Yogini: *Rakini*	Chakra/Physical Gland: Thymus
Chakra Program: the challenge of self-analysis and self-control to correctly influences all the pranas.		
Siddhi Powers: (when developed) Acquires Divine powers, ability to make miracles		
Indian God: The 4-armed god of air rides a black antelope, holding 3-eyed *Isha* on his lap, offering protection and boons		
Indian goddesses: *Kakini* has 3 eyes and four arms and is yellow-skinned. She grants boons and dispels fear. She dwells in an downward triangle containing a gold *Siva* linga in which dwells Laksmi, the goddess of prosperity.		
Element Name: Air	Elemental State: Gaseous	Elemental Action: Surrounds
Elemental Function: Bouncy	Elemental Motion: Outward	Elemental Nature: Erratic
Elemental Power: control of details, emotions	Elemental Quality: Hot, Wet, Moving	Elemental Strength: to connect with others
Energy Type: Electrical	Manifests through: Gaseous Vapors	Quantum Force: Strong Nuclear Force
Emotional Characteristic: Compassion	Emotional Desires: to act, love, move, serve	Emotional Drive: sharing, devotion, service
Emotional Family Role: Son	Emotional Nature: self-control, balance	Emotional/Psychological Level: Imagination
Emotional reaction: envy, boastful, fickle, restless	Emotional/Sensory Block: Habits from past lives	
Emotional/Sexual Identity: Feminine, active, projective	Emotional Strength: unselfish worker	Emotional weakness: agitated, empty-headed
Mind Action: *Chitta* (Feeling, Psychic Content)	Mind Function: Direct Cognition, Insight	Mind State: Beyond Waking
Physical/Action Organ: Hands	Physical/Action Form: Grasping	Physical/Action Effect: Reductive

Physical/Astral Sense: Touch, Feeling	Physical/Astral Sense (Cognition) Organ: Skin	Physical Body Functions: muscular, respiration
Physical Energy Correlations between physical/etheric & astral bodies—Fingers of Hand: Ring Finger		
Psychic Powers: OBE, mental healing, powerful speech	Psychic/Astral Work: visualize a blue lotus floating on a lake in a hexagram in heart center	
Alchemical Metal: Gold	Alchemical Planet: Venus	Alchemical Quality: ?
Alchemical Symbolic Season: Spring	Alchemical Symbolic Time of Day: Sunset	Astrological Lunar Phase: Three-Quarter Moon
Astrological Types: Gemini, Libra, Aquarius	Astrological Qualities: flexibility, harmony, balance	
Astrological Planetary Expression: ?	Astrological Ruling Planet: Jupiter, Venus	
Egyptian Divinities: *Maat, Nu*	Greek God Form: Hermes (travel)	Greek goddesses: Aphrodite
Hebrew God Name: Yod He Vav He	Runes: Ansuz, Eihwaz, Raidho, Tiwaz	
Magical Angel: Chassan	Magical Animals: birds, flying insects	Magical Archangel: Raphael
Magical Mythical Beings: Gryphons, gremlins	Magical Colors: light blue, pastels, yellow, white	Magical Day: Wednesday
Magical Direction: East	Magical Elemental King: Paralda	Magical Elemental Spirits: Sylphs
Magical Energy: ?	Magical Enochian Watchtower: Eastern	Magical God Name: Shaddai El Chai
Magical Herbs: almond, caraway, jasmine, mint, parsley	Magical Incense: galbanum, lavender; Rose Oil	Magical/Kerub: Man
Magical Metals: copper	Magical/Musical Note: F#; Musical Scale: Fa	Magical Places: mountain peaks, towers
Magical Planet: Venus ?	Magical Plants: acacia, aspen, anise, lavender, birch	
Magical Power: To Know, Divination	Magical Ruler: Ariel	
Magical Rulerships: abstract thinking, air, beginnings, communications, divination, drug addictions, freedom, groups, intellectualizing, joy, laughter, memory, organizations, organizing, schoolings, teaching, tests, theorizing, travel, writing		
Magical Season: Spring	Magical States: Spiritual Empowerment	
Magical Stones: aventurine, emerald, mica, mottled jasper, pumice, rose quartz, watermelon tourmaline		
Magical Symbols:	Magical Time of Day: Dawn	Magical Time of Life: Infancy, Childhood
Magickal Tool: broom, incense, scourge, sword	Magical Work: high divination, visualization	

Tarot Court: King	Tarot suit: Swords	Tarot Trumps: Fool
Tree of Life Path: 11th from 1 to 2	Tree of Life Sphere: Tiphareth	Tree of Life Soul Level: Ruach-Middle Consciousness
*OBE stands for Out-of-Body Experience, or Astral Projection. In common usage, OBE describes spontaneous experiences, Astral Projection describes active projection.		
*The Mental Body is also called the Intelligence Sheath, and in Theosophy is the Lower Mental Body while the Higher is the Causal Body.		
Note: The various magical correspondences are only minimal selections. More complete information can be found in the resources listed at the end of the book.		
For serious study, you should add to this list, & other lists you may be building. Correspondences build your inter-relationships between Inner & Outer, Subconscious & Conscious, Cosmic & Personal. All magical systems inter-relate and add to your personal memory/library.		

Air—Seed of Air

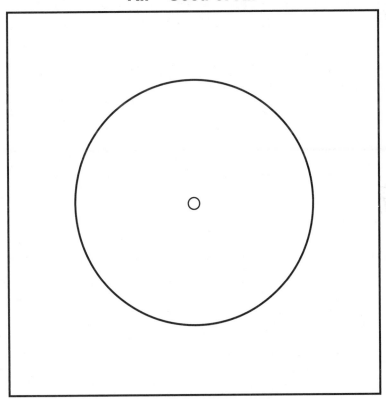

Color the tiny inner bindu circle white,
the inner circle blue,
and the outer square orange

Air—Seed of Air: Vayu YAM

The Tattvic Connection Meditation & Visualization Program #4: Air/Air
Vayu: Air—Seed of Air

Introduction. The Purpose & Function of this Procedure.

This procedure is intended to bring **Vayu**, the **Air** Element, into a particular state of psychic awareness. While the procedure is directed by your conscious mind, the main operation occurs in the subconsciousness and in the autonomic system. In itself it does not bring about dramatic changes, but allows certain changes to happen and bring the personal element into balance with its cosmic equivalent.

Throughout life we create changes in the complex of physical and subtle bodies that combine in our vehicle of manifestation and experience for this life time. Some changes represent positive growth and others are negative and even destructive depending on your reactions to and understanding of their emotional nature.

This exercise and those that follow are specifically intended for balancing and harmonizing the inner Tattvic Matrix of Body and Soul with the universal Cosmic Matrix and "Spirit." The result is a purification of the inner matrix so that clairvoyant visions will not be distorted by "accumulated psychic and emotional garbage" left over and unresolved from childhood and past lives.

Nothing is ever forgotten in our subconsciousness, but the emotional "flavor" that accompanied the original experience can be recognized as such when seen with a new and wiser perspective.

You can repeat this entire procedure often, but not more than once daily. And I suggest that you allow a week between each exercise.

Summary of Purpose & User Benefits.

With this meditation we purify, balance, and harmonize the **mental and psychic** elemental force in our body and soul as contained in the **Air** tattva. As this is completed, along with other elemental meditations, you will be better equipped to follow on with specific stimuli of particular psychic centers to accomplish your projected goals.

Step 1. Preliminaries.

Always start with Physical Relaxation.

Read through the entire procedure before beginning so that further reference is not needed. Mostly it is identical with the other *Tattva Connection Meditation & Visualization Programs* except for specific references to the **Air** Element, which I have placed in boldface for ease of recognition.

Time & Space: Allow a period of at least 30 minutes (an hour is better) for the actual 16 step procedure to be conducted in a comfortably warm, quiet, and safe setting free of interruptions. While a darkened room is not required, freedom from both sound and visual distractions is advisable.

Personal Preparations: Remove shoes and keep clothing or covering minimal to reduce the effects of external stimuli.

Posture & Position: It is not desirable to lie flat for this procedure, but a relaxed posture in a chair or recliner is helpful.

Special Lighting: You should arrange a small desk or reading light next to your chair that you can comfortably reach to turn it on and off as required, and focus as directed.

Breathing: It is always desirable to establish a deep but natural, rhythmic flow of your breath, mostly balanced between inhalation and exhalation.

Vocalization: Vocalize, either silently stated or voiced aloud, your affirmations and the name of the tattva and then the sounding of the mantra in Step 9.

With each step 5 through 13, it is helpful to vocalize the words describing any particular feelings or even visions you experience.

Vibration: This is very important. In Step 9 you should chant or hum the Sanskrit name of the tattva, and then the tattvic mantra as instructed. You want to draw these words out and feel the *vibration.* "Vibration" means to actually lightly *warble* the words at the back of your throat, and as you do, you may want to raise or lower the "musical note" until it feels right. The same approach applies to the volume: initially you may want to chant loudly but later reduce the volume. You want to feel the words *vibrate* throughout your skull, and then in the location of the corresponding chakra—with experience you will be able to move the vibration to other designated places inside your body, and then—in advanced work—intentionally into external objects.

The yantra, the name, and the mantra are your means to connect the inner tattva with the external tattva for purification and balance.

Step 2. Goal Statement.

Your goal is three-fold:

• To become fully familiar with the feelings associated with the **Air** Element. You've read about it, you've seen the characteristics and correspondences, but now we want you to *feel* the **Air** in you, under you, around you, and *through* your entire inner being, to become aware of Elemental **Air** as one of the primal *foundational* elements of the outer material universe.

- To identify inner **Air** with outer **Air**, and feel yourself purified and balanced through the *harmonizing of inner with outer.*

- *To address particular concerns:* As an example, we have suggested two areas—your **ability to make rational and ethical choices** and **to control your awareness of other people's ideas and needs.** You must determine the goals yourself and then *affirm* them simply and concisely in as few words as possible. Write them down, fix them in your mind, but do not consider them as the primary function of the exercise which is the balancing and purification of personal elemental **Air.** (Note: particular concerns must relate to the Element being addressed—see the Overview Table.)

Step 3. Affirmations.

These affirmations may be spoken as goals at the beginning, and then as confirmations at the ending of the procedure. In addition to these, add the affirmation you wrote as one of your goals.

*I feel **Air** everywhere within me.*

*I feel **Air** everywhere around me.*

*I feel purified and in harmony with all that is **Airy & Moving** everywhere.*

Step 4. Mental Imagery.

Imagery, like vocalization, can increase the effectiveness of the procedure.

Visualization: Visualizing the tattvas as described is essential.

Spontaneous Imagery: Other images may appear at the end of the procedure—and that is alright *unless you have negative feelings about them—in which case you should willfully "banish" them.* (There is value in relating your banishing technique to the element involved. Of course, nothing can ever be completely forgotten, but we can isolate them and make them so difficult to find that they never will be. In the case of elemental earth, we buried our locked box of negativities deeply in the ground, for water we sank it deeply in the ocean, for fire we tossed it into an active volcano—so for air let us shoot it by rocket to the top of the tallest mountain where it will be soon frozen in the deepest ice.)

Recording: Other images that may appear spontaneously at the end of the procedure should be noted along with any particular feelings or ideas, and then recorded in your journal for later analysis.

Analysis: Always let a day or two pass before reading and analyzing your journal entries.

Step 5. Preparation.

Preparing the Yantra Card.

It is recommended that you photocopy the illustration on page 217, preferably on heavier paper or card stock, or draw it yourself in exactly the same sizes using a ruler and black pen. If you can manage it, using a drawing compass or a template, draw a tiny ⅛" inch diameter circle in the exact center. Leave the inside of the circle white. This inner circle or point aids your steady focus. It is not essential, but it is helpful. Make the outer square 4" x 4" and the inner Circle should be about 2½" wide and centered, and the little circle in the exact center should be ⅛" in diameter and have a heavy black border around it but not quite as thick as those around the Circle and the outer square.

Coloring the Yantra Card.

It will be beneficial to you to color the image as follows: (a) Leave the tiny circle white; (b) color the **Circle Sky Blue,** and the surrounding larger square **Bright Orange**. Each square and the tiny inner circle are bordered with bold black lines.

Cutting the Yantra Card.

If you have reproduced the image on the heavy card stock as recommended, now measure off either one or two inches (your choice) on each side and cut away the surplus so you have a square 6" x 6" or 8" x 8" *card* with the colored image in the center.

This preparation will be repeated for all the additional images during which you will have constructed a set of 25 Tattva Cards that can be used again and again in the clairvoyance process discussed in this book, and in many other functions to be discussed later.

Position & Lighting.

Holding the tattvic yantra card, recline in a comfortable chair in a quiet room where you will not be disturbed for a minimum of 30 minutes (preferably, an hour). Prior to doing so, arrange the lighting to focus on the card so that you can turn it on and off.

Note the preferred direction for placing the chair indicated in Step 9 (a and b).

Breathing & Relaxation.

Become fully relaxed, combining slowed rhythmic breathing, and progressive tension and release of muscles from your toes to your brow and scalp if you have not

already followed the Empowerment Tension & Release Procedure described in the Addendum to Chapter 1.

Step 6. Pranic Breathing Pattern.

With eyes closed; engage in a pattern of rhythmic breathing involving equally spaced —*without any stress*—in-breaths, holding, out-breaths, holding, and repeating throughout the process.

Step 7. White Light Circulation.

Then, with each in-breath visualize White Light flowing into the body; while holding the breath visualize the light circulating throughout the body; while breathing out see the light being excreted, knowing that it is carrying out impurities; and while holding the out breath realize that you have energized and cleansed the inner energy body.

Step 8. Psychic Shield.

While continuing the breathing pattern and the flowing light, turn your imagination outward and visualize an absolutely clear field around you, one that is as transparent as the clearest glass. Know that this is a shield that protects you from external influences while containing the tattvic meditation program's benefits.

Step 9a. Yantra Card Focus.

If you have constructed the tattva yantra card as described, turn on the light and focus it on the card held or positioned comfortably about a foot to a foot and a half in front of you.

If possible, arrange your chair to face the tattvic direction: **East.** Otherwise—think and feel *East*.

Vibrate the name of tattva: **Vayu.** Repeat three times.

Chant or hum the tattva element mantra **YAM** (pronounced **YA-UUM**). Vibrate the mantra as instructed in Step 1, preliminaries. Repeat three times. Later, you can do more but always in groups of three. And feel the mantra vibrate over the **heart,** the corresponding physical location of the psychic **Anahata** chakra.

Focus on the small white *bindu* circle at the center of the image, and stare at it for as long as you can without blinking. When you can't continue the "burning" feeling any longer, turn off the light, close your eyes and focus your inner sight on the space in front of your brow chakra (between your eyebrows and on the ridge you can feel just above your nose), and you will soon see floating in space before you the tattva image. See the **Blue Circle** vibrate within the outer **Orange** Square. Soon it will change to the complementary yantra colors: the Circle becoming **Orange** over a **Blue** background.

Absorb this image! Identify with it, become one with it. As you repeat the exercise, often, you will reach a point when you will be able to recall this image at will. For now, just know that there will be practical applications for this ability—but that's a big subject for a different book.

Step 9b. Yantra Visualization.

Alternatively, if you haven't made a **Vayu** tattva card, immediately in front of you, visualize a large **Orange Square**, inside of which is a **Blue Circle** approximately half the size of the **Orange Square**. See the **Blue Circle** gently vibrate within the **Orange Square**. The colors will then reverse to their complementary yantra colors.

Step 10. Experiencing Elemental Air.

Feel yourself becoming totally *absorbed* in the **Blue Circle** while retaining awareness of the surrounding **Orange** Square. Feel *your* **Airy** nature harmonize with the Cosmic **Air** Tattva, and feel all impurities in your **Air** Tattva—all emotional garbage and unconscious psychic attachments—dissipate.

*In particular: feel the **Airy** nature of your physical body become free of adverse thoughts and feelings. Feel your physical body becoming ideally healthy, strong, and energized. Feel and see your **Astral** and **Mental** bodies in clear and bright colors. Know your **Mental** body to be clear and free of **distorting emotions** and **irrational thoughts**. See your physical/etheric body as perfectly healthy, feel your whole being energized and clear of **emotional** and **mental** pain and illness, and charged with **Love** and **High Ideals**.*

Step 11. Knowing Elemental Air.

Allow yourself to receive any information or messages from you're experiencing of Elemental **Air**. *In particular: receive information involving your **Psychic** and **Mental** health, strength, and security.* Receive the information without any emotional reaction.

Step 12. Dissipation of Images.

Slowly dissipate the **Circle** and the surrounding **Square**, return to the clear field around you, continuing the breathing pattern of Step 6 above.

Step 13. Letting Go of Evoked Feelings.

Let go of all the particular feelings evoked by the imagery, slowly change your breathing to its natural rhythm, and feel the physical relaxation achieved in Step 1 above.

Step 14. Completion & Self-Realization.

Feel yourself fully relaxed and fully self-contained. Feel yourself to be healthy, energized, cleansed, and refreshed. Know yourself to be strong and secure.

Step 15. Return to Normality.

Open your eyes, return to the physical world knowing all is well. Stand up and move about. Have some refreshment and engage in some normal activity.

Step 16. Review, Record & Analyze.

Record in a journal all messages and feelings received in Step 11 above. At this point, merely record—do not analyze. After a few days, read what you've recorded and then write down an analysis of what you believe the messages mean for you at this time. Realize that when you repeat the exercise at another time, the messages are likely to change to meet new circumstances in your life.

Conclusion: This exercise has demonstrated the particular usefulness of clairvoyance focused on the single areas of Mental, Emotional, and Psychic health, strength and security in Steps 10 and 11 At the same time the relaxation program and light circulation procedure provide physical health and healing benefits.

However, the entire 16-step Meditation is a basic program that can be modified by changes in the tattvic element and then particular modifications in Steps 10 and 11. You should explore these ideas on your own.

Sources & Suggested additional reading:

Judith, A. *The Illuminated Chakras: A Visionary Journey into Your Inner World*, DVD.

Pond, D. *Chakras for Beginners: A Guide to Balancing Your Chakra Energies*, 4 audio CDs with 28-page booklet.

CHAPTER SEVEN

Shamanism & Religion, Spiritualism & Channeling, and Clairvoyance

He Who Has the Power . . .

In the long history of humanity, paranormal powers were first associated with the lonely role of the shaman, and then later they became mostly associated with religious practices. In substance, they were perceived as a function of a special spiritual consciousness inaccessible by "ordinary" men and women. The person who could see where to find the best hunting was a natural leader; the person who could foresee danger and lead away from it became recognized as a wise man; the person who could perceive the cause of disease became a healer.

Conscious & Subconscious—The Split between

At the beginning, there were instances of natural clairvoyance before mind became split into conscious and subconscious. Then natural paranormal powers "retreated" into the subconscious mind under the onslaught of intensifying conscious perceptions and demands. Only those few who learned how to access the subconscious could call upon instinctive levels of clairvoyance.

Shamanic "Techniques" to access the Subconscious

These people with their special talents became separated from the ordinary people, and began to learn the "technology" to access the subconscious and then develop and enhance their skills. They found—aided by their natural clairvoyance—special practices and techniques to train even those who may not have shown a natural talent so that their special status could be handed down to their descendants, or separately to apprentices.

The Shaman as "Outsider"

First we had the role of shamanism in which the shaman (usually—as the word suggests—a man) undertook special disciplines and practices in order to gain or strengthen such powers as clairvoyant Seeing at a Distance, clairvoyant Seeing the Future, clairvoyant Seeing a Disease, and clairvoyant Seeing the Enemy. Added to shamanic powers came the ability to heal a disease, the ability to interpret dreams and omens, the ability to see beyond physical reality, and—sometimes—the ability to kill at a distance.

But the early shamans were usually not ordinary men but often were born with something setting each aside from others in family or tribe. Sometimes the shaman-to-be had a physical disability or disfigurement, or there had been extraordinary phenomena surrounding his birth and early childhood. Being set apart, his conscious mind was less active and he was a candidate for shamanic training that might include a special diet, periodic fasting, ecstatic dancing, magical chanting, the use of hallucinogenic substances (that became sacraments reserved for the shamen), special practices that induced altered consciousness including isolation, flagellation, and prolonged (often self-bound) bondage in particular postures.

Shamanism predates all organized religions by many thousands of years, and while sometimes is itself called a primitive indigenous religion that may not really be accurate as we will see later.

Shamanism: "Technique of Ecstasy"

Mircia Eliade* defines it with no reference to religion: "A first definition of this complex phenomenon, and perhaps the least hazardous, will be: shamanism = *technique of ecstasy,*" which itself is defined variously as suspension of the physical senses, a trance state by which an individual can go out-of-body to transcend normal consciousness, and also as a state of consciousness bringing expanded spiritual awareness and visions from beyond the physical world.

> *Mircea Eliade, *Shamanism: Archaic Techniques of Ecstasy*, Bollingen Series LXXVI, Pantheon Books, NY, 1964.

Using the word "Spirit"

It is important in this stage of our study to carefully distinguish our discussion of spirits, the spirit world, spirit guides, spirit companions, spiritual consciousness, and spiritual practices from later discussions of the same terms in religion. The undistinguished use of these words can be misleading. Shamanism is "man-made" and the world of spirits is not the world of *divinely* inspired religions.*

> *The word "religion" is derived from *relig* (*re*) to tie, fasten, or (*re-re-+ ligāre*) to bind, tie; in other words to bind together in a common belief system and moral code, a shared world-view and program of action in relation to others not sharing that belief system, and even an enforced legal system of property ownership and human relations.

A religion binds people together, whereas a shaman is always an "outsider" even as he serves the tribal community. Like the village "wise women" (or men) of later times who lived outside the village, the shaman often lived apart from his community. His function and special practices necessitated it.

The Shaman as Intermediary between the Worlds

Shamans see themselves as intermediaries between the human (physical) and spirit worlds. They enter non-physical dimensions of consciousness to discover solutions to the problems afflicting their physical (human, animal and plant) community. Other than induced trances and out-of-body experiences, shamans gain specific information through dreams and visions.

Spirit Guides

Shamans are almost always in contact with spirit guides who enable their entry into the spirit world and guide them in their journeys, during which they may receive specific information and instruction as to what is needed to heal a diseased person. It should be noted that such healing is not always accomplished by means of medicines but often by the performance of acts of penance to balance previous harmful actions. Other times, the shaman "enters the body" (the subtle body by means of his own subtle body) to confront the spiritual infirmity, or energy imbalance, and banish it from the body.

The Shaman's Technology of the Sacred

The shaman's knowledge of healing and hallucinogenic plants is obtained directly from the plants via his inner vision of clairvoyance. Among the common ecstasy-producing psycho-active plants used are Psilocybin mushrooms, Cannabis, Tobacco, San Pedro Cactus, Peyote, Ayahuasca, Cedar, Matura, Deadly Nightshade, Fly Agaric, Iboga, Morning Glory, Sage. Salvia Divinorum, and Hawaiian Baby Woodrose.

In addition to the sacred plants, various prolonged (often to the point of collapse and trance) physical activities: drumming, shaking the rattle, shaking and trembling of the practitioner's own body, singing, chanting, dancing, and costumes* are used to enable the shaman and his followers to enter other worlds. In this connection, public rituals and performances add to the shaman's mystique and his political power within the tribe. In many cases, these included demonstrations of clairvoyance and other paranormal powers: prophecy, healing, levitation, feats of strength, summoning of animals, séances with spirits of the deceased, revealing crimes, solving mysteries, etc.

*It should be noted that the shamanic "costume" was often both symbolic and more than symbolic. For the person unaware of subtle (beyond the physical) energies, the shaman's wearing of a bearskin, for example, is assumed to be *just a symbolic assumption* of the bear's physical strength—but it is more. The bear's skin is filled with the subtle energies of the bear—which add to those of the shaman—and the bear's "spirit" which connects to the group soul of all bears. Often the shamanic costume is a complex of feathers, skins, bones, teeth, and claws related to those creatures common in the shaman's community and providing subtle links between the shaman and the living creatures making up the food supply of the community. Many of the shaman's songs and dances are imitative and likewise connect him to the living creatures. In other instances, we would recognize these same elements and actions as "magical."

The Shaman as Keeper of Myth and Tradition

Within the history of the tribe and its culture, the shaman was often the keeper of the traditions and myths, and the story teller who transmitted them to his current generation. A final function was as a psycho-pomp—a guide of souls—to guide the souls of the deceased to their spiritual resting place.

But it was the earlier "pre-shaman" looking for answers on the origin of the universe, of his people, and other questions who invented the myths in the first place—looking for answers and finding them in the deep Unconscious as stories and symbols slowly taking more sophisticated shape in the form of geographically based mythology and traditions meeting the needs imposed by environment.

The inductive and transforming techniques of the shaman were primarily physical—drugs and stressful activities to induce altered states. In all probability the first experiences were accidental and then developed into a kind of technology that could be duplicated. It may well be that these early *scientists of the paranormal* were the first to discover and understand the role of the psychic centers (the chakras) and currents (meridians) in the etheric and astral bodies. We will discuss the role of the chakras as "psychic switches" in a later chapter, but it should be noted that the stress-inducing physical techniques of shamanism are today replaced by Mental Focus.

Originally, the shaman felt "called" to his spiritual role, but in latter times, one shaman trained another, sometimes transferring his "Power" by a ritual initiation, and still later the power and role was transferred through inheritance accompanied by ritual.

The Appearance of Religion

The appearance of religion to assume the role of the paranormal facilitator probably started with this inherited role of the shaman justifying his status through recounting the mythic origins of the world, of humanity, and the universe as seen in his out-of-body visions. This was perhaps even more important to the shaman's descendants—whether by family or apprenticeship. Thus the shaman was transformed from "medicine man" to "prophet" and priest, and the tribal myth was codified and transformed into religious doctrine suited for increasingly urban cultures within nation states where religion became a binding, unifying, and ultimately a controlling *political* force forever locked into history by its founding myths.

"Calling Down" the Power

Rituals were codified by function into magical acts controlled by the priesthood. At some point the ritual became more than physical and "called down" spiritually transforming power from higher dimensions identified as the abode of spirits, spirit guides, and then higher spiritual entities, the Gods and Goddesses specializing in particular powers.

The difference between shamanism and religion lies in this codification and established structure of authority derived from a hierarchy of spiritual powers inhabiting a heaven world to which well-behaved humans could be admitted upon death if certain sacraments were performed for them by the priests.

Paranormal Power Denied to Common People

Over many millennia, first shamanism and then even more rigidly—backed with political and economic power—organized religion and its priesthood denied paranormal powers to the "common" people and restricted them to "certified" professionals. Worse, the appearance of the paranormal among the commoners was seen as proof of diabolism and people demonstrating paranormal ability were punished and often executed: so-called "Witches" were burned at the stake.

Faced with torture and execution, people denied any "symptoms" of the paranormal in their own lives.

The Coming of Change

But the program of human evolution and the progression of the zodiacal cycle called for change. And the coming changes were marked by—among others—the 18th century activities of the Swedish scientist and clairvoyant, Emanuel Swedenborg, who wrote more than forty books both scientific and theological in which he recounted his clairvoyant visions of non-physical dimensions and life-after-death.

Swedenborg was a noted clairvoyant. While dining with friends in Gothenburg on July 29, 1759, he suddenly announced that there was an immense fire in Stockholm

(250 miles, or 405 kilometers away) that was threatening his own home. Two hours later he announced that the fire had been contained just three doors from his home. It was two days later that news reports were received confirming every detail of Swedenborg's vision.

Swedenborg's Call to Reform Christianity

But our main interest centers on Easter weekend in April, 1744, when he had a spiritual awakening during which Jesus Christ appeared and appointed him to write the doctrine of a *reformed* Christianity based on the visions that would follow. Swedenborg wrote eighteen books of this new theology describing heaven, hell, angels, demons, and other spirits, and the true nature of the Trinity as existing in one person: the One God Jesus Christ. This was substantially at variance with traditional Christian teachings, and rejected the doctrine of salvation through faith alone but rather claimed that both faith and acts of charity are necessary.

The Church of the New Jerusalem

Swedenborg himself made no effort to found a new Christian Church, but about 15 years after his death in 1772, small groups starting forming to study his books. Among the prominent names over the years were Immanuel Kant, William Blake, Arthur Conan Doyle, Ralph Waldo Emerson, Henry James Sr., Helen Keller. D. T. Suzuki, W. B. Yeats, Jorge Luis Borges, August Strindberg, and Dr. Carl Jung. It was King Carl XIII (the grand master of Swedish Freemasonry) who wrote the unique system of degrees and rituals that become incorporated into the Swedenborgian Church of the New Jerusalem.

Everyman's Potential to see Spiritual Realities

Swedenborg's experience and teaching are grounded in everyman's potential to see spiritual realities that include the role of a hierarchy of spiritual entities. Even though presented within a Christian structure, it was a severe break from the Church's dogmatic intolerance of contact between man and God without the intermediary of its established clergy. But as a famous scientist, Swedenborg's display of paranormal power outside the bounds of the Church was a further step on the path toward individual psychic empowerment.

The Fox House

The Coming of Spiritualism

The advent of the modern renaissance started on March 31, 1848, in the Fox family home in Hydesville, a small town in upper New York State. Shortly after the family moved into this home, there was an outbreak of bangs and rapping on the walls. Of course, many older houses, particularly wood structures, make noises as the seasons change and as the house settles into the ground. And, of course, there are often earth movements—mostly subtle and hardly noticed in themselves but having a cumulative effect on buildings—even in areas not known for earthquakes.

Before the family moved into the home it already had a reputation for being haunted. Even the nearby neighbors admitted to similar phenomena, but what was different about March 31 is that two young Fox sisters thought it would be interesting to ask questions of the rapping, to *which they started getting intelligent answers.* And the phenomenon was not limited to the two girls, Maggie and Kate.

Neighbors were called in to witness the strange goings on and likewise asked questions and received satisfactory answers. Because such a large group soon gathered, the girls and their mother left to sleep elsewhere that first night—and the questions and answers continued—refuting later claims by doubters that it was the girls themselves producing raps by cracking their finger and toe joints and contradicting later "confessions" by one of the girls that it was fakery!

The news of these non-vocal communications spread and soon the news media invaded the countryside. Among them were two people, Colonel Henry Olcott and Helena Blavatsky who later, in 1875, founded the Theosophical Society in New York.

Murder, They Said

More rapping and communications followed, with the rapper claiming to have been murdered in the basement of the home. Bones were indeed found buried under the basement floor and in 1904 a complete human skeleton was found sealed in a basement wall.

This new interest in spirit communication spread from America to Great Britain, and then to Europe, the religion of Spiritualism was born with professional mediums serving as intermediaries between the living and those "on the other side." Famous scientists of the day investigated and some mediums were exposed as frauds while others under close observation produced paranormal phenomena that could not be explained in the purely materialistic terms standard at the time. While spiritualism as a religion older than its new daughter (the Swedenborg church itself was founded in 1787), the new American Spiritualism rapidly became mainstream and even President Lincoln consulted mediums in the White House not merely to contact the spirit of his son Willie but on military matters. The news media of the day had a great time over that!*

> *Fleckless, E. V. *Willie Speaks Out—The Psychic World of Abraham Lincoln*, 1974, Llewellyn.

While Spiritualism was recognized as a phenomenon, it did not become formalized into a religious movement until the early 20th century. As a spiritual movement it was adopted by a number of Quakers, freethinkers, and many reformist-minded people breaking away from established religion because of the churches' failure to fight slavery and advance the cause of women's rights.

The Women's Movement

Women were particularly attracted to the movement for its freethinking environment that provided them one of the first public forums in which women could openly speak to a mixed gender audience, and many became mediums, trance lecturers, and organizers of spiritualist events and séances.

Fundamental to Spiritualism is the belief that spirits of the dead, residing at least temporarily in the spirit world, have the ability and desire to communicate with the still living. Most communication is received through an entranced "medium" during a séance. Spirits continue to evolve in the afterlife and thus may be capable of providing moral and ethical guidance as well information about the purpose of life. There is also a belief in "spirit guides" who may provide both worldly and spiritual guidance to the living, and the dead.

By the 1850s, when a popular song was titled "Spirit Rapping's," Spiritualist phenomena was so widely accepted that afternoon tea parties among the wealthy and fashionable women often included table-turning and tilting.

"Automatic Writing," another method for spirit communication, was popularized by William Stanton Moses, an Anglican clergyman writing in the 1870s. Moses also demonstrated the ability to "channel" spirit energy for healing, and offered further evidence of the power in this spirit energy by levitating a large table simply by touching it.

Parapsychology and Metaphysics

Truly the spirits have always been with us, and equally there has always been interest in the non-material worlds by thoughtful people. Priests and shamans, long before the Fox Sisters and before Swedenborg, were communicating with spirits, and throughout the world there were non-religious groups—sometimes organized into *Secret Initiatory Orders*—studying the larger universe beyond the purely physical world—just as there were scientists probing the heavens above despite repression and persecution by religious authorities .

What was new was the sudden popular awareness of these spiritual dimensions leading to "uncontrolled" research and participation into these areas once the exclusive domain of a special class of people operating within religious institutions.

We forget that it is only a few centuries ago that astronomers were burned at the stake for claiming that the Earth rotated about the Sun, and that Earth was not the center of a Universe existing only for its inhabitants. We forget that it was only a few centuries ago that so-called Witches, otherwise known as herbalists and natural healers, were burned at the stake during the "Dark Ages" when knowledge outside the Church was proscribed.

America & Freedom from Religious Repression

What America brought to the world was not only freedom of religion but freedom _from_ religion that claimed exclusivity of knowledge and the definition of what was "true." March 31, 1848, was truly the beginning of a New Age of spiritual and scientific freedom, and—even just as importantly—the birth of mass communication.

Today, knowledge once hidden away for fear of persecution and misunderstanding is widely available through our schools and universities, books and the Internet, and is freely researched in laboratories and by ordinary people. However, this freedom is increasingly threatened by the demands for sectarian Christian Bible teachings to replace modern secular public education, and for a purely Koran-based teaching (for boys only) in many Islamic countries.

The New Age of Spirit

In all their wide-ranging manifestations, spirit communications are consistently purposeful and empowerment driven. As other-dimensional sources, they can provide insight into the nature of our existence as spiritual beings. They can expand our awareness of ourselves and offer insight into our past, present, and future as evolving souls. At times of adversity, sorrow, and disappointment, they can generate hope and positive expectations. They persistently invite us to acknowledge them as reassuring sources of comfort, knowledge, and power while never imposing themselves upon us.

Spirit resources, like any other, *can* be useful and helpful but it is we who make them so. We have to turn experience into understanding, and understanding into knowledge and practice. *We, individually, have to become active partners in developing and applying new technology to the spiritual opportunity opened for us.*

The Nature of Spiritual Communication

As spiritual beings, each of us is intimately connected to the spirit world. It's a dimension from which we came and to which we will return. It is our home between lifetimes. In each lifetime, our ties to that realm, including our interactions with many entities and with spirits of the departed, offer both enlightenment and power. Through our interactions with the spirit dimension, we have constant access to its limitless powers. We enrich our lives and find solutions to the most difficult of personal problems.

Activating the Spiritual Medium Within

Your best personal medium exists within yourself as an essential part of your being. That medium is your personal link to the spirit realm with its abundance of empowering resources. When you connect to that medium, you will have full access to the spiritual enlightenment you need at the moment and all the critical growth resources required for your spiritual fulfillment.

To interact with the medium within, one of the most effective approaches is the *Medium Activation Lift* that raises your awareness of that medium and connects you to its powers. With that connection, you have full access to all the spiritual resources you need, including those existing in the spirit world.

The Spiritual Medium Activation Lift Program

To begin the Medium Activation Lift, find a quiet place (see later section on the *Astral Room*) and take a few moments to relax and clear your mind of active thought. With eyes closed, visualize the bright core at the center of your being. Let the brightness of that core expand and infuse your whole being with the bright energy and life force that sustains your existence as a soul being.

Visualize the spirit realm as a bright energy source, possibly taking shape as a series of colorful planes of energy. Sense your connection to them and allow yourself to interact with them. You can facilitate that process by visualizing beams of energy connecting you to the energies of the spirit realm. At this stage of the exercise, you may experience your consciousness rising to embrace the spirit realm with its intelligent guides, helpers, growth specialists, and gathering of souls, including certain of the departed and significant others. Certain entities may capture your attention and communicate important messages related to your present concerns or situation.

When this stage of the program runs its course, shift your attention again to the inner medium situated at the innermost core of your being. Listen to the messages emerging from that knowing part of your inner self. At this stage, solutions to pressing problems, such as conflicts and difficult relationships, will often unfold.

Clairvoyance and Trance

Because both the spiritual "medium" and the more contemporary "channeler" often utilize clairvoyance in their practice, we want to explore both in relation to it and accompanying paranormal phenomena. Following our historic formula, we start with the mediumship, and then channeling, but we will also explore "trance" as—to some degree—it is intrinsic to both.

One of the practical difficulties we face both in paranormal research and in writing about it for general understanding is the historic ambiguity of terms. "Clairvoyance" has often been applied indiscriminately to nearly all spiritualist phenomena excepting only the Out-of-Body Experience and Trance Induction. However, one important factor in our discussion is the entire matter of how the clairvoyant faculty is produced and controlled—and modern parapsychological research largely neglects that because the presumption is that all such abilities are purely physical in origin.

The Role of the Medium

The Oxford English Dictionary defines a medium as "a person believed to be in contact with the spirits of the dead and to communicate between the living and the dead."* The role of the medium was seen as an intermediary to bring messages from the spirits to the living present in the séance circle. The medium facilitates communication "between the worlds" by listening to and then relaying conversation.

> *Oxford English Dictionary (3rd on-line version ed.). 2011.

It was common for the medium to enter into a trance, usually aided by the séance group singing hymns, praying out-loud, listening to soothing recorded music in a dimly lit room and sometimes in darkness. For many mediums, the first spirit encountered was that of her "control" who then may *seemingly* enter the medium's body and allow the spirits to speak though her.*

> *It can become cumbersome in writing to always reference to both genders. While the standard grammar accepts the male reference as meaning either gender, because the medium was and is so often female, we are simply going to refer to the medium as of feminine gender from this point forward.

Many times the control was a Native American (Indian) who sometimes produced paranormal phenomena including levitation of objects and other times of the medium's body, apports (objects transported through space from other locations), the materialization of spirits using ectoplasm drawn from the medium's body, and sometimes the voices of spirits speaking through a levitated trumpet.

As Spiritualism "matured" into a religion, it became a matter of record to use descriptive terminology, and we try to clarify the new terms by highlighting them in the following text.

Developing Mediumship

In *How to Develop Mediumship,** Rev. Simeon Stefanidakis defines **"clairvoyance"** as the ability to see, with the inner vision, that which is not perceived by the physical eyes. This can include perception of spirits, auras, energy fields, visions, etc. When a spirit communicator links with a medium he gives the medium some visual image which can be related to the sitter.

> *Stefanidakis, S. *How to Develop Mediumship and Channeling,* 2002, First Spiritual Temple.

How does the medium actually see a spirit? Since a spirit is, by definition, "other-worldly," the medium has to alter her consciousness and focus beyond the physical plane. Yet, such is the power of _imag-in-ation_ (the mind's power to make mental images) that the medium can construct a rudimentary image of her impression that is then completed by the spirit to reflect his or her one-time earthly appearance. Even though we've described it as a process initiated by the medium and ending in a vision, that **"vision"** is what we otherwise call clairvoyance.

Physical Mediumship

A physical medium is a living person able to provide the vital, magnetic energy used by a spirit entity as a **"vehicle"** to act on the physical plane. In addition, some mediums can provide **"ectoplasm"** (an etheric substance) which **"spirit"*** can use for physical manifestation.

> *"Spirit" as a word is itself used somewhat indiscriminately. Without going into all unrelated usage (such as alcoholic spirits, or the symbolic spirit of the thing), "spirit" in the context of Spiritualism primarily relates to:
> (a) When used with a pronoun it means a spirit entity.
> (b) When used without a pronoun it means an abstract but intelligent force.
> (c) When capitalized, and especially if accompanied by a positive adjective like "Great," it refers to "a" or "The" creative power.
> (d) When used as an adjective accompanied by a noun, such as "Spirit World" it generally refers either to the Astral World (or Plane) or to all the non-physical worlds together.
> (e) It can also spirit as "substance" or as a component of a compound such as "ectoplasm" is believed to be.

In a child, if there is a proclivity toward physical mediumship, the signs usually appear around the time of puberty and may include typical poltergeist activity such as unexplained sounds, movements, and strange events taking place in the vicinity. These happenings may intensify as the child matures, but more often they subside and disappear unless encouraged.

"Physical mediumship" involves the manipulation of energies and energy systems by spirits, including loud raps and other noises, voices (sometimes spoken through a trumpet), apports (materialized or transported objects), materialized spirit bodies, or body parts such as hands, and physical levitations. The medium's body is the source of power for such spirit manifestations, combining energy with ectoplasm.

Physical mediumship requires a lot of vital energy, and unless the medium learns how to develop and replenish the physical and etheric sources for it, and how to "budget" its expenditure, she can suffer serious depletion and physical harm. However, there are techniques by which physical phenomena can be supported. Since this type of energy is not fully understood, and has various names, research by each individual should be undertaken to determine that most suitable to her needs. Reference should be made to both quality nutrition and to psychic energies (under many names, but *chi* and *kundalini* probably have the most resources). See recommendations at the end of this chapter.

The Spirit Cabinet

The Spirit Cabinet

Most physical mediumship occurs in a darkened or dimly lit room. Some mediums make use of a "**spirit cabinet,**" essentially a sort of curtained off corner or partially closed closet isolating the seated medium from the group so that her energies could condense and then extrude through the opening. In some rather flamboyant demonstrations there was an actual furniture cabinet designed like a modern steam cabinet to allow the medium's head to protrude, seeming to prove that there were no tricks involved.

"**Ectoplasm**" is only *semi*-physical, composed of etheric and astral substance most commonly believed to primarily originate from the medium's etheric body. In addition, some believe that the medium's ectoplasm can be unknowingly reinforced with energy and substance from other members' present in the room. The actual operation producing forms of ectoplasm may resemble the creation of a "familiar" through magical ritual.

"Mental Mediumship" involves Telepathy and Clairaudience when the medium hears the spirit's message: Clairvoyance when the message is seen, and Clairsentience when the message is felt. Often it was a **"Spirit Guide"** helping the spirit to communicate through the medium. The person receiving the message is called the **"Recipient,"** unless the entire communication (a **"Reading"**) was between the medium and a client then known as the **"Sitter."**

A Spiritualist Church service normally includes the singing of hymns, a lecture on spiritualist philosophy, and the **"Affirmation:"** *We affirm that the precepts of Prophecy and Healing are Divine attributes proven through Mediumship*, ending with a **"Demonstration"** of mediumship through contact with spirits of deceased relatives or friends of those present.

The Spiritual Mediumship Development Circle

A group of people who meet regularly for the purpose of developing mediumship is known as a spirit circle or development circle. There are several reasons why sitting with a group is helpful in developing your mediumship:

- The group provides nurturing and stability in the shared pursuit of developing mediumship.
- The group provides a sharing of support and experience leading towards understanding of both principles and practice.
- The group provides an environment of continuity and discipline.
- The group provides mutual assistance in the development of each others' mediumship.
- The group, when one is available, offers the assistance of an experienced teacher and guide.

Spirit Guides and Controls

Generally in the practice of both mediumship and channeling there have been one or more kinds of guide or "control" on the spirit side assisting the medium in various ways. In the case of mediumship, these are described as follows:

- **Spirit Guide:** Helps teach, guide, and inspire the medium in her development.
- **Spirit Controller:** Protects the medium while working as a channel for spirit by helping control the energy field of the medium, the sitter(s), and any communicating spirit.

- **Spirit Control:** Controls and protects the consciousness of the medium during the condition of trance.

"Direct Voice" involves the creation of a "voice-box" out of the ectoplasm extracted from the medium's body, and probably with contributions from other participants in the séance room. Spirits are enabled to speak through the voice-box to the **"communicants"** in the room.

Direct voice "Evidential" message work is spontaneous: you never know how the message will come out until it begins. This can be difficult, yet—realize—we do it all the time in normal conversation. Even an experienced lecturer or public speaker can be surprised at what comes out, especially in response to questions. As writers, we are often astonished to see some of the things we didn't know we knew—such are the workings of the subconscious mind relating to the needs and questions of the conscious mind when engaged in our work.

Trance Mediumship

For years this was the hallmark of the séance, enabling the spirits to speak through the medium as the medium's personality was put aside to be temporarily replaced by that of the spirit.

The trance is actually an **"*altered-state-of-consciousness*"** either self-induced by the medium or sometimes through **"magnetic passes"** by another person. In the typical *deep* trance, the medium is generally unconscious and unaware of the messages being conveyed through her.

"Trance phenomena" results from an intense focusing of attention—whether through personal effort or as aided in hypnosis—and that it is this *focus* that is the key mechanism of trance induction that results in some *entrainment* of neural networks in the brain.

More often in modern séances the medium enters a light trance and remains conscious of the spirit's communications. It is as if a kind of telepathy is involved wherein the medium's mind responds to the spirit's thoughts, but then the medium's *ego* steps aside to facilitate delivery of the spirit's message. But, it must be acknowledged that because the medium is aware of the spirit's thoughts, she may influence the messages with personal bias or attempt to clarify those that seem confusing.

Three Phases of Spirit Communication

1. The message begins. The spirit communicator links with you through your energy field. At first, the information from the communicator may lack clarity because

the link, initially, may be weak. Pass the information on to your recipient, and the channeling link becomes stronger and additional information is communicated.

2. The link becomes stronger and the message becomes more substantive. When the communicator is satisfied that the message is complete, he will withdraw.

3. The final phase occurs while the communicator withdraws, and the energy fields separate. The message is complete.

The first phase challenges the medium and the communicator to establish a stronger link. Without this, nothing further can really happen. As a developing medium, you have the greater responsibility. The spirit communicator is trying to blend with your energy field and you need to strengthen the link with verbal interaction in order to pass on to the next stage bringing the communicator into a stronger linkage.

Working with Spirit

As a channel for a spirit communicator, you are opening your consciousness to the consciousness of another. The sharing of consciousness with another entity can be as intimate as accepting another presence into your body. There are hazards to consider as well as benefits and shared obligations. And the relationship has to be mutual: you have to know that your personhood is respected and you have to do the same.

In view of the challenges, you need to review why you want to develop mediumship, and what kind of medium you want to be. And how great a part of your life you want to devote to mediumship. As in all things, balance is vital to health and to a meaningful and fulfilling life. Mediumship, in particular, cannot go on 24 hours a day and seven days a week.

In addition, the primary way mediumship functions is through your spirit guide: another consciousness to know and respect in a genuine working relationship. As your guide he (or she—if indeed gender continues in the spirit world) is involved in your mediumistic development. Meditate and become sensitive to his interests. Ask questions. Set forth your goals and find out his.

Your Journal

As a student (and you are always a student so long as you want to grow and develop particular abilities—no matter what they are), you *must* write things down. The process of journaling is also the process of "objectifying" to bring all the elements of your consciousness together to focus on the matter at hand. Make notes of your studies, the books you read, the classes and lectures you attend, the lessons learned, the opinions and questions you have. Record your goals and your feelings about them; record the questions you ask and the answers you receive; record your "experiments" and practice sessions and what you learn; if you become a "professional" serving others, record every session and what was accomplished.

Even as a professional, *never stop being a student!* As a professional you have even greater opportunities and obligations to learn. Journaling, through its recording and objectifying functions, is your life-long learning tool and companion. If you are computer literate (and, if not, *learn* and make it a natural extension of your mind and body), develop your own journal format and open that file several times daily.

Women Activists

Particularly in the earlier years, spiritualism attracted many women, and many mediums were women thus placed in a key position of responsibility and authority unusual at that historic period.

Many women attracted by this were also involved in such matters of social justice as the ending of slavery and child abuse in the workplace, and working for women's rights *and* the right to vote. Spiritualism offered women a platform from which they spoke out in passionate speeches on the abolition of slavery and concern for the entrance of former slaves into the mainstream; on the quality of education for all; on the terrible toll of alcohol abuse; and the absolute need for women to have political and economic equality with men.

Spiritualism played a powerful role in American history in the last half of the 19th century and early decades of the 20th.

The Nature of Spirit Mediumship and Spirit Channeling

In the 20th century, the nature of spiritual communication developed into two basic scenarios (not counting the roles in religious and magical rituals, and personal direct contact through meditation practices):

1. The Spiritualist medium as a particular kind of "sensitive" able to speak with spirits (and sometimes with other entities) and then communicate their messages to the intended recipients—whether an individual client or an assembled group. The medium may or may not go into a deep or light trance in order to facilitate this communication, but it still needs to be said that the communication is mostly "personal" rather than a "universal" message for all humanity.

2. Channeling. The trance state is as fundamental as it was in early Spiritualism, but the communication comes through the entranced "channel" from high-

er entities than the recently departed and is generally treated as "knowledge" intended for a wide or even universal audience.

3. Three characteristics distinguish Spiritualist Communication and Channeling:

    a. In Spiritualism the facilitator is called a "medium;" In Channeling the facilitator is called a "channel."

    b. In modern Spiritualism, the facilitator may or may not go into trance, and rarely goes into a truly deep trance; In Channeling a very deep trance is apparently necessary during which a specific spirit "possesses" the facilitator and talks through him. Alternatively, the channeler goes out-of-body to contact the teaching entity.

    c. In Spiritualism, the communication is usually personal between one who is living and one who is deceased; In Channeling, the communication is often between a group of seekers and a higher entity giving advanced spiritual knowledge. If the facilitator is in deep trance, an interrogator is necessary to organize questions being asked and then to record and organize the answers.

Channeling and mediumship—whether in trance or not—require a focusing of consciousness toward a specific target. The target could be a deceased person by name, or an entity by name, or a particular "vibrational frequency" or level of consciousness. It has been described as connecting through an "information network" to the target 1) by his correct address or 2) by asking a question and/or describing the information desired. In the first case you reach the person named, in the second you reach a source for the information desired.

The Use of Self-Determination

Today we largely use Self-Hypnosis to focus consciousness towards the desired target, but here we simply point the way to self-determination—you're determined to act to engage your consciousness with those of the Spirit Realm ready to work with you. We offer two scripts—one for Mediumship and one for Channeling.

INTERACTION WITH SPIRIT GUIDES PROCEDURE

This script is based on the two-fold concept that the spirit dimension exists and that you, as a spirit being, can interact with it. It recognizes that you are more than mind and body, you are also spirit. Without the spirit, the mind and body would not exist.

As a soul, your existence is forever—from everlasting to everlasting. While all things physical have a beginning and therefore an end, you as a soul existed forever before your first lifetime and will exist forever beyond your last. Within that endless spectrum, you are inextricably linked to the spirit realm. You came from that realm, and you will return to it. Rather than a distant realm, it is a non-physical dimension of power available to you at any moment. As a soul, you are integrally connected to it.

Through interactions with that dimension, you become increasingly empowered to fulfill the basic purpose of your existence in this physical realm—to learn and grow while also helping others to do the same. This script is designed to promote empowering interactions with those spirit guides ready to help you fulfill that all-important purpose.

(This script makes no presumptions about the form your Spirit Guide may assume in your consciousness, and neither should you. Spirit is multi-dimensional and non-dimensional. Your Guide will manifest as most beneficial to your needs: as a wise person, a loving animal, an angelic being, or a mere presences. You may experience your guide in vision, as a voice, or in just knowing. There may be dialogue or there may just be a flash of knowledge. Spirit knows no boundaries and your spirit, too, is without bounds.)

Step 1. Goal Statement. Begin the script by stating in your own words your goal of interacting with spirit guides. You may wish to include other specific goals related to that interaction, such as solving a particular personal problem, achieving career success, building self-esteem, or coping with a difficult life situation.

Step 2. Focused Attention & Receptivity. Induce a state of focused attention and receptivity to suggestion through deep relaxation or the drowsy state preceding sleep, and self-hypnosis or meditation.

Step 3. Self-Empowerment Dialogue: While in the deeply receptive state, initiate positive self-dialogue related to your stated goal. Here are a few examples:

I am a more than mind and body, I am also spirit—the essential essence of my existence.

As a spirit being, I am intimately connected to the spirit realm and its wealth of empowerment resources.

I am at this moment empowered to engage the spirit realm and interact with spirit guides that make up that bright dimension.

My interactions with the spirit realm are essential to my growth as an evolving soul.

Step 4. Visualization. As you remain in the deeply focused and receptive state, visualize a beam of light connecting you to the spirit realm as a glowing dimension of unparalleled beauty. Rather than some distant, untouchable realm, think of it as spiritually present with spirit guides in clear view.

Step 5. Affirmation. Affirm your resolve to engage in on-going interaction with your personal spirit guides as sources of enlightenment, support, and fulfillment. As you continue the interaction, you can again state your personal goals and ask the support of spirit guides in achieving them. (At this step, a particular guide will sometimes come forward, and its name will become known.)

Step 6. Post-script Cue. Affirm that by simply visualizing the bright beam of light connecting you to the spirit dimension you can instantly generate an interaction with your spirit guide(s) and activate the full empowering effects of this script.

Step 7. Exit and Conclusion. End the script by giving yourself permission to exit the trance or other receptive state. Take as long as you need to reflect on the experience and its empowering relevance.

The script now complete, reaffirm in your own words the spiritual essence of your existence and the supremacy of the spiritual over the physical. Express your appreciation of the guiding presence you came to know through this script. Take time to enjoy that presence as a source of comfort, power, and joy. Record it in your Journal.

DEVELOPING YOUR MEDIUMISTIC POTENTIALS

The mediumistic potential is the capacity to directly communicate with entities in the spirit realm. The skilled medium is anyone who has developed that potential and applies it, communicating, for example, with a departed relative or friend, or—at another level—interacting with highly advanced spirit beings who can be important sources of spiritual enlightenment and knowledge.

This script is based on the premise that the mediumistic potential exists to some degree in everyone. The best medium is, in fact, already a part of your innermost self. Through this script, that personal medium can become an invaluable source of spiritual insight and personal power. These mediumistic communications will promote inner balance and attunement and inspire your higher spiritual growth.

Here's the script:

Step 1. Goal Statement. Formulate your goal of developing your mediumistic potentials and using them to empower your life. In stating your goal, you may wish to specify the discovery of advanced spirit teachers who will facilitate your mediumistic development.

Step 2. Focused Attention and Receptivity. Induce a state of focused attention and receptivity to suggestion through deep relaxation or the drowsy state preceding sleep, and follow with either self-hypnosis or meditation.

Step 3. Self-Empowerment Dialogue. While in the deeply focused and receptive state, initiate positive self-dialogue related to the development and application of your mediumistic potentials. Here are a few examples:

I am a spiritual being, and my destiny is spiritual evolvement.

By interacting with the spirit dimension, I am fulfilling that destiny and bringing deeper meaning into my life.

By developing my mediumistic powers, I am becoming empowered to communicate and interact with spirit entities existing in the spirit dimension.

My mediumistic interactions are critical to my understanding of myself and my destiny.

I am committed to using my mediumistic powers to accelerate my spiritual evolvement while contributing to the greater good.

Step 4. Visualization. Visualize a gateway to the spirit realm and see yourself open it to reveal a dimension of indescribable beauty. Sense peace and harmony flowing from there to permeate your whole being. See the presence of others beyond the gate and the bright glow enveloping them. You may recognize certain departed loved ones, friends, and familiar spirit guides who have been with you in the past. Give yourself permission to communicate and interact with them. Notice that beings on the other side can come and go through the gateway to interact with souls on this side. Clearly, it's a spiritual gateway of interaction, not separation. You too can briefly slip through that gate to interact with the spirit realm. Adding to the beauty of the spirit realm is the presence of animals and plant life—could it be heaven without them? To conclude this step, see yourself closing the gateway, thus ending this mediumistic interaction with the other side.

Step 5. Affirmation. Affirm your strong commitment to use your mediumistic powers to gain knowledge of spiritual relevance and use it as needed to promote your spiritual evolvement while contributing to the higher good.

Step 6. Post-script Cue. Give yourself the post-script cue that you can at any moment activate your mediumistic powers by simply visualizing the gateway to the spirit realm and yourself opening it.

Step 7. Exit and Conclusion. Conclude this script by giving yourself permission to exit the trance or other receptive state. Reflect on the information gained during the experience and your sense of spiritual empowerment. Record your experience.

This script opens an exciting gateway to the spirit realm as an unlimited source of power and knowledge. Through repeated practice you will fine tune your ability to use your mediumistic powers. You will discover ways of applying them at will to increase your understanding of your present and future existence. You will discover that the other side is a rich dimension of continuing growth and fulfillment. You will see your present life as filled with wondrous opportunities for growth and fulfillment. You will see death, not as a sad ending, but as a marvelous beginning in another dimension filled with limitless possibilities.

Tools and Techniques

Although we can interact with the spirit realm purely through the medium within, we also have a wide range of tools and techniques to access that realm's abundant growth resources. Equipped with spiritual insight through such programs as the séance, table tipping, and other mediumistic approaches, we can experience profound spiritual interactions that energize us with new insight and growth potential. The following tools and techniques of spiritual empowerment can facilitate that all-important process.

The Table Tapping (or Tipping) Strategy

Table tapping is an excellent approach to activate the medium existing within oneself. Once a mediumistic connection is established, the possibilities reach far beyond the constricted information provided by the taps of the table.

This technique is based on the concept that a tangible object can be used as an extension of the human energy system to "tap into" sources of spiritual knowledge and power. Typically, a group of four persons is seated around the table with their fingertips (the body's antennae) resting lightly upon the table top. Following a brief meditation in which spirit sources are invited to communicate through the table, the group with hands continuing to rest on the table awaits a signal of a spirit presence.

Within moments, the table will typically signal a presence, first by subtle vibrations followed by increased movement and finally by the tilting of one side of the table as the group's hands continue to rest upon it. With the table in the tilted position, a member of the group invites the table to respond to the group's questions by tapping once upon the floor to signify a "yes" response, twice to signify "no," and thrice to signal the unavailability of a "yes" or "no" answer. The table then typically resumes a rest position and awaits questions from the group. A permissive, non-demanding approach by the group throughout the program is essential to the success of the exercise.

Questions can range from the nature of the spirit realm to personal issues and concerns. They can include questions regarding future events, distant happenings, financial matters, career concerns, and the well-being of the departed. While departed souls are not "called up" or summoned, they sometimes do communicate through the table if they wish. Sometimes a departed friend or relative will communicate personally with a member of the group.

To end the table tilting session, the participants, with hands still resting upon the table, give thanks for the opportunity to interact with the spirit realm and for the spirit communications that emerged during the sessions.

Here are a few other applications of table tipping:

Table Tipping Applications

- To promote attunement to the spirit realm.
- To communicate with spiritual guides.
- To relate information concerning past lives, including the relevance of past-life experiences to the present.
- To gain important information related to lost articles.
- To relate information on personal concerns and relationships.
- To relate information about health issues, including physical fitness and longevity,
- To relate information on financial affairs, investments and financial management.
- To communicate with the departed and allow them to communicate with us.
- To predict future happenings and events of both personal and global relevance.
- To identify career opportunities and gain information related to career success.

The Séance

The Séance is defined as a group activity opening communications with a spirit source, or with the departed, spirit guides and teachers. The séance group consists of at least three people seated around a table in a room free of distractions, typically with subdued lighting. (See later reference to your Astral Room) Any of the group can serve as the group's contact with the spirit realm, or any can exercise the "medium within" for the mediumistic potential exists in everyone.

To initiate the mediumistic interaction, the group together invites sources from the spirit realm to manifest their presence and communicate with the group. A focused state of receptiveness is then formed by the group by clearing the mind and with eyes closed, mentally expressing openness to impressions and specific messages of spiritual origin.

Once contact is established, mediumistic interactions with spirit beings are welcomed. The typical séance experience will include both informational and emotional exchanges, many of which can have significant empowering effects. Interactions with departed friends, family members, and personal spirit guides are common. Spontaneity within the group facilitates the interaction and adds to the relevance of the experience.

To end the séance, members of the group join hands and give thanks for their interactions with the spirit realms. Members then share their experiences and impressions, and the entire group explores their empowering possibilities.

The modern séance, which recognizes the medium existing in everyone, is based on the synergistic concept that several mediums working together are more effective than one medium working alone. The effect of working together can overcome our personal limitations and tear down the walls that too often separate us from the other side.

Ouija and Pendulum: Spirit Communication for just One or Two

Other familiar tools besides the séance and table tapping that may be used include the Ouija Board accommodating two people and the Pendulum easily used by a single person. As always, what is important in all practice and research is a certain basic discipline—even when, as is often the situation, people at first engage with psychic tools for personal and party entertainment. To get results, here is a reminder of the basic rules of engagement:

Rules of Engagement: Your Tools & Actions

1. Respect. Every tool is an extension of your whole physical and energetic body and you will always get better results through respect for the equipment.
2. Planning. Know what you need to do in the way of preparation, including:
   a. Physical relaxation gets rid of the tension that can stand between you and the subconscious and other consciousness.

b. Preliminary ritual sets the stage. It can be as formal or informal as you desire: it can be just a prayer or simply a statement of your intention.

c. Frame your questions in writing. It really is only when you put something on paper that it starts the process of physical manifestation.

3. Engage. Ask your questions and work with the chosen tool.

4. Gratitude. Always express appreciation for the results. For every established tool or technique, there is a psychic entity formed that has grown with the practice and that works with your subconscious mind. Give it respect and appreciation.

5. Record your results. Even if your participation was entertaining, write down the answers to your questions accompanied by any observations and feelings.

6. Conclude. Return your tools to their container and place. Again, give them respect and protect them from casual handling.

The Automatic Writing Strategy

This is a well recognized method of spirit and psychic communication which may be experienced as a direct communication from a deceased person's spirit, or sometimes a higher spirit channeling through the writer, or as a communication from the personal subconscious. In most cases it starts as a kind of involuntary process where the writer is unaware of the communication until it is completed.

Automatic writing is based on two important concepts: first, information existing in the subconscious regions of the mind persistently seeks manifestation in conscious awareness; and second, indirect channels, including automatic writing, can activate inner psychic faculties and access hidden sources of knowledge when more direct channels are either unavailable, or if available, are less efficient.

Automatic writing is a psychic accessing strategy in which spontaneous or involuntary writing is used to bring forth information from the subconscious mind. The technique is believed by some to tap into other sources of knowledge as well, including those of higher planes. Usually, the only materials required are a writing pen and paper. The pen is held in the writing position with the point resting lightly on the writing surface, as meaningful written messages are permitted to unfold.

A brief relaxation and mental-clearing exercise, in which physical tension is released and active thought is minimized or banished altogether, can increase the effectiveness of automatic writing.

The initial products in automatic writing are often illegible; but once meaningful writing emerges, the technique can provide important messages about the past, present, and future. Automatic writing can consist of a single but significant word, sentence, or phrase; and occasionally the technique will produce a drawing or a meaningful symbol. Although the technique often is used in an open-ended fashion, as a completely spontaneous expression of the self, it can be used to gather answers to specific questions or to find solutions to particular problems. At advanced levels, it can access highly significant sources of psychic knowledge.

Because of its capacity to tap into the psychic mind and channel messages, automatic writing, as a psychic accessing tool, has almost unlimited applications. Among them is precognition that can tap into the future to provide information needed for planning and decision making. At the advanced level of this technique's clairvoyant and precognitive applications, no reality can escape the penetrating probe of the psychic pen.

As already noted, automatic writing as a psychic empowerment procedure is more effective when preceded by a brief period of meditation with affirmations designed to prepare oneself for the exercise and to explore the psychic sources of knowledge.

When automatic writing is used to discover a specific answer, the question is usually written at the top of the page before beginning the process.

The effectiveness of automatic writing as a psychic tool is directly related to the spontaneity of the process. Any conscious intent to influence the process can negate its psychic significance. With conscious functions subdued and the physical body sufficiently relaxed, our psychic channels can be activated, and the sources of psychic insight can be accessed through this empowering technique.

One of the most important empowering applications of automatic writing is its therapeutic role in probing the subconscious for strivings, motives, and conflicts buried within the self. Knowledge and insight can be brought forth as a new surge of personal awareness and power.

A major advantage of automatic writing over other psychic accessing strategies concerns the nature of the information the procedure can produce. The information yielded by some psychic tools is highly constricted, and in some instances limited to simple "yes" or "no" responses. Automatic writing, on the other hand, can address such concerns as what, when, where, why, and how. At its most advanced level, automatic writing is limited only by our willingness to yield to our subconscious faculties, and by the capacity of written language to communicate. Achieving that optimal level requires skill in consciously surrendering to the inner, knowing part of the self and allowing its written expression.

Because it is not subject to the screening and suppressive functions of consciousness, automatic writing, once mastered, offers a direct line to the vast powers of the subconscious mind. The super-intelligent part of our inner self is accessed and liberated, resulting in a full and free expression of our inner powers.

Automatic writing can overcome the language barriers that often thwart inner communication. Among its major functions is the translation of subconscious images into a meaningful conscious reality: the written word. Imagery is the native language of the sub-conscious mind, and as such, it is the most powerful language known. Imagery can convey an almost unlimited range of emotions and knowledge. Incipient imagery has been the embryo of major scientific inventions, new discoveries, and even global change. Seminal imagery can provide us with a challenging vision of our highest destiny, and empower us to achieve our loftiest goals. Through imagery we can get a glimpse of the vast regions of our inner world of awareness and stored experience. Automatic writing can tap into that inner powerhouse to permit direct, undisguised written expressions of empowering insight.

Automatic writing can enrich our psychic faculties and expand our capacity to actively communicate and interact with the inner self. Inner psychic communication channels—dreams, intuitions, and psychic impressions—can be supplemented and clarified. Many psychic communications occur in disguised or symbolic forms that require a concentrated effort to glean the essential substance of the message. Automatic writing is a powerful tool for disrobing the disguised figure of psychic communication. An impression of a rose can symbolize a developing romantic relationship; whereas a psychic impression of a whirlpool can represent a social relationship spinning out of control and overwhelming us. Automatic writing can be applied to glean the true meaning of these symbols from among the many possibilities.

Aside from its complementary role in facilitating psychic processes, automatic writing can function independently of other psychic channels. It can directly probe the future, activate repressed faculties, initiate empowering dialogue, and generate new psychic knowledge and understanding. In its ultimate form, automatic writing can connect us to the central core of our existence; it can channel universal wisdom and manifest it materially as a visual, written message.

Any skill that unleashes our capacity for self-expression and discovery is essentially self-empowering. Automatic writing is valued as a psychic empowerment tool because it achieves that important goal. All the references to accessing the psychic faculties apply equally and more famously to Automatic Writing's use in Spirit Communication.

In addition, various books have been written, or claimed to have been written, while the authors were in trance with their hands guided by spiritual entities. Among the more famous are the writings of the American Andrew Jackson Davis, including *The Principles of Nature, Her Divine Revelations, and a Voice to Mankind* published in

1847. Another is the "New Bible," *Oahspe, by* John Ballou Newbrough, published in 1882 and reported to have been written on a typewriter at enormous speeds.

While perhaps not the same as Automatic Writing, the receipt of information while in a trance state is, at least, similar. Two of the most important writers of dictated material are Alice Bailey and H. B. Blavatsky. Perhaps the most famous contemporary work claimed to have been dictated by an inner voice is *The Course in Miracles* published in 1976 with sales of over two million copies.

Prophets as Channels of God

It's easy to overlook the role that spirit communication has had in all the major religions. We tend to think that there was something special about the past that can't be duplicated in the present—and perhaps that is true. Nevertheless, it was human beings who received—*channeled*—the sacred teachings that are the foundation of at least the three major religions of the West and the major philosophies of India and China.

Subsequent teachers—who were also prophets—are within the range of historic recording, but they themselves credited their own messages to divine sources—either to God or to Archangels and spiritual intermediaries.

Why only in the distant past?

One answer is that our modern times are filled with distraction, with interference, and with "over-load" making psychic and spiritual communication more difficult. Another answer as that instead of turning within for guidance, we look to external experts and authorities for answers. Another answer is that we commonly "lack faith" that such direct experience is possible for people who have been conditioned to not only ignore the divinity within but to deny it. God is beyond, and even those who believe in a personal intermediary see that being as likewise distant. People within religious practice are taught to *worship* rather than *communicate*. Even prayer is seen as impersonal—like the purchase of a lottery ticket that might be a winner, but we all know that's unlikely.

Spirits are a step away, on the "other side," and other beings—prophets, angels, archangels, etc.—are still more steps away, but there is no barrier between living people and the spiritual realities of this "other side."

Perhaps, like spirits of your loved ones, they are only waiting for you to reach toward them to make contact.

The Emergence of Popular Metaphysics

Coincidental with the growing popularity of spiritualism among the middle and upper educated classes in America was the emergence of Theosophy, Rosicrucian groups, New Thought, and other occult, metaphysical, and philosophical movements— all characterized by open gender participation and belief in direct access to the spiritual dimensions, communication with spiritual guides and teachers, paranormal powers and healing, and the legitimacy of divinatory practices.

One of the early proponents of New Thought was Phineas Parkhurst Quimby who wrote and taught that physical illness originates from false beliefs in the individual's mind. His work laid the foundation for such movements as Divine Science, Christian Science, Unity, Religious Science, and many more. He believed disease is an error in the mind and could be corrected by the understanding of the right relation between the divine and the human.

Quimby taught that 1) Beliefs are fundamental to the life we live, and to our happiness, or the lack of it; 2) Beliefs can be changed, and Life responds to our changed beliefs; 3) We exist within the One Spirit, and are forever in its Presence; 4) We have access to the One through prayer and intention.

He was joined by a Swedenborgian minister and healer, Warren Felt Evans, explaining the healing process in terms of Swedenborgian doctrines of the Mind/Body relationship and the important role of "correspondences"* (natural but inner connections) between the physical, spiritual, and divine worlds. His first book, *The Mental Cure*, published in 1869, developed a thoroughly consistent philosophy of mental healing at the core of the New Thought movement.

> *Correspondences are based on similarities between "things" which may be based on numerous factors from appearances to numerical relations to color, smell, taste, astrological signs, placements on the Kabalistic Tree of Life, etc. From simple to sophisticated, from natural to esoteric, from earthly to heavenly from inner to outer, the logic is that if one thing is like another, they will share in some kind of inner energy. Thus, an herb that resembles the male sexual organ may be a sexual enhancer of some sort. Words in Hebrew with identical numerical values are identical in other ways. Anything white suggests purity, hence cleanliness, health, innocence, virginity; while anything black suggests things hidden, hence secrets, poisons, evil, perversion, and so on. Such similarities must be used only as "starting points" to explore the real meanings within a particular situation. It's a tool for the imagination to draw from the subconscious to the conscious.

Mesmerism, the Scientific Study of Hypnotism, and Modern Self-Hypnosis

All life, and the phenomena of life, originates in Consciousness. Over time, in the process of evolution and then in the advent of humanity, a split developed between what we now experience as the Conscious Mind and the Subconscious Mind. With the conscious mind we connect to the outer world; with the subconscious mind we connect to the inner world, and then through the subconscious with the Collective Unconscious and Universal Consciousness in a two-way communication.

We think as a conscious mind, and we feel and dream as a subconscious mind. But, more than that by far, the subconscious mind is a hidden doorway into the Unconscious that is largely closed to conscious awareness. While always accessible to us through dreams, meditation and shamanic practices, it was the development of hypnosis that brought realization that access to the subconscious mind was voluntary and controllable. The door to other worlds slowly began to open.

Franz Anton Mesmer (1734–1815) developed the use of hypnosis to induce trances enabling people to contact spirits, communicate with spirit entities, and to demonstrate clairvoyance. While Mesmer's theories of animal magnetism and magnetic fluids were largely disproved, it was one of his students, the Abbe Faria, who pioneered the scientific study of hypnotism and in 1814 concluded that hypnosis worked purely by the power of suggestion and "autosuggestion" (self-hypnosis) and that everything takes place in the imagination of the subject.

Swedenborg had claimed to communicate with spirits while awake (not through dreams or a trance state) and described the spirit world as multi-dimensional and stated that spirits are intermediaries for communications between God and humans.

An American combining the methods of Swedenborg and Mesmer was Andrew Jackson Davis, clairvoyant, healer, and hypnotist. His *Hamonial Philosophy* is a concise exposition of the broad spiritualist beliefs of the early 19th century.

All of these developments—from Swedenborg through the birth of Spiritualism and the attendant psychic phenomena, the discovery of Self-Hypnosis and the practices of Mental Healing, the popularizing of Esotericism and Eastern Philosophy, etc., on to the 20th century scientific studies of the paranormal led like an arrow fired from a cross bow to today's understanding of Clairvoyance (and other paranormal powers) as natural to the ordinary human being and readily accessible through Mind Training, Discipline and Focused Attention.

As Swedenborg personally experienced, clairvoyance was not restricted to Christian clergy under papal authority. The practice of Mesmerism and then of hypnosis brought more experience of trance-induced clairvoyance. With the coming of Spiritualism in the early 19th century, the "medium" entered into a self-induced trance state to communicate with spirits, who in turn delivered messages, clairvoyant visions and various psychic phenomena.

As the public interest in Spiritualism and New Thought increased in the late 19th century, the spread of Esotericism also developed—particularly in relation to Theosophy and Eastern practices of yoga, meditation, and the teachings of advanced spiritual guides variously called "the Masters," "Mahatmas," and "Inner Plane Adepti."

The writings of H. P. Blavatsky and Alice Bailey are channeled from these advanced guides. Other writers in the same period: Rudolph Steiner, Annie Besant, C. W. Leadbeater, Dion Fortune, among others, combine those teachings with their own direct communications and clairvoyance. Leadbeater's clairvoyant-based writings on the aura, the astral world, the inner side of ritual, the amazing views of atoms and sub-atomic particles presented in "Occult Chemistry" (written more than 100 years ago and being confirmed in today's quantum physics), all remain classics well worth serious study.

Again, in this same exciting period of the late 19th century we had a public appearance of Masonic and Magical Orders teaching the nature of the inner worlds, the inner nature of the human person and various methods for direct study through personal empowerment. The Masonic Orders were also concerned with ethical behavior, honest business practices, and political ideals well represented in the actions of America's "founding fathers," many of them including President Washington were Masons. The ethical influence of Masonry continues to this day through lodges in every city.

There are numerous books bringing these teachings of the Golden Dawn, Aurum Solis, and other orders by Israel Regardie, Chic and Tabatha Cicero, Denning and Phillips, Donald Tyson, Donald Michael Kraig, Jean-Louis de Biasi, Dion Fortune, and many, many, many others providing a solid intellectual foundation for understanding and *working with* the tools and techniques of growth and transformation.

Along with the teachings of Mental and Spiritual Healers, Christian Science, Unity and Psychic Science, more people were experiencing degrees of inner vision through practices of guided meditation, and personal practices of spirit contact through table tipping, the Ouija Board, Automatic Writing and various practices of divination.

With the coming of the 20th century and new turns in the direction of psychology and physics toward deeper understanding of the Subconscious Mind and sub-atomic matter and energy, the scientific study of the paranormal moved from superficial physical interpretations to genuine metaphysics. Non-physical dimensions took on supra-physical reality in which the "spirit world" was only a part of a still larger picture of a

Greater Universe in which the human "soul" played a much different role than previously believed.

The Age of Enlightenment is for Everyone!

But like everything in life, effort, know-how, and self-discipline are necessary to "Open the Doors to Opportunity." On the other side there may be fields for exploration and self-discovery. Or there may be such sources called "the Akashic Records" and the "Collective Unconsciousness" where everything there has ever been is recorded. Or there may be advanced spiritual beings with names like St. Germain, Djwhal Khul and Kuthumi, or others called Ascended Masters and Secret Chiefs, Gods and Goddesses, Angels, Space Aliens, and one's own Higher Self or Holy Guardian Angel.

The "Key" to Successful Channeling

The "Key" to successful and safe channeling is to be specific about your target and then focus on it as you proceed through meditation, self-hypnosis, or even as you are walking, listening to relaxing music, or just reading and studying. "Trance" is something that can be deep after you have learned more, or it can be light as when you just lose awareness of anything external to your internal search. Focus your awareness and be receptive only within that targeted area.

There are additional factors to successful and safe spirit communication we will discuss later, but do remember the importance of this particular Key—that of focus on a specific target or targets involving both an entity and a subject. The Spirit World, also known as the Astral World, is no place for beginners to wander idly about like stoned-out hippies on San Francisco's Folsom Street. Later, with knowledge and experience, exploration is to be encouraged—but not yet!

Where Do Spirits Live?

The response: "Right next door" may be true, but it's also wrong. When we say that we live in a *multi-dimensional universe* we are moving beyond the confines of the 3-dimensional physical universe in which things can be measured, weighed, and defined in universally accepted physical terms.

But when we say "right next door" speaking of non-physical spirits and psychic phenomena, all the satisfactory terminology used to describe physical phenomena is turned upside down and sideways and replaced. "Next door" normally signifies closeness in physical space and time which have no place in the higher planes of the Greater Universe levels of consciousness.

Access to "Other Worlds" is entirely through your Own Consciousness

When you open the doors to "other worlds" their access is entirely through your own consciousness, which you ultimately share with every being in the universe. The real spirit is as close to you as an image from your own imagination. But what is in your imagination is personal to you, while the real spirit moves from dimensions of the Unconscious through your subconsciousness before manifesting in your own conscious mind.

This should raise a very BIG question for you. If the real spirit comes to you through your subconscious mind, where do the physical phenomena of the séance room come from? As with the ectoplasm emitted from your etheric body to facilitate physical manifestations comes from you so does all the physical phenomena of the séance, of channeling, and all paranormal phenomena including poltergeist activity, psychic or spiritual healing, and more.

What this ultimately means is that YOU HAVE THE POWER but you don't have the knowledge to produce, control, and skillfully to intentionally use that power for healing and other applications until you development it.

And, that's our goal through all the books we write and the lessons we teach—to provide more and more knowledge, but it's up to each of us—your authors included—to learn how to develop the ability to raise that power at will, to see the power in the greater universe, and to skillfully apply that power to good cause.

Clairvoyance and Empowerment

It isn't a matter of "seeing is believing" but of "seeing before acting!" All seeing beyond the physical dimension is clairvoyance. All the tools and methods of divination, all the communications and visions of the medium and the channel, all the alterations of consciousness achieved by shamans and priests, and everything we do in the paranormal lab is directed toward developing higher and higher levels of clairvoyance operating in increasingly wider and higher dimensions so we *see* better and act intelligently. The point is that we must learn to "clear see" in order to best apply the power. What can a surgeon skillfully do without the benefit of an X-ray or MRI to see inside the body? What can the "pilot" of a drone aircraft do without the benefit of satellite guidance and radar systems to see and focus on the target? What can the medical analyst say about your blood sample unless he can see the tiny cells through his microscope?

That ability to see is clairvoyance. While we still may use many tools (as in forms of divination and scrying) to enable our clairvoyance, increasingly we will know that "psychic power" is a blending of mental and astral partially functioning through the human brain. We will experience it consciously as a mental power and be able to exercise our clairvoyance through our mind.

Before we are able to do that, we have to undertake some training exercises in visualization and memory work.

Illusion is present Reality

The Buddha taught that all was illusion, but that illusion is also the present reality that we know. It is a two-way street between the Physical and Astral Plane—from the astral to the physical and from the physical to the astral. What you imagine is in the astral and what you visualize is in the astral. They are almost the same: to "imagine" is to create a mental image in astral substance; to visualize is also to create a mental image in the astral. The difference is that the imagination is mainly spontaneous and creative while visualization is a purposeful creating reinforced with memorization.

The Astral World where Spirits Live

The astral world is where spirits live, and is more than right next door because it is truly in your mind, but also beyond your mind because it is part of the Greater Universe that is all inclusive. The astral images that you create are part of the astral world, but they are also *your* astral images and like with a computer "firewall" you can control who enters into your astral room.

Procedure for Establishing Your Astral Room and Work Place

And it is here, in your astral room that your divinatory, your mediumistic, your magical and your spiritual activities take place. It is the place of your clairvoyance, and your paranormal actions. It is your psychic lab and workshop.

Note, it's your astral room and only you can create it. And here's how.*

> *Some of the wording and the ideas that follow are developed from Donald Tyson's excellent *Scrying for Beginners—Tapping into the Supersensory Powers of Your Subconscious*, 1997, Llewellyn.

Always remember that an astral room is not limited by space, and yet your room is centered in your space. The Greater Universe is infinite in all directions and—as a result—its center is everywhere and anywhere you want it. But because you, yourself, are anchored in your physical body, the center of your astral room is your center. It's a geometric center and its boundaries are limitless but nevertheless defined by you so that control access to your room.

We start with establishing the infinite extension and the place of the geometric center:

1. Standing, or sitting in what is or will be your work room, extend your arms straight out from the sides and know that a straight line continues from each hand to the "infinite no-ends" of the universe.

2. From the point in your body where that line changes from left to right, see a vertical line extend up through your head and down through your feet to the infinite no-ends of the universe.

3. From that same point in your body see a line extending forward and another backward to the infinite no-ends of the universe.

Let those three infinite lines become three infinite planes and where they intersect at the center of your body you will visualize a globe of white, pulsing light becoming larger and larger to become infinite, but within that infinite globe is your personal globe just comfortably enclosing your work room. See this personal globe become a translucent silvery demarcation of your personal space from infinite space, a demarcation of your consciousness from the universal consciousness, a demarcation of your spirit from the infinite Holy Spirit. This is the space you control, into which you can admit spiritual entities as you wish, but not those whose intentions are out of harmony with yours.

The Declaration of Intent to Establish

Say these words:

> By my act of will I establish this sacred space.
> The Light of Spirit creates it.
> The Fire of Spirit surrounds it.
> The Air of Spirit expands it.
> The Water of Spirit cleanses it
> The Earth of Spirit sustains it.

Within this silvery globe are the astral reflections of your physical room, furniture and tools. It is now your job to examine the walls, ceiling, and floor of the room and each one of the objects and commit their feature to your memory. Then close your eyes and create them in your visual memory. One by one, check and verify the accuracy of your vision, and repeat until you can knowingly see only the astral reproductions within which the physical ones are mere shadows.

Next you should choose a scent, either of incense or an essential oil, and memorize that scent so that you can reproduce it astrally to purify both physical room and the astral room. Whether working in ritual, or inducing an altered state through trance, use the astral and physical scent to purify the atmosphere of your astral room and establish it as your domain where only the "invited" gain entrance. You can also establish guardians to enforce "your rule" at the four quarters and above and below.

The Question of Security

The Astral Room's security against negative energies and entities is entirely dependent on your Strength and Detail of Visualization. If you have done a good job, nothing more is needed. Yet, there is considerable value to invoking your Higher Self, or Holy Guardian Angel. In addition, there is a long tradition regarding adding Guardians at the quarters. We will provide suitable rituals for either.

Invoking Your Holy Guardian Angel

Seated in your Work Space at the foundation of your Astral Room, place a single lighted candle before you. While gazing at the candle flame, visualize and sense a human-like presence standing several feet behind you. Build a complete and sustained *mental impression* of this, your Guardian Angel. As a mental impression, do not <u>impose</u> your ideas of his appearance. If your Guardian Angel presents an image of himself in your mind, accept it. *Do not turn your head or attempt to look at this entity in any manner, including the use of a mirror to see behind you!*

Mentally invite your Guardian Angel to step forward and visualize him raising his hands to place them very lightly on your shoulders. Feel the shape of his fingers, their weight, their pressure, their warmth.

Say these words:

By my act of will, I welcome the illuminating radiance of my Holy Guardian Angel into this sacred sphere and into this Astral Room.

From his hands, feel an energy flow into your body like a cooling Fluid Fire. This vitalizing energy is known by many names: *chi, mana, kundalini, the quintessence, the occult virtue.* We most often call it Psychic Energy or Kundalini.

Opening the Third Eye*

Allow the Fluid Fire to circulate throughout your body, feeling every part tingle with vitality. Mentally, direct it to concentrate in the space on your forehead above your nose and between your eyebrows. This is the place of your third eye, the *Ajna Chakra* that is the means to spiritual vision and clairvoyance.

> *This particular Third Eye Opening is just one of the several techniques that will be developed separately in the next chapter on Chakras as on-off switches for clairvoyance. As mentioned previously, it is such activation and control of clairvoyance that has marked the transition from the old parapsychology studying physical phenomenon to the "New Science of the Paranormal."

Visualize an eye opening in this place on your forehead. This eye is smaller than your physical eyes (about the size of an almond), and it is *vertical* rather than horizontal.

Say these words:

By my act of will, with the holy fire of my Guardian Angel, I open and illuminate my third eye of second sight.

You astral sight, clairvoyance, will seem the same as physical sight because third eye visions are automatically translated into images acceptable to your ordinary consciousness. Often these images come in the form of symbols and representations of the archetypes requiring *in situ* interpretation.

Closing The Third Eye

Because you live in the physical world, you should close down your astral vision at the end of your session.

Say these words:

By my act of will, I withdraw the illuminating fire of my holy guardian angel and close my third eye of second sight.

Mentally, feel the kundalini energy flow out of your Ajna chakra and out of your body though the hands still resting on your shoulders. Visualize the energy returning to the unseen body of the Guardian Angel standing behind you.

Say these words:

By my act of will, I release the illuminating radiance of my Holy Guardian Angel from this place of spirit, my Astral Room and work space.

Feel your Angel's hands leave your shoulders as he withdraws away from your chair.

The Act of Withdrawal

At this point, some advocate a complete withdrawal of the Astral Room by reversing your visualizations in creating. Otherwise, if you feel that your workspace is going to be used for spiritual work nearly every day, than a simple act of closure would be sufficient.

Say these words:

THE DECLARATION OF INTENT TO CLOSE

The Earth of Spirit sustains it.
The Water of Spirit cleanses it.
The Air of Spirit expands it.
The First of Spirit surrounds it.
The Light of Spirit creates it.
By my act of will I close this sacred space.

The act of closure is completed as you snuff out the candle, respectfully put away your divination tools, clean up any incense or oil residues, actually dust and clean the furniture and put everything away. Such closure is a principle that should be observed in all your activities, whether in the kitchen or the office, the garage or the barn, no matter what your work or play, never leave the things at "loose ends" and open to negative energies or entities—even if it is just flies feeding on food leftovers. Take seriously the admonition that "Cleanliness is next to Godliness."

THE MAGICAL WAY

A tried and true traditional method for opening and closing sacred space comes from the Magician's "tool box."

The Lesser Ritual of the Pentagram
Part One: The Qabalistic Cross

1. Stand in the center of an imagined circle itself at the center of your Astral Room. Face East. Bring both hands upward in a wide sweeping movement to your brow and place the palms together as in prayer. Vibrate the word *Atah* (To Thine, the Essence). Visualize White Light descending to form a sphere of white brilliance above the crown of your head.

2. Lower your Hands, still together as in prayer, to chest over the heart centre. Vibrate the word *Malkuth* (The Kingdom, the Earth). Visualize a beam of Light extending downward from your crown centre through your heart centre and continuing to the center of the Earth.

3. Place both Hands together to your right shoulder. Vibrate the words *Ve Geburah* (Divine Strength). Visualize a beam of Light extending to the ends of the Universe from below your right shoulder.

4. Place both Hands together to your left shoulder. Vibrates the words *Ve Gedulah* (Divine Magnificence). Visualize a beam of Light extending to the ends of the Universe from below your left shoulder.

5. Cross both arms over your chest. Vibrate the word *Le-Olahm* (To the Ages of Ages, so be it).

6. Clasp both hands together firmly over your heart centre. Vibrate *Amen*. See yourself at the center of a great cross of white light.

You have formed the Qabalistic Cross.

Part Two: Forming the Pentagrams

7. Still standing, facing east, form a "wand" with the first two fingers of your right hand, and draw a full-size banishing pentagram of Earth in the air before you. Begin the pentagram from outside your left hip, then up to a point that is level with the top of your head, and down to outside the right hip. Then straight up diagonally to outside of your left shoulder, and horizontally across to outside your right shoulder, and then down and across to the point of beginning. The two lower points are roughly outside the left and right hips, the apex level with the crown of your head, the other two points outside the left and right shoulders. See the pentagram burning and flaming before you. Bring the point of your "wand" to the center, project energy as if you were "stabbing" it, and vibrate the Divine Name *Yod He Vau He*. See the Pentagram become even more energized.

Forming the Pentagram

8. Continue to hold your arm and hand extended for the entire Circle. *Do not lower the point throughout the ritual.* You are visualizing and energizing the Circle of Light, with the fiery Pentagrams marking each quarter.

9. Turn 90 degrees to your right to face South, draw another Pentagram and "stab" it in its center while vibrating *Adonai.*

10. Again turn 90 degrees to your right, keeping your arm straight, to face West. Draw the Pentagram, stab it, and vibrate *Eheieh.*

11. Again turn 90 degrees to your right, keeping your arm straight, to face North. Draw the Pentagram, stab it, and vibrate *Agla.*

12. Complete the circle to face East and stand in the Tau Posture, arms extended so as to make a T-cross with the whole body, palms upward. You should now see a circle of brilliant light around you, studded with four bright flaming pentagram stars.

Part Three: Evocation of the Archangel Guardians

13. Standing as described in No. 12 above, Speak forcefully and vibrate the divine names of the Archangels: *Before me <u>Raphael</u>, behind me <u>Gabriel</u>, on my right hand <u>Michael</u>, on my left hand <u>Auriel</u>. For about me flames the pentagram, and in the column stands the six-rayed star!* Pronounce the Archangel names: *Rah-Fah-el, Gah-bree-el, Mee-kah-el, Or-ee-el.*

14. See the archangels clearly, standing before their Pentagrams. Raphael wears robes of yellow and violet, while golden rays of the Air element pour through the pentagram from the East.

15. See Michael in robes of scarlet and emerald, while red rays of the Fire element pour through the pentagram from the South.

16. See Gabriel in robes of blue and orange, while the blue rays of Water element pour through the pentagram from the West.

17. See Auriel in robes of citrine, olive, russet, and black, while the green rays of the Earth element pour through the pentagram from the North.

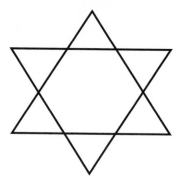

The Golden Hexagram

18. See yourself surrounded by a circle of light studded with four flaming pentagrams, with the Archangels (very tall and towering) guarding the quarters. Above you and below you appears the six-rayed star, **the golden hexagram**. It is the floor and roof of the palace for the Indwelling Spirit that you have built.

19. Repeat the Qabalistic Cross as at the beginning.

In Summary

With the Qabalistic Cross, you invoked the divine presence into your heart, mind and body, and then placed yourself at the center of the Universe. You have cleansed the four quarters of the Universe with pentagrams of fire, affirming that Man is mirror of the Divine Image, Microcosm to Macrocosm, and hence with the ability to control the elements through spirit.

The deity names are sent thundering through to the Ends of the Universe and back again. *Your* Magical Universe is then defined by the circle of light.

The drawing of the four pentagrams automatically invokes spirit, the fifth point, and so raises the microcosmic consciousness to the level of the macrocosm, having completely sealed the circle against the Outer Darkness.

The column is the shape of the space that is created by the circle extending vertically above and below the magician. The construction of the circle banishes the four Elements and thus the column is the Element of Spirit extending into the infinite above and the infinite below.

Clairvoyance & the Astral World

In this chapter, and in general discussions of Spiritualism and what is loosely called "spirituality," the only distinction generally made is between physical and spiritual, and in this everything non-physical is generally lumped together with no understanding of the real nature and potential of this "spiritual" dimension of the person.

Yes, we talk about the physical world, the astral world, and the mental world, but we need to understand that we are—ultimately—Soul who projects a newly created spirit that manifests as a total being composed of physical, etheric, astral, mental, and causal bodies altogether anchored initially in just the physical body. We can refer to that as the "physical person," but in truth that physical person is dominated by emotionality and until emotionality is controlled by our mental self we lack the ability to act with true purpose.

This is a long chapter in which we have seen a continuous inter-relationship between the physical world and a spiritual world. In this, we have witnessed communication, healing, and various paranormal phenomena—including clairvoyance which is the subject of this book. We have touched upon the astral world and drawn upon its resources to create a safe environment for our psychic and spiritual work. We've made a point that there are astral counterparts to everything physical, and we've shown how to strengthen those astral counterparts until they dominate the original physical objects.

And this "dominance" of the physical by astral imagery is a key to mental control of psychic power and phenomena, and to mental domination of the physical-emotional personality. Without mental domination, we are whip-lashed by emotion—and the astral body is very open to massive waves of emotional energy and imagery generated by crowds of excited people at rock concerts, sports events, religious revivals, and political rousers. And we have learned that physical presence at these events is not necessary—raw emotion is "broadcast" by radio, television, and even the Internet.

As the physical person grows, there is more and more involvement with the higher bodies but the emotional personality still dominates all. As children, our physical bodies become further entwined with the etheric body, and as we more and more express our feelings the astral body is vivified and personalized. As we learn things year-by-year, and particularly as we go through our schools from lower to higher grades, our mental body becomes more active but still cannot dominant the astral-emotional personality.

As we grow, particular physical activities that are not competitive but "unifying" (gymnastics, expressive dance, martial arts, full-body exercise, etc.) bring the physical and etheric bodies into a singular unity. But with puberty the astral/emotional body is flooded with hormonal and sex-based emotions. Those, along with the primal "reactive" feelings (hate, fear, ambition, desire, lust, pain, hunger) can drive the physical-emotional personality into irrational behavior and bad decisions.

With increasing maturity and fewer competitive activities, we experience and project "subjective" feelings (love, empathy, sympathy, obligation, loyalty). We begin the long process of organizing our astral-emotional nature. Every intentional act is mental, and when combined with feeling, it is unifying with the astral and when extended into physical actions that express feelings, it is unifying to the whole system.

An esoteric principle (whether called magical or spiritual) is that the *higher controls the lower.* It is essential that Mind becomes the dominant partner in the person complex. Thus we continue our journey to Self-Empowerment.

Sources and Suggested Additional Reading:

Andrews, T. *How to Meet & Work with Spirit Guides,* 2002, Llewellyn.

Buckland, R. *Buckland's Book of Spirit Communication,* 2004, Llewellyn.

Dale, C. *Everyday Clairvoyant: Extraordinary Answers to Finding Love, Destiny and Balance in Your Life,* 2010, Llewellyn.

Dale, C. *Kundalini: Divine Energy, Divine Life,* 2011, Llewellyn.

Van den Eynden, R. *Ask a Medium: Answers to Your Frequently Asked Questions About the Spirit World,* 2010, Llewellyn.

Fleckless, E. V. *Willie Speaks Out: The Psychic World of Abraham Lincoln,* 1974, Llewellyn.

Paulson, G. L. *Kundalini and the Chakras,* 2002, Llewellyn.

Slate, J. H. & Weschcke, C. L. *The Llewellyn Complete Book of Psychic Empowerment: A Compendium of Tools & Techniques for Growth & Transformation,* 2011, Llewellyn.

Slate, J. H. & Weschcke, C. L. *Psychic Empowerment for Everyone: You Have the Power, Learn How to Use It,* 2009, Llewellyn.

Slate, J. H. & Weschcke, C. L. *Self-Empowerment through Self-Hypnosis: Harnessing the Enormous Potential of the Mind,* 2010, Llewellyn.

Stefanidakis, S. *How to Develop Mediumship and Channeling,* 2002, First Spiritual Temple.

Tyson, D. *Scrying for Beginners: Tapping into the Supersensory Powers of Your Subconscious,* 1997, Llewellyn.

ADDENDUM #7 TO CHAPTER SEVEN
Microcosm to Macrocosm & Macrocosm to Microcosm

The Tattvic Connection—
Meditation & Visualization Program #5: Ether/Ether

Ether—Seed of Ether: New Birth

In some ways, that which we call "metaphysics" both complicates and simplifies the "physics" perception of universe and the cosmos in which we live. I use those two words—"universe" to describe the apparent reality of the physical world and "cosmos" to describe the much more complex and much larger reality inclusive of physical and subtle structures that used to be called "occult."

"Occult" means *hidden,* but metaphysical realities are not so much hidden as they are not commonly perceived and generally ignored. Why is this? For the most part these greater realities are outside the predominant view we grew up with, but anything "outside the norm" makes people uncomfortable: they threaten the status quo, they ask you to think, and they may even call upon you to act in different ways, to accept greater responsibility for actions that you could take if you were to see things from a larger perspective.

At the same time, these metaphysical realities are matched by current developments in Quantum Theory, in new directions of medical and longevity research, in the challenges between academic disciplines challenging past authoritarian views, and widening the gap between the "real world" and the distorted views of political and religious establishments.

Where do we go from here? The point is that as we undertake such balancing and purification meditation programs as these five Tattva Connection Meditation & Visualization Programs, we have the opportunity to see more clearly. As it says in I Corinthians 13:11: "When I was a child, I spoke as a child, I understood as a child, I thought as a child: but when I became a man, I put away childish things." That's our goal—in developing clairvoyance we need to be sure we see clearly and accurately, free of childish misunderstanding and distortions.

TATTVA OVERVIEW TABLE #5: Chakras

Tattva Name	Element Name	Chakra Name	Common Name	Chakra Location
Prithivi	Earth	Muladhara	Base	Pelvis
Apas	Water	Svadhisthana	Sex	Below Navel
Tejas	Fire	Manipura	Solar Plexus	Above Navel
Vayu	Air	Anahata	Heart	Heart
Akasha	Ether	Vishuddha	Throat	Throat
Manas	Light	Ajna	3rd Eye	Brow
Bindu	Thought	Sahasrara	Crown	Crown

While we are not discussing the chakras to any detail in this book, most people are aware of their importance, and that commonly we recognize seven or eight major chakras. Likewise, in this book we are not discussing Kundalini, or the major channels Sushumna, Ida, and Pingala. These, and techniques for their activation and application will be developed in later books, over assignments of glands, order of unfoldment, specifics of location, and other questions.

The element discussed in this addendum, Ether (also spelled Aether), and also called Spirit, is the fourth dimensional source of the other four Primal Elements. Both names are appropriate, although conveying slightly different meanings. Closely related to Ether/Aether/Spirit is *Space*—not as a "location" but as a kind of Spiritual Substance within which all physical particles are formed and all forces flow.

Spirit is most commonly symbolized as an "egg" through which one kind of life is transformed into another and appearing as a new birth. It is the psychic power to *channel* communication from the subtle realms into the physical, and to *prophetically* see the future. Alternatively, Spirit is symbolized as an "8-spoked wheel" whose constant rotation is fundamental to all manifestation.

Another way to think about this is that Spirit is the *transitional phase* between the physical/material level and the subtle planes, between this world and the worlds beyond the physical plane. This "spirit" is not a thing or an entity but an "interdimensional" *function* through which things and entities seem to appear and disappear with a change in their nature, one aspect of which is life-to-death and death-to-rebirth and another may be a kind of interdimensional space flight.

THINK ELEMENTAL ETHER (SPIRIT)

When approaching a subject referred to as a "transitional phase," we start by realizing that we must make a shift in our thinking process away from definitive and

TATTVA OVERVIEW TABLE #5: Chakras

Seed Mantra	Chakra Color	Chakra Gland	Tattva Form	Alchemical Planet
LAM	Red	Gonads	Square	Saturn
VAM	Orange	Adrenals	Crescent	Pluto
RAM	Yellow	Pancreas	Triangle	Sun
YAM	Green	Thymus	Hexagram	Venus
HAM	Bright Blue	Thyroid & Parathyroid	Oval	Jupiter
AUM	Indigo	Pineal	Winged Globe	Moon
H	Violet	Pituitary	Rose	Uranus

purely rational as applied in the familiar physical world to something we call *meta-physical* and understand that our language has to be looser, more speculative, more poetic and symbolic and without the logical and mathematical precision possible on the physical plane.

Think "spiritual," and think of the "space" *between* physical beings and objects that energizes their substance and the force of their self-expression. When we think "spiritual" we think in terms of something closer to the *Divine Source* of being. We relate to particular concepts called gods and goddesses, or angels and archangels, or to saints and other beings that express or represent specific forces of creation and continued manifestation.

The Akasha Tattva is associated with the Alchemical and Magical Element named "Spirit" in the Western Tradition and symbolized by an egg representing the womb of the Universal Mother. That symbol represents the point where Imagination empowers change from one reality into the miraculous. Akasha is the fundamental Tattva from which all forms come and in which all forms "live" and have their being.

Akasha is "every color" or "clear." Its tattvic color, black or indigo, is the absorption of all other colors, and its complimentary (or "flashing") yantric color is luminous white. This rather well illustrates Akasha's role in New Birth and in Re-birth. There is a constant emergence of the other tattwas from Akasha and a constant re-absorption of them back into Akasha.

When Akasha is used as a "doorway" for scrying, the clairvoyant can scan for information within the Akashic Records (also known as the "collective unconscious" in Jungian psychology) containing all memories of human experience, personal and universal. In a personal "reading" these memories bring clarity and perspective to the visions rising out of the psychic field, and can place them within a larger context of greater relevance.

The Collective Unconscious also contains *potential* future "history" in what esoterics call *seed* form. It's what is most likely to happen under current circumstances, but not what will necessarily happen because changes made today will affect what happens tomorrow. The challenge is to know the many connections between the details making up present reality as well as those contributing to the potential future so you better understand what changes are possible, always presuming you have the power to make the necessary changes and have sufficient confidence in your knowledge of "right and wrong."

The operations of any individual tattva extend beyond the location of the specific chakra involved and include various major and minor glands. In the case of Akasha, the glandular secretions—in balance—are more feminine than masculine, thus in a woman we will find more of such qualities as love, affection, unselfishness, and reliability.

In every way, the expanded metaphysical view brings new clarity, new understanding, and new dimensions to everything physical as well as giving us the foundations for actually understanding more of the subtle worlds than merely accepting them as "mysteries." We are in a New Age where those Mysteries are now revealing their meaning.

> Note: The following Elemental Overview Table #5 for Ether is exactly what the title says—an "overview" intended to give you a fundamental awareness of the Elemental Qualities and Characteristics. You may notice some seeming conflicts but these represent particular sources and intended usage from Meditational and Magickal perspectives. An excellent source book for all this is David Hulse's *The Eastern Mysteries*, which can be supplemented by the same author's *The Western Mysteries*.

ELEMENT OVERVIEW TABLE #5: Ether
Ether—Seed of Ether: New Birth

Tattva Name: *Akasha*	Tattva Form: Oval or 8-spoked wheel	Tattvic Color: Indigo, black
Tattva/Primary Sheath: *Anandamaya* (causal body, bliss)	Tattvic Animal: White Elephant	Tattvic Taste: Bitter
Yantra Color: Luminous White	Yantra Form: Egg	Cosmic Plane: *jana*, higher mental, causal
Chakra Name: *Vishuddha* (purity centre)	Chakra Common Name: Throat Chakra	Chakra Bija Mantra: *HAM*
Chakra Body Location: throat	Chakra Body Space: mid-eyebrows to top of head	Chakra Body Zone: pharyngeal plexus
Chakra Color: Bright Blue, Smoky Purple	Chakra Function of astral & etheric centers: communication, creativity, etheric & astral hearing	

Chakra Goal: sympathetic vibration	Chakra God (*Shiva*) Energy: *Ardhvanarisvara*	Chakra Goddess (*Shakti*) Energy: *Sakini* with 5 heads
Chakra Meditation: gives knowledge of past, present & future along with freedom from disease & sorrow.	Chakra Petals (Spokes): 16	Chakra Power: rejuvenation, health, longevity, creative thinking, sympathetic communication
Chakra Problem: thyroid problems, sore throat, colds, stiff neck, hearing problems		
Chakra Symbol: 16 smoky purple petals inscribed with mantras am, am, im, im, um, um, rm, rm, lrm, lrm, em, aim, om, aum, am, and ah, surrounding a blue circle with a white inverse triangle inside of which is a circle representing the full moon, inside of which is a white elephant and the goddess *Gauri* and god *Shiva*. Picture yourself riding the elephant, chanting HAM.		
Chakra Vital Air: *Samana Vayu*	Chakra Yogini: *Dakini*	Chakra/Physical Gland: Thyroid & Parathyroids
Siddhi Powers: (when developed) freedom from the infirmities of old age and death, freedom from need to eat.		Chakra Verbal Expression: I speak
Indian God: Ambera sits on a white elephant holding a noose and a goad. On his lap sits Sadashiva who is white-skinned, has 10 arms, 5 faces with 3 eyes, dressed in a tiger pelt, embracing Parvati.		
Indian goddesses: Dwelling within the lotus is white-skinned Sakini, dressed in yellow, holding a bow, arrow, noose & goad. Also Chhinnamasta & Dakini.		
Element Name: Spirit, Ether, Aether	Elemental State: Space	Elemental Action: Unlimited Potentials
Elemental Function: Insight	Elemental Motion: Outward	Elemental Nature: Mixed
Elemental Power: Innovation, and change	Elemental Quality: Space	Elemental Strength: to transform, to transition
Energy Type: Nuclear	Manifests through: Stellar Space	Quantum Force: Super Force
Emotional Characteristic: Communication	Emotional Desires: to know, think, understand	Emotional Drive: Creativity, to work alone
Emotional Family Role: Patriarch, Wise Grandmother	Emotional Nature: Future "memories"	Emotional/Psychological Level: deep unconscious*
Emotional Reaction: Fascination	Emotional/Sensory Block: Visible form	
Emotional/Sexual Identity: union—matter with spirit	Emotional Strength: Transformation	Emotional weakness: feeling lost & alone
Mind Action: *Jivataman* (Individual Self)	Mind Function: Intuition, Mystical Vision	Mind State: Pure Consciousness
Physical/Action Organ: Mouth, vocal cords	Physical/Action Form: Speaking, Chanting, Singing	Physical/Action Effect: Uniting
Physical/Astral Sense: Hearing	Physical/Astral Sense (Cognitive) Organ: Ears	Physical Body Function: vocalization, emotions

Physical Energy Correlations between physical/etheric & astral bodies—Fingers of Hand: Little Finger	Psychic Powers: know past & future, prophecy, telepathy.	Psychic/Astral Work: focus on your throat, on inbreaths visualize energy rising from each of lower chakras
Alchemical Metal: Copper	Alchemical Planet: Jupiter	Alchemical Quality: Source of All
Alchemical Symbolic Season: Ever Present	Alchemical Symbolic Time of Day: Timeless	Astrological Lunar Phase: Full Moon
Astrological Types: none known	Astrological Qualities: none known	Astrological Ruling Planet: Jupiter
Astrological Planetary Expression: Neptune		
Egyptian Divinities: Seshat	Greek God Form: Iacchus, Hermes	Greek goddesses: none known
Hebrew God Name: Yehoshuah	Runes: none known	
Magical Angel: none known	Magical Animals: spiders	Magical Archangel: Metatron. Sandalphon
Magical Mythical Beings: phoenix, dragon, sphinx	Magical Colors: White, Black, Purple, All colors	Magical Day: Thursday
Magical Direction: Center, Above AND Below	Magical Elemental King: none known	Magical Elemental Spirits: none known
Magical Energy: everything potential, start up	Magical Enochian Watchtower: Tablet of Union	Magical God Name: AHIH
Magical Herbs: artemisia, vervain	Magical Incense: benzoin, frankincense,	Magical Kerub: none known
Magical Metals: iron, mercury	Magical Musical Note: G; Musical Scale: So	Magical Places: none known
Magical Planet: Mercury, Neptune	Magical Plants: Flowering Almond, apple,	Magical Ruler: Kerub
Magical Power: Akashic Records, Invisibility		
Magical Rulerships: alchemy, change, divinity, infinity, magic, spacelessness, timeliness, transformation, unification		
Magical Season: none known	Magical States: Rebirth	
Magical Stones: Aquamarine, black diamond, celestite, lapis lazuli, meteorite, quartz, sodalite, turquoise		
Magical Symbols: none known	Magical Time of Day: none known	Magical Time of Life: Full circle, from birth to death
Magickal Tool: crystal, voice, cord, witches cradle	Magical Work: Transformation, invisibility	
Tarot Court: none known	Tarot suit: Major Arcana	Tarot Trumps: All Trumps
Tree of Life Path: 31st (alternate)	Tree of Life Sphere: Chesed & Geburah	Tree of Life Soul Level: Yechidah-Divine Self

Note: The various magical correspondences are only minimal selections. More complete information can be found in the resources listed at the end of the book. For serious study, you should add to this list, and other lists you may be building. Correspondences build your inter-relationships between Inner & Outer, Subconscious & Conscious, Cosmic & Personal. All magical systems inter-relate and add to your personal memory/library.

Ether—Seed of Ether

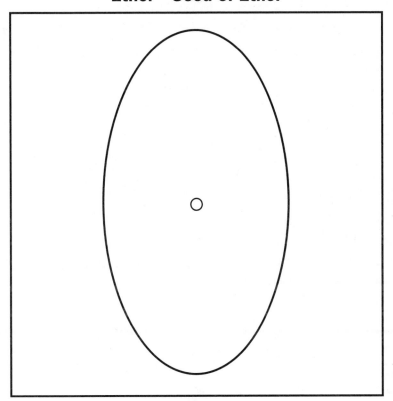

Color the tiny inner bindu circle white,
the inner oval indigo,
and the outer square yellow/orange

Ether—Seed of Ether: Akasha *HAM*

The Tattvic Connection Meditation & Visualization Program #5: Ether/Ether
Ether—Seed of Ether: New Birth

Introduction. The Purpose & Function of this Procedure.

This procedure is intended to bring *Akasha*, the Ether (and Spirit) Element, deeply into your psychic awareness. While the procedure is directed by your conscious mind, the main operation occurs in the subconscious mind and the autonomic system. It does not bring about dramatic conscious changes, but allows the personal element to balance with its cosmic equivalent.

Throughout life you have created changes in the complex of physical and subtle bodies that combine in your vehicle of manifestation for this life time. Some changes represent positive growth and others are negative and even destructive depending on childhood misunderstanding of things seen and heard, resulting in misperceptions distorting their emotional nature.

This program and those that follow are specifically intended to balance and harmonize the inner Tattvic Matrix of Body and Soul with the universal Cosmic Matrix and Spirit. The result is a purification of the inner matrix so that clairvoyant visions will not be distorted by "accumulated psychic and emotional garbage" from childhood and past lives.

Nothing is ever forgotten in our subconsciousness, but the emotional "flavor" that accompanied the original experience can be recognized as such and now seen with a new and wiser perspective that brings about change in adult perception.

You can repeat this entire procedure often, but not more than once daily, and I suggest that you allow a week between each exercise.

Summary of Purpose & User Benefits.

With this meditation we purify, balance, and harmonize the emotional and psychic elemental force in our body and soul as contained in the **Akasha** tattva. As this is completed, along with other elemental meditations, you will be better equipped to follow on with specific stimuli of particular psychic centers to accomplish your projected goals.

Step 1. Preliminaries.

Always start with Physical Relaxation.

Read through the entire procedure before beginning so that further reference is not needed. Mostly it is identical with the other *Tattva Connection Meditation & Visualization Programs* except for specific references to the **Ether** Element, which I have placed in boldface for ease of recognition.

Time & Space: Allow a period of at least 30 minutes (an hour is better) for the actual 16 step procedure to be conducted in a comfortably warm, quiet, and safe setting free of interruptions. While a darkened room is not required, freedom from both sound and visual distractions is advisable.

Personal Preparations: Remove shoes and keep clothing or covering minimal to reduce the effects of external stimuli.

Posture & Position: It is not desirable to lie flat for this procedure, but a relaxed posture in a chair or recliner is helpful.

Special Lighting: You should arrange a small desk or reading light next to your chair that you can comfortably reach to switch on and off as required, and focus as directed.

Breathing: It is always desirable to establish a deep but natural, rhythmic flow of your breath, mostly balanced between inhalation and exhalation.

Vocalization: Vocalize, either silently stated or voiced softly aloud, your affirmations and the name of the *tattva* and then the sounding of the *mantra* in Step 9.

With each step, 5 through 13, it is helpful to vocalize the words describing any particular feelings or even visions you experience.

Vibration: This is very important. In Step 9 you should chant or hum the Sanskrit name of the *tattva*, and then the *tattvic mantra* as instructed. You want to draw these words out and feel the *vibration.* "Vibration" means to softly *warble* the words at the back of your throat, and as you do, you may want to raise or lower the "musical note" until it feels right. The same approach applies to the volume: initially you may want to chant loudly but later reduce the volume. You want to feel the words *vibrate* throughout your skull, and then in the location of the corresponding *chakra*—with experience you will be able to move the vibration to other designated places inside your body, and then—in advanced work—intentionally into external objects.

The *yantra*, the name, and the *mantra* are your means to connect the inner *tattva* with the external *tattva* for purification and balance.

Step 2. Goal Statement.

Your goal is three-fold:

1. To become fully familiar with the feelings associated with the **Ether** Element. You've read about it, you've seen the characteristics and correspondences, but now we want you to *feel* the Ether in you, under you, around you, and *through* your entire inner being.

2. To become aware of Elemental **Ether** as the primary *foundational element* of the outer material universe.

3. To identify inner **Ether** with outer **Ether**, and feel yourself purified and balanced through the *harmonizing of inner with outer.*

- *To address particular concerns:* As an example, we have suggested two areas —your ability to innovate and stimulate change in your environment and to feel and respond appropriately to other people's feelings and needs. You must determine the goals yourself and then *affirm* them simply and concisely in as few words as possible. Write them down, fix them in your mind, but do not consider them as the primary function of the exercise which is the balancing and purification of personal elemental ether. (Note: particular concerns must relate to the Element being addressed—see the Overview Table.)

Step 3. Affirmations.

These affirmations may be spoken as goals at the beginning, and then as confirmations at the ending of the procedure. In addition to these, add the affirmation you wrote as one of your goals.

*I feel **Ether** everywhere within me.*

*I feel **Ether** everywhere around me.*

*I feel purified and in harmony with all that is **Etheric** & **Unlimited** everywhere.*

Step 4. Mental Imagery.

Imagery, like vocalization, can increase the effectiveness of the procedure.

Visualization: Visualizing the tattvas as described is essential.

Spontaneous Imagery: Other images may appear at the end of the procedure—and that is alright *unless you have negative feelings about them—in which case you should willfully "banish" them.* (If you wish, you might work with the nature of this element, **Space.** Following the concept of seeing all those negativities flow into a box that can be then locked, let's place the box on a space rocket and send it to get lost in the farthest space where it will freeze solid.)

Recording: Other images that may appear spontaneously at the end of the procedure should be noted along with any particular feelings or ideas, and then recorded in your journal for later analysis.

Analysis: Always let a day or two pass before reading and analyzing your journal entries.

Step 5. Preparation.

Preparing the Yantra Card.

It is recommended that you photocopy the illustration on page 275, preferably on heavier paper or card stock, or draw it yourself in exactly the same sizes using a ruler and black pen. If you can manage it, using a drawing compass or a template, draw a tiny ⅛" diameter circle in the exact center. Leave the inside of the circle white. This inner circle or point aids your steady focus. It is not essential, but it is helpful. Make the outer square 4" x 4" and the inner Oval (length up) should be about 2" wide by 3¼" tall and centered, and the little circle in the exact center should be ⅛" in diameter and have a heavy black border around it, but not quite as thick as those around the Oval and outer square.

Coloring the Yantra Card.

It will be beneficial to you to color the image as follows: (a) Leave the tiny circle white; (b) color the **Oval Egg Indigo**, and the surrounding larger square **Yellow/Orange**. Each square and the tiny inner circle are bordered with bold black lines.

Cutting the Yantra Card.

If you have reproduced the image on the heavy card stock as recommended, now measure off either one or two inches (your choice) on each side and cut away the surplus so you have a square 6" x 6" or 8" x 8" *card* with the colored image in the center.

This preparation will be repeated for all the additional images during which you will have produced a set of 25 Tattva Cards that can be used again and again in the clairvoyance process discussed in this book, and in many other functions to be discussed later.

Position & Lighting.

Holding the tattvic yantra card, recline in a comfortable chair in a quiet room where you will not be disturbed for a minimum of 30 minutes (preferably, an hour). Prior to doing so, arrange the lighting to focus on the card so that you can switch it on and off as desired.

Note the preferred direction for placing the chair indicated in Step 9 (a and b).

Breathing & Relaxation.

Become fully relaxed, combining slowed rhythmic breathing, and progressive tension and release of muscles from your toes to your brow and scalp if you have not

already followed the Empowerment Tension & Release Procedure described in the Addendum to Chapter 1.

Step 6. Pranic Breathing Pattern.

With eyes closed; engage in a pattern of rhythmic breathing involving equally spaced —*without any stress*—in-breaths, holding, out-breaths, holding, and repeating throughout the process.

Step 7. White Light Circulation.

Then, with each in-breath visualize white light flowing into the body, while holding the breath visualize the light circulating throughout the body, while breathing out see the light being excreted knowing that it is carrying out impurities, and while holding the out breath realize that you have energized and cleansed the inner energy body.

Step 8. Psychic Shield.

While continuing the breathing pattern and the flowing light, turn your imagination outward and visualize an absolutely clear field around you, one that is as transparent as the clearest glass. Know that this shield protects you from external influences while containing the tattvic meditation program.

Step 9a. Yantra Card Focus.

If you have constructed the tattva yantra card as described, turn on the light and focus it on the card held or positioned comfortably about a foot to a foot and a half in front of you.

If possible, recline your chair so you face upward while thinking of the tattvic direction: **Centered**. Otherwise—think and feel **Centered**.

Vibrate the name of tattva: *Akasha*. Repeat three times.

Chant or hum the tattva element mantra **HAM** (pronounced **HA-UUM**). Vibrate the mantra as instructed in Step 1, preliminaries. Repeat three times. Later, you can do more but always in groups of three. And feel the mantra vibrate over the **Throat**, the location of **Vishuddha** chakra.

Focus on the small white circle* at the center of the image, and stare at it for as long as you can without blinking. When you can't continue the "burning" feeling any longer, turn off the light, close your eyes, and focus your inner sight on the space in front of your brow chakra (between your eyebrows and on the ridge just above your nose), and you will soon see floating in space before you the tattva image. See the

Indigo Oval vibrate within the outer **Yellow/Orange** Square. And then it will slowly reverse to the complementary reverse yantra colors.

Absorb this image! As you repeat the exercise, often, you will reach a point when you will be able to recall this image at will.

Step 9b. Yantra Visualization.

Alternatively, if you haven't made an **Akasha** tattva card, immediately in front of you, visualize a large **Yellow/Orange** Square, inside of which is an **Indigo Oval**. See the Indigo Oval gently vibrate within the **Yellow/Orange** Square. The colors will soon reverse to their complementary yantra colors.

Step 10a. Experiencing Elemental Ether.

Feel yourself becoming totally *absorbed* in the **Indigo Oval** while retaining awareness of the surrounding **Yellow/Orange** Square. Feel *your* **Etheric** nature harmonize with the Cosmic **Ether** Tattva, and feel all impurities in your **Ether** Tattva—all emotional garbage and unconscious psychic attachments—dissipate.

Becoming absorbed. Enter into the **Ether Oval** and become one with it and feel surrounded by it. Moving outward from the bindu point to the outer edge of the large square become the **Ether** element in your body and feel it become harmonized and purified as it is balanced with the Cosmic **Ether,** with **Cosmic Spirit** from which the other tattvas emerge and to which they return.

*In particular: feel the **Etheric** nature of your physical body become free of adverse thoughts and feelings. Feel your body becoming ideally healthy, strong, and energized. See your Etheric, Astral, and Mental bodies in clear and bright colors and your Spirit as clear crystal. See your body as perfectly healthy, feel your whole being energized and clear of emotional pain and illness, and charged with **Universal Love**.*

Step 11. Knowing Elemental Ether.

Allow yourself to receive any information or messages from your experience of Elemental **Ether.** *In particular: receive information involving your Spiritual, Mental, Emotional & Psychic health, strength, and security.* Receive the information without any emotional reaction.

Step 12. Dissipation of Images.

Slowly dissipate the **Oval** and the surrounding Square, return to the clear field around you, continuing the breathing pattern of Step 6 above.

Step 13. Letting Go of Evoked Feelings.

Let go of all the particular feelings evoking by imagery, slowly change your breathing to its natural rhythm, and feel the physical relaxation achieved in Step 1 above.

Step 14. Completion & Self-Realization.

Feel yourself fully relaxed and fully self-contained. Feel yourself to be healthy, energized, cleansed, and refreshed. Know yourself to be strong and secure.

Step 15. Return to Normality.

Open your eyes, return to the physical world knowing all is well. Stand up and move about. Have some refreshment and engage in some normal activity.

Step 16. Review, Record & Analyze.

Record in a journal all messages and feelings received in Step 11 above. At this point, merely record—do not analyze. After a few days, read what you've recorded and then write down an analysis of what you believe the messages mean for you at this time. Realize that when you repeat the exercise at another time, the messages are likely to change to meet new circumstances in your life.

Conclusion: This exercise has demonstrated the particular usefulness of clairvoyance focused on the single areas of Spiritual, Mental, Emotional and Psychic health, strength and security in Steps 10 and 11 At the same time the relaxation program and light circulation procedure provide physical health and healing benefits.

However, the entire 16-step Meditation is a basic program that can be modified by changes in the tattvic element and then particular modifications in Steps 10 and 11. You should explore this concept of using elemental and other symbols yourself. We will further address this technology in another book.

Sources & Suggested Additional Reading:

Crowley, A. (with Introduction by Regardie, I.) *The Qabalah of Aleister Crowley— Gematria, Liber 777, Sepher Sephiroth*, 1973, Weiser.

CHAPTER EIGHT
"Techno-Shamanism"

Inducing Clairvoyance with Consciousness Altering Aids of Sensory Deprivation & Sensory Isolation:

The Witches Cradle and Meditation Masks

What Can We Learn from History?

Strangely enough (and this will anger historians and those benefiting from the new *status quo*), history is less factual than *what we make of it.* Two axioms illustrate the challenge we have:

1. The *Victors always write (and re-write) history* to match their goals and ideals. While this particularly applies to large scale wars, it equally applies to the surviving cultures of all massive social change and to the empowered institutions.

2. The Past is (or can be) *Prologue to the Future,* but "prologue" only sets the stage and is not the play itself nor the limits of where we will go.

What Do We <u>Want</u> to Learn from History?

That's the more important question. Rather than just repeating the mistakes others have made we want to learn from those mistakes, and build on their successes. We want to analyze their actions and their results, and then try to make something better. Re-written and biased history deprives us of an honest and factual picture. It doesn't matter whether we are talking about things physical or techniques esoteric and spiritual. From our position in present time we see the past as experimental, reduce it to theory, and then create something we expect to work better. Mostly we do this more-or-less unconsciously—feeling and knowing that present day actions are building blocks for the future. But we should want to do better by making wiser decisions and conscious choices.

For some strange reason, most people are reluctant to realize that "we" continually evolve, and that change is a constant feature of life. *Evolution* is not limited to biological "survival of the fittest" but applies to all dimensions of life. Even for those who "religiously" refuse to recognize the evidence of evolution, the remains of Cro-Magnon and Neanderthal people, and even earlier ancestors reaching back to the very ancient past, should at least remind them that modern humanity and modern culture is very recent and yet we do, literally, walk on the bones of our ancestors.

Neanderthal Man

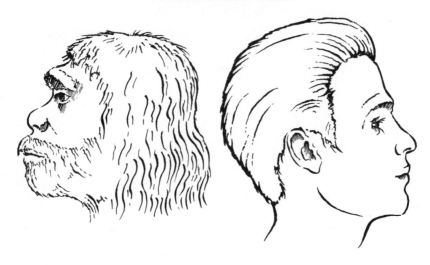

Change, Adaptation, & Building the Future

We have changed, and our world has changed, and everything and everyone in it must change and adapt to the ever-changing circumstances that surround us—*like it, or not!* And, unless we learn from the past in our adaptations, we *may* neither survive nor prosper—nor continue to evolve and grow into the empowered whole persons for which we are destined.

Along with slow physical and biological evolution, our modern world is characterized by a vast and accelerating explosion of *technological* development (a kind of "evolution" of its own) reflecting our increased real world knowledge ranging beyond the plane of physical matter and energy into those planes that are actually composed of emotional substance and energy, mental substance and energy, and spiritual substance and energy.

Yes, there is "Esoteric Technology" too

All of this, physical and *beyond* into the non-physical, is the subject of "esoteric technology." *Everything in the Cosmos is intertwined and all actions are limited only by understanding and purpose.* Understanding the nature of things is crucial to the realization of our purpose, no matter how expressed. Lack of real knowledge is why many plans go wrong, most "prayers" are unanswered, most "spells" do nothing, and the best of "intentions" often backfire. *Wishful thinking is no substitute for knowledge-able action.*

Technology is systematic knowledge applied to purposeful action. There is "technology" specific to every plane and dimension of the Cosmos, and there is function, substance, energy, and rules for each that must be understood and appropriately and intentionally directed from those "inner" bodies that make up the Whole Person.

Esoteric Technology—East and West

For nearly two thousand years, Westerners have practically been *conditioned* to look to the East for "spiritual" technologies of change, growth, and transformation because much of Western spiritual knowledge was suppressed and repressed by the Church, and what was left hidden away for its preservation and then referred to in a denigrating way as the "occult" (a word simply meaning *hidden* and *obscured)* and its practitioners persecuted and often executed for deviance from Establishment theology.

In reality, outside of the confining walls of the medieval churches, present day researchers have recovered a complex understanding of an evolving universe, and the history and presence of transformational sciences like Alchemy, Ceremonial and Ritual Magick, natural and developed levels of Clairvoyance along with associated forms of Divination (Crystal Gazing, Geomancy, Rune-casting, Tarot Cards, and more), Herbalism in Healing as well as Consciousness Alterations, Spirit Invocation and Communication, and Witchcraft (vastly mis-understood and mis-represented, and its adherents victimized).

Yes, there is a history of these or similar subjects in the East as well, and we need to clarify that the "East" generally referred to in esoteric discussion is mostly limited to India and Tibet. China, Japan, the Middle East, along with Africa and the Americas are largely ignored with only passing references to Ancient Egypt, Greece, and mythic Atlantis and Lemuria. In other regions, many spiritual practices took form as folk magic and lore, and as shamanism, and were generally ignored by the white European explorers as too "primitive" to study. (See a previous chapter on Shamanism & Religion)

Self-Reliance, not External Authority

But there are some fundamental differences with the older forms of Esoteric practices, East and West, that are important to our understanding of contemporary variants and modern needs. Again, it is emphasized that we must knowingly adapt to the changes around us. The world changes, and life and consciousness evolve, and our technologies adapt and lead to new ways of developing and using particular powers and skills. Life is constantly bringing us new challenges and new opportunities leading to personal growth and advancement of human-kind.

The most important reason and defining factor in our transformation into what we call "modernity" across the entire spectrum of the coming Global Civilization is reflected throughout modern culture in our increasing *reliance on personal knowledge rather than blind acceptance of external authority,* and with that comes the necessity for the acquisition of required information and unbiased knowledge, for disciplined self-study and self-responsibility, and—as may be desirable or necessary—partnership with experts and specialists in our personal actions.

The Modern World in Perspectives of Past, Present, and Future, and the Role of Personal Clairvoyance

There are twelve important factors in our evolving and changing world that should be understood as we explore and adapt the Perennial and Modern forms of both Esoteric and Shamanic Technologies to contemporary needs:

The 12 Factors of Revolution, Challenge, Evolution & Solution

<u>Number 1:</u> The **"Population Revolution"**—We've had an explosive increase in human population with little real acknowledgment of the resultant and forthcoming stresses. Consider the following:

- In 1700, India's population was about 100 million, today it is about 1.2 billion.

China's population in 1700 was also about 100 million, but today it is about 1.4 billion.

- In 1700, the population of all of Europe totaled 83 million and today is about 750 million.
- The United States' population in 1700 is estimated at 250 <u>thousand</u>, today is about 300 <u>million.</u>
- The world population in 1700 was only 610 <u>million</u> and today it is 7 <u>billion.</u>

So far, agricultural, industrial and technological innovation has enabled us to mostly meet the accelerating demands for food, and other of life's necessities and—depending on regional economics and politics—provide many comfortable luxuries. In many countries (mostly outside of Africa and the Middle East), wealth is increasingly distributed beyond the ruling elites.

But we are beginning to fall behind in meeting the health crisis of fast spreading epidemics and medically resistant diseases. Along with changing climate and weather patterns, we are facing water problems of sufficiency to provide both for drinking and to meet irrigation needs for increased food production, and of pollution of water resources from agricultural and industrial runoff. We are not recognizing and responding to the popular demand and real need for political and economic change in most of the Middle East along with much of Africa. Even in most of the "developed world" we are failing to meet the increasing critical needs to adjust their unique financial, economic, and political realities with appropriate new systems and new methodologies.

Likewise, in advanced countries where the birth rate is declining the tax base is unable to provide for the increasing economic and medical needs of aging populations.

Can we have cultural changes that will bring population growth under a fair and balanced control and at the same time fulfill the promise of Gender Independence and meet other challenges of future development? (See #10 below)

The development of Personal Clairvoyance will increase comprehension of "Disasters in the Making" and suggest ways to circumvent the often deadly corruption and corrosive actions of the Middle East's Ruling Elite, and the failures of "populist" dictators in North Korea, Africa, and Latin America. And, indeed, we are also seeing collusion between Big Corporations & Moneyed Elite and government regulators in advanced countries where there is a re-distribution of wealth from the most in need to those with the least need.

<u>Number 2:</u> The **"Knowledge Revolution"**—Only a few hundred years ago the scientist Giordano Bruno was burned alive for teaching that our Sun was a star among many stars, and the astronomer Nicholaus Copernicus nearly met the same fate until he recanted his teaching that the Earth revolved around the Sun. While we know much more today, *ignorance is costly*. Our actual knowledge of the Earth is superficial, and yet it is the *source* for our material resources, the *foundation* of our food chain, the *platform* for our homes, and the *launching pad* for our entry into space. We have a minimal understanding of earth movements, and a near zero ability to forecast earthquakes—yet, in just one year (2010) they killed 226,000 people. Likewise, our knowledge and ability to forecast extreme weather is improving, but storm-related deaths and damages during 2010–2019 decade should have been preventable. Our understanding of sub-atomic physics is increasing but the potential value in terms of energy and material welfare is beyond present intellectual comprehension and political acceptance of appropriate action.

The development of Personal Clairvoyance will augment other techniques of forecasting through expanded vision and give us increased psychic sensitivity to earth changes, to weather extremes, and to the ramifications of human preparedness and response.

<u>Number 3:</u> The **"Technology Revolution"**—Until very recent historical times, the major "technology" was *Human Slave Labor.* In just the last few hundred years we moved rapidly from Man and Horse Power to Mechanical Power; from small Wind Power to Steam Power; from Wood to Fossil Fuels for Heat and Transportation, and currently from Fossil to Nuclear for Electrical Power, and we're on our way to economical and geographic independent Solar Power and large Wind Power installations; from the Town Crier to Print to Broadcast to the Internet for News and Entertainment; from hand-delivered Written Letters to the Telephone to the Internet for Communication; from hand-copies book in monastery libraries to Print-books in Bookstores and e-commerce to E-books on the Internet for Information and Knowledge; and so on with lots in between.

The global impact of the internet is still only vaguely acknowledged and the far-reaching Transforming Power of access to immense amounts of current Information and Knowledge in all areas of life available immediately and personally on-line is barely understood by even the most ardent enthusiasts, and the practical economics are barely in minimal development.

A faster implementation of the Internet's potentials is critical to all areas of Human Welfare and its Advancement, and is the acknowledged foundation for World Peace. With the development of Personal Clairvoyance, entrepreneurs will have a better vision of these potentials and investors greater confidence of success for their business models, and users will discover transforming applications and means of communication bypassing the restrictions of dictatorial censorship and propaganda.

<u>Number 4:</u> The **"Urban Revolution"**—in one century we have moved from primarily rural culture to primarily urban . . . *Worldwide!* Population density has facilitated the broad spread of basic education and (to a lesser extent) of realistic vocational, higher and advanced education, and more efficient distribution of food and manufactured products.

But we are encountering critical challenges in areas of cross-cultural migrations, in environmental stresses, and in meeting the increased demands for energy production and distribution, in criminal apprehension and prosecution, in the increasing abuse of political power and "crony capitalism" and in the terrifying ethical acceptance of greed and corruption as justifiable and even beneficial "normal human behavior!"

The disastrous effects of intellectual stupidity and arrogance in political and other leadership positions (religious, corporate, labor, education, etc.), along with the all-pervasive destructiveness of short-term goals with a lack of *structural* vision, must be corrected if we are to avoid obvious disastrous consequences.

Can the Internet and other high-technological innovations be quickly applied to adapt urban culture to environmentally favorable practices that will reduce transportation costs (highways and fuel) by creating virtual offices with self-responsible free-lance entrepreneurial staffs, develop alternatives to fossil fuels, make manufacturing still more efficient through more computer controlled processes, stimulate pertinent education and vocational re-training, and develop new business applications and models to broaden the economic base, etc.?

We need to broaden the industrial economic base and add new employment and entrepreneurial opportunities in areas not even being thought about today, and be able to rapidly adjust our social, governmental, and economic thinking to meet and facilitate new realities.

To put it simply, people need to "grow up" and we need more people to recognize, develop, and employ Personal Clairvoyance in daily practice in order to better see factors related to their work and activities, and to perceive their potential effects.

Number 5: The **"Industrial Food Revolution"**—in a half-century we have moved from locally and regionally grown foods by family farms to massive "factory" farming based on chemical, hormonal, and genetic developments that increase growth rates and resistance to some parasites. One contra indication is that it is increasingly apparent that such "unnaturally" grown food (most particularly meat and poultry) have negative effects starting with child development, early sexual maturation, increases in obesity, diabetes, asthma, allergies, and the occurrences of early diabetes, autism, attention deficit hyperactivity disorder (ADHD), depression, cancers and coronary diseases, etc. One possible positive side benefit is the ability to supply an international market with grains and even fruit grown on one continent and moved by air to another, balancing surpluses and shortages resulting from weather and climate aberrations. At the same time it is recognized that many foods grown outside the United States could be grown "at home" for a positive contribution to the local economy and better food safety inspections.

Good food is fundamental to good health, and with the growth of industrial foods, we may not always have good food. But because of the increasing lobbying connections between industry and governmental agencies (*crony capitalism*), the public is left in doubt as to what is and what is not safe. *Can the Governmental Process change from greed to ethics and honesty?*

The development of Personal Clairvoyance may give some people actual warnings about food dangers while leading to visions of helpful and healing alternatives.

<u>Number 6:</u> The **"Natural Food Revolution"**—in the last quarter-century we are moving toward culturally select crops that are increasingly local and home grown under organic and even lunar-timed conditions, reflecting a developing Nature-Harmonious, Self-sufficiency New Age movement. Such small and home-scale, and even hobby-time gardening, is creating a counter-revolution to the industrial food questions raised in the previous point. Yet, we are left with the questions: *Can we produce enough quantity of locally grown, organic quality, food to supplementally meet the population driven needs of an urban civilization? Or, can the Industrial Food Revolution fast-forward to producing the needed quantity and quality of food from algae and oceanic sources?*

The development of Personal Clairvoyance may give people new answers to such pressing questions with a long-term perspective. Increased psychic sensitivity may also lead to a broadening vision of our Human interconnectedness with Nature and the Cosmos.

Never before has there been such potential for massive employment of esoteric technology to solve critical problems. And, the need for solutions is immediate and not just for futuristic speculations.

<u>Number 7:</u> The **"Climate & Weather Change Challenge"**—in which man-made factors are responsible for extreme weather and climate aberrations that are becoming more and more threatening to global health and wealth, peace and welfare. While scientific evidence for the involvement of pollutions, industrial gases and wastes, CO_2, etc., is nearly overwhelming in substance, short-sighted political and even religious forces are in actual denial and claim the expense of "saving the Earth" is unaffordable. In the meantime, the Ice Caps melt, sea levels rise, tornadoes and extreme weather destroy property and kill people, weather extremes produce flooding in some areas and drought in others, moisture shortages in the American Heartland threaten future crops, and all this is faced by increased popular demands and the threat of economic recessions.

Longer range climate & weather forecasting augmented with astrology and Personal Clairvoyance could give individuals some guidance to personal actions, but is unlikely to have sufficient popular support to make any substantial difference. It appears that it may take even greater catastrophes than those of this decade to awaken politicians to the need for global action.

<u>Number 8:</u> The **"Economic & Political Challenge"**—All the factors listed previously are not being addressed under the current national and regional financial and governance systems, revealing the failures of both leaders and citizens to perceive what is happening and have the "guts" and sense and maturity to assume responsibility to resolve critical trends now at both local and global levels. We elect politicians who are

mostly untrained in law to make laws, with no training or experience in economics to deal with economic matters, and whose primary goals are not those of public service but of political and financial connections that can be turned into profitable lobbying work upon leaving office.

We have a system today where politics "trump" economics while destroying the very fabric of our national and regional economies with failures of fair regulation, the pursuit of "crony capitalism," and the failure to advance towards global solutions.

A clear vision (Personal Clairvoyance) affirms the need for globalism in contrast to present day financial chaos, personal greed and political gamesmanship oblivious to the international dimensions of real world economic activity fundamental to the health and wealth of all nations and peoples.

Number 9: The **"Irrational Beliefs Challenge"**—With financial and political greed reaching towards catastrophic levels, "crowd psychology" turns toward the Irrational for impossible solutions and emotionally dependent people are easily mis-led by bigoted, unscrupulous and under-educated leaders determined to bring the world under domination to their biased representation of Divinity. So long as sectarian "Religion" remains politically untouchable, spiritual ignorance will reign and pervert the very essence of spirituality common to genuine world religions. (This statement should not be misinterpreted as any rejection of the First Amendment to the U.S. Constitution, but seen as an affirmation of it and the need to include non-sectarian world religion and philosophy in today's schools.)

The three major monotheistic religions all "preach our way is better than their way" leading the way toward bigoted behavior and inevitable conflict. Religious Terrorism is on the increase, and Religious War, unfortunately, is increasingly likely.

Despite their mystical foundations, the leaders of these religions reject personal mystical (paranormal) practices and generally condemn Personal Clairvoyance because it might lead towards vision and belief different from their own time-frozen theology.

Number 10: The **"Gender Independent Evolution"**—We have moved to gender equality in Labor, Politics, Education, and even in Sexuality. In the West, and especially in the United States, women have been freed of previous legal and cultural restraints, and both men and women have become able to be sexually expressive in dress, adornment, behavior, and more Holistic Relationships inclusive of gender and role play experimentation. Among the benefits is employment based on Skill and Training, flexibility in Employment Practices that recognize the roles of parents and that encourage advanced job-related education and training, a cultural encouragement of Independent and Creative Thinking, Intelligent Family Planning and Child Care, increased exposure to Nature and a growing understanding and practice of a harmonious relationship with Nature.

Increased leisure time and increasing freedom from repressive religions (particularly in so-called religious education of children) have brought about greater exposure to Esoteric and Spiritual practices, which in turn are leading to Self-responsibility, and Psychic and Self Empowerment—including developing Personal Clairvoyance.

Unfortunately, we have lost recognition and understanding of archetypal imagery and the natural and functional differences in feminine and masculine energies regardless of gender—if we ever did have it. Personal Clairvoyance will lead to actually seeing these differences and how they function on the different planes in alternating polarities. It is these differences and the actual positive and negative sexual energies that bring about "sexual empowerment" and transform the energetic exchanges into a spiritual dynamic long unrecognized outside of the Tantric practices of India and China.

Number 11: The **"Home/Work" Evolution"**—Initially recognized under the categories of Part-Time Employment, then of Free-Lance Employment, and now often as Self-employed Consultants and Independent Contractors. Working-at-Home (or "Working-Out of Home") is one of the fastest growing areas of employment. Sometimes these "non-organization" entrepreneurially-spirited people rapidly evolve into consulting firms, independent sales agencies, and start-up businesses often involved in new technologies.

But, it is important not to limit our focus to the glamorous new technology start-ups and instead see the growing trend to *out-source* regular "office work" to the "home-work" force each responsible for his or her own work hours (sometimes with certain set availability requirements) and work furniture, equipment and tools.

No matter how it is handled (along with presumed honesty), such programs call upon individual entrepreneurial spirit, encourage personal subject expertise, and are more efficient, producing capital savings, reducing overhead costs, and reducing the environmental impact, of large office buildings, the related costs of police and fire protection, the costs of related infrastructure (highways, parking lots, traffic control, pollution, etc.

Of course, not all work can be out-sourced to the home worker, but often we also see examples of individual "light manufacturing" going home: cutting and sewing of garments, small assembly operations, customer and technical telephone service, fund-raising and various political and social appeals, various "support" services related to publicity and marketing (valet service, personal guides, setting retail displays, doing hand-outs, and so on.

The human benefits are enormous as the individuals involved are more at home with families, learn self-responsibility, develop ambition, practice personal time management, learn particular skills and are often encouraged and helped to take advanced training and professional education.

The more personal responsibility and self-management there is, the greater is the natural growth and development of the Whole Person, including the natural induction of paranormal powers otherwise nearly impossible in a crowded work and social environment. Personal Clairvoyance facilitates the perception of opportunity and the ways of innovation.

<u>Number 12:</u> The **"Global Solution"**—*These are critical times*. On the one hand, we have never before enjoyed the levels of Wealth, Health, Education, and Individual Freedom of expression as we have today. But, the three challenges described above are leading toward Global Catastrophe that can only be addressed by:

• Global Institutions

• Vertically Integrated Economics

• Individual Education and Enlightenment

• A Renewed educational system that teaches the value of rational ethical behavior in relation to a modern, scientifically sound, world view.

Since World War II ended when the United States dropped two atomic bombs on Japan, eight nations currently are known to have nuclear weapons, a ninth nation is believed to have them, and one nation is eagerly developing them. Of these ten nations, <u>two regularly express their intention of using them against designated enemies</u>.

Eight of the ten nations have to varying degrees become democratic, semi-capitalist/ free enterprise, and "modern" in most ways. The two who are not democratic are the two bellicose nations mentioned above. There's no need to name them. Of those two, the one that is still developing nuclear capacity is currently threatening military actions, and that nation is ruled by a religious dictator openly declaring his ability and willingness to sacrifice millions of lives in pursuit of ideological goals. No amount of diplomacy has reduced tensions, and that one situation threatens world peace.

Can this nation be defeated in case of attack?

Yes, of course, but at a tremendous cost in human life.

What will happen?

Can War be Avoided?

Frankly, we don't know. Hope, optimism, and an ultimate belief in rationalism lead us to believe that war can be avoided—but accidents happen and emotion clouds clairvoyant sight as well as rational thinking and perception.

If a 21st century World War III war is avoided, there are still many problems and challenges as previously outlined. *Are the dominant five or six nations willing, and politically able, to pursue the course of true global civilization?* There seem to be two possible answers:

1. That only a truly global disaster actually occurs, or is barely avoided as the result of concerted actions by these same five or six dominant nations. Turning to science fiction for an example, this would have to be something like an immense asteroid barely pushed away from direct impact by the deployment of every available nuclear armed missile—thus *proving the value of global action using modern technology.*

2. That enough people "grow up" into higher consciousness and clairvoyant vision, accept their role as global citizens, and deploy sufficient people power to force reluctant politicians to move to a global reorganization. The world needs international standards for economic, educational, commercial, financial, and other activities in accordance with international law enforced by a single global military force dominant over national police forces.

***

What does all of this political umbrage and speculations about global challenges have to do with the induction of Clairvoyance and Techno-Shamanism's tools of Sensory Isolation and Deprivation?

This is not a book about Globalism or rational economics, and these historic trends and contemporary challenges are raised only to show the transitions in life style and culture that should be recognized even in esoteric practices.

Spirituality cannot Avoid Worldly Concerns

Spirituality is not isolated from worldly matters, but all aspects of Body, Feeling, Mind, and Spirit are integral to the Whole Person and to our Life Work. We function at all levels, even though most people remain unaware of the non-physical and others ignore the call to Wholeness through denial that there is anything non-physical.

Anyone can become Psychically Empowered

Today we believe that anyone, hence *everyone*, should have opportunities for spiritual growth and psychic empowerment, and our writing always has broad potential readership in mind. While our programs are developed under strict laboratory conditions in the objective and scientific manner acceptable at professional and academic levels, we want them to be fully understandable by everyone, and useful—even enjoyable—by *anyone*.

In early India—in relative terms—a person was either rich or poor, and very few people had the time or circumstance to practice yoga or other esoteric technologies, and those that did (mostly men) devoted all the mature years of their lives to it, living in isolation, and dependent on the charity of people really barely able to provide for their own selves and families.

Anyone can live a "Spiritual Life"

Yes, anyone in modern culture can practice a "spiritual life" that may include vegetarianism, meditation, prayer, a few yoga stretches, study of astrology and other esoteric subjects, or carry on side activities of Tarot readings, participate in Pagan events, have an herbal garden, and other activities along with a steady job, keeping a household, raising a family, participating in the kids' school events and support groups, and many other activities all worthy and all part of *the "good life" with spiritual qualities.*

Our modern systems allow a life of many activities because so many of life's necessities and many relative luxuries are provided and facilitated economically through advanced technologies. And with good personal time management we are enabled to do more than casual meditation and a few esoteric studies. Today's Western developed psychic practices include very efficient techniques using self-hypnosis and guided meditations that are *transformative* and *empowering*—which is the cumulative and ultimate goal of all esoteric practice.

Controlled Sensory Input

Included with these practices are many tools of transformation ranging from divination aids to powerful audio and video products that complement such techniques through *controlled* sound and image effects.

Generally, we use sensory input of *external* origin involving <u>moving</u>* sounds and images in our audio self-hypnosis CDs, and even when we are not using external sensory input we tend to duplicate these through *internally* originating visualization and imagination.

*By "moving," we mean that visualized images, symbols, and even fields of color are pictured as objects, people or entities <u>in motion</u>, and as images that vibrate and move forward and backward, in and out, enlarging and diminishing, and sounds that travel as well as words often spoken with effect. <u>Nothing is static</u>. This is aside from sounds and lights that bombard and overload the senses as with loud drumming, bright flashing lights, and discordant music.

In our *private, personal, individual* and unaided practice, we use <u>silent</u> "self talk" in our self-hypnosis sessions; we may silently sound mantras and prayers; we visualize symbols and powerful images including those of gods and goddesses, angels, saints and other spiritual beings moving through expressive stories and roles.

Looking back over these few paragraphs, you should note the emphasis on "controlled" sound and image for "personal" and "individual" use in "private" practice. It's what we imagine "Quiet Time" to be in a private, light-proof, sound-insulated room.

Constant "Sensory Bombardment"

But one of the consequences of our very successful technologically empowered, and constantly-in-motion, very busy and socially involved, modern life style, is constant *sensory bombardment*. Our practice of yoga is usually with a group or class in a studio or gym; our meditation is usually with a group in a church or temple; many of our studies are in groups. Despite the potential for self-empowering study and practice provided to us by books, CDs and the Internet, we are overly dependent on others to provide opportunity and discipline.

Individual, or Group, Possession

Most shamanic practices are individual and sometimes solitary. Sometimes it involves group activities that support the role of the individual shaman. Others may be solitary or involve a single support person. All shamanism is directed toward some form of "Divine Possession" or *Communion* which may include out-of-body journeys.

Most shamanic activities have non-specific goals and rather just seek ecstatic and mystical experience. Others may have such defined goals as clairvoyant visions or out-of-body journeys seeking specific information or answers to specific questions, or *defined experiences to stimulate particular growth & development of the subtle body parts.* (You might well want to re-read that italicized part of the last sentence as it summarizes much about Techno-Shamanism that we will be discussing in this chapter.)

Traditional vs. Techno-Shamanism

In reality, there is very little difference other than the choices of the "tools" to aid the experience. Drums are very traditional, while Light Shows are very modern; Herbal Hallucinogens are traditional whereas psychedelic drugs are modern. Chanting is chanting, although the words and songs have changed. Dancing, ritual bondage, and flagellation may be common to both, but the *styling* is different. Sex is universal but the roles and relationship between the sexes have changed as masculine "dominance" is no longer universal in experience or fantasy.

But, when we say "Techno" we know that we are not relating to something antique and perhaps not applicable to modern ways and needs. As the world revolves and changes, so must we evolve and adapt to differing circumstance.

Sensory Overload

To put it specifically, the more familiar techniques of Techno-Shamanism directly employ Rock Concert-like sensory overload of sound, light, and movement as in loud rhythmic drumming with *intentional brakes,* very bright rhythmic flashing lights with *intentional brakes,* and very energetic body movements and ecstatic dancing with *intentional brakes.* (Note the mention of "intentional brakes;" their occurrence in the midst of intense sensory "movement" causes a kind of "falling forward" that often induces trance.)

Usually, but not always, these shamanic activities take place in a controlled environment of specific stage-setting, sometimes the dancers and performers are ritually costumed, and there commonly is a "stage manager" or ritual director singing and calling out specific words of power and invoking particular deities by their "sacred" names.

Call up in your imagination a picture of a Haitian Voudoun ceremony, or of Sufi Dervishes, or a Pentacostalist service, or of other ecstatic religions seeking possession by a higher presence, and you will gain some understanding of "controlled" sensory overload.

Sensory Denial

There is a different technique that employs the absence of sensory input to allow mind and spirit to move into other dimensions of altered states of consciousness not dependent on hallucinatory drugs, ecstatic dancing, and forms of sensory overload. Like certain form of meditation that clear the mind of all thought and emotion, the goal of sensory denial's physical aids is to facilitate the *surrender* of self to Self, *submission of*

Lower Ego to domination by Higher Self, and to replace the *struggle* of the physical body with the unblocked bliss of free-flowing energies.

By *encasing* our sensory organs and thus *blanking* the sensory bombardment normal to everyday life, the tools of sensory denial enable us to return—temporarily—to the comforting physical embrace and emotional security of the womb before our entry into physical life. The goal is not oblivion, and not sleep or physical restoration but *to use the unencumbered fully alert awareness for a focused and empowered opening of the inner senses to the Cosmic Light and the Cosmos' Message.*

Floatation Tank

Floatation Tanks

In the 1950s, research related to the subjects of "brain washing" and the potential problems of "men in space" opened two areas of research. There was concern that the lack of sensory stimulation—the normal daily experience not that of overload—would "drive men mad," lead soldiers and spies' held in solitary confinement to confess either real military secrets or make false confessions which would then be used in propaganda.

There was plenty of evidence to support these fears, but the analysis of these experiences neglected one single over-riding factor: as prisoners, many already subjected to torture, these men's thoughts and fantasies while in isolation centered on fear and expectation of more torture. While there was indeed an absence of sensory overload there was "emotional overload" on top of the physical torture that did result in confessions.

For further research in genuine sensory isolation, Dr. John C. Lilly created the Floatation Tank in which he stripped naked, put on a skin-diver's mask with attached air tube for breathing, and was suspended face down in a tank of comfortably warm (94°F), barely circulating water. He could see nothing, and hear nothing except his own breathing and faint water sounds. He felt nothing other than the face mask and the straps holding him in place. However, despite his intention to remain perfectly still, he found himself making small swimming movement,s and stroking one finger against another. *When he restrained himself from such movement, he became very tense* and had to get out of the tank. Eventually, he and others trained themselves not to move, and began to experience fantasies "too personal to be related publicly." After several hours he seemed to enter a "three-dimensional dark, empty space," and then a tunnel whose "inside space seem to be emitting a blue light."

Unfortunately, his mask started leaking and he had to get out of the tank. Later tanks had the occupant floating upwards in supporting saline water with the head held above the water with flotation pillows so a breathing mask was not necessary. Initially, the tanks were located in dark, quiet rooms; later the tanks themselves became isolation rooms with an entry door that closed from the inside by the occupant.

Others continued the floatation tank experiments, but only a few common points of interest can be noted:

Flotation Tank Common Experience

- Many occupants relieved their isolation by speaking and singing out loud.
- Others simply fell asleep in the absence of external stimuli.
- Most started hallucinating, some within 15 minutes. Some hallucinations were pleasant, others frightening.
- Logical organized thinking becomes difficult.
- Others were able to visualize themselves in physical activities like running, ballet, lifting, etc.—finding that the visualized work-outs were effective in strengthening muscles and perfecting these activities.

Flotation tanks became a fashionable thing to do during the 1980s: you could go to a public "tankatoria" and "tank" for $14 an hour.

Isolation Rooms

Another set of isolation experiments involved the use of "Silent Rooms"—some very elaborately designed to accomplish a truly silent mission. In England, one such lightproof room was suspended by nylon cords inside another soundproof room to prevent vibrations from passing trains and trucks reaching the occupants.

The periods of voluntary isolation ranged from 5 hours to 92 hours.

In another experiment, the occupants additionally had eyes and ears covered, but communicated to researchers via a live microphone. Another experiment involved persons placed in an inactive "iron lung."

The results were not substantially different than the floatation experiments, and the general conclusion of these experiments was that short-term sensory deprivation can be psychologically beneficial but longer term deprivation could be detrimental.

Factors in Failed Research In Floatation Tank & Isolation Rooms

- there was no actual restraint of movement and
- no repression of external communications either incoming or outgoing.
- Sound and Sight suppression was environmental rather than personal. And,
- there was no designated purpose other than participation in an experiment.

Note these factors in what we might call "failed research": *No restraint on personal movement, no restraint on personal communication, no restraint on personal hearing, no restraint on personal sight, no barrier to external touch, and there was nothing purposeful (such as vision seeking).* When we consider the Witches Cradle, these failures will be seen as important to the device's success.

We have two further examples to study before moving on to our main theme. Neither of these involves scientific study but each is a report of real life experience.

Restraint of Movement: the Eskimo Shaman

Peter Freuchen worked and lived among Eskimo people for about 50 years and once witnessed a shamanic technique of severe bondage restraining physical movement. Inside an ice igloo, surrounded by many fully dressed villagers, the shaman stripped himself naked, sat on a ledge where his arms and legs were tightly bound so no movement was possible. A drum was placed nearby along with a piece of dried sealskin, and the room was darkened leaving only one dim lamp to provide minimal light.

The shaman began to chant and with time his voice grew stronger and stronger, and seemed to emanate from different parts of his body. Then the chanting began to be accompanied by the beating of the drum and rattling of the dried sealskin with those sounds seeming to emanate from above the watchers' heads and beneath their feet—all the time neither the drum nor the sealskin was or could be touched by the shaman and was not touched by anyone in the igloo.

Suddenly, the shaman vanished!

The villagers present in the igloo became ecstatic—screaming, singing, swaying, danc-ing, and ripping clothes off—and this lasted some time. But when it stopped, the still chanting voice of the shaman could be heard approaching from a distance outside of the igloo! And then the drum beat started again, and grew so loud that the whole ice igloo was shaking. The piece of sealskin was flying about, and when Peter tried to grab it he said it nearly broke his arm. Sudden Silence. The remaining lamps were lit, the exhausted sha-man reappeared, still sitting, completely bound. He spoke of guidance received from the Spirits during his journey.*

*Paraphrased from the August 1962 issue of *Fate* magazine.

Restraint of Movement: The Shrink-Wrapped Prisoner

The second example relates to a case of modern torture practiced at the Arizona State Penitentiary in which the prisoner was repeatedly bound first in one straight jacket and then a second was tightly laced over the first. Water was then poured over both, soaking the canvas completely so that as it dried it shrank.

"Morell has himself told how he suffered inconceivable agonies for about a half hour. Then a strange peace would descend upon him, and he would find himself roaming freely outside the prison walls. Much of what he saw in the outside world was later checked and found to be true, though he himself was confined in an underground cell with no windows."*

*Hunt, D. *Exploring the Occult,* 1964, Pan Books.

This case was fictionalized in Jack London's *The Star Rover.*

TOOLS & TECHNIQUES OF SHAMANIC WITCHCRAFT

In personal correspondence between Gerald Gardner (the founder of modern Wic-ca), Charles Clark, and this co-author, **the "Eightfold Path to the Centre"** was stated to include:

1. Meditation or concentration, accompanied by the firm knowledge that you can and will succeed—forming a clear picture in your mind of your goal.
2. Trance states, Clairvoyance, Projection of the Astral Body, etc.
3. Drugs, Wine, Incense.
4. Dance, Performing Rites with a purpose.

5. Chants, Spells, etc.

6. Blood control (Cords, etc.), Breath control.

7. Scourging.

8. The Great Rite.

It is obviously necessary to explain some of these things. First, however, a caution: all these activities were actually guided and "supervised" by an experienced leader—the High Priest or Priestess. Second, the stated intention of the "endeavor" was trance to invoke the Great Mother Goddess to descend into the body of the person, in other words the goal is Divine Possession. In other words, the goal was not personal pleasure—not even in the sexual intercourse of the Great Rite. All shamanic action—indeed, all magical action—is done with a "higher purpose."

Because there are similarities between elements of these shamanic rituals and those of modern "concerts," we feel the need to interject what should be common sense warnings regarding the use of drugs, scourging, bondage, breath control, and unprotected sex. Things taken out of context are never quite right, and can be dangerous.

In the Gardnerian writing, it was also clearly stated that:

the great thing is to combine as many of these paths into the one operation. No. 1 must be in all—for if you have no clear picture of what you wish and no certainty you will succeed—'tis useless. No. 2 can be combined with this easily. Nos. 3, 4, & 5 are all good preliminaries—also 6 & 7; but No. 3 is dangerous and therefore to be avoided, except for incense, which is harmless if too much is not used.

The best combination is Nos. 1, 4, 5, & 7, for small purposes—with No. 8 if great force is necessary. Also a combination of 1, 6 & 7 is good if more can not be done—this if properly performed leads to No. 2

"No. 6 Blood control, (Cords, etc.), Breath Control" is ritual bondage itself used as a minor adjunct to Consciousness Alteration and as symbolic "submission" to the Deity, inviting possession of the body. The form of bondage is rather specific—the arms are pulled behind the back, and the wrists bound and pulled upward nearly to the neck in what looks like a reversed prayer position. Sometimes additional cords were used to bind the arms tightly to the body from just above and just below the breast/chest area. Artistic Japanese rope bondage calls this position "Ushiro Takatekote." The position does result in "blood control," i.e. reduced circulation and resultant numbness which psychologically opens the questor to trance and possession. Again, note that this form of bondage was ritualistic, or—in the case of Japanese rope bondage—an actual art form.

"Breath Control" involved two different things. The one is self-regulated breathing as in many yoga practices. The other was ritual suffocation—either self-induced or aided by another person (safer of the two)—to bring near-loss of consciousness as an invitation to possession or a precursor to trance. Again, *unless performed under experienced supervision, it can be dangerous!*

"Scourging" is ritual flagellation used for several purposes: 1) is symbolic surrender and submission to Deity and invitation to possession. 2) The physiology of light but rhythmic whipping on the buttocks draws blood to that area and away from the brain, inducing trance, 3) as a prelude to the "Great Rite"—ritual sex—the same light whipping induces sensual and sexual feeling.

"Chants" are a traditional rhythmic repetition of particular "mantra-like" words and deity names, leading toward trance and possession by the deity.

"Dance" is rhythmic movements usually in relation to chanting and perhaps to drumming, the flute, and other musical sources.

Trance & Possession

The goal of all these tools and techniques is trance, and possession by a "higher power." Sex is an element common to shamanism—not for itself but for it arousal of energy and surrender to the invoked deity.

We can sum it up simply into **the three objectives of Ritual Sex:**

1. The arousal of energy, physical and psychic, through any or all the above techniques, including sex in which at least one partner is actively managing the action and directing the energy to a single "higher" purpose;

2. The actual invocation and "surrender" to being possessed by the Deity (or Higher Power)—which, strangely enough, can include one's own Higher Self;

3. The return to "normality" with either the particular knowledge associated with the Deity, or particular messages from the Deity to the participant and the immediate community or audience.

Shamanism is (or was, depending on your perspective) the core of all "primitive" religious experience. The use of the word, "Primitive," here is not pejorative in any sense but rather is simply descriptive of its fundamental simplicity and its role as the foundation for the more complex religions that followed the initial experience of union with the "Source," the "Mother," the Father," "the God," the Goddess, the "Higher Power," etc.

It is also recognition that the "Son of the Father" is the "Son of Man," and that we are all "Children of the Goddess" by whatever names we prefer to use. Here, simply, there is no intermediary between the Deity and Man. That came only with "organized religion" and the professionalism of clergy who themselves no longer had the power to invoke and experience Deity but only to interpret and serve an established theology. The experience of Deity was placed to one side, and those persons are referred to as Mystics and Saints, basically "out of the loop."

But with the ending of the Church's monopoly on religious experience, many "sects" have risen in which direct experience is encouraged, although frowned upon by mainstream society.

Tools are not "necessary," but are often helpful and thus practical.

The emphasis in Techno-Shamanism is on a small range of "tools and techniques," alone or in combination. *We want to emphasize that we are only providing information, not recommendations. And with most of these techniques that point must be made that these all involved "assistance" and observation to avoid harm.*

This is a discussion of "technology" applying knowledge of body and spirit to the accomplishment of trance along with deity possession and/or the attainment of the major psychic powers of Clairvoyance and Astral Projection. It is not a discussion of morality, which is a personal and not a religious matter.

Of course, none of this is necessary as anything can be accomplished through Mind Control. But a life devoted to the pure and prolonged meditation—like a life devoted to prayer—is a life separated from any kind of active lifestyle and one that basically requires "support" to secure life's minimal necessities of food and shelter, and an environment free of distraction.

Shamanism offers one kind of alternative. In this book we also explore other forms for the induction of Clairvoyance—primarily Self-Hypnosis and Guided Meditation. Our goal is to offer the reader choices, and to provide sufficient instruction and information for all these different forms.

THE WITCHES CRADLE

The "Witches Cradle" comes down to us from medieval times through the practice of Traditional Witchcraft as a technique and tool to induce clairvoyance.

The Witches Sack

It has been described as a torture device used by the Inquisition to force confessions, but it was simply a large sack used to suspend the occupant from a tree or scaffold and then spin her about (medieval Witches were always believed to be women by the male Catholic clergy in charge of their torture). We want to clarify this mis-identification because of the association with pain and torture. The real Witches Cradle was not a burlap sack.

The Witches Sack Today

Various Pagan events today, and even some entertainment venues, provide such a sack and let people experience the sensations of mild sensory deprivation and spatial distortion. In *The Astral Projection Workbook* (see source material at the end of this chapter) J. H. Brennan gives instructions on "How to Make a Witch's Cradle" that is actually this type of sack.

> *You can construct a [witches sack] by finding, or making, a sack large enough to hold you while you are standing upright and strong enough to support you if it was lifted while you were inside. Since you will be inside when the cradle [sack] is in use, it is well to stress that plastic or any other air-tight material should be avoided because of the danger of suffocation. Coarse, strong, loose-weave sacking is probably the most ideal . . . . The neck of the sack should be fastenable by a draw string and the whole thing arranged so that it may be suspended safely with a subject inside. (Brennan, J. H.: The Astral Projection Workbooks*

It must be pointed out that for safety consideration; there should always be an assistant or observer present to assure that the occupant's breathing is not impaired, or that other hazards have not arisen. This "team" approach should be seen as necessary for one reason or another in all forms of Techno-Shamanism.

The "Real" Witches Cradle

But, these sacks are not the real thing as we will show though correspondence and illustrations provided by an English Witch, Margaret Bruce, for an article this co-author wrote back in 1964.

In a letter dated July 17, 1962, Mrs. Bruce wrote:

The "Witches Cradle" is an exercise based upon the fact that isolation of the senses from outward stimuli tends to produce clairvoyance and "lifts the veil of matter" as effectively as the use of the Unguentum Sabbatti or similar forms of drugs.

The Basics of the Cradle

The cradle itself could have any variety of forms but in general pattern it was always designed to bind the limbs firmly in a rigid position so that movement was impossible. The canvas, leather, or other material that enveloped the body of the person seeking entrance to one or other of the "Aethyrs" was thick enough and adjusted to the degree where no other sensation but the even supporting pressure of the material itself could be felt. A thick hood covered the head muffling the hearing and keeping the indrawn air at the body temperature or as near as possible in order to reduce even the sensation of breathing* to a minimum.

> *Note that the thick hood did not prevent breathing—that would be contradictory to the intent of a "living" experience of trance and possession by Deity—but it does introduce the element of "Breath Control" mentioned earlier as among the Eightfold Paths to the Centre. The slowed breath helped bring about trance.

There seems to have been no standard design for a "witches cradle." In some cases the person was hung by straps attached to the wrists in a similar manner to the sleeves of a straightjacket. Pressure of the upper arms at the side of the head, through the thickness of the hood, impeded the flow of blood to the brain and [physical] unconsciousness* followed. An alternative method was to twist the suspending cord in such a way that, when suspended, the body would spin rapidly back and forth producing dizziness and sometimes lack of consciousness.*

> *Such unconsciousness may been purposeful, i.e. marking the Out-of-Body Experience. Nevertheless, we need to emphasize the need for experienced supervision to detect anything hazardous. While sleep is also a state of unconsciousness, it is not the object of sensory deprivation.

Movement

It is this back and forth rocking or twisting movement which dulls the awareness of material surroundings in the case of the "witches cradle." There was probably a spell or ritual mantra to go with the cradle method of reaching the astral or exploring the Aethyrs.

The "Self-Hug"

The first illustration shows the Witch laced into a leather garment similar to a straight jacket, arms crossed beneath the chest,* and the head covered with a hood. The occupant is strapped into a suspended iron frame that swings and rotates freely. The second illustration shows how her head is firmly secured in place to prevent nodding—likely to produce undesired sleep.

> *This "self-hug" crossing of the arms is a proven posture inducing relaxation and feelings of security.

What we see here is a means to total sensory deprivation along with complete restraint of any physical movement. Because of the complete wrapping of the body and the support of the device itself, there is no discomfort interfering with the absence of all sensation. The occupant can literally "float" in an ocean of consciousness.

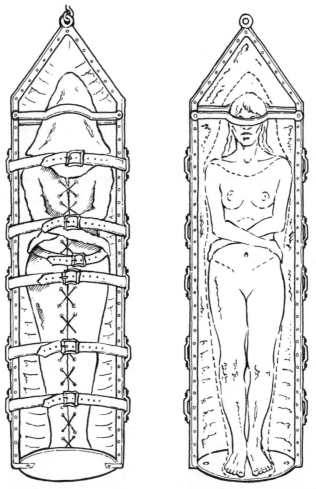

Traditional Witches Cradle (left) Inside the Witches Cradle (right)

Floating in an Ocean of Consciousness

Floating in an Ocean of Consciousness opens up two pathways: one of undirected openness to—**what?** *Can it be defined at all or only experienced?* The other pathway is one of *vision*—the focus on a single question or desired information. The absence of all sensation opens the occupant to the clear vision of Clairvoyance, perhaps along with Astral Projection. A question asked with focused purpose is almost always answered.

Altered States of Consciousness Induction Device

Another modern Consciousness Altering device was invented by the husband and wife founders of the Foundation for Mind Research, Drs. Jean Houston and Robert Masters, after my 1964 article on the Witches Cradle was published. They patented it as "The Altered States of Consciousness Induction Device" for use in research and psychotherapy.

The device, known by the then (1970s) fashionable acronym of ASCID, was manufactured by the Erickson Educational Foundation for professional use only, and it was demonstrated on many college campuses and at professional conferences.

The device as shown in the accompanying illustration consists of a metal frame supporting a metal swing suspended from a single pivot so that it can freely swing in all directions. The occupant stands upright on a platform, held in place against the supporting metal bars by wide sheets of canvas. Padded goggles render him blind.

The pivot is so sensitive that any movement at all sets the device in motion. Masters and Johnson describe it as a method for inducing a non-hypnotic trance with much vivid imagery and responsive to suggestion or guidance. In other words, the device induced a trance which opened the occupant to external therapeutic guidance just like regular hypnosis.

Note that neither hearing nor speech is inhibited—a possible drawback to its usefulness for inducing clairvoyance and cosmic exploration. Note, too, that the concept of professional use contradicts the use as a means to Personal Clairvoyance and the goal of self-understanding and self-empowerment.

Sensory Deprivation and Personal Clairvoyance

Can Sensory Deprivation produce Extra Sensory Perception, or does it merely lead to Illusion and Self-Deception?

This question may lead to a very important consideration in any study of the various methods that have been used in all cultures to go beyond-the-normal perception of the day-to-day world. It may be, as various investigators have suggested, that we experience or see more or less what we expect to see or have been conditioned to expect.

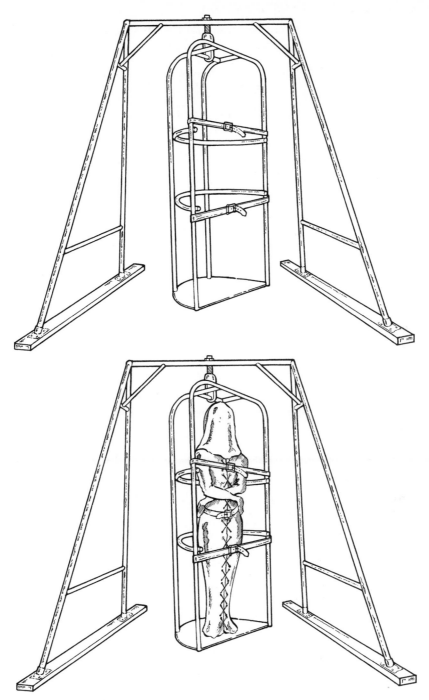

Altered States of Consciousness Induction Device (top)
and the ASCID in use (bottom)

The Limitations of Ordinary Vision

Such a possibility is not to be considered lightly when you realize that much of what we do see or experience through the normal physical senses is also in the realm of what we have become conditioned to expect. The artist learns to see certain things that the layman misses; the super patriot finds menace under every imported tree; the trained naturalist sees a city of life at his feet where another only sees dirt.

Personal Clairvoyance

Throughout this chapter and elsewhere in this book, we have given specific attention to "personal" clairvoyance in contrast to general clairvoyance, and higher clairvoyance.

As scientists and writers, we can come up with a multitude of distinctions for any power or skill, and readily invent new names for them. Too many, however, just becomes too confusing. Still there are some basic distinctions. When you consult with a professional clairvoyant, we are calling that "general clairvoyance" in distinct contrast to "personal clairvoyance."

Both "personal" and "general" clairvoyance refer to the *clear seeing* of visions, pictures, symbols, etc., in relation to *mundane* matters. But the word "personal" means that not only is the vision seen by you, alone, but its application is to you, alone. Even when the vision is of something that involves other people—as in the sinking of a cruise ship you were thinking about for your vacation—the message is fully personal applying to you, for you, and by you. Yes, you can share it with others, but the reason for the vision was to warn you!

"Higher" Clairvoyance is mostly impersonal and deals more with the "inner side" of things—seeing and interpreting the several Auras we all have, gaining insight into the ways of Reincarnation, the Age of the Cosmos, the History of the Great Pyramid, the Great Plan of Evolution, etc. It's generally about the "Esoteric" in contrast to the "Mundane"—but we have to be careful with such distinctions because deeper understanding of things Esoteric is helpful in every aspect of your present and future lives.

The 1960s Drug Culture

In the early 1960s there were many sensational articles dealing with hallucinogenic drugs, including LSD-25, mescaline, and "magic" mushrooms. In many of these articles it was pointed out that the "researchers"— often college students tripping out on excessive quantities of the drugs in question and turning them into recreational and party drugs—seemed to suffer a loss of contact with the social world along with emotional and mental deterioration.

Others who have studied these drugs can equally point to people who have used mescaline, or peyote, for years without ill effects. The difference may well lie in the fact that those who have used hallucinogens in connection with religious ceremonies are conditioned to expect a certain kind of experience, and are subjected to the psychological and perhaps psychosomatic effects of rituals with chanting, dancing, gestures, music, etc., that give direction to the flow of psychic energy released by the drugs.

"Psychic energy" may be a misleading term to use in the above context, but we use it to represent whatever factor is involved in the indisputable alterations of consciousness accompanying the use of psychoactive substances. It may be only that certain areas of normal brain function are 'shut off', and others are 'turned on' to a greater than normal degree.

Seeing "Beyond the Normal"

In contrast, Isolation, or Sensory Deprivation, is primarily used to induce the state of clairvoyance, or what we have already called a "beyond-the-normal" experience. That Sensory Deprivation also functions under the same laws as the drug experience—that altered states may be affected by the expectation of the seeker, or given direction by ritual and psychological factors, is logical.

The Limitations of Earlier Research

In many of the experiments conducted in connection with the space program, the experimental subjects also experienced disorganization, loss of social contact, fear, etc. There are two factors in particular that we want to emphasize in regard to these experiments: (1) the lack of any preconditioning that would give direction to the new level of consciousness experienced; and (2) the comparative freedom of movement allowed the persons being subjected to sensory deprivation.

The first factor is obviously a necessary one, at least for some percentage of the experiments, to give meaning to the research of the experimenters. The second factor is one that has generally been overlooked, perhaps out of concern that it would be difficult to secure persons to participate in the experiments who would be willing to subject themselves to a complete restraint of body movement. There was some research along this line in academic programs, but it was been extremely limited by a fear of misunderstanding and possibilities of mis-use of restraints leading to harmful incidents.

Movement as Sensory Experience

As any dancer well knows, body movement is itself a sensory experience as well as a means of expression. By allowing movement of the body, even as limited a movement as in some of the research involving submersion of a rubber-suited man in a tank of water where his movements were limited to waving of arms and legs there has not been a full deprivation of normal sensory input. The normal pattern of living has taught us to seek some degree of sensation at all waking moments, and so long as we have an opportunity for such sensory experience, we are likely to take it. The fears and erotic fantasies experienced by many in those isolation experiments may have been the result of this partial deprivation of sensory input creating a desire for more in the same way that a little candy makes you want more of the same thing!

The Witches Cradle is a device that not only effectively isolates a person from his physical environment but makes body movement completely impossible. Under such conditions, consciousness is forced to move in new channels, and for some this results in Extra Sensory Perception—and *more so when that is the pre-determined intent of the operation.*

The "X-ray" view of the witches cradle illustrated in this chapter shows the body of the person seeking entry to other planes of consciousness bound in a mummy-like sheath of leather with the arms are fastened straitjacket fashion. Straps firmly hold the body in the iron frame of the cradle, a leather hood cuts off vision and sound, and an iron band holds the head in position. The cradle itself is suspended from a single pivot so that it can swing and rotate freely.

Sensory Deprivation PLUS Restraint of Movement

Sensory Deprivation can and does produce conditions conducive to ExtraSensory Perception. Restraint further reduces actual physical sensory experience, and, as stated in a letter received from a member of a witch coven, ". . . one of the witch secrets is that restraint will produce powers."

The main purpose of complete sensory isolation and restraint of movement is to induce Personal Clairvoyance. A further purpose is of aiding the projection of consciousness beyond the physical body. As one correspondent expressed it:

"The 'Witches Cradle' is not so much the name of an instrument as the name of an exercise for 'getting out of the body.'"

People who have *recreationally* experimented with it for short periods have not had beyond-the-normal experiences other than pleasurable relaxation. Essentially the same technique has been in medical use for years to bring about relaxation—as the familiar strait jacket which is used as much for its sedative value as it is for a restraint, and as the wet sheet that is wrapped around the body tightly to prevent any movement at all.

One occupant wrote:

Being strapped into the garment-like cradle, you feel as if you are entering into a world all your own. The straps are the only things holding me in the cradle. After this a mask is put over the head shutting off all sound and light. The cradle was raised, and I was left suspended in mid-air—completely and wonderfully alone.

This was my first time in the cradle but I know it cannot be my last for the feeling of seclusion itself is almost unbelievably relaxing. Many things go through the mind at first, but most common problems are forgotten. Then the feeling of this new world comes which no words can express.

The following is excerpted from a long letter reporting on a series of nearly thirty informal experiments with four subjects using the cradle to achieve ESP abilities, and experiencing successful telepathy between the occupant and a receiver. The occupants were also aware of activities beyond the immediate environment:

. . . the time spent in the cradle is all important. It takes several hours for the subject to lose all physical sensation. . . . Although the subject loses all physical sensation she retains a strong mental perception of the snug confinement of the cradle which induces a relaxed impression of complete security. The taut confinement causes that subject to lose all desire for any kind of muscular movement.

. . . We had some fear that the cradle might create a loss-of-touch with reality but the subjects emerge with an increased sense of perception with their physical surroundings.

It should be noted that the report is anonymous and claims that some of the sessions were continuous for more than twenty-four hours.

Rise of the "Serpent Fire"

Relaxation of the physical body and of emotional and mental tension is an important factor in establishing the conditions conducive to ESP phenomena. Another factor that may be involved in the witches cradle relates to the study of Yoga. In Hatha Yoga, and in Raja Yoga which utilizes the bodily positions and exercises of Hatha Yoga, much concern is given to the spine being kept straight. In the witches cradle this condition is naturally met, and it may be that the feeling of isolation causes a spontaneous movement of the "Serpent Fire" (aka Kundalini) mentioned in Laya Yoga.

Scientific and Academic Parapsychology studies has actually discovered very little about the mechanisms of ESP phenomena because of their fixation on the physical brain, and generally ignored in most parapsychology laboratories—except for some investigation of spirit mediums—the techniques actually used by persons trained in traditional ways to attain clairvoyance, projection of the astral body, etc. As we move into a new era—with the *New Science of the Paranormal*—we will see an active and more *subjective* study of the traditional methods and the non-physical factors involved. The results will hopefully lead to improved techniques adapted to contemporary needs and conditions.

Experience of "Ritual Death"

If the witches cradle is one of these techniques, it should also be studied as an exercise that is something more than an instrument. It is a symbolic experience of ritual death. To experience the sensory deprivation of the witches cradle is to experience the separation of consciousness from the physical environment that is death: to experience the restraint of the cradle, the enforced rigidity that is like the rigor mortis of death, is to experience the freedom of the soul, the expansion of awareness that is beyond death.

Through the experiences gained by the use of such symbols, through the living myths, through such rituals, we come to understand the deeper truths of universal life. In the experience of isolation, of immobility, of suspension in space, perhaps the apprentice witch sees herself as she really is—not the body, or the daily-life personality, not the 'shadow' made up of fears and denials, nor the 'animus' of her projected ideal but as a bit of the nothing that is everything.

Through Ritual & Symbol to Archetypal Truths

Through ritual, through symbol, we contact the archetypal truths that lie deep in our Unconscious and that are the wisdom of the entire race. We experience in condensed form the entire history of human consciousness. And in one moment, we can see the panorama of our entire life.

While a witches cradle itself may be comparably rare, the experience is not so rare. It has occurred to persons temporarily confined to bed, to persons out of contact with society, to fliers and astronauts.

The Witches Cradle Today

A modern variant, quite modified, is called a "Sleepsack."

Sleepsacks generally have a pocket at the bottom for the occupant's feet, and then zippers from below the knees to a neck collar. Most sleepsacks have internal arm sleeves either in strait-jacket self-hug style or straight down at the side of the body.

Some sleepsacks have straps along each side to loop at the shoulders so that the occupant can be comfortably and safely suspended from overhead, thus fully duplicating the Witches Cradle.*

*Wikipedia. *Sleepsack (BDSM)*

Sleepsacks either include a complete hood to provide sensory deprivation along with restricted movement or are complimented with a mask for that purpose.

There are numerous blogs on the Internet regarding out-of-body experiences during prolonged use of tight Sleepsacks. Researchers could contact these and other sites inviting response to questionnaires that could be helpful to deeper understanding of this OOBE technique and the possibilities for its refinement and improvement.

THE MEDITATION MASK

There are many methods that have been used to stimulate psychic phenomena of one type or another. Some methods are primarily chemical and physiological, such as psychogens like peyote, the amanita muscaria mushroom, certain incenses, fasting, etc. Others might be said to be primarily emotional, as demonstrated in the reports of visions by mothers of their dying sons, the psychic manifestations surrounding great emotional mystics, the use of light, color, music, and drama in ritual and in Rock and Rave concerts. Still other methods may be termed mental, involving extreme discipline of the mind and intense development of the powers of concentration and visualization as found in Raja Yoga and in certain practices of western Magick.

All these methods have certain common denominators. They all bring about a concentration of consciousness at the same time that a separation of the consciousness from the domination of the physical body and environment is obtained.

Precognitive Experiences

In his book, *Witchcraft: Its Power in the World Today*, William Seabrook wrote about his experiences with a young woman he called "Justine." Justine had the power of precognition, the perception of events in future time, but could only evoke this power when prolonged fatigue and strain seemed to bring about a separation of the "self" from the physical body.

Seabrook's first experiments were adapted from the "dangling" of the Arabian Dervishes. The Dervish mystics pass one wrist through a soft rope hanging from the ceiling, and then revolve their bodies until the rope shortens enough to leave only their toes in contact with the floor. Dangling in this manner is first of all a discipline, but second it is a means for inducing *melboos,* a state in which consciousness is experienced separately from the physical body. Seabrook modified the Dervish's dangling so that both wrists were fastened to create a psychological condition in which the subject knew she could not quit the experiment because of boredom or fatigue, and hence would give herself up to the experience.

While hanging this way in a darkened New York studio-apartment, Justine "saw" and described to Seabrook detailed scenes and events that both of them personally experienced months later.

No impersonal "predictions" were ever made—such as what the stock market might do, or who would win an election. The personal nature of Justine's visions seemed to suggest that precognition, or at least these precognitive experiences, were a 'welling up' of material from the sub-conscious, or the Un-conscious mind of the subject, rather than actual objective vision that can be focused at will on objects and events independent of ourselves in the way we can focus our physical vision.

Past, Present, and Future

In other words, *it may be that the future, in a personal sense, is as present with each of us as is the past.* Perhaps we do not normally perceive past and future time because we are captives of our present-time sense impressions.

A Leather Mask

A blind person often develops a vastly intensified sense of touch and of hearing in seeming compensation for the loss of physical sight. Seabrook devised a leather mask for Justine that blanked out the normal physical senses. The mask of soft, smooth, glace kid covered Justine's entire head and laced down the back to fit skin-tight. The only opening was for breathing. The wide open eyes inside the mask stared into utter blackness. The hearing was dulled, and the sense of touch—the tactile sensitivity of the cheeks to air currents and temperature—was also blanked.

Justine enjoyed being in the mask, and would spend as much time thus freed from her physical senses as she could. Here is perhaps an important observation to be made—she looked forward to these masked meditations: she did not experience boredom, pain, fatigue, fear, or loneliness. The mask seemed to relieve her of the need for physical sensation just as much as it deprived her of it.

ESP Testing

Seabrook and Justine in her mask conducted a series of ESP experiments using an ordinary deck of playing cards. Most of the time, Justine's scores were not very impressive —although statistically they were as good as many of the scores accepted by Dr. J. B. Rhine as positive—but on rare occasions, she had *actual visions* of the correct card Seabrook was holding while she was in the mask. She would *see* the card in the same way that you *see a* remembered object—i.e., there was a visual image seen as if it were projected in front of her eyes.

Always the precognitive experiences were highly detailed, and these details always actually occurred. But, none of Justine's visions were ever of a serious nature, but rather they concerned unimportant incidents, sometimes comical ones. One such vision came to Justine when she had been in the mask all day. What she saw was the delivery of a barrel of fish to her cousin's apartment. Months later, Justine was with her cousin when this barrel of fish, which had been sent as a joke by a vacationing friend in Canada, was delivered. The actual event occurred in all the exact details that Justine described in her precognitive experience.

Personal Visions

More often, Justine's visions were of the distant past. Again, these visions were always of a personal nature, as if Justine—separating her "self" from the physical limitations of present time and space—was able to relive lives past. Perhaps there was a "welling up" of actual memories of past lives from some level of the sub-conscious mind. Perhaps these experiences were just the racial memories of the Collective Unconscious common to all of us and not experiences of any previous lives of Justine's soul.

Many have experimented with deprivation, but most just repeat endlessly what we already know. However, Sanford Freedman in *Perceptual and Cognitive Change in Sensory Deprivation in SENSORY DEPRIVATION* noted that those subjects who relaxed and gave themselves to the experimental situation found it pleasant and were willing to return for further sessions.

Those who fought against the condition of isolation found it unpleasant and terminated the experiment before the designated time. We have already noted that Justine enjoyed wearing the mask.

Benefits of Temporary Sensory Deprivation

Subjects that have repeated the experiments have come to enjoy sensory deprivation and feel refreshed and relaxed by it. Smokers generally lose the need for cigarettes, and nervous habits disappear. The person experiencing isolation comes to appreciate the deeper layers of his own personality and finds less need for external stimulation.

It has been suggested that sensory deprivation, as is involved in the wearing of a mask such as Justine's, can be a healthy and therapeutic act neutralizing rigid or over-developed egos. As a demonstration of this, it has been shown that persons who are highly inhibited or sexually frigid often will become naturally expressive when wearing a mask. It seems as if the experience of separating the "self" from the physical present enables one to integrate emotional and mental complexes into the whole personality.

"The Journey into the Wilderness"

The temporary loss of self-identification with the body and its immediate physi-cal and social surroundings might be likened to the journey into the "wilderness" commonly found in the lives of great religious leaders and mystics. Such a "retreat" restores the body as well as the mind, bringing about a normalization of physical and nervous processes. In this context, it is interesting to find that there is commonly a loss of body weight during the isolation experiments, even though food intake is main-tained at normal levels despite the reduction of physical activity.

Sensory deprivation—whether by journey into the "wilderness," isolation in cells or rooms away from noise and disturbance, practices of mental discipline, "witch's cradle," or meditation mask—is found to be a common element in many magical practices.

There is nothing magical in the mask itself, but sensory deprivation is a technique that has been used in various forms to bring about a change in consciousness. Some-times this temporary change in consciousness is accompanied by types of extra sensory perception. While one would naturally judge that methods of mental discipline to attain isolation through control of the physical senses would be the best, such control of the mind and body is difficult and perhaps impractical in our present way of life subject to constant sensory bombardment and social togetherness.

In other words, with use of sensory isolation devices, it is possible to aid the devel-opment of paranormal skills without having to totally give up a normal life. Tech-nology brings us many experiences and opportunities once—not so long ago—near unobtainable and very expensive. Today you can readily see the latest motion pictures on your living room television, you can connect with the equivalent of a vast library with a few clicks, you can secure the advice of experts at minimal or no cost whatsoev-er and whenever needed, and with a relatively inexpensive mask or sleepsack you can control your sensory environment to benefit from deprivation and isolation within a busy, even noisy, urban existence.

Masking as a Method

The use of a mask covering the entire head to blank sight and sound is probably the most convenient and least troublesome of all the methods for accomplishing sensory deprivation. Such a mask can obviously be made of other materials than leather, but leather is satisfactorily light proof and "breathes" with the skin. The mask should not press upon the eyes as would a blindfold, since pressure on the eyeballs causes certain physical visual phenomena and would prevent the feeling of isolation that is an essential feature of these methods.

As with the Sleepsack substitute for the manufactured ASCID modernized Witches Cradle, you will find a practical and inexpensive substitute for a made-to-measure Meditation Mask for sensory deprivation available from many on-line retailers.

A Closing Note

Obviously, these devices and other physical aids are not *necessary* to the development of Clairvoyance or any other psychic power. Neither is a Crystal Ball but crystal gazing is a long established practice and the crystal ball a valid physical aid to Clairvoyance. Equally it could be said that divinatory tools—Tarot Cards, Runes, Geomantic sand boxes, Tea Leaf Reading, etc., are not *necessary* to Clairvoyance even though they are as essential to their particular technique as a Dowsing Rod or Pendulum is to dowsing for water or mineral resources.

Dowsing, Divination, Tarot, Runes, Crystal Gazing, etc., are all physical aids to various forms and practices of Clairvoyance. A highly developed psychically empowered person presumably does not need any physical aids. In the right environment, with the right training and discipline, objectless meditation can bring about whatever altered state of consciousness is necessary.

And some very developed people can "switch gears" without the need even for meditation.

Some men have been buried alive for days in underground coffins with the most minimal air support. It proves that amazing things can be done. Others can sleep on a bed of nails, sit naked in freezing mountain temperatures, walk on burning coals, lick white hot steel bars, and many more demonstrations of mind-over-body control.

But, this is a book on Clairvoyance for Psychic Empowerment, and this is one chapter dealing with just one form of technological aid in inducing clairvoyance for practical benefit in everyday life without a lifetime effort.

Psychic Empowerment as part of your Life Plan

We consider that there are **two aspects to psychic empowerment:**

1. That it is part of a program of accelerated growth.
2. That psychic power can and should be as readily used as any other power or skill for a better life.

Both should be part of your life plan, and it is our intention to provide you with tools and techniques for your personal growth and transformation into an empowered person. Your choice of tools and techniques is yours alone. That some choices may have additional or alternative uses should be no more controversial than drinking the tea in which the tea leaves used in a reading was brewed.

Sources & Suggested Additional Reading:

Baron, the (pseudonym for Weschcke, C. L). MinuteScope article *The Girl in the Leather Mask*. December 1963, Llewellyn.

Baron, the (pseudonym for Weschcke, C. L): MinuteScope article *The Witches Cradle and ESP,* January 1964, Llewellyn.

Brennan, J. H. *The Astral Projection Workbooks: How to Achieve Out-of-Body Experiences,* 1989, Aquarian Press, reprinted 1990 Sterling Publishing.

Buckland, R. *Buckland's Complete Book of Witchcraft,* 1986, Llewellyn.

Heron, W. *Cognitive and Physiological Effects* in SENSORY DEPRIVATION, A Symposium, 1961, Harvard University Press.

Houston, J. & Masters, R. *Mind Games: The Guide to Inner Space,* 1998, Quest.

Llewellyn. For information and application of Lunar timing in horticultural practice, see Llewellyn's annual *Moon Sign Book: Conscious Living by the Cycles of the Moon,* (2013), Llewellyn.

Seabrook, W. *No Hiding Place,* 1942, Harcourt Brace.

Seabrook, W. *Witchcraft: Its Power in the World Today,* 1940, Harcourt, Brace.

Woodburn, H. *Cognitive and Physiological Effects in Sensory Deprivation,* A Symposium, 1961, Harvard University Press, Cambridge.

ADDENDUM #8 TO CHAPTER EIGHT
Microcosm to Macrocosm & Macrocosm to Microcosm
THE ART OF COMPOUNDING

Nothing manifest can exist in a pure state. Everything we objectively experience is combined with other elements in various forms channeling various energies. Even as we meditate with the primal tattvas to balance and purify our subtle bodies and energies, we have to acknowledge the fact of their compounding.

In many ways we can use this knowledge of compounding to better understand the world as it is and to make our own experience better—in our well-being, in our relationships in and to the world around us, and in deliberate strengthening of the bonding of elements and forces for strategic purposes.

The "Bonds of Matrimony"

Think of the phrase: "Bonds of Matrimony"—meaning, of course, the bonding, or compounding, of husband and wife, of male and female, man and woman to change two singles into a duality, and then to a trinity as each relates the new entity of institutional marriage (having legal, social, economic and even *tax & insurance benefits* recognition). And then, as "two become one," uniting in procreation to parent a child, three people now unite in a new unity of a family, "three become one" in the archetypal *Trinity,* and the process of compounding further changes and *expands our reality.* The "Real World" consists of compounds.

Just as you may have asked what the first level of the Tattvic Connection Meditation & Visualization Program (involving the five primal elements) had to do with Clairvoyance, the question may arise again of this second level involving compounded elements. The answer remains the same: the Goal of Clairvoyance is *clear & accurate seeing* and thus of better interpreting and understanding the resultant vision as it applies to the information sought in the clairvoyant reading. Our reality, both objective and subjective, is complex and it is by deliberately invoking a controlled inner experience of that complexity that we develop and enlarge our psychic capacity.

The Nature of "Worship" as Invocation

Just as Marriage is a bonding between two separate entities, so is "worship." For most people, the act of worship is a purely external relationship between a single person and a proclaimed Deity. Forget, at least for a moment, any reference to a *named* Deity—whether Christian, Hebrew, Hindu, Pagan, Egyptian, Greek, Chinese, or other—and rather than thinking in terms of prayer or supplication TO that Deity, or of any kneeling or groveling before any statute or representation—think instead of your practice of meditation and visualization and the experience of *Becoming One* with the Primal Element through absorption in its name and mantra, and color and form.

Maybe you have yet to experience such union in its fullness, but if you persist in these programs, that visualization will become an inner reality and realization of the substance & force of the element involved. Now, just consider that every historic Deity is an established repository of a specific or—more often—a compound of psychic forces represented by the nature of that Deity—whether of that of an agricultural goddess or of a fertility goddess, or of a god of the hunt or one of prosperity, or one of universal love.

Also, think how the nature of each Deity is represented through various symbolisms involving name (and "mantra"), color and form. Yes, there is almost always a mantra of some sort associated with the Deity, whether formal prayers, chant, hymn, song, or repeated names and titles. Sometimes these will be called "Words of Power" but their identification with particularized Force is always defined.

The nature of worship itself has always been one of *exchange*: worship the goddess in her established ways, and receive her grace in the form of her specific psychic force. Rather than experiencing Deity as external, through our meditation and visualization we internalize the experience and unite with the "Force" *within* represented by the Deity. All that exists manifests through Force and Substance perceived through Consciousness.

But, realize that the operation of "worship" is little different than the operation of Magick: it is a set of specific formulae of compounded substances invoking particular forces to accomplish a determined goal. Likewise, in our visualization of a primal element we are invoking the primal force behind that element. Incorporating it, becoming one with it, we are awakening it and "perfecting" our inner nature by *consciously uniting with a specifically identified Force.*

"Worship" of a deity is really a form of temporary and conscious SELF-*IDENTIFICATION* with the special character and power of compounded deific forces in the chosen form and name of a god or goddess, or even of an abstract ideal. However, this differs from both what we might call "unconscious awareness" where people feel touches of the sacred from visiting shrines or seeing artifacts, and from what is called "worship" in the major monotheistic religions which is mostly an emotional (rather than mental and/or spiritual) involvement between the worshipper and the image presented in the rousing sermons of the minister. In both these cases there is no conscious connection between the High Self of the worshipper and the deific force invoked.

To avoid confusion, we will henceforth refer to this conscious connection by the magical term of "invocation"—which must be clearly seen as different from the similar term "evocation." At the same time, we must point out that most if not all Tantric and Hindu based literature refers to "worship" for what we refer to as "Invocation." And the same problem is also experienced in the study of most Pagan and Shamanic religions in which deity is invoked, even as it is referred to as "worship."

From that starting point, we can take many directions—some of which will be explored later.

In mystical traditions, this concept moves beyond such "practical" applications as crop and cattle management to what is termed *theosis,* union with the Absolute. In Christian doctrine, this was expressed by St. Athanasius: "God became man so that men might become gods." Other names for this mystical union are "Self-realization" (Hinduism), "enlightenment" (Buddhism), and also as "awakening." St. Basil the Great stated that "becoming a god is the highest goal of all."

I suggest that in New Age thought, each step in psychic empowerment (as in developing and improving clairvoyance) is a *Next Step* toward realization of our Higher Self. The meditation and visualization exercise that we have been using in these addenda appears to be a psychic technology thousands of years old, and that has been adapted in many esoteric, self-improvement, and religious practices.

The only "certainty" we have is that of continuing evolution. We are here to grow, to become more than we are, and to realize the wholeness to which we are intended.

Why "Compound?"

As already discussed, everything manifest exists in combination. But, there are differences between accidental compounding and intentional compounding. Contact with poison ivy results in a painful accidental compounding; while applying a healing salve to the irritated skin is intentional compounding. Through experience and knowledge we are enabled to intelligently bring about intentional compounding for specific benefit. We call these "science and technology" and it is through intentional application of "compounding" that we continually benefit life, expand culture, extend longevity, and some day bring peace and prosperity to all.

Just as nothing manifests in purity, so nothing exists in isolation. Even is the privacy of meditation, in spiritual retreat, in the silence of forest and mountain, we are forever connected with one another, and every intentional act has dynamic repercussions throughout our entire world.

CLAIRVOYANCE: DIVINATION, MAGICK, TRANCE, and INVOCATION (aka "worship")

Clairvoyance

We've said it again and again: the purpose of Clairvoyance is "Clear, and *Accurate*, Seeing"—but *seeing what?*

For most people, that "what" is an answer to specific questions about love, money, security, health, and . . . the FUTURE. But, we also more properly call this "divination"—often associated with such tools and techniques as Tarot, Runes, Astrology, Palmistry, Dream Interpretation, Geomancy, the I Ching, the use of Divining Rod & Pendulum, the Crystal Ball, etc. In fact, almost anything can be used to aid clairvoyance, and likewise it can be said that almost nothing is needed because the power & skill is internal. Even so, like all tools, their use can extend, multiply, and both define and refine the power and skill of the operator. And each such tool is as specific as is a hammer, a telescope or a surgeon's scalpel.

A very well developed clairvoyant may have little use for tools, and yet we need to say that clarity and accuracy of vision can be improved both by expertise in the choice and use of the tool and in the development, refinement and purification of clairvoyant's own internal resources—physical and subtle—and the training and experience that comes with continued developmental exercises and real-life applications.

In this book we see Clairvoyance as inclusive of any manner of securing "information about an object, person, location or physical event through means other than the known human senses." (Wikipedia) However, we have also to distinguish between the physical senses and the corresponding *subtle* senses that seem to act as extensions or expansions of physical perception.

Included in what we might refer to as "pure clairvoyance"—such as aura reading, past-life memories, pre-cognition, remote viewing, etc.—we must specifically mention "direct seeing" by which well-known clairvoyant writers such as Annie Besant, H. P. Blavatsky, Geoffrey Hodson, C. W. Leadbeater, Swami Panchadasi, Rudolph Steiner, and others seem to be able to switch-on an inner vision to see the "invisible" sides of man and nature. We generally refer to that as "Higher Clairvoyance" and it is that which particularly benefits from such programs as the *Tattva Connection Meditation & Visualization Program.*

Nevertheless, all techniques for gaining information outside of standard physical resources, or in augmenting such information through spontaneous intuition, fall into the general discussion of clairvoyance even though they are treated in detail in sources beyond this book.

Divination

The Merriam-Webster Dictionary defines it as: *the art or practice that seeks to fore-see or foretell future events or discover hidden knowledge usually by the interpretation of omens or by the aid of supernatural powers.* Wikipedia, however, gives us much more—so much so that I can only excerpt and paraphrase for this work:

Divination (from Latin *divinare* "to foresee, to be inspired by a god," related to *divinus*, divine) is the attempt to gain insight into a question or situation by way of an occultic standardized process or ritual. Used in various forms for thousands of years, diviners ascertain their interpretations of how a quer-ant should proceed by reading signs, events, or omens, or through alleged con-tact with a supernatural agency.

Divination can be seen as a systematic method with which to organize . . . random facets of existence . . . [to] provide insight into a problem at hand. If a distinction is to be made between divination and fortune-telling, divination has a formal or ritual and often social character . . . while fortune-telling is a more everyday practice for personal purposes. Particular divination methods vary by culture and religion.

Divination is often dismissed by skeptics, including the scientific commu-nity, as being mere superstition . . . It is considered a sin in Islam, most Chris-tian denominations and Judaism, though some methods, especially dream interpretation, do appear in Scripture. [And, today, dream interpretation is often used by psychologists].

In Ancient Greece, Oracles were the conduits for the gods on earth; their prophecies were understood to be the will of the gods verbatim. Because of the high demand for oracle consultations and the oracles' limited work schedule, they were not the main source of divination for the ancient Greeks. Seers were not in direct contact with the gods; instead, they were interpreters of signs provided by the gods. Seers used many methods to explicate the will of the gods includ-ing [examine entrails], bird signs, etc. They were more numerous than the oracles and did not keep a limited schedule; thus, they were highly valued by all Greeks, not just those with the capacity to travel to Delphi or other such distant sites.

Divination was considered a pagan practice in the early Christian church. Later the church would pass canon laws forbidding the practice of divination. In 692 the [Church], passed canons to eliminate pagan and divination prac-tices. Soothsaying and forms of divination were widespread through the Middle Ages. In the constitution of 1572 and public regulations of 1661 of Kur-Saxony, capital punishment was used on those predicting the future. Laws forbidding divination practice continue to this day.

[In the Hebrew Bible] Deuteronomy 18:10-12 clearly forbids any acts of divination, describing them as something detestable to God, and Leviticus 19:26 says "You must not practice either divination or soothsaying."

Divination was a central component of ancient Mesoamerican religious life. Many Aztec gods, including central creator gods, were described as diviners and were closely associated with sorcery. Tezcatlipoca is the patron of sorcerers and practitioners of magic. His name means "smoking mirror," a reference to a device used for divinatory scrying. In the Mayan _Popol Vuh_, the creator gods Xmucane and Xpiacoc perform divinatory hand casting during the creation of people.

Every civilization that developed in Ancient Mexico, from the Olmecs to the Aztecs, practiced divination in daily life, both public and private. Scrying through the use of reflective water surfaces, mirrors, or the casting of lots were among the most widespread forms of divinatory practice. Visions derived from hallucinogens were another important form of divination, and are still widely used among contemporary diviners of Mexico.

From this it can readily be seen that the Diviner, regardless of _objective_ tools and techniques, benefits from paying attention to the _subjective_ aspects of divinatory practice. If you are already reading this book, it seems doubtful that you are concerned that "divination"—even though it contains the word _divine_—is called sinful by all three of the major monotheistic religions of Christianity, Islam and Judaism. And likewise that it is considered superstition by the so-called scientific community that often has its own set of prejudices inhibiting an "open mind."

Divination was the original inspiration for Dr. Mumford's book, _Magical Tattwas,_ and the accompanying deck of _Magical Tattwa Cards_—the first ever publication of the 25 cards in color. The earlier use of self-colored tattwa cards was part of the teaching program of the original Hermetic Order of the Golden Dawn and there the student was expected to draw his own for use in skrying and magic. We will be developing both the divinatory and magical applications in subsequent addenda

Magick

Also spelled "magic" (without the "K"), but we want to distinguish this application from the common trickery and illusion of the entertaining stage magician. Let's start with a simple question. After you, the clairvoyant or the diviner has answered your question about love, money, security, health, and . . . the FUTURE, *what do you want to do about it?*

No, we are not talking about fairy tales in which a fictional "magician" simply waves a wand and produces the perfect lover, oodles of money, loads your pension fund, cures any health problem including "old age," and gives you promises or warnings about your future, but "Real Magick" through which you organize and then energize elements of the physical and subtle worlds to function as a "matrix of manifestation" so that your stated goal will more easily materialize.

Notice: Nothing is absolute. We don't promise that your divination will be absolutely correct down to the most finite detail, and we don't promise that your magickal working will produce exactly what you have programmed. The universe is too big and too complex and forever changing for you to be able to know and factor in every possible variable to manifest exactly what you hope for. Nevertheless, giving direction to these possibilities is reason for the age-old warning: *Be careful what you wish for!*

Elsewhere I've told the story of one elderly magician who—over many years—constantly visualized himself in a Rolls Royce automobile. After those many years, he phoned to tell me that he was finally sitting in his own Rolls Royce. The problem was that it was an old derelict that didn't run and was currently sitting on blocks in his back yard. He got what he wished for, but it was not what he wanted. I don't know what eventually happened to the old car but he was able to laugh at his own naiveté. Magickal operations alone will not produce material results, but they will aid your physical working toward a material goal.

As I had to tell one author: *just because you've written a book, don't quit your day job!*

Magick, psychic powers, spiritual ideals, high moral standards, academic degrees, love and devotion to deity, may all be no better than wishful thinking unless you put them all together through hard work guided by both common sense and solid knowledge about what you are doing. Magick and Clairvoyance just improve the odds for material success and are not necessarily the reason for your psychic development and magickal study.

Your real goal is to *become more than you are* and *all you can be.*

Trance

We include this subject because both spiritualist trance and shamanic trance have a long history of enabling clairvoyance. Mediums have often described visions of other beings and dimensions, delivered messages from the other side, as well as messages from the departed.

Shamanic trances are more varied, usually requiring some degree of "physical over-load"—ecstatic dancing, exhaustion, flagellation, drugs, bondage, sensory bombard-ment, sensory deprivation, etc.—to bring about an externally *imposed* altered state of consciousness, following which the shaman or an assistant direct the shaman's "flight" to other dimensional destinations to obtain and bring back desired information.

Trances are also part of the hypnotic experience in which attention is focused on a single goal and all other sensory impressions are blocked by the hypnotized person him-self. In the case of self-hypnosis, as with meditation, an altered state of consciousness is internally *self*-imposed. The constant goal of "the new science of the paranormal" is consciously directed experience or invocation of phenomena outside of the limited and limiting "normal" world.

Trances likewise occur in meditation, especially in "moving meditation" in which the visualized "path-working" involves a symbolic trip that accomplishes an inner realization of the symbolized "truth."

In Tantric practice Trance is usually produced in connection with the use of spe-cific Mantras and Yantras that tightly control the entranced consciousness, usually in relation to a specified deity as in Invocation and Worship.

Invocation and Worship

Here we must carefully distinguish between the external and the internal experience. It is tempting, but mis-leading, to refer to the external as Western and the internal as Eastern, yet the most familiar examples of each are largely experienced in Christianity and Hinduism. And terminology itself can be very misleading. Many Western "religious experiences" are basically shamanic as in Pentecostal Protestantism, Catholic Mysticism, Spiritist religions like Voudoun, Brujeria, and Candomble, and others that involve a direct personal experience of the deity.

The more familiar external form of worship distances the person from personal experience and requires adherence to a particular theology sometimes associated with such symbols as Bible or Koran, Star, Cross or Crescent, statutes and images, and includes responsive but not participatory ritual.

In Hinduism, particularly in Tantra (and it is important to distinguish "tradition" from "religion") there are many gods and goddesses—all richly endowed with names, ornaments, colorful costumes, positions, movements, stories, etc., that are largely unique to each and serve as complex "living symbols" that could be called "formulae." In addition, there are many specific and complex symbols called "yantras" and spe-cific voiced "mantras" also uniquely associated with many of these deities, and others associated specifically with such cosmic/personal forces as we've described for each of the five primal tattvas/elements, and also with the chakras, and various other primal factors.

In a sense, these deities are extreme but very powerful (because they are "living" complex symbols) examples of "compounding."

The Inner Experience of Compounding

We live in a complex world, and even as we may attempt to simplify our own experience—as in our *TattvIc Connection Meditation & Visualization Programs* involving the individual primal elements—we are using a procedure to enhance our ability to consciously "clearly see" material reality and also to better see and understand subtle realities. Nevertheless, what we see is a compounded reality.

By purifying our personal elements, getting rid of distorting emotional and psychic "garbage," we can better see the individual elements in our experience of compounded reality. Just as we used the cosmically pure primal elements to purify our inner personal elemental structure, now we reverse that process to better perceive and understand the outer world. It's as if we were to analyze the separate elements in a chemical compound to better understand their multiple effects in the "real world"—as how the elements of sodium and chlorine (as chloride) united in common table salt affect human health positively or negatively (only partially in relation to quantity) as well as in so many other applications.

We more clearly perceive our experiences through our now unconscious analysis of compounds as exercised in divination, but we can also deliberately enhance our inner experiences by compounding the outer *correspondences* as listed in our Elemental Tables in magickal operations, or by identifying with the complex "living symbols" of the cosmic forces we know as gods and goddesses that transform us inwardly in spiritual growth.

In the next several chapter addenda we will proceed with practical applications of the Art and Experience of Compounding of the Primal Elements.

Sources & Suggested Additional Reading:

Auset, B. *The Goddess Guide: Exploring the Attributes and Correspondences of the Divine Feminine,* 2009, Llewellyn.

Endredy, J. *Shamanism for Beginners: Walking with the World's Healers of Earth & Sky,* 2009, Llewellyn.

Lembo, M. A. *Chakra Awakening: Transform Your Reality Using Crystals, Color, Aromatherapy & the Power of Positive Thought,* 2011, Llewellyn.

Penczak, C. *The Temple of Shamanic Witchcraft: Shadows, Spirits & the Healing Journey, 2005*, Llewellyn.

Walsh, R. *The World of Shamanism: New Views of an Ancient Tradition*, 2007, Llewellyn.

Williams, M. *Follow the Shaman's Call: An Ancient Path for Modern Lives*, 2010, Llewellyn.

Wolfe, A. *In the Shadow of the Shaman: Connection with Self, Nature & Spirit*, 2002, Llewellyn.

CHAPTER NINE
Clairvoyant Viewing of Documents, Events, and Criminal Evidence

When all pleasure is lost, cry the "tears of freedom" that release the pain. Regain pleasure in yourself. You really may be all you have. Once regained, you have yourself

Soul Bilbo

New Knowledge & Empowerment

Knowledge, application, and empowerment—they go hand in hand. Through clairvoyance, you can acquire new knowledge and discover more effective ways of using it to empower your life while contributing to the greater good. Locating lost persons or animals, viewing distant events as they occur, intervening in situations of urgency, and gathering important evidence related to crime, to list but a few of the possibilities, are all within the scope of clairvoyance.

Clairvoyance in Viewing of Documents & Events.

The clairvoyant viewing of important documents and events can provide an information base unavailable from any other source. It is beyond the limitations of even the most advanced technology in that it can access information in its formative stage and compile important concepts as they evolve. It can monitor unfolding events and follow their advancement and materialization. In its finest form, clairvoyant viewing literally becomes the cutting edge of advanced awareness and modern technology. It can, in fact, contribute to the evolvement of technology itself.

As an extrasensory skill, clairvoyance perceives but does not intervene. It does, however, empower us with the knowledge required for effective intervention, whether individually or on a global scale. Personal awareness of the forces that presently shape our expectations and plans can empower us to make better decisions and take responsibility for them. The viewing of unfolding events and the documents related to them can dramatically enlarge our world of awareness while empowering us with the knowledge required to shape outcomes in ways that bring forth desired change.

Clairvoyance in Criminal Investigations

The importance of clairvoyant insight and the application of it is perhaps nowhere better illustrated than in the criminal justice setting. Fortunately, criminal justice experts have in recent years becoming increasingly aware of the relevance of clairvoyance, especially in the investigative situation. Although such terms as a "hunch", "gut feeling," "instinct," "intuition," and "sixth sense" remain common, they imply advanced awareness far beyond ordinary sensory perception alone.

In a recent survey conducted by the Parapsychology Research Institute and Foundation (PRIF), 62 percent of criminal investigative respondents reported openness to clairvoyance in the criminal justice setting. That receptiveness included not only the "unexplained" impressions that are often experienced by professional investigators but the contributions of consultant clairvoyants as well. Several criminal justice professionals noted that they are "open to any information source" that could facilitate the criminal investigative process. Among the specific examples of clairvoyance cited by respondents in our survey were the discovery of weapons used in the commission of crimes such as robberies, assaults, and murders; the location of missing persons including children; and the discovery of stolen money and merchandise. In one striking instance, a cache of valuable jewelry taken during an armed robbery was discovered in an insulated shipping bag hidden at a construction site on the outskirts of the city where the robbery had occurred. The source of the information was an investigative clairvoyant with previous experience as a criminal justice consultant.

Automatic Writing in Criminal Investigations

In an unusual instance of clairvoyance as an investigative strategy, a detective whose academic background included an elective college course in parapsychology used *automatic writing* to gather critical information related to the abduction of a child. With a writing pen in hand and resting lightly on paper, he identified through both his drawing and writing the exact location of the child as well as the full name of the abductor. As a result of information gathered through automatic writing, the child was safely rescued.

Automatic writing as a clairvoyant investigative strategy requires simply a writing pen or pencil and a standard sheet of white paper. With pen or pencil resting lightly upon the paper in writing position, the objective is stated either silently or audibly, whereupon writing is allowed automatically to occur. A period of inactivity often precedes writing, which may at first appear as meaningless scribble, but given time, significant writing will usually emerge. It is important to allow plenty of time for automatic writing to unfold. Any effort to rush the procedure or deliberately intervene as writing unfolds can interrupt the clairvoyant process.

Automatic writing can be used either individually or as a group activity. In an unusual application of the strategy in the criminal justice setting, two investigators used the technique simultaneously to identify the location of a valuable oil painting. The painting, which had hung in the city's museum for many years, mysteriously disappeared during a busy holiday season and remained missing for several months. After an exhaustive investigation that included interviews with museum personnel and certain "persons of interest," the two detectives assigned to the case decided to use automatic writing in their joint effort to locate the painting. Although their academic background in automatic writing was limited to a college course in experimental parapsychology at Athens State University, the two detectives used automatic writing separately and then compared notes. Somewhat to their surprise, each of their separate writings identified the exact location of the painting—a remote storage facility on the outskirts of the city. To their own amazement, the investigators each identified not only the location of the facility, but the correct storage unit number. The lead investigator noted, "Immediately following automatic writing and viewing the results, a clear image emerged concurrently in our minds detailing the position of the painting against the unit's back wall." The painting was retrieved from the storage unit and returned undamaged to the museum. Exactly how the painting ended up at the storage facility remains unknown. Perhaps another session of automatic writing might solve that mystery.

Clairvoyance Applied in Manufacturing, Construction, & Business Settings

Equally as important as its role in criminal investigation is the application of clairvoyance in the industrial setting. Here are a few examples based on studies conducted by PRIF:

- Clairvoyance can identify hazardous conditions that, if gone unnoticed, can result in the loss of life and property.
- Clairvoyance can uncover errors in blueprints and equipment designs.
- In the construction setting, clairvoyance can facilitate planning and promote more accurate cost estimates and construction timelines.
- In the manufacturing setting, clairvoyance can identify more efficient operational procedures while promoting employee safety.
- In business planning, clairvoyance can identify the most desired location and promotional procedures for a new business.

- In the retail setting, clairvoyance can identify consumer preferences for products and services.
- Clairvoyance can assess the appeal of specific product characteristics, including the product name as well as the size, color, and design of packaging.

The relevance of clairvoyance to industry was poignantly illustrated by a clairvoyant industrial consultant who identified an error in the blueprints for a large manufacturing facility under construction. In the consultant's own words, "Immediately upon viewing the drawing, I noted a small area enveloped in a violet glow, the color often associated with either urgency or a spirit presence." The blueprint was promptly inspected by the contractor and found to contain a critical error in the specified area. Fortunately, the early detection of the error allowed adequate time for corrective action in construction to be undertaken. According to the contractor, the error if gone undetected could have resulted in a costly failure of the structure and possible loss of lives. The violet glow was, incidentally, visible only to the consulting clairvoyant.

Further illustrating the relevance of clairvoyance to industry is the report of a plant security guard who, upon reporting for night-shift duty, experienced a powerful impression that something was awry. Here's his report: "A certain building near the back of the plant stood out among all the others as a place of unusual activity. When I entered the building, I noticed at once a large tank unleashing a massive flow of contaminated liquid that had flooded the building and was overflowing into an outside water stream. I immediately called for assistance and the emergency situation was quickly corrected." According to the plant's manager, a potentially serious environmental situation was effectively corrected and precautions were taken to prevent any further environmental breaches. Thanks to clairvoyant insight and the security guard's responsiveness to it, a disaster in the making was promptly averted. In the absence of the guard's receptiveness to clairvoyance, the consequences of environmental contamination could have been far-reaching.

Clairvoyant Objectology

Among the most effective strategies designed to activate clairvoyant viewing are those that use tangible objects, an approach called *clairvoyant objectology*. Gathering information related to criminal acts, locating missing persons and animals, and viewing hidden documents as well as distant happenings are all within the scope of clairvoyant objectology. Included in this concept are a wide range of strategies that apply a physical object to activate certain emotional, cognitive, and psychical functions through simply touching or viewing the object. *Psychometry, dowsing,* and the *wrinkled sheet technique* are among the common examples of clairvoyant objectology.

Psychometry & Clairsentience

Perhaps the most widely used form of clairvoyant objectology is *psychometry* in which physical touch as a *clairsentience phenomenon* is used to activate clairvoyant viewing. As a relevant object such as a piece of jewelry, article of clothing, or other personal object is touched or held in the hand, spontaneous impressions of clairvoyant significance will frequently unfold. Psychometry can be facilitated by first clearing of the mind while touching the object and then, with eyes closed, allowing sufficient time for relevant images to emerge. It should be noted that simply viewing an object can alone initiate impressions of clairvoyant significance. The object alone seems often to become a critical link to distant realities of important relevance to urgent situations and concerns.

In the criminal justice setting, psychometry can be highly effective as clairvoyant investigative technique, not only when used by consulting clairvoyants but by professional criminal investigators as well. In a remarkable example of psychometry as an investigative strategy, a detective discovered, by his own report, the exact location of a missing child as he held in his hand the child's photograph. While viewing the photograph, the detective experienced a clear image of a beach scene with the child playing in the sand. He then closed his eyes and intentionally expanded the image to generate an overhead view of the city, to include the beach scene. With that information, the five-year old child who had been abducted by a distant relative was located and safely returned to his parents.

In another remarkable instance of psychometry as a clairvoyant viewing technique, a criminal investigator used a city map to locate a missing body. As he viewed the map in his office, a small area of darkness, by his report, literally formed upon the map. He searched the location designated by the unusual darkness on the map and found the body in the dark basement of an abandoned building. This example raises the interesting possibility of the psychokinetic (PK) capacity of the clairvoyant mind, in this case, to form an area of darkness on a map that was visible not only to the investigator but others as well. Does clairvoyant awareness, once experienced subconsciously, have power to communicate meaningful messages through the materialization of subconscious thought energy? Given the enormous power of the subconscious mind, why not? Clairvoyance is indeed a purposefully empowering phenomenon that goes far beyond the ordinary constrictions of conventional thought.

Map Dowsing & Pendulums in Criminal Investigation & Surveillance

In contrast to psychometry, dowsing typically consists of the use of forked twigs or metal rods that, when properly positioned in the hands and held over an object or setting, accesses relevant information through their movements. Aside from rods, dowsing can also include the use of a pendulum, typically a weight suspended on a string or chain. When properly held in the hand and suspended over an appropriate object, the pendulum can accesses an extensive range of relevant information by its movements.

Case studies have shown a wide range of successful applications of the pendulum as an investigative tool. When held over a map, the pendulum has been used to gather information of criminal investigative relevance but of global significance as well. An investigative consultant used the pendulum over a map determine the central location of a drug dealer whose operation included an organization that distributed drugs throughout a Midwestern city. The pendulum, when used with a map of the city and in response to questions posed, identified the central location of the organization as well as several distribution points throughout the city. The location of five distribution points was accurately identified through the use of the pendulum.

Aside from its application as a criminal investigative tool, the pendulum has reportedly been used as a surveillance strategy to gather important information on a global scale. In a rather unusual military application of this technique, the pendulum was reportedly used to identify through its movements the location of a secret enemy facility where an advanced weapons research and development program was in progress. Through information gathered clairvoyantly, a successful military operation was conducted. The operation based primarily on the findings of the pendulum resulted in the discovery of an advanced weapons program that proved highly relevant to later space research and development.

The Crumpled Paper Technique Adapted for Viewing
of Documents, Events, and Criminal Evidence

The *crumpled paper technique,* which was developed in our labs at Athens State University, is a multi-functional procedure that includes stimulation of the clairvoyant faculty and its development. Aside from its clairvoyant application, it has been used as a practice exercise to promote development of other extrasensory faculties, including telepathy and precognition. It is often during practice of this step-by-step procedure that spontaneous awareness of important future events will unfold as well as insight related to past-life experiences.

In the controlled lab setting, the techniques as a self-empowerment exercise showed a high degree of effectiveness in promoting creativity, improving problem-solving skills, increasing short-term memory, and generating a highly positive state of personal well-being. College students who participated in our development of the procedure often reported dramatic improvements in their academic performance along with enriched social relationships. Here are a few specific examples of the wide ranging **applications of the crumpled paper technique:**

- A college professor used the technique to locate his dog companion that had days earlier strayed from his residence.
- A defense attorney discovered through his use of the technique an important document of relevance to a trial in progress. The document was critical in proving the innocence of his client, a financial adviser who was charged with a white collar crime.
- A psychologist used the technique to discover a serious fault in the foundation of a house he was about to purchase. The fault, as it turned out, had been documented years earlier but was allegedly unknown to the present owner.
- A graduate student in physics used the technique in his research to identify critical principles related to the so-called *multiverse*, to include its formation, evolvement, structure, and dynamics.
- A clairvoyant consultant used the technique to successfully identify the exact location of a prison escapee convicted of drug trafficking.
- As a self-empowerment technique, the procedure has been used for such diverse goals as breaking unwanted habits, overcoming phobias, managing stress, overcoming depression, accelerating learning, and improving memory. (See *The Llewellyn Complete Book of Psychic Empowerment* by Carl Llewellyn Weschcke and Joe H. Slate).

Here's an adapted version of the wrinkled sheet technique specifically formulated for clairvoyant viewing of documents, events, and criminal evidence. The only material required for this procedure is a standard blank sheet of 8½ x 11 inch paper.

The Crumpled Paper Technique in Applied Clairvoyance

Step 1. In a quiet, comfortable place free of distractions, settle back and with the sheet of paper in hand, crumple it into a mass just as you would if you intended to throw it away.

Step 2. While holding the crumpled mass of paper loosely in your cupped hands, note its characteristics, such as weight, shape of the mass, and any unusual feature related to it.

Step 3. Remind yourself that the crumpled mass of paper resting in your hands is a unique creation. It is unlike any other crumpled mass, whether past, present, or future.

Step 4. As the crumpled mass continues to rest in your hands, clear your mind of active thought and then focus your full attention upon it. With your eyes closed, visualize the crumpled mass and remind yourself that it is a repository of the energy required to create it.

Step 5. As your eyes remain closed, sense your connection to the crumpled mass as a unique energy form. Sense its attuning and balancing effects. Let the crumpled mass become a dynamic link to other dimensions of awareness and power.

Step 6. Clearly specify your goals and affirm your complete success in achieving them. It is at this stage that clairvoyant viewing is activated. Allow plenty of time for clairvoyant viewing to unfold.

Step 7. For clairvoyant viewing of sensitive or secretive documents, on-going events, and criminal evidence, carefully unfold the crumpled paper and place it between your hands and allow relevant images and impressions to spontaneously occur. For directed viewing of specific documents, visualize the now spread out crumpled paper as a copy of the document upon which relevant information becomes clearly visible. For viewing of on-going events, think of the unfolded sheet of paper as a screen upon which the unfolding actions appear.

Step 8. Place the unfolded sheet of crumpled paper aside and reflect on the experience. Affirm: The information, insight, and power I need at the moment are now available to me.

Step 9. In your clairvoyant journal, record the session and any subsequent developments related to it.

The crumpled paper technique has been extensively used as an investigative procedure for gathering crime-related information. On a broader scale, it has been used as an effective espionage technique. It has, for instance, been used on a global scale to clairvoyantly monitor weapons development programs and secret military operations. A major advantage of the technique is its applications from a safe distance and beyond the limitations of conventional approaches. Also, the accuracy of information gathered through the procedure, according to validation results, is often superior to other more conventional approaches.

Conclusion: The Cutting Edge

In his groundbreaking book, *The Law of Psychic Phenomena*, Thomas J. Hudson concluded in 1893: *In the field of psychological investigation, a satisfactory working hypothesis has never been formulated. That is to say, no theory has been advanced which embraces all psychological phenomena* (p. 22).* More than a century later, such a working hypothesis and comprehensive theory have yet to come forth in unified scientific and practical form. Hopefully, recent advancements in our understanding of clairvoyance and related phenomena will rapidly accelerate our progress in achieving that important goal.

Sources & Additional Suggested Reading:

*Hudson, Thomas J. *The Law of Psychic Phenomena.* Chicago: A. C. McClurg & Co., 1893.

ADDENDUM #9 TO CHAPTER NINE
Microcosm to Macrocosm & Macrocosm to Microcosm

*THE PRACTICES OF APPLICATION:
DIVINATION, MAGICK & INVOCATION*

*and
The Tattvic Connection—
Meditation & Visualization Program #6: Earth/Earth*

Earth in Divination, Magick & Invocation

Earth—Seed of Earth

While the primary discussion in regard to the Character, Quality, and Power of the individual Primal Tattvas has related to the Meditation Exercises to bring clarity and accuracy to clairvoyant vision, we have also introduced the compounding of those Tattvas (better discussed here as "Elements") to more clearly distinguish between a primarily *subjective* meditation practice and the forthcoming more *objective* application practices involving the compounded elements.

These practices specifically involve the chakras, the subtle energy centers within which the tattvic elements function.

Please also note that the locations given for the chakras become very important in various applications. See the following chart to guide your work in this regard.

Body Locations of Chakras, Tattvas, & Endocrine Glands

Chakra	*Gland*	*Tattva/Element*

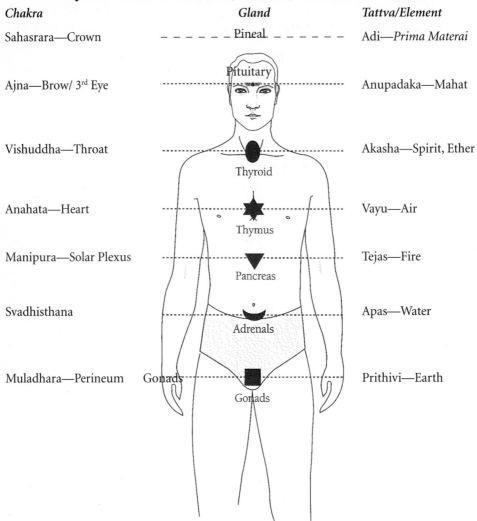

Sahasrara—Crown — Pineal — Adi—*Prima Materai*

Ajna—Brow/ 3rd Eye — Pituitary — Anupadaka—Mahat

Vishuddha—Throat — Thyroid — Akasha—Spirit, Ether

Anahata—Heart — Thymus — Vayu—Air

Manipura—Solar Plexus — Pancreas — Tejas—Fire

Svadhisthana — Adrenals — Apas—Water

Muladhara—Perineum — Gonads — Gonads — Prithivi—Earth

You will want to refer to this chart often, so you might want to make a photocopy to keep around as you work with the later chapters and addenda.

Earth—Seed of Earth

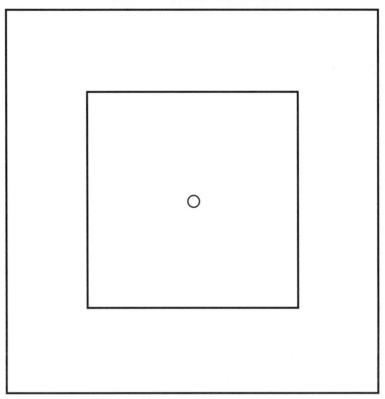

Color the tiny inner bindu circle white,
the inner square bright yellow,
and the outer square bright purple

Earth—Seed of Earth: Prithivi *LAM*

Earth—Seed of Earth
Now! Planting the Seed of Beginning

Earth: Culminating in Creation as we know it, BUT Just Our Beginning

Planet Earth is our Family Home. It is our Place of Work (Farm, Factory, Office, Studio) and our Play Ground. Standing before us there is a "ladder reaching to heaven"—but we have a "long row to hoe" before we climb that first step. There are many, many steps, but each step we take builds on the growth and achievements of the previous and with each one the *Ascension* is a little faster. Planetary, Human, and Personal Evolution is a long process but it's our job and it is the source of meaning in each and every life.

Elemental Earth is one of the five Primal Elements, and while it is the foundation and starting point, all the Elements function together in a constant interplay. This Earth is not a pile of physical dirt and rock—although at the astral level there are energetic images of all that is seen as Physical Earth. In addition there are images of Earthy things imagined and desired, things dreamed of by architects and artists, things pictured by inventors and scientists, monsters created in children's imagination, seductive women in men's fantasies, seductive fashions in women's imagination, etc. Everything that exists on the Physical Plane is represented by images composed of Elemental Earth in the Astral.

These are "energy images" that can be manipulated and transformed by disciplined creative visualization, or their physical equivalents can themselves be traced, perceived, moved, and transformed through operations of dowsing, alchemy, geomantic divination, and magickal operations. At a higher level of occult symbols, geometric yantras, and religious images, their special powers can be brought into material manifestation through psychic techniques.

Elemental Earth is much more than even astral dirt and rock. Through your meditation program you will come into contact with Elemental Earth primarily in Divination, but also in Magick.

Earth—Seed of Earth

Please refer back to Addendum #3, page 107, and in particular to the Tattvic Meditation & Visualization Program #1 on page 108 where you fully visualized the Earth Tattva image in shape, colors, and size and hopefully also reproduced that image as a Tattva Card following the detailed instructions.

You should refresh that image by repeating the exercise and placing the Tattva Card before you (or visualize that image) as we discuss Earth from this more advanced perspective of particular applications of Divination, Dream Interpretations, Invocation, and Magick.

In particular, in the case of Earth—Seed of Earth, we are seeing the difference between our earlier *more passive* purification programs in regard to achieving more accurate clairvoyance free of distortion from past memories to recognition of our *more active* impact on both external and internal worlds through our "intentional" work.

Quantum Theory provides scientific verification, and thus better understanding, of the ancient wisdom teachings showing that even looking at something at the fundamental energy level brings changes. The impact we have varies with the intensity of our *psychic* actions. Clairvoyance is at one level, whereas Divination with a particular question in mind is at a greater level of impact. Invocation and Magick are at still greater levels of impact.

This recognition is important, for the greater the impact—i.e. the greater the exercise of *power*—the greater personal responsibility we have for intelligent actions. It has long been part of ethical training not to approach anything "psychic" purely for amusement or entertainment. Be responsible. Recognize that you are a being of great power, even if it is still mostly unrecognized and unconscious potential.

The message of "Earth—Seed of Earth" is that of a substantial increase of Astral level Earth Energy being brought into application.

The following table is a simple summary of basic Earth factors drawn from the more complete Element Overview Table on page 104 which you should review.

ELEMENT SUMMARY TABLE # 9
Earth, Divinatory Background Application

Element Name: Earth	Tattva Form: Square	Tattva Color: Yellow
Tattvic Animal: Black Elephant with 7 trunks	Chakra: Root Chakra	Cosmic Plane: Physical/Etheric
Chakra Goal: Awaken Kundalini, vivify each center	Chakra God (Shiva) Energy: Brahma	Chakra Goddess (Shakti) Energy: Dakini
Chakra Bija Mantra: *LAM*	Element State & Action: solid support, foundation	Element Function: Survival & Evolution
Element Nature: Initiative, Start-Up	Element Power: to create a new reality	Element Strength: focus, determination
Emotional Desires: comfort & survival	Emotional Nature: passive, stable	Emotional Strength: instinct, care
Emotional/Psychological Level: Deep Unconscious	Emotional/Sexual Identity: feminine, active, receptive	
Energy: mechanical	Energy Manifests Through: congealment	Quantum Force: gravity
Mind Function: knowledge, memory	Mind State: waking intelligence	Physical/Action Organ: feet
Physical/Action Form: locomotion	Physical/Action Effect: lasting	Physical Body Function: building, moving
Astrological Qualities: hardworking, disciplined, persevering, patience	Astrology—Ruling Planet: Saturn, Mercury	
Astrological Planetary Expression: Mercury— communication, business, mathematics, practical matters		
Magical Animals: owl, bear, boar, bull, stag	Magical Colors: Brown, Black, Green	Magical State: Physical Perception
Magical Rulership: agriculture, animals, antiques, buildings, business, conservation, construction, death/rebirth, ecology, fertility, food, grounding, health foods, investments, jobs, material things, money, museums, nature, old age, progress, promotions, prosperity, stock markets , structural foundations		
Tarot Court: Page, Princess	Tarot Suite: Pentacles	Tarot Trumps: Emperor, World

Table #9, above, is selected entirely from Element Overview Table #1, page 104, to illustrate the principle involved of providing and reviewing data believed most pertinent to the divinatory operation. Note, however, there is greater value when you, yourself, review the complete Element Overview Table for the Element (and both elements when they are compounded) because your own subconscious mind will subtly bring the appropriate datum into your conscious awareness. Whenever you are employing your psychic powers—whether for divination, magick, or invocation—you are calling your subconscious mind into play.

Bearing that in mind, do it intentionally rather than otherwise.

THE PRACTICE OF DIVINATION

In our previous addendum for Chapter 8, we simply outlined five particular applications of Tattvic Meditation beyond the vitally important *purification* work with the first five. Each of these—Clairvoyance, Divination, Magick, Trance, and Invocation (Worship)—has a long history which has been discussed in the main text. However, three applications have practical applications easily pursued—Divination, Magick, and Invocation. Each of these is a valuable adjunct to your clairvoyant work.

With Divination, you ask a question and look for an answer; with Magick you look at the answer and decide to act upon it to accomplish a particular goal; with Worship (Invocation) your goal becomes an inward quest for psychic empowerment and spiritual growth through a process of self-identification with the "personality" of the elemental force or "being" associated with it (more about this later). Each of these could be the subject of one or more extensive studies but we are only concerned here with their relation to Clairvoyance.

For some readers, a question will naturally occur: *What's the difference between clairvoyance and divination?* While a professional clairvoyant reading may be broad in its coverage, it is often related directly to specific questions involving relationships, career, children, money, etc. Divinations should be specific—one question per reading, even if not framed specifically as such. In developing your own clairvoyance—and that's the primary purpose of this book—your "reading" will typically become more like physical vision. Just as physical vision can be narrowly focused on to a specific object to answer a specific question related to that object, so can clairvoyant vision—only more so. The clairvoyant can see as if with a powerful microscope or a powerful telescope, or get close-up to an object or travel to a distant one. The "view" can be expanded to give you historic information at a cosmic level or at a personal level. It can give you information that is almost experiential of even the most subjective "targets"—like the nature of the goddess Kali or an understanding of your own or another person's needs and desires. Clairvoyance can function in other dimensions—astral, mental, causal, spiritual—while divination is pretty much limited to the physical and lower astral plane.

And, sometimes that focus on the physical plane is exactly what you want and a divination focused on a specific question may serve your needs better than clairvoyance. With Divination, you ask a question and look for an answer.

Traditionally, divination involves the use of dedicated aids or tools often chosen either by the user's affinity and expertise with the particular device, or by the nature of the operation. Divination often makes use of crystal balls, divining rods, cards of various types, dice, yarrow sticks, pendulums, etc. A person may be able to use any or several of these in a personal or even professional divinatory practice, but more often a person specializes in the use of one or another of these tools. A Tarot reader, a "Water Witch" (person using a divining rod to locate the best place for a well), an Astrologer, Palmist, Graphologist, etc., typically becomes expert in just one divinatory "science." (I use that word deliberately and correctly even though there is always an "art" to every psychic exercise involving communication between two or more people as well as between conscious and subconscious minds.)

Dr. Jonn Mumford pioneered the development of "Magical Tattwa Cards" for use primarily in divination—but these same tattvic symbols or yantras can also be employed in magick, invocation, and deific worship through specialized ritual and/or forms of meditation. And, indeed, even divination can be accomplished in a similar meditative manner. Many people enjoy working with the "mechanical side of things" while a few people are getting into the purely "mental" or psychic working.

Whether or not you have made a set of Tattva Cards as described, you should have become familiar with the five primal tattvas, and you will become familiar with the additional twenty compounded tattvas as we progress in the book.

For now, we need only work with the five primal tattvas.

While the paragraph that follows is just for Primal Earth, it illustrates the entire process. You are already familiar with the Earth Element from the addendum to Chapter Three. Even more important is your growing understanding of all the Primal Elements and your *experiential realization of Earth within your own body and psyche*. Your meditation practice has *awakened* and *purified* this core foundation to body and soul.

Just as you have five *physical* senses, so you have five *subtle* senses that are working for you all the time—but more so now that their tattvic "homes" are awake and the "windows and doors" washed. And the psychic and emotional "garbage" has been taken out and disposed of. This is, of course, just a simile, but a simile is like a symbol that summarizes and represents an entire reality. Simile and symbol function as *psychic switches and levers to increase our comprehensive awareness in multiple dimensions.*

We've emphasized that—through consciousness—everything is connected. In certain situations "connections" are particularly evident. Here, the simple and cursory word paragraph readily connects us to the previous material on the Earth Element, and—additionally—to our memories, to our knowledge, to experiences, and more. As you become more attuned to your expanding psychic awareness, those connections open the way to providing specific answers to your specific questions asked in a divination whether or not you are using an aid or tool. In no way are you limited to the information presented in our tables or even the seemingly infinite resources of the World Wide Web. Instead, as you progress in "becoming more than you are" you are increasingly accessing the Cosmos Wide Web that is Universal Consciousness. The challenge is to know when you are connected and when you are merely fantasizing. The time will come when you know that with surety.

While the "Divination Guide" below summarizes a particular "signal" that it's a good time to *start,* and adds a reminder that a new beginning needs to be *nurtured,* the reality is that of the five primal tattvas you will have either picked this or found yourself spontaneous attracted to it because is embodies the answer to your question.

That's the nature of psychic empowerment. By one means or no means, you will find the right answer to your question, particularly when you open the door to the subconscious mind. **The key factors in asking the psychic question** are to:

1. State the question,
2. Open yourself to become aware of the answer.

You can use tools, rituals, meditations, prayers, and other techniques that are personally attractive—and hence empowering—that may give you the answers faster and in symbolic detail, but always remember that *you have the power*—not in the tool. The tool works in your hands to extend and often magnify your power, and can be a wonderful aid, but it works because of your expanding awareness and the mobilization of energies that bring the answer to you.

DIVINATION GUIDE TO EARTH—SEED OF EARTH
Earth—Seed of Earth: Foundation, * or Stagnation

From ending to new beginning, Earth is the culmination of *the* Creation and the start of the re-creation we call evolution. Earth is the foundation, the platform, the support upon which we walk, sleep, eat, procreate, and *individually* and as a species evolve. Earth is solid, reliable, and dependable and is our home and the firm foundation upon which we build our dreams and new realities. Earth is the soil upon which plants and crops grow. While most life, including humanity, evolves unconsciously in the Darwinian mode of "Survival of the Fittest," the individual human person learns to act consciously and responsibility and thus becomes an active instrument of evolution in the fulfillment of the "Great Plan." Knowledge brings responsibility, and action requires balance within nature's laws. Earth is both matter and energy. When we plant an idea, we need nurture and balance for growth: Too little Earth makes a poor foundation, too much Earth can be deadening and result in stagnation. Beginnings determine outcomes. A successful beginning requires knowledge as well as appropriate action.

In a divination, Earth signals a good time to "start up," but reminds you of the need to carefully tend and nurture your new beginning.

> *Some or these "keywords" and quotations are taken from Dr. Mumford's "Magical Tattwas."

Often, the "answer" is all you need to move forward to the manifestation of your goal. Other times, in the case of mundane matters, you will want to move the process along. So you know the answer, *what are you going to do about it?* Your question & answer process may have set things in motion, but are all the factors for successful manifestation available to you within a desired time frame?

You are not likely to get the job of your dreams without suitable education and training. You can't win the lottery without a ticket. You can't find the love of your life if you are hiding in the closet.

That's all common sense. Presuming you have all the prerequisites in place, but want action now, you can turn to simple magick as described below.

THE PRACTICE OF MAGICK

Magick and Worship/Invocation both may use incenses, ceremonial dress, controlled gestures, chants, symbols, and more to raise specific energies and establish a particular state of consciousness, and then to give direction in the case of magick to the accomplishment of an external goal and in the case of worship to identification with a particular cosmic force usually identified with a particular deity.

There are many books on the traditional forms of divination and magick, and an increasing understanding of worship and *invocating meditation* through studies of Vedic and Tantric Yoga and other practices. We will include some suggested reading resources but here we are only going to deal with the mind directed meditational forms.

The Three Essential Actions for all Divinatory & Magickal Operations

1. To establish the goal;
2. To choose the pertinent associations;
3. To focus consciousness meditation or ritual with particular intent.

The form of meditation exercise is the same as you've already undertaken in the five primal tattva exercises, and you can and now should easily adapt them to these new programs in the first and third actions listed above. However, we will describe one particular Meditation & Visualization Program for the Earth Personality that can be adapted to use with the compounded Elements.

With regard to the second essential, refer back to the earlier tables and select from them for your working. Here is one example for a first step in Clairvoyant Divinatory Meditation. We have selected certain points from Earth Element Overview Table #1 104 for this purpose. In your previous meditation on the Earth Element your purpose was that of bringing the pure cosmic element into your subtle body as a means of cleansing the accumulated emotional and psychic garbage. In this exercise your goal is to *invoke* the Earth Energy and Consciousness and become one with the cosmic principle of Earth. The difference is subtle but real.

ELEMENT SUMMARY TABLE #10:
Earth/Water, Magickal Background Application

Element Name: Earth	Element Action: support	Element Function: survival, evolution
Element Nature: initiative, start-up	Element Power: to create a new reality	Element Strength: focus, determination
Tattva Name: *Prithivi*	Tattva Form: square	Tattva Color: yellow
Chakra Name: *Muladhara*	Chakra Location: base of spine, perineum	Chakra Bija Mantra: *LAM*
Goddess Energies—Greek: Gaia, Demeter, Hestia, Rhea	Tantric Goddess: Dakini, Kundalini	
Mind Function: knowledge, memory	Mind State: waking intelligence	Psychological Level: deep unconscious
Physical Sense: smell	Psychic Function: to awaken Kundalini	Psychic Powers: pain control, psychometry
Ruling Planet: Saturn, Mercury	Planetary Expression: communication	Sexual Identity: feminine, active, and receptive

Tarot Trump: World	Tree of Life Path: 32nd	Tree of Life Sphere: Malkuth
Magical Colors: brown, black, green	Magical Day: Friday	Magical Direction: North
Magical Incense: cedar, storax	Magical Place: cave, forest, garden, wilds	Magical Planet: Venus
Magical Rulerships: agriculture, animals, buildings, business, death/rebirth, food, nature, promotions, prosperity, stock market		
Magical Stones: emerald, hematite, jade	Magical Symbols: Pentacle	Magical Time of Day: Midnight
Magical Tools: crystal ball	Magical Work:: alchemy, geomancy, talismanic magic	

These selections are just examples. The purpose is to create an environment—material and/or imaginative—that "speaks" to you of Earth. We have included a listing of a few Greek and Tantric Earth Goddesses because they are among the most familiar to readers, and it is psychologically easier to identify with a "personality" clothed in colors and symbols appropriate to the energy being invoked than with mere lists and abstract principles. It's *Human Nature* to personalize most things in our personal world—material and otherwise/

For a fresh start or a new beginning, Consciousness, acting with intention, plants the masculine seed in the Unconscious, feminine and receptive Earth. "To become pregnant with a thought can give birth to mental progeny . . . Mother Earth is the womb from which all our creations and projects can be born, for *Terra Firma* provides a secure foundation which, if carefully tended, can support a crop of projects."

Magickal Operations

Resolute imagination is the beginning of all magical operations.

Paracelsus, 1493–1543

Magick is the process for imposing change in accordance with the intention ("Will") of the operator upon particular possibilities *before they happen!* This must be carefully understood—you cannot change current material reality but based on your clairvoyant vision of the astral circumstances surrounding that material reality you may be able to impose your vision of change on the energies affecting the future relating to the current reality.

Clairvoyance and Magick work hand-in-hand: you need vision before you operate!

Look at the following simple list of points taken from both the Earth and Water Elemental Overview tables as found on pages 104 and 131, selected to represent factors involved with the purpose of a magickal working—seeking inspiration for an adverting campaign to improve business for a health food store.

ELEMENT SUMMARY TABLE #11:
Earth/Water, Magickal Working for Success

Purpose of Work: Inspiration for an Advertising Daughter's Campaign	Magical Rulership: Business Promotion & Partnership	Magickal Goal: Success in Health Food Store
Tattva Names: *Prithivi & Apas*	Tattva Forms: Square & Crescent	Tattva Colors: Yellow & Silver
Element Names: Earth & Water	Element Action: Support & Adapting	Element Function: Survival & Reproduction
Element Nature: Initiative & Flowing	Element Powers: to create a new Reality & Co-operation	Element Strength: Focus, Determination & Feeling, Relationships, and Fantasy
Emotional Character: Solidarity & Flexibility	Emotional Desires: Comfort, Survival	Emotional Drive: Security, Saving & Pleasure, Fantasies
Emotional Strength: Instinct, Care & Will	Family Roles: Daughter & Mother	Mind Function: Knowledge & Analysis
Chakra Names: *Muladhara & Svadhisthana*	Chakra Locations: Perineum & Genitals	Chakra Bija Mantras: *LAM & VAM*
Magical Colors: Brown, Black, Green, Silver	Magical Days: Friday & Monday	Magical Incense: Storax, Cedar, Gardenia
Magical Metals: Lead & Copper, Silver	Magical Places: Caves, Forest, Garden,	Magical Planet: Venus & Moon
Magical State: Physical & Psychic Perception	Magical Stones: Hematite & Quartz	Magical Symbols: Pentacle & Cup
Magical Tool: Crystal Ball & Chalice of Water	Magical Work: Talismans & Spells	Magical Results: A Talisman for Success

In this example, you have established a magickal goal of helping your daughter's health food store with a new advertising campaign. Recognizing that business is largely an elemental Earth matter, you have referred to The Element Overview Table #1 for Earth found on page 104 of the addendum to Chapter 3 and listed the items that seemed more pertinent to you. But, because of the relationship of Mother and Daughter and other factors you have included some points taken from the table for Water on page 131 that add further dimension to the forthcoming operation.

The Power of Sound

In all three of these Element Summary Tables, we have included the Chakra *Bija* Mantra, *LAM (pronounced LAuuummm*—and vibrated at a lower tone of voice than your natural speaking voice). *Do not "sing" this mantra!* The sound is primarily directed internally into the back of the skull, and then it can also be projected to the chakra's body location, and in situations involving a material object, such as making a talisman, then into the object.

Sight and Sound, Vision and Hearing, are the two most powerful sensory energy systems we possess. They—even Sight—are both projective and receptive. We are used to projecting sound in speech, song, chanting, screams, etc., and perhaps less so in magickal workings—but we rarely perceive the power of projecting visual energy. It is, nevertheless real and it is the destiny and obligation of the evolving human person to perceive all these powers and to be aware and care in their use.

The Practice of Invocation

Invocation is a very powerful technique with many applications—in practical Magick, in religious and non-religious Worship, in personal Self-Development, and in Spiritual Divination, and probably others that are more esoteric. I will try to give a concise overview of the subject and then narrow it down to just a few applications and suggestions for your own research.

Invocation is often confused with *evocation,* and there is a lot of similarity that offers a fruitful field of debate and discussion, but we are only touching upon the subject in this book to demonstrate the Tattvic Connection.

"Invocation" simply means to *bring within,* and can be applied to images representing energies or principles. It can also be applied to images of deities and there can be called *assumption of a god-form* or be a form of *worship* in which the practitioner (or devotee) "becomes one with the god, goddess, saint or other spiritual entity. The particular point to be emphasized is that this form of worship is *internal* and does not involve praying or kneeling before a statute or other image.

To some Westerners this idea that a god can be brought within is *sacrilegious;* to many Easterners, it is a more familiar practice. In Western ceremonial magick, the identification with a god is slightly different and involves putting oneself *inside* the image of the god by *assuming the god form* much like an actor dressing as a character in a drama. Of course, *there is more to it than just a costume change!*

In this exercise, we are only concerned—as we have already been doing in the previous "visualization and meditation" programs—with *awakening* the tattva force within and identifying with the universal cosmic tattva that is <u>not</u> outside us, but neither is it inside us in the familiar way we think. In essence, the very important factor is involved with the actual "vitality" of the image. In the case of the Tattvic geometric Yantras, it is the energetic construction of the form in accordance with a mathematically certain symbolic logic that has thousands of years of precedence that bridges personal consciousness with universal consciousness.

Such union is the objective of nearly all forms of meditation, but it is only through experience that it becomes "real" to the user. So, let us begin.

The Tattvic Connection Magickal Application Program #6: Earth/Water
Earth—And its Compounds: Water
A Magickal Application

Introduction. The Purpose & Function of this Procedure.

The following program involving the manufacture of a magickal talisman is an example of working with Earth compounding with Water to demonstrate one application. Based on the object of a magical operation your choices of the primal and secondary elements would be dictated by the nature of the operation.

In this case, the goal was material, hence the primal element chosen was Earth, and because of the secondary goal of helping a relative, Water was chosen.

How you proceed is largely a matter of choice.* First, using either a physical or a visualized image of the yellow square with a silver crescent in its center, carefully list both the purpose of the work and your goal, noting that you want to "create a new reality" by means of a talisman developed as inspired by your meditation which your daughter will keep with her until the goal is achieved. You may augment your meditation by using an incense of cedar, holding a piece of hematite in your left (feminine) hand, performing the operation on Friday at midnight while facing north. You could gaze in a crystal ball or a chalice of pure water to aid your vision for a talisman design but you might base it on a pentacle with a crescent in its center, perhaps using brown and green colors.

> *This emphasis on personal choice may seem strange to most people trained in Western science and technology, but "Real" Magick brings the Unconscious Mind into play and hence we are working at both *subjective* and *objective* levels: thus, let the Mind speak to you! Your Unconscious has deeper and broader knowledge than will ever be possible to the Conscious Mind alone which is forever busy with ordinary material reality. Your goal is to *become more than you,* and to *become all you can be* through integration of Unconscious with Conscious, and *SuperConscious.*

Some Western Magicians will take umbrage with such "looseness," missing the point of Unconscious Wisdom where appropriate. In contrast, other kinds of Magickal operations can be very demanding and involve very specific choices of Words, Symbols, and other correspondences mostly derived from the Kabbalistic Tree of Life with at least hundreds of years of proven usage.

The more you integrate Unconscious with Consciousness while invoking the authority of your own Higher Self, the more you become!

Use your regular meditation exercise for Earth described previously starting on page 108 (as the primary element for such an operation), visualizing the Tattvic symbol and allowing a talisman image and any associated messages to occur. However, you will strengthen the operation by using the new *compound* Tattvic symbol illustrated in the drawing at the beginning of the addendum to Chapter Four (page 134). Ideally, follow the directions to create a Tattva Card, otherwise visualize it according to the instructions for content and color.

Having created the design, now *materialize* it on paper, cardboard, or a small piece of metal. Referring to the Earth table you see that the correspondence of Magical Metal is lead. Lead is soft and easy to engrave, and can even be painted and then sprayed to protect the image from being rubbed off.

In all practice of serious magick—East or West, North or South—there is recognition that all of material reality is itself a manifestation of the "Feminine Force,"* otherwise known as the Goddess in any of her forms and names or just the pure feminine deity in Tantra known as "Shakti." To bring our magical ritual—whether a physical script, a visualized play, or active meditation—into material manifestation, the magician must <u>invoke</u> the Goddess Energy (becoming *at one* with it as in "worship") and direct it into the vision of the goal.

Sometimes this is referred as "Drawing down the Moon" as a scenario of a priest calling the *Shakti* goddess energy into the body and soul of a priestess and then together they visualize the transmission of the manifesting power into the image of accomplishment.

*While references to Feminine and Masculine or Goddess and God can lead to considerable controversy, in which politics, religion, science and even grammar and the "style manual" all have their say, it really is a matter of common sense and psychological efficacy. Nearly all esoteric traditions recognize three basic factors are involved in the universe at the point of creation and continued and forever evolving existence. Often we call these factors *Consciousness, Energy,* and *Matter* but in "practice" over thousands of years Energy and Matter through many cultures are seen to manifest together as God and Goddess, Father and Mother, Masculine and Feminine, Positive and Negative, while Consciousness is perceived as their origin and the constant Source of All in the background. The Source, too, is often called "God" and sometimes "Father/Mother" but is not the same as the "lesser "gods of energy who accompany the goddesses of matter.

Remember that Matter and Energy are convertible, and both are particularized expressions of Consciousness. Because we are part of material reality, it is the Goddess who is dominant in this partnership with her companion God. It is She who "calls the shots."

This cosmology, whether addressed in esoteric science, ancient traditions, or the many polytheistic religions is much too complex to address in this small book. Goddess and God each are associated with names, chants, gestures, costumes, ornaments, colors, positions, movements, and other complex symbolisms all contained in a single image that then becomes a means to contact and receive further intuition through acts called worship, invocation, and self-identification.

Consciousness is in all things; hence all things can be given "personality." Through our active imagination, we endow the Earth's things, places, and FORCES with a *Humanized Personality.* Because the Earth is feminine, we recognize all Earth Energies and Forces as Goddesses—and each specific force is a Goddess with a different name, form, costume, and accessories—all with symbolic meaning that can be used in our invocation.

In meditation, and prayer, and in dreams, we can commune with these personalities.

How you carry this principle out is your decision. You must be the magician, the priest or priestess, or implementer. The less you follow other people's rules, the better you are able to accomplish your own reality—*once you understand the principles!*

As the final act, hold the talisman in your "power" hand (the one you write with), visualize it as radiating an increasing amount of yellow or golden light as you chant the Bija Mantra for Earth, **LAM**, three times (or multiples of three) followed by that for Water, *VAM* three times, while feeling the talisman becoming charged with SUCCESS energy. Place it in a coin envelope (representing the Water Magical Tool of a Cup or Chalice) and give it to your daughter to place in her purse or in the store cash register.

You have performed an act of magick employing the principles of the *Prithivi* and *Apas Tattvas* to inspire a new advertising campaign that will fulfill your stated magical goal: **Success in Daughter's health food store.**

You can adapt this example for other magical goals. Depending on the nature of the goal, you may work with any of the five primal elemental forces or the twenty compound forces, selecting the points corresponding to your goal from the appropriate elemental overview tables, and making necessary adjustments. Use your common sense. You are not going to make a talisman out of fire, water, air, or spirit, but your use of the Tattvic Form incorporates those energies.

Sources & Suggested Additional Reading:

Cunningham, S. *Encyclopedia of Crystal, Gem & Metal Magic,* 1998 & 2002, Llewellyn.

Cunningham, S. *Encyclopedia of Magical Herbs,* 1985, Llewellyn.

Frawley, D. *Tantric Yoga and the Wisdom Goddesses,* 1994, Passage Press.

Mumford, J. *Magical Tattwas: A Complete System for Self-Development,* 1997. Llewellyn.

CHAPTER TEN
Clairvoyance and Espionage in War & Peace

Remote Viewing, Map Dowsing and Psychokinesis

<u>News Report:</u>

CHINESE REPORTED TO BE HACKING INTO AMERICAN COMPUTERS
Not limited to Military Targets and "Enemy Combatants"

"Hacking" is defined as the use of a computer or other technological device or system in order to gain unauthorized access to data in order to steal information, or/and injure the software and hardware assets of the other party.

"Espionage" is just plain old-fashioned spying.

The Two Objectives of Espionage

1. Gain real knowledge about what an enemy, or potential enemy, or a commercial or political competitor is doing in specific areas of interest, activity, or geography;

2. Develop on-going strategies to combat, undermine, steal, destroy, or distort the other party's specific assets in the specified areas.

Hacking & Espionage: Today's Targets & Objectives

Do note that the targets and objectives of espionage & hacking are not limited to "enemy combatants" but—in today's fast-changing, competitive and greedy world—is likely to include current friends as well as foes, partners & allies of today and potential enemies & competitors of tomorrow, military as well as commercial secrets, scientific & technological developments, as well as academic research of unknown value, private lives & sexual predilections, beliefs & prejudices, health & biological factors, uses of drugs & chemicals, along with any information that could be twisted and used in programs of lies, deceit, distortion, negative advertising or propaganda, and anything else that could be hurtful to the other party while benefiting the first party.

In other words, to use the current jargon, *everything's on the table, and everyone's in the game!*

Today's espionage targets "butter" as well as "guns."

Today, the world is largely at peace compared to past centuries where major armies confronted each other on land, at sea, and then also in the air. Today, even space and cyberspace are potential theatres of war. And, as indicated in the news headlines quoted in this chapter's opening, those bytes and bits of data on computers everywhere are currently the actual objects of search, theft, and damage requiring increasing investments in defense, and—we can only guess—counter-attacks.

Biological, Mental, and Psychic (?) Manipulations

But we have also to consider that the men and women who program and operate these systems may be subjected not only old-fashioned espionage but to modern and futuristic biological and mental manipulations of one sort or another—whether through direct contact and offers of money, or psychological and—perhaps as we can only speculate—psychic manipulations as well.

And, perhaps there may still be programs of "remote viewing" by trained psychics, and that opens the doors of possibilities to psychic attacks and manipulations totally outside the geographic and physical limitations of the past.

Perceptions and Realities of Wars Today

No matter what the past history of psychic spying and wars may have been, we have to focus on what we know about military and commercial warfare today, about the known and speculative realities and limits of remote viewing and other forms of paranormal powers may be.

We will summarize what has been claimed in the past, but the reality is that we know very little other than that there is nearly as much science-fiction fantasy about paranormal warfare as there is about futuristic military weapons to be found in research laboratories around the world, as captured UFO and space aliens' may have provided, and that may exist in undiscovered German bunkers left over from World War II.

A Single Person's Powerful Weaponry

Today (January, 2012), there is only one major army in a conflict that is not against another army but a highly motivated guerilla force aiming its guns at "occupiers" rather than a territorial enemy. It's a new world where a single person can kill and injure hundreds of people, destroy massive amounts of property, and even bring down a huge bomber with a single shoulder-fired missile.

Religious Idolatry

Past wars were mostly between nations seeking to gain territory. Today's military conflicts are mostly ideological, and the ideologies involved are less political and more religious, less organized and more personal, and increasingly one side of the conflict is openly defenseless, and its population is being abused, starved, murdered, and enslaved, while women are raped and tortured for sadistic gratification, while children are murdered as a matter of course to eliminate them as future soldiers.

Even those few nations whose constitutional laws forbid war now train their police for conflict. Yet, military "accidents"—a *test* missile that kills people, an *unacknowledged* torpedo or mine that sinks a ship, *drones* that miss their targets but still kills untargeted children, etc.—don't trigger the national wars that resulted from similar accidents in the past.

Rational Choices

Why? For the simple reason that "rational" leaders recognize that the only way to fight a modern nation-against-nation war is to seek total obliteration of the enemy. That was the recognized dogma of the "Cold War" that ended when one side couldn't keep up with the ever increasing expense of "total" weaponry that *only might* destroy the enemy's ability and will to retaliate from a first strike. The power of offensive weapons is so great that no rational mind can contemplate their use in a massive war. The greatest danger comes from irrational religious fanaticism which is why there is so much effort concentrated on denying nuclear weapons to those willing (perhaps eager) to destroy every person of a contrary belief.

Instead, more people are being killed in drug wars than in regular military conflicts. Civilians are being killed by their country's dictators. Religious terrorist kill "unbelievers" on a scale beyond the loss of lives in the last "World" War.

Fortress Mentality

Still, there are immense military budgets—termed "defense" although most of the expenditure are for offensive weapons and training that are equally effect for deterrence and can be re-programmed for actual defense of the "homeland." The most rational and practical approach for national defense may be a "fortress" mentality that provides both maximum protection from attack and threatens massive and total retaliation should any attack be made.

"Black Budget," Futuristic Weapons, & Psychic Possibilities

And, more importantly although mostly unacknowledged are the "Black Budget" (meaning "off the budget" and disguised) expenditures for the development of ever more sophisticated hi-tech "weapon of tomorrow." Some secret items are provided for in the "research budget" and Special NSA (National Security Agency) Programs, Intelligence Support to Information Operations, and the Cyber Security Initiative that even though they have names show no numbers. Monies are, however, listed for "Directed Energy Technology," "Prompt Global Strike Capacity," "Global Hawk drones," "Landfill Gas Energy Capture," "Tactical Deployable Micro-Grid," and "Maui Space Surveillance System." And newly added are the "Imagery Satellite Way Ahead" and "Electro-optical satellites" programs.

Yes, the defense budgets of a few nations are immense, and increasingly unaffordable in terms of any thought of aggression. *Defense* against attack or invasion is still the goal of new super weapons. There is one nation totally dedicated to the support of a military as its civilian population starves and is subjected to massive and continuous propaganda supportive of its leader. Another nation is dedicated to the acquisition of nuclear weapons with the avowed intention to "wipe (a nation of a different religion) totally off the face of the earth," and to return world culture to the time of 700 AD dominated by a single, all-pervasive, religion.

Is "Psychic" included in the "off budget research? Probably, yes, but let's clearly state two probably "facts" about such matters:

The Two Important Facts about Psychic Spies

1. All "forward thinking," whether military or not (and probably more so when not), involves some degree of clairvoyance. So, for any general or admiral, or Defense employee above the "Just Follow the Rules" grade level is, knowingly or more often unknowingly, calling about his or her psychic abilities.

2. Regardless of "rank," very few such personnel unless tested and demonstrating proven psychic skills, are going to have seriously developed psychic skills no matter what and how much training they may be given. Yes, everyone has innate psychic powers, but they are like other "talents" so even though most can be taught to make some kind of simple sketch, few will become real artists. No amount of training will produce a genius.

In reality, we will never really know to what degree "Psychic Spies" have been used or are being used, nor will we know how effective or accurate their work has been.

Today's Espionage is as much Commercial as Industrial, Technological and Scientific, as well as Military

Today, China, Russia, and other countries, corporations, and individuals—including major American and International corporations and even private parties—are engaged in an assault on intellectual property rights including those supposedly protected by patents, copyrights, trademarks and other legal notices of asset identification and protection. It's often as much just plain theft as it is high-class espionage or even ordinary spying. The spies themselves look less like "moles" and "lurkers" and more like glamorous models and well-dressed professionals.

Property Rights fundamental to personal freedom and growth

Property rights are among the most fundamental of personal rights, intrinsic to liberty and personal choice. And it is *Intellectual Property* that honors those rights and encourages ambition, growth and development. Intellectual property is legally recognized in patents and copyrights. These, in particular, are under assault by pirates from countries like China who are stealing American and other nations' developments, counterfeiting products and technology, cheating their way to economic growth at the expense of those who invented and perfected new and better products.

The new technology that enables any entity to *cheaply* scan any document or book results is an expensive burden for copyright owners to constantly monitor their properties for pirated versions offered on the Internet. Challenging such intellectual thievery often results in the stolen property quickly showing up on another site.

Patents offer little more protection because to secure a patent the claimed property has to be described in sufficient detail that a competitor is often able to *backwards engineer,* or "replicate" the process of production and sometimes even to secure a patent on the slightly modified replicating method.

In other words, *greed* has replaced ethics in the market place: Greed for money, social position, academic recognition, and political power.

Greed, and "Normal Human Behavior"

It is, unfortunately, "normal human behavior" and it is not really as new as it is universally pervasive and openly encouraged. Read your history books and you will never find a time or place of universal peace and altruism other than in myth, fairy tales, false propaganda and misinformation. Such misinformation and propaganda has been particularly evident in modern dictatorships: Nazi Germany, the Soviet Union, North Korea and Iran, and any of the institutionalized religions in which historic theology dominates and distorts historic truth, current science, and personal freedom.

Realize that "normal human behavior" doesn't just apply to overt wars, whether cold or hot, and is not limited to matters of defense, military actions, corporate competitiveness, or actions recognized as "criminal" or even as "illegal."

Realize that "normal human behavior" is instinctively competitive as we become individuals rather than merely parts of groups of various sizes and intensities—family, clan and tribe.

Realize that "normal human behavior" is in your "daily grind." While rarely are you the intended target for acts of theft and injury, you are nevertheless the victim of their "Unintended Consequences," and need to protect and defend yourself and your employer from these abuses.

Realize that this "normal human behavior" actually leaves us all vulnerable—but that doesn't mean we are defenseless. As we have grown in consciousness and have become true individuals benefiting from quality education, we are likewise developing stronger personal auras with natural defenses against external pressures of conformity. And it is as individuals that we start to build greater defenses by strengthening the personal aura against psychological and psychic aggression. (See Slate, J. H.: *Aura Energy for Health, Healing & Balance*)

It doesn't have to be that way! "Normal" is not necessarily "Right"

Just because Greed is part of "normal human behavior" doesn't mean that every individual has to be greedy to survive and progress in modern society. *Quite the contrary!* No matter what the name: Arab Spring, Occupy Wall Street, Revolt of the Masses, the New Age, etc., we are seeing an assertion of idealism in place of accepting the abuse of power that became "normal human behavior." What someone else calls "normal" doesn't mean you can't choose to be different.

Individual Choice fundamental to growth and freedom

Individual choice is how we grow as a person, and perhaps never before in history has such individual choice become such a force for societal, political, and economic change. This is change disassociated from political, military, religious, and other forms of institutionalized "leadership" without regard for "Establishment" definitions of *normality*, political or religious *correctness*, or even for *personal safety and security*.

The process is far from complete—there are still legal and political battles being fought over sexual preferences, marital and partnership rights, medical choices, language, and keeping institutional religion out of schools and public life. On the other hand in the industrialized world, there is almost bewildering freedom in regard to dress and personal "adornment" that was unthinkable less than fifty years ago, more opportunity for life style choices, more variable choices of education, employment, belief, association, etc., and the exercise choices are not only free of legal restrictions but increasingly free of societal "frowns" and religious bigotry and hostility.

Constitutional Rights, Self-Awareness and Self-Defense

No matter how large or powerful a group, tribe or nation may be, personal defense is an expression of individual strength. We may stand arm-in-arm with our neighbor, but group strength is never stronger than the weakest link. Your defense against "normal human behavior" is your personal responsibility. You can never assume that someone else will provide for you even when you have the legal right to demand it.

In Unity there is Strength, but . . .

Yes, but . . . remember that the union is never stronger than its weakest link. Yes, even when we are talking about defense against acts of espionage we have to build our individual defenses. We started this chapter talking about news stories that Chinese individuals are hacking into American computers to gain access to secrets of various kinds. This author is using a personal computer that has software defending it from various forms of attack. At the same time, this computer is part of a network likewise protected by "firewalls" and other lines of defense, but the network is part of a larger network, etc., and networks can be attacked, subverted, and its members' secrets (credit card and bank numbers, personal interests and correspondence, business secrets and practices, etc.) can be violated, stolen, or erased.

Don't be a Victim

We defend ourselves at multiple levels, but our actual defense comes from the breadth of our awareness. The more you know, the greater your real strength. Ignorance is not "bliss," but an open invitation to exploitation and victimization. *Don't be a victim! Defend yourself through Awareness, Knowledge, Know-how, and Determination. And Know, and Exercise, Your Constitutional Rights.*

Awareness is like Radar, like Satellite Observation, like . . .

Yes, even like Clairvoyance. "Hacking" can be seen as an act of aggression, but it is also like "normal human behavior" in today's world. Our national borders are defended though layers of radar and satellite observation, and—no doubt—by technicians analyzing all sorts of data from many computers, actual spies on the grounds, and many things few of us have any knowledge about.

But, each of us is also being "spied upon" by security cameras, the analysis of our daily purchases whether on-line or in stores, by the news and the entertainment we watch, the Internet sites we surf, where we work and where we shop, what we eat and what we drink. Individually we expose our personal interests and entertainment choices by our presence on various social media, blogs, the catalogs and information we request, the "friends" we relate to, the books we read and the hobbies we enjoy.

The net result: there is no genuine privacy while at the same time there is far greater acceptance and respect for who we are. Your religious views may be rejected by others, but there is no denial of your right of belief in modern civilized societies. Your fashion and adornment choices may be seen as weird but you are less likely to be fired from your job because of them. (Note, however, that these remarks apply more or less universally—except for the Islamic North Africa and Middle East where fundamentalist Islam seems intent on restoring the world view at the time of the Prophet Mohamed. The prospects for world peace diminish accordingly.)

What has all of this to do with Clairvoyance and Espionage?

Strangely enough, quite a bit. We have to see that the old methods and ideas about military and industrial spying have changed, just as technologies have also changed. We have to learn a new lexicon, and see the world with a different understanding of the assets and rights to be protected.

Yes, some of the same awful weapons are still with us, but the old motivations of using them have changed. In a world where trade is more important than territory there is no logical justification for an invasion. In a world where wealth is stored as bytes and bits, even gold and gems becomes just another commodity increasingly impractical to steal and transport.

Instead of threats involving bombing in its attempts to deter Iran's religious dictators from developing nuclear weapons, America and its allies impose trade embargoes and financial restraints. At the same time, the "West" must recognize that it cannot *impose* cultural change on nations of the Middle East even as within the United States local governments must be stopped from trying to impose sectarian Christianity (no matter how defined) in public schools and public venues.

Good values mature from "within" and not authoritarian imposition from without—no matter what guise it comes under.

What's left? Knowledge and Know How, and while those are being stolen today, it's far less expensive and ultimately more beneficial for those sponsoring nations to invest in education and intellectual development, and far cheaper to license a patent than even to backwards-engineer a product. As for corporate theft, we need to remove corruption from the regulators' equation and allow members of the United States Congress to once again be subject to the criminal laws they have exempted themselves from.

The best means of personal and national defense come from universal economic and social development beyond national borders, improved secular education, greater access to a faster world-wide Internet, and rewards for personal accomplishments beyond purely monetary ones.

Know what to look for!

This preliminary dialogue is necessary in order to establish what we must look for in order to discover, counter, and prosecute those real acts and threats of espionage, terrorism and criminality from outside the regular military defense and criminal justice systems.

For the most part, America's sophisticated satellite and aerial surveillance systems, along with spies-on-the ground, have revealed the location of weapons everywhere in the world, so we won't waste our time with "Remote Viewing" and other paranormal techniques specifically for that purpose. Remote Viewing for other purposes may be useful, but itself has never been fully defined as either distance-clairvoyance or geographic-specific astral projection.

And, while it is helpful to have geographic targets, it isn't necessary. What is necessary is to define the *intention* of your paranormal effort. *Are you looking for the location of a major stash of illegal drugs? Are you looking for the location of a particular drug lord, or the whereabouts of a kidnapped child? Are you looking for Elizabeth Taylor's stolen or lost famous ruby necklace?* When goals are not well defined, you cannot expect good results.

Don't mix the purely Physical with the Non-Physical!

Always, the more *intellectually* descriptive the target or the question is the more effective will be your *non-physical* "search and rescue" efforts. *Why?* Because a purely physical object cannot be found by purely non-physical means! By changing the object of your search to one that is richly described in intellectual and non-emotional terms you have moved outside the physical parameters.

Note, too, the framing of the above directions, summed up in the last phrase of "search and rescue." The more *benevolent* the intention, the more energy *free of moral or ethical conflict* you have applied to the work at hand.

There is an old adage: *Don't mix the planes!*—essentially meaning to keep emotions out of the equation. Strangely enough, the polarity of the planes alternate, so physical and mental, correctly applied, can be mutually supportive, while emotional and "spiritual" likewise can be mutually supportive but are conflictive with physical and mental. But, that's a subject for an entirely different book!

TECHNIQUES AND TOOLS FOR DISTANCE CLAIRVOYANCE

We are including a short historic review of Cold War psychic espionage as background for understanding present-day challenges and opportunities. While the Cold War was seen as a conflict between two economic and social systems that sometimes took on a nearly "religious" fervor, it was not an actual "Religious War" with purported religious goals or the promises of heavenly rewards for warriors and martyrs.

Remote Viewing

Remote Viewing is defined as the purported ability to gather information about a distant or unseen physical target by means of non-physical perception (generally called ESP for Extra Sensory Perception). Typically a remote viewer is expected to give information about an object that is hidden from physical view and separated at some distance. The term was introduced by physicists-turned-parapsychologists Russell Targ and Harold Puthoff in 1974.

The modern history of *Remote Viewing* started during the Cold War between the Soviet Union and the Western Allies that existed from the end of World War II in 1945 to the Communist-based Soviet Union's economic collapse in 1991.

While there was never a direct military confrontation between the two sides, there was constant competition through military and economic aid to their various satellite states, conventional force deployments facing each other, various proxy wars, espionage, the nuclear arms race, outrageous propaganda, and then as technological competition and the Space Race.

The Cold War: A War of Ideas & Ideals

The Cold War was mainly a "War of Ideas," and American intelligence agencies funded projects countering Communism's appeal among the intellectuals in Europe and the developing world. The Soviets were more centered on technological competition and were the first to develop long-range intercontinental ballistic missiles (August 1957) capable of reaching the continental United States, and then in October the same year, they launched the first Earth satellite, Sputnik, inaugurating the Space Race that culminated in the American Apollo Moon Landings.

Lies, Damned Lies, & Everything Else

Since there was no openness between the two sides separated not only by a military-enforced physical border (the Iron Curtain) but by an ideology of near religious bellicosity, there was instead a constant flow of rumor, lies, false news stories, alleged conspiracies, and mutual paranoia attached to every kind of mystery—UFOs & Aliens, Crop Circles & Weird Weather, Abominable Snowmen & Bigfoot, Psychic Phenomena & Powers, etc.—to variously insinuate the superiority of one or the other of the two conflicting political systems.

While many articles were published and conferences organized under the pretense of stimulating intellectual exchange, actual psychic research was being carried on undercover mostly in Russia and the United States.

The Psychic Arms Race

In 1960 the psychic arms race intensified when the United States conducted successful telepathy exchanges between a man at a Duke University laboratory and a man submerged at sea aboard the nuclear-powered submarine, *Nautilus*. (Note: Normal communications from *under water* is impossible, so reliable psychic communication would provide a considerable strategic advantage.)

The Soviets countered with new studies of telepathy, and in the mid-1960s, the sensationally successful book *Psychic Discoveries Behind the Iron Curtain* by Ostrander & Schroder claimed that the U.S. was "fifty years behind the Russians," resulted in government funding of psychic research at Stanford University.

In 1972, physicist Harold Puthoff tested psychic Ingo Swann's remote viewing ability at Stanford Research Institute (SRI), and the experiment quickly resulted in a visit from the CIA's Directorate of Science and Technology.

In 1974, Puthoff and Dr. Bonnar Cox drove aimlessly about for 30 minutes and then stopped at an unplanned destination. Back in an electrically shielded room in SRI's engineering sciences building, Pat Price, a retired police commissioner, then described the scene where the two had stopped.

Even before the 30 minutes were up, Pat Price, proceeded for 20 minutes to tell physicist Russell Targ about the scenes he was seeing while the two were still driving, and then predicted where they would stop and accurately described that scene. Targ and Puthoff continued their remote viewing experiments with Pat Price and psychic Ingo Swann for ten more years at SRI with similar positive results.

In 1979 the Army's Intelligence and Security Command was ordered to develop its own program. First it evaluated research in the Soviet Union and China, and concluded that their programs were better funded and supported than U. S. research.

Stanford continued its research in remote viewing, with Pat Price whose reported description of a new class of a strategic submarine and the location of a downed Soviet bomber in Africa again was verified.

Psychic Abilities lack Specifics Reliability

But, one problem encountered in this research was its seeming unreliability, varying from day to day. The CIA released a paper called the AIR Report by Edwin C. May, Ph.D., explaining that though there was an observable phenomenon, it was not reliable enough in specifics to continue. Swann and Puthoff then developed a remote-viewing training program meant to enable any individual with a suitable background to produce useful data. It has been claimed that 22 military officers and civilians were trained and formed a military remote viewing unit based at Fort Meade, Maryland.

Weapons Systems & Mind Power

In December 1980, Lt. Col. John B. Alexander stated that "there are weapons systems that operate on the power of the mind and whose lethal capacity has already been demonstrated." He further said that illness or death had been successfully induced in lower organisms such as flies and frogs by mentally transmitting disease over distance and (Page 144 *Psychic Powers,* Time-Life series on "Mysteries of the Unknown," 1987.)

"Voodoo Warfare"

In response to this article, nationally syndicated columnist Jack Anderson reported that the U.S. was using psychics "to spy on the Soviets by projecting their minds outside their bodies" and that "the CIA was considering deploying 'psychic shields' to protect American secrets from the Soviets." Ron McRae, Anderson's associate ridiculed this as "Voodoo Warfare."

At its peak, the Stargate Project was a twenty million dollar program before it was terminated in 1995. Many documents have been released that show that there were indeed programs of "psychic spying," but there are suggestive indications that "spying" on military installations could not be verified to the extent necessary—to put it bluntly—to authorize someone to launch a Third World War. However, it was suggested that psychic attacks on people could be psychologically and even biologically effective. Further, *unofficial* information suggests that such biological attacked were more effective when the attacker and attackee were of opposite sex.

The Current Situation

Although the London Sunday Times, in November 2011, reported that remote viewers are being recruited by the U.S. government, we can only speculate about current military involvement in any form of psychic research in the United States or in other countries. With the rise of the Fundamentalist Far Right, it is doubtful that any Republican and perhaps not many Democrat politicians are going to endorse and support "the Occult" in any form, whether as the science of parapsychology or as the natural psychic power of any healthy person.

Still, it must be admitted that "psychic spies" can go anywhere and leave no footprints behind. One difficulty is that the accuracy of spy work cannot be reported and analyzed in the same manner as other investigative work, and without feedback provided to the psychics it is difficult for them to improve their methodology.

The public website presence for STARstream Research, STARpod.org, has posted a declassified 72-page Defense Intelligence Agency SECRET on-line briefing reports that paranormal "psychic vision," referred to as "remote viewing" by the Department of Defense, is, to quote from the document, "a real phenomenon," and that "an unusual mechanism may have been observed" with "significant application implications

Other documents show that following 9/11, American intelligence sought the use of psychics to locate Saddam's rumored nuclear locations in Iraq. Of course, those nuclear facilities never existed and their premise proved to be just an excuse for the American invasion of Iraq and, unfortunately, removed the established deterrent to Iranian power.

PK affect on Electronic Systems

Other STAR GATE files showed the Missile Intelligence Agency of the U.S. Army feared that psychokinesis might be used by an enemy to affect sensitive electronic systems and funded research to "document that psycho-energetic phenomena are real and reproducible, to determine the underlying mechanisms, and to bring psychoenergetics research into the mainstream of human performance research."

This research was eventually moved to Science Applications International Corporation (SAIC), a major defense contractor whose technical analysis noted that "approximately 1 percent of the general population appears to meet strict statistical criteria for exhibiting a robust AC [psychic] ability," the report then notes that SAIC "may have discovered the source of an AC [psychic] signal."

"Recent experimental data from the former Soviet Union and similar experiments conducted in this country suggest that the peripheral nervous system may be susceptible to AMP [psychic] influence."

In 2011 STARpod reported that Mike McConnell, former National Intelligence Director and other intelligence officials have stated for the record that Chinese and Russian intelligence collection efforts are approaching Cold War levels.

Astral Projection or Clairvoyance

The natural powers closest to the remote viewing experience are astral projection and clairvoyance. Whether it is one or the other, or both, may be activated by the techniques of its employment.

It is Dr. Slate's opinion that remote viewing can involve clairvoyance, out-of-body travel, or combinations of both. Some of his most successful research subjects first entered the out-of-body state, and while in that state, viewed the distant reality but did not travel to it. In that state, they gave highly detailed and accurate information.

Other students felt they entered a spiritually liberated state in which they had access to new information as needed—the information came typically in imagery form. Yet other subjects explained the experience as a manifestation of self-contained higher mental functions that exist to some degree in everyone. These findings and views reaffirm the concept that any phenomenon (like any act of behavior) can have multiple explanations; furthermore, the more complex the phenomenon, the more varied the explanations.

Among the most effective techniques for remote viewing started with a progressive relaxation program with included suggestions of a "sub-conscious" link to other selected realities. Using that approach, a location is selected and visualized. Detailed mental images are then allowed to appear.

Preparing for Remote Viewing & Astral Projection
Relaxation Procedure for Remote Viewing & Astral Projection

For either approach to self-induced remote viewing, arrange for a period of one hour of more of uninterrupted time in a comfortable room where you will not be disturbed. A recliner is recommended so you can find a position most conducive to physical relaxation.

The essential elements of a relaxation program include:

• A posture or position that you will be comfortable in for an hour or more.

• A light covering providing sufficient warmth for the inactive body.

- Breathing that is slow and regular, proceeding from a series of deep breaths to the resumption of a natural rhythm.

- Deliberate relaxation of the body. This may effectively include progressive relaxation from feet to head, or it may involve "tensing and relaxing" muscle groups progressing from left foot up to groin, and then right foot up to groin, then the groin and abdominal areas, up through stomach and chest, then the left hand up to the shoulder followed by the right hand up to shoulder, and then particular attention on the shoulders themselves, the neck, and the facial and back of the skull muscles.

- As desired, this can be followed by self-hypnosis procedures leading toward either astral projection or clairvoyance.

- In any case, let the procedure end in either natural sleep or a deliberate "return" of progressive awakening, comfortable stretching, and a few moments to record your experience.

The Astral Projection Program:

Astral projection and remote viewing are similar in that they both provide information concerning spatially distant realities. They differ, however, in that astral projection incorporates disengagement of the *astral body* from the physical and usually leads to a wider range of experiences.

There are numerous programs for astral projection induction, and many will be found in the books recommended at the end of this chapter. The following is provided as a sample of one program called the "Eye Blink Procedure" that utilizes eye blinks and innovative orientation techniques to induce the out-of-body state and facilitate travel to either physical or non-physical destinations.

It is important to read the entire procedure before starting. The steps are well defined and easy to follow. Here's the procedure.

The "Eye Blink" Procedure for Remote Viewing & Astral Projection
Step 1. The Setting

Select a safe, quiet area that facilitates walking among a variety of items, such as tables, chairs, sofas, appliances, and plants. The typical home setting with living room, dining room, family room, and kitchen connected provides an excellent situation. If a large area is unavailable, a single room or office with space for walking around furnishings is sufficient. The setting should include a comfortable recliner or couch for use during astral projection. Select the specific path you will follow while walking, preferably a circular route that includes a variety of things to view.

Step 2. Physically Walking

Walk slowly through the path you selected, paying special attention to what you see on either side.

Step 3. Viewing and Eye Blink

After walking through your selected area several times, stop and pick a well-defined object, such as a lamp or vase. Gaze at the object for a few seconds and then snap your eyes shut. Rather than closing them slowly, snap them as you would if blinking. *Think of taking a snapshot of the item with your eyes.* With your eyes closed, you will note that the afterimage of the object will remain briefly. When the image disappears, open your eyes and repeat the exercise. You will note that when you first start this process, the image may turn negative. This will change with practice.

Step 4. Forming Mental Impressions

As you continue to practice Step 3, you will notice that the afterimage of the select-ed object stays with you longer. As the duration of the image increases, you will note that a mental impression of the image remains for a few moments even after the image itself fades. Developing this awareness requires practice, possibly for several minutes. Test your effectiveness by turning your head to see if the mental impression remains. When the impression of the image remains, you are ready to go on to the next step.

Step 5. Walking and Eye Blink

Resume walking around the area you selected as your chosen path. As you continue to walk, repeatedly snap your eyes shut for about a second and then open them for about a second while always facing forward. Carefully adjust your eye-blink rate and step so as not to stumble or collide with anything. Upon beginning this routine you will prob-ably see the images in your mind's eye as stationary. After several times around and possibly more than one session, you will notice that when your eyes are shut, the items continue to move so that your eyes can be closed longer before the movement stops. You will know when you have this mastered when the objects you envisioned are adjacent to you when you open your eyes.

Step 6. Mental Walking

Having mastered Step 5, find a comfortable place to recline or lie down with your legs uncrossed and your hands resting at your sides. As you relax, make the entire trip mentally with your eyes closed. While mentally walking through your selected space, pay special attention to the familiar details along your pathway. Observe them from different viewpoints as you sense yourself walking among them.

Step 7. Remote Viewing

As you remain relaxed with your eyes closed, select a familiar distant place and view it remotely. Pay particular attention to the specific details of the distant setting you are viewing. Take plenty of time for the setting to emerge in full detail.

Step 8. Astral Projection

Having remotely viewed a distant setting, you are now ready to travel out of body. With your eyes remaining closed, mentally walk around your selected path once more. View in detail the setting as you move among its furnishings. As you continue this mental exercise, you will begin to sense yourself literally walking out-of-body through the room, maneuvering among pieces of furniture and noticing objects in even greater detail. You will then sense that you can travel out-of-body beyond the room to experience firsthand other surroundings, including the place you remotely viewed in Step 7. You are now ready to walk out the door and travel to that place. Take plenty of time to travel to that place, and once there, add to your awareness such sensations as hearing and touch. Remain in that place long enough to get a full sense of your presence there.

Step 9. Distant Travel

You can now travel to places you have not physically been before. Note your sense of freedom and control. By intent alone, you can travel in any direction to any location you choose. Your destination can include both physical and spiritual realities. You can travel to familiar distant settings or to places totally unknown to you. You can observe others, including other astral travelers, and possibly interact with them. You can engage the spirit realm, again by intent alone. You can interact with your *spirit guides* and other entities in the spirit realm. You can experience the magnificent beauty of that dimension and the empowerment resources it offers.

Step 10. The Return

To return to your physical body and re-engage it, give yourself permission to first return to the familiar setting you visited earlier, and from there to your physical body at rest. Allow plenty of time for yourself to slip into your body, full re-engaging it. When you notice such sensations as breathing, heart rate, and weight, you will know you are back in your body.

Step 11. Resolution and Verification

Take a few moments to reflect on your out-of-body experiences. Explore the relevance of the experiences, particularly your visitations to the spirit realm. Verify as far as possible that what you experienced during astral travel was accurate.

Step 12. Journal

Finally, write down important observations made during your Out-of-Body Experience and your conclusions as to what you have learned.

The Clairvoyance "Third Eye" Program:

Repeat the preparation program of relaxation, and then refer to the Chapter on Chakras and repeat the exercise for the Brow Chakra. Keeping your physical eyes closed, visualize the image of the Winged Eye firmly in your mind's eye, reach up and touch your brow with you index and middle fingers at that point above and between your eyes where the "Third Eye" is located, and feel that your inner vision is now open.

Keeping your joined two fingers in contact with the Third Eye, visualize anything that links you to the location desired. Calmly let images appear in your vision.

Either of the above procedures could be used with voice guidance or hypnosis with a second person.

Set Your Goals

Before you proceed with either astral projection or clairvoyance techniques, determine your goal—the location for your remote vision using whatever knowledge of it that you can bring together. That may be as little as the name of a person residing there, the longitude & latitude, the physical address, a photograph or an image, etc., along with an approximation of what you anticipate seeing there. *What are you looking for, what do you want to discover, what information do you want to bring back from your trip? You could be checking on the health of a relative. You might be visiting the site of a future sales call. You may want to check out a vacation destination. You may be viewing the road ahead for a driving trip.*

All of these are logical examples, but the real point is to keep your goal specific and your focus narrow. And, always, the better your preparation, the more likely your success.

ANOTHER WAY OF SEEING
Map Dowsing

Looking for Information

What are we looking for in these fields of Espionage and Criminal Investigation?
Information!

We are always looking for specific information in answer to specific questions, concerns, and interests. Clairvoyance is defined as "clear seeing," but it is really an alternative to physical (and, usually, on-site) seeing. Information, however, is mostly *intelligence* about something, and while it may come in the form of physical photographs, files, drawings, maps, reports, etc., what we are really looking for is non-physical "intelligence" about physical things.

Many times the intelligence about what we are looking for is hidden away, even *beneath the surface!* A bomb-making or storage facility may be buried underground beneath layers of concrete or hidden in mountain caves. But since we are really concerned with *intelligence* we may want to know where the computer and servers are located that contain the intelligence about those bombs, or about troop locations, or fuel storage, or other information resources. Intelligence is *information* about the target.

Intelligence is Information about Assets and Resources

Let's refine our thinking. Whether in war or peace, we are interested in assets and resources of many kinds, and usually we want to find their location. We go on-line with our computers and employ a search engine to find sources for intelligence of interest. But sometimes that source is presently undeveloped but still of great value and importance, future or present.

Map Dowsing is commonly used to locate resources like water and other earth resources, or lost or missing persons, or for finding a person in hiding.

Dowsing, itself, is a technology thousands of years old. 4000 year old Chinese and Egyptian artwork shows dowsing with forked tools; the Biblical Moses used a rod to locate water; dowsing was used to locate coal deposits in Europe's middle ages; in 17th Century France criminals were tracked by means of dowsing. During the Vietnam War, U.S. Marine Corps engineers were trained to use dowsing rods to locate booby traps and sunken mortar shells.

Lyall Watson in *Supernature* writes , "experiments in all countries suggest that, whatever the dowsing force may be, it cannot work on the rod alone. A living being has to act as a 'middleman.' The Dutch geologist Solco Trump has shown that dowsers are unusually sensitive to the earth's magnetic field, and respond to changes in the field that can be verified with magnetometers.

About that image of an old farmer guy in bib overalls looking for water with a forked stick? That's only one of the benefits of dowsing, and the forked stick is only one familiar tool of many that are used today to search for water, oil, minerals, gems, buried pipelines, pirate treasures, electrical wiring, archaeological sites and artifacts, and more. While the natural freshly cut forked stick is still preferred by some, many dowsers use Y-shaped and L-shaped *divining rods*—some as simple as bent coat hangers and others complicated devices of exotic metals and coiled springs. And some dowsers called "hand tremblers" use only their unaided hands or their *entire body* as divining instruments.

Dowsing's Many Practical Applications

As a technique for gathering information, dowsing has been successfully applied to science and technology, business and industry, forensics, and the military. Valuable subterranean resources including oil, coal, water, minerals, and natural gas have been located through dowsing. In industrial settings, dowsing has been effective in locating buried cables, water, gas lines and valuable resources. Before excavating, some contractors routinely engage dowsers to determine certain geological characteristics of the site, including water sources, bedrock formations, and the existence of any hazardous conditions.

Although metal detectors are sometimes used for locating objects such as lost coins, jewelry, and buried metal pipe lines or cables, dowsing is often preferred because of its higher sensitivity and effectiveness in locating metal and specific non-metal materials from a greater distance.

Dowsing with a Pendulum

In addition, the same functional usage is accomplished with a simple pendulum for dowsing earth resources with maps, for finding sources of illness, locating lost objects, and even in forensic applications to trace the human history of objects pertinent to a crime scene. While there are many theories offered to explain the phenomena of dowsing, its greatest value is *communication between the subconscious mind and the conscious mind, and actually going beyond to the universal consciousness in which all memories and all knowledge resides.*

Test it Yourself

Sit in a comfortable chair next to a table on which you have several small objects, relax your mind and body, and then hold either hand about six inches above one of those objects, and then another, and so on. Perhaps you won't detect anything at first, but you will as you continue your developmental exercise. Change hands, change objects, let your conscious change and slide into different modes.

Try other objects like something battery powered, then something connected to household current, and perhaps a cell phone. Add a natural crystal, a small magnet, a photograph, an old heirloom piece of jewelry, perhaps a child's small favorite toy, and similar objects to expand your range of experience.

You are extending your own energy field and awareness to comprehend the energy fields of these objects. At some point you will *feel* their radiant energy, and will be able to detect differences among the objects. You might label them, shuffle them about with your eyes closed, and then with eyes still closed see if you can identify each object by name and move it aside for the next. Next try holding your hand above small household plants, and then outdoors over different flowers and small vegetable plants.

Note your results in a journal.

The whole purpose of the exercise is to actually experience your own unaided hand as a *sensitive instrument* detecting different energies, and perhaps—in the case of crystals and plants—different kinds of consciousness. With some personal objects, like a grandmother's ring or a grandfather's watch, you may get impressions of the person to whom the object belonged. While the ability to detect such impressions is the subject of a separate study called "Psychometry," the ability to use the physical body to detect invisible subtle energies is the same as used in Dowsing and working with the Pendulum.

Dowsing with the Pendulum

The pendulum—simply a small weight suspended by a chain or string—is an important psychic-empowerment tool primarily because of its capacity to gather highly objective information not available by non-psychic means. In its empowerment applications, the pendulum, suspended from the hand, can be used to answer questions and convey meaningful information by its simple movements.

The advantage to the pendulum as an information-gathering tool is its capacity to respond to very mild energy stimuli. As an extension of the physical body when suspended from one's hand, the pendulum can amplify minute, involuntary muscle activity and thus function as a highly sensitive recording instrument.*

> *It's important to remind the reader that human person & human body are part of an energy system that functions as a kind of "middleman" in the psychic exchange between divining tool and goal. The power is not in the tool but in the operator, so the very fact that the arm and hand may be seen

to "twitch" and seem to cause the motion of the pendulum (or the dowsing rod) should in no way be perceived to negate the efficacy of the system.

The hand-held pendulum's psychic empowerment role includes its capacity to probe sources of knowledge outside the self. In its clairvoyant application, the pendulum engages externally charged stimuli to assert a mild but significant influence on either the pendulum or our inner psychic faculties to produce meaningful movement—perhaps psychokinetically—in the pendulum.

The pendulum is a valuable psychic tool for gathering information regarding personal concerns. For that purpose, the pendulum is usually suspended over one's own hand or, when applicable, that of another individual, as questions are posed regarding financial investments, relationships, career decisions, and other issues.

Center Pendulum Here

The Pendulum Alphabet Chart

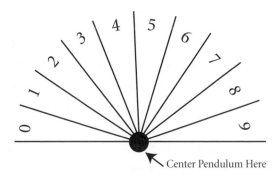

Center Pendulum Here

The Pendulum Number Chart

As both a precognitive and clairvoyant tool, the pendulum has demonstrated accuracy in gathering information on regional and world events. For this application, the pendulum is held over any relevant object, such as a map for national events or a globe for world affairs. The pendulum can also be used as a dowsing tool gathering archaeological data or researching historical artifacts, by suspending it over the object being studied.

The pendulum can provide highly specific and complex information when used with alphabet and number charts. Suspended from the hand and appropriately centered over the chart, the pendulum can spell out detailed messages regarding the past, present, and future.

As a simple information-gathering tool, the hand-held pendulum can accurately explore our inner motives, abilities, interests, and potentials. As a probe of external realities, the pendulum can tap distant sources of psychic insight and connect us to a vast wealth of empowering psychic knowledge.

Pendulum Prospecting with Maps

The pendulum can be used as part of a dowsing program by holding the pendulum over maps to locate targets for prospecting specific natural and human resources. We can start with large scale maps, and even aerial surveys, and then as target areas show up we move on to aerial photos and local maps specific to those areas. We can continue with our map dowsing using more localized maps, photos, drawings augmented with written details, of switch over to field dowsing with L or Y rods, if practical.

Many operators using pendulums and dowsing rods often make use of "specimen samples" held in one hand or incorporated into compartments on the pendulum bob or handle area of a dowsing rod. The sample is of the material objective to the outer physical dowsing work—water, oil, gold, nickel, etc.—and functions as a *focus* for the inner psychic, part of the operation. Other operators simply keep the objective in mind during the mechanical process with either pendulum or dowsing rod.

Map Dowsing is a particular combination of the dowsing ability with the use of a pendulum over a map to locate the defined target well suited to espionage work and criminal investigations.

Map Dowsing Procedure

Obviously, we start with three basic things:

1. Knowledge about the target—as much information about the objective of our search as possible.
2. Maps and/or aerial photographs suitable for the search.
3. The Pendulum, sometimes augments with specimens or even small photos of the objective.

In addition, you will need a straight edge (short ruler) and a pencil.

Lay all your equipment out on a flat surface, and then clear you mind of "clutter" and think about and even visualize the objective and whatever you know about the locale.

There are three approaches you can use, and sometimes you will find it helpful to start with the one, and then continue with another.

1. Topical. Simply move the hand holding the pendulum over the map until a "hit" is experienced. Continue with more localized maps to refine the targeted location.

2. Triangulation. Holding the pendulum in one hand beside the map, and use the other hand to move the straight edge slowly across the map until you feel a hit. Lightly draw a line. Now, holding the straight edge at a 90° angle to the first line, repeat the process until you get a second hit, and draw a line. Where the two lines intersect should be the location of the target.

3. Quartering. Divide the map into quarters, and move the pendulum over one quarter, and then another, etc., until you get a hit. Divide the positive quarter into small quarters, and repeat the process until you have localized the target as much as possible.

Combining Map Dowsing with Distance Clairvoyance

Map Dowsing can be combined with Distance Clairvoyance by holding one hand on or over the identified target, and then using any of the techniques for clairvoyance described elsewhere in this book.

All forms of divination are specific tools & techniques of Clairvoyance. Even though many people practice these specific forms of divination—whether reading Tea Leaves or Tarot, reading Auras or interpreting Dreams, analyzing Handwriting or casting Runes, Crystal Gazing or Geomancy, etc.—without thought of clairvoyance, they are methods of using that particular kind of psychic sensitivity that we call "clear seeing," and those practices can be improved with that realization.

HYPNOSIS FROM FAR, FAR AWAY

Cold War Paranoia

During the Cold War following the end of World War II, the Soviet Union took the lead in developing new technologies to counter American superiority in Atomic Bombs, heavy military hardware, the numbers of naval and air war craft, and forward bases.

It took awhile for America and its Western allies to fully realize the extent and consequences of the "Iron Curtain" that slammed down in Europe, and then elsewhere across the globe as Communist China became as active partner with Russia and its Soviet satellites. And the intellectual appeal of socialism in India, many European countries, and developing nations in Africa, the Middle East, and Latin America gave the Soviets' the feeling that "History is on our side."

When the Soviets matched the American nuclear advantage, and then added the threat of long-range missiles and the launch of the first artificial satellite, compounded by the placement of Russian missiles in Cuba (a mere 80 miles from the United States), the Americans finally realized they were losing the war and plunged into programs of building alliances, building military hardware, and building new technology.

All the while, the conflict intensified via massive propaganda work, economic and political alliances, massive gifts of military and economic aid, heavy investments in new technologies, and science programs that resulted in the American's Lunar Landings and spending programs that finally brought about the economic and political collapses of the old Soviet Union and of Communist economics.

The revolutionary appeal of political and economic individualism continues, but already is changing to meet new challenges. The Past may be prologue to the Future, but the Vision of the Moment is never clear and precise. Tomorrow is always Another Day.

Illusions, East and West, during the Cold War

The isolation and news restrictions characteristic of the Soviet's top-down control of information led to many rumors and government directed propaganda. Old scientific studies of paranormal phenomena were revived, studies of telepathy and hypnosis given new funding, individuals demonstrating psychokinetic powers were given celebrity status, and the rumor mills ground speedily and crudely to give the illusion that Soviet sciences were 50 years in advance of anything in the Western World.

Cold War paranoia on both sides of the Iron Curtain led to stories and claims about long distance hypnosis via telepathy leading to murder, suicides, disease, etc. East and West both worried that telepathy or clairvoyance could be combined with psychokinesis to manipulate physical actions upon military weapons or simply to use PK itself to destroy weapons. Many of the fears expressed reached the dimensions of fantastic science fiction.

"Sleep-Wake Hypnosis"

In 1886, the French psychiatrist, Pierre Janet, demonstrated the telepathic induction and termination of hypnosis with the subject located a distance away. This work was taken up in the 1930s by Leonid Vasiliev and proclaimed as a Russian invention called "Sleep-Wake Hypnosis".

A Ukrainian, Albert Ignatenko, was able to raise or lower the pulse rate of people distant from him. Russian experimenters were able to stop the hearts of test animals and this led to claims of remote killing ability.

Vladimir Zironosvky, on BBC television, claimed that Russia had psychics who could remotely kill anyone up to a thousand kilometers away. Such Russian boasts of remote killings were treated seriously in the Cold War era when fiction often was claimed as fact. (See reports "Paraphysics R & D—Warsaw Pact Countries" U.S. Air Force/Air Force Systems Command/ Foreign Technology Division and "Soviet and Czechoslovakian Parapsychology" Research" Army Medical Intelligence Branch

Hypnosis and Psychic Powers

In the early history of Mesmerism and Hypnosis, psychic phenomena and psychic powers were sometimes observed together. One common phenomenon was called "community of sensation" and referred to a hypnotized subject having the same sensations (taste, for example) as a distant person.

In our recent history, hypnosis has been found to facilitate clairvoyance, telepathy, and precognition. It is suggested that it is the combination of physical and mental relaxation with the sensory isolation normal to either a hypnotic or self-hypnosis session.

Dr. Charles Tart has reported experiments in which two people mutually hypnotize each other and then further reinforce the hypnosis between them. Here it should be remarked that the potentials of mutually reinforced hypnosis resemble the shared empathy of a group in ritual and other shared experience.

Two (or more) people working together to deepen their shared hypnotic state could, theoretically at least, enhance shared psychic practice as sometimes reported in healing work, visions (usually presumed to be hallucinatory), distance clairvoyance and telepathy, demonstration of PK, and spiritual communication.

PSYCHOKINESIS:
Mind over Matter

Perhaps nothing more vividly illustrates the far-reaching power of the mind than psychokinesis (PK). Also known as telekinesis, PK is defined as the ability to mentally influence objects or conditions without intervening physical energy or intermediary contact. In plain words, *PK is the ability to move or influence physical objects and internal conditions without physical intervention.*

The current view of PK, influenced by the contributions of quantum mechanics, includes concepts related to the teleporting of tangible objects and the transmitting of matter to distant destinations (*The Futurist,* September-October 2008). It is increasingly conceivable that the teleportation of materials and matter to distant destinations is a reasonable reality awaiting discovery and development.

Additionally, the expanding view of paranormal science recognizes the assumed capacity of PK to influence not only external conditions but also physiology, including critical systems and organ functions. The capacity of PK to intervene physiologically has been dramatically illustrated in the biofeedback setting where increased awareness of biological processes led to the ability to mentally control them, including such functions as blood pressure, muscular tension, migraine and tension headaches, heart rate, and brainwave patterns. Given these powers of the mind over the body, PK interventions that promote wellness and healing become reasonable possibilities. Unfortunately, that means PK interventions could also be used to promote disease and accelerated aging.

Like other paranormal phenomena, PK can be either spontaneous or deliberately induced.

PK in the Laboratory.

The deliberate induction of PK has been repeatedly demonstrated at Athens State University in experiments designed to initiate motion in stationary objects. A group of ten volunteer subjects were instructed to induce movement in a pendulum suspended inside a bell jar. With the bell jar and its suspended glass pendulum situated on a table before the group, the group was instructed simply to gaze at the pendulum and try to bring it into motion. Within moments, the pendulum began a slow turning movement followed by a swinging motion that increased until the pendulum struck the sides of the bell jar. The students were then instructed to bring the pendulum to rest and, again within moments, the pendulum returned to its slow turning. Other groups duplicated the results in a variety of situations.

When we consider the many manifestations of PK, whether spontaneous or deliberate, the empowering potential of this interactive phenomenon becomes increasing evident. PK should be considered an on–going mental phenomenon, constantly influencing both internal and external physical realities. Even though the complexities of PK are far from fully understood, the following four progressive stages characterize induced PK targeting a specific goal:

Stages of Induced PK

1. **Alert Stage.** The inner PK potential enters a state of mental alertness and empowerment readiness. The following three essential conditions are effective in alerting the PK potential and placing it in a readiness mode: (1) formulating clear objectives; (2) envisioning desired results; and (3) generating positive expectations of success. A positive mental state invariably increases PK readiness whereas doubt dilutes the PK potential.

2. **Centering Stage.** This is a critical stage at which PK energies are generated, typically through concentration, and then mentally assembled into an appropriate image, such as a ray of bright energy or an orb with an enveloping glow.

3. **Focusing Stage.** The mind is cleared of distractions as the energies are mentally aimed at the target. For distant, unseen targets, the eyes are typically closed to form a clear mental image of the target.

4. **Releasing Stage.** The focused energies are mentally released. For either seen or unseen targets, images of desired effects are combined with brief but strong one-word affirmations such as *move, heal, repair, correct, make whole,* and even *levitate* are presented verbally. *The sound of your own voice almost always increases the effectiveness of empowering affirmations.*

As with other psychic empowerment programs, practice is essential to the development of your PK potentials. Practice that exercises your PK powers can energize each of the progressive stages of PK previously discussed. Beyond that, it can build your self-confidence and increase your expectations of success, both of which are critical to the development of your psychic skills.

Developed in the labs at Athens State University, this simple drill is a coin-flipping exercise designed to influence the fall of a coin. Here's the exercise.

The PK Bombardment Drill

Step 1. While holding the selected coin prior to each toss, clear your mind, and with your eyes closed, visualize the designated outcome (heads or tails). Stroke the coin as you continue to visualize the designated outcome. Affirm: *I will influence the fall of this coin.*

Step 2. Toss the coin and assume firm control by focusing you attention upon it. Bombard the coin with clear imagery and verbal commands of the selected outcome.

Step 3. Continue bombarding the coin until it comes to rest.

Step 4. Repeat the drill and keep a record of your progress

The PK Bombardment Drill can be easily adapted to other PK practice exercises, including the tossing of dice and bringing a pendulum into motion. It is also readily adaptable to the group setting. Group PK is based on the premise that the combined PK faculties of a group can be organized to produce a synergistic PK effect in which the PK power of the whole group is greater than the sum of its individual parts. *Critical to group PK are a positive and cooperative group interaction, consensus of purpose within the group, and a fusion of the group's psychic energies,* all of which can be facilitated by group participation in goal setting and practice in a variety of preliminary visualization exercises prior to the PK activity.

PK and Wellness

Repeated observations of PK in both the laboratory setting and real-life situations suggest a phenomenon with near-unlimited empowerment possibilities. Given the capacity of PK to mentally influence external processes and conditions, it requires no quantum leap to assume the potential of PK to influence complex inner processes and conditions, including those related to our mental and physical health and well-being.

The capacity of mental factors to influence the physical body as indicated earlier in our discussion of biofeedback suggests profound empowering possibilities. Unfortunately, the same capacity of the mind, if misdirected, also suggests potentially disempowering consequences. Many physical and mental illnesses are associated with disempowering stress that chips away at our biological systems, depletes our psychological resources, and weakens our ability to adjust to the demands of daily life. Given time, excessive stress can lead to serious tissue damage, organ dysfunctions, and even death. Almost every major category of illness can, in fact, be affected by psychological factors.

The mind and body are in a state of constant interaction. If disempowering mental factors—stress, conflict, fear, inferiority, and inadequacy feelings, to list but a few—can contribute to the initiation or exacerbation of illness, it would follow that the alleviation of negative stress and disempowering mental states should promote tissue repair and normal physiological functioning. Wellness programs are designed to tap into that interaction and influence it in ways that meet the goals of health and fitness. The psychic concept of wellness is based on the twofold premise that (1) inner wellness resources exist in a form that can be mentally accessed and, (2) those resources are at a state of constant readiness to distribute wellness energies throughout the body.

Mind Body Interaction for Wellness

This program is designed to promote a mental and physical state conducive to wellness by activating the PK potential to infuse the body with wellness energy. The critical elements are positive affirmations of personal well-being accompanied by related wellness imagery. The program requires a relaxed state and consists of six essential steps. Each step, however, can be altered to include additional affirmations required to specific wellness needs. Here's the program.

The Wellness Activation Program

Step 1. Settle back into a comfortable position and with eyes closed, slow your breathing and let yourself become increasingly relaxed by mentally scanning your body from your head downward as your let all tension dissolve away. Once relaxed, affirm:

I am day by day becoming a more confident, secure person. I am increasing aware of my inner potential for wellness and well-being. The powers of my conscious mind are now merging with hidden energies deep in my subconscious mind to influence my total being with vibrant health. I am now empowered with positive energy and new vigor.

Step 2. With your eyes remaining closed, envision a glowing wellness core as the empowerment generator situated in your solar plexus region. Affirm:

My potential for wellness centered at the luminous core of my being is now at its peak. I am fully permeated with the inner and outer glow of wellness.

Step 3. Further activate the wellness core by envisioning an expansive, luminous field of energy surrounding it as you affirm:

The empowering wellness core at the innermost part of my being is now saturated with brilliant, healthful energy, pulsating with potential and power.

Step 4. Mentally disperse wellness energy as rays of light throughout your body. Visualize your body enveloped in a glowing aura of wellness as you affirm:

My empowerment potential for wellness, now fully activated, is radiating powerful wellness energies through my total being. My mind and body are absorbing soothing, invigorating, and rejuvenating wellness. The glow of wellness now envelops my body as a brilliant aura of health and vitality.

Step 5. Imagine your circulatory system as a conveyor of powerful wellness energy. Mentally permeate the organs and systems of your body with the glow of wellness. Affirm:

I now direct wellness to each system, organ, and function of my body, strengthening and fortifying them with powerful energy.

Step 6. Conclude with the following affirmation:

By simply visualizing the luminous core of wellness energy within, I will become instantly empowered to disperse wellness throughout my total body and being.

The self-affirmations presented in this program are flexible and can be revised as needed to meet your personal preferences and specific applications. They can be presented either silently or audibly. Remember: *The sound of your own voice almost always increases the effectiveness of empowering affirmations.*

Wellness PK is a promising and developing field of personal empowerment. We now know that constricting PK to external conditions alone is both contradictory and limiting. Our personal empowerment rests largely on our commitment to liberate our thinking, eliminate constricted thinking, and embrace new possibilities, including those related to wellness and well-being.

PK and Rejuvenation

Possibly no other human developmental phenomenon is more complex than aging and its counterpart, rejuvenation. Physical, social, cultural, environmental, psychological, and psychical factors all interact to influence both aging and rejuvenation. The application of PK to rejuvenation suggests a state of empowered control over physiology, including systems typically considered autonomous. Through the appropriate direction of our inner PK faculty, we alter crucial aging variables and activate our rejuvenating potentials, thus restoring the natural flow of youthful energy and, in some instances, literally reversing the aging process.

Psychic rejuvenation recognizes the aging effects of negative mental states including depression, hostility, and insecurity. More importantly, psychic rejuvenation emphasizes the constructive effects of positive mental states to eliminate their negative opposites. Love neutralizes hate—its negative counterpart that is physically and mentally destructive and disempowering. Such positive states as self-confidence, self-esteem, and self-acceptance are both empowering and rejuvenating. They inject rejuvenating energies into the self system, eradicating those disempowering states which contribute to aging.

From the self-empowerment perspective, the application of PK to rejuvenation recognizes the following three important principles.

PK Rejuvenation Principles

1. Aging is primarily a physical-mental interactive phenomenon. Any alteration of aging must engage the mind's power to influence physiology.

2. Aging is a complex process with many influencing factors. Some of those factors, such as genetic makeup and biological dispositions, resist intervention and direct alteration. Others are psychosocial and highly receptive to the empowered self, thus allowing their functions to be altered or extinguished altogether. Equally important, new functions affecting aging can be introduced by the empowered self into the self system.

3. Any alternation of the psychosocial influences related to aging will invariably alter the underlying physiology associated with aging.

Together, these principles suggest profound empowerment possibilities. The complex factors related to aging are clearly within reach of the empowered self, and when we embrace the positive elements conducive to rejuvenation into the self system, the physical aging process is altered. Dominant aging forces are eliminated or minimized while rejuvenating forces are activated and strengthened. As a result, the negative energies and interactions underlying accelerated aging are extinguished altogether.

Rejuvenation PK

The extension of PK to include rejuvenation suggests the possibility of living younger, longer, and better while literally reversing the physical signs of aging. The following exercise is designed to activate the body's rejuvenation potentials and unblock the flow of rejuvenating energies from the inside out. Developed at Athens State University, the exercise involves empowering imagery and affirmations. Through it, physical functions, including those once considered autonomic or involuntary, are linked to mental functions in a positive rejuvenating interaction. The results are actual and observable changes in the physical body. Here's the exercise.

Rejuvenation PK Program

Step l. Relaxation. Physical relaxation sets the stage for PK intervention into the physical body's many functions. For this exercise, breathing is slowed and muscles are allowed to relax from the forehead downward as the following affirmation is presented:

I am now fully in charge of my physical body. I am empowered to influence every function, mental and physical. All the rejuvenating energy of my being is now at my command.

Step 2. Stress Expiation. Relaxation procedures are intended to reduce stress, but even when stress is reduced, the residual wear-and-tear effects of stress can linger. The goals of stress expiation are to extinguish stress and all its residual effects, and to infuse the physical body with positive, rejuvenating energy. To achieve these goals, the physical body's systems and organs are visualized and mentally energized. This energizing process is accomplished by centering your full awareness on various body regions and mentally bathing them with glowing energy accompanied by the following affirmation:

Youthful, invigorating energy is now flowing through my body. All organs, systems, and functions are now fully revitalized. The wear-and-tear of stress is now replaced by the flow of youth and vigor

Step 3. Attunement and Balance. The goal of this step is to establish a state of mental and physical attunement and balance which are the most powerful rejuvenation forces known. With the body physically relaxed and the effects of stress expiated, an empowering state of full attunement and balance is possible through the *Finger Engagement Procedure.* This procedure is based on the premise that the complex functions of the mind and body seek not only balance, but rejuvenation and efficiency as well. Beyond that, they seek simplicity. To implement the procedure, simply bring the tips of your fingers together and with your eyes closed, imagine your hands as antennae for your brain. Imagine your left brain actively generating positive energy that flows into your right hand as the extension of that hemisphere. Next, imagine your right brain actively generating positive energy that flows into your left hand as the extension of that hemisphere. Allow the energies flowing into your hands and merging at your fingertips to engage in a powerful interaction that balances you mentally, physically, and spiritually. To end the exercise, disengage your finger tips and allow your hands to relax, palm sides up. Imagine your hands as your body's antennae to the universe as you affirm:

My total being is now fully balanced and attuned mentally, physically, and spiritually. The energies of youth are now unleashed to flow throughout my being. I am now at one, both within myself and with the universe.

It is important to note that, although left- or right-hemisphere dominance in brain functions is considered normal, balancing the functions of the two hemispheres increases the efficiency of both without affecting their functional asymmetry.

Step 4. PK Illumination. At this final step in Rejuvenation PK, the rejuvenation process reaches its peak. PK illumination is initiated by viewing a photograph of yourself at your youthful prime. If no photo is available just create one mentally which can be equally effective. Study the picture (either real or imagined), carefully noting your youthfulness, especially in your facial features. Now close your eyes and imagine yourself at your peak of youth standing, preferably nude, before a full-length mirror. Study your eyes and note the youthful gleam. Next, allow a colorful glow of rejuvenating energy to envelop your full body. While breathing slowly, soak in the colorful rejuvenating glow while affirming:

My inner powers of rejuvenation are now being unleashed to permeate my total being with the glow of youth and vigor. Every system within is now being revitalized with the infusion of rejuvenating power. Tired, worn tissue is being renewed with glowing youthfulness. Every function of my body is now fully infused as sparkling, youthful energy is absorbed into every cell and fiber. Surrounded by a colorful aura of rejuvenating energy, I am now secure in the present, bathed in vitality and the glow of youth. My inner rejuvenating powers are fully unleashed to flow freely throughout my total being. Each day, my mind and body will absorb the abundance of youthful energy that is constantly being unleashed within my being. Whenever I envision myself enveloped with the colorful glow of radiant energy, I will become instantly invigorated and fully empowered.

These affirmations recited either silently or audibly, can be revised to fit your personal preferences or needs. A small, self-adhesive start or dot of color consistent with the rejuvenation glow seen enveloping your body during the exercise can be strategically situated—on a mirror or computer for instance—as a cue to promote the inner flow of rejuvenating energy.

The complete PK Rejuvenation procedure can be practiced daily or as often as desired to maximize its rejuvenation effects. You can use the star or dot at frequent intervals throughout the day to instantly infuse your mind and body with rejuvenation. With practice of this exercise, you will discover that relevant imagery and accompanying affirmations become a natural, spontaneous, and continuous function of the psychically empowered self.

Together, positive affirmations and empowering imagery form a powerful two-component system of wellness and rejuvenation. In that system, PK assumes a critical role as the essential vehicle for physical change and well-being, and a vital defense against any form of psychic and psychological attack.

Sources & Suggested Additional Reading:

Austin, J. & Guiley, R. *ESP, Psychokinesis, and Psychics: Mysteries, Legends, and Unexplained Phenomena,* 2008, Checkmark Books.

Cheung, Theresa. *The Element Encyclopedia of the Psychic Worlds,* 2006, Harper/Element.

Department of Defense. *20th Century U.S. Military Defense and Intelligence Declassified Report: Soviet and Czechoslovakian Parapsychology Research, Telepathy, Energy Transfer, . . . the Paranormal, Psychokinesis (PK),* (CD-ROM), 2004, Progressive Management.

Department of Defense. *20th Century U.S. Military Defense and Intelligence Declassified Reports: Paraphysics, Controlled Offensive Behavior, and Parapsychology Research—Extrasensory . . . Psychokinesis (PK), Levitation (CD-ROM),* (CD-ROM), 2004, Progressive Management.

Hewitt, W. *Psychic Development for Beginners: An Easy Guide to Developing & Releasing Your Psychic Abilities,* 1996, Llewellyn.

McTaggart, L. *The Intention Experiment: Using Your Thoughts to Change Your Life and the World,* 2008, Free Press.

Slate, J. *Aura Energy for Health, Healing and Balance,* 1999, Llewellyn.

Slate, J. *Psychic Empowerment for Health and Fitness: Strategies for Success,* 1996, Llewellyn.

Slate, J. *Rejuvenation: Strategies for Living Younger, Longer, and Better,* 2001, Llewellyn.

Slate, J. & Weschcke, C. L. *Psychic Empowerment for Everyone: You Have the Power, Learn How to Use It.,* 2009, Llewellyn.

Watson, L. *Beyond Supernature: A New Natural History of the Supernatural,* 1988, Bantam.

Watson, L. *Supernature: An Unprecedented Look at Strange Phenomena and Their Place in Nature,* 1973, Anchor/Doubleday.

Webster, R. *Dowsing for Beginners: The Art of Discovering: Water, Treasure, Gold, Oil, Artifacts,* 1996, Llewellyn. Note: A free dowsing tool is available with purchase of the book. It's a transparent disk with a circle with degree indications around the circle's edge and yes/no cross lines inside the circle that divide the circle into quadrants marking four important areas of your life: Physical, Social, Spiritual, and Mental. It can be easily positioned over maps or documents, or used alone in question and answer sessions.

Webster, R. *Pendulum Magic for Beginners: Power to Achieve All Goals, Tap Your Inner Wisdom, Find Lost Objects, Focus Energy for Self-Improvement,* 2002, Llewellyn.

Wilson, C. *Strange Powers: Astral Projection, Reincarnation, Dowsing, Spirit Writing,* 1973, Random House.

World Spaceflight News: *21st Century U.S. Military Documents, Teleportation Physics Study: Analysis for the Air Force Research Laboratory of Teleportation of Physical Objects . . . Psychokinesis (PK), Levitation (CD-ROM),* 2005, Progressive Management.

ADDENDUM #10 TO CHAPTER 10
Microcosm to Macrocosm & Macrocosm to Microcosm

The Tattvic Connection—
Meditation & Visualization Programs #7 to #10
Earth—And its Compounds

Earth—Seed of Water:
Timing is the Key to Success

Earth—good Solid Earth, but not always

Because of our terminology we tend to forget that the "Earth" we are discussing is not really the dirt in our garden or the rock in our neighbors' wall. It's the astral Earth, subtle energy patterns that pre-exist the manifestation that results when energy is converted into matter.

Astral Earth is conditioned by our feelings and our thoughts, and even more so by the causal level where we believe the "Great Plan" behind all creation and manifestation function.

Astral Earth is only "solid" in concept and "out of habit," by which we mean you can't readily change what has been manifest for a long time. On our home planet we call "Earth," the World *in* which we live, I live in an area called the "Laurentian Shield"—basically a lot of granite formation that has been here for 500 million years. In contrast, the wet land around New Orleans is in constant flux but still the basic geography has changed in slow motion compared to the Laurentian Shield.

This short introduction is a reminded about Astral Earth that is the concern in our developmental and conditioning exercises, and that is the foundation for our clairvoyant visions and psychic operations. We are looking "behind the scenes" where things in the process of manifesting are—to varying degrees—still affected by thought and emotion, and our clairvoyant vision colored by our own memories and even personal desires. The goal of our meditation and visualization exercises has been to "purify" our own elemental sources, and to "inner experience" their compounding to better see their effect in the manifesting world.

Earth—Seed of Water

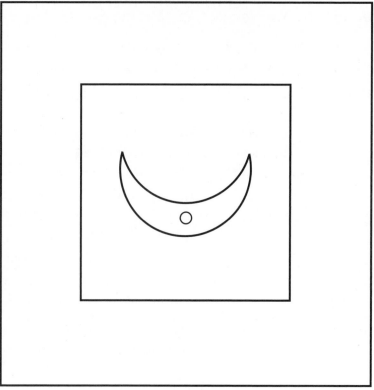

Color the tiny inner bindu circle white,
the inner crescent metallic silver (or white),
the inner square bright yellow,
and the outer square bright purple

Earth—Seed of Water: Prithivi & Apas *LAM & VAM*

Review

We urge you to review the Element Overview Table #1 for Earth on page 104 and Element Overview Table #2 for Water on page 131 in preparation for this procedure and the Divination and other applications involved with this compound.

The Tattvic Connection Meditation & Visualization Compound Program #7: Earth/Water
Earth—Seed of Water

<u>*Introduction. The Purpose & Function of this Procedure.*</u>

While this exercise is similar to those for the five Primal Elements in Addenda #3 through #7, this is the first involved with the "construction" of a compounded image of a *primary* tattva/element with a *secondary* tattva/element. In this case the elements are **Earth** and **Water**, but the procedure is basically the same for those compounds that will follow throughout this addendum and those that follow.

In a very real sense, it can be said that the act of compounding through these exercises is *evolutionary.* As emphasized elsewhere, nothing manifests in purity but always in compounds with other elements. In the first set of exercises our goal was to restore "purity" to your internal *personal* core of the subtle energy forms in order to eliminate accumulated psychic and emotional "garbage" that is part of all growth—in this life and past lives. *It's part of life!* But such garbage complicates things because it carries emotionally reactive primitive and childish memories inappropriate to your adult life—and thus distorting of your current perceptions, feelings, and thinking. It's a problem in daily life, and even more in your clairvoyant visions—which, by definition, must be "clear seeing."

Because of the fundamental nature of those five primal exercises, it can be beneficial to repeat them from time to time, and the same is true for the compounding exercises that follow. They will aid your clairvoyance in divination and other psychic work ranging from astral project and aura reading to magickal and self-realization work.

Summary of Purpose & User Benefits

The primary purpose is to harmonize the inter-connections of between the identified compounded elements and to create a single geometric yantra of their inter-related functions that can be reproduced in card form and visualized to aid in divination and other psychic level work.

Step 1. Preliminaries.

Always precede meditation exercises with complete physical relaxation.

Read through the procedure before beginning to avoid need for further reference.

Time & Space: Allow approximately 30 minutes for the procedure. Work in a comfortably warm, quiet, and safe setting free of interruptions. A darkened room is not necessary. Freedom from sound and visual distractions is advisable.

Personal Preparations: It's best to remove shoes and keep clothing or covering minimal to minimize the effects of external stimuli from tight clothing or rough fabric.

Posture & Position: It's preferable to sit in a relaxed posture in a recliner chair.

Special Lighting: Have a small desk or reading light next to your chair within easy reach to turn on and off as required, and focus as directed.

Breathing: Establish a comfortably deep and natural rhythm in your breathing, mostly balanced between inhalation and exhalation.

Vocalization : Vocalize, either silently stated or voiced aloud, your affirmations and the name of the tattvas/elements, the sounding of the mantras in Step 9, and—if the operation is for a magickal or other purpose, state that purpose.

With each step 5 through 13, it is helpful to vocalize the words describing any particular feelings or even visions you experience.

Vibration: This is very important. In Step 9 you should chant or hum the Sanskrit name of the tattvas, and then the tattvic mantras as instructed. You want to draw these words out and feel the *vibration.* "Vibration" means to softly *warble* the words at the back of your throat, and as you do, you may decide to raise or lower the "musical note" until it feels right. Do the same with the volume of sound. You want to feel the words *vibrate* throughout your skull, and then in the location of the corresponding chakras. With experience you will be able to move the vibration to designated places inside your body, and then—in advanced work—intentionally into external objects.

The yantra (geometric image), the names, and the mantras are your means to connect the inner compounded nature of two tattvas with the external tattvas for the unique energization and connection with the Universal wisdom and power the compounded yantra expresses and connects with.

Step 2. Goal Statement.

You've already become familiar with the feelings associated with the two compounding elements, in this case **Earth** and **Water,** now we want you to:

- Feel the nature of their compounding—two elements functioning together.
- Feel the difference as one element is primary over the secondary other. *This is important because their roles will be reversed in a later exercise.* Think how it can be in a relationship between two persons who switch leader and support roles under differing functions and circumstances of their union.
- Think how this *particular compound functions* in different operations—divinatory and magickal, and perhaps in particular communications with spiritual entities.
- Think also how this *particular combination functions* within your own physical & subtle bodies in matters of health, healing, daily work, relationships with family and others.

- Try to imagine how this *particular combination* is reflected in the functioning of your unconscious mind, in the shaping of archetypal experiences, in your perception of myth and in your emotional and mental reaction to events.

Step 3. Affirmations.

Affirmations are important!

They are specific, condensed, statements of your goals in <u>active "feeling" or "realized" format</u>. In other words, they are a variation of "I am" confirmations of the desired accomplishment. Because of the work you are presently engaged in, I feel that the best example I can offer here is drawn from ordinary life:

I am Slim, becoming Slimmer!

Note how it is a positive statement as if your goal was already accomplished, but it also avoids conflict with what may be reality by adding an action statement. You state it with feelings that charge it and the accompanying image with emotional energy. *Why?* Because the reality of emotion is "E-MOTION," i.e. *Energy-in-Motion.* That's what you want to accomplish in any affirmation.

It's up to you to <u>write</u> these affirmations, and then to state them silently, or—better—aloud at the beginning and then as a confirmation at the ending of the exercise. And record them in you journal. Writing and Speaking with purpose are true acts of Magick in which chosen words are literally *charged* with the energy of intention. Don't let my references to Magick fill your mind with silly images of a magician waving a wand: realize that *magick is anything we do with the willed intention of accomplishment.*

Step 4. Mental Imagery.

Intentional Imagery, like vocalization, increases the effectiveness of the exercise.

Visualization: Visualizing the tattvas as described is essential.

Spontaneous Imagery: Other images may appear at the end of the procedure—and that is alright *unless you have negative feelings about them—in which case you should willfully "banish" them.* (If you wish, you can simply visualize a box, you can imagine all those negative feeling going into the box, close the box tightly, and imagine burying it in the earth and pouring cement over it. Then smooth clean dirt over the cement, seed it with grass, and know that those negativities are gone forever.)

Recording: Other images that may appear spontaneously at the end of the procedure should be noted along with any particular feelings or ideas, and then recorded in your journal for later analysis.

Analysis: Always let a day or two pass before reading and analyzing your journal entries.

Step 5. Preparation.

Preparing the Yantra Card.

It is recommended that you photocopy the illustration on page 396, preferably on heavier paper or card stock, or draw it yourself in exactly the same sizes using a ruler and black pen. If you can manage it, using a drawing compass or a template, draw a tiny ⅛" inch diameter circle in the exact center. Leave the inside of the circle white. This inner circle or point aids your steady focus. It is not essential, but it is helpful. Make the outer **Earth Square** 4" x 4" and the inner **Earth Square** 2¼" x 2 ¼", the inner **Water Crescent** 1⅛" wide, and the little **Bindu Circle** in the exact center should be ⅛" in diameter and have a black line around it but not quite as thick as those around the **Crescent** and the two **Squares.**

Coloring the Yantra Card.

It will be beneficial for you to color the image as follows: (a) color the tiny inner **Bindu Circle White**; (b) the **Water Crescent Metallic Silver** (or White); (c) the smaller **Earth Square Bright Yellow**, and (d) the surrounding larger **Earth Square Bright Purple.** Each square is bordered with bold black lines, the **Water Crescent** is bordered with a less bold black line, and the tiny inner circle is bordered with a thinner black line.

Cutting the Yantra Card.

If you have reproduced the image on the heavy card stock as recommended, now measure off either one or two inches (your choice) on each side and cut away the surplus so you have a square 6" x 6" or 8" x 8" card with the colored image in the center.

Step 6. Pranic Breathing Pattern.

With eyes closed; engage in a pattern of rhythmic breathing involving equally spaced—_without any stress_—in-breaths, holding, out-breaths, holding, and repeating throughout the process.

Step 7. White Light Circulation.

Then, with each in-breath visualize white light flowing into the body, while holding the breath visualize the light circulating throughout the body, while breathing out see the light being excreted knowing that it is carrying out impurities, and while holding the out breath realize that you have energized and cleansed the inner energy body.

Step 8. Psychic Shield.

While continuing the breathing pattern and the flowing light, turn your imagination outward and visualize an absolutely clear field around you, one that is as transparent as the clearest glass. Know that this shield protects you from external influences while containing the benefits of your tattvic meditation program.

Step 9a. Yantra Card Focus.

If you have constructed the tattva yantra card as described, turn on the light and focus it on the card held or positioned comfortably about a foot to a foot and a half in front of you.

If possible, arrange your chair to face the primary tattvic direction: North for **Earth.** Otherwise—think and feel North. (To the extent you feel the secondary element's importance to the operation, you can finish with an acknowledgment of *West* for **Water.**

Vibrate the name of the two tattvas: ***Prithivi*** and ***Apana***, alternating one after the other. Repeat three times.

Chant or hum the tattva element mantras *LAM* and *VAM* (pronounced *LA-UUM* and *VA-UUM),* alternating. Vibrate the mantras as instructed in Step 1, preliminaries. Repeat three times. Later, you can do more but always in groups of three. And feel the mantra vibrate in the *Pelvis*, the location of **Muladhara** chakra and then in *above the genitals and below the navel,* the location of **Svadhisthana** chakra.

Focus on the small **White Bindu Circle*** at the center of the image, and stare at it for as long as you can without blinking. When you can't continue the "burning" feeling any longer, turn off the light, close your eyes and focus your inner sight on the space in front of your brow chakra (between your eyebrows and on the ridge you can feel just above your nose), and see the **Silver Crescent** in the **Yellow Square** floating in the space before you and vibrating within the **Purple Square**. And, then, you will soon see the tattva image change into the complementary yantra colors of **Black**, **Purple** and **Yellow.**

Again vibrate the names to the tattvas and chant or hum the mantras three times.

Absorb this image! As you repeat the exercise often, you should reach a point when *you will be able to recall this image at will.*

> *The small white circle is called a "Bindu," and focus on it is comprehensive of the entire tattvic image and all its energies. There is a small spot on the back of your head that likewise serves as a comprehensive psychic center used in certain meditational exercises. A Bindu is also the name of a single drop of semen, the focal point of a new life. And "bindu" is likewise the single point from which all creation began "in the union of divine forces,

Male and Female, God and Goddess, Siva and Shakti in all their names and images—i.e., the "Big Bang."

Bindu is a point of leverage where force applied becomes force multiplied and directed to accomplish your particular goal.

Step 9b. Yantra Visualization.

Alternatively, if you haven't made an **Earth/Water** card, immediately in front of you, visualize the image as described for making the card. See the image gently vibrating. And then the colors will reverse to their complementary yantra colors.

Step 10a. Experiencing Compounded Elemental Earth and Elemental Water.

Feel yourself becoming totally *absorbed** in the image while retaining awareness of the surrounding large tattvic **Purple Square**. As the smaller tattvic **Yellow Square** changes to the complementary yantra **Purple** feel *your* **Earthy** nature harmonize with the Cosmic **Earth** Tattva, and feel all impurities in your **Earth** Tattva—all emotional garbage and unconscious psychic attachments—dissipate. The tattvic **Silver Crescent** will change to the complementary yantra **Black** as your **Watery** nature harmonizes with the Cosmic **Water** Tattva and the impurities of your **Water** tattva dissipate.

> **Becoming absorbed.* Enter into the **full image** and become one with it and feel surrounded by it. Moving inward from the outer **Earth square** become one with the **Earth** Element, and then move inward to become one with the **Water** Element, and then further in to the **Bindu** to become one with **All**. Now, moving outward from the **Bindu** point to the **Water Crescent** and then to the **Earth Square** and to its outer edge feel the balanced **Earth** and **Water** elements in your body become harmonized and purified as they are balanced with their **Cosmic Source**.

In particular: feel the **Earthy** and **Watery** nature of your physical body become free of adverse thoughts and feelings. Feel your body becoming ideally healthy, strong, and energized. See your body in perfect health, free of any excess weight, free of pain and disfigurement, free of illness, and fully energized. Feel your **emotional self** free of **imposed inhibitions, irrational fears**, and fully able to give and receive **love**.

Step 11. Knowing Elemental Earth compounded with Elemental Water.

Allow yourself to receive any information or messages from you're experiencing of these Elemental Forces. *In particular: receive information involving your **Physical** and **Emotional** health & strength at both **material** and **astral** levels.* Receive the information without any emotional reaction and know that the knowledge is fully activated within your psyche.

Step 12. Dissipation of Images.

Slowly dissipate the images, return to the clear field around you, continuing the breathing pattern of Step 6 above.

Step 13. Letting Go of Evoked Feelings.

Let go of all the particular feelings evoked by the imagery, slowly change your breathing to its natural rhythm and feel the physical relaxation achieved in Step 1 above.

Step 14. Completion & Self-Realization.

Feel yourself fully relaxed and fully self-contained. Feel yourself to be healthy, energized, cleansed, and refreshed. Know yourself to be strong and secure. These feeling should be part of your self-realization at the end of each of the Tattvic Meditation Exercises regardless of the Elements involved. Your healthy body is the foundation of all your life and work.

Step 15. Return to Normality.

Open your eyes, return to the physical world knowing all is well. Stand up and move about. Have some refreshment and engage in some normal activity.

Step 16. Review, Record & Analyze.

Record in a journal all messages and feelings received in Step 11 above. At this point, merely record—do not analyze. After a few days, read what you've recorded and then write down an analysis of what you believe the messages mean for you at this time. Realize that when you repeat the exercise at another time, the messages are likely to change to meet new circumstances in your life.

Conclusion:

This exercise is challenging because of its focus on two elements simultaneously, but in reality we do it all the time. In a way it's like driving a car where you have to focus on many things at once. A little practice and it becomes easy—perhaps deceptively easy. We really lose the potential value of the many things we let pass by without conscious awareness.

Don't let things become too easy as the result of the technological power available to us. We grow through experience, and without "paying attention" we only experience things when they slap us in the face, or the car crashes into a bridge abutment—and then we may have lost life too.

It is the first paragraph of the Introduction and in steps 5, 9, 10, and 11 that are the central factors that change as we move on to the other compounded elements. Rather than repeat the entire exercise for the coming 19 variations, we will just describe those steps and refer you back to this exercise for their execution.

Diversity is the Law, and the Law is for All

In everything we experience, we find endless variety. And through everything that each of us does, we add still more variety. Throughout all Manifestation, throughout all of Nature, we see diversity beyond comprehension.

Despite the amazing accumulation of scientific knowledge over the last few centuries of time, science still uncovers life and things previously unknown. And even life in such harsh conditions as previously believed impossible. Life forms live within sulfur vents at the deepest depths of the ocean—life without oxygen, life under extremes of pressure and heat, life that is not carbon-based. Life that is impossible according to the science of the 20th century.

Nature seems to abhor conformity and rigid rules—where there is Space, there is Life in some form. Even where there is nothing else—if such is possible—there is consciousness manifesting life, perhaps even new forms not yet known to us. Such infinity and such diversity has purpose and meaning beyond present human comprehension but our very awareness of this awakens our ever-growing capability of understanding and appreciation for the glory of being in which we participate.

The Primal Elements do not manifest in a pure state but always compounded. And despite the human tendency to classify everything in narrow and specific categories, *we do not live that way!* We do not function only on the Physical Plane, and then in our Astral Body or on to Mental Plane; nor do we find *pure* Elemental Earth, or *pure* Elemental Water and so on, *ad infinitum!* We function, consciously and unconsciously in all our bodies and on all planes and levels at all times. Our primary perception is physical but we are not limited to just one narrow window of experience defined by Elemental Earth.

Instead, think of Nature as a master chef, adding spices to enhance the flavor of our Earthy meal. She adds a bit of Water, or a bit of Fire, maybe some Air, and certainly a touch of Ether. Each combination is unique, and is reflected in our Human and Cosmic experiences. We perceive Earth—Seed of Water; Earth—Seed of Fire; and so on.

Through their Tattvic geometric representations, we perceive and experience certain realities, and then we ourselves *become* differently. With every vision we seen not only past and present, but in seeing also into the future we bring about changes in ourselves and in the World around us and the Cosmos beyond us.

For our divinations, we open our subconsciousness to select the appropriate concepts, formulae, and symbol to divine the message being signaled from the Unconscious to the Conscious Mind. As we manipulate our divinatory and magickal tools and the images and visions rising into our awareness, interpretations and new understandings filter into our conscious mind for translation into action.

Pick a Card, any Card, or none at all

If you have created a set of Magical Tattva Cards, shuffle them or spread them out and follow your instinctive attraction to any one card. If, not, let the images flow through your mind and again let your instinct make choices. *Trust your subconscious.*

Perhaps you have only the five Primal Tattva images. Let yourself choose any two for the next workings. Here we just will proceed to compound Earth with Water to illustrate the process.

Here we provide a summary of the data seemingly most pertinent for this divination.

ELEMENT SUMMARY TABLE #12:
Earth/Water, Divinatory Background
Nature of Compound: Life & Growth, Stability & Flexibility

Element Names: Earth & Water	Tattva Forms: Square & Crescent	Tattva Colors: Yellow & Silver or White
Tattvic Animals: black elephant with 7 trunks & crocodile	Chakra Names: root & sex Chakra Locations: perineum & genitals	Cosmic Planes: physical/etheric & lower astral
Chakra Goddess (Shakti) Energy: *Dakini & Rakini, Varuni*	Chakra Goals: awaken Kundalini & gain control over root chakra	Chakra God (Shiva) Energy: *Brahma & Vishnu*
Chakra Bija Mantras: *LAM & VAM*	Element States & Actions: solid support, foundation & fluidity and adapting	Element Function: Survival & Evolution and Reproduction
Element Natures: initiatives, start-ups, & cool and & flowing	Element Powers: to create new realities establish relationships & Cooperation	Element Strengths: focus, determination, feeling relationships, and fantasy
Emotional Character: solidarity & flexibility	Emotional Desires: comfort, survival & new meetings, procreation, family	Emotional Drives: security, saving & pleasure, sex, and fantasies

Emotional Strengths: instinct, care & will	Family Roles: Daughter & Mother	Mind Functions: knowledge, memory, & Intellect, analysis, reason, logic
Physical/Action Forms: locomotion, & Procreation, nutrition	Physical/Action Effect: lasting & transitory	Physical Body Functions: building, moving & body fluids, generative center
Astrological Qualities: hard-working, disciplined, persevering, patience & Imaginative, sharp intelligence, diplomatic, sensitive		
Astrology—Ruling Planet: Saturn, Mercury & Pluto; Magical Planets: Venus. Moon		
Astrological Planetary Expressions: Mercury—communication, business, mathematics, practical matters, & pre-conscious memories, alien life, dark mysteries		
Magical Animals: owl, bear, boar, bull, stag, & dolphins, fish, sea-life, whales	Magical Colors: Brown, Black, & aqua, gray, green, silver	Magical Days: Friday & Monday
Magical Incense: Storax, Cedar, Gardenia	Magical Metals: Lead & Copper, Silver	Magical Places: Caves, Forest, Gardens, & beeches, lakes, marshes, oceans
Magical Rulership: agriculture, animals, antiques, buildings, business, conservation, construction, death/rebirth, ecology, fertility, food, grounding, health foods, investments, jobs, material things, money, museums, nature, old age, progress, promotions, prosperity, stock markets, structural foundations, & affection, ancestors, astral travel, beauty, childbirth, children, contract negotiation, emotions, family, fishing, friendship, healing, home, hospitals, love, medicine, nursing, partnerships, recuperation, scuba & other diving, receptivity, restoration, spirituality, swimming pool, unions, water professions		
Magical States: Physical Perception, & psychic energy & psychic perception	Sexual Identity: Feminine, Active, Receptive, & Feminine, Passive, & Receptive	
Magical Stones: amazonite, bloodstone emerald, fire agate, hematite, jade, jasper, jet, lodestone, peridot, serpentine, smoky quartz, tiger's eye, tourmaline, & amethyst, beryl, carnelian, chalcedony, citrine, coral, geodes, holey stones, moonstone, mother of pearl, pearl, quartz, sapphire		
Magical Symbols: Pentacle & Cup	Magical Tool: Crystal Ball & Chalice of Water	Magical Work: Talismans & Spells
Tarot Court: Page, Princess, & Queen	Tarot Suite: Pentacles, & Cups	Tarot Trumps: Emperor, World, & Moon, Death, Lovers

In their Tattvic geometric representations, we experience and become differently. In our divinations, we moved to select the appropriate symbol to divine the message being signaled from the Unconscious to the Conscious Mind.

THINK EARTH; THINK WATER

When fluid Water is added to solid, dry Earth, changes begin. Out of the mud, life happens. Of course, there are many forces at work but we need only to imagine Earth and Water as deities coming together, missing their unique individualities to reproduce themselves in new forms and individualities.

What was begun, continues. We are both Product and now part of the continuing Process. Every action produces something new combining Earth and Water in multiple forms and dimensions. As humans, we introduce our own consciousness into the process and initiate our own changes, and plan new progeny, new careers, new combinations, and new products. We have gone forth and multiplied, and with multiplicity, we have added to the Diversity that is Nature's own Law.

Based on our work with these concepts and symbols, we have produced the following divination guide for Earth—Seed of Water.

DIVINATION GUIDE TO EARTH—SEED OF WATER
Earth—Seed of Water: Boldness, * or Caution

Fluid Water when added to solid Earth sponsors life and growth. The oceans, lakes, and rivers rest upon the Earth and provide means of transportation, recreation, and serve as home to aquatic life and sea food. Water was the first element added to Earth and thus symbolizes first steps and new enterprises. The ocean depths, however, hide many secrets: sunken battleships and sunken treasures, sea monsters and strange life forms living without oxygen in plumes of sulfuric acid under extreme pressure, exotic and rich mineral nodules and fields of oil and gas to provide humanity with energy resources. And the oceans provide cover to submarines in defensive and offensive warfare.

In a divination, this suggests a good time to make changes and launch a new career or project. Because still waters can run deep they hide secrets and may indicate hidden dangers or unexpected resources. Starting something new calls for a solid plan and right timing. The Moon waxes and wanes with increase or decrease, encouragement or caution. Timing is always of essence whether in planting or harvesting, in forming new relationships or renewing established ones, in matters mundane or magickal. The Moon is the Goddess who can guide you through the darkness.

> *These "keywords" and quotations are taken from Dr. Mumford's "Magical Tattwas."

Dream Interpretation

Dream interpretation is one form of active divination. Most divinations are active in the way cards are shuffled or pulled from a spread after a question or goal is stated. Cards are just one tool used in this way. Other divinations search among existing choices such as the use a divining rod to locate water or minerals, while still others—such as a crystal may passively wait for a vision to spontaneously arise.

Dreams are unique. While some people actively practice *Dreaming True*—by asking a question or stating a problem, and then "sleeping on it" to induce a dream containing an answer (which still must be interpreted), most dreams happen and then we ask what they mean. The Unconscious never "sleeps" but sends us messages in a language of symbols that begs for interpretation.

There is an old adage that promises: *If you pay attention to your dreams, they will pay attention to you!* Our dream-time is approximately one-third of our life, so it behooves us to take dreams seriously,

Your dreams can be "divined" just as can other questions or problems.

To Divine

Think about that word. To divine invokes the Divinity that lies within as part of our being. Without that Divine Spark, we die. With it, we live—and the more attention we pay to that Divinity within the more integrated are we consciously with it. We move into a higher and new form of consciousness and the practice of all forms of divination facilitate our spiritual growth.

Earth—Seed of Fire:
Human Ambition & Resource Potential

Earth—Seed of Fire

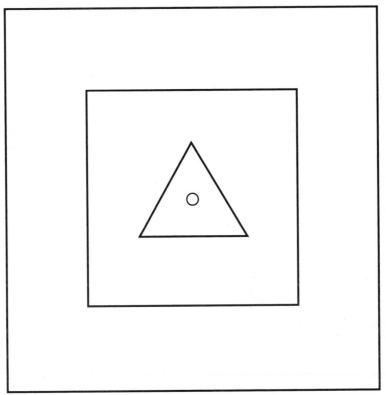

Color the tiny inner bindu circle white,
the inner triangle bright red,
the inner square bright yellow,
and the outer square bright purple

Earth—Seed of Fire: Prithivi & Tejas *LAM & RAM*

Review

We urge you to review the Element Overview Table #1 for Earth on page 104 and the Element Overview Table #3 for Fire on page 189 in preparation for this procedure and the Divination and other applications involved with this compound.

The Tattvic Connection Meditation
& Visualization Program #8: Earth/Fire
Earth—Seed of Fire

Introduction. The Purpose & Function of this Procedure.

Rather than repeating the procedure in its entirety, we are asking you to kindly refer to page 396 for the complete *Tattva Connection Meditation & Visualization Compound Program #7 and make your own adjustments to substitute "Fire" for "Water" in steps 2 (goal statement), 3 (affirmations), we are here providing content for Steps 5 (preparing and coloring the yantra card), 9a (yantra card focus),10a (experience the compounded elements and 11 (knowing the compounded elements).*

The Program's Variables:

Steps 2. Goal Statement.

Note your need to consider how to express your goals to reflect the particular natures of the two elements in their primary and secondary combination in relation to your physical, emotional, mental, and spiritual well-being, and their functions in divination, magick, and self-growth.

Step 3. Affirmations.

You need to write positive affirmations to accomplish your goals.

Step 5. Preparation.

Preparing the Yantra Card.

It is recommended that you photocopy the illustration on page 409, preferably on heavier paper or card stock, or draw it yourself in exactly the same sizes using a ruler and black pen. If you can manage it, using a drawing compass or a template, draw a tiny ⅛" inch diameter circle in the exact center. Leave the inside of the circle white. This inner circle or point aids your steady focus. It is not essential, but it is helpful. Make the outer **Square** 4" x 4" and the inner **Earth Square** 2¼" x 2 ¼", the inner equal-sided upright **Fire Triangle** 1" wide, and the little **Bindu Circle** in the exact center should be ⅛" in diameter and have a black line around it but not quite as thick as those around the **triangle** and the two **squares.**

Coloring the Yantra Card.

It will be beneficial for you to color the image as follows: (a) color the tiny inner **Bindu Circle White**; (b) the **Fire Triangle Bright Red**; (c) the smaller **Earth Square Bright Yellow**, and (d) the surrounding larger **Square Bright Purple.** Each square is bordered with bold black lines, the **Fire Triangle** is bordered with a less bold black line, and the tiny inner circle is bordered with a thinner black line.

Step 9a. Yantra Card Focus.

If you have constructed the tattva yantra card as described, turn on the light and focus it on the card held or positioned comfortably about a foot to a foot and a half in front of you.

If possible, arrange your chair to face the primary tattvic direction: *North* for **Earth**. Otherwise—think and feel *North.* (To the extent you feel the secondary element's importance to the operation, you can finish with an acknowledgment of *South* for **Fire.**

Vibrate the name of the two tattvas: ***Prithivi*** and ***Tejas,*** alternating one after the other. Repeat three times.

Chant or hum the tattva element mantras ***LAM*** and ***RAM*** (pronounced *LA-UUM* and *RA-UUM),* alternating. Vibrate the mantra as instructed in Step 1, preliminaries. Repeat three times. Later, you can do more but always in groups of three. And feel the mantra vibrate in the *Pelvis,* the location of **Muladhara** chakra and then *at the solar plexus over the heart,* the location of **Manipura** chakra.

Focus on the small **White Bindu Circle*** at the center of the image, and stare at it for as long as you can without blinking. When you can't continue the "burning" feeling any longer, turn off the light, close your eyes and focus your inner sight on the space in front of your brow chakra (between your eyebrows and on the ridge you can feel just above your nose), and see the **Red Triangle** in the **Yellow Square** floating in the space before you and vibrating within the **Purple Square.** And, then, you will soon see the tattva image change into the complementary yantra colors of **Green, Purple** and **Yellow.**

Again vibrate the names to the tattvas and chant or hum the mantras three times.

Absorb this yantra image! As you repeat the exercise, often, you will reach a point when you will be able to recall this image at will.

Step 9b. Yantra Visualization.

Alternatively, if you haven't made an **Earth/Fire** card, immediately in front of you, visualize the image as described for making the card. See the image gently vibrating. And then the colors will reverse to their complementary yantra colors.

Step 10a. Experiencing Compounded Elemental Earth and Elemental Fire.

Feel yourself becoming totally *absorbed** in the image while retaining awareness of the surrounding tattvic purple square. As the tattvic **Yellow** changes to the complementary yantra **Purple** feel *your* **Earthy** nature harmonize with the Cosmic **Earth** Tattva, and feel all impurities in your **Earth** Tattva—all emotional garbage and unconscious psychic attachments—dissipate. The tattvic **Red Triangle** will change to the complementary yantra **Bright Green** as your **Fiery** nature harmonizes with the Cosmic **Fire** Tattva and the impurities of your **Fire** tattva dissipate.

> *Becoming absorbed.* Enter into the **full image** and become one with it and feel surrounded by it. Moving inward from the outer **Earth Square** become one with the **Earth** Element, and then move inward to become one with the **Fire** Element, and then further in to the **Bindu** to become one with **All.** Now, moving outward from the **Bindu** point to the **Fire Triangle** and then to the **Earth Square** and to its outer edge feel the balanced **Earth** and **Fire** elements in your body become harmonized and purified as they are balanced with their **Cosmic Source.**

In particular: feel the **Earthy** and **Fiery** nature of your physical body become free of adverse thoughts and feelings. Feel your body becoming ideally healthy, strong, and energized. See your body in perfect health, free of any excess weight, free of pain and disfigurement, free of illness, and fully energized. Feel your **passionate self** free of **reactive compulsions** and **desires to impose your will** on others but rather to help **inspire** them to discover their **own truth** and have the **will to live it.**

Step 11. Knowing Elemental Earth compounded with Elemental Fire.

Allow yourself to receive any information or messages from you're experiencing of these Elemental Forces. *In particular: receive information involving your* **Physical** *and* **Mental** *health and strength at both* **material** *and* **mental** *levels.* Receive the information without any emotional reaction and know that the knowledge is fully activated within your psyche.

Continue on with the Programs to Conclusion.

DIVINATION GUIDE TO EARTH—SEED OF FIRE
Earth—Seed of Fire: Potential—Use it or Lose it!

Fire is hot and transformative, and placed upon an Earthy foundation provides warmth in cold environments and heat for cooking and baking of food. Fuel for Fire is extracted from Earth and enables processing natural resource into new products.

Ores, sand and other resources are mined from Earth and transmuted by Fire into glass, steel, and other resources used in construction and manufacturing.

In a divination, this combination symbolizes ambition and upward movement and the light that opens up dark places to reveal secrets. It signals that this is the time and place to be creative, original, and innovative with what you already have.

Earth—Seed of Air:
Mind, & Matter

Earth—Seed of Air

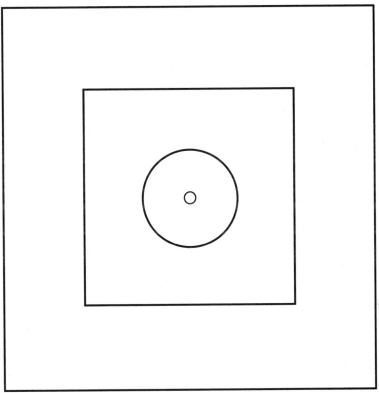

Color the tiny inner bindu circle white,
the inner circle blue,
the inner square bright yellow,
and the outer square bright purple

Earth—Seed of Air: Prithivi & Vayu *LAM & YAM*

Review

We urge you to review the Element Overview Table #1 for Earth on page 198 and the Element Overview Table #4 for Air on page 214 in preparation for this procedure and the Divination and other applications involved with this compound.

The Tattvic Connection Meditation
& Visualization Program #9: Earth/Air
Earth—Seed of Air

Introduction. The Purpose & Function of this Procedure.

Rather than repeating the procedure in its entirety, we are asking you to kindly refer to page 396 for the complete *Tattva Connection Meditation & Visualization Compound Program #7 and make your own adjustments to substitute "Air" for "Water" in steps 2 (goal statement), and 3 (affirmations), We are here providing content for Steps 5 (preparing and coloring the yantra card), 9a (yantra card focus), 10a (experience the compounded elements and 11 (knowing the compounded elements).*

The Program's Variables:

Steps 2. Goal Statement.

Note your need to consider how to express your goals to reflect the particular natures of the two elements in their primary and secondary combination in relation to your physical, emotional, mental, and spiritual well-being, and their functions in divination, magick, and self-realization

Step 3. Affirmations.

You need to write positive affirmations to accomplish your goals.

Step 5. Preparation.

Preparing the Yantra Card.

It is recommended that you photocopy the illustration on page 413, preferably on heavier paper or card stock, or draw it yourself in exactly the same sizes using a ruler and black pen. If you can manage it, using a drawing compass or a template, draw a tiny ⅛" inch diameter circle in the exact center. Leave the inside of the circle white. This inner circle or point aids your steady focus. It is not essential, but it is helpful. Make the outer **Earth Square** 4" x 4" and the inner **Earth Square** 2¼" x 2¼", the inner **Air Circle** 1" wide, and the little **Bindu Circle** in the exact center should be ⅛" in diameter and have a black line around it but not quite as thick as those around the **Circle** and the two **Squares.**

Coloring the Yantra Card.

It will be beneficial for you to color the image as follows: (a) color the tiny inner **Bindu Circle White**; (b) the **Air Circle Bright Blue**; (c) the smaller **Earth Square Bright Yellow**, and (d) the surrounding larger **Earth Square Bright Purple.** Each

Square is bordered with bold black lines, the **Air Circle** is bordered with a less bold black line, and the tiny inner **Bindu Circle** is bordered with a thinner black line.

Step 9a. Yantra Card Focus.

If you have constructed the tattva yantra card as described, turn on the light and focus it on the card held or positioned comfortably about a foot to a foot and a half in front of you.

If possible, arrange your chair to face the primary tattvic direction: *North* for **Earth.** Otherwise—think and feel *North.* (To the extent you feel the secondary element's importance to the operation; you can finish with an acknowledgment of *East* for **Air.**

Vibrate the name of the two tattvas: ***Prithivi*** and ***Vayu,*** alternating one after the other. Repeat three times.

Chant or hum the tattva element mantras ***LAM*** and Y***AM*** (pronounced ***LA-UUM*** and Y***A-UUM),*** alternating. Vibrate the mantra as instructed in Step 1, preliminaries. Repeat three times. Later, you can do more but always in groups of three. And feel the mantra vibrate in the *Pelvis,* the location of **Muladhara** chakra and then *over the heart,* the location of **Anahata** chakra.

Focus on the small **White Bindu Circle*** at the center of the image, and stare at it for as long as you can without blinking. When you can't continue the "burning" feeling any longer, turn off the light, close your eyes and focus your inner sight on the space in front of your brow chakra (between your eye brows and on the ridge you can feel just above your nose), and see the small **Blue Circle** within the larger **Yellow Square** floating in the space before you and vibrating within the **Purple Square.** And, then, you will soon see the tattva image change into the complementary yantra colors **Orange**, **Purple** and **Yellow.**

Again vibrate the names to the tattvas and chant or hum the mantras three times.

Absorb this yantra image! As you repeat the exercise, often, you will reach a point when you will be able to recall this image at will.

> *The small white circle is called a "Bindu," and focus on it is comprehensive of the entire tattvic image and all its energies. There is a small spot on the back of your head that likewise serves as a comprehensive psychic center used in certain meditational exercises. A Bindu is also the name of a single drop of semen, the focal point of a new life. And "bindu" is likewise the single point from which all creation began "in the union of divine forces, Male and Female, God and Goddess, Siva and Shakti in all their names and images—i.e., the "Big Bang."
>
> Bindu is a point of leverage where force applied becomes force multiplied and directed to accomplish your particular goal.

Step 9b. Yantra Visualization.

Alternatively, if you haven't made a **Earth/Air** card, immediately in front of you, visualize the image as described for making the card. See the image gently vibrating. And then the colors will reverse to their complementary yantra colors.

Step 10a. Experiencing Compounded Elemental Earth and Elemental Air.

Feel yourself becoming totally *absorbed** in the image while retaining awareness of the surrounding large tattvic **Purple Square**. As the smaller tattvic **Yellow Square** changes to the complementary yantra **Purple** feel *your* **Earthy** nature harmonize with the Cosmic **Earth** Tattva, and feel all impurities in your **Earth** Tattva—all emotional garbage and unconscious psychic attachments—dissipate. The tattvic **Blue Circle** will change to the complementary yantra **Bright Orange** as your **Airy** nature harmonizes with the Cosmic **Air** Tattva and the impurities of your **Air** tattva dissipate.

> *Becoming absorbed.* Enter into the **full image** and become one with it and feel surrounded by it. Moving inward from the outer **Earth Square** become one with the **Earth** Element, and then move inward to become one with the **Air** Element, and then further in to the **Bindu** to become one with **All**. Now, moving outward from the **Bindu** point to the **Fire Circle** and then to the **Earth Square** and to its outer edge feel the balanced **Earth** and **Air** elements in your body become harmonized and purified as they are balanced with their **Cosmic Source**.

In particular: feel the **Earthy** and **Airy** nature of your physical body become free of adverse thoughts and feelings. Feel your body becoming ideally healthy, strong, and energized. See your body in perfect health, free of any excess weight, free of pain and disfigurement, free of illness, and fully energized. Feel your **mental self** free of **imposed authoritarian ideas** and **ideologies,** and confident in your own **logically derived ethics.**

Step 11. Knowing Elemental Earth compounded with Elemental Air.

Allow yourself to receive any information or messages from you're experiencing of these Elemental Forces. *In particular: receive information involving your* **Physical** *and* **Mental** *health & strength at both* **material** *and* **higher astral** *and* **mental** *levels.* Receive the information without any emotional reaction and know that the knowledge is fully activated within your psyche.

Continue on with the Programs to Conclusion.

DIVINATION GUIDE TO EARTH—SEED OF AIR
Earth—Seed of Air: Aspiration, or Desperation?

Air is gaseous, moving and surrounding things, and also connecting them to one another. It rests on Earth and reaches toward the Sky as our atmosphere. While often erratic and even "bouncy," it expresses love and compassion through touch on skin. While Earth is solid it is also supportive while Air is imagination, insight and inspiration, joined together in aspiration to share and serve.

In a divination, this combination often signals a good starting point but may also be warning us that we are being held back in our present situation. Caution: do not act out of desperation but with deliberation.

Earth—Seed of Ether: *A Time of Transition*

Earth—Seed of Ether

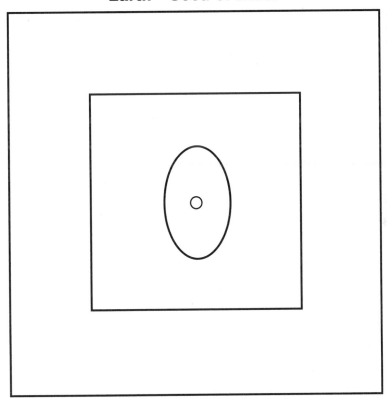

Color the tiny inner bindu circle white,
the inner oval indigo,
the inner square bright yellow,

Earth—Seed of Ether: Prithivi & Akasha *LAM & HAM*

Review

We urge you to review the Element Overview Table #1 for Earth on page 104 and the Element Overview Table #5 for Ether on page 272 in preparation for this procedure and the Divination and other applications involved with this compound.

The Tattvic Connection Meditation & Visualization Program #10: Earth/Ether
Earth—Seed of Ether

Introduction. The Purpose & Function of this Procedure.

Rather than repeating the procedure in its entirety, we are asking you to kindly refer to page 396 for the complete *Tattva Connection Meditation & Visualization Compound Program #7 and make your own adjustments to substitute "Ether" for "Water" in steps 2 (goal statement), and 3 (affirmations), We are here providing content for Steps 5 (preparing and coloring the yantra card), 9a (yantra card focus),10a (experience the compounded elements and 11 (knowing the compounded elements).*

The Program's Variables:

Steps 2. Goal Statement.

Note your need to consider how to express your goals to reflect the particular natures of the two elements in their primary and secondary combination in relation to your physical, emotional, mental and spiritual well-being, and their functions in divination, magick, and self-realization

Step 3. Affirmations.

You need to write positive affirmations to accomplish your goals.

Step 5. Preparation.

Preparing the Yantra Card.

It is recommended that you photocopy the illustration on page 417, preferably on heavier paper or card stock, or draw it yourself in exactly the same sizes using a ruler and black pen. If you can manage it, using a drawing compass or a template, draw a tiny ⅛" inch diameter circle in the exact center. Leave the inside of the circle white. This inner circle or point aids your steady focus. It is not essential, but it is helpful. Make the outer **Earth Square** 4" x 4" and the inner **Earth Square** 2¼" x 2¼", the inner **Ether Egg** ¾" wide by 1¼" tall, and the little **Bindu Circle** in the exact center should be

⅛" in diameter and have a black line around it but not quite as thick as those around the **Egg** and the two **Squares.**

Coloring the Yantra Card.

It will be beneficial for you to color the image as follows: (a) color the tiny inner **Bindu Circle White**; (b) the **Ether Egg Bright Indigo**; (c) the smaller **Earth Square Bright Yellow**, and (d) the surrounding larger **Earth Square Bright Purple.** Each **Square** is bordered with bold black lines, the **Ether Egg** is bordered with a less bold black line, and the tiny inner **Bindu Circle** is bordered with a thinner black line.

Step 9a. Yantra Card Focus.

If you have constructed the tattva yantra card as described, turn on the light and focus it on the card held or positioned comfortably about a foot to a foot and a half in front of you.

If possible, arrange your chair to face the primary tattvic direction: *North* for **Earth**. Otherwise—think and feel *North*. (To the extent you feel the secondary element's importance to the operation; you can finish with an acknowledgment of *Skyward* for **Ether**.

Vibrate the name of the two tattvas: ***Prithivi*** and ***Akasha,*** alternating one after the other. Repeat three times.

Chant or hum the tattva element mantras ***LAM*** and ***HAM*** (pronounced ***LA-UUM*** and ***HA-UUM),*** alternating. Vibrate the mantra as instructed in Step 1, preliminaries. Repeat three times. Later, you can do more but always in groups of three. And feel the mantra vibrate in the *Pelvis,* the location of **Muladhara** chakra and then *above the navel and at the throat,* the location of **Vishuddha** chakra.

Focus on the small white **Bindu Circle** at the center of the image, and stare at it for as long as you can without blinking. When you can't continue the "burning" feeling any longer, turn off the light, close your eyes and focus your inner sight on the space in front of your brow chakra (between your eyebrows and on the ridge you can feel just above your nose), and see the small **Indigo Egg** within the **Yellow Square** floating in the space before you and vibrating within the **Purple Square**. And, then, you will soon see the tattva image change into the complementary yantra colors of **Yellow/Orange, Purple** and **Bright Yellow**.

Again vibrate the names to the tattvas and chant or hum the mantras three times.

Absorb this yantra image! As you repeat the exercise, often, you will reach a point when you will be able to recall this image at will.

Step 9b. Yantra Visualization.

Alternatively, if you haven't made an **Earth/Ether** card, immediately in front of you, visualize the image as described for making the card. See the image gently vibrating. And then the colors will reverse to their complementary yantra colors.

Step 10a. Experiencing Compounded Elemental Earth and Elemental Ether.

Feel yourself becoming totally *absorbed** in the image while retaining awareness of the surrounding tattvic purple square. As the tattvic **Yellow** changes to the complementary yantra **Purple** feel *your* **Earthy** nature harmonize with the Cosmic **Earth** Tattva, and feel all impurities in your **Earth** Tattva—all emotional garbage and unconscious psychic attachments—dissipate. The tattvic **Indigo Egg** will change to the complementary yantra **Yellow/Orange** as your **Ether/Spirit** nature harmonizes with the Cosmic **Ether/Spirit** Tattva and the impurities of your **Ether/Spirit** tattva dissipate.

> **Becoming absorbed.* Enter into the **full image** and become one with it and feel surrounded by it. Moving inward from the outer **Earth Square** become one with the **Earth** Element, and then move inward to become one with the **Ether** Element, and then further in to the **Bindu** to become one with **All.** Now, moving outward from the **Bindu** point to the **Ether Egg** and then to the **Earth Square** and to its outer edge feel the balanced **Earth** and **Ether** elements in your body become harmonized and purified as they are balanced with their **Cosmic Source.**

In particular: feel the **Earthy** and **Ether/Spirit** nature of your physical body become free of adverse thoughts and feelings. Feel your body becoming ideally healthy, strong, and energized. See your body in perfect health, free of any excess weight, free of pain and disfigurement, free of illness, and fully energized. Feel your **spiritual self** free of the **restrictions of past karma** and other **limitations upon your truly unlimited potential,** and increasingly able to **communicate your deeper insights** to others.

Step 11. Knowing Elemental Earth compounded with Elemental Ether.

Allow yourself to receive any information or messages from you're experiencing of these Elemental Forces. *In particular: receive information involving your **Physical** and **Spiritual** health and strength at both **material** and **higher mental and causal** levels.* Receive the information without any emotional reaction and know that the knowledge is fully activated within your psyche.

Continue on with the Programs to Conclusion.

DIVINATION GUIDE TO EARTH—SEED OF ETHER
Earth—Seed of Ether: Complacency, or Renewal?

Ether is Space, and Ether is Spirit. Ether is not limited by its place upon Earth but offers unlimited potentials in overcoming complacency and apathy.

In a divination, it is time for renewal but more than a fresh start it's the opportunity to transform and even to transmute present circumstances into a transcendent future. It is time to "speak out" with tree vision from deep within your Unconscious.

CHAPTER ELEVEN
Clairvoyance & Astral Projection

... The ability to undertake astral journeys therefore involves considerable expansion of one's scope for experience. It brings opportunities for promoting one's own spiritual advancement, which begins with the involution of consciousness.

M. Baba, *God Speaks*

Here we come to a parting of the seas!
Or of the Ocean of Consciousness in which we have our being.

The Foundation for Spiritual Knowledge

Clairvoyance and Astral Projection are together the most dynamic and distinctive extensions of human consciousness and the real foundation for all that we know of the non-physical (spiritual) dimensions of life and Cosmos. Because their visions are non-physical, they have also served as the foundations (recognized or not) of all *visionary* art, poetry, literature, music, and—of course—vastly misunderstood mythology (which represents a metaphysical expression of history and science as seen by clairvoyance).

Increase in Sensitivity

Most of the tools and techniques for the "awakening" of Clairvoyance—even the most aggressive forms of Shamanism and the use of Self-Hypnosis—are directed toward the increase of *Sensitivity*. The Clairvoyant is sensitive to incoming information either in response to a specific request or in a general "casting of the net" hoping to land the right fish, i.e. helpful guidance in response to need.

Incoming, or Outgoing

In Astral Projection, we exchange "incoming" for "outgoing." We project consciousness beyond the body in the same way a news editor sends an investigative reporter out to uncover the story, or the chief of detectives sends his top investigator to solve the mystery.

Many Bodies

In both clairvoyance and astral projection we recognize the "mechanics" of consciousness in which we see that whole person consisting of multiple bodies or levels: physical, etheric, lower and higher astral, mental and causal—while knowing that beyond the delineation of "person" the soul has still further dimensions that will be awakened in future evolutionary development.

At the same time, we don't really know that there is a separation of consciousness in which the astral body *actually* leaves the environment of the person, or if it is more a matter of "swimming" within the ocean of a universal and all pervading consciousness without anything ever being projected or leaving home!

More than one type of Out-of-Body Experience

Or, do we have more than one type of Out-of-Body Experience just as we have more than on type of clairvoyance? The answer appears to be that we do as will be later described, and in addition we have forms of consciousness projection other than of the astral body involving the etheric and mental bodies. Nevertheless, it is astral projection that is most common and it is astral projection that is experienced spontaneously as during sleep, meditation, accidents, near-death, sensory deprivation, shamanic sensory overload, mystical ecstasy, etc.

The Right Connections

Everything is connected, and at the higher levels of consciousness those connections can be more real than telephone lines stretching across continents and cables under the sea. Either way—receptive sensitivity or projective seeking—the greatest importance remains in asking the right questions and establishing the goals. You have to ask for what you get—"Ask and it shall be given unto you"—and there will always be an answer, the accuracy of which is highly dependent upon the sufficient detail of the question.

"Active" Sensitivity & Seekers

The "question and the goal" affirm that our paranormal science is not passive but is indeed active. "Sensitivity" is best understood as an active technique even for the wearer of a leather meditation mask. *Looking, Listening, Feeling* are actions of the physical organs (inclusive of etheric and astral "particles") in the same way as the actions of the sensitive opening the doors and windows of consciousness and the action of projection through those doors and windows as the occupant of the Witches Cradle has an Out-of-Body Experience. The exercises of clairvoyance and astral projection are active—even if minimally so—and the degree of the activity largely determines the nature of the experience.

Ultimately, we are all "Seekers." And seeking is a reaching forward from the ordinary to the extraordinary of the human person.

Vibrations

"Vibes!" Yes, everything does vibrate, and things have levels of vibration. And we are told that we can *raise* our vibrations and that in doing so we reach higher levels of consciousness. We measure all sorts of things by their vibratory frequency—from brain waves to light and sound spectrums, and to feelings and thoughts themselves.

Sometimes vibrations are bad—as when moving parts of a machine are "out of synch," causing vibrations that can shake things apart. When vibrations are synchronized, then there is harmony. Sound and Music can be harmonious or discordant. Dance movements can be harmonious or broken. Our inner energies can be harmonious or "out of sorts." We can have harmonious politics or anarchy. With harmonious actions, we introduce balance and healing. When our body, mind, and spirit are in balance, our vibrations throughout the whole person rise; but we can also raise vibration through distinct techniques involving mantras and visualizations specific to the chakras, and by specific programs of self-hypnosis.

Some astral projectors encounter a "vibrational state" in which they experience a separation of the etheric double (discussed later) from the physical in a series vibrating waves moving from foot to head and back. With practice, the waves can be made stronger and be pushed up and out of the head into a full and conscious projection.

Kundalini & the Chakras, East & West

With the raising of Kundalini up through the chakras we introduce greater control of the subtle bodies, and with this we increase the range of our response to stated goals for higher forms of clairvoyance and astral projection. Famed clairvoyant, C. W. Leadbeater points to "the existence in both the astral and the etheric bodies of man of certain centres of force which have to *vivified* in turn by the sacred serpent-fire as the man advances in evolution."

"Up, up, and away!"

Is the "raising of Kundalini" the same as "raising vibrations"? There are arguments pro and con from separate philosophies, but if not the same they are so similar that a *concerted* action for either may amount to the same thing. The important guideline, as always, is to establish the goal and complete the program. *Up, up, and away! a*s the superhero Superman said—and, indeed—it is our evolutionary goal to all become superheroes.

In some situations, Clairvoyance and Astral Projection emerge together as a single function while in others going out of body is a necessary and vital extension of the clairvoyant action. During such projections, information may be secured through communication with other entities or observations of astral replicas and of the Akashic Records.

Physical, Etheric, Astral, Mental . . .
A Vehicle for the Soul

For many people, these references to vibrations, chakras, and other than physical bodies can be a challenge. It is easier for them to think of the astral body as a kind of vehicle for the soul after death than to believe that they function through a composite of several subtle bodies in addition to the physical base. If they believe in "life after death," it is easier to think of an astral body than of something nebulous and vaporous. Physical life comes to an end, but life and consciousness moves on to an astral body. And there are many reports of people seeing something rise up out of the physical body at the time of death.

The astral body isn't "born" at the death of the physical body—it has been part of the complex that is the whole person of which we know so little for the simple reason that all our instruments only measure the physical and our sense organs have not learned to look for or see things that are not physically *solid*. Yet, we now know that nothing physical is solid but rather consists of tiny molecular or atomic particles that are in constant vibratory motion only held in place by various gravity-like electro-magnetic forces.

"Particle" Metaphysics

During life, every part of the physical body contains not only physical particles but also etheric, astral, and mental particles—all in constant vibratory motion. In particular, our physical sense organs not only contain these other particles but the forces holding them together are structured to "reach out" to *sense* things in accordance with particular programming related to the vibrations of the particles making up the organs and the things being sensed.

Among those particles are those of the finer non-physical bodies. Upon death, we lose the physical particles and now sense only non-physical realities which do include replicas of physical things as well as things that are "solid" in the astral and mental planes. However, during life we do have the capacity to use those etheric, astral, and mental particles to sense these non-physical realities, but only to the degree that we learn to focus on these higher vibratory levels.

As C. W. Leadbeater has written:*

A man's etheric body is in reality merely the finer part of his physical frame, and that therefore all his sense-organs contain a large amount of etheric matter of various degrees of density, the capacities of which are still practically latent in most of us.

With development, we can have,

. . . a steady and progressive extension of our senses, so that both by sight and by hearing we may be able to appreciate vibrations far higher and far lower than those which are ordinarily recognized. . . . Such impressions will still be received through the retina of the eye; of course they will affect its etheric rather than its solid matter, but we may nevertheless regard them as still appealing only to an organ specialized to receive them, and not to the whole surface of the etheric body.

. . . any given organ of the physical body must always have as its counterpart a certain amount of astral matter, it does not retain the same particles for more than a few seconds at a time, and consequently there is nothing corresponding to the specialization of physical nerve-matter into optic or auditory nerves, and so on.

Clairvoyance, 1899, Theosophical, London (public domain).

Expanding Sensory Capacities to Perceive Higher Reality

In other words, as we learn to raise our ability to sense higher vibration, we expand our abilities to see, hear, feel, smell, and even taste. We now know that we can thus expand our sensory capacities to perceive higher reality by willful focus. The older Theosophical literature taught that raising vibrations was only possible by extracting things of lower vibration from the physical body through lifestyle changes—becoming vegetarian, not smoking tobacco, not drinking alcohol, not having sex, not associating with "bad company," and thinking only noble thoughts, etc., In a sense, that still left the focus on the physical whereas willful change perhaps aided by self-hypnosis or particular meditations or utilizing sensory helps such as incense, mantras, visualization, etc., moved the focus in a targeted manner.

Projections of the Astral Body

Bishop Leadbeater describes **four forms of clairvoyance extended with astral methods,** plus one of mental projection—which expands our subject:*

1. *By means of an astral current.* A kind of temporary telephone connection to convey vibrations by means of which all that is going on at the other end of it may be seen. Such a line is established by visualizing the transmission of energy

until the line is formed, or the "astral current" may be established by a strong emotional thought at the other end of the line.

2. *By the projection of a thought-form.* The ability necessitates a certain amount of control upon the mental plane. Thought takes form upon its own plane, and in then on the astral plane as well. If a person strongly visualizes himself as present at any given place, a thought form of his/her likeness will appear at that place. This form must be composed of the matter of the mental plane, and then it will draw astral substance around itself. This type of clairvoyance requires a considerable exercise of power to retain the image and its connection to the desired place to receive impressions by means of it. Impressions made upon the form will be transmitted to the thinker—not along an astral telephone line, as before, but by sympathetic vibration almost as though the seer projected a part of his consciousness into the thought-form, and used it as a personal observer able to transfer those observations.

3. By *traveling in the astral body in which the person's "consciousness" is transferred to the distant scene.* It is the most satisfactory form of clairvoyance available as it enables the traveler to take part in those scenes, and even conversing with various astral entities. If in addition he can learn how to materialize himself, he will be able to take part in physical events or conversations at a distance.

4. *By traveling in the mental body.* Here the vehicle used for projection is no longer the astral body, but a substitute formed from the substance of the mind-body, a vehicle belonging to the mental plane. The vision of the mental plane is totally different, not involving separate senses such as sight and hearing, but rather one general sense which responds so fully to the vibrations reaching it that any object is at once comprehended fully—knowing everything about it by the one instantaneous operation.

*Paraphrased from his 1899 edition of *Clairvoyance.* See Sources at end of chapter.

Astral Projection is neither a common experience nor a unique and bizarre matter. Various surveys from the 1960s on have reported as few as 8 percent of the population to as many as 50 percent (at least within surveyed groups) has had Out-of-Body Experiences. (Wikipedia)

But, such surveys don't distinguish between spontaneous and induced astral projections. While some people claim that we all go out-of-body when the physical body sleeps that is not the same thing as being "awake" and actively conscious in the astral body.

Even ordinary sleep dreams (in contrast to "lucid dreaming) are said to be unconscious projections, generally with little value and only occasionally having any pertinent meaning. Lucid dreaming is believed to be partial astral projections during which it is possible for the dreamer to take control and turn them into true projections. But, even those lack the value of truly conscious projections during which the projector can explore the astral world which is in a "non-spatial" sense much larger than the physical dimension. Conscious astral projections provide a substantial expansion of personal consciousness and the active exploration of the astral world (also known as the "emotional plane").

Projection of the Etheric Double

Nevertheless, as indicated previously, the phrase "astral projection" does not give us a complete picture of Expanded Consciousness. Early writers largely failed to distinguish astral projection from etheric and mental projections. Today, it is more common to call those out-of-body experiences of the physical world as projections of the "etheric double" where sight and action is limited to just the physical and "higher physical" (etheric) dimension. It is with etheric projection that the person can "walk through brick walls" and "leap tall buildings," but will not communicate with angels and astral beings.

The Etheric Double is also known as the "Energy Body" and is the intermediary between the physical and astral bodies transferring "vital force" (*prana*) through the chakras to the physical and otherwise manifesting the energies involved in most paranormal phenomena, martial arts, energy healing, and in a variety of magical and religious phenomena.

Projection of the Mental Body

Just as the etheric double is "below" (vibrationally) the Astral Body, so is the Mental Body above the Astral. The mental body is our intellectual consciousness and is not an actual *body* so much as a place or state of consciousness—yet, it is definitive and has its own substance and functions according to its own rules. It is at the border between the astral and mental planes that the "Akashic Records" have their place.

The Mental Thought Form as Vehicle

We all too commonly speak one way when we are should be speaking in another way. We don't actually project a mental body, but instead create a thought form that then appears on the astral plane and can function as a "container" for magical and healing operations. The power of imagination/visualization is enormous, and the creation of a Thought Form and then using it as a vehicle to function in higher dimensions is a truly advanced, but attainable, psychic skill.

Vibrational Power and Astral Projection

As mentioned earlier, some people spontaneously experience a "vibrational state" in which they experience a separation of the etheric double (also discussed above) from the physical in a series vibrating waves moving from foot to head and back. With practice, the waves can be made stronger and be pushed up and out of the head into a full and conscious projection.

Such *vibrational projection* can also be thought of as an "energy projection" because it is experienced as intensely energizing and sometimes initially accompanied by pulsating blue light—much like that of electric sparks—that intensifies as the vibrational waves reach toward the head (crown chakra).

Here is a program designed to facilitate this projection.

ASTRAL PROJECTION AND VIBRATIONAL POWER
The Vibratory Power Projection Program

Entering the out-of-body state is often accompanied by a *vibrational state* which is characterized by a series of pulsating movements, typically upward from the feet to the head region and then downward. Through a progression of these up and down movements, the vibrating waves generate an energized integrative state of balance and synchronicity that embraces not only physical reality but the non-physical as well. Typically accompanying the series of vibrational waves is a spontaneous state of heightened psychic awareness that can include both clairvoyance and precognition along with past-life enlightenment. Although much remains to be known about these waves and the dynamics underlying them, they are often seen as precursors to the out-of-body state in which the astral body is liberated from the physical and energized to travel to distant destinations.

Aside from the spontaneously empowering effects of both vibrational waves and the synchronicity they generate is their receptiveness to stated objectives including those related to clairvoyant viewing, precognitive awareness, and distance traveling. With the formulation of specific objectives prior to the vibrational experience, the empowering potential of the vibration is magnified by its capacity to integrate the stated objectives into the out-of-body experience. Adding to the power of vibration waves is its capacity to generate a heightened sense of self-confidence and a positive expectancy effect related to previously stated goals. Following the out-of-body experience, the integrated nature of vibrational waves generates a state of balance and a powerful expectancy effect that ensures success in achieving personal goals.

As an integrative energy force, the vibrational waves are believed by some to provide protection for the duration of the out-of-body experience. They are believed to facilitate astral travel and interactions with other realities, including distant planes and dimensions of energy as well as personal guides and guardians. They are likewise believed to ensure a safe return to the physical body.

Energy Waves and PK Power

The psychokinetic (PK) powers of energy waves are believed to include the capacity not only to generate an integrative state of synchronicity, but in some instances to literally influence other realities. Here are a few examples of PK power associated with the focusing of energy waves:

- Promote health, fitness, and rejuvenation by targeting healthful energy on specific internal organs and functions.
- Intervene in emergency situations, including the influencing of objects in motion, removing blockages to escape, and initiating warning signals.
- Influence global realities in ways that facilitate progress and peace.

These functions of energy waves can be implemented either during the vibrational state preceding astral projection or during the out-of-body state. The formulation of PK goals prior to the vibrational state is essential to the success of this application.

The Vibrational State and Ascending to Sleep

The vibrational state is often described by astral projectors as similar in some ways to the hypnagogic stage of sleep—that brief interval between wakefulness and sleep. One popular view holds, in fact, that hypnagogic sleep is itself a vibrational state that either facilitates or actually induces the out-of-body state. A variation of that view holds that the astral body remains disengaged from the physical body, often hovering over it, for the duration of sleep. The vibrational state, rather mystical or paranormal, thus becomes a normal psycho-physiological phenomenon experienced to some degree by everyone. Thus "falling asleep" becomes more accurately *ascending to sleep*.

The ascending to sleep view holds that the astral body does indeed remain suspended over the physical body and in close proximity to it for the duration of sleep. This view further holds that during that projected state, the astral body is liberated to travel to distant destinations, both physical and non-physical. The ascending to sleep view also holds that the dream experience, rather than simply a physically based experience, can include profound out-of-body experiences, to include those related to travel to temporal as well as non-temporal travel. The lucid dream, in particular, is believed to consist of perceptions related to interactions with other realities.

Among the most effective techniques for inducing out-of-body projection are those that incorporate the hypnagogic stage of sleep. The Hypnagogic Arrest Strategy is specifically designed to arrest hypnagogic sleep by holding the fingers of either hand in a tense spread position and then slowly relaxing them as goals related to astral travel are affirmed (See Slate, J., *Beyond Reincarnation*. Woodbury, MN: Llewellyn, 2008). The technique, according to some, temporarily slows the vibrational waves characteristic of hypnagogic sleep while facilitating the out-of-body experience, to include travel to specified destinations including the spirit realm. The technique often initiates awareness of a familiar spirit presence who becomes a "travel guide" throughout astral travel.

The Vibratory Power Program

The Vibratory Power Program is designed not only as an out-of-body induction approach but also a facilitative program that focuses on the integrative functions of astral waves to generate a multi-functional state of self-empowerment. The procedure generates an inverse relation between the body's vibratory waves and their integrative effects. As the upward and downward movements of vibratory waves become slower, their integrative effects become increasingly powerful. The result is a mental and physical state that not only facilitates astral projection but activates a host of dormant potentials.

As a self-administered holistic approach, this program incorporates personal goals, positive suggestions, and post-procedure gestures into a fully integrated state of mind and body. It is one of the most powerful procedures known for activating both clairvoyance and precognition. Profound awareness in vivid imagery form often unfolds as the vibratory waves become increasingly balanced and integrated into the body's mental and physical functions. Tension is released and thinking processes become clearer as the body becomes progressively relaxed. Vivid imagery of present situations and future events often emerge in great detail. Subconscious potentials related to specific goals become activated and empowered. Conflicts are often resolved during the integrative process in which the energy waves seem to literally generate new insight related to past, present, and future concerns.

Once the integrative functions of this program reach their peaks, a spontaneous out-of-body state of readiness often occurs. Upon reaching a state of full integrated readiness, your capacity for astral projection and travel is at its peak. The choice of whether to engage the out-of-body experience, however, rests with you alone. You can choose to remain in the state of readiness which is independently empowering, or you can engage astral projection by simply embracing it. The program requires a safe, comfortable setting free of distractions. Loose fitting clothing with shoes removed is recommended. The duration of the program depends of whether the astral projection option is included.

Step 1. Settle back into a comfortable reclining or lying down position with your hands resting at your sides. Take a few moments first to clear your mind and then to affirm your personal goals in positive terms using the "I am empowered" approach.

Step 2. While resting comfortably, take in a few deep breaths, exhaling slowly. Develop a slow, rhythmic breathing pattern and give your body permission to become increasingly relaxed, attuned, and balance.

With your eyes closed, visualize your full body resting comfortably. Take a few moments to allow a clear image to fully emerge.

Step 3. Slowly scan your body, beginning at your toes and gradually progressing upward. Notice such sensations as warmth, coolness, tingling, and so forth. Take plenty of time to scan your full body, pausing at areas of tension and allowing the relaxation and attunement to go deeper and deeper. Give special attention to body joints including ankles, knees, hips, and so forth. Sense the balancing effects of relaxation and attunement going deeper and deeper into the muscles and joints.

Step 4. Upon reaching your abdomen, momentary slow your scan as tension is replaced with relaxation and attunement going deeper and deeper within.

Step 5. Upon reaching your chest, again momentarily slow your scan as you sense fresh air soaking deeply into your lungs.

Step 6. Upon reaching your shoulders, visualize the joints and allow relaxation to flow downward into your arms, right through to the tips of your fingers.

Step 7. Allow the relaxation in your shoulders to flow upward into your neck and head region. Sense the balancing and attuning effects of vibratory power flowing upward from the tips of your toes right though the top of your head.

Step 8. Take a few moments to reflect of the flow of attuning energy progressing upward from the tips of your toes right through the top of your head. Affirm: "I am relaxed, balanced, and attuned from the tips of my toes right through the top of my head."

Step 9. Reverse the body scan by progressing slowly downward from the top of your head to the tips of your toes. As with the upward scan, take a few moments along the way to allow relaxation, balance, and attunement to permeate your body.

Upon reaching your toes, affirm: "I am relaxed, balanced, and attuned from the top of my head right through the tips of my toes.

Step 10. Slowly repeat the upward scan, and upon its completion, note the heightened state of empowerment readiness. It's at this stage that profound clairvoyant and precognitive insight often emerges. By re-affirming your personal goals as earlier stated, you can readily access the power required for your complete success. You can, at this step, choose either to conclude the program or to enter the out-of-body state.

Step 11. (Optional). Entering the out-of-body state is a natural progression of the heightened state of readiness generated by this program. Should you decide to enter the out-of-body state upon completion of the second upward scan, restate your goals and affirm your intent to achieve them through the out-of-body experience. Affirm in your own words that you are protected and secure throughout the experience, to include travel to designated destinations. Further affirm that you are empowered to successfully return to your physical body at any time and re-engage it by the power of intent alone. To initiate the out-of-body state, begin by giving yourself permission to enter it. You can facilitate that process through imagery of the astral body gently disengaging the physical and rising above it. It is important to flow with the disengagement process. Allow plenty of time for disengagement to occur. Upon full disengagement, again affirm your goals and your intent to use the out-of-body experience to achieve them. While astral travel during the out-of-body state can be spontaneous, it can be deliberately induced, typically through intent combined with so-called "destination imagery". To end the out-of-body experience, view your physical body at rest and state your intent to re-engage it. You can immediately before re-engagement formulate a post-procedure cue, such as simply joining the hands, which you can use on demand to activate the full empowering effects of the experience.

Step 12. Conclude the program by taking time to reflect on the experience and its relevance to your stated goals.

Conclusion

Clairvoyance, vibratory power, and astral projection—they each facilitate the other. By working together as an integrative force, they generate the power required for you to actualize your highest potentials, realize your loftiest goals, and reach your highest destiny. Who could ask for more than that?

Sources & Suggested Additional Reading:

Baba, M. *God Speaks,* 1997, Walnut Creek.

De Long, D. *Ancient Teachings for Beginners,* 2000, Llewellyn.

Leadbeater, C. W. *Clairvoyance,* 1899, Theosophical, London.

Slate, J. H. *Beyond Reincarnation,* 2008, Llewellyn.

ADDENDUM #11 TO CHAPTER 11
Microcosm to Macrocosm & Macrocosm to Microcosm

The Tattvic Connection—
Meditation & Visualization Programs #11–#15

Water—And its Compounds

Water, Water, Everywhere—but not a drop to drink!

You can't drink Astral Water to quench physical body thirst, but you can imagine yourself drinking imaginary water or other imagined fluids. With the power of your imagination you can psychically *charge* wine and other physical fluids with emotional and mentally developed *intentions*.

Like Earth, and like the other primal Elements, Water has unique characteristics that are simply listed in the Element Overview Table on page 131 which you should review, and even photocopy as a handy reference for the work in this Addendum.

Water is a "fluid Solvent and Carrier" enabling the transfer of many substances from one place to another enabling the application of the transferred substance's own characteristic to a different person, place, another substance, etc. Sometimes, the enabled *compound* has greater powers and different functions that either the carrier or the transferred substance as a result of Water's Solvent capability.

All that is true of physical Water is even more so in the case of Astral Water and is further intensified in the compounding with its own element and the other primal elements.

Water—Seed of Water:
Fluidity, Flexibility, & the Universal Solvent

Water—Seed of Water

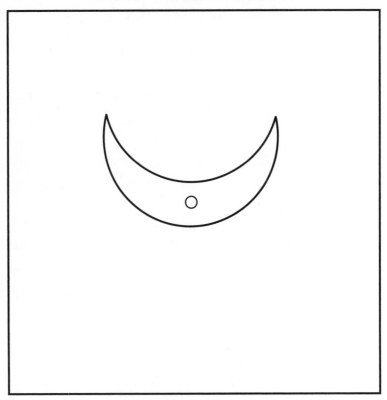

Color the tiny inner bindu circle white,
the inner crescent bright metallic silver,
and the outer square black

Water—Seed of Water: Apas VAM

Rather than repeat the content of the earlier Element Overview Tables from pages 104 for Earth, 131 for Water, 189 for Fire, 214 for Air, and 272 for Ether, we simply ask that you refer to them individually as called for in the following exercises.

In particular, we urge you to review the Element Overview Table #2 for Water on page 131 in preparation for this procedure and the Divination and other applications involved with this compound.

The Tattvic Connection Meditation
& Visualization Program #11: Water/Water
Water—Seed of Water

Introduction. The Purpose & Function of this Procedure.

Rather than repeating the procedure in its entirety, we are asking you to kindly refer to page 396 for the complete *Tattva Connection Meditation & Visualization Compound Program #7 and make your own adjustments to substitute for "Water" in steps 2 (goal statement), and 3 (affirmations), We are here providing content for Steps 5 (preparing and coloring the yantra card), 9a (yantra card focus), 10a. (experience the compounded elements and 11 (knowing the compounded elements).*

The Program's Variables:

Steps 2. Goal Statement.

Note your need to consider how to express your goals to reflect the particular natures of the two elements in their primary and secondary combination in relation to your physical, emotional, mental and spiritual well-being, and their functions in divination, magick, and self-realization

Step 3. Affirmations.

You need to write positive affirmations to accomplish your goals.

Step 5. Preparation.

Preparing the Yantra Card.

It is recommended that you photocopy the illustration on page 438, preferably on heavier paper or card stock, or draw it yourself in exactly the same sizes using a ruler and black pen. If you can manage it, using a drawing compass or a template, draw a tiny ⅛" inch diameter circle in the exact center. Leave the inside of the circle white. This inner circle or point aids your steady focus. It is not essential, but it is helpful. Make the outer **Square** 4" x 4" and the inner **Water Crescent** 2¼" wide and centered, horns up, the inner, and the little **Bindu Circle** in the exact center should be ⅛" in diameter and have a black line around it but not quite as thick as those around the **Crescent** and the two **Squares**.

Coloring the Yantra Card.

It will be beneficial for you to color the image as follows: (a) color the tiny inner **Bindu Circle White**; (b) the **Water Crescent Metallic Silver** (or White); (c) and the surrounding larger **Square Black**. The large outer **Square** is bordered with bold black lines, the **Water Crescent** is bordered with a less bold black line, and the tiny inner **Bindu Circle** is bordered with a thinner black line. Of course, the lines for the Square and Crescent will be invisible because of the surrounding black, but it helps your psychic perception to draw them in.

Step 9a. Yantra Card Focus.

If you have constructed the tattva yantra card as described, turn on the light and focus it on the card held or positioned comfortably about a foot to a foot and a half in front of you.

If possible, arrange your chair to face the primary tattvic direction: *West* for **Water**. Otherwise—think and feel *West*.

Vibrate the name of the tattva: *Apas.* Repeat three times.

Chant or hum the tattva element mantra *VAM* (pronounced *VA-UUMO.* Vibrate the mantra as instructed in Step 1, preliminaries. Repeat three times. Later, you can do more but always in groups of three. And feel the mantra vibrate between the *Genitals & Navel*, the location of **Svadhisthana** chakra.

Focus on the small white **Bindu Circle** at the center of the image, and stare at it for as long as you can without blinking. When you can't continue the "burning" feeling any longer, turn off the light, close your eyes and focus your inner sight on the space in front of your brow chakra (between your eyebrows and on the ridge you can feel just above your nose), and see the **Silver Crescent** floating in the space before you and vibrating within the **Black Square**. And, then, you will soon see the tattva image change into the complementary yantra colors of **White** and **Black**.

Again vibrate the names to the tattvas and chant or hum the mantras three times.

Absorb this yantra image! As you repeat the exercise, often, you will reach a point when you will be able to recall this image at will.

Step 9b. Yantra Visualization.

Alternatively, if you haven't made a **Water** card, immediately in front of you visualize the image as described for making the card. See the image gently vibrating. And then the colors will reverse to their complementary yantra colors.

Step 10a. Experiencing Compounded Elemental Water and Elemental Water.

Feel yourself becoming totally *absorbed* in the image while retaining awareness of the surrounding tattvic black square. As the tattvic **Silver** changes to the complementary yantra **Black** feel *your* **Watery** nature harmonize with the Cosmic **Water** Tattva, and feel all impurities in your **Water** Tattva—all emotional garbage and unconscious psychic attachments—dissipate. The tattvic **Silver Crescent** will change to the complementary yantra **Black** (and the larger surrounding Black Square to White) as your **Water** nature harmonizes with the Cosmic **Water** Tattva and the impurities of your **Water** tattva dissipate.

In particular: feel the **Watery fluid** nature of your **physical** body become ideally healthy, strong, and energized, free of obstruction and constrictions and any excess weight. Feel your **Emotional Self free of imposed** and **irrational inhibitions**, **open to sensory pleasure** and **emotional enjoyment** in **positive relationships** of **Family** and of **Romance** & **Intimacy**.

Step 11. Knowing Elemental Water compounded with Elemental Water.

Allow yourself to receive any information or messages from you're experiencing of these Elemental Forces. *In particular: receive information involving your **Physical** and **Emotional** health & strength at both **material** and **astral** levels.* Receive the information without any emotional reaction and know that the knowledge is fully activated within your psyche.

Continue on with the Programs to Conclusion.

DIVINATION GUIDE TO WATER—SEED OF WATER
Water—Seed of Water: *Procrastinating, or Partnering for Progress?*

Water, Water, Everywhere, and plenty to drink. Water with Water: working together bring fluidity and flexibility to every situation. The "universal solvent" flows, washes, adapts and transports people, foods, and goods across the Earth to nurture life, commerce, and industry. Water is the second element upward on the "path of return" and reminds us of the power of e-motion—defined as "energy in motion."

In a divination, it signals the need and timely opportunity to solve problems through cooperation, interaction and "networking" with others. It tells us to build and work with and in communities, gaining communal support for even personal goals. And, It's also time to "let go" and release guilt from past failures that you have allowed to hold you back. Don't be "wishy-washy" and procrastinate—move forward, and upward. The

Moon symbolizes feminine intuition and reminds us of the importance of "right timing." *Timing is the ultimate Key to Success!*

Water—Seed of Earth:
Initiation & Realization of Higher Potential

Water—Seed of Earth

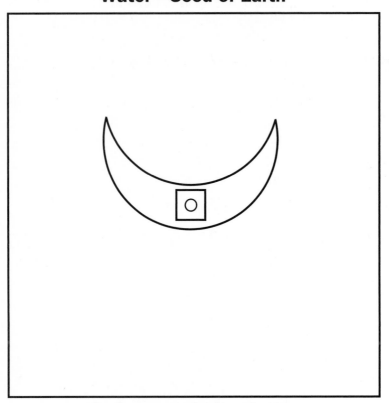

Color the tiny inner bindu circle white,
the inner little square yellow
the inner crescent bright metallic silver,
and the outer square black

Water—Seed of Earth: Apas & Prithivi VAM & LAM

Review

We urge you to review the Element Overview Table #2 for Water on page 131 and the Element Overview Table #1 for Earth on page 104 in preparation for this procedure and the Divination and other applications involved with this compound.

The Tattvic Connection Meditation & Visualization Program #12: Water/Earth
Water—Seed of Earth

Introduction. The Purpose & Function of this Procedure.

Rather than repeating the procedure in its entirety, we are asking you to kindly refer to page 580 for the complete *Tattva Connection Meditation & Visualization Compound Program #7 and make your own adjustments to substitute "**Water**" for "**Earth**" and "**Earth**" for "**Water**" in steps 2 (goal statement), 3 (affirmations. (I know that seems redundant, but in the psychic world little things count for a lot.) We are here providing content for Steps 5 (preparing and coloring the yantra card), 9a (yantra card focus),10a. (experience the compounded elements and 11 (knowing the compounded elements).*

The Program's Variables:

Steps 2. Goal Statement.

Note your need to consider how to express your goals to reflect the particular natures of the two elements in their primary and secondary combination in relation to your physical, emotional, mental and spiritual well-being, and their functions in divination, magick, and self-growth.

Step 3. Affirmations.

You need to write positive affirmations to accomplish your goals.

Step 5. Preparation.
Preparing the Yantra Card.

It is recommended that you photocopy the illustration on page 442, preferably on heavier paper or card stock, or draw it yourself in exactly the same sizes using a ruler and black pen. If you can manage it, using a drawing compass or a template, draw a tiny ⅛" inch diameter circle in the exact center. Leave the inside of the circle white. This inner circle or point aids your steady focus. It is not essential, but it is helpful. Make the outer square 4" x 4" and the inner **Water Crescent** (horns up) 2¼" wide and centered, the inner **Earth Square** ⅝" x ⅝", and the little **Bindu Circle** in the exact center should be ⅛" in diameter and have a black line around it but not quite as thick as those around the **Crescent** and the **Square**.

Coloring the Yantra Card.

It will be beneficial for you to color the image as follows: (a) color the tiny inner **Bindu Circle White**; (b) the small **Earth Square Bright Yellow** ; (c) the **Water Crescent Metallic Silver** (or White); and (d) the surrounding larger square **Black.** The square and **Water Crescent** are bordered with bold black lines, the small **Earth Square** is bordered with a less bold black line, and the tiny inner circle is bordered with a thinner black line.

Step 9a. Yantra Card Focus.

If you have constructed the tattva yantra card as described, turn on the light and focus it on the card held or positioned comfortably about a foot to a foot and a half in front of you.

If possible, arrange your chair to face the primary tattvic direction: *West* for **Water.** Otherwise—think and feel *West.* (To the extent you feel the secondary element's importance to the operation; you can finish with an acknowledgment of *North* for **Earth.**

Vibrate the name of the two tattvas: *Apas* and *Prithivi*, alternating one after the other. Repeat three times.

Chant or hum the tattva element mantras *VAM* and *LAM* (pronounced *VA-UUM* and *LA-UUM),* alternating. Vibrate the mantra as instructed in Step 1, preliminaries. Repeat three times. Later, you can do more but always in groups of three. And feel the mantra vibrate *between the genitals and the navel,* the location of **Svadhisthana** chakra and then *in the pelvis,* the location of **Muladhara** chakra.

Focus on the small white circle* (see note on next page) at the center of the image, and stare at it for as long as you can without blinking. When you can't continue the "burning" feeling any longer, turn off the light, close your eyes and focus your inner sight on the space in front of your brow chakra (between your eye brows and on the ridge you can feel just above your nose), and see the small **Yellow Square** in **Silver Crescent** floating in the space before you and vibrating within the **Black Square.** And, then, you will soon see the tattva image change into the complementary yantra colors **Purple, Black** and **White.**

Again vibrate the names to the tattvas and chant or hum the mantras three times.

Absorb this yantra image! As you repeat the exercise, often, you will reach a point when you will be able to recall this image at will.

Step 9b. Yantra Visualization.

Alternatively, if you haven't made a **Water/Earth** card, immediately in front of you, visualize the image as described for making the card. See the image gently vibrating. And then the colors will reverse to their complementary yantra colors.

Step 10a. Experiencing Compounded Elemental Water and Elemental Earth.

Feel yourself becoming totally *absorbed** in the image while retaining awareness of the surrounding tattvic blue square. As the tattvic **Yellow** changes to the complementary yantra **Purple** feel *your* **Earthy** nature harmonize with the Cosmic **Earth** Tattva, and feel all impurities in your **Earth** Tattva—all emotional garbage and unconscious psychic attachments—dissipate. The tattvic **Silver Crescent** will change to the complementary yantra **Black** (and the larger surrounding Black Square to White) as your **Watery** nature harmonizes with the Cosmic **Water** Tattva and the impurities of your **Water** tattva dissipate.

> **Becoming absorbed*. Enter into the **full image** and become one with it and feel surrounded by it. Moving inward from the outer **Square** become one with the **Water** Element, and then move inward to become one with the **Earth** Element, and then further in to the **Bindu** to become one with **All.** Now, moving outward from the **Bindu** point to the **Earth Square** and then to the **Water Crescent** and to its outer edge feel the balanced **Water** and **Earth** elements in your body become harmonized and purified as they are balanced with their **Cosmic Source.**

In particular: feel the **Watery fluid** nature of your **physical** body become ideally healthy, strong, and energized, free of obstruction and constrictions and any excess weight. Feel your **Physical Self free of imposed** and **irrational ideals of excessive muscular development and the sportsman personality.** Be open to the **"fix-it" approach to life's little problems,** but don't transfer that to the world's big problems.

Step 11. Knowing Elemental Water compounded with Elemental Earth.

Allow yourself to receive any information or messages from you're experiencing of these Elemental Forces. *In particular: receive information involving your **Physical** and **Emotional** health and strength at both **material** and **astral** levels.* Receive the information without any emotional reaction and know that the knowledge is fully activated within your psyche.

Continue on with the programs to Conclusion.

DIVINATION GUIDE TO WATER—SEED OF EARTH
Water—Seed of Earth: *Right Timing or Missed Opportunity?*

Earth lovingly cups Water, and Water lovingly nourishes Earth through its power as a carrier of needed substances. Seeds planted in Earth are "initiated" by Water into a higher dimension, first sprouting and then blooming. And all plants and aquatic life become nourishment for higher and more complex life-forms. Water on top of Earth begins the great pyramid of evolving life into Spirit.

In a divination, the message is loud and clear: "Act Now, but watch the forecast." It may also signal a new partner to help your plans, or a new relationship may be developing. The Moon moves Water on Earth and fluids in our body in patterned tides that become critical cycles of life. However, too much Water floods Earth into mud and loss. With careful planning, timing and choice of action, we grow and succeed. Shakespeare wrote:

> *"There is a tide in the affairs of men*
> *Which, taken at the flood, leads on to fortune."*
>
> William Shakespeare, *Julius Caesar*, Act iv, Scene 3

Never neglect the importance of Right Timing, for Wrong Timing can lead to disaster!

Water—Seed of Fire:
Opposites Fire-Up Romance & Ambition!

Water—Seed of Fire

Color the tiny inner bindu circle white,
the inner little triangle red,
the inner crescent bright metallic silver,
and the outer square black

Water—Seed of Fire: Apas & Tejas VAM & RAM

Review

We urge you to review the Element Overview Table #3 for Fire on page 189 and that for Earth on page 104 in preparation for this procedure and the Divination and other applications involved with this compound.

The Tattvic Connection Meditation & Visualization Program #13: Water/Fire
Water—Seed of Fire

Introduction. The Purpose & Function of this Procedure.

Rather than repeating the procedure in its entirety, we are asking you to kindly refer to page 396 for the complete *Tattva Connection Meditation & Visualization Compound Program #7 and make your own adjustments to substitute "**Water**" for "**Earth**" and "**Fire**"* *for "**Water**" in steps 2 (goal statement), 3 (affirmations. (I know that seems redundant, but in the psychic world little things count for a lot.) We are here providing content for Steps 5 (preparing and coloring the yantra card), 9a (yantra card focus), 10a. (experience the compounded elements and 11 (knowing the compounded elements).*

The Program's Variables:

<u>Steps 2. Goal Statement.</u>

Note your need to consider how to express your goals to reflect the particular natures of the two elements in their primary and secondary combination in relation to your physical, emotional, mental, and spiritual well-being, and their functions in divination, magick, and self-growth.

<u>Step 3. Affirmations.</u>

You need to write positive affirmations to accomplish your goals.

<u>Step 5. Preparation.</u>

Preparing the Yantra Card.

It is recommended that you photocopy the illustration on page 446, preferably on heavier paper or card stock, or draw it yourself in exactly the same sizes using a ruler and black pen. If you can manage it, using a drawing compass or a template, draw a tiny ⅛" inch diameter circle in the exact center. Leave the inside of the circle white. This inner circle or point aids your steady focus. It is not essential, but it is helpful. Make the outer square 4" x 4" and the inner **Water Crescent** (horns up) 2¼" wide and centered, the inner **Fire Triangle** ¾" on each side, and the little **Bindu** circle in the exact center should be ⅛" in diameter and have a black line around it and the Triangle but not quite as thick as those around the **Crescent** and the **Square**.

Coloring the Yantra Card.

It will be beneficial for you to color the image as follows: (a) color the tiny inner **Bindu Circle White**; (b) the small **Fire Triangle Bright Red**; (c) the **Water Crescent Metallic Silver** (or White); and (d) the surrounding larger **Square Black.** The outer **Square** and **Water Crescent** are bordered with bold black lines, the **small Fire Triangle** is bordered with a less bold black line, and the tiny inner **Bindu Circle** is bordered with a thinner black line.

Step 9a. Yantra Card Focus.

If you have constructed the tattva yantra card as described, turn on the light and focus it on the card held or positioned comfortably about a foot to a foot and a half in front of you.

If possible, arrange your chair to face the primary tattvic direction: *West* for **Water.** Otherwise—think and feel *West.* (To the extent you feel the secondary element's importance to the operation; you can finish with an acknowledgment of *South* for **Fire.**

Vibrate the name of the two tattvas: **Apas** and **Tejas,** alternating one after the other. Repeat three times.

Chant or hum the tattva element mantras **VAM** and **RAM** (pronounced **VA-UUM** and **RA-UUM),** alternating. Vibrate the mantra as instructed in Step 1, preliminaries. Repeat three times. Later, you can do more but always in groups of three. And feel the mantra vibrate *between the genitals and the navel,* the location of **Svadhisthana** chakra and then *between the navel and the heart,* the location of **Manipura** chakra.

Focus on the small white circle* at the center of the image, and stare at it for as long as you can without blinking. When you can't continue the "burning" feeling any longer, turn off the light, close your eyes, and focus your inner sight on the space in front of your brow chakra (between your eyebrows and on the ridge you can feel just above your nose), and see the small **Red Triangle** in the **Silver Crescent** floating in the space before you and vibrating within the **Black Square.** And, then, you will soon see the tattva image change into the complementary yantra colors of **Green, Black,** and **White.**

Again vibrate the names to the tattvas and chant or hum the mantras three times.

Absorb this yantra image! As you repeat the exercise, often, you will reach a point when you will be able to recall this image at will.

Step 9b. Yantra Visualization.

Alternatively, if you haven't made a **Water/Fire** card, immediately in front of you, visualize the image as described for making the card. See the image gently vibrating. And then the colors will reverse to their complementary yantra colors.

Step 10a. Experiencing Compounded Elemental Water and Elemental Fire.

Feel yourself becoming totally *absorbed** in the image while retaining awareness of the surrounding tattvic blue square. As the tattvic **Red** changes to the complementary yantra **Green** feel *your* **fiery** nature harmonize with the Cosmic **Fire** Tattva, and feel all

impurities in your **Fire** Tattva—all emotional garbage and unconscious psychic attachments—dissipate. The tattvic **Silver Crescent** will change to the complementary yantra
Black (and the larger surrounding Black Square to White) as your Watery nature harmonizes with the Cosmic **Water** Tattva and the impurities of your **Water** tattva dissipate.

> *Becoming absorbed.* Enter into the **full image** and become one with it and
> feel surrounded by it. Moving inward from the outer **Square** become one
> with the **Water** Element, and then move inward to become one with the **Fire**
> Element, and then further in to the **Bindu** to become one with **All.** Now,
> moving outward from the **Bindu** point to the **Fire Triangle** and then to the
> **Water Crescent** and to its outer edge feel the balanced **Water** and **Fire** ele-
> ments in your body become harmonized and purified as they are balanced
> with their **Cosmic Source.**

In particular: feel the **Watery fluid** nature of your **physical** body become ideally
healthy, strong, and energized, free of obstruction and constrictions and any excess

weight. Feel your **Fiery Passionate Self free of imposed** and **irrational extraverted images and competitive ideals.** Be open to **natural enthusiasm** and **passion** in **positive relationships** of **Family** and of **Romance** and **Intimacy.**

Step 11. Knowing Elemental Water compounded with Elemental Fire.

Allow yourself to receive any information or messages from you're experiencing of these Elemental Forces. *In particular: receive information involving your **Physical** and **Emotional** health and strength at both **material** and **astral** levels.* Receive the information without any emotional reaction and know that the knowledge is fully activated within your psyche.

Continue on with the Programs to Conclusion.

DIVINATION GUIDE TO WATER—SEED OF FIRE
Water—Seed of Fire: *Creative Tension—Good or Bad?*

Fire and Water don't mix, yet Fire warms water for bathing and heating, boils water for cooking and cleaning, turns Water into steam for power and high-powered cleansing and sterilization. Water extinguishes out-of-control Fires. Working together, the Intuitive properties of Water and the cognitive faculties of Fire can lead to material success. Romantically, and sexually, "Fire and Ice"—frozen Water—can be an affair of passion or one of disaster. In every relation, there is friction but not necessarily conflict if intelligence is applied to balance emotion with drive.

In a divination, it is more often a warning of dangerous attraction but can be indicative of power if combined with mutual understanding and careful planning to benefit from the attributes of both—neither to drown the fire nor boil away the water. Verify the signal with the Moon's signs.

Water—Seed of Air:
The Moon Rules the Motion of Water

Water—Seed of Air

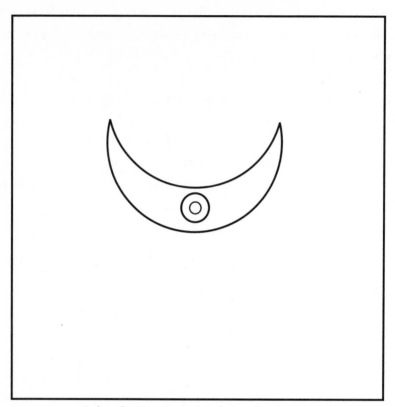

Color the tiny inner bindu circle white,
the inner little circle blue
the inner crescent bright metallic silver,
and the outer square black

Water—Seed of Air: Apas & Vayu VAM & YAM

Review

We urge you to review the Element Overview Table #4 for Air on page 214 and the Element Overview Table #1 for Earth on page 104 in preparation for this procedure and the Divination and other applications involved with this compound.

The Tattvic Connection Meditation & Visualization Program #14: Water/Air
Water—Seed of Air

<u>Introduction. The Purpose & Function of this Procedure.</u>

Rather than repeating the procedure in its entirety, we are asking you to kindly refer to page 396 for the complete *Tattva Connection Meditation & Visualization Compound Program #7 and make your own adjustments to substitute "**Water**" for "**Earth**" and "**Air**"* *for "**Water**" in steps 2 (goal statement), 3 (affirmations. (I know that seems redundant, but in the psychic world little things count for a lot.) We are here providing content for Steps 5 (preparing and coloring the yantra card), 9a (yantra card focus), 10a. (experience the compounded elements and 11 (knowing the compounded elements).*

The Program's Variables:

Steps 2. Goal Statement.

Note your need to consider how to express your goals to reflect the particular natures of the two elements in their primary and secondary combination in relation to your physical, emotional, mental and spiritual well-being, and their functions in divination, magick, and self-growth.

Step 3. Affirmations.

You need to write positive affirmations to accomplish your goals.

Step 5. Preparation.

Preparing the Yantra Card.

It is recommended that you photocopy the illustration on page 451, preferably on heavier paper or card stock, or draw it yourself in exactly the same sizes using a ruler and black pen. If you can manage it, using a drawing compass or a template, draw a tiny ⅛" inch diameter circle in the exact center. Leave the inside of the circle white. This inner circle or point aids your steady focus. It is not essential, but it is helpful. Make the outer square 4" x 4" and the inner **Water Crescent** (horns up) 2¼" wide and centered, the inner **Air Circle** ⅝" in diameter, and the little **Bindu** circle in the exact center should be ⅛" in diameter and have a black line around it and the **Circle** but not quite as thick as those around the **Crescent** and the **Square.**

Coloring the Yantra Card.

It will be beneficial for you to color the image as follows: (a) color the tiny inner **Bindu Circle White**; (b) the small **Blue Circle Bright Blue ;** (c) the **Water Crescent Metallic Silver** (or White); and (d) the surrounding larger square **Black.** The **square** and **crescent** are bordered with bold black lines, the small **Blue Circle** is bordered with a less bold black line, and the tiny inner **circle** is bordered with a thinner black line.

Step 9a. Yantra Card Focus.

If you have constructed the tattva yantra card as described, turn on the light and focus it on the card held or positioned comfortably about a foot to a foot and a half in front of you.

If possible, arrange your chair to face the primary tattvic direction: *West* for **Water**. Otherwise—think and feel *West*. (To the extent you feel the secondary element's importance to the operation, you can finish with an acknowledgment of *East* for **Air**.

Vibrate the name of the two tattvas: **Apas** and **Vayu**, alternating one after the other. Repeat three times.

Chant or hum the tattva element mantras **VAM** and **YAM** (pronounced **VA-UUM** and **YA-UUM),** alternating. Vibrate the mantra as instructed in Step 1, preliminaries. Repeat three times. Later, you can do more but always in groups of three. And feel the mantra vibrate *between the genitals and the navel,* the location of **Svadhisthana** chakra and then *over the heart,* the location of **Anahata** chakra.

Focus on the small white circle* at the center of the image, and stare at it for as long as you can without blinking. When you can't continue the "burning" feeling any longer, turn off the light, close your eyes and focus your inner sight on the space in front of your brow chakra (between your eye brows and on the ridge you can feel just above your nose), and see the small **Blue Circle** in the **Silver Crescent** floating in the space before you and vibrating within the **Black Square**. And, then, you will soon see the tattva image change into the complementary yantra colors of **Orange**, **Black**, and **White**.

Again vibrate the names to the tattvas and chant or hum the mantras three times.

Absorb this yantra image! As you repeat the exercise, often, you will reach a point when you will be able to recall this image at will.

Step 9b. Yantra Visualization.

Alternatively, if you haven't made a **Water/Air** card, immediately in front of you, visualize the image as described for making the card. See the image gently vibrating. And then the colors will reverse to their complementary yantra colors.

Step 10a. Experiencing Compounded Elemental Water and Elemental Air.

Feel yourself becoming totally *absorbed** in the image while retaining awareness of the surrounding tattvic blue square. As the tattvic **Blue** changes to the complementary yantra **Orange** feel *your* **Airy** nature harmonize with the Cosmic **Air** Tattva, and feel all impurities in your **Air** Tattva—all emotional garbage and unconscious psychic attachments—dissipate. The tattvic **Silver Crescent** will change to the complementary yantra **Black** (and the larger surrounding Black Square to White) as your Watery nature harmonizes with the Cosmic **Water** Tattva and the impurities of your **Water** tattva dissipate.

> **Becoming absorbed.* Enter into the **full image** and become one with it and feel surrounded by it. Moving inward from the outer **Square** become one with the **Water** Element, and then move inward to become one with the **Air** Element, and then further in to the **Bindu** to become one with **All.** Now, moving outward from the **Bindu** point to the **Air Circle** and then to the **Water Crescent** and to its outer edge feel the balanced **Water** and **Air** elements in your body become harmonized and purified as they are balanced with their **Cosmic Source.**

In particular: feel the **Watery fluid** nature of your **physical** body become ideally healthy, strong, and energized, free of obstruction and constrictions and any excess weight. Feel your **Mental Self free of imposed** and often **irrational & authoritative ideas.** Be open **to new intellectual pleasures** and **emotional enjoyment** of **debate** and **discovery,** and the satisfaction of **compassion** and **service** to **Family** and **Community.**

Step 11. Knowing Elemental Water compounded with Elemental Air.

Allow yourself to receive any information or messages from your experiencing of these Elemental Forces. *In particular: receive information involving your **Physical** and **Mental** health & strength at both **material** and **higher astral & mental** levels.* Receive the information without any emotional reaction and know that the knowledge is fully activated within your psyche.

Continue on with the Programs to Conclusion.

DIVINATION GUIDE TO WATER—SEED OF AIR
Water—Seed of Air: *Effervescence or Dissipation?*

The crescent moon symbolizes a cup filled with bubbly liquid—perhaps champagne? Air constantly rises up, so Champagne will rapidly lose its fizz, so act quickly before bubbles burst and liquid things go flat. Water symbolizes relationships and fantasy, while Air represents connections and enthusiasm: exercise care and discretion so that too much excitement doesn't cause things to bubble over and leave the relationship high and dry, and your glass empty.

In a divination, this signals a time to make social contacts while expressing your natural fun and animated self. But, remember: not everyone is the same so don't let your own enthusiasm overcome that rational basis for a business relationship, or blind you to another's needs in a romantic or family relationship. In everything involving the essence of Water, refer to the Moon for understanding and timing. It's the Moon that makes the tides.

Water—Seed of Ether:
Feeling, Guided by Intuition

Water—Seed of Ether

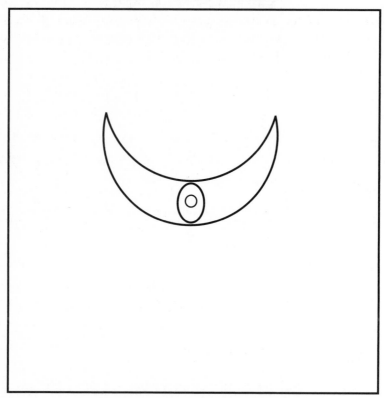

Color the tiny inner bindu circle white,
the inner little oval indigo,
the inner crescent bright metallic silver,
and the outer square black

Water—Seed of Ether: Apas & Akasha VAM & HAM

Review

We urge you to review the Element Overview Table #5 for Ether on page 272 and that for Earth on page 104 in preparation for this procedure and the Divination and other applications involved with this compound.

The Tattvic Connection Meditation & Visualization Program #15: Water/Ether
Water—Seed of Ether

Introduction. The Purpose & Function of this Procedure.

Rather than repeating the procedure in its entirety, we are asking you to kindly refer to page 396 for the complete *Tattva Connection Meditation & Visualization Compound Program #7 and make your own adjustments to substitute "**Water**" for "**Earth**" and "**Ether**" for "**Water**" in steps 2 (goal statement), 3 (affirmations. (I know that seems redundant, but in the psychic world little things count for a lot.) We are here providing content for Steps 5 (preparing and coloring the yantra card), 9a (yantra card focus), 10a. (experience the compounded elements and 11 (knowing the compounded elements).*

The Program's Variables:

Steps 2. Goal Statement.

Note your need to consider how to express your goals to reflect the particular natures of the two elements in their primary and secondary combination in relation to your physical, emotional, mental and spiritual well-being, and their functions in divination, magick, and self-growth.

Step 3. Affirmations.

You need to write positive affirmations to accomplish your goals.

Step 5. Preparation.

Preparing the Yantra Card.

It is recommended that you photocopy the illustration on page 455, preferably on heavier paper or card stock, or draw it yourself in exactly the same sizes using a ruler and black pen. If you can manage it, using a drawing compass or a template, draw a tiny ⅛" inch diameter circle in the exact center. Leave the inside of the circle white. This inner circle or point aids your steady focus. It is not essential, but it is helpful. Make the outer square 4" x 4" and the inner **Water Crescent** (horns up) 2¼"wide and centered, the inner **Ether Egg** ⁷⁄₁₆" wide and ¹¹⁄₁₆" tall, and the little **Bindu** circle in the exact center should be ⅛" in diameter and have a black line around it and the **Egg** but not quite as thick as those around the **Crescent** and the **Square**.

Coloring the Yantra Card.

It will be beneficial for you to color the image as follows: (a) color the tiny inner **Bindu Circle White**; (b) the small **Egg Indigo** ; (c) the **Water Crescent Metallic Silver** (or White); and (d) the surrounding larger square lack. The square and crescent are bordered with bold black lines, the small Indigo Egg is bordered with a less bold black line, and the tiny inner circle is bordered with a thinner black line.

Step 9a. Yantra Card Focus.

If you have constructed the tattva yantra card as described, turn on the light and focus it on the card held or positioned comfortably about a foot to a foot and a half in front of you.

If possible, arrange your chair to face the primary tattvic direction: *West* for **Water**. Otherwise—think and feel *West*. (To the extent you feel the secondary element's importance to the operation, you can finish with an acknowledgment of *Skyward* for **Ether.**

Vibrate the name of the two tattvas: *Apas* and *Akasha*, alternating one after the other. Repeat three times.

Chant or hum the tattva element mantras *VAM* and *HAM* (pronounced *VA-UUM* and *HA-UUM),* alternating. Vibrate the mantra as instructed in Step 1, preliminaries. Repeat three times. Later, you can do more but always in groups of three, and feel the mantra vibrate *between the genitals and the navel,* the location of **Svadhisthana** chakra and then *at the Throat,* the location of **Vishuddha** chakra.

Focus on the small white circle* at the center of the image, and stare at it for as long as you can without blinking. When you can't continue the "burning" feeling any longer, turn off the light, close your eyes and focus your inner sight on the space in front of your brow chakra (between your eye brows and on the ridge you can feel just above your nose), and see the small **Indigo Egg** in the **Silver Crescent** floating in the space before you and vibrating within the **Black Square**. And, then, you will soon see the tattva image change into the complementary yantra colors.

Again vibrate the names to the tattvas and chant or hum the mantras three times.

Absorb this yantra image! As you repeat the exercise, often, you will reach a point when you will be able to recall this image at will.

Step 9b. Yantra Visualization.

Alternatively, if you haven't made a **Water/Ether** card, immediately in front of you, visualize the image as described for making the card. See the image gently vibrating. And then the colors will reverse to their complementary yantra colors.

Step 9b. Yantra Visualization.

Alternatively, if you haven't made a **Water/Ether** card, immediately in front of you, visualize the image as described for making the card. See the image gently vibrating. And then the colors will reverse to their complementary yantra colors.

Step 10a. Experiencing Compounded Elemental Water and Elemental Ether.

Feel yourself becoming totally *absorbed** in the image while retaining awareness of the surrounding tattvic blue square. As the tattvic **Indigo** changes to the complementary yantra **Yellow/Orange** feel *your* **Ether** nature harmonize with the Cosmic **Air** Tattva, and feel all impurities in your **Ether** Tattva—all emotional garbage and unconscious psychic attachments—dissipate. The tattvic **Silver Crescent** will change to the complementary yantra **Black** (and the larger surrounding Black Square to White) as your Watery nature harmonizes with the Cosmic **Water** Tattva and the impurities of your **Water** tattva dissipate.

> **Becoming absorbed.* Enter into the **full image** and become one with it and feel surrounded by it. Moving inward from the outer **Square** become one with the **Water** Element, and then move inward to become one with the **Ether** Element, and then further in to the **Bindu** to become one with **All.** Now, moving outward from the **Bindu** point to the **Ether Egg** and then to the **Water Crescent** and to its outer edge feel the balanced **Water** and **Air** elements in your body become harmonized and purified as they are balanced with their **Cosmic Source.**

In particular: feel the **Water** and **Ether** nature of your physical body become free of adverse thoughts and feelings. Feel your body becoming ideally healthy, strong, and energized. See your body in perfect health, free of any excess weight, free of pain and disfigurement, free of illness, and fully energized.

Step 11. Knowing Elemental Water compounded with Elemental Ether.

Allow yourself to receive any information or messages from you're experiencing of these Elemental Forces. *In particular: receive information involving your Physical and Emotional health and strength at both material and astral levels.* Receive the information without any emotional reaction.

Continue on with the Programs to Conclusion.

precedes Ether, suggesting that flexibility as well as intuition and inspiration will lead to innovation and possibly new sources of wealth.

In a divination, this signals the value of synergy in relationships (Water) for the discovery and development of limitless opportunities (Ether—Space)—but without the material limitations imposed by the cup holding the water Ether's innovations could become freely accessed without benefit to the creator. Common sense and good business practices are necessary in even the most spiritually inspired enterprise. Yes, "Reach for the Moon," but let the "Moon be your Guide in action and timing."

CHAPTER 12

Self-Hypnosis & Clairvoyance: The Journey Inward & Beyond

Go to your bosom; Knock there, and ask your heart what it doth know.
William Shakespeare, *Measure for Measure*

The Power of Together

When equipped with self-hypnosis and clairvoyance, you have at your command two of the most powerful forces known. Although each can be used separately to gain new knowledge and power, *when used together they can generate an interactive state of personal empowerment that is unparalleled in quality and scope.*

Achieving Your Highest Personal Goals

Fortunately, the potential for self-hypnosis and clairvoyance exists in everyone, but it's up to you to develop that potential and apply it as needed. Through the combined powers of self-hypnosis and clairvoyance, you can achieve your highest personal goals and reach advanced levels of personal growth available through no other means. Best of all, reaching that state of personal empowerment is at this moment within your reach. It begins with a self-directed journey inward through which you will discover the most highly advanced personal hypnotist and the best personal clairvoyant—they are each an essential part of your innermost self. You now can embrace them as your personal empowerment specialists. They welcome your engagement and they challenge you to uncover their powers and apply them to enrich your life as never before. As specialized growth partners, they are poised to accompany you step-by-step on your journey of discovery and self-empowerment.

Inner Potentials of Self-Hypnosis & Clairvoyance Used Together

When used to generate clairvoyance awareness, self-hypnosis spontaneously sets into motion the inner potentials related to it. Given that interaction, we experience a unified state of self-empowerment in which we can take control and make important changes.

- We can identify dormant growth potentials and find ways of developing them.
- We can activate creativity, accelerate learning, and generate a powerful state of adequacy and self worth.
- We can encounter crisis situations and efficiently resolve them.
- We can identify blockages to our growth and successfully dismantle them.
- We can identify the best options for success and fulfillment in complex social and career situations.

These are only a few of the possibilities available to us when we are equipped with the unification of power available to us through clairvoyance and self-hypnosis.

The Unification of Power

The Unification of Power is a self-hypnosis program designed to activate clairvoyance and the subconscious powers related to it. Developed in our labs at Athens State University, the program is a goal-directed approach that is both flexible and multi-functional. It introduces the Knee Press Procedure to induce a trance state conducive to clairvoyance. Once a successful trance state has been achieved, the program introduces the Blue Moon Technique which is used as an imagery mechanism with a three-fold function: 1) to generate during hypnosis a state of consciousness that's conducive to both spontaneous and induced clairvoyance; 2) specifically target clairvoyance upon designated goals; and 3) exercise our clairvoyant faculties in ways that promote their continued development. The program includes a post-hypnotic cue that can be used on demand to re-activate certain designated effects of the program as needed.

Our combined use of the Knee Press Procedure and the Blue Moon Technique is based on rigorously controlled laboratory research in which various trance induction procedures were explored to determine their conduciveness to clairvoyance. From among the various induction approaches investigated, including eye fixation, progressive relaxation, hand levitation, and EM/RC (eye movement/reverse counting), the Knee-press Procedure emerged as the most effective when applied to promote clairvoyance. The clairvoyant tasks investigated included the use of hypnosis to identify concealed objects, containers of contaminated liquid placed among other identical containers, cards drawn from a deck, and photos concealed in envelopes.

The Blue Moon Technique

The Blue Moon Technique used during the trance state is the centerpiece of this program. As a clairvoyant mechanism specifically designed for use in this program, it utilizes images of a full blue moon upon which appears information of clairvoyant significance. In our preliminary lab studies designed to determine the relevance of color imagery, a moon of blue consistently emerged as the most effective in activating clairvoyance.

Although the Blue Moon Technique has wide ranging applications, it is especially useful as a problem-solving strategy. It can clairvoyantly identify relevant factors and organize them in ways that lead to solutions. At the same time, it can provide spontaneous enlightenment relevant to an endless range of concerns including relationships, career opportunities, health and fitness, and financial planning, to list but a few.

The Unification of Power Self-hypnosis Program

Here's the Unification of Power procedure which requires approximately 45 minutes in a comfortable setting free of distractions:

Step 1. Preliminaries. Settle back into a comfortable seated position with legs uncrossed and your hands resting upon your thighs.

Step 2. Goal Designation. Designate your clairvoyant goal(s), including general and/or specific. Goals including the discovery of lost objects, the viewing of concealed documents, the solution to complex problems, and the development of your clairvoyant ability (to list but a few) are all within the scope of this program.

Step 3. Cognitive Clearing. With your eyes closed, clear you mind of active thought by visualizing your thoughts as having wings, soaring upward and away into the distance. Take plenty of time for your mind to become clear like a blue sky, and then silently affirm,

I am now free of all active thought.

Note the relaxation that accompanies this process.

Step 4. The Knee Press. With your mind now clear, bring your knees together and gently press them against each other. Hold the press position as you sense tension building above and below your knees. Next, relax your knees and note the tension giving way to relaxation, first in your knees and then spreading into your legs, both above and below your knees. Take a few moments for your knees and legs to become fully relaxed, and then press your knees together even more firmly and for a longer period than before as you note the tension again building above and below your knees. Continue to hold the knee-press position until the tension seems to have reached its peak, and then, as before, slowly relax your knees and note the relaxation spreading above your knees into your thighs and hips and below your knees right into your ankles and feet. With your knees and legs relaxed, notice the relaxation spreading deeper and deeper, from your hips into the tips of your toes. Finally, bring your knees together once again and hold the position until the tension builds even higher than before. Hold that position and tense the muscles in your hips and abdomen to intensify the pressure between your knees. Hold that tense position until it seems to have reached it highest level, then very slowly relax the pressure between your knees. Once your knees are fully relaxed, you will note the relaxation spreading upward and downward from your knees to permeate your full body with very deep relaxation.

Step 5. Successful Hypnosis. As you remain deeply relaxed, you are now prepared to enter successful hypnosis. With your eyes closed, begin by counting slowly downward from ten to one with interspersed suggestions of going deeper and deeper. Affirm in your own words, either silently or audibly, that as you count downward you will become even more fully relaxed and responsive to each of your suggestions. Further affirm that on the count of one, you will enter a state of successful hypnosis whereupon you will be fully receptive to clairvoyant enlightenment that unfolds during the trance state. Upon the count of one, you can further deepen hypnosis, should you decide to do so, through relaxing imagery, such as a tranquil moonlit lake with a white sail drifting slowly at a distance or a leisurely stroll through a park in the calming shadows of trees or along a pathway beside a gentle stream. At this stage, imagery of oneself slowly descending a stairway accompanied by suggestions of going deeper into hypnosis with each step can be used if needed to further deepen the trance state.

Step 6. The Blue Moon Technique. As you remain in a state of successful hypnosis, visualize a blue moon as a clairvoyant sphere with power to activate your clairvoyant potentials. Take plenty of time for the moon to appear as a bright blue image. Sense the wondrous serenity that accompanies the emergence of the bright blue sphere. Think of it as your connection to all that exists, including not only the world around you but the most distant reaches to the universe. Let the blue moon become a force that activates your highest clairvoyant potentials. As you continue to focus on the moon, affirm:

All that I need to know is now available to me. I am empowered to use that knowledge to accelerate my growth and reach my highest goals.

Note the building sense of connection to the clairvoyant powers within and your capacity to use them at will. It's at this stage that clairvoyant enlightenment typically unfolds, often as images projected upon the blue moon.

Step 7. Post Hypnotic Cue. Upon concluding the Blue Moon Technique, affirm in your own words that by simply visualizing the blue moon, you can at any time activate your subconscious clairvoyant capacities to expand awareness and provide clairvoyant insight as needed.

Step 8. Conclusion. Conclude the experience by again visualizing the blue moon and affirming its empowering effects in promoting clairvoyance and the activating your clairvoyant faculties.

Step 9. Journaling. Keep a hypnosis journal and record in it a detailed account of each hypnosis session, including the clairvoyant information that emerged during hypnosis. Keep a record of your post-hypnosis experiences that suggest clairvoyant relevance.

The Unification of Power program is a highly flexible procedure which can be adapted to meet your personal preferences, both for entering hypnosis and deepening the trance state. Such techniques as reverse counting, finger anesthesia, hand levitation, and appropriate imagery can be readily incorporated into the procedure to promote induction and facilitate deepening of the trance state.

This program assumes the existence of subconscious clairvoyant faculties that are relevant to an extensive range of personal goals. The focusing of the program on the activation and development of clairvoyance does not in any way inhibit its direct application to highly specific personal goals.

When we first began our pioneering research related to the Unification of Power program in the 1970s and '80s at Athens State University, the classic song, Blue Moon,* was wildly popular. In the song's lovely lyrics, the personification of the blue moon is described as the appearance of the seeker of perfect love* standing alone and seen by the object of affection, followed by the sudden appearance of the image of the beloved person suggested excellent application of moon imagery as a clairvoyant technique. Students who participated in the development of the program connected instantly to our incorporation of the blue moon into the program. They, in fact, often left the lab singing the ballad, *Blue Moon*. Once developed, the Blue Moon Technique was so effective and appealing to students of various majors that they began using it for a variety of their personal goals, from finding love to improving their GPA. Although those early years proved to be an opportune time for studying the unexplained, our more recent research, while validating those pioneering efforts, offers totally new evidence that there is no better time than *now* to discover the power of the paranormal!

> *Written in 1934 by Richard Rogers and Lorenz Hart, the song was recorded by a number of artists over the next eighty years, including Billie Holiday, Vaughan Monroe, Nat King Cole, Dizzie Gillespie, Elvis Presley, Julie London, Louis Armstrong, The Ventures, Jo Stafford, Harpo Marx, Frank Sinatra, Mel Tormé, Dean Martin, Tony Bennett with Ella Fitzgerald, Bob Dylan, The Supremes, and others, and was featured in several films—*Unfortunately,*

copyright law prevents us from quoting the exact lyrics but you can readily find them online searching for "Blue Moon Lyrics."

The Blue Moon Technique as applied during hypnosis is highly flexible and can be easily modified if preferred. For instance, the blue moon can be of any preferred size or brightness. It can be positioned as a rising moon or anywhere else in the sky to facilitate easy viewing. If preferred, the moon can be situated within a frame to facilitate viewing. Among additional possibilities is the substitution of other geometric designs for the blue moon. Some of our subjects found that the imagery of a triangle with a bright blue interior could promote awareness of spiritual realities, including the presence of ministering guides. In another instance of the technique's flexibility, a scuba diver substituted imagery of a blue underwater vista as a screen upon which clairvoyant information could be easily depicted. For her, imagery of the underwater vista provided a panoramic view with greater movement and detail than the fixed moon. In one instance, she observed unfolding upon the screen a clear image of her misplaced Ph.D. diploma that had fallen from its hanging onto the floor behind an office bookcase. A search the next day confirmed the accuracy of the image.

The Blue Sapphire

Further illustrating the flexibility of the Blue Moon Technique is the use of a tangible object rather than imagery of the blue moon as a post-hypnotic cue. For instance, stroking a blue sapphire gemstone was among the preferred post-hypnotic cues for college students who participated in our research. They, in fact, concluded that simply wearing a blue gemstone ring or pendant increased their receptiveness to clairvoyance. In their opinion, the blue sapphire was a convenient, tangible representation of the blue moon and the empowering clairvoyant nature of the color blue. For them, simply stroking the blue gemstone when worn as a pendant or ring facilitated imagery of blue which they considered relevant to the initiation of clairvoyance. In one unusual account of this application, a psychology doctoral student with practice in the Unification of Power program found that stroking her blue sapphire ring as a post-hypnotic cue during course examinations seemed to significantly improve her test performance. Following graduation, she attributed her outstanding performance on a stringent professional licensure examination to her frequent stroking of the gem during the testing session. Stroking the gem, by her account, activated "subconscious clairvoyant retrieval" of information relevant to the examination.

Past-life Experiences

The Unification of Power program has demonstrated a remarkable capacity to identify past-life experiences with important relevance to present-life behavior. Rather than regressing to the past-life, the program simply uncovers past-life experiences as present subconscious realities and projects them upon the blue screen., Although the capacity of clairvoyance to uncover subconscious realities of past-life origin may seem to some an excessive codicil to the conventional definition of the phenomenon, it nevertheless retains the basic conceptual structure of clairvoyance. At the same time, *it takes clairvoyance to a totally new level of relevance:* A unification of past-life realities, present-life conditions, and self-empowering applications.

Applications in Advancing Technology

In the scientific research and development setting, the Unification of Power has shown unusual effectiveness when applied toward advancing technology related to space exploration. Identifying relevant concepts, structuring equipment testing procedures, diagnosing technical malfunctions, and identifying optimal intervention measures are all within the scope of that application. In a remarkable example of clairvoyance related to space exploration, an existing malfunction in a critical system was clairvoyantly identified prior to a flight and in advance of any objective evidence of the malfunction. The engineer, a technical advisor in our development of the Unification of Power program, concluded that clairvoyant insight related to the space program may have been instrumental in not only promoting the program but saving lives as well.

Any situation of special concern at the moment is usually receptive to this program. It can identify causative factors underlying problem relationships and personal conflicts. Complementing that function, the program almost always suggests appropriate coping options. Perhaps even more importantly, the program builds feelings of adequacy and strong expectations of success, both of which are intrinsically empowering in almost any challenging life situation.

Self-hypnosis: The Liberation of Perception

We experience our lives within a perceived field of personal existence. That field, which is unique to each of us, consists of both sensory and extrasensory perception. We now know that both sensory and extrasensory experiences interact within that field to facilitate greater awareness and accelerate our personal growth. Aside from the potential of hypnosis to directly facilitate clairvoyance and other forms of ESP, there is strong evidence that the limits of our perceptual field can be deliberately expanded through self-hypnosis. This concept called "the liberation of perception" holds that, with the removal of conventionally prescribed limits for perception, the possibilities for both sensory and extrasensory perception are significantly expanded.

Expanding Awareness

The Liberation of Perception Program was specifically designed and developed in our labs at Athens State University to expand the perceptual field of awareness through the liberation of sensory and extrasensory perception. Our preliminary studies showed that extrasensory perception, including clairvoyance, is almost always accompanied by a liberated state of expanded sensory awareness. Following controlled practice of the step-by-step program, our subjects showed a dramatic increase in their performance on laboratory tasks designed to measure not only clairvoyance but telepathy and precognition as well. Even more remarkably, similar improvements were noted in their performance on tasks related to psychokinesis (PK) and out-of-body experiences (OBEs). Not unlike ESP, PK, and OBEs, significant improvements were also noted among our research participants on experiments designed to measure accuracy and relevance on sensory perception exercises following their participation in the program. For instance, dramatic improvements were noted in their attention to detail as well as recall related to their viewings of pictures, blueprints, and tangible objects, including historic artifacts.

The Liberation of Perception Program

The Liberation of Perception is a self-hypnosis program developed in our labs for a three-fold purpose: (1) Transcend the ordinary, conventional limits for sensory perception, (2) increase the capacity for extrasensory perception, and (3) promote an expansive state of personal empowerment. The program is based on the premise that the sensory as well as extrasensory capacities existing in everyone can be liberated in ways that expand their limits and fortify their empowerment functions. Throughout our development of this program, it became increasingly clear that the old, self-imposed limits of human experience no longer apply. We can now reach far beyond them through the liberation of our sensory capacities and the consequent extension of our extrasensory faculties.

Occurring throughout our development of this program were instances in which our participants experienced clairvoyant awareness related to not only the physical realm but the non-physical realm as well. Even more interestingly, they often experienced the merging of the two realms. Many of our participants, for instance, experienced the presence of a spirit guide who, according to them, offered both comfort and support, particularly during their clairvoyant viewing of distressful situations. Many of them likewise observed distant colorful planes of power from which they drew specialized energy and power related to personal concerns, including stressful life situations.

Self-Empowerment through Psychic Empowerment Accomplishments

Here are a few examples of the program's empowering possibilities:

- It can expand our awareness of our natural surroundings and ways of interacting with them to bring forth desired change.
- It can be an effective stress management technique that includes observations of tranquil, natural settings.
- It can promote mental, physical, and spiritual enlightenment.
- It can be a source of inspirational and creative ideas related to art, music, science, and writing, to list but a few.
- It can be an effective investigative strategy for locating missing persons and animals.
- It can identify potentially dangerous conditions in the work setting.
- It can be a source of information regarding investment options.
- It can provide information relevant to academic and career planning.
- As an espionage strategy, it can provide direct observations of covert conditions, sensitive documents, and classified research activities.
- It can gather evidence related to crime.
- It can be a source of information regarding impending danger.
- It can investigate unsolved mysteries and unexplained phenomena.
- In its most advanced form, it can include observations of realities unavailable for viewing by other means, such as overhead viewings of our universe.
- It can accelerate development of other mental faculties, including telepathy, precognition, PK, and astral projection.

Included in this program is a modified version of the so-called *Finger Interlock Technique*. The technique as adapted for use in this procedure is multi-functional in its capacity not only to promote induction of the successful trance state but to envelop the individual during self-hypnosis in a protective shield called the *Shield of Power* that extends far beyond the physical body. One view of that shield holds that it reaches to infinity as an extension of the life force that characterizes our existence.

A Protective Shield

There is substantial evidence that, once we are enveloped in the Shield of Power through self-hypnosis, we become empowered not only to experience distant realities, but to intervene in ways that bring forth needed change. That possibility suggests a near-unlimited range of possibilities, including both personal and global empowerment. It would seem to follow that activating the Shield of Power could be among the best ways of developing our psychokinetic potentials. Here's the program.

The Shield of Power Program

Step 1. Preliminaries. Set aside approximately 45 minutes for the program which requires a comfortable, quiet setting free of distractions or interruptions.

Step 2. Goals. Clarify your self-hypnosis goals and write them down. Your goals may range from simply experiencing a liberated state of sensory perception to the extrasensory awareness of distant realities through self-hypnosis. Your goals can include interactions with both physical and non-physical realms.

Step 3. Sensory Perception. Take a few moments to view a tangible object, such as a picture, painting, or article of jewelry. Note its identifying characteristics, and then, with your eyes closed, form a detailed mental picture of the object. Open your eyes and again view the object. Check the accuracy of your mental picture. Repeat the procedure and note the improvements in your ability to form an accurate mental picture of the object.

Step 3. Energy Infusion Exercise. Following the sensory perception exercise, settle back into a comfortable seated or reclining position and with your eyes closed and legs uncrossed, rest your hands, palm sides upward, in your lap. Notice the relaxation in your hands spreading upward into your arms, shoulders, and throughout your full body. Form a mental picture of a distant dimension of energy sending forth empowering beams of bright energy entering your palms and from there, fully infusing your body. Affirm:

I am fully infused with energy and power.

Step 4. Self-hypnosis through Finger-tip Engagement. Bring the fingertips of your hands together to generate a state of energy balance and attunement throughout your full body. As your sense of physical balance and attunement spreads, slowly relax your hands and allow them to return to a position of rest. Affirm in your own words your intent to enter successful hypnosis by counting slowly downward from ten. Further affirm that upon the count of one you will be in a successful state of hypnosis in which your field of perceptual awareness is expanded and liberated. You can increase the effectiveness of reverse counting by interspersing suggestions such as "going deeper" and "becoming more and more relaxed." Upon the count of one, affirm in your own words that you are now in a state of successful hypnosis. Further affirm that you are in full charge of the experience and can exit it at will.

Step 4. Liberated Awareness. Upon reaching successful hypnosis, you can use the so-called Finger Interlock to generate a *Shield of Power* that is without limits. To form the Finger Interlock and generate the Shield of Power, bring together the tips of your thumb and middle finger of each hand to form two circles, and then bring your hands together to form interlocking circles. While holding the Finger Interlock position, note the progressive infusion of power. Sense yourself at the center of the vast perceptual field of power as you affirm:

> *My sensory and extrasensory potentials are now fully activated. I am now empowered to experience distant realities, whether tangible or intangible, sensory or extrasensory. All that I need to know is now available to me. Nothing is beyond my reach.*

Step 5. Perception Without Limits. As perceptual awareness unfolds, center your attention upon the emerging details, such as actions, persons, objects, and settings. Give special attention to specific aspects of the experience that command your attention. Note your impressions and emotions that accompany the experience. It is at this step that clairvoyant insight related to spatially distant conditions often unfolds. Also common at this stage is the appearance of distant planes or dimensions of power as well as the emergence of helping entities or ministering guides.

Step 6. Conclusion. Conclude the trance state by counting slowly from one to five. Upon the count of five, open your eyes and affirm either audibly or silently that you are now empowered with the knowledge and other resources you need at the moment.

Step 7. Post-hypnosis Review. Review the experience and record it in your journal, paying special attention to features that stand out as distinctly different from others. That phenomenon, called *perceptual distinctiveness*, is often the key to successful goal achievement.

The insight gained through this program can unleash the potentials required to achieve a wide range of personal goals. Aside from its capacity to expand our sphere of both sensory and extrasensory experience, it can connect us to higher sources of power, such as ministering guides as well as advanced planes or dimension of power that invite our interaction. Given the expansive insight available to us through this program, we become empowered not only to advance our own personal growth beyond our old perceptual limits, but to contribute to the development of others as well. Here are a few anecdotal reports of university students who participated in our liberation of perception research program:

An Elementary Education Major, female, age 21, Recovery of Lost Ring:

"I was skeptical from the start regarding the concept of *perceptual liberation*. Nevertheless, I decided to volunteer for the study. Following a single session, I became a staunch believer. During the first session, I viewed a familiar outdoor campus area with a bench where I often studied. I saw under the bench a squirrel scurrying about and occasionally nibbling at a ring he held in his paws. Although I did not recognize the ring, I recalled having lost a class ring several weeks before. Following the session, I immediately searched under the bench and found the ring partially hidden in the grass. I continue to regularly practice the program which has been the source of several clairvoyant experiences, including the identification of a teaching opportunity in an area elementary school."

A Criminal Justice Major, male, age 19, Extended Sensory Awareness & ESP in Criminal Investigations:

"My experience as a volunteer research participant expanded my capacity for perceptual detail, a characteristic that's important to my field of career interest. I learned through the program to give special attention to even minor details in situations involving criminal investigations. Aside from that, my participation in the program convinced me that extrasensory awareness is often a concomitant to extended sensory awareness. I'm now fully convinced that a criminal investigation effort is minimized when we arbitrarily eliminate the possibility of the liberation of perception, whether sensory and extrasensory."

A Physics Major, female, age 21, Extended Perception & Science Discoveries:.

"Science is the story of my life. My interest in science, especially physics, reaches into my earliest childhood. In fact, my earliest memory is that of dismantling a mechanical toy to analyze how it worked. When I volunteered for Dr. Slate's research project, I thought it would be far-removed from my interest in physics. But I soon discovered that the liberation of perception is critical to science. My participation led directly to an explanation of several unexplained observations in physics. It suggested ways of not only validating existing concepts, but discovering totally new ones as well. I consider this program to be a major breakthrough because of its relevance to scientific research. I think I've convinced one of my physics professors to experiment with it."

An Art Major, female, age 24, Extended Perception & Artistic Creativity:

"As an art major, developing my creativity potentials is essential to career success. The liberation of perception concept unlocks a treasure of creative ideas, techniques, and applications. Practicing the Liberation of Perception Program uncovered a wealth of creative ideas, techniques, and applications. It equipped me with a new level of insight and attentiveness to detail that is critical to my artistic expressions. My art professor noted a marked improvement in my art and what he called, "a dramatic twist in artistic expression" following my participation in the program.

Opening New Doors to Knowledge, New Opportunities for Growth

Self-hypnosis and clairvoyance—they go hand in hand with each contributing to the other. They open not only new doors to knowledge; they offer new opportunities for growth unavailable through any other source. Best of all, they are at this moment available to everyone. Through them, you can unveil new dimensions of power that will enrich your life, often in an instant. You not only have the potential, you now have the power to use it to its fullest.

ADDENDUM #12 TO CHAPTER 12
Microcosm to Macrocosm & Macrocosm to Microcosm

The Tattvic Connection—
Meditation & Visualization Programs #16 to #20

Fire—And its Compounds

Fire—the Element of Transformation

Each Step in Human Evolution as seen from the material level was marked by Man learning to control and use the primal physical elements in historical sequence.

With Earth, we learned to harvest natural bounty, and then to dig and shape dirt, and then to build with dirt and stone. The beginnings of agriculture came as we organized natural growth into plots and gardens—weeding out the unwanted plants to concentrate desirable plants conveniently in relation to "home."

With Water, we learned to wash and clean, and to locate "home" near reliable sources of water: permanent creeks, rivers, ponds, lakes, and—best of all and seemingly most miraculous—bubbling springs. At some point we learned that we could bring water to our garden plots and improve their growth.

But, with learning to control Fire—first by grabbing a burning "torch" from fire ignited by lightning and then always to keep a tribal *sacred* fire and a "home fire burning" we learned to boil water and then to cook with it. Suddenly, a *technology was born* when someone discovered that rubbing two pieces of flint together produced sparks that could ignite tinder, and then someone else discovered that rapidly rubbing two sticks together in the presence of tinder could also ignite fire. Now people could travel away from home and always have access to this powerful technology.

The Birth of Civilization

It was with the control of Fire, that what we call "civilization" was born. This was the step with which Man asserted control over his own destiny.

Still, we are only looking at the physical forms of the Elements. It's the *ASTRAL* form where these elemental powers begin the process of manifestation and physical form. It was at the astral level of consciousness that humans developed the ideas that brought the primal elements under control—from digging in the Earth to irrigating the garden to boiling the water for cooking. All that we call "Creation" started somewhere "up" in the subtle planes and *devolved* into physical manifestation with a "Big Bang."

That was the start of *evolution*—the movement back upward but carrying all of humanity—every individual person—into ever-expanding awareness, ever-growing consciousness.

Astral Fire

It is the goal of this element in its compounding and their applications to develop the individual's *Will Power* and accelerate the development of higher consciousness, healing power, and to transform. Fire—astral and physical—transforms all that it touches, and changes the essential nature of what it compounds with to itself become more active and transformative.

The Importance of Applications

It is in applying these compounded elements that you accomplish the overall goals of accelerated expansion of awareness and growth in consciousness. While we provide you with a short Divination Guide to each of the Fire Compounds, it is to your benefit to develop your own applications in Dream Interpretation, Invocation, Magick, and others following—if necessary—the examples provided earlier.

We evolve through both inner transformation and by external application. It is through both that we support the process of planetary and universal growth and *becoming* in fulfillment of the Great Plan summarized in that word "evolution." It is this that ultimately gives meaning to each life.

Fire—Seed of Fire

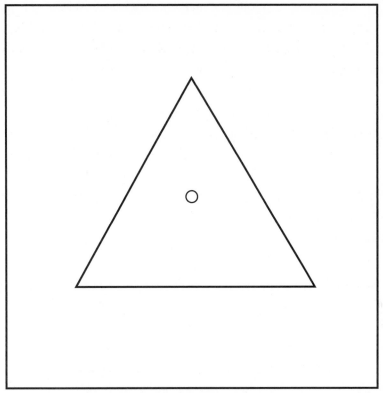

Color the tiny inner bindu circle white,
the inner triangle bright red,
and the outer square bright green

Fire—Seed of Fire: Tejas *RAM*

Fire—Seed of Fire:
Human Control over Primal Power & Passion

Review

We urge you to review the Element Overview Table #3 for **Fire** on page 189 in preparation for this procedure and the Divination and other applications involved with this compound.

The Tattvic Connection Meditation
& Visualization Program #16: Fire/Fire
Fire—Seed of Fire

Introduction. The Purpose & Function of this Procedure.

Rather than repeating the procedure in its entirety, we are asking you to kindly refer to page 396 for the complete *Tattva Connection Meditation & Visualization Compound Program #7 and make your own adjustments to substitute "**Fire**" for "**Earth**" and "**Fire**" for "**Water**" in steps 2 (goal statement), 3 (affirmations. (I know that seems redundant, but in the psychic world little things count for a lot.) We are here providing content for Steps 5 (preparing and coloring the yantra card), 9a (yantra card focus), 10a. (experience the compounded elements and 11 (knowing the compounded elements).*

The Program's Variables:

Steps 2. Goal Statement.

Note your need to consider how to express your goals to reflect the particular natures of the two elements in their primary and secondary combination in relation to your physical, emotional, mental, and spiritual well-being, and their functions in divination, magick, and self-growth.

Step 3. Affirmations.

You need to write positive affirmations to accomplish your goals.

Step 5. Preparation.

Preparing the Yantra Card.

It is recommended that you photocopy the illustration on page 477, preferably on heavier paper or card stock, or draw it yourself in exactly the same sizes using a ruler and black pen. If you can manage it, using a drawing compass or a template, draw a tiny ⅛" inch diameter circle in the exact center. Leave the inside of the circle white. This inner circle or point aids your steady focus. It is not essential, but it is helpful. Make the outer square 4" x 4" and the inner **Fire Triangle** (apex up) about 2½" wide and centered, and the little **Bindu** circle in the exact center should be ⅛" in diameter and have a black line around it and the **Triangle** but not quite as thick as those around the **Square**.

Coloring the Yantra Card.

It will be beneficial for you to color the image as follows: (a) color the tiny inner **Bindu Circle White;** (b) the large **Triangle Bright Red;** and **(c)** the surrounding larger **Square Bright Green.** The outer square and the **Triangle** are bordered with bold black lines, and the tiny inner circle is bordered with a thinner black line.

Step 9a. Yantra Card Focus.

If you have constructed the tattva yantra card as described, turn on the light and focus it on the card held or positioned comfortably about a foot to a foot and a half in front of you.

If possible, arrange your chair to face the primary tattvic direction: *South* for **Fire**. Otherwise—think and feel *South*.

Vibrate the name of the tattva: *Tejas*. Repeat three times.

Chant or hum the tattva element mantra *RAM* (pronounced *RA-UUM*. Vibrate the mantra as instructed in Step 1, preliminaries. Repeat three times. Later, you can do more but always in groups of three. And feel the mantra vibrate *between the Navel and the Heart*, the location of **Manipura** chakra.

Focus on the small white circle* at the center of the image, and stare at it for as long as you can without blinking. When you can't continue the "burning" feeling any longer, turn off the light, close your eyes and focus your inner sight on the space in front of your brow chakra (between your eye brows and on the ridge you can feel just above your nose), and see the **Red Triangle** in the floating in the space before you and vibrating within the **Green Square**. And, then, you will soon see the tattva image change into the complementary yantra colors to **Green** and **Red.**

Again vibrate the names to the tattvas and chant or hum the mantras three times.

Absorb this yantra image! As you repeat the exercise, often, you will reach a point when you will be able to recall this image at will.

> *The small white circle is called a "Bindu," and focus on it is comprehensive of the entire tattvic image and all its energies. There is a small spot on the back of your head that likewise serves as a comprehensive psychic center used in certain meditational exercises. A Bindu is also the name of a single drop of semen, the focal point of a new life. And "bindu" is likewise the single point from which all creation began "in the union of divine forces, Male and Female, God and Goddess, Siva and Shakti in all their names and images—i.e., the "Big Bang."
>
> Bindu is a point of leverage where force applied becomes force multiplied and directed to accomplish your particular goal.

Step 9b. Yantra Visualization.

Alternatively, if you haven't made a **Fire** card, immediately in front of you, visualize the image as described for making the card. See the image gently vibrating. And then the colors will reverse to their complementary yantra colors.

Step 10a. Experiencing Compounded Elemental Fire.

Feel yourself becoming totally *absorbed** in the image while retaining awareness of the surrounding tattvic blue square. As the tattvic **Red** changes to the complementary yantra **Green** feel *your* **Fire** nature harmonize with the Cosmic **Fire** Tattva, and feel all impurities in your **Fire** Tattva—all emotional garbage and unconscious psychic attachments—dissipate. The surrounding **Green** square changes to yantra **Red.**

> **Becoming absorbed.* Enter into the **full image** and become one with it and feel surrounded by it. Moving inward from the outer **Square** become one with the **Fire** Element, and then move inward to the **Bindu** to become one with **All.** Now, moving outward from the **Bindu** point to the **Fire Triangle** to the outer square's edge and feel the balanced **Fire** and the other elements in your body become harmonized and purified as they are balanced with their **Cosmic Source.**

In particular: feel the **Fire** nature of your physical body become free of **energy blockages** and any excessive feelings of **anger** or **lust**. Feel your body becoming ideally healthy, strong, and energized, and give free reign to your natural **enthusiasm** and **expansiveness**. See your body in perfect health, free of any excess weight, free of pain and disfigurement, free of illness, and fully energized.

Step 11. Knowing Elemental Fire.

Allow yourself to receive any information or messages that you're experiencing of these Elemental Forces. *In particular: receive information involving your Physical and Emotional health and strength at both material and astral levels.* Receive the information without any emotional reaction and know that the knowledge is fully activated within your psyche.

Continue on with the Programs to Conclusion.

DIVINATION GUIDE TO FIRE—SEED OF FIRE
Fire—Seed of Fire: *Control or Burning Passions?*

Fire burns! Fire reinforced with Fire presents the challenge of control over the most primal power in our life. Out of control Fire burns and scorches all in its path. Controlled with understanding and purpose, Fire transforms and transmutes material reality into something higher and newer.

In a divination, this can signal "a Hot Time Tonight,"—a time of "burning passions"—almost always transitory and hence "proceed with caution"! It calls for resolve and self-discipline to assert the necessary control to guide passion and enthusiasm for productive and progressive purposes. It signals the need for knowledge about the matters at hand, and the methodology for integrating different energy resources.

Most important, it requires understanding of the nature of our internal fires that power life but that can burn the circuits with overload. That same "Serpent Fire" can open spiritual paths to "Illumination," but all power must be handled with care—else, it can corrupt the source.

Fire—Seed of Earth:
The Human Powers to Initiate Transmutation & Cause Change

Fire—Seed of Earth

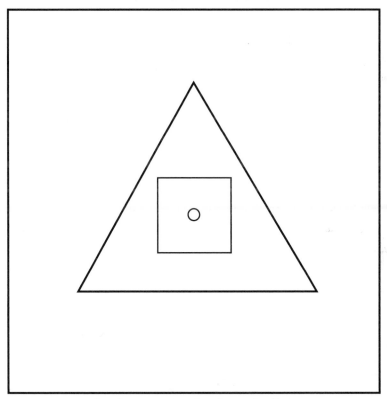

Color the tiny inner bindu circle white,
the inner little square yellow,
the inner triangle bright red,
and the outer square bright green

Fire—Seed of Earth: Tejas & Prithivi *RAM & LAM*

Review

We urge you to review the Element Overview Table #3 for **Fire** on page 189 and the Element Overview Table #1 for Earth on page 104 in preparation for this procedure and the Divination and other applications involved with this compound.

The Tattvic Connection Meditation & Visualization Program #17: Fire/Earth
Fire—Seed of Earth

Introduction. The Purpose & Function of this Procedure.

Rather than repeating the procedure in its entirety, we are asking you to kindly refer to page 396 for the complete *Tattva Connection Meditation & Visualization Compound Program #7 and make your own adjustments to substitute "**Fire**" for "**Earth**" and "**Earth**" for "**Water**" in steps 2 (goal statement), 3 (affirmations. (I know that seems redundant, but in the psychic world little things count for a lot.) We are here providing content for Steps 5 (preparing and coloring the yantra card), 9a (yantra card focus), 10a. (experience the compounded elements and 11 (knowing the compounded elements).*

The Program's Variables:

Steps 2. Goal Statement.

Note your need to consider how to express your goals to reflect the particular natures of the two elements in their primary and secondary combination in relation to your physical, emotional, mental, and spiritual well-being, and their functions in divination, magick, and self-growth.

Step 3. Affirmations.

You need to write positive affirmations to accomplish your goals.

Step 5. Preparation.

Preparing the Yantra Card.

It is recommended that you photocopy the illustration on page 481, preferably on heavier paper or card stock, or draw it yourself in exactly the same sizes using a ruler and black pen. If you can manage it, using a drawing compass or a template, draw a tiny ⅛" inch diameter circle in the exact center. Leave the inside of the circle white. This inner circle or point aids your steady focus. It is not essential, but it is helpful.

Make the outer square 4" x 4" and the inner **Fire Triangle** (apex up) 2¼" wide and centered, the inner **Earth Square** ⅞" x ⅞" and the little **Bindu** circle in the exact center should be ⅛" in diameter and have a black line around it and the little **Square** but not quite as thick as those around the **Triangle** and the outer S**quare.**

Coloring the Yantra Card.

It will be beneficial for you to color the image as follows: (a) color the tiny inner **Bindu Circle White**; (b) the small **Earth Square Bright Yellow**; (c) the **Fire Triangle Bright Red**; and (d) the surrounding outer square **Bright Green.** The outer **Bright Green Square** and the **Bright Red Fire Triangle** are bordered with bold black lines, the small **Yellow Earth Square** is bordered with a less bold black line, and the tiny inner **Bindu Circle** is bordered with a thinner black line.

Step 9a. Yantra Card Focus.

If you have constructed the tattva yantra card as described, turn on the light and focus it on the card held or positioned comfortably about a foot to a foot and a half in front of you.

If possible, arrange your chair to face the primary tattvic direction: *South* for **Fire.** Otherwise—think and feel *South.* (To the extent you feel the secondary element's importance to the operation; you can finish with an acknowledgment of *North* for **Earth.**

Vibrate the name of the two tattvas: *Tejas* and *Prithivi,* alternating one after the other. Repeat three times.

Chant or hum the tattva element mantras *RAM* and *LAM* (pronounced *RA-UUM* and *LA-UUM),* alternating. Vibrate the mantra as instructed in Step 1, preliminaries. Repeat three times. Later, you can do more but always in groups of three. And feel the mantra vibrate *between the Navel and the Heart,* the location of **Manipura** chakra, and then *at the Pelvis,* the location of **Muladhara** chakra.

Focus on the small white circle* at the center of the image, and stare at it for as long as you can without blinking. When you can't continue the "burning" feeling any longer, turn off the light, close your eyes and focus your inner sight on the space in front of your brow chakra (between your eye brows and on the ridge you can feel just above your nose), and see the small **Yellow Square** in the **Red Triangle** floating in the space before you and vibrating within the **Black Square.** And, then, you will soon see the tattva image change into the complementary yantra colors of **Purple, Green,** and **Red.**

Again vibrate the names to the tattvas and chant or hum the mantras three times.

Absorb this yantra image! As you repeat the exercise, often, you will reach a point when you will be able to recall this image at will.

> *The small white circle is called a "Bindu," and focus on it is comprehensive of the entire tattvic image and all its energies. There is a small spot on the back of your head that likewise serves as a comprehensive psychic center used in certain meditational exercises. A Bindu is also the name of a single drop of semen, the focal point of a new life. And "bindu" is likewise the single point from which all creation began "in the union of divine forces, Male and Female, God and Goddess, Siva and Shakti in all their names and images—i.e., the "Big Bang."
>
> Bindu is a point of leverage where force applied becomes force multiplied and directed to accomplish your particular goal.

Step 9b. Yantra Visualization.

Alternatively, if you haven't made a **Fire/Earth** card, immediately in front of you, visualize the image as described for making the card. See the image gently vibrating. And then the colors will reverse to their complementary yantra colors.

Step 10a. Experiencing Compounded Elemental Fire and Elemental Earth.

Feel yourself becoming totally *absorbed** in the image while retaining awareness of the surrounding outer tattvic **Bright Green Square**. As the tattvic **Red** changes to the complementary yantra **Bright Green** feel *your* **Fire** nature harmonize with the Cosmic **Earth** Tattva, and feel all impurities in your **Fire** Tattva—all emotional garbage and unconscious psychic attachments—dissipate. The tattvic **Yellow** will change to the complementary yantra **Purple** as your **Earthy** nature harmonizes with the Cosmic **Earth** Tattva and the impurities of your **Earth** tattva dissipate. The surrounding **Green Square** changes to yantra **Red.**

> **Becoming absorbed.* Enter into the **full image** and become one with it and feel surrounded by it. Moving inward from the outer **Square** become one with the **Fire** Element, and then move inward to become one with the **Earth** Element, and then further in to the **Bindu** to become one with **All.** Now, moving outward from the **Bindu** point to the **Earth Square** and then to the **Fire Triangle** and to its outer edge feel the balanced **Fire** and **Earth** elements in your body become harmonized and purified as they are balanced with their **Cosmic Source.**

In particular: feel the **Fire** and **Earth** nature of your **physical** body become free of **Energy Blockages** and **Circulatory Problems**. Feel your body becoming ideally healthy, strong, and energized. See your body in perfect health, free of any excess weight, free of pain and disfigurement, free of illness, and fully energized. Feel your **Emotional/Mental** body free of **Depression** or **Over-extension.**

Step 11. Knowing Elemental Fire compounded with Elemental Earth.

Allow yourself to receive any information or messages that you're experiencing of these Elemental Forces. *In particular: receive information involving your **Physical** and **Emotional/Mental** health and strength at both material and higher **astral** and lower **Mental** levels.* Receive the information without any emotional reaction and know that the knowledge is fully activated within your psyche.

Continue on with the Programs to Conclusion.

DIVINATION GUIDE TO FIRE—SEED OF EARTH
Fire—Seed of Earth: *Transmutation, or Fantasy?*

When Fire is primary and Earth secondary, we have Alchemy—the transmutation of base matter into higher values symbolized by gold. But remember, even gold is matter, so this symbolizes human action to transform the physical world (symbolized by a square) into the higher ideal (symbolized by the upright triangle). But, the transforming power of Fire can be misapplied or poorly directed. Fire burns and brings change—desired or not. Without the practicality of our Earthy nature, Fire can leave behind only a cinder instead of gold.

In a divination, it signals both time and opportunity to support imagination and emotional drive with rational guidance to avoid fantasy without direction. Earth offers both support and "tempered" guidance. The Earth Goddess endures, while Sun and Moon and the Starry Heaven pass overhead. Root your feet to the Earth, let your imagination soar, but have both a steady hand and steady vision. Combined, they bring Empowerment.

Fire—Seed of Water:
Unleashing Potential—
Empowering of Natural & Human Resources

Fire—Seed of Water

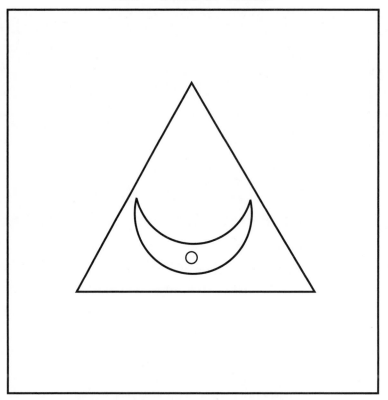

Color the tiny inner bindu circle white,
the inner little crescent metallic silver,
the inner triangle bright red,
and the outer square bright green

Fire—Seed of Water: Tejas & Apas *RAM & VAM*

Review

We urge you to review the Element Overview Table #3 for **Fire** on page 189 and the Element Overview Table #2 for **Water** on page 131 in preparation for this procedure and the Divination and other applications involved with this compound.

The Tattvic Connection Meditation & Visualization Program #18: Fire/Water
Fire—Seed of Water

Introduction. The Purpose & Function of this Procedure.

Rather than repeating the procedure in its entirety, we are asking you to kindly refer to page 396 for the complete *Tattva Connection Meditation & Visualization Compound Program #7 and make your own adjustments to substitute "**Fire**" for "**Earth**" and "**Water**" for "**Water**" in steps 2 (goal statement), 3 (affirmations. (I know that seems redundant, but in the psychic world little things count for a lot.) We are here providing content for Steps 5 (preparing and coloring the yantra card), 9a (yantra card focus), 10a. (experience the compounded elements and 11 (knowing the compounded elements).*

The Program's Variables:

Steps 2. Goal Statement.

Note your need to consider how to express your goals to reflect the particular natures of the two elements in their primary and secondary combination in relation to your physical, emotional, mental and spiritual well-being, and their functions in divination, magick, and self-growth.

Step 3. Affirmations.

You need to write positive affirmations to accomplish your goals.

Step 5. Preparation.
Preparing the Yantra Card.

It is recommended that you photocopy the illustration on page 486, preferably on heavier paper or card stock, or draw it yourself in exactly the same sizes using a ruler and black pen. If you can manage it, using a drawing compass or a template, draw a tiny ⅛" inch diameter circle in the exact center. Leave the inside of the circle white. This inner circle or point aids your steady focus. It is not essential, but it is helpful. Make the outer square 4" x 4" and the inner **Fire Triangle** (apex up) 2¼" wide and centered, the inner **Water Crescent** (horns up) 1⅛" wide, and the little **Bindu** circle in the exact center should be ⅛" in diameter and have a black line around it and the little **Crescent** but not quite as thick as those around the **Triangle** and the outer S**quare**.

Coloring the Yantra Card.

It will be beneficial for you to color the image as follows: (a) color the tiny inner **Bindu Circle White**; (b) the small **Water Crescent Metallic Silver**; (c) the **Fire Triangle Bright Red**; and (d) the surrounding outer square **Bright Green.** The outer **Bright Green Square** and the **Bright Red Fire Triangle** are bordered with bold black lines, the small **Silver Water Crescent** is bordered with a less bold black line, and the tiny inner **Bindu Circle** is bordered with a thinner black line.

Step 9a. Yantra Card Focus.

If you have constructed the tattva yantra card as described, turn on the light and focus it on the card held or positioned comfortably about a foot to a foot and a half in front of you.

If possible, arrange your chair to face the primary tattvic direction: *South* for **Fire.** Otherwise—think and feel *South.* (To the extent you feel the secondary element's importance to the operation; you can finish with an acknowledgment of *West* for **Water.**

Vibrate the name of the two tattvas: *Tejas* and *Apas,* alternating one after the other. Repeat three times.

Chant or hum the tattva element mantras *RAM* and *VAM* (pronounced *RA-UUM* and *VA-UUM),* alternating. Vibrate the mantra as instructed in Step 1, preliminaries. Repeat three times. Later, you can do more but always in groups of three. And feel the mantra vibrate *between the Navel and the Heart,* the location of **Manipura** chakra, and then *between Genitals and Navel,* the location of **Svadhisthana** chakra.

Focus on the small white circle* at the center of the image, and stare at it for as long as you can without blinking. When you can't continue the "burning" feeling any longer, turn off the light, close your eyes and focus your inner sight on the space in front of your brow chakra (between your eye brows and on the ridge you can feel just above your nose), and see the small **Silver Crescent** in the **Red Triangle** floating in the space before you and vibrating within the **Green Square**. And, then, you will soon see the tattva image change into the complementary yantra colors of **Black, Green,** and **Red**.

Again vibrate the names to the tattvas and chant or hum the mantras three times.

Absorb this yantra image! As you repeat the exercise, often, you will reach a point when you will be able to recall this image at will.

> *The small white circle is called a "Bindu," and focus on it is comprehensive of the entire tattvic image and all its energies. There is a small spot on the

back of your head that likewise serves as a comprehensive psychic center used in certain meditational exercises. A Bindu is also the name of a single drop of semen, the focal point of a new life. And "bindu" is likewise the single point from which all creation began "in the union of divine forces, Male and Female, God and Goddess, Siva and Shakti in all their names and images—i.e., the "Big Bang."

Bindu is a point of leverage where force applied becomes force multiplied and directed to accomplish your particular goal.

Step 9b. Yantra Visualization.

Alternatively, if you haven't made a **Fire/Water** card, immediately in front of you, visualize the image as described for making the card. See the image gently vibrating. And then the colors will reverse to their complementary yantra colors.

Step 10a. Experiencing Compounded Elemental Fire and Elemental Earth.

Feel yourself becoming totally *absorbed** in the image while retaining awareness of the surrounding outer tattvic **Bright Green Square**. As the tattvic **Red** changes to the complementary yantra **Bright Green** feel *your* **Fire** nature harmonize with the Cosmic **Earth** Tattva, and feel all impurities in your **Fire** Tattva—all emotional garbage and unconscious psychic attachments—dissipate. The tattvic **Silver** will change to the complementary yantra **Black** as your **Watery** nature harmonizes with the Cosmic **Water** Tattva and the impurities of your **Water** tattva dissipate. The surrounding **Green Square** changes to yantra **Red.**

> *Becoming absorbed.* Enter into the **full image** and become one with it and feel surrounded by it. Moving inward from the outer **Square** become one with the **Fire** Element, and then move inward to become one with the **Water** Element, and then further in to the **Bindu** to become one with **All.** Now, moving outward from the **Bindu** point to the **Water Crescent** and then to the **Fire Triangle** and to its outer edge feel the balanced **Fire** and **Water** elements in your body become harmonized and purified as they are balanced with their **Cosmic Source.**

In particular: feel the **Fire** and **Water** nature of your **physical** body become free of **excessive appetite** and **indigestion** & problems of **constipation**. Feel your body becoming ideally healthy, strong, and energized. See your body in perfect health, free of any excess weight, free of pain and disfigurement, free of illness, and fully energized. Feel your **Emotional/Mental** body becoming **decisive** but also **accepting** and **comfortable in relationships.**

Step 11. Knowing Elemental Fire compounded with Elemental Water.

Allow yourself to receive any information or messages from you're experiencing of these Elemental Forces. _In particular: receive information involving your_ **Physical** _and_ **Emotional/Mental** _health and strength at both material and_ **higher astral** _and_ **lower mental** _levels._ Receive the information without any emotional reaction and know that the knowledge is fully activated within your psyche.

Continue on with the Programs to Conclusion.

DIVINATION GUIDE TO FIRE—SEED OF WATER
Fire—Seed of Water: Passion over Emotion—
A Steamy Romance or a Powerful Partnership

Fire and Water; Water and Fire—there's a difference because one is predominant over the other, and the other tattvas present in lesser "quantities." In every compound, proportion counts. Here, Fire is predominant and Water is secondary. Fire burns and leaves behind a residue mostly of ashes. Even the ashes left from burning can become a valuable resource when dissolved in Water and carried into a process of vaporization and transformation powered by Fire. Fire, with Water, also symbolizes empowerment through emotional transformation—just like Fire transforming Water into steam to drive a locomotive or to generate electrical power. But, boiling water can bubble over and steam can escape in a loss of power if not intelligently and properly managed.

In a divination, this signals time and opportunity for engagement, for nourishment, and enterprise, but warns of possible waste if your time and energy is diverted away from your established goals. You always have a choice: reaction leading to distraction, or action leading to accomplishment.

Fire—Seed of Air:
Energized, and Driven, Inspiration—
A Powerful Combination, but Might does not Make Right!
TAKE CARE THAT AMBITION ISN'T BLINDING

Fire—Seed of Air

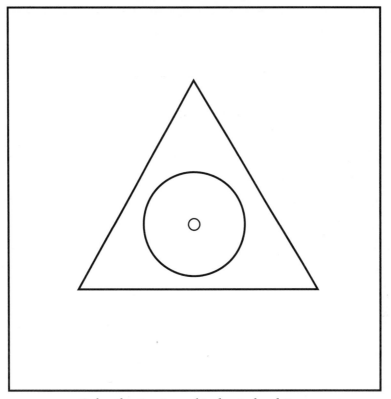

Color the tiny inner bindu circle white,
the inner little circle bright blue,
the inner triangle bright red,
and the outer square bright green

Fire—Seed of Air: Tejas & Vayu *RAM & YAM*

Review

We urge you to review the Element Overview Table #3 for **Fire** on page 189 and the Element Overview Table #4 for **Air** on page 214 in preparation for this procedure and the Divination and other applications involved with this compound.

The Tattvic Connection Meditation & Visualization Program #19: Fire/Air
Fire—Seed of Air

Introduction. The Purpose & Function of this Procedure.

Rather than repeating the procedure in its entirety, we are asking you to kindly refer to page 396 for the complete *Tattva Connection Meditation & Visualization Compound*

*Program #7 and make your own adjustments to substitute "**Fire**" for "**Earth**" and "**Air**" for "**Water**" in steps 2 (goal statement), 3 (affirmations. (I know that seems redundant, but in the psychic world little things count for a lot.) We are here providing content for Steps 5 (preparing and coloring the yantra card), 9a (yantra card focus), 10a. (experience the compounded elements and 11 (knowing the compounded elements).*

The Program's Variables:

Steps 2. Goal Statement.

Note your need to consider how to express your goals to reflect the particular natures of the two elements in their primary and secondary combination in relation to your physical, emotional, mental and spiritual well-being, and their functions in divination, magick, and self-growth.

Step 3. Affirmations.

You need to write positive affirmations to accomplish your goals.

Step 5. Preparation.

Preparing the Yantra Card.

It is recommended that you photocopy the illustration on page 491, preferably on heavier paper or card stock, or draw it yourself in exactly the same sizes using a ruler and black pen. If you can manage it, using a drawing compass or a template, draw a tiny ⅛" inch diameter circle in the exact center. Leave the inside of the circle white. This inner circle or point aids your steady focus. It is not essential, but it is helpful. Make the outer square 4" x 4" and the inner **Fire Triangle** (apex up) 2¼" wide and centered, the inner **Air Circle** 1" in diameter centered within the Triangle, and the little **Bindu** circle in the exact center should be ⅛" in diameter and have a black line around it and the little **Circle** but not quite as thick as those around the **Triangle** and the outer S**quare.**

Coloring the Yantra Card.

It will be beneficial for you to color the image as follows: (a) color the tiny inner **Bindu Circle White**; (b) the small **Air Circle Bright Blue;** (c) the **Fire Triangle Bright Red**; and (d) the surrounding outer square **Bright Green.** The outer **Bright Green Square** and the **Bright Red Fire Triangle** are bordered with bold black lines, the small **Blue Circle** is bordered with a less bold black line, and the tiny inner **Bindu Circle** is bordered with a thinner black line.

Step 9a. Yantra Card Focus.

If you have constructed the tattva yantra card as described, turn on the light and focus it on the card held or positioned comfortably about a foot to a foot and a half in front of you.

If possible, arrange your chair to face the primary tattvic direction: *South* for **Fire.** Otherwise—think and feel *South.* (To the extent you feel the secondary element's importance to the operation; you can finish with an acknowledgment of *East* for **Air.**

Vibrate the name of the two tattvas: ***Tejas*** and ***Vayu,*** alternating one after the other. Repeat three times.

Chant or hum the tattva element mantras ***RAM*** and ***YAM*** (pronounced ***RA-UUM*** and ***YA-UUM),*** alternating. Vibrate the mantra as instructed in Step 1, preliminaries. Repeat three times. Later, you can do more but always in groups of three. And feel the mantra vibrate *between the Navel and the Heart,* the location of **Manipura** chakra, and then *over the Heart,* the location of **Anahata** chakra.

Focus on the small white circle* at the center of the image, and stare at it for as long as you can without blinking. When you can't continue the "burning" feeling any longer, turn off the light, close your eyes and focus your inner sight on the space in front of your brow chakra (between your eye brows and on the ridge you can feel just above your nose), and see the small **Blue Circle** in the **Red Triangle** floating in the space before you and vibrating within the **Green Square.** And, then, you will soon see the tattva image change into the complementary yantra colors. The surrounding **Green Square** changes to yantra **Red,** the **Red Triangle** to Green, and the **Blue Circle** to **Orange.**

Again vibrate the names of the tattvas and chant or hum the mantras three times.

Absorb this yantra image! As you repeat the exercise, often, you will reach a point when you will be able to recall this image at will.

> *The small white circle is called a "Bindu," and focus on it is comprehensive of the entire tattvic image and all its energies. There is a small spot on the back of your head that likewise serves as a comprehensive psychic center used in certain meditational exercises. A Bindu is also the name of a single drop of semen, the focal point of a new life. And "bindu" is likewise the single point from which all creation began "in the union of divine forces, Male and Female, God and Goddess, Siva and Shakti in all their names and images—i.e., the "Big Bang."
>
> Bindu is a point of leverage where force applied becomes force multiplied and directed to accomplish your particular goal.

Step 9b. Yantra Visualization.

Alternatively, if you haven't made a **Fire/Air** card, immediately in front of you, visualize the image as described for making the card. See the image gently vibrating. And then the colors will reverse to their complementary yantra colors.

Step 10a. Experiencing Compounded Elemental Fire and Elemental Air.

Feel yourself becoming totally *absorbed** in the image while retaining awareness of the surrounding outer tattvic **Bright Green Square**. As the tattvic **Red** changes to the complementary yantra **Bright Green** feel *your* **Fire** nature harmonize with the Cosmic **Earth** Tattva, and feel all impurities in your **Fire** Tattva—all emotional garbage and unconscious psychic attachments—dissipate. The tattvic **Blue** will change to the complementary yantra **Orange** as your **Airy** nature harmonizes with the Cosmic **Air** Tattva and the impurities of your **Air** tattva dissipate. The surrounding **Green Square** changes to yantra **Red.**

> **Becoming absorbed.* Enter into the **full image** and become one with it and feel surrounded by it. Moving inward from the outer **Square** become one with the **Fire** Element, and then move inward to become one with the **Air** Element, and then further in to the **Bindu** to become one with **All.** Now, moving outward from the **Bindu** point to the **Air Circle** and then to the **Fire Triangle** and to its outer edge feel the balanced **Fire** and **Air** elements in your body become harmonized and purified as they are balanced with their **Cosmic Source.**

In particular: feel the **Fire** and **Air** nature of your **physical** body become free of **muscular tension** and **respiratory problems**. Feel your body becoming ideally healthy, strong, and energized. See your body in perfect health, free of any excess weight, free of pain and disfigurement, free of illness, and fully energized. Feel your **Emotional/ Mental** body gaining **endurance** and **confidence.**

Step 11. Knowing Elemental Fire compounded with Elemental Air.

Allow yourself to receive any information or messages from you're experiencing of these Elemental Forces. *In particular: receive information involving your **Physical** and **Emotional/Mental** health and strength at both **material** and **higher astral** levels and **lower mental** levels.* Receive the information without any emotional reaction and know that the knowledge is fully activated within your psyche.

Continue on with the Programs to Conclusion.

DIVINATION GUIDE TO FIRE—SEED OF AIR
Fire—Seed of Air: *Finish what you start—*
one way or another!

Fire and Air are interdependent. Air "vitalizes" Fire: without it Fire is smothered no matter how much fuel is available. Moving Air—as with wind—drives Fire to greater intensity and heights. Fire is expansive, Air is movement. Too much Fire is dangerous; too much Air with movement is dangerous—but the right amount of each in combination is just right and energizes the parties involved to move on, to persevere, and to reach higher.

In a divination, it often signals a time of testing—of relationships, of judgment for future actions, and of decisions regarding perseverance or discontinuance—but it is also a reminder to avoid rash decisions and impulsive actions that may result in loss of the potential gain from previous actions. Avoid haste. Think before you leap. Analyze carefully. One way or another, *finish what you start!*

Fire—Seed of Ether:
Energized Enthusiasm, Empowered Intuition
Fire—Seed of Ether

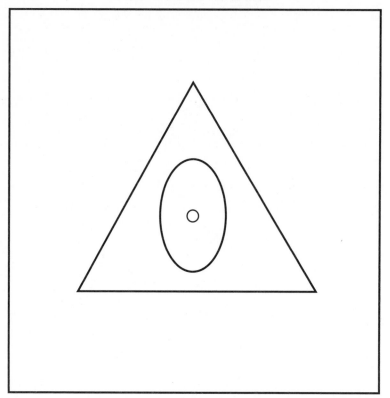

Color the tiny inner bindu circle white,
the inner little oval indigo,
the inner triangle bright red,
and the outer square bright green

Fire—Seed of Ether: Tejas & Akasha *RAM & VAM*

Review

We urge you to review the Element Overview Table #3 for **Fire** on page 189 and that for **Ether** on page 272 in preparation for this procedure and the Divination and other applications involved with this compound.

The Tattvic Connection Meditation
& Visualization Program #20: Fire/Ether
Fire—Seed of Ether

Introduction. The Purpose & Function of this Procedure.

Rather than repeating the procedure in its entirety, we are asking you to kindly refer to page 396 for the complete *Tattva Connection Meditation & Visualization Compound Program #7 and make your own adjustments to substitute "**Fire**" for "**Earth**" and "**Ether**" for "**Water**" in steps 2 (goal statement), 3 (affirmations. (I know that seems redundant, but in the psychic world little things count for a lot.) We are here providing content for Steps 5 (preparing and coloring the yantra card), 9a (yantra card focus), 10a. (experience the compounded elements and 11 (knowing the compounded elements).*

The Program's Variables:

Steps 2. Goal Statement.

Note your need to consider how to express your goals to reflect the particular natures of the two elements in their primary and secondary combination in relation to your physical, emotional, mental and spiritual well-being, and their functions in divination, magick, and self-growth.

Step 3. Affirmations.

You need to write positive affirmations to accomplish your goals.

Step 5. Preparation.

Preparing the Yantra Card.

It is recommended that you photocopy the illustration on page 396, preferably on heavier paper or card stock, or draw it yourself in exactly the same sizes using a ruler and black pen. If you can manage it, using a drawing compass or a template, draw a tiny ⅛" inch diameter circle in the exact center. Leave the inside of the circle white. This inner circle or point aids your steady focus. It is not essential, but it is helpful. Make the outer square 4" x 4" and the inner **Fire Triangle** (apex up) 2¼" wide and centered, the inner **Ether Egg** ¹¹⁄₁₆" wide by 1³⁄₁₆" tall centered within the Triangle, and the little **Bindu** circle in the exact center should be ⅛" in diameter and have a black line around it and the little **Egg** but not quite as thick as those around the **Triangle** and the outer S**quare.**

Coloring the Yantra Card.

It will be beneficial for you to color the image as follows: (a) color the tiny inner **Bindu Circle White**; (b) the small **Ether Egg Bright Indigo**; (c) the **Fire Triangle Bright Red**; and (d) the surrounding outer square **Bright Green.** The outer **Bright**

Green Square and the **Bright Red Fire Triangle** are bordered with bold black lines, the small **Indigo Egg is** bordered with a less bold black line, and the tiny inner **Bindu Circle** is bordered with a thinner black line.

Step 9a. Yantra Card Focus.

If you have constructed the tattva yantra card as described, turn on the light and focus it on the card held or positioned comfortably about a foot to a foot and a half in front of you.

If possible, arrange your chair to face the primary tattvic direction: *South* for **Fire.** Otherwise—think and feel *South.* (To the extent you feel the secondary element's importance to the operation; you can finish with an acknowledgment of *Skyward* for **Ether.**

Vibrate the name of the two tattvas: ***Tejas*** and ***Akasha,*** alternating one after the other. Repeat three times.

Chant or hum the tattva element mantras ***RAM*** and ***HAM*** (pronounced ***RA-UUM*** and ***HA-UUM),*** alternating. Vibrate the mantra as instructed in Step 1, preliminaries. Repeat three times. Later, you can do more but always in groups of three. And feel the mantra vibrate *between the Navel and the Heart,* the location of **Manipura** chakra, and then *over the Throat,* the location of **Vishuddha** chakra.

Focus on the small white circle* at the center of the image, and stare at it for as long as you can without blinking. When you can't continue the "burning" feeling any longer, turn off the light, close your eyes and focus your inner sight on the space in front of your brow chakra (between your eye brows and on the ridge you can feel just above your nose), and see the small **Indigo Egg in** the **Red Triangle** floating in the space before you and vibrating within the **Green Square.** And, then, you will soon see the tattva image change into the complementary yantra colors. The surrounding **Green Square** changes to yantra **Red,** the **Red Triangle** changes to **Green,** and the Egg changes to **Yellow/Orange.**

Again vibrate the names of the tattvas and chant or hum the mantras three times.

Absorb this yantra image! As you repeat the exercise, often, you will reach a point when you will be able to recall this image at will.

> *The small white circle is called a "Bindu," and focus on it is comprehensive of the entire tattvic image and all its energies. There is a small spot on the back of your head that likewise serves as a comprehensive psychic center used in certain meditational exercises. A Bindu is also the name of a single drop of semen, the focal point of a new life. And "bindu" is likewise the single point from which all creation began "in the union of divine forces,

Male and Female, God and Goddess, Siva and Shakti in all their names and images—i.e., the "Big Bang."

Bindu is a point of leverage where force applied becomes force multiplied and directed to accomplish your particular goal.

Step 9b. Yantra Visualization.

Alternatively, if you haven't made a **Fire/Ether** card, immediately in front of you, visualize the image as described for making the card. See the image gently vibrating. And then the colors will reverse to their complementary yantra colors.

Step 10a. Experiencing Compounded Elemental Fire and Elemental Ether.

Feel yourself becoming totally *absorbed** in the image while retaining awareness of the surrounding outer tattvic **Bright Green Square**. As the tattvic **Red** changes to the complementary yantra **Bright Green** feel *your* **Fire** nature harmonize with the Cosmic **Fire** Tattva, and feel all impurities in your **Fire** Tattva—all emotional garbage and unconscious psychic attachments—dissipate. The tattvic **Indigo** will change to the complementary yantra **Yellow/Orange** as your **Ether** nature harmonizes with the Cosmic **Ether** Tattva and the impurities of your **Ether** tattva dissipate. The surrounding **Green Square** changes to yantra **Red**.

> **Becoming absorbed.* Enter into the **full image** and become one with it and feel surrounded by it. Moving inward from the outer **Square** become one with the **Fire** Element, and then move inward to become one with the **Air** Element, and then further in to the **Bindu** to become one with **All**. Now, moving outward from the **Bindu** point to the **Air Circle** and then to the **Fire Triangle** and to its outer edge feel the balanced **Fire** and **Air** elements in your body become harmonized and purified as they are balanced with their **Cosmic Source**.

In particular: feel the **Fire** and **Ether** nature of your **physical** body become free of the **adversity of aging** and **blessed with longevity**. Feel your body becoming ideally healthy, strong, and energized. See your body in perfect health, free of any excess weight, free of pain and disfigurement, free of illness, and fully energized. Feel your **Emotional/Spiritual** body become **Light** and filled with **Bliss**.

Step 11. Knowing Elemental Fire compounded with Elemental Ether.

Allow yourself to receive any information or messages from you're experiencing of these Elemental Forces. *In particular: receive information involving your **Physical** and*

Emotional and *Spiritual* health and strength at both **material** and **higher astral** and **Causal** levels. Receive the information without any emotional reaction and know that the knowledge is fully activated within your psyche.

Continue on with the Programs to Conclusion.

DIVINATION GUIDE TO FIRE—SEED OF ETHER
Fire—Seed of Ether: *Limitless Potential, or Over-extension?*

Primary Fire combined with secondary Ether beneficially transforms and transmutes present circumstances. Fire is desire, motivation, enthusiasm, and combined with Ether the potential is limitless.

In a divination, this signals probable beneficial changes that—with correctly inspired action—will lead toward beneficial changes, creative actions, and spiritual growth. It can indicate sales and promotion opportunities in career management. But, remember that Fire needs fuel for this also is a reminder not to overextend your energies or resources. Neither Fire nor Ether is restrained by rationality or common sense.

CHAPTER THIRTEEN
Clairvoyance & Sleep

*". . . nearly every one who tries his powers touches the wall of his being occasion-
ally, and learns about how far to attempt to fling."*
> Charles Dudley Warner, *"Third Study," Backlog Studies, 1873*

Sleep & Spontaneous Clairvoyance,
and the "need-to-know" Factor

Clairvoyance and sleep—they each facilitate the other. Sleep provides the ideal mental
and physical state for spontaneous clairvoyance to occur. Clairvoyance in turn facilitates
a healthful sleep state that is highly conducive to increased awareness on a need-to-know
basis. A simple flash of clairvoyant insight during the earliest stages of sleep can generate a detailed framework in which more comprehensive insight unfolds. Beyond that,
clairvoyance during sleep can activate the higher creative powers of the subconscious and
organize them as goal-related resources.

Principle of Multiple Causation

The principle of multiple causation holds that for any given act of behavior, there
exist multiple causes. Causative factors can include our conscious perceptions along
with a host of subconscious influences and motives. In clairvoyance, for instance,
clairvoyantly viewing of a present condition, situation, or event may be strongly influenced by our past development, specific training, motivational factors, and our perceptions of both present circumstances and upcoming events. These same factors can
influence sleep, dreaming, and clairvoyance.

The principle of multiple causation, as it relates to clairvoyance and sleep is illustrated by a doctoral student with a background in military intelligence that included
training in the clairvoyant viewing of documents. As a student enrolled in a course on
rational-emotive psychotherapy, he disclosed during a class discussion of clairvoyance
that he regularly viewed in a vivid dream each scheduled weekly test for the course.
The tests, he claimed, were usually situated on the instructor's office credenza the day
before the test. Somewhat skeptical of the student's claim, the professor decided to
remove the next scheduled test from his office credenza and place it in the trunk of
his car on the night before the exam. In a brief discussion with the professor before

class, the student commented: *Though it was rather dark, I viewed inside a car trunk last night the test scheduled for today. I hope that's not considered cheating!*" Although either precognition or out-of-body viewing could explain the student's experience, he firmly held that it was clairvoyant viewing during sleep. Having been trained in clairvoyance as an intelligence agent, he valued the skill and the importance of perfecting it through continuous practice. In his words, "I can't imagine not having this skill. I've become so accustomed to it that, without it, I would feel almost disabled."

Principle of Multiple Possibilities.

Balancing the principle of multiple causation as it relates to clairvoyance and sleep, is the *principle of multiple possibilities* which recognizes the many potentially empowering applications of the clairvoyance during sleep. Clairvoyant perception during sleep is never a happenstance event—it is consistently purposeful and multi-functional. It can work in conjunction with precognitive dreams to generate a mental state conducive to success in achieving important personal goals. It can activate the subconscious resources required to resolve conflicts and find solutions to pressing problems. It can identify hidden potentials and uncover ways of developing them. It can dissolve growth blockages and identify conditions that can accelerate successful personal development, improved social relationships, and academic achievement, and even better financial management, to list but a few. It can uncover past-life experiences that are relevant to your present growth and personal empowerment. It can identify hidden sources of phobias, obsessions, and self-defeating habits while unleashing the resources required for overcoming them. On a larger scale, it can work with the subconscious to promote positive social relationships, happiness, and success. While it may seem as a stretch to some, clairvoyance in its highest, most spontaneous form could uncover during sleep new knowledge and generate global enlightenment that would contribute to the common good and make the world a better place for all.

Based on our case studies over several years, here are a few other examples of the empowering possibilities of clairvoyance during sleep:

Empowering Possibilities in Spontaneous Sleep Clairvoyance
- It can organize our strivings in ways that promote an empowering self-concept while generating positive feelings of worth and personal well-being.
- It can be a gateway to the subconscious that generates totally new growth possibilities.

- It can work together with sleep to connect us to the very essence of our being and add meaning to our lives.

- It can connect us to higher dimensions of reality, including the spirit realm, with abundance new resources.

- It can manage the dream experience in ways that empower us with enlightenment available from no other source.

- It can liberate dormant subconscious resources that can be applied to break unwanted habits and overcome growth blockages.

- It can activate our creative powers.

- It can lead to solutions of common everyday problems.

- It can be a therapeutic force that enriches our daily lives and empowers us to meet the challenges of every day living.

- It can expand our awareness of reality, including that of the universe and multi-verse.

These are only a few of the empowering possibilities of clairvoyance and sleep. When we add to these examples the vast range of personal reports of clairvoyance during sleep, the possibilities become seemingly unlimited. For instance, a college student majoring in business administration viewed on the night before his graduation an unfamiliar administration building with the name of the company boldly appearing over the front entrance. He followed up on the dream and discovered that a highly attractive administrative position with the company had just become available. He applied for the position and was promptly accepted. He attributed his success to clairvoyance during sleep, including the perfect timing of the experience.

In another example of the extensive empowering possibilities of clairvoyance during sleep, a well-known race car driver reported viewing his race car "from all angles" while sleeping on the night before an important race. In the dream, he identified a certain potential malfunction that, if left uncorrected, could result in a breakdown during the race. Early the next morning, he checked the car and with the assistance of an attending mechanic, made the necessary corrections. Incidentally, he won the race which he attributed largely to clairvoyance during sleep.

The Interactive Nature of Clairvoyance

Adding to the extensive range of clairvoyance during sleep is the interactive nature of the experience, including its capacity to stimulate both precognition and retro-cognition which are then incorporated it into the dream experience. As a result, the clairvoyant dream becomes a comprehensive problem solving or information gathering strategy that often organizes past events and existing conditions into a form that brings forth new knowledge and positive change.

While clairvoyant awareness is empowering in its own right, its power is almost always amplified when the experience is applied or acted upon to achieve a personal goal. Here is an example of a college student's clairvoyant dream and his application of it:

> *Because I've always been interested in mountain climbing, I often have dreams in which I climb unfamiliar mountains. Recently, however, I experienced a dream in which I climbed a mountain I had previously climbed and discovered a cave hidden by shrubs about midway to the mountain's top. A few days later, I decided to investigate the dream. I again climbed the mountain and found the cave exactly as seen in my dream. I decided to explore the cave and discovered to my surprise a Civil War sword in pristine condition resting on a stone ledge deep inside the cave. Upon researching the sword, I discovered that it could have belonged to an ancestor who had been a soldier in the Civil War. The sword is now displayed on a wall in my dorm room, not only as a valued historic relic, but as a symbol of the power of clairvoyant dreams. Questions remain, however, as to exactly how the sword ended up in the cave. Perhaps a future clairvoyant dream will fill in the missing links.*

This example of the interactive nature of clairvoyance illustrates the capacity of clairvoyant dreaming to incorporate personal interest and activities (such as mountain climbing) into the dream in ways that uncover new realities (a cave and sword) with important personal relevance (a possible family heirloom). Perhaps even more importantly, the student's experience validated for him the clairvoyant potential of dreams as well as his personal clairvoyant skills.

Daytime Residue and Clairvoyant Symbolism

The sleep state can organize our daytime experiences, often labeled *day residue*, in ways that spontaneously activate our subconscious clairvoyant faculties during sleep. As a result, personal empowerment objectives stated immediately before falling asleep can become powerful incentives for related clairvoyance to occur, often in vivid dream-like form. Complementing that process is the emergence of totally new clairvoyant awareness with personal empowerment relevance related to our stated goals. The sleep experience thus becomes a gateway to clairvoyant awareness that is unavailable to us during our waking hours.

Although resistance to clairvoyant perception is typically minimized during sleep, resistance does often occur, often as a mechanism to protect sleep. Fortunately, when resistance is present, the dream can employ symbols to manifest important subconscious elements while protecting sleep, a phenomenon called *clairvoyant symbolism*. Consequently, the dream experience often uses *clairvoyant symbolism* not only to convey important clairvoyant insight but to reduce any discomfort of day residue related to it. For instance, a college student troubled by the impending divorce of his parents experienced during sleep a peaceful scene in which two birds in flight gently parted as if in slow motion and flew in opposite directions. The dream, rather than distressful, was a comforting message in which each bird followed its own path. Upon awakening and reflecting on the dream, the student experienced a peaceful acceptance of her parents' separation and future divorce. In her words, "I realized that relationships can run their course and from there begin separate but rewarding journeys."

In another example of the capacity of clairvoyant symbolism to convey important new information while alleviating the discomfort of day residue related to it, a candidate in a losing race for mayor of a progressive Alabama city experienced during sleep an overhead view of the city in which certain areas were highlighted in blue, the color of his campaign signs. Upon awakening, he knew in an instant the importance of reorganizing his campaign to include those areas of the city that he had largely overlooked. The clairvoyant experience eliminated his fear of losing the race and motivated him to generate a highly positive campaign that focused on all areas of city. He won the election in a landslide. By his report, "My campaign took on new life because of a simple dream."

Clairvoyance Facilitators

Fortunately, we can facilitate clairvoyance during sleep through a variety of intervention techniques. Our research showed that the same factors that promote quality of sleep tend to likewise promote clairvoyance during sleep. Consequently, pre-sleep concerns, to include our perceptions and expectations of present life situations, can become guiding forces that shape our clairvoyant experiences during sleep. Clairvoyance during sleep then becomes an energy force that can eliminate growth blockages and facilitate achievement of personal goals.

Our case studies of clairvoyance during sleep repeatedly suggested that generating a positive mental state immediately prior to sleep can set the stage for not only restful sleep but clairvoyance as well. Positive pre-sleep suggestions that include optimistic expectations and peaceful dreams tend to promote clairvoyance during sleep as a self-empowerment vehicle for change. Feelings of insecurity, rejection, and inadequacy that interrupt productive sleep and inhibit clairvoyance tend to yield to a positive pre-sleep state that builds positive expectations.

Pre-sleep Guidance Program to Facilitate Clairvoyance

The Pre-sleep Guidance Strategy is a step-by-step program developed in our labs for the two-fold purpose of promoting restful sleep and facilitating clairvoyant enlightenment. In our studies, a positive mental state when combined with specific clairvoyant goals during the pre-sleep state was found to stimulate the subconscious sources of clairvoyance to unleash relevant clairvoyant information, often in lucid dream form. Here's the procedure which is administered while resting comfortably before falling asleep:

Step 1. Holistic Clearing. While resting comfortably before falling asleep, take a few moments to clear your mind of active thought and relax your physical body from your forehead to the tips of your toes. As the relaxation spreads deeply into every joint and fiber of your body, sense your total being flowing gently into a state of complete attunement and balance.

Step 2. Energy Focusing. Turn your attention to your solar plexus and focus on it as your personal center of mental, physical, and spiritual energy. Allow the bright glow of that center to permeate your total being, mentally, physically, and spiritually.

Step 3. Visualizing. Visualize the glow of energy enveloping you being to stream upward and outward to join the highest realms of power. Sense the essence of your being as an energy force merging with the highest dimensions of power. Remind yourself that noting is impossible for you in that balanced, attuned, and connected state.

Step 4. Affirming. Affirm in your own words: *As I drift into restful sleep, my clairvoyant potentials will be activated as needed. I will be receptive to clairvoyant messages and their empowering effects as I sleep. I will become empowered to overcome all blockages to my growth. I will become equipped with the knowledge I need for complete success.* At this point, you can add other affirmations related to such specific goals as academic and career success, social enrichment, personal improvement, and even financial independence, to list but a few.

Step 5. Engaging. Engage restful and productive sleep by simply repeating Step 1 in which you generate a state of balance and attunement conducive to sleep. Conclude with the simple affirmation, *I am now entering restful and productive sleep.*

Step 6. Awakening and Reflecting. Upon awakening from sleep, reflect on the sleep experiences, including those that relate specifically to your stated goals.

Step 7. Journaling. Record the experience in your sleep journal.

The Pre-sleep Guidance Program was used by a doctoral student in her efforts to overcome serious obstacles in her dissertation research designed to quantify certain emotional states, including anxiety, depression, anger, and grief. In the drowsy state preceding sleep, the student who had participated in our development of the program stated her goal of developing a workable plan. As drowsiness deepened, she continued to reflect upon her goal until finally a highly detailed plan began to emerge in lucid dream form. As she slept, she developed a highly specific assessment plan that included a controlled interview guide, objective tests, and physiological assessments. Upon awakening, she documented the step-by-step plan which would receive recognition by her doctoral research committee as a major contribution to the science of quantifying emotions. The student upon completing her doctorate accepted a faculty position in neuroscience at the university.

Therapeutic Power of Clairvoyance During Sleep

Clairvoyance during sleep often provides important insight of therapeutic relevance. Whether related to past-life experiences or present-life situations, the subconscious exist as a storehouse of knowledge unavailable from other sources. Through clairvoyance, we can often tap into that domain and retrieve information of advanced therapeutic relevance. That possibility was illustrated by a college freshman who reported a life-long fear of both darkness and confined places. Here's his account of a clairvoyant dream experience that became a turning point in his life:

> I had been up most of the night cramming for an early morning physics exam. After the exam, I decided to take a quick nap and almost instantly drifted into sleep during which I experienced a vivid dream of mountain skiing. An avid skier, I flowed with the experience which was like reality rather than a dream. Suddenly, I became caught in a snow slide, but felt confident that I could somehow manage it. Soon, however, I became trapped by a sliding cascade of snow. Buried deeply in the snow, I struggled to enlarge the dark cubicle I was trapped in, but the more I struggled the smaller the space became. I then realized that escape was impossible. In that of state of panic, I finally became aware that I was dreaming, but that awareness did not reduce the terror of the experience. Once fully awake, I knew that the dream had tapped into the past-life source of my phobias of darkness and confined places. The power of that awareness generated in an instant a sense of freedom and personal empowerment unlike anything I had experience in the past. Clairvoyance had transformed the panic of the experience into life-changing

enlightenment. The phobias were no longer mine. Through clairvoyance, they had both vanished once-and-for-all.

All knowledge is consistently empowering. We now know that knowledge of clairvoyant origin is power in its finest form. Its effects can be instant and enduring.

Even awareness of a personal spirit guide has been known to occur through clairvoyance during sleep with results that are often instantly therapeutic. An elementary school teacher with a long history of inferiority feelings experienced during sleep the comforting presence of a personal spirit guide who reached forth with the simple message, "You are not alone." Immediately, she awakened from sleep and experienced powerful feeling of self-esteem and confidence unlike any she had felt before. By her report, "I was instantly empowered. My life changed in a moment of enrichment and enlightenment that continues till this day." A fringe benefit of the experience was the complete extinguishment of stage fright, a condition that had hounded her for years.

In another example of the therapeutic power of clairvoyance during sleep, an assistant professor experienced a "dream-like" clairvoyant viewing in which her professional life took a dramatic turn. She had recently been advised of a budget cutback that would eliminate her position with the college. Adding to the stress of that situation was the recent death of her mother in an automobile accident. With these extreme stressors bearing heavily upon her, she experienced during sleep a clairvoyant intervention that would become a turning point in her life. In the "dream-like experience," as she described it, she viewed just before awakening a red rose that had been placed at her front door with the unsigned note: *When life becomes complex, nothing is as simplifying as a flower from a lover.* Upon awakening, she checked the front door and found a red rose with the identical note: *When life becomes complex; nothing is as simplifying as a flower from a lover.* She recognized the writing as that of her fiancé who had left the rose earlier that night.

Within days following the experience, she was informed by the college that her job was secure due to budget revisions. She was further informed that she had been promoted to the position of associate professor. As a footnote, timing is critical in classifying a so-called "paranormal experience" as clairvoyant or precognitive. Had the instructor's dream occurred before the rose had been placed at the door, it would have been categorized as pre-cognitive rather than clairvoyant. But does the exact classification of the dream really matter? The fact that dreaming, whether clairvoyant or precognitive, can be empowering is what truly counts.

Clairvoyant PK During Sleep

When viewed as a manifestation of mental energy, clairvoyance during sleep suggests the possibility of not only psychic viewing but even more importantly, psychic energy intervention which we could call *clairvoyant psychokinesis (PK)*.

In striking instance of apparent clairvoyant PK during sleep, a college student who had previously demonstrated outstanding clairvoyant abilities viewed during sleep his father's office and discovered an important document situated on the floor underneath his father's desk. He called his father early the next day to inform him of the dream experience. His father responded that upon entering his office early that morning, the document commanded his attention, but rather than being located under his desk, it was situated on the floor just inside the office door. In the student's own words, "I am convinced that during sleep, I clairvoyantly viewed the misplaced document, and as a result of my concern, I spontaneously targeted PK energy to re-locate it either during direct viewing or immediately following it." Could clairvoyant situations of perceived urgency during sleep activate PK, either during the clairvoyance experience of immediately following it? Whatever our explanation of the experience, it clearly suggests the remarkable capacity of clairvoyance during sleep, not only to view the otherwise unseen, but even more remarkably, to influence it through PK intervention.

Though it may seem a quantum leap, clairvoyance during sleep that includes *clairvoyant PK* suggests a near unlimited range empowering possibilities to include psychic healing. That possibility was illustrated by a psychologist whose beloved dog companion had sustained a serious leg injury when hit by a car. As she clairvoyantly viewed the animal during sleep, she used "positive thought energy" to relieve the animal's pain and promote healing. She described the dog's rapid recovery as "miraculous". While this example could be seen as astral travel during sleep in which the psychologist interacted out-of-body with the dog, she is convinced that it was clairvoyant healing from a distance.

Future Oriented Clairvoyance

While clairvoyance during sleep does not directly view the future, it does often view existing conditions with important future relevance. When future oriented, clairvoyance during sleep can empower us either to either shape the future or to become better prepared for it. As a problem-solving process, clairvoyance during sleep can identify existing conditions that could have catastrophic consequences. As a result, we become equipped with enlightenment that, once applied, generates positive change. Among the examples is clairvoyant awareness of existing environmental contamination that once identified results in increased public awareness and corrective intervention. Other examples include clairvoyant insight into acts of violence in their formative stages. The results could result in the correction of conditions that foster violent behaviors on both an individual and mass scale.

Through future oriented clairvoyance during sleep, the future becomes a function of choice and decision making rather than pre-determined. Given the knowledge available to us through clairvoyance, we can assume greater command of the future and thus make the world a better place for present and future generations.

Conclusion

Becoming self-empowered is a never-ending process of growth and self-discovery. Among the major purposes of this chapter is to make the self-empowering techniques of clairvoyance during sleep available to everyone. We are now entering a new stage of consciousness that is both self-contained and universally oriented. In our transition to universal awareness, it becomes increasing important not only to know ourselves, but to be who and what we are. Through clairvoyance during sleep, we can facilitate that important process. We experience empowerment that validates our being and authenticates our existence in the universe.

ADDENDUM #13 TO CHAPTER 13
Microcosm to Macrocosm & Macrocosm to Microcosm

The Tattva Connection—
Meditation & Visualization Programs #21 to #25

Air—and its Compounds

AIR: It's a CONDITIONER!

"A *Cold Front* is moving in bringing some relief from the recent storms," says the Weather Person. "You're so full of *Hot Air that* you're floating right out of the real world," says your loving spouse. "This morning's *Cold and Thin Air* in the high mountain area did not provide enough lift for the small propeller driven plane resulting in its crash at lift-off," said the news announcer.

Yes, we know we can't live without *physical* Air, but we have little understanding of the function of *ASTRAL* Air or of the astral form of the other primal elements or of their compounds—*but we should!* It is the astral energy patterns that actually CONDITION material reality in *advance* of their material manifestation.

With Elemental Water and Fire, we are mostly dealing with emotional factors (very broadly defined and meaning much more than feelings of love, hate and fear); with Elemental Air we are mostly dealing at the Mental level. BUT, don't let this confuse matters! What has Mind or Thought to do with a *Cold Front, Hot Air,* or *Thin Air?* What we are *mentally* realizing is how the astral elements "condition" factors affecting coming events.

It is with such mental perception that psychic applications of clairvoyance, divination, dream interpretation, invocation, and magick themselves become understandable and specific rather than vague and "Oh, that's what that dream meant" after the fact. With understanding of the *conditioning* affect, knowledge of a Cold Front or of Thin Air enables us to take appropriate material world actions that may save lives and reduce property damage, etc.

In other words, our study of the Tattvas is more than "a lot of Hot Air!" Much more, and important to the purpose and meaning of our lives and the roles we play in the human and cosmic drama.

Air—Seed of Air:
Intuition, Inspiration, Discovery & Invention

Air—Seed of Air

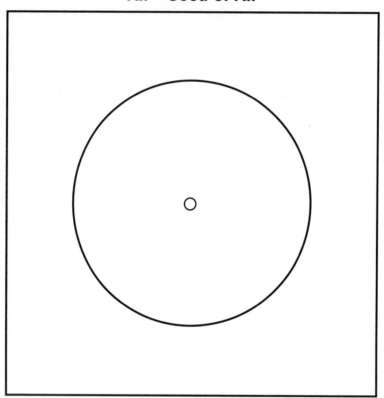

Color the tiny inner bindu circle white,
the inner circle blue,
and the outer square orange

Air—Seed of Air: Vayu YAM

Review

We urge you to review the Element Overview Table #4 for **Air** on page 214 in preparation for this procedure and the Divination and other applications involved with this compound.

The Tattvic Connection Meditation
& Visualization Program #21: Air/Air
Air—Seed of Air

Introduction. The Purpose & Function of this Procedure.

Rather than repeating the procedure in its entirety, we are asking you to kindly refer to page 396 for the complete *Tattva Connection Meditation & Visualization Compound Program #7 and make your own adjustments to substitute "**Air**" for "**Earth**" in steps 2 (goal statement), 3 (affirmations. I know that seems redundant, but in the psychic world little things count for a lot.) We are here providing content for Steps 5 (preparing and coloring the yantra card), 9a (yantra card focus), 10a. (experience the compounded elements and 11 (knowing the compounded elements).*

The Program's Variables:

Step 2. Goal Statement.

Note your need to consider how to express your goals to reflect the particular natures of the two elements in their primary and secondary combination in relation to your physical, emotional, mental, and spiritual well-being, and their functions in divination, magick, and self-growth.

Step 3. Affirmations.

You need to write positive affirmations to accomplish your goals.

Step 5. Preparation.

Preparing the Yantra Card.

It is recommended that you photocopy the illustration on page 512, preferably on heavier paper or card stock, or draw it yourself in exactly the same sizes using a ruler and black pen. If you can manage it, using a drawing compass or a template, draw a tiny ⅛" inch diameter circle in the exact center. Leave the inside of the circle white. This inner circle or point aids your steady focus. It is not essential, but it is helpful. Make the outer square 4" x 4" and the inner **Air Circle** about 2½" wide and centered, and the little **Bindu** circle in the exact center should be ⅛" in diameter and have a black line around it and the **Circle** but not quite as thick as those around the **Square.**

Coloring the Yantra Card.

It will be beneficial for you to color the image as follows: (a) color the tiny inner **Bindu Circle White;** (b) the large **Air Circle Bright Blue;** and (c) the surrounding larger square **Bright Orange.** The outer **Square** and the **Circle** are bordered with bold black lines, and the tiny inner circle is bordered with a thinner black line.

Step 9a. Yantra Card Focus.

If you have constructed the tattva yantra card as described, turn on the light and focus it on the card held or positioned comfortably about a foot to a foot and a half in front of you.

If possible, arrange your chair to face the primary tattvic direction: *East* for **Air**. Otherwise—think and feel *East*.

Vibrate the name of the tattva: ***Vayu***. Repeat three times.

Chant or hum the tattva element mantra **YAM** (pronounced **YA-UUM**. Vibrate the mantra as instructed in Step 1, preliminaries. Repeat three times. Later, you can do more but always in groups of three. And feel the mantra vibrate *over the Heart*, the location of **Anahata** chakra.

Focus on the small white circle* at the center of the image, and stare at it for as long as you can without blinking. When you can't continue the "burning" feeling any longer, turn off the light, close your eyes and focus your inner sight on the space in front of your brow chakra (between your eye brows and on the ridge you can feel just above your nose), and see the small **Blue Circle** floating in the space before you and vibrating within the **Orange Square**. And, then, you will soon see the tattva image change into the complementary yantra colors of **Orange** for the Circle and **Blue** for the surrounding Square.

Again vibrate the names to the tattvas and chant or hum the mantras three times.

Absorb this yantra image! As you repeat the exercise, often, you will reach a point when you will be able to recall this image at will.

> *The small white circle is called a "Bindu," and focus on it is comprehensive of the entire tattvic image and all its energies. There is a small spot on the back of your head that likewise serves as a comprehensive psychic center used in certain meditational exercises. A Bindu is also the name of a single drop of semen, the focal point of a new life. And "bindu" is likewise the single point from which all creation began "in the union of divine forces, Male and Female, God and Goddess, Siva and Shakti in all their names and images—i.e., the "Big Bang."
>
> Bindu is a point of leverage where force applied becomes force multiplied and directed to accomplish your particular goal.

Step 9b. Yantra Visualization.

Alternatively, if you haven't made an **Air** card, immediately in front of you visualize the image as described for making the card. See the image gently vibrating. And then the colors will reverse to their complementary yantra colors.

Step 10a. Experiencing Compounded Elemental Air.

Feel yourself becoming totally *absorbed** in the image while retaining awareness of the surrounding tattvic **Orange Square**. As the tattvic **Blue Circle** changes to the complementary yantra **Orange** feel *your* **Air** nature harmonize with the Cosmic **Air** Tattva, and feel all impurities in your **Air** Tattva—all emotional garbage and unconscious psychic attachments—dissipate. The surrounding **Orange Square** changes to yantra **Blue.**

> *Becoming absorbed.* Enter into the **full image** and become one with it and feel surrounded by it. Moving inward from the outer **Square** become one with the **Air** Element, and then move inward to the **Bindu** to become one with **All.** Now, moving outward from the **Bindu** point to the **Air Circle** to the outer square's edge and feel the balanced **Air** and the other elements in your body become harmonized and purified as they are balanced with their **Cosmic Source.**

In particular: feel the **Air** nature of your **physical** body become free of **Fever** and **Inflammation**. Feel your body becoming ideally healthy, strong, and energized. See you body in perfect health, free of any excess weight, free of pain and disfigurement, free of illness, and fully energized. Feel you **Mental** body become filled with **Compassion** for others and able to **Communicate** your thoughts and feelings to them.

Step 11. Knowing Elemental Air

Allow yourself to receive any information or messages from you're experiencing of these Elemental Forces. *In particular: receive information involving your **Physical** and **Mental** health and strength at both **material** and **mental** levels.* Receive the information without any emotional reaction and know that the knowledge is fully activated within your psyche.

Continue on with the Programs to Conclusion.

DIVINATION GUIDE TO AIR—SEED OF AIR
Air—Seed of Air: *Growth & Profit, or a Flash in the Pan?*

Air carries Light, Moisture, and Seed to Earth; Air is the vehicle for rain clouds, fog, and mists that convey Water to Earth; Air is the medium bringing Fire as lightening to Earth; Air supports Birds and Insects that in turn carry Life to Earth; Air moves over the Earth, transferring seed and moisture across the surface of the Earth; and Air stirs the oceans moving the surface and even the depths. Movement is Mind and Intelligence and without Air all would stagnate. Air brings Life-sustaining Oxygen to Earth's life-forms—without which we would die. Air reinforced with Air is doubly powerful and intellectually stimulating.

In a divination, it represents the potential for rapid change. Pay attention to your feelings as Air can signal the calm before the storm, the potential for growth and profit, the opportunity for learning and intelligence, and the flash of energy and power signaling an evolutionary leap. But, too much Air can lead to imbalance, lack of discretion, hasty decisions, failure to carefully analyze details of a situation, and overlooking emotional and practical factors.

Air—Seed of Earth:
Turning Inspiration into Realization

Air—Seed of Earth

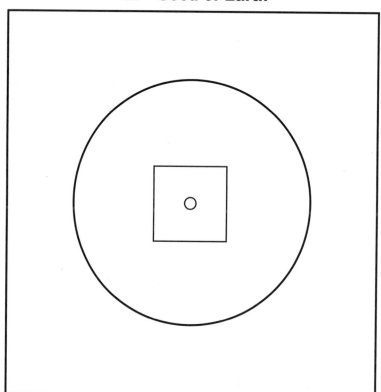

Color the tiny inner bindu circle white,
the inner square yellow,
the inner circle blue,

Air—Seed of Earth: Vayu & Prithivi YAM & LAM

Review

We urge you to review the Element Overview Table #4 for **Air** on page 214 and that for Earth on page 104 in preparation for this procedure and the Divination and other applications involved with this compound.

The Tattvic Connection Meditation & Visualization Program #22: Air/Earth
Air—Seed of Earth

Introduction. The Purpose & Function of this Procedure.

Rather than repeating the procedure in its entirety, we are asking you to kindly refer to page 396 for the complete *Tattva Connection Meditation & Visualization Compound Program #7 and make your own adjustments to substitute "**Air**" for "**Earth**" and "**Earth**" for "**Water**" in steps 2 (goal statement), 3 (affirmations. (I know that seems redundant, but in the psychic world little things count for a lot.) We are here providing content for Steps 5 (preparing and coloring the yantra card), 9a (yantra card focus), 10a. (experience the compounded elements and 11 (knowing the compounded elements).*

The Program's Variables:
Steps 2. Goal Statement.

Note your need to consider how to express your goals to reflect the particular natures of the two elements in their primary and secondary combination in relation to your physical, emotional, mental and spiritual well-being, and their functions in divination, magick, and self-growth.

Step 3. Affirmations.

You need to write positive affirmations to accomplish your goals.

Step 5. Preparation.
Preparing the Yantra Card.

It is recommended that you photocopy the illustration on page 516, preferably on heavier paper or card stock, or draw it yourself in exactly the same sizes using a ruler and black pen. If you can manage it, using a drawing compass or a template, draw a tiny ⅛" inch diameter circle in the exact center. Leave the inside of the circle white. This inner circle or point aids your steady focus. It is not essential, but it is helpful. Make the outer square 4" x 4" and the inner **Air Circle** should be 2½" wide and centered, the inner **Earth**

Square ⅞" x ⅞", and the little **Bindu** circle in the exact center should be ⅛" in diameter and have a black line around it and the little **Square** but not quite as thick as those around the **Circle** and the outer **Square.**

Coloring the Yantra Card.

It will be beneficial for you to color the image as follows: (a) color the tiny inner **Bindu Circle White;** (b) the small **Earth Square Bright Yellow; (c)** the **Air Circle Bright Blue;** and (d) the surrounding outer square **Bright Orange.** The outer **Bright Orange Square** and the **Bright Blue Circle** are bordered with bold black lines, the small **Yellow Earth Square** is bordered with a less bold black line, and the tiny inner **Bindu Circle** is bordered with a thinner black line.

Step 9a. Yantra Card Focus.

If you have constructed the tattva yantra card as described, turn on the light and focus it on the card held or positioned comfortably about a foot to a foot and a half in front of you.

If possible, arrange your chair to face the primary tattvic direction: *East* for **Air.** Otherwise—think and feel *East.* To the extent you feel the secondary element's importance to the operation; you can finish with an acknowledgment of *North* for **Earth.**

Vibrate the name of the two tattvas: **Vayu** and **Prithivi,** alternating one after the other. Repeat three times.

Chant or hum the tattva element mantras **YAM** and **LAM** (pronounced **YA-UUM** and **LA-UUM),** alternating. Vibrate the mantra as instructed in Step 1, preliminaries. Repeat three times. Later, you can do more but always in groups of three. And feel the mantra vibrate *over the Heart,* the location of **Anahata** chakra, and then *at the Pelvis,* the location of **Muladhara** chakra.

Focus on the small white circle* at the center of the image, and stare at it for as long as you can without blinking. When you can't continue the "burning" feeling any longer, turn off the light, close your eyes and focus your inner sight on the space in front of your brow chakra (between your eye brows and on the ridge you can feel just above your nose), and see the small **Yellow Square** in the **Blue Circle** floating in the space before you and vibrating within the **Orange Square.** And, then, you will soon see the tattva image change into the complementary yantra colors of **Purple, Orange,** and **Blue.**

Again vibrate the names to the tattvas and chant or hum the mantras three times.

Absorb this yantra image! As you repeat the exercise, often, you will reach a point when you will be able to recall this image at will.

*The small white circle is called a "Bindu," and focus on it is comprehensive of the entire tattvic image and all its energies. There is a small spot on the back of your head that likewise serves as a comprehensive psychic center used in certain meditational exercises. A Bindu is also the name of a single drop of semen, the focal point of a new life. And "bindu" is likewise the single point from which all creation began "in the union of divine forces, Male and Female, God and Goddess, Siva and Shakti in all their names and images—i.e., the "Big Bang."

Bindu is a point of leverage where force applied becomes force multiplied and directed to accomplish your particular goal.

Step 9b. Yantra Visualization.

Alternatively, if you haven't made an **Air/Earth** card, immediately in front of you, visualize the image as described for making the card. See the image gently vibrating. And then the colors will reverse to their complementary yantra colors.

Step 10a. Experiencing Compounded Elemental Air and Elemental Earth.

Feel yourself becoming totally *absorbed** in the image while retaining awareness of the surrounding outer tattvic **Bright Orange Square**. As the tattvic **Blue** changes to the complementary yantra **Bright Orange** and the outer square to **Blue** feel *your* **Air** nature harmonize with the Cosmic **Earth** Tattva, and feel all impurities in your **Air** Tattva—all emotional garbage and unconscious psychic attachments—dissipate. The tattvic **Yellow** will change to the complementary yantra **Purple** as your **Earthy** nature harmonizes with the Cosmic **Earth** Tattva and the impurities of your **Earth** tattva dissipate.

> **Becoming absorbed.* Enter into the **full image** and become one with it and feel surrounded by it. Moving inward from the outer **Square** become one with the **Air** Element, and then move inward to become one with the **Earth** Element, and then further in to the **Bindu** to become one with **All.** Now, moving outward from the **Bindu** point to the **Earth Square** and then to the **Air Circle** and to its outer edge feel the balanced **Air** and **Earth** elements in your body become harmonized and purified as they are balanced with their **Cosmic Source.**

In particular: feel the **Air** and **Earth** nature of your **physical** body become free of **muscular problems** and **weakness**. Feel your body becoming ideally healthy, strong, and energized. See your body in perfect health, free of any excess weight, free of pain and disfigurement, free of illness, and fully energized. Feel your **mental** body overcome tendencies to **erratic thought** and excessive **fantasies.**

Step 11. Knowing Elemental Air compounded with Elemental Earth.

Allow yourself to receive any information or messages from you're experiencing of these Elemental Forces. *In particular: receive information involving your **Physical** and **mental** health and strength at both **material** and **mental** levels.* Receive the information without any emotional reaction and know that the knowledge is fully activated within your psyche.

Continue on with the Programs to Conclusion.

DIVINATION GUIDE TO AIR—SEED OF EARTH
Air—Seed of Earth: *Squaring the Circle, or Flying off on a Tangent?*

Air's Circle symbolizes the *kingdom of mind*—home to ideas, imagination, fantasy, intelligence and freedom for Air is all of these and the means to rational decisions and behavior. But, ideas to have to be brought down to Earth to become realized!

Earth's square symbolizes the *womb* in which ideas and flights of fantasy are materialized and then can be acted upon to transfer a mental concept for physical reality. "To square the Circle means to bring sense to what could be nonsense. It means to test imagination with reality. It means to contain flights of fantasy with healthy objectivity.

In a divination, it marks the time to translate thoughts into action, words into deeds, theory into practice. But, the presence of Earth is also a reminder to check thought and imagination for practicality and thus avoid for flying off on a tangent! Ideas are like seeds—they must be brought to earth and properly planted to bring forth a deserved harvest. An inspiration is nothing but wind if not processed into solid plan that withstands the test of analysis.

Air—Seed of Water:
Stormy Weather, or a Lovely Affair, OR Plenty of Mental Excitement!

Air—Seed of Water

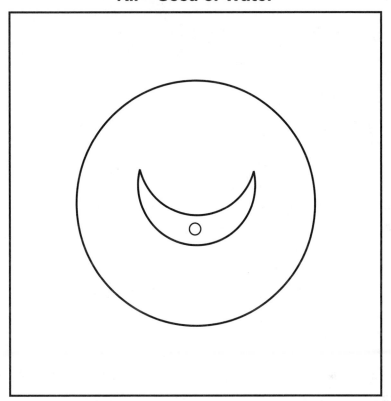

Color the tiny inner bindu circle white,
the inner crescent silver,
the inner circle blue,
and the outer square orange

Air—Seed of Water: Vayu & Apas YAM & VAM

Review

We urge you to review the Element Overview Table #4 for **Air** on page 214 And the Element Overview Table #3 for Water on page 131 in preparation for this procedure and the Divination and other applications involved with this compound.

The Tattvic Connection Meditation
& Visualization Program #23: Air/Water
Air—Seed of Water

Introduction. The Purpose & Function of this Procedure.

Rather than repeating the procedure in its entirety, we are asking you to kindly refer to page 396 for the complete *Tattva Connection Meditation & Visualization Compound Program #7 and make your own adjustments to substitute "**Air**" for "**Earth**" and "**Water**" for "**Water**" in steps 2 (goal statement), 3 (affirmations. (I know that seems redundant, but in the psychic world little things count for a lot.) We are here providing content for Steps 5 (preparing and coloring the yantra card), 9a (yantra card focus), 10a. (experience the compounded elements and 11 (knowing the compounded elements).*

The Program's Variables:

Steps 2. Goal Statement.

Note your need to consider how to express your goals to reflect the particular natures of the two elements in their primary and secondary combination in relation to your physical, emotional, mental and spiritual well-being, and their functions in divination, magick, and self-growth.

Step 3. Affirmations.

You need to write positive affirmations to accomplish your goals.

Step 5. Preparation.

Preparing the Yantra Card.

It is recommended that you photocopy the illustration on page 521, preferably on heavier paper or card stock, or draw it yourself in exactly the same sizes using a ruler and black pen. If you can manage it, using a drawing compass or a template, draw a tiny ⅛" inch diameter circle in the exact center. Leave the inside of the circle white. This inner circle or point aids your steady focus. It is not essential, but it is helpful. Make the outer square 4" x 4" and the inner **Air Circle** should be 2½" wide and centered, the inner **Water Crescent** 1⅛" wide (horns up and centered) and the little **Bindu** circle in the exact center should be ⅛" in diameter and have a black line around it and the little **Crescent** but not quite as thick as those around the **Circle** and the outer **S**quare.

Coloring the Yantra Card.

It will be beneficial for you to color the image as follows: (a) color the tiny inner **Bindu Circle White**; (b) the small **Water Crescent Metallic Silver** (or White); (c) the **Air Circle Bright Blue**; and (d) the surrounding outer square **Bright Orange.** The outer **Bright Orange Square** and the **Bright Blue Circle** are bordered with bold black lines, the small **Silver Water Crescent** is bordered with a less bold black line, and the tiny inner **Bindu Circle** is bordered with a thinner black line.

Step 9a. Yantra Card Focus.

If you have constructed the tattva yantra card as described, turn on the light and focus it on the card held or positioned comfortably about a foot to a foot and a half in front of you.

If possible, arrange your chair to face the primary tattvic direction: *East* for **Air.** Otherwise—think and feel *East.* (To the extent you feel the secondary element's importance to the operation; you can finish with an acknowledgment of *West* for **Water.**

Vibrate the name of the two tattvas: *Vayu* and *Apas,* alternating one after the other. Repeat three times.

Chant or hum the tattva element mantras *YAM* and *VAM* (pronounced *YA-UUM* and *VA-UUM),* alternating. Vibrate the mantra as instructed in Step 1, preliminaries. Repeat three times. Later, you can do more but always in groups of three. And feel the mantra vibrate *over the Heart,* the location of **Anahata** chakra, and then *between Genitals and Navel,* the location of **Svadhisthana** chakra.

Focus on the small white circle* at the center of the image, and stare at it for as long as you can without blinking. When you can't continue the "burning" feeling any longer, turn off the light, close your eyes and focus your inner sight on the space in front of your brow chakra (between your eye brows and on the ridge you can feel just above your nose), and see the small **Silver Crescent** in the **Blue Circle** floating in the space before you and vibrating within the **Orange Square.** And, then, you will soon see the tattva image change into the complementary yantra colors of **Black, Orange** and **Blue.**

Again vibrate the names to the tattvas and chant or hum the mantras three times.

Absorb this yantra image! As you repeat the exercise, often, you will reach a point when you will be able to recall this image at will.

> *The small white circle is called a "Bindu," and focus on it is comprehensive
> of the entire tattvic image and all its energies. There is a small spot on the

back of your head that likewise serves as a comprehensive psychic center used in certain meditational exercises. A Bindu is also the name of a single drop of semen, the focal point of a new life. And "bindu" is likewise the single point from which all creation began "in the union of divine forces, Male and Female, God and Goddess, Siva and Shakti in all their names and images—i.e., the "Big Bang."

Bindu is a point of leverage where force applied becomes force multiplied and directed to accomplish your particular goal.

Step 9b. Yantra Visualization.

Alternatively, if you haven't made an **Air/Water** card, immediately in front of you, visualize the image as described for making the card. See the image gently vibrating. And then the colors will reverse to their complementary yantra colors.

Step 10a. Experiencing Compounded Elemental Air and Elemental Water.

Feel yourself becoming totally *absorbed** in the image while retaining awareness of the surrounding outer tattvic **Bright Orange Square**. As the tattvic **Blue** changes to the complementary yantra **Bright Orange** and the outer square to **Blue** feel *your* **Air** nature harmonize with the Cosmic **Water** Tattva, and feel all impurities in your **Water** Tattva—all emotional garbage and unconscious psychic attachments—dissipate. The tattvic **Silver** will change to the complementary yantra **Black** as your **Watery** nature harmonizes with the Cosmic **Water** Tattva and the impurities of your **Water** tattva dissipate.

> **Becoming absorbed.* Enter into the **full image** and become one with it and feel surrounded by it. Moving inward from the outer **Square** become one with the **Air** Element, and then move inward to become one with the **Water** Element, and then further in to the **Bindu** to become one with **All**. Now, moving outward from the **Bindu** point to the **Water Crescent** and then to the **Air Circle** and to its outer edge feel the balanced **Air** and **Water** elements in your body become harmonized and purified as they are balanced with their **Cosmic Source.**

In particular: feel the **Air** and **Water** nature of your **physical** body become free of **respiratory problems** and **allergies**. Feel your body becoming ideally healthy, strong, and energized. See your body in perfect health, free of any excess weight, free of pain and disfigurement, free of illness, and fully energized. Feel your **emotional** and **mental** bodies become free of **constricting** feelings and **thoughts**, particularly those arising from childhood memories.

Step 11. Knowing Elemental Air compounded with Elemental Water.

Allow yourself to receive any information or messages from you're experiencing of these Elemental Forces. *In particular: receive information involving your **Physical** and **Emotional/Mental** health and" strength at both **material** and **astral** & **mental** levels.* Receive the information without any emotional reaction and know that the knowledge is fully activated within your psyche.

Continue on with the Programs to Conclusion.

DIVINATION GUIDE TO AIR—SEED OF WATER
Air—Seed of Water: *Excitement, or Delusion?*

Air normally moves over the surface of Water, but strong winds can whip the depths into a froth of airy bubbles, empty of substance and potentially blinding. Sometimes the stronger movements of Air over Water produce rain or snow, or blinding fog. Air is the kingdom of Mind; Water is the kingdom of Emotion. An abundance of Air mixed into Emotion can result in fantastic relationships, or delusional fantasies. Air and Emotion can lead to enchantment or to loss of perspective leading to an emotional crash.

In a divination, it may signal a quick romantic affair or exciting sexual encounter, or an end to excitement as when champagne goes flat, an affair or other relationship plateaus. Or, it may be a time of watch your step until the vision clears, a time to step back from the action and clear the head, to take a needed change of scene in a vacation.

Air—Seed of Fire:
The Power of Inspiration

Air—Seed of Fire

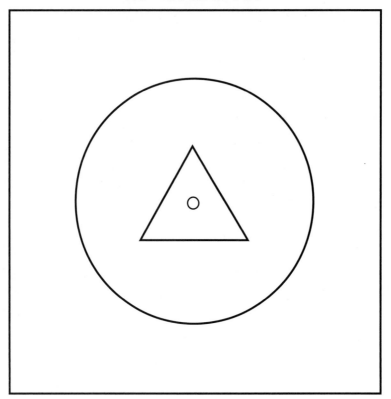

Color the tiny inner bindu circle white,
the inner triangle red,
the inner circle blue,
and the outer square orange

Air—Seed of Fire: Vayu & Tejas YAM & RAM

Review

We urge you to review the Element Overview Table #4 for **Air** on page 214 and Table #3 for Fire on page 189 in preparation for this procedure and the Divination and other applications involved with this compound.

The Tattvic Connection Meditation & Visualization Program #24: Air/Fire
Air—Seed of Fire

Introduction. The Purpose & Function of this Procedure.

Rather than repeating the procedure in its entirety, we are asking you to kindly refer to page 369 for the complete *Tattva Connection Meditation & Visualization Compound Program #7 and make your own adjustments to substitute "**Air**" for "**Earth**" and "**Fire**" for "**Water**" in steps 2 (goal statement), 3 (affirmations. (I know that seems redundant, but in the psychic world little things count for a lot.) We are here providing content for Steps 5 (preparing and coloring the yantra card), 9a (yantra card focus), 10a. (experience the compounded elements and 11 (knowing the compounded elements).*

The Program's Variables:

Steps 2. Goal Statement.

Note your need to consider how to express your goals to reflect the particular natures of the two elements in their primary and secondary combination in relation to your physical, emotional, mental and spiritual well-being, and their functions in divination, magick, and self-growth.

Step 3. Affirmations.

You need to write positive affirmations to accomplish your goals.

Step 5. Preparation.
Preparing the Yantra Card.

It is recommended that you photocopy the illustration on page 526, preferably on heavier paper or card stock, or draw it yourself in exactly the same sizes using a ruler and black pen. If you can manage it, using a drawing compass or a template, draw a tiny ⅛" inch diameter circle in the exact center. Leave the inside of the circle white. This inner circle or point aids your steady focus. It is not essential, but it is helpful. Make the outer square 4" x 4" and the inner **Air Circle** should be 2½" wide and centered, the inner **Fire Triangle** 1" one each side (apex up and centered) and the little **Bindu** circle in the exact center should be ⅛" in diameter and have a black line around it and the little **Triangle** but not quite as thick as those around the **Circle** and the outer **Square.**

Coloring the Yantra Card.

It will be beneficial for you to color the image as follows: (a) color the tiny inner **Bindu Circle White**; (b) the small **Fire Triangle Bright Red**; (c) the **Air Circle Bright Blue**; and (d) the surrounding outer square **Bright Orange.** The outer **Bright Orange Square** and the **Bright Blue Circle** are bordered with bold black lines, the small **Red Fire Triangle** is bordered with a less bold black line, and the tiny inner **Bindu Circle** is bordered with a thinner black line.

Step 9a. Yantra Card Focus.

If you have constructed the tattva yantra card as described, turn on the light and focus it on the card held or positioned comfortably about a foot to a foot and a half in front of you.

If possible, arrange your chair to face the primary tattvic direction: *East* for **Air.** Otherwise—think and feel *East.* (To the extent you feel the secondary element's importance to the operation; you can finish with an acknowledgment of *South* for **Fire.**

Vibrate the name of the two tattvas: *Vayu* and *Tejas,* alternating one after the other. Repeat three times.

Chant or hum the tattva element mantras *YAM* and *RAM* (pronounced *YA-UUM* and *RA-UUM),* alternating. Vibrate the mantra as instructed in Step 1, preliminaries. Repeat three times. Later, you can do more but always in groups of three. And feel the mantra vibrate *over the Heart,* the location of **Anahata** chakra, and then *between Navel and Heart,* the location of **Manipura** chakra.

Focus on the small white circle* at the center of the image, and stare at it for as long as you can without blinking. When you can't continue the "burning" feeling any longer, turn off the light, close your eyes and focus your inner sight on the space in front of your brow chakra (between your eyebrows and on the ridge you can feel just above your nose), and see the small **Red Triangle** in the **Blue Circle** floating in the space before you and vibrating within the **Orange Square.** And, then, you will soon see the tattva image change into the complementary yantra colors of **Green**, **Orange**, and **Blue.**

Again vibrate the names to the tattvas and chant or hum the mantras three times.

Absorb this yantra image! As you repeat the exercise, often, you will reach a point when you will be able to recall this image at will.

> *The small white circle is called a "Bindu," and focus on it is comprehensive of the entire tattvic image and all its energies. There is a small spot on the back of your head that likewise serves as a comprehensive psychic center used in certain meditational exercises. A Bindu is also the name of a single

drop of semen, the focal point of a new life. And "bindu" is likewise the single point from which all creation began "in the union of divine forces, Male & Female, God & Goddess, Siva & Shakti in all their names and images—i.e., the "Big Bang.""

Bindu is a point of leverage where force applied becomes force multiplied and directed to accomplish your particular goal.

Step 9b. Yantra Visualization.

Alternatively, if you haven't made a **Air/Fire** card, immediately in front of you, visualize the image as described for making the card. See the image gently vibrating. And then the colors will reverse to their complementary yantra colors.

Step 10a. Experiencing Compounded Elemental Air and Elemental Fire.

Feel yourself becoming totally *absorbed** in the image while retaining awareness of the surrounding outer tattvic **Bright Orange Square**. As the tattvic **Blue** changes to the complementary yantra **Bright Orange** and the outer square to **Blue** feel *your* **Air** nature harmonize with the Cosmic **Fire** Tattva, and feel all impurities in your **Fire** Tattva—all emotional garbage and unconscious psychic attachments—dissipate. The tattvic **Red** will change to the complementary yantra **Green** as your **Fiery** nature harmonizes with the Cosmic **Fire** Tattva and the impurities of your **Fire** tattva dissipate.

> **Becoming absorbed.* Enter into the **full image** and become one with it and feel surrounded by it. Moving inward from the outer **Square** become one with the **Air** Element, and then move inward to become one with the **Fire** Element, and then further in to the **Bindu** to become one with **All.** Now, moving outward from the **Bindu** point to the **Fire Triangle** and then to the **Air Circle** and to its outer edge feel the balanced **Air** and **Fire** elements in your body become harmonized and purified as they are balanced with their **Cosmic Source.**

In particular: feel the **Air** and **Fire** nature of your **p**hysical body become free of **circulatory** and **respiratory weaknesses**. Feel your body becoming ideally healthy, strong, and energized. See your body in perfect health, free of any excess weight, free of pain and disfigurement, free of illness, and fully energized. Feel your **Emotional** and **Mental** strengths in your **career** and **romance relationships**.

Step 11. Knowing Elemental Air compounded with Elemental Fire.

Allow yourself to receive any information or messages from you're experiencing of these Elemental Forces. *In particular: receive information involving your* **Physical** *and* **Emotional/Mental** *health & strength at both* **material** *and* **astral** *and* **mental** *levels.* Receive the information without any emotional reaction and know that the knowledge is fully activated within your psyche.

Continue on with the Programs to Conclusion.

DIVINATION GUIDE TO AIR—SEED OF FIRE
Air—Seed of Fire: *Evolution, or Revolution?*

Without Air, Fire dies. Without Air, all Life dies. Air enables Fire to burn more warmly and more brightly—as long as balance and harmony are maintained. Air enables Life to continue as the body's internal fires provide the energies of metabolism and other life professes—including the senses and the brain. Air brings intelligence and understanding; Fire brings enthusiasm and ambition. Don't let Fiery passion overcome common sense and rational decision. Take care to balance innovation with awareness of all that is involved; reinforce perception with enthusiasm and desire. "You"—the whole personality—have the power to bring balance to all the primal elements and thus negotiate Life with purpose and success. Air, the Mind, is your instrument to control passions, instincts, hungers, emotions. Use your "common sense, and live well and wisely.

In a divination, it signals time to move forward from passion only to compassion, supported by idealism and wisdom. To build a bridge, you need an idea, desire, faith, and work—but it gets you from the end of one road to the beginning of another on the other side—giving you the choice of staying where you are or moving ahead. Don't let your vision of the road ahead blind you to the road past: Innovation should be evolutionary and not revolutionary. Past supports Future.

Air—Seed of Ether:
Planning for Change

Air—Seed of Ether

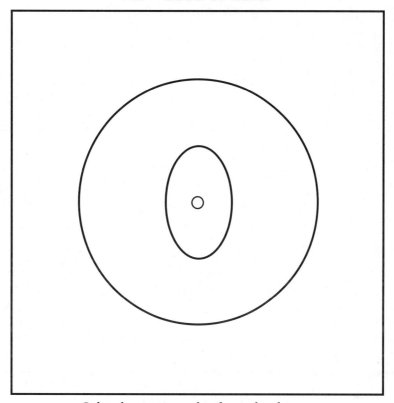

Color the tiny inner bindu circle white,
the inner triangle red,
the inner circle blue,
and the outer square orange

Air—Seed of Ether: Vayu & Akasha YAM & VAM

Review

We urge you to review the Element Overview Table #4 for **Air** on page 214 and Table #5 for Ether on page 272 in preparation for this procedure and the Divination and other applications involved with this compound.

The Tattvic Connection Meditation
& Visualization Program #25: Air/Ether
Air—Seed of Ether

Introduction. The Purpose & Function of this Procedure.

Rather than repeating the procedure in its entirety, we are asking you to kindly refer to page 396 for the complete *Tattva Connection Meditation & Visualization Compound Program #7 and make your own adjustments to substitute "**Air**" for "**Earth**" and "**Ether**" for "**Water**" in steps 2 (goal statement), 3 (affirmations. (I know that seems redundant, but in the psychic world little things count for a lot.) We are here providing content for Steps 5 (preparing and coloring the yantra card), 9a (yantra card focus), 10a. (experience the compounded elements and 11 (knowing the compounded elements).*

The Program's Variables:

Steps 2. Goal Statement.

Note your need to consider how to express your goals to reflect the particular natures of the two elements in their primary and secondary combination in relation to your physical, emotional, mental and spiritual well-being, and their functions in divination, magick, and self-growth.

Step 3. Affirmations.

You need to write positive affirmations to accomplish your goals.

Step 5. Preparation.

Preparing the Yantra Card.

It is recommended that you photocopy the illustration on page 531, preferably on heavier paper or card stock, or draw it yourself in exactly the same sizes using a ruler and black pen. If you can manage it, using a drawing compass or a template, draw a tiny ⅛" inch diameter circle in the exact center. Leave the inside of the circle white. This inner circle or point aids your steady focus. It is not essential, but it is helpful. Make the outer square 4" x 4" and the inner **Air Circle** should be 2½" wide and centered, the inner **Ether Egg** ¹¹⁄₁₆" wide and 1¹³⁄₁₆" tall, and the little **Bindu** circle in the exact center should be ⅛" in diameter and have a black line around it and the little **Egg** but not quite as thick as those around the **Circle** and the outer **Square**.

Coloring the Yantra Card.

It will be beneficial for you to color the image as follows: (a) color the tiny inner **Bindu Circle White**; (b) the small **Ether Egg Bright Indigo**; (c) the **Air Circle Bright Blue**; and (d) the surrounding outer square **Bright Orange.** The outer **Bright Orange Square** and the **Bright Blue Circle** are bordered with bold black lines, the small **Indigo Egg** is bordered with a less bold black line, and the tiny inner **Bindu Circle** is bordered with a thinner black line.

Step 9a. Yantra Card Focus.

If you have constructed the tattva yantra card as described, turn on the light and focus it on the card held or positioned comfortably about a foot to a foot and a half in front of you.

If possible, arrange your chair to face the primary tattvic direction: *East* for **Air.** Otherwise—think and feel *East.* (To the extent you feel the secondary element's importance to the operation; you can finish with an acknowledgment of *Skyward* for **Ether.**

Vibrate the name of the two tattvas: ***Vayu*** and ***Akasha,*** alternating one after the other. Repeat three times.

Chant or hum the tattva element mantras ***YAM*** and ***HAM*** (pronounced ***YA-UUM*** and ***HA-UUM),*** alternating. Vibrate the mantra as instructed in Step 1, preliminaries. Repeat three times. Later, you can do more but always in groups of three. And feel the mantra vibrate *over the Heart,* the location of **Anahata** chakra, and then *at the Throat,* the location of **Vishuddha** chakra.

Focus on the small white circle* at the center of the image, and stare at it for as long as you can without blinking. When you can't continue the "burning" feeling any longer, turn off the light, close your eyes and focus your inner sight on the space in front of your brow chakra (between your eye brows and on the ridge you can feel just above your nose), and see the small **Indigo Egg** in the **Blue Circle** floating in the space before you and vibrating within the **Orange Square.** And, then, you will soon see the tattva image change into the complementary yantra colors of **Yellow/Orange, Bright Orange,** and **Blue.**

Again vibrate the names to the tattvas and chant or hum the mantras three times.

Absorb this yantra image! As you repeat the exercise, often, you will reach a point when you will be able to recall this image at will.

*The small white circle is called a "Bindu," and focus on it is comprehensive of the entire tattvic image and all its energies. There is a small spot on the

back of your head that likewise serves as a comprehensive psychic center used in certain meditational exercises. A Bindu is also the name of a single drop of semen, the focal point of a new life. And "bindu" is likewise the single point from which all creation began "in the union of divine forces, Male and Female, God and Goddess, Siva and Shakti in all their names and images—i.e., the "Big Bang."

Bindu is a point of leverage where force applied becomes force multiplied and directed to accomplish your particular goal.

Step 9b. Yantra Visualization.

Alternatively, if you haven't made an **Air/Ether** card, immediately in front of you, visualize the image as described for making the card. See the image gently vibrating. And then the colors will reverse to their complementary yantra colors.

Step 10a. Experiencing Compounded Elemental Air and Elemental Ether.

Feel yourself becoming totally *absorbed** in the image while retaining awareness of the surrounding outer tattvic **Bright Orange Square.** As the tattvic **Blue** changes to the complementary yantra **Bright Orange** and the outer square to **Blue** feel *your* **Air** nature harmonize with the Cosmic **Ether**, and feel all impurities in your **Ether** Tattva—all emotional garbage and unconscious psychic attachments—dissipate. The tattvic **Indigo** will change to the complementary yantra **Yellow Orange** as your **Ether** nature harmonizes with the Cosmic **Ether** Tattva and the impurities of your **Ether** tattva dissipate.

> **Becoming absorbed.* Enter into the **full image** and become one with it and feel surrounded by it. Moving inward from the outer **Square** become one with the **Air** Element, and then move inward to become one with the **Ether** Element, and then further in to the **Bindu** to become one with **All.** Now, moving outward from the **Bindu** point to the **Ether Egg** and then to the **Air Circle** and to its outer edge feel the balanced **Air** and **Ether** elements in your body become harmonized and purified as they are balanced with their **Cosmic Source.**

In particular: feel the **Air** and **Ether** nature of your physical body become free of **nervous agitation** and **feelings of isolation**. Feel your body becoming ideally healthy, strong, and energized. See your body in perfect health, free of any excess weight, free of pain and disfigurement, free of illness, and fully energized. Feel your **Mental** and **Spiritual** selves becoming **Connected** and **Creative.**

Step 11. Knowing Elemental Air compounded with Elemental Ether.

Allow yourself to receive any information or messages from you're experiencing of these Elemental Forces. *In particular: receive information involving your **Physical** and **Mental/Spiritual** health and strength at both material and astral levels.* Receive the information without any emotional reaction and know that the knowledge is fully activated within your psyche.

Continue on with the Programs to Conclusion.

DIVINATION GUIDE TO AIR—SEED OF ETHER
Air—Seed of Ether: *Evolution, or Revolution?*

"Air over Ether," as in a mathematical formula, suggests an impossibility of Elemental Air dominating Elemental Space (Ether, Spirit). Air is atmosphere, rising and thinning into nothingness to disappear into Space. But Space is also everywhere—between things, in things, and beyond things. Ether is the Beginning and the Culmination of the other primal elements. But we are not dealing with mathematics but with powerful symbols that are not limited by material or even intellectual realities. "Air—Seed of Ether" is a reminder that you are without limit; you can be anything you want to be. Everything is before you, so Change is upon you.

In a divination, it is a signal to plan for change with intelligence and intuition. This change may have been brought on by past actions and failures, but it is nevertheless an open field of opportunity that may "Knock but Once" in a lifetime, and perhaps not at all for most people. You now can "grasp the brass ring" and reach for the higher prize. What you want to do is tie up all loose ends so you can move freely without the drag of the past. It's the "Chance of a Lifetime"—your lifetime.

CHAPTER FOURTEEN

Clairvoyance in Business, in Work & Career, and Education

INTRODUCTION

The content of this book is the work of both Joe Slate and myself, Carl Llewellyn Weschcke, who is also its "Managing Editor" responsible of integrating text, producing the various tables as well as the Tables of Contents, of Illustrations and Photographs, of Charts, Lists and Tables, and of Programs and Procedures, the Index and Glossary, and the "etc." of those little things that support the content in its delivery to the reader.

In most cases, a chapter is written totally by one or the other author, in a few cases by both of us without any separation, but in this particular case I felt that the two parts were so distinctive as to warrant our separate authorship credit.

It's not that the distinction is particularly overt—as it would be in an *anthology*—but in Part One Joe's material is absolutely unique and his *Multiversal Power Program* so effective that I just felt the authorship should be specifically credited. In addition, we will be making the *Multiversal Power Program* also available as an Audio CD product.

Part One: Clairvoyance is Purposeful and Empowerment Driven, by Joe H. Slate

Be thy own palace or the world's thy jail.

John Donne
"To Sir Henry Wotton" (1633)

Clairvoyance as an etheric extension of sensory perception is consistently purposeful and empowerment driven. Whether spontaneous or induced, it is valued primarily because of its capacity to unveil realities otherwise unavailable to us. By increasing our awareness of existing conditions of both present and future relevance, clairvoyance becomes a powerful force that empowers us to more effectively manage present realities and facilitate achievement of our personal goals. Pursuits related to all areas of our lives, including educational, business, work, and careers, are all enriched through clairvoyant insight and our readiness to apply it.

Clairvoyance is both multifunctional and global in its capacity to reach beyond "what is." It can probe our innermost being and activate potentials related to all areas of life. In that role, it can be a source of enlightenment that dissolves growth block-ages, inspires motivation, and promotes success. On a much larger scale, clairvoyance can provide a three-dimensional picture of physical reality without limits. It can reach beyond the range of our most advanced space technology to encompass the full uni-verse. There is, in fact, compelling evidence that clairvoyance can reach beyond our known universe to reveal the multiverse. As later discussed, that capacity was illustrat-ed in our labs in which volunteer participants used clairvoyance to view the universe and its position among other universes within a comprehensive cosmic pattern.

Bridging the Gap between Known and Unknown

The capacity of clairvoyance to effectively bridge the gap between the known and unknown was further illustrated in our labs by even so-called "lower" animals. For instance, in the structured maze setting with all appropriate controls in place, a group of mice chose significantly beyond chance the maze that led to escape rather than to punishment by mild electrical shock. In another experiment, even fruit flies demon-strated their capacity to choose a maze that led to escape rather than to entrapment. Admittedly, more research is needed to further verify the results of these pioneer-ing efforts, but even without further validation, these studies suggest the existence of clairvoyance as a universal phenomenon with possibilities related to all areas of life. Situations involving choice, however, seem to be particularly conducive to clair-voyance, a finding that suggest a powerful relevance of clairvoyance to such areas as choosing a career and succeeding in business

Clairvoyance: The Integrative Science of Learning and Success

From the cradle to the grave, we are here to learn and grow, often through prac-tice and experience. Without learning, we are minnows trapped is a shallow, isolated stream, darting aimlessly to-and-fro. Through learning that expands the borders of our existence, we become liberated from all self-constricting thoughts, beliefs, and expectations. Learning becomes the key that unlocks the door to progress and success, whether in education, business, work, career pursuits, or any other area of life. Satis-faction, happiness, and success become available to everyone through the integrative power of learning that includes clairvoyance.

Clairvoyance as a learning process is a source knowledge, insight, and power unavailable to us from any other source. But beyond that, it is an integrative force that incorporates sensory awareness, cognition, and affect into a broader spectrum which embraces the totality of reality. Though it may seem extreme to some, it is only through the integrative power clairvoyance that all limitations to success, both professionally and personally, are finally extinguished. Only through the integrative power of clairvoyance can we become fully self-empowered.

The Fourfold Awareness of Unseen Realities

Over recent years, the study of clairvoyance has progressively become recognized as an important body of systematized knowledge due in part to controlled research that verified its existence as an integrative science of learning and success. The developmental role of clairvoyance as a self-empowering science is at least fourfold:

1. It can focus awareness outward to view otherwise unseen realties. These can include not only the physical but the spiritual as well, including other planes and higher dimensions of reality.

2. It can focus awareness inward to identify dormant potentials and ways of developing them. In that role, it can accelerate our personal growth and promote our achievement of stated goals.

3. It can uncover conditions that inhibit our growth, including the possibility of unresolved past-life experiences.

4. It can integrate our perceptions and concepts in ways that expanded awareness of our uniqueness as persons of dignity and incomparable worth.

The evidence is clear: There exists absolutely no substitute for clairvoyance as a self-empowering integrative force. Here are a few other examples of the critical relevance of clairvoyance to learning and success.

The Critical Relevance of Clairvoyance to Learning & Success

- Clairvoyance can build self-confidence and increase motivation to learn and grow.
- It can generate a state of inner balance that builds feelings of security and well-being.
- It can promote the positive transfer of learning in which acquired skills are transferred to other areas of learning.
- It can increase motivation and dissolve growth blockages.
- It can generate a positive state of readiness to learn and grow.
- It can add meaning to life unavailable from any other source.

Clairvoyance, learning, and success are clearly interrelated. Together, they work hand-in-hand to generate totally new growth possibilities along with a powerful expectancy effect that increases the probability of success in all areas of life, including education, business, work, and careers. *Through clairvoyance, we accelerate learning; and through learning, we increase our clairvoyant skills.* The results are not only success but quality of life without limits.

Clairvoyance in the Real World

In the real world of work, clairvoyance is often the deciding factor that ensures success. That function is especially evident in competitive business situations in which clairvoyant insight related to such areas as production, advertising, consumer preference, and product appeal can be essential to success. Even in competitive sports and recreational activities, our studies showed that performance was enhanced through training in clairvoyance. In such games as poker, chess, and bridge, participants with formal training in clairvoyance typically performed better than subjects with no formal training.

Improved Management Programs

Along another line, our case studies of business managers found that mastery of clairvoyance skills dramatically increased their efficiency. The results included more effective management programs related to *employee selection, advertising, product marketing,* and *expansion.* In larger business settings, clairvoyance was found to be effective in *identifying problems* and *providing insight* on how to solve them. More specifically, it often identified more effective *production procedures* and ways of implementing them.

Among the interesting findings of our research was the fact that workers in high risk occupations were typically altruistic in their concerns for the safety of co-workers. It was not unusual for workers in high risk settings to clairvoyantly sense potentially danger and ways to effectively intervene. They were typically attentive to the welfare of others and showed a strong willingness to immediately help co-workers caught in danger situations, even at their own risk. That characteristic often resulted in a powerful bond among workers in high-risk job settings, a factor that could help explain their remarkably high level of job satisfaction.

As in the business and other work settings, clairvoyance has shown important relevance as a multifunctional skill in the educational setting. Our case studies of college students enrolled in various courses of study showed that participation in a clairvoyant development program *increased motivation, accelerated learning,* and *improved retention.* Clairvoyance was also shown to promote *effective decision making* involving both social and career goals. Students with undeclared majors or who were ambivalent regarding their career goals were successful in using clairvoyance to clarify their academic majors and career pursuits.

Aside from its application by students, clairvoyance can be effective when used by educators to facilitate *development of new programs and courses* of study designed to meet student needs. It can be especially effective when used in preliminary planning toward establishing new interdisciplinary programs in which each discipline contributes to the other. On a broader scale, clairvoyance as a planning strategy can help identify important global needs and the employment prospects related to them. In its integrative role, clairvoyance can help *identify global trends and career prospects* for new academic specialties. That possibility was illustrated in the university setting by the development of a new program in environmental technology. Once implemented, the program received enthusiastic reception by students and became among the university's most popular majors.

The Multiversal Power Program

Possibly the ultimate clairvoyant experience is that of viewing the multiverse with its array of universes, each functioning separately but in synchronization with the others. The Multiversal Power Program was developed in our labs specifically for that purpose. The program was designed first to initiate clairvoyant viewing of the planet and from there, to facilitate viewing of the full universe. Finally, clairvoyant viewing is expanded to encompass the multiverse with its multiple universes, including our own, all functioning within a pattern of *multiverse synchronicity*. Through the Multiverse Power Program, you can experience the multiverse with its diversity of characteristics, including those of relevance to your personal existence. You will not only increase your world view, your will broaden your awareness of your existence within the multiverse. Here's the eight-step program that can be administered as either an individual or group exercise:

Step 1. Set aside approximately one hour for the program which is administered in a quiet, comfortable setting free of any distraction. The affirmations presented throughout the program can be presented either silently or audibly. Here's the program which can be implemented as either an individual or group exercise.

Step 2. Mind/body/spirit Synchronicity. Let your mind, body, and spirit merge to generate a balanced state of mental, physical, and spiritual harmony. With your eyes closed, take in a few deep breaths and exhale slowly as relaxation flows throughout your body. Affirm: *I am at complete harmony, both within myself and with all that exists.*

Step 3. Planetary Orientation. Visualize the planet and sense your connection to it. Let you awareness of the planet expand to take in its fullness, to include continents, oceans, islands, deserts, plains, mountains, rivers and so forth. Continue to focus on the planet and your existence upon it. Allow a clear *clairvoyant planetary map* to emerge as you affirm: *I am at one with the world.*

Step 4. Universal Orientation. Visualize the universe and sense your connection to it. Note its stars, galaxies, and intergalactic spaces. Take plenty of time to view its features, including its central region and outer reaches. Give special attention to specific parts of the universe that command your awareness. Let a complete picture of the universe emerge as a *clairvoyant universal map.* Affirm: *I am now at one with the universe.*

Step 5. Multiversal Orientation. Think of our universe as one among many universes. As you continue to view our universe, let images of other universes emerge. Note differences among universes in size, brightness, structure, motion, patterns, and other features along with distances separating universes. Pay particular attention to the position of our universe among other universes. Allow a clear *clairvoyant multiversal map*s to emerge. Focus your full attention on the map as you affirm: *I am now at one with the multiverse. The multiversal map will remain clear in my mind.*

Step 6. Multiversal Liberation. Allow clairvoyant enlightenment related to the multiverse to unfold. Give particular notice to the various universes that command your attention. Note any unusual features among universes, particular unique identifying features that set a particular universe apart from others. Notice any sense of personal connectedness to a particular universe, including the possibility of a past-life linkage or other association with it.

Step 7. Empowering Affirmation. Turn your attention again to the planet and your position upon it. As in Step 2, let your mind, body, and spirit again merge to generate a balanced state of mental, physical, and spiritual harmony as you again affirm: *I am at complete harmony, both within myself and with all that exists.*

Step 8. Documentation. Document the experience by recording it in a personal clairvoyant journal. Include in your documentation the clairvoyant maps that emerged during the program. Give special attention to specific details and patterns along with personal impressions that unfolded during the experience.

In our development of this program, both objectivity and flexibility were emphasized as essential to the clairvoyant perceptions related not only to our planet but the universe and the multiverse as well. Although no effort was made to shape the specific perceptions of our participants, strong similarity was noted in their personal reports of the experience. To document their experience, they each drew a map after the exercise depicting the universe with other universes surrounding it as perceived during clairvoyant viewing. A comparison of their maps revealed amazing consistency regarding the location of our planet in the universe as well the location of our universe in the multiverse. The earth, for instance, was typically found near the center of the upper left quadrant of the universe; whereas the location of our universe was typically found in the upper right quadrant of the multiverse. A strong consistency was also noted in the documentation maps regarding the locations and comparative sizes of the multiple universes.

Further efforts to validate the accuracy of the Multiversal Power Program included the use astral projection with a group of volunteer participants who had no experience in multiversal viewing. The results were in some instances highly consistent with the experiences of our research participants who used the Multiversal Power Program, a finding that raises the possibility that astral projection could have occurred during the application of that program. Our research participants with past experience in astral projection, however, were convinced that the Multiversal Power Program experience was distinctly unlike astral projection.

The documentation reports of our research participants often noted areas of color occurring during their clairvoyant viewing, particularly of our planet. They concluded that the color red typically suggested adversity or a potential catastrophe such as revolution, warfare, widespread abuse of human rights, and environmental threats. In one remarkable instance, a bright area of red over Ecuador was observed by several of our research participants a few days before a volcano erupted in that exact area, an event that required the evacuation of scores of families. Rather than a precognitive signal, the area of red was a "hot spot" that commanded clairvoyant awareness. Another hot spot that grabbed the attention of our research subjects appeared over Wellington, New Zealand a few days before an earth quake occurred. Other hot spots have recently been observed over New York City and Nashville, Tennessee. In contrast to red hot spots, areas of bright light typically signified peace and progress. Interestingly, the earth as clairvoyantly viewed was typically enveloped in radiant blue, a hopeful feature that, according to our research subjects, signaled the potential for global advancement. Here are a few other conclusions based on the documentation reports of our research participants:

Movement Patterns characterizing the Universe & Multiverse

- Aside from color features, the clairvoyant viewings of our research participants revealed a variety of movement patterns characterizing both the universe and multiverse.

- Highly active circular movements within either the universe or multiverse were typically accompanied by rapid expansion of the external limits.

- The movements among certain universes, however, were constrictive inward patterns that suggested a "dying universe".

- Vast fixed areas of darkness were typically seen as the "seat of an extinguished or imploded universe". Such a "cosmic grave site" was common within the vast multiverse.

- Our universe and the multiverse are in a state of constant expansion.

- At present, there exists no clear evidence of a parallel universe.

- Once the outer edges of both our universe and others reach their limits, constriction and enfoldment will occur with resultant implosion.

- Constricted areas of darkness in the universe and multiverse indicate possible areas of *extinction by implosion.*

- A particular universe, once imploded, no longer exists.

- There exists intelligent life beyond.

Reaching Upward and Beyond

Clairvoyance is a driving force that can empower you not only to lean forward but to reach upward and beyond. Through clairvoyance related to education, business, work, and career along with all other areas of life, you can "power up" with new knowledge and success. You can expand your perceptions of "what exists" and your horizons for unlimited achievements. A new world of possibilities becomes a present reality in your life. Through the power of clairvoyance, you can become, in a word, *empowered!*

Part Two: Clairvoyance is part of Your Life, by Carl Llewellyn Weschcke

We've said it many times: *Clairvoyance can be an ever-present function in your daily life.* Everyone has some clairvoyant ability, and that ability manifests in different ways, in varying degrees, and at different levels in the course of nearly all your activities—at home, at work, at play, at school. It's particularly prominent in the relationship between family members, between fellow students, workers, and associates, with team players, and any time you are "looking ahead" whether driving an automobile or spying on the enemy, or recognizing and solving a problem, inventing, innovating and being creative, and in sports activities where split-second decisions must be made with "that-moment" awareness of all the action around you.

Clairvoyance is Innate to Everyone

Clairvoyance, as with all "psychic powers," is innate to everyone. As a result it cannot be "learned" in the same way you can learn an academic subject or professional skill. Clairvoyance must be developed thorough (1) your recognition of it in your life and (2) its exercise with or without the particular aids we otherwise refer to as "tools and techniques."

But, clairvoyance benefits from everything you learn through study, development, exercise, and accumulating experience. And, with only a few bizarre exceptions, your psychic development benefits from everything that's "good for you"—for your body, mind, and spirit.*

> *"Spirit." Please do not identify spirit with religion! Spirit is part of your being in the same way that body, emotions, and mind are. It's become a generalized term for things that are *beyond* physical including etheric energies, psychic powers, and various manifestations of our astral, mental and causal levels of our greater being.

> There have been bizarre incidents where serious brain injuries have led to clairvoyance, where mal-nourishment has led to increased sensitivity to spiritualist phenomena and communications, where physical torture has led to out-of-body experiences, and so forth. While we can learn from these and adapt what we learn from those experiences to our paranormal technology—as in the cases of sensory deprivation and other examples found in the chapter on techno-shamanism—never make the mistake of identifying the skill with the tool. A hammer and saw does not make one a carpenter nor does a crystal ball turn a person into a clairvoyant.

Extended Awareness

Think about all the activity going on in a big pro football game at any crucial moment and consider whether "normal" awareness is sufficient for a player whose vision is partially obscured by helmet and face guard, whose hearing is overwhelmed by the roar of the crowd, all the players are in constant (and spontaneous) motion, lights flashing from cameras in every direction, and probably many other factors a non-player knows nothing about. Without the extended awareness of clairvoyance at these moments, *success would be impossible.*

And that word, "success," is a measure of clairvoyant involvement. Any success beyond the "norm" is at least partly the result of the expanded "vision" of clairvoyance at work. *We can all become successful!*

Where everything is above normal

It's like Garrison Keillor's fictional Minnesota community, Lake Wobegone, where it's always nice and warm even when there's a little snow on the ground, and "the women are all strong, the men are all good looking and the children are above average." *Why not? Set your goals and a new reality starts happening.*

Clairvoyance is so normal that you rarely recognize it when it is happening. Rarely is there a dramatic ray from the sky above or halo of great light surrounding you, a sound of trumpets or an angelic choir, or other announcement that you are having a commanding vision that will make all the difference in the situation.

"Tools of the Trade"

Yes, we can make use of particular *aids*—such as a crystal ball or diving rod, or practice powerful programs of self-hypnosis or go into deep meditation, or deliberately raise our vibrations and enter into an altered state of consciousness—but such actions are exactly just "aids" to develop and exercise your innate psychic ability called clairvoyance. Never credit them for more than that, but don't disregard their value as "tools of the trade." Tools and aids are very important and without their use your development and "perfection" of any skill—psychic or otherwise—is slowed.

Anytime you are exercising your native talents, your vocational or professional training, calling upon your accumulating experience and expertise, or just trying to "do better," you are *extending* your awareness towards a particular goal, *expanding* your consciousness and *focusing* it upon its attainment.

Etheric Extensions of Sensory Organs

Clairvoyance is a function of particular aspects of your "whole being complex"—including actual physical organs of sensory perception and their etheric extensions, and in varying degrees astral and mental involvement. Generally we can establish three levels of clairvoyance roughly corresponding to involvement of particular chakras. For the moment, just call them *Lower, Middle,* and *Higher* Clairvoyance.

Lower Clairvoyance—Gut Feelings

(It would be helpful if you would review information in Chapter Five about the Chakras and Clairvoyance, and the methods for their activation.)

When you have that sudden feeling that's something's not right, that you might be danger, and sometimes instinctively know what to do for your own safety, you are experiencing Lower Clairvoyance. It often centers itself right in your "gut"—that lower part of your abdomen corresponding to the "Base" and "Sacral" chakras, *Muladhara* and *Swadhisthana,* which are strongly concerned with your physical health, security, and well-being. The psychic warning may manifest itself in uncomfortable intestinal upset.

The base chakra may signal dangers of sexual abuse, and the sacral chakra may signal relationship problems. Distinct information may be obtained through Dowsing, Pendulum Work, and Psychometrics.

Sometimes these two are joined by the "Solar Plexus" chakra, *Manipura,* when the endangerment is of a "higher" but *personal nature* such as hopes and concerns over financial, social or political matters. Then the feelings may manifest in stomach upset and even ulcers. Because the threats to your well-being are more "social" than physical (*Will your 401-K retirement fund be sufficient? Is your medical insurance adequate? Will you be able to afford living in your present home? How can I nurture important relationships?*), their understanding and distinction may also be more social and aided with such tools as the Tarot or Tea Leaf Reading.

Middle Clairvoyance—"Feelings," Good or Bad

Middle Clairvoyance is mostly associated with the "Heart" chakra, *Anahata,* and may also involve the "Throat" chakra, *Vishuddha.* Here we are less concerned with fears and dangers and more so with insights and creative opportunities. Now, we're "getting down to Business," and not just commercial, industrial, or financial *business* but to the *operational aspects* of the practices of Law, Healing, Counseling, Science, Teaching, Soldiering, Designing, Advertising, Innovating, and Entrepreneurial Technology.

At the same time that we are discussing the "higher" chakras, we are moving up the vibratory scale from base fears and desires to more abstract emotions and ideas, to hopes, loves, and actual vision. Even more importantly, we are moving upward from passive reaction to active actions.

Action is at the core of being Alive

No matter how minute a life-form may be, or how ill or near death it might be, as long as there is life, there is action. Even the phrase, "passive reaction" contains the word, and concept, of *action.* Living bacteria is active, living cells are active, the heart of dying person is active until the end.

Consciousness is part of all being. Even though it may at a level beneath our ability to perceive without aid, the activity of bacteria, of cells and even of a dying organ, is consciously driven by the life-form's inner purpose. But that purpose is limited by the boundaries of what the life-form is. *Consciousness is what is.*

Goals are <u>Beyond</u> "what is."

Even *desire* is an expression of "what is," but a Goal is set for "what is not" and moving beyond "what is" to "what can be." A Goal is a determination to *Become more than you are!* Working to fulfill goals is how we grow. Goal-driven action involves more of the Whole Person than reaction-driven action reflecting mostly biological needs of the lower chakras.

When we become sensitive to what is happening around us, that is reaction-driven clairvoyance. When we reach out beyond our present limits, we are using goal-driven clairvoyance.

"Reaching beyond" is the nature of being Human!

In lower education, we are taught that we are more than biologically defined animals. Along with Body, we have Mind and Spirit, and we also have Feelings and Emotions that reach out towards other people, other beings with Hopes and Loves.

As children and then as young adults, we want more things—more toys, more indulgences, more entertainment, and then more food, more fashionable clothing, a bigger home, a fancier car, more expensive jewelry and furniture, longer vacations, and more, more, and more of what modern culture—and no longer just Western or "Capitalist" culture—creates and trades as the foundation of the world economy.

In the 20th century we found that even those societies that claimed to be "classless" and dedicated only to "the common good and well-being of all citizens" instead wanted more goods, more weapons, more power, more land, and more subservience to the "command and control" of the leaders at the top. From political dictators whether called socialist or communist, to theocratic dictators claiming to know the "will of God," and democratic leaders claiming to represent the "will of the people," the message was the same: produce more to grow our wealth giving us more power to protect us from those who want to take from us, to limit us, and destroy our leadership.

But the *abuse of power* is not a determinant of the value of the economic and political system that has brought about the greatest material good the world has even seen along with the greatest distribution of wealth and of its redistribution in the form of education, health, science, knowledge, and personal empowerment to more people than ever before even imagined.

As we grow, we learn that the very essence of being human is not to just to want and have more, but to *become and be more.*

The Method of Achievement is called "Business"

No matter that we may be involved in such "non-profit" activities as medical and scientific research and development, of charitable and benevolent operations, of police and military management, education and the spread of information and knowledge, or of such service fields as healing and medical care, news and weather information and forecasts, entertainment, and all the forms of good government, *the method of their achievement are those systems, practices, and organization of resources that we know as "business," or*—sometimes—as the "back office."

In each of these, we establish and direct our efforts to the accomplishment of GOALS. The fulfillment of those goals may be measured by profit in the case of commercial, industrial and financial enterprises or by other criteria as the case may be, but the reality is that success is only possible through the applications of the "science of business administration" which brings together all the resources for successful operations within budgetary constraints.

Achievement is called "Success"

The full accomplishment of any Goal is called "Success."

And like the folks of mythical Lake Wobegone mentioned earlier, we practitioners of the new Science of the Paranormal are—of course—all above average, even above normal, so we can do things smarter and that's how we will *successfully* meet the challenges of our times.*

> *Of course, we are trying to introduce a little light humor into what otherwise may seem a heavy approach to the subject that is sometimes considered too "spiritual" to be practical. Business organization and practice is practical, and so is the development and application of clairvoyance to business. The important point is that success in any activity is a serious matter and should have practical application. If not, it is a waste of time and human resources, and is usually a one-person ego trip generally acknowledged by the wearing of fancy robes and hats.

"All achievements, all earned riches, have their beginning in an idea."

Napoleon Hill

One of the most distinctive forms of business style clairvoyance was popularized by Napoleon Hill (1883–1970) in his 1937 classic, *Think and Grow Rich.* He served as an advisor to President Franklin Delano Roosevelt from 1933 to 1936 during the worst years of the Great Depression. He wrote, and then popularized this important principle: **"What the mind of man can conceive and believe, it can achieve."**

Hill developed his "Achievement Philosophy" through interviews with over 500 of the most successful people* of his times and the study and analysis of their methods.

> *He started with Andrew Carnegie, and, at Carnegie's urging, went on to interview Thomas Edison, Alexander Graham Bell, George Eastman, Henry Ford, John D. Rockefeller, F. W. Woolworth, William Wrigley, John Wannamaker, William Jennings Bryant, U.S. Presidents Theodore Roosevelt and William H. Taft, and many others.

The Source of Personal Empowerment

Hill considered this system more than one of business success and believed that it was the responsibility of every human being to learn and practice it in daily life as a source of Personal Empowerment no matter their position or vocation. **"First comes thought; then organization of that thought, into ideas and plans; then transformation of those plans into reality. The beginning, as you will observe, is in your imagination." "Reduce your plan to writing. The moment you complete this, you will have definitely given concrete form to the intangible desire."**

Essentially Hill's Achievement Philosophy is a restatement of Business Science in esoteric terms recognizing that the whole human person is a complex of esoteric energies, principles and abilities as well as a physical, emotional and mental being. It is through such a restatement that we have a more complete Art and Science of Business Organization and Principles to meet our needs today and tomorrow. It's an Art and Science that is neither abstract nor difficult to apply to any situation, small or large. **"There is one quality which one must possess to win, and that is definiteness of purpose, the knowledge of what one wants, and a burning desire to possess it."**

Business Science

We require knowledge of our market (those who benefit from our service), knowledge of our product (what we provide to the market), the methods of its development and its production (creating the product or service), the channels of distribution (how we get our product to the user), advertising and promotion (how the product benefits the market), financing the operation (raising and applying capital), and administering the details (capital and human resources, benefits, taxes, etc.).

All of this requires a Vision (the Business Plan), Management (turning Vision into Reality), Application (What for Who), Forecast and Budget (What and When), Facilities (Where for What), Personnel (Who for What), and Training (the right Skills for what Job).

Training for Success

No matter what the business or service, no matter whether for-profit or non-profit, private or public, personal or corporate, governmental or academic, etc. pertinent skills make or break any enterprise.

The Four Factors for Success

Number 1. Of course, the most pertinent—and often the most overlooked—the #1 factor is specific subject expertise in the product or service being provided. In the modern business and financial climate, the MBA belief became that anything could be "managed by the numbers," through statistical analysis and spreadsheet comparisons. This false understanding eventually led to the detrimental practice of "leveraged buy-outs" of sound businesses, overloading them with debt, paying the fund investors huge dividends out of the borrowed money, and then—in many cases—the result was bankruptcy because it was now "over-leveraged." Financial shenanigans are not a substitute for management skill.

Number 2. The #2 factor—and often equally ignored—is specific management skills. There is both a science and an art to management, whether of a business, a non-profit, a charity, a governmental body, or any other organization functioning for a purpose. "Happy Fellowship" will not get the job done. And while "numbers" and "spreadsheets are tools of good management, they are only supplemental to the human factor.

Number 3. The #3 factor is specific financial skills. Yes, of course, money is the fluid that lubricates every organization. It is the "blood" necessary to nourish the organs and the people who create, produce, promote, sell, distribute, deliver, operate the "back office" (where the accounting, billing, collecting, customer service, etc., is carried on. Rather than "back office" it should be called the "back bone" for without it no organization can long stand). And money is also the reward to the people for a "job well done."

Number 4. The most forgotten factor is that of **ethics**. Amazingly, the most noble of intentions is often the most abused through greed for money, for power, for prestige, and for public recognition. Unless specific ethical rules are developed and adopted for the enterprise, and made omnipresent in everyone's conscience, it will eventually fail at great cost and suffering to those very people it was supposed to serve. (The worldwide financial crises of 21ˢᵗ Century provide amble examples of this.)

These skills are all beyond the purpose of this book and can be readily found in other books. What we do here is to describe what is pertinent to the development and application of "middle" clairvoyance to any chosen "business." And all of them— except two—are fully covered elsewhere in this book in specific applications of Self-Hypnosis.

The Science of Futurology

The first of these is the science of Futurology,* and an entire industry has developed to teach and apply technique to forecast the future by analysis of trends through professional courses enabling the student to choose from various methods when facing a particular challenge, to develop critical thinking, listening, and observational skills. And to learn about primary and secondary research methodologies and examine classical "futuring" techniques, including scenario planning, trend and product forecasting, crisis preparedness, transformation, and hyper-change sensitivity. Examples of courses currently being offered by the Futurist Society include:

- _Technology Transformations in Society, Work, and Higher Education_—reviewing current trends and shifts in the workforce that change the way that educators and employers need to service today's modern workforce;
- _The Human Dynamics of Creation to Effect Change_—tools and tips for overcoming barriers, anticipating opportunities, and unleashing new pathways to knowledge, leveraging research honoring the human spirit and creative problem solving;
- _Identifying and Exploring Security's Futures and What Can Be Done to Prepare_—How strategic foresight can shed light on and promote understanding of the challenges and opportunities provoked by the new security environment (national defense and public safety;
- _An Insider's Guide to Foresight Consulting_—Using a case-study approach, this course will illustrate the range of techniques and contexts in which using the future can make a difference for what people see and do in the present.
- _Scenario Planning: How to Build and Use Scenario_—teaching the best practices in extracting the value from scenarios—using them to test and improve decision making and distilling from competing scenarios the optimal decisions a specific organization in a particular sector at a given time should make;

- *Weak Signals and Minitrends: Foundations for Truly Innovative Organizations*—identifying weak signals and minitrends, analyzing their value, and taking full advantage of attractive opportunities.

  *Further information available from the World Future Society, 7910 Wood-mont Ave., Suite 450, Bethesda, MD 20814. www.wfs.org.

Aside from Futurology, knowledge of what is going in your chosen field is essential—read the journals and the trade publications, the news media, and In business, any business—commercial or otherwise—the more you know current information and trends, the better your chances of success. *Bloomberg's Businessweek* should be read weekly. And we feel it important to mention the very valuable daily intelligence reports available from STRATFOR, 221 W. 6th Street, Suite 400, Austin, TX 78701 US, www.stratfor.com.

In addition, of course, we suggest the very pertinent study of "real" astrology, and particularly such specialties as Mundane Astrology, Astro-meteorology, Financial Cycles, and others dealing with specific geographic areas and countries, with earth changes, and the natal horoscopes of current leaders.

The Group Mind

A "Group Mind" is mostly a spontaneous happening whenever a small group of people regularly comes together under the guise of either common interest or a shared purpose. Mostly it is an informal happening at a regular time and place—like meeting at Harry's Sports Bar every Tuesday evening—to mostly discuss a common interest such as Bass Fishing.

It can have a more serious shared purpose, as in developing a new business line or solving an accounting problem, but it rarely has a permanent existence, unless—for example—it continues on to develop another business line or to solve another accounting problem. In either example, the people involved may be changed to draw upon others within the business who have pertinent knowledge or experience for the new project. It's technically referred to as an *ad hoc* committee.

The Master Mind

The second skill pertinent to Business Clairvoyance is that developed by Napoleon Hill called "The Master Mind" also sometimes mistakenly referred to as the Group Mind. The difference is that the Master Mind is deliberately created by a small group of people, while a Group Mind spontaneously comes into being whenever a small group of people regularly come together.

The difference is important, and is defined by two concepts: 1) Common Interest, and 2) Shared Purpose. While the Group Mind is often a temporary or transitional function of a small number of people coming together with a common interest, OR a shared purpose, The Master Mind is a deliberate function of a small group of people, often on a long term or permanent basis with both a Common Interest and a Shared Purpose.

Today, it is commonly known as "the Board" or as a "Permanent Committee."

Even though a committee or board is commonly formed of a small group of people charged with a particular purpose, there is little awareness of the technique and potential of "The Master Mind."

Give it a NAME and a Statement of Purpose

It is important that the group endures at the astral and mental levels between meetings, and this is easily accomplished by giving it an identity by means of a name, a symbol or picture, and a written statement of purpose. The name might be obvious—such as "the Board of Directors for the Humongous Corporation," and the symbol might be the Corporate Logo, and there might be a portrait of the Company's founder on the meeting room wall.

The statement of purpose is the *raison d'être*—the reason for its existence. Rather than a mere repetition of the legal statement found in the corporate charter or minute book, it should define the purpose of both the entity and the function of the board or committee. Even though both are intended to "continue forever," the statement of purpose should be readily amended to adjust for the times.

What's this got to do with Clairvoyance?

As we wrote earlier, "Middle Clairvoyance" is mostly associated with the "Heart" chakra, Anahata, and may also involve the "Throat" chakra, Vishuddha. Here we are less concerned with fears and dangers and more so with insights and creative opportunities. Here we are really *"getting down to Business"*, and not just business per se but to the very nature of what people actively do in modern life everywhere on planet Earth.

Too often, the very word "corporate" suggests *not applicable to me!* Even if your business is small and unincorporated, perhaps employing only a very few people, or just yourself part time, and is operated out of personal desire or necessity, it is a business, and—depending on size and location—may be subject to various governmental rules and regulations you need to understand. It can be a small retail store, a summer time Vegetable & Fruit Garden, just a temporary freelance writing or reporting activity, but once you are in business the special factors and benefits of Middle Clairvoyance are also working.

Are they working for you?

Most probably, yes. But with awareness and understanding, the answer is not just probable but becomes firmly positive. The more of "self" that you *sink into the business,* the more of your total being is at work. And that's what you want, not only for the success of your business but also because it is a growth and developmental opportunity for yourself *to become more than you are.*

Heart Feelings

In this "business world"—whether working as a casual laborer or a school teacher, a social worker or a scientist, a soldier or police detective, a lawyer or a banker or writer of romance novels—you are actively employing the Heart Chakra in your daily life. Whether you are *sensing* or *seeking,* the special nature and energies of *Anahata* are working for you. Unlike occasional *Gut Feelings, Heart Feelings* are constantly at work except when you are sleeping, making love, or being entertained watching sports events, and even then your passive "social senses" are at work.

Your Heart is your constant companion—sensing information relating to your work, or responding to your active seeking with information and knowledge enabling you to creatively solve problems and make improvements in your work projects.

Heart Feelings are an extension of your whole being.

"Your Voice, Your Vote"

At the time of this writing, Americans were in the midst of Presidential campaigning, and ABC television had coined this phrase under which to present political news. But is also the perfect phrase to describe the clairvoyance of the Throat Chakra. (In a democracy, we are always voting, at one level or another, so your voice is always pertinent and far more important than most people realize who instead say: *What can I do about it?* You owe it to yourself, to your community, and to the "system" to think, study, speak out, and vote. It's part of the Self-responsibility I mention in all my writing. It's how you grow, and how you become more than you are.)

When we talk, we reach out for answers. Just as some people say that they "think with their fingers" as at the computer keyboard, others "think when they talk." It's not just asking questions, but in saying things we define what we are thinking about and the information we want. And, yes, the Throat Chakra is very sensitive to incoming data by means of clairaudience (the "hearing" variation of clairvoyance), telepathy, and channeling.

"Ask, and Ye shall Receive"

Because in talking we are constantly reaching out, the throat chakra is an active psychic organ constantly sensing things in our environment and particularly things of human origin. It is the "Creativity Center" in our work world. You can *talk* your way into finding solutions to your problems and answers to your questions.

"Talk is cheap" should not be perceived in a derogatory manner, but rather understood as an inexpensive technology and a personal "search engine" of a very high order.*

> *Note: In our *Llewellyn Complete Book of Psychic Empowerment: A Compendium of Tools & Techniques for Growth & Transformation* (Llewellyn, 2011) we provide very concise techniques to activate specific chakras.

Talk, and "Self-Talk" as Technology

One of the "techniques" that we write about throughout this book is that of Self-Hypnosis. Whether words are spoken out loud or silently, talk is involved. It can be called Active Meditation, Self-Hypnosis, Self-Talk, or Auto-Suggestion. It can include Visualization of Goals or of special symbols, it can include familiar words or Words of Power, and be Spoken, Chanted, or Sung. It can be accompanied by gestures or foot and body movements—all of which can be valid methods to further invoke, activate and deploy energies of the body and the Cosmos.

All of these can be studied as expansions of the fundamental technique, but there is one fundamental principle that was well and simply described in Napoleon Hill's writing:

"Your ability to use the principle of autosuggestion will depend, very largely, upon your capacity to concentrate upon a given desire until that desire becomes a burning obsession."

The Heart Chakra, along with the Solar Plexus and the other lower chakras, is a resource and a transformer of energies that be simply and effectively aroused and directed towards the accomplishment of your established goal exactly as Hill describes. The technology has other names, including Magick, Tantra (not sexual), Shamanism, and many others East and West, North and South, but many times people presume or fail to grasp that this principle, and the entire concept of energy arousal and direction, cannot and even should not be applied in business and every day matters.

There is nothing wrong, evil, or unethical in bringing all your knowledge and strength to bear to accomplish an objective so long as that objective itself is ethical. Being successful in business by honest methods is not unethical.

Higher Clairvoyance—"Power Up!"

Please note that we discuss Higher Clairvoyance in greater detail in Chapter Eighteen, where we write:

Clairvoyance at the higher level is not just a psychic skill but a culmination of a developmental process involving the Whole Person. It's not merely the awakening of a dormant psychic power but the purposeful evolution of innate clairvoyant power brought about by a deliberate and personal program of "spiritual" practice.

Here we limit the discussion only to the business applications. The two Higher Chakras of *Ajna* at the Brow and *Sahasrara* at the Crown are those involved in Higher Clairvoyance. The powers associated with *Ajna* are Clairvoyance, Telepathy, Telekinesis, Precognition, Remote Viewing, and Aura Reading, and those of *Sahasrara* are Astral Projection and Prophecy.

At the same time, the exercises given in Chapter Five and intended to specifically awaken *Intuition*, and it is this particular aspect of Clairvoyance that is pertinent as the broad vision we want to employ at the highest level in business. It is this, presumably, that led to Steve Jobs greatest and most transformative products at Apple, to Bill Gates' great innovation of Windows and Office Applications at Microsoft, to Mark Zuckerberg's achievement at Facebook, to Larry Page and Sergey Brin vision of Google, and to the other notable achievements by such single entrepreneurs as Andrew Carnegie, Thomas Edison, Henry Ford, and other great names in American industry.

The "Visionaries"

These are the people in business that we refer to as "Visionaries," the founders of great innovative enterprises. Mostly these visionaries have pioneered new technologies. None of them are "capitalists" per se. They are not the people who buy and sell businesses and assemble them into "empires."

Yes, of course, such high level visionaries have appeared elsewhere—America's "founding fathers" like Thomas Jefferson, George Washington, and Ben Franklin; great scientists like Galileo, Leonardo da Vinci, and Carl Jung; philosophers like Confucius, Plato, Plotinus, and Socrates; and many, many others in all fields and cultures throughout history, but our concern is with the immediate potential for you to become a visionary.

Great Answers to Great Problems

You can develop high level clairvoyance through the methods described in Chapter Five and elsewhere in this book, but you also have to be a Great Mind searching for Great Answers to Great Problems. To achieve Greatness you have to seek Greatness. Not for the rewards of money and power, but for the Insights, and the Service to Mankind. Great Wealth was not the goal for Steve Jobs or Bill Gates; Great Wisdom was not the goal for Plotinus or Carl Jung; Marvelous Inventions were not the goal of Da Vinci.

In our *Llewellyn Complete Book of Psychic Empowerment: A Compendium of Tools & Techniques for Growth & Transformation* (Llewellyn, 2011) we provide very concise techniques to activate specific chakras along with a short chapter on clairvoyance. Also, guidance to the employment of many tools and aids to your employment of clairvoyance.

Higher Clairvoyance brings its own rewards

Sources and Suggested Additional Reading:

Bloomberg's Businessweek.

Hill, N. *The Law of Success,* 1928.

Hill, N. *Think and Grow Rich,* 1937.

Slate, J. H. & Weschcke, C. L. *Llewellyn Complete Book of Psychic Empowerment: A Compendium of Tools & Techniques for Growth & Transformation,* 2011, Llewellyn.

STRATFOR, 221 W. 6th Street, Suite 400, Austin, TX 78701 US, www.stratfor.com.

World Future Society, 7910 Woodmont Ave., Suite 450, Bethesda, MD 20814. www.wfs.org.

ADDENDUM #14 TO CHAPTER 14

Microcosm to Macrocosm & Macrocosm to Microcosm

The Tattvic Connection—
Meditation & Visualization Programs #26–#30

Ether—and its Compounds

Ether, Aether, Aethyr, Spirit, Space, and "Clear Sky": Source & Resource, Start & Finish

It's all these things, and more. It's the Source for the other four Primal Elements but it's also one of the five Primal Elements. They all flow into one another and into Ether to become Universal Ether, and then flow out to again become Ether, Air, Fire, Water and Earth. It's like a constantly moving ladder going up and down, up and down, and then down and up.

And, remember there is no such thing as *Physical* Ether just as the other elements, despite their familiar names, are best understood as Astral rather than Physical.

From Spirit all things come; To Spirit all things return

In the case of this, the 5th Element, we will get further calling it "Spirit" and thinking of it as non-local—like Space—existing in things and between things. We have Spirit/Space, and we things suddenly appearing out of Space/Spirit and eventually disappearing back into Spirit/Space. It's also a matter of *dimensions*: the Physical/Etheric Plane has the familiar three, while the Astral adds Time and has four. The Mental/Causal Plane has five, the Buddhic six, and the Spiritual Plane has seven.

Essentially, that's intellectually incompressible, and meaningless from a practical perspective. And Spirit, our fifth Element, is not the same as the Spirit Body or the Spiritual Plane. The Sanskrit and Hebrew languages do a better job on having more definite words for these higher concepts. But, the fact is that neither you nor I presently go to these higher realms—they are in our evolutionary future. Our job is here and now, not "up there" and then.

Elemental Spirit is not the same thing as "spirits" of the departed. Nor is it the "Holy Spirit" of the Christian and other Trinities. Just think of it as the "Spirit behind things" because it is the element from which the other four primal elements appear and into which merge and again appear in a constant flux of renewal.

But, Spirit—like the other Primal Elements—has its own unique characteristics and functions, and its own Chakra and other relationships and correspondences as you see partially listed and summarize in the Elemental Overview Table #5 on page 272. It functions through the sense of hearing and the action of speech—communicating, singing, chanting, praying, invoking, and spontaneous expression of pain and other emotions (as in screaming).

Astral Senses and Actions

Like all the Primal Elements, Spirit/Ether is *Astral* and not Physical, but guides physical manifestations. All the physical senses and actions extend into the Astral and even higher planes. Physical Sight extends into the Astral and becomes *Clairvoyance;* Physical Hearing extends into the Astral and becomes *Clairaudience;* Physical Touch extended into the Astral becomes *Clairsentience;* the Physical senses of Smell and Taste extended into the Astral have their *Psychic Senses;* Physical Speaking extends into the Astral and becomes *Telepathy, Prophecy,* and the foundation for *Magickal Action.*

It is important to remember the No Thing is only One Thing but instead always exists and functions in and through the other planes but it is the Physical Plane (which is not the same thing as Elemental Earth!) that is the ultimate level of manifestation. We can act—as we become more aware of them—on the Higher Planes to influence and even change the process of physical manifestation.

Ether—Seed of Ether:
Renewal, Rebirth & Time to Move Forward

Ether—Seed of Ether

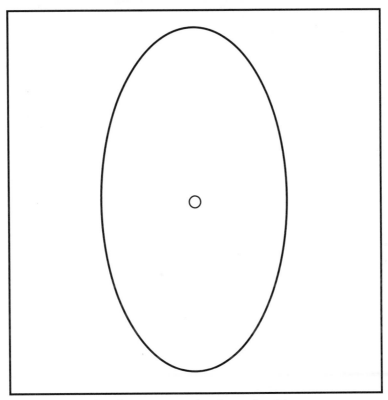

Color the tiny inner bindu circle white,
the inner oval indigo,
and the outer square yellow/orange

Ether—Seed of Ether: Akasha HAM

Review

We urge you to review the Element Overview Table #5 for **Ether** on page 272 in preparation for this procedure and the Divination and other applications involved with this compound.

The Tattvic Connection Meditation
& Visualization Program #26: Ether/Ether
Ether—Seed of Ether

Introduction. The Purpose & Function of this Procedure.

Rather than repeating the procedure in its entirety, we are asking you to kindly refer to page 396 for the complete *Tattva Connection Meditation & Visualization Compound Program #7 and make your own adjustments to substitute "Ether" for "Earth" in steps 2 (goal statement), 3 (affirmations. (I know that seems redundant, but in the psychic world little things count for a lot.) We are here providing content for Steps 5 (preparing and coloring the yantra card), 9a (yantra card focus), 10a. (experience the compounded elements and 11 (knowing the compounded elements).*

The Program's Variables:

Steps 2. Goal Statement.

Note your need to consider how to express your goals to reflect the particular natures of the two elements in their primary and secondary combination in relation to your physical, emotional, mental and spiritual well-being, and their functions in divination, magick, and self-growth.

Step 3. Affirmations.

You need to write positive affirmations to accomplish your goals.

Step 5. Preparation.

Preparing the Yantra Card.

It is recommended that you photocopy the illustration on page 561, preferably on heavier paper or card stock, or draw it yourself in exactly the same sizes using a ruler and black pen. If you can manage it, using a drawing compass or a template, draw a tiny ⅛" inch diameter circle in the exact center. Leave the inside of the circle white. This inner circle or point aids your steady focus. It is not essential, but it is helpful. Make the outer square 4" x 4" and the inner **Ether Egg** about 1¹⁵⁄₁₆" wide by 3³⁄₁₆" tall and centered, and the little **Bindu** circle in the exact center should be ⅛" in diameter and have a black line around it and the **Egg** but not quite as thick as those around the **Squar**e.

Coloring the Yantra Card.

It will be beneficial for you to color the image as follows: (a) color the tiny inner **Bindu Circle White;** (b) the large **Ether Egg Bright Indigo;** and (c) the surrounding larger square **Yellow Orange.** The outer **Square** and the **Egg** are bordered with bold black lines, and the tiny inner circle is bordered with a thinner black line.

Step 9a. Yantra Card Focus.

If you have constructed the tattva yantra card as described, turn on the light and focus it on the card held or positioned comfortably about a foot to a foot and a half in front of you.

If possible, arrange your chair to face the primary tattvic direction: In this case, just lean back and look *Skyward* for **Ether.** Otherwise—think and feel *Skyward.*

Vibrate the name of the tattva: *Akasha.* Repeat three times.

Chant or hum the tattva element mantra *HAM* (pronounced *HA-UUM.* Vibrate the mantra as instructed in Step 1, preliminaries. Repeat three times. Later, you can do more but always in groups of three. And feel the mantra vibrate *between over the Throat,* the location of **Vishuddha** chakra.

Focus on the small white circle* at the center of the image, and stare at it for as long as you can without blinking. When you can't continue the "burning" feeling any longer, turn off the light, close your eyes and focus your inner sight on the space in front of your brow chakra (between your eyebrows and on the ridge you can feel just above your nose), and see the small **Indigo Egg** floating in the space before you and vibrating within the **Yellow/Orange Square.** And, then, you will soon see the tattva image change into the complementary yantra colors.

Again vibrate the names to the tattvas and chant or hum the mantras three times.

Absorb this yantra image! As you repeat the exercise, often, you will reach a point when you will be able to recall this image at will.

> *The small white circle is called a "Bindu," and focus on it is comprehensive of the entire tattvic image and all its energies. There is a small spot on the back of your head that likewise serves as a comprehensive psychic center used in certain meditational exercises. A Bindu is also the name of a single drop of semen, the focal point of a new life. And "bindu" is likewise the single point from which all creation began "in the union of divine forces, Male and Female, God and Goddess, Siva and Shakti in all their names and images—i.e., the "Big Bang."
>
> Bindu is a point of leverage where force applied becomes force multiplied and directed to accomplish your particular goal.

Step 9b. Yantra Visualization.

Alternatively, if you haven't made an **Ether** card, immediately in front of you, visualize the image as described for making the card. See the image gently vibrating. And then the colors will reverse to their complementary yantra colors.

Step 10a. Experiencing Compounded Elemental Ether.

Feel yourself becoming totally *absorbed** in the image while retaining awareness of the surrounding tattvic **Yellow/Orange Square**. As the tattvic **Indigo Egg** changes to the complementary yantra **Yellow/Orange** feel *your* **Ether** nature harmonize with the Cosmic **Ether** Tattva, and feel all impurities in your **Ether** Tattva—all emotional garbage and unconscious psychic attachments—dissipate. The surrounding **Yellow/Orange Square** changes to yantra **Indigo.**

> **Becoming absorbed.* Enter into the **full image** and become one with it and feel surrounded by it. Moving inward from the outer **Square** become one with the **Ether** Element, and then move inward to the **Bindu** to become one with **All.** Now, moving outward from the **Bindu** point to the **Ether Egg** to the outer square's edge and feel the balanced **Ether** and the other elements in your body become harmonized and purified as they are balanced with their **Cosmic Source.**

In particular: feel the **Ether** nature of your physical body become free of adverse thoughts and feelings of **"Aloneness"**—of being **unconnected with the World**. Feel your body becoming ideally healthy, strong, and energized. See your body in perfect health, free of any excess weight, free of pain and disfigurement, free of illness, and fully energized. Feel your **Spiritual Self** becoming secure in your **Higher Consciousness and Understanding.**

Step 11. Knowing Elemental Ether

Allow yourself to receive any information or messages from you're experiencing of these Elemental Forces. *In particular: receive information involving your **Physical** and **Spiritual** health & strength at both **material** and **causal** levels.* Receive the information without any emotional reaction and know that the knowledge is fully activated within your psyche.

Continue on with the Programs to Conclusion.

DIVINATION GUIDE TO ETHER—SEED OF ETHER
Ether—Seed of Ether: *Rebirth, or Stagnation*

Ether is both the source and beginning of the other four primal elements, and their culmination and continuous rebirth. As Space, it is pregnant with possibilities, and calls for an open mind to see them. As Spirit it is renewal and rebirth, and the faith to willingly and eagerly move on. Growth requires that we have the self-discipline to develop new strengths.

In a divination, it signals the time to harvest past work, to see opportunities for expansion of business or personal pursuits, to embark on a new career, to experience a genuine "change of life." It is also a time for regeneration and rejuvenation through wise choices, and a time to let go of the past and be "born again" into the *Next Step* in human evolution that is individual to you.

Ether—Seed of Earth:
The Past is Prologue to the Future

Ether—Seed of Earth

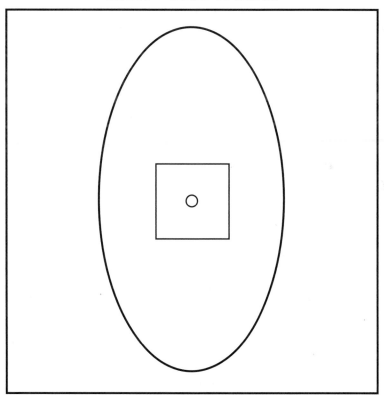

Color the tiny inner bindu circle white,
the inner square bright yellow,
the inner oval indigo,

Ether—Seed of Earth: Akasha & Prithivi HAM & LAM

Review

We urge you to review the Element Overview Table #5 for **Ether** on page 272 And the Element Overview Table #1 for Earth on page 104 in preparation for this procedure and the Divination and other applications involved with this compound.

The Tattvic Connection Meditation & Visualization Program #27: Ether/Earth
Ether—Seed of Earth

Introduction. The Purpose & Function of this Procedure.

Rather than repeating the procedure in its entirety, we are asking you to kindly refer to page 396 for the complete *Tattva Connection Meditation & Visualization Compound Program #7 and make your own adjustments to substitute "**Ether**" for "**Earth**" and "**Earth**" for "**Water**" in steps 2 (goal statement), 3 (affirmations. (I know that seems redundant, but in the psychic world little things count for a lot.) We are here providing content for Steps 5 (preparing and coloring the yantra card), 9a (yantra card focus), 10a. (experience the compounded elements and 11 (knowing the compounded elements).*

The Program's Variables:
Steps 2. Goal Statement.

Note your need to consider how to express your goals to reflect the particular natures of the two elements in their primary and secondary combination in relation to your physical, emotional, mental, and spiritual well-being, and their functions in divination, magick, and self-growth.

Step 3. Affirmations.

You need to write positive affirmations to accomplish your goals.

Step 5. Preparation.

Preparing the Yantra Card.

It is recommended that you photocopy the illustration on page 565, preferably on heavier paper or card stock, or draw it yourself in exactly the same sizes using a ruler and black pen. If you can manage it, using a drawing compass or a template, draw a tiny ⅛" inch diameter circle in the exact center. Leave the inside of the circle white. This inner circle or point aids your steady focus. It is not essential, but it is helpful. Make the **Outer Square** 4" x 4" and the inner **Ether Egg** should be about 2" wide by

3¼" tall and centered, the inner **Earth Square** ⅞" x ⅞", and the little **Bindu** circle in the exact center should be ⅛" in diameter and have a black line around it and the little **Square** but not quite as thick as those around the **Circle** and the outer **Square.**

Coloring the Yantra Card.

It will be beneficial for you to color the image as follows: (a) color the tiny inner **Bindu Circle White**; (b) the small **Earth Square Bright Yellow; (c)** the **Ether Egg Bright Indigo**; and (d) the surrounding outer square **Bright Yellow/Orange.** The outer **Bright Yellow/Orange Square** and the **Bright Indigo Egg** are bordered with bold black lines, the small **Yellow Earth Square** is bordered with a less bold black line, and the tiny inner **Bindu Circle** is bordered with a thinner black line.

Step 9a. Yantra Card Focus.

If you have constructed the tattva yantra card as described, turn on the light and focus it on the card held or positioned comfortably about a foot to a foot and a half in front of you.

If possible, arrange your chair to face the primary tattvic direction: In this case, simply lean back and look *Skyward* for **Ether**. Otherwise—think and feel *Skyward.* (To the extent you feel the secondary element's importance to the operation; you can finish with an acknowledgment of *North* for **Earth.**

Vibrate the name of the two tattvas: *Akasha* and *Prithivi*, alternating one after the other. Repeat three times.

Chant or hum the tattva element mantras *HAM* and *LAM* (pronounced *HA-UUM* and *LA-UUM),* alternating. Vibrate the mantra as instructed in Step 1, preliminaries. Repeat three times. Later, you can do more but always in groups of three. And feel the mantra vibrate *over the Throat*, the location of **Vishuddha** chakra, and then *at the Pelvis,* the location of **Muladhara** chakra.

Focus on the small white circle* at the center of the image, and stare at it for as long as you can without blinking. When you can't continue the "burning" feeling any longer, turn off the light, close your eyes and focus your inner sight on the space in front of your brow chakra (between your eye brows and on the ridge you can feel just above your nose), and see the small **Yellow Square** in the **Indigo Egg** floating in the space before you and vibrating within the large outer **Yellow/Orange Square**. And, then, you will soon see the tattva image change into the complementary yantra colors of **Purple, Yellow/Orange,** and **Indigo.**

Again vibrate the names to the tattvas and chant or hum the mantras three times.

Absorb this yantra image! As you repeat the exercise, often, you will reach a point when you will be able to recall this image at will.

> *The small white circle is called a "Bindu," and focus on it is comprehensive of the entire tattvic image and all its energies. There is a small spot on the back of your head that likewise serves as a comprehensive psychic center used in certain meditational exercises. A Bindu is also the name of a single drop of semen, the focal point of a new life. And "bindu" is likewise the single point from which all creation began "in the union of divine forces, Male and Female, God and Goddess, Siva and Shakti in all their names and images—i.e., the "Big Bang."

> Bindu is a point of leverage where force applied becomes force multiplied and directed to accomplish your particular goal.

Step 9b. Yantra Visualization.

Alternatively, if you haven't made an **Ether/Earth** card, immediately in front of you, visualize the image as described for making the card. See the image gently vibrating. And then the colors will reverse to their complementary yantra colors.

Step 10a. Experiencing Compounded Elemental Ether and Elemental Earth.

Feel yourself becoming totally *absorbed** in the image while retaining awareness of the surrounding outer tattvic **Bright Yellow/Orange Square**. As the tattvic **Indigo Egg** changes color to the complementary yantra color of **Bright Yellow/Orange** and the large outer square to **Indigo,** feel *your* **Ether** nature harmonize with the Cosmic **Ether** Tattva, and feel all impurities in your **Ether** Tattva—all emotional garbage and unconscious psychic attachments—dissipate. The tattvic **Yellow** will change to the complementary yantra **Purple** as your **Earthy** nature harmonizes with the Cosmic **Earth** Tattva and the impurities of your **Earth** tattva dissipate.

> *Becoming absorbed.* Enter into the **full image** and become one with it and feel surrounded by it. Moving inward from the outer **Square** become one with the **Ether** Element, and then move inward to become one with the **Earth** Element, and then further in to the **Bindu** to become one with **All.** Now, moving outward from the **Bindu** point to the **Earth Square** and then to the **Ether Egg** and to its outer edge feel the balanced **Ether** and **Earth** elements in your body become harmonized and purified as they are balanced with their **Cosmic Source**.

In particular: feel the **Ether** and **Earth** nature of your physical body become free of feelings of **heaviness** and at the same time of unbearable **Lightness**. Feel your body becoming ideally healthy, strong, and energized. See your body in perfect health, free of any excess weight, free of pain and disfigurement, free of illness, and fully energized. Feel **Physical Wellness** and **Spiritual Wholeness.**

Step 11. Knowing Elemental Ether compounded with Elemental Earth.

Allow yourself to receive any information or messages from you're experiencing of these Elemental Forces. *In particular: receive information involving your **Physical** and **Spiritual** health and strength at both **material** and **causal** levels.* Receive the information without any emotional reaction and know that the knowledge is fully activated within your psyche.

Continue on with the Programs to Conclusion.

DIVINATION GUIDE TO ETHER—SEED OF EARTH
Ether—Seed of Earth: *Been there, Done that; Now, be Born Again, or New Birth?*

Earth is the last step down and the first step up in our earthy incarnations and Ether is the last step up and the Next Step beyond earthy incarnation. But, it's a long road and we are not there yet. The Past is prologue to the future, giving you a map for wise decisions in choosing a new route. You are being called to "Go forth and multiply" for the evolutionary change upon you now is filled with greater potentials.

In a divination, it's a signal that you need to make new choices and fresh decisions because you are entering into a time of rapid growth. Open your heart and mind for the near future is NOW! You need to erect a new edifice upon firm foundations based upon the accumulation of past wisdom from previous incarnations. *Up, up, and away!*

Ether—Seed of Water:
The Higher Dimensions of Emotion

Ether—Seed of Water

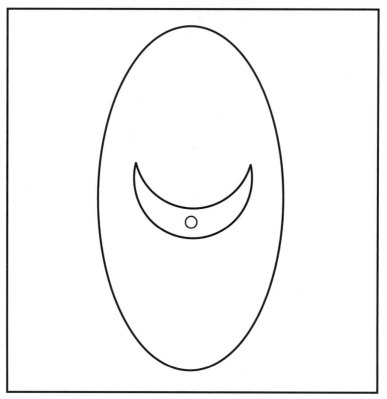

Color the tiny inner bindu circle white,
the inner oval indigo,
and the outer square yellow/orange

Ether—Seed of Water: Akasha & Apas HAM & VAM

Review

We urge you to review the Element Overview Table #5 for **Ether** on page 272 And the Element Overview Table #2 for Water on page 131 in preparation for this procedure and the Divination and other applications involved with this compound.

The Tattvic Connection Meditation & Visualization Program #28: Ether/Water
Ether—Seed of Water

Introduction. The Purpose & Function of this Procedure.

Rather than repeating the procedure in its entirety, we are asking you to kindly refer to page 396 for the complete *Tattva Connection Meditation & Visualization Compound Program #7 and make your own adjustments to substitute "**Ether**" for "**Earth**" and "**Water**" for "**Water**" in steps 2 (goal statement), 3 (affirmations. (I know that seems redundant, but in the psychic world little things count for a lot.) We are here providing content for Steps 5 (preparing and coloring the yantra card), 9a (yantra card focus), 10a. (experience the compounded elements and 11 (knowing the compounded elements).*

The Program's Variables:

Steps 2. Goal Statement.

Note your need to consider how to express your goals to reflect the particular natures of the two elements in their primary and secondary combination in relation to your physical, emotional, mental and spiritual well-being, and their functions in divination, magick, and self-growth.

Step 3. Affirmations.

You need to write positive affirmations to accomplish your goals.

Step 5. Preparation.

Preparing the Yantra Card.

It is recommended that you photocopy the illustration on page 570, preferably on heavier paper or card stock, or draw it yourself in exactly the same sizes using a ruler and black pen. If you can manage it, using a drawing compass or a template, draw a tiny ⅛" inch diameter circle in the exact center. Leave the inside of the circle white. This inner circle or point aids your steady focus. It is not essential, but it is helpful. Make the **Outer Square** 4" x 4" and the inner **Ether Egg** should be about 2" wide by 3¼" tall and centered, the inner **Water Crescent** 1⅛" wide and centered within the **Egg,** and the little **Bindu** circle in the exact center should be ⅛" in diameter and have a black line around it and the little **Water Crescent** but not quite as thick as those around the **Ether Egg** and the **Outer Square**.

Coloring the Yantra Card.

It will be beneficial for you to color the image as follows: (a) color the tiny inner **Bindu Circle White**; (b) the small **Water Crescent Metallic Silver**; (c) the **Ether Egg Bright Indigo**; and (d) the surrounding outer square **Bright Yellow/Orange.** The outer **Bright Yellow/Orange Square** and the **Bright Indigo Egg** are bordered with bold black lines, the small **Silver Water Crescent** is bordered with a less bold black line, and the tiny inner **Bindu Circle** is bordered with a thinner black line.

Step 9a. Yantra Card Focus.

If you have constructed the tattva yantra card as described, turn on the light and focus it on the card held or positioned comfortably about a foot to a foot and a half in front of you.

If possible, arrange your chair to face the primary tattvic direction: In this case, simply lean back and look *Skyward* for **Ether.** Otherwise—think and feel *Skyward.* (To the extent you feel the secondary element's importance to the operation; you can finish with an acknowledgment of *West* for **Water.**

Vibrate the name of the two tattvas: *Akasha* and *Apas,* alternating one after the other. Repeat three times.

Chant or hum the tattva element mantras *HAM* and *VAM* (pronounced *HA-UUM* and *VA-UUM),* alternating. Vibrate the mantra as instructed in Step 1, preliminaries. Repeat three times. Later, you can do more but always in groups of three. And feel the mantra vibrate *over the Throat,* the location of **Vishuddha** chakra, and then *between the Genitals and the Navel,* the location of **Svadhisthana** chakra.

Focus on the small white circle* at the center of the image, and stare at it for as long as you can without blinking. When you can't continue the "burning" feeling any longer, turn off the light, close your eyes and focus your inner sight on the space in front of your brow chakra (between your eye brows and on the ridge you can feel just above your nose), and see the small **Silver Water Crescent** in the **Indigo Ether Egg** floating in the space before you and vibrating within the large outer **Yellow/Orange Square.** And, then, you will soon see the tattva image change into the complementary yantra colors of **Black, Yellow/Orange,** and **Indigo.**

Again vibrate the names to the tattvas and chant or hum the mantras three times.

Absorb this yantra image! As you repeat the exercise, often, you will reach a point when you will be able to recall this image at will.

> *The small white circle is called a "Bindu," and focus on it is comprehensive
> of the entire tattvic image and all its energies. There is a small spot on the

back of your head that likewise serves as a comprehensive psychic center used in certain meditational exercises. A Bindu is also the name of a single drop of semen, the focal point of a new life. And "bindu" is likewise the single point from which all creation began "in the union of divine forces, Male and Female, God and Goddess, Siva and Shakti in all their names and images—i.e., the "Big Bang.""

Bindu is a point of leverage where force applied becomes force multiplied and directed to accomplish your particular goal.

Step 9b. Yantra Visualization.

Alternatively, if you haven't made an **Ether/Water** card, immediately in front of you, visualize the image as described for making the card. See the image gently vibrating. And then the colors will reverse to their complementary yantra colors.

Step 10a. Experiencing Compounded Elemental Ether and Elemental Water.

Feel yourself becoming totally *absorbed** in the image while retaining awareness of the surrounding outer tattvic **Bright Yellow/Orange Square**. As the tattvic **Silver Crescent** changes to the complementary yantra color of **Black** and the tattvic **Indigo Egg** changes color to the complementary yantra color of **Bright Yellow/Orange** and the large outer square to **Indigo,** feel *your* **Ether** nature harmonize with the Cosmic **Ether** Tattva, and feel all impurities in your **Ether** Tattva—all emotional garbage and unconscious psychic attachments—dissipate. The tattvic **Silver** will change to the complementary yantra **Black** as your **Watery** nature harmonizes with the Cosmic **Water** Tattva and the impurities of your **Water** tattva dissipate.

> **Becoming absorbed.* Enter into the **full image** and become one with it and feel surrounded by it. Moving inward from the outer **Square** become one with the **Ether** Element, and then move inward to become one with the **Water** Element, and then further in to the **Bindu** to become one with **All.** Now, moving outward from the **Bindu** point to the **Water Crescent** and then to the **Ether Egg** and to its outer edge feel the balanced **Ether** and **Water** elements in your body become harmonized and purified as they are balanced with their **Cosmic Source.**

In particular: feel the **Ether** and **Water** nature of your **physical** body become free of **light-headedness** and **fluid retention**. Feel your body becoming ideally healthy, strong, and energized. See you body in perfect health, free of any excess weight, free of pain and disfigurement, free of illness, and fully energized. Feel your **Emotional** and **Spiritual** selves become **Whole** and **Alive, connected** to the **Whole of Life.**

Step 11. Knowing Elemental Ether compounded with Elemental Water.

Allow yourself to receive any information or messages from you're experiencing of these Elemental Forces. *In particular: receive information involving your **Physical** and **Emotional/Spiritual** health and strength at **material**, **astral** and **causal** levels.* Receive the information without any emotional reaction and know that the knowledge is fully activated within your psyche.

Continue on with the Programs to Conclusion.

DIVINATION GUIDE TO ETHER—SEED OF WATER
Ether—Seed of Water: *Dare Greatness*

Ether is boundless Space. Water, naturally seeking the lowest level, is cupped by Earth and in return brings nourishment to Earth, and together they support life upon Earth. The Moon symbolizes Water, but Water also symbolizes the Unconscious forces within us seeking security, stability, and the comfort of home. Even aided by Fire and Air, Water cannot escape the physical dimension but aided by Ether can move higher and higher into the Astral and beyond.

In a divination, it signals that we should look within to uncover repressions and suppressions that manifest as inhibitions and depression. It is time to overcome fears and step beyond a limited comfort zone to stimulate inner growth and psychic empowerment. Water, the Unconscious Mind, is freed to evolve upward into the fourth dimension of Space and the Astral World.

Ether—Seed of Fire:
The Drive for Greatness

Ether—Seed of Fire

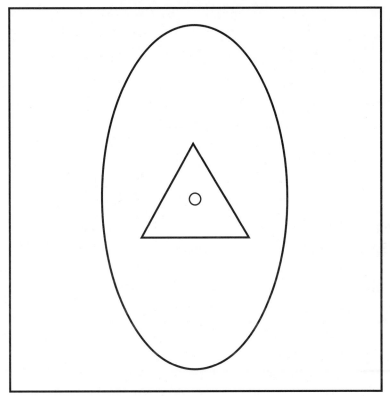

Color the tiny inner bindu circle white,
the inner triangle red,
the inner oval indigo,
and the outer square yellow/orange

Ether—Seed of Fire: Akasha & Tejas HAM & RAM

Review

We urge you to review the Element Overview Table #5 for **Ether** on page 272 And the Element Overview Table #3 for Fire on page 189 in preparation for this procedure and the Divination and other applications involved with this compound.

The Tattvic Connection Meditation
& Visualization Program #29: Ether/Fire
Ether—Seed of Fire

Introduction. The Purpose & Function of this Procedure.

Rather than repeating the procedure in its entirety, we are asking you to kindly refer to page 396 for the complete *Tattva Connection Meditation & Visualization Compound Program #7 and make your own adjustments to substitute "**Ether**" for "**Earth**" and "**Fire**" for "**Water**" in steps 2 (goal statement), 3 (affirmations. (I know that seems redundant, but in the psychic world little things count for a lot.) We are here providing content for Steps 5 (preparing and coloring the yantra card), 9a (yantra card focus), 10a. (experience the compounded elements and 11 (knowing the compounded elements).*

The Program's Variables:

Steps 2. Goal Statement.

Note your need to consider how to express your goals to reflect the particular natures of the two elements in their primary and secondary combination in relation to your physical, emotional, mental and spiritual well-being, and their functions in divination, magick, and self-growth.

Step 3. Affirmations.

You need to write positive affirmations to accomplish your goals.

Step 5. Preparation.

Preparing the Yantra Card.

It is recommended that you photocopy the illustration on page 575, preferably on heavier paper or card stock, or draw it yourself in exactly the same sizes using a ruler and black pen. If you can manage it, using a drawing compass or a template, draw a tiny ⅛" inch diameter circle in the exact center. Leave the inside of the circle white. This inner circle or point aids your steady focus. It is not essential, but it is helpful. Make the **Outer Square** 4" x 4" and the inner **Ether Egg** should be about 2" wide by 3¼" tall and centered, the inner **Fire Triangle** should be 1" on each side, apex up and centered within the **Egg,** and the little **Bindu** circle in the exact center should be ⅛" in diameter and have a black line around it and the little **Fire Triangle** but not quite as thick as those around the **Ether Egg** and the **Outer Square.**

Coloring the Yantra Card.

It will be beneficial for you to color the image as follows: (a) color the tiny inner **Bindu Circle White**; (b) the small **Red Fire Triangle Bright Red;** (c) the **Ether Egg Bright Indigo**; and (d) the surrounding outer square **Bright Yellow/Orange.** The outer **Bright Yellow/Orange Square** and the **Bright Indigo Egg** are bordered with bold black lines, the small **Red Fire Triangle** is bordered with a less bold black line, and the tiny inner **Bindu Circle** is bordered with a thinner black line.

Step 9a. Yantra Card Focus.

If you have constructed the tattva yantra card as described, turn on the light and focus it on the card held or positioned comfortably about a foot to a foot and a half in front of you.

If possible, arrange your chair to face the primary tattvic direction: In this case, simply lean back and look *Skyward* for **Ether.** Otherwise—think and feel *Skyward.* (To the extent you feel the secondary element's importance to the operation; you can finish with an acknowledgment of *South* for **Fire.**

Vibrate the name of the two tattvas: *Akasha* and *Tejas,* alternating one after the other. Repeat three times.

Chant or hum the tattva element mantras *HAM* and *RAM* (pronounced *HA-UUM* and *RA-UUM),* alternating. Vibrate the mantra as instructed in Step 1, preliminaries. Repeat three times. Later, you can do more but always in groups of three. And feel the mantra vibrate *over the Throat,* the location of **Vishuddha** chakra, and then *between the Navel and the Heart,* the location of **Manipura** chakra.

Focus on the small white circle* at the center of the image, and stare at it for as long as you can without blinking. When you can't continue the "burning" feeling any longer, turn off the light, close your eyes and focus your inner sight on the space in front of your brow chakra (between your eye brows and on the ridge you can feel just above your nose), and see the small **Red Fire Triangle** in the **Indigo Ether Egg** floating in the space before you and vibrating within the large outer **Yellow/Orange Square**. And, then, you will soon see the tattva image change into the complementary yantra colors of **Green, Yellow/Orange**, and **Indigo**.

Again vibrate the names to the tattvas and chant or hum the mantras three times.

Absorb this yantra image! As you repeat the exercise, often, you will reach a point when you will be able to recall this image at will.

> *The small white circle is called a "Bindu," and focus on it is comprehensive of the entire tattvic image and all its energies. There is a small spot on the

back of your head that likewise serves as a comprehensive psychic center used in certain meditational exercises. A Bindu is also the name of a single drop of semen, the focal point of a new life. And "bindu" is likewise the single point from which all creation began "in the union of divine forces, Male and Female, God and Goddess, Siva and Shakti in all their names and images—i.e., the "Big Bang."

Bindu is a point of leverage where force applied becomes force multiplied and directed to accomplish your particular goal.

Step 9b. Yantra Visualization.

Alternatively, if you haven't made an **Ether/Fire** card, immediately in front of you, visualize the image as described for making the card. See the image gently vibrating. And then the colors will reverse to their complementary yantra colors.

Step 10a. Experiencing Compounded Elemental Ether and Elemental Fire

Feel yourself becoming totally *absorbed** in the image while retaining awareness of the surrounding outer tattvic **Bright Yellow/Orange Square**. As the tattvic **Red Fire Triangle** changes to the complementary **Green** and the **Indigo Egg** changes color to the complementary yantra color of **Bright Yellow/Orange** and the large outer square to **Indigo,** feel *your* **Ether** nature harmonize with the Cosmic **Ether** Tattva, and feel all impurities in your **Ether** Tattva—all emotional garbage and unconscious psychic attachments—dissipate. The tattvic **Red** will change to the complementary yantra **Green** as your **Fire** nature harmonizes with the Cosmic **Fire** Tattva and the impurities of your **Fire** tattva dissipate.

> **Becoming absorbed.* Enter into the **full image** and become one with it and feel surrounded by it. Moving inward from the outer **Square** become one with the **Ether** Element, and then move inward to become one with the **Fire** Element, and then further in to the **Bindu** to become one with **All.** Now, moving outward from the **Bindu** point to the **Fire Triangle** and then to the **Ether Egg** and to its outer edge feel the balanced **Ether** and **Fire** elements in your body become harmonized and purified as they are balanced with their **Cosmic Source.**

In particular: feel the **Ether** and **Fire** nature of your physical body become free of adverse thoughts of **aggression** and feelings of being "**spaced out.**" Feel your body becoming ideally healthy, strong, and energized. See your body in perfect health, free of any excess weight, free of pain and disfigurement, free of illness, and fully energized.

Feel your **Emotional/Mental** self become **calm and deliberate,** and you **Causal** self become **Confident and Aware of the Higher Self.**

Step 11. Knowing Elemental Ether compounded with Elemental Fire.

Allow yourself to receive any information or messages from you're experiencing of these Elemental Forces. *In particular: receive information involving your* **Physical** *and* **Emotional/Mental** *health and strength at the* **material, high astral** *and* **causal** *levels.* Receive the information without any emotional reaction and know that the knowledge is fully activated within your psyche.

Continue on with the Programs to Conclusion.

DIVINATION GUIDE TO ETHER—SEED OF FIRE
Ether—Seed of Fire: *Unlimited Potential & the Need for Self-Discipline!*

Ether, boundless Space and Spirit—symbolized by the Cosmic Egg—brings change and insight to each of the primal elements and opens unlimited potentials. Ether is everywhere and in all things. Fire is desire, passion, ambition, drive, aspiration, enthusiasm. Enthusiasm means "filled with God." Fire filled with Ether is a veritable supernatural force. If you, yourself, can and will impose discipline and control over your own emotions and passions, then you become a force for positive change. Equally important is the need to employ your understanding of your own passions to defuse the reactions of people around you

It's equally important to understand the feelings of people around you and not accept rage and anger whether of the "crowd" or specifically directed towards you. Self-discipline is one of the basic "secrets" to success in every operation you undertake.

In a divination, it signals a change coming that will arrive with great energy, and even great drama. But such change may not be welcomed by you unless you are able to greet it with optimism and calm acceptance, allowing it to "incubate" and produce new meaning in your life.

Ether—Seed of Air:
The Power of the Word

Ether—Seed of Air

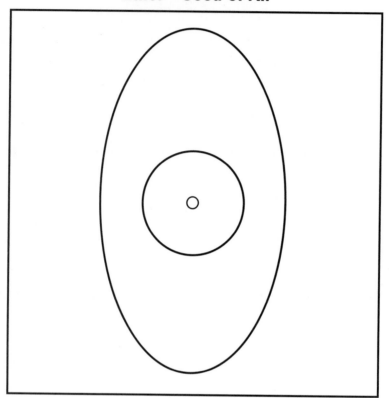

Color the tiny inner bindu circle white,
the inner circle blue,
the inner oval indigo,
and the outer square yellow/orange

Ether—Seed of Air: Akasha & Vayu HAM & YAM

Review

We urge you to review the Element Overview Table #5 for **Ether** on page 572 And the Element Overview Table #4 for Air on page 214 in preparation for this procedure and the Divination and other applications involved with this compound.

The Tattvic Connection Meditation & Visualization Program #30: Ether/Air
Ether—Seed of Air

Introduction. The Purpose & Function of this Procedure.

Rather than repeating the procedure in its entirety, we are asking you to kindly refer to page 396 for the complete *Tattva Connection Meditation & Visualization Compound Program #7 and make your own adjustments to substitute "**Ether**" for "**Earth**" and "**Air**" for "**Water**" in steps 2 (goal statement), 3 (affirmations. (I know that seems redundant, but in the psychic world little things count for a lot.) We are here providing content for Steps 5 (preparing and coloring the yantra card), 9a (yantra card focus), 10a. (experience the compounded elements and 11 (knowing the compounded elements).*

The Program's Variables:

Steps 2. Goal Statement.

Note your need to consider how to express your goals to reflect the particular natures of the two elements in their primary and secondary combination in relation to your physical, emotional, mental and spiritual well-being, and their functions in divination, magick, and self-growth.

Step 3. Affirmations.

You need to write positive affirmations to accomplish your goals.

Step 5. Preparation.

Preparing the Yantra Card.

It is recommended that you photocopy the illustration on page 580, preferably on heavier paper or card stock, or draw it yourself in exactly the same sizes using a ruler and black pen. If you can manage it, using a drawing compass or a template, draw a tiny ⅛" inch diameter circle in the exact center. Leave the inside of the circle white. This inner circle or point aids your steady focus. It is not essential, but it is helpful. Make the **Outer Square** 4" x 4" and the inner **Ether Egg** should be about 2" wide by 3¼" tall and centered, the inner **Air Circle** should be 1" in diameter and centered within the **Egg,** and the little **Bindu** circle in the exact center should be ⅛" in diameter and have a black line around it and the little **Air Circle** but not quite as thick as those around the **Ether Egg** and the **Outer Square**.

Coloring the Yantra Card.

It will be beneficial for you to color the image as follows: (a) color the tiny inner **Bindu Circle White**; b) the small **Air Circle Bright Blue**; (c) the **Ether Egg Bright Indigo**; and (d) the surrounding outer square **Bright Yellow/Orange.** The outer **Bright Yellow/Orange Square** and the **Bright Indigo Egg** are bordered with bold black lines, the small **Blue Air Circle** is bordered with a less bold black line, and the tiny inner **Bindu Circle** is bordered with a thinner black line.

Step 9a. Yantra Card Focus.

If you have constructed the tattva yantra card as described, turn on the light and focus it on the card held or positioned comfortably about a foot to a foot and a half in front of you.

If possible, arrange your chair to face the primary tattvic direction: In this case, simply lean back and look *Skyward* for **Ether.** Otherwise—think and feel *Skyward.* (To the extent you feel the secondary element's importance to the operation; you can finish with an acknowledgment of *East* for **Air.**

Vibrate the name of the two tattvas: *Akasha* and *Vayu,* alternating one after the other. Repeat three times.

Chant or hum the tattva element mantras *HAM* and *YAM* (pronounced *HA-UUM* and *YA-UUM),* alternating. Vibrate the mantra as instructed in Step 1, preliminaries. Repeat three times. Later, you can do more but always in groups of three. And feel the mantra vibrate *over the Throat,* the location of **Vishuddha** chakra, and then *over the Heart,* the location of **Anahata** chakra.

Focus on the small white circle⋆ at the center of the image, and stare at it for as long as you can without blinking. When you can't continue the "burning" feeling any longer, turn off the light, close your eyes and focus your inner sight on the space in front of your brow chakra (between your eye brows and on the ridge you can feel just above your nose), and see the small **Blue Air Circle** in the **Indigo Ether Egg** floating in the space before you and vibrating within the large outer **Yellow/Orange Square.** And, then, you will soon see the tattva image change into the complementary yantra colors of **Bright Orange, Yellow/Orange,** and **Indigo.**

Again vibrate the names to the tattvas and chant or hum the mantras three times.

Absorb this yantra image! As you repeat the exercise, often, you will reach a point when you will be able to recall this image at will.

⋆The small white circle is called a "Bindu," and focus on it is comprehensive of the entire tattvic image and all its energies. There is a small spot on the

back of your head that likewise serves as a comprehensive psychic center used in certain meditational exercises. A Bindu is also the name of a single drop of semen, the focal point of a new life. And "bindu" is likewise the single point from which all creation began "in the union of divine forces, Male and Female, God and Goddess, Siva and Shakti in all their names and images—i.e., the "Big Bang."

Bindu is a point of leverage where force applied becomes force multiplied and directed to accomplish your particular goal.

Step 9b. Yantra Visualization.

Alternatively, if you haven't made an **Ether/Air** card, immediately in front of you, visualize the image as described for making the card. See the image gently vibrating. And then the colors will reverse to their complementary yantra colors.

Step 10a. Experiencing Compounded Elemental Ether and Elemental Air.

Feel yourself becoming totally *absorbed** in the image while retaining awareness of the surrounding outer tattvic **Bright Yellow/Orange Square**. As the tattvic **Indigo Egg** changes color to the complementary yantra color of **Bright Yellow/Orange** and the large outer square to **Indigo,** feel *your* **Ether** nature harmonize with the Cosmic **Ether** Tattva, and feel all impurities in your **Ether** Tattva—all emotional garbage and unconscious psychic attachments—dissipate. The tattvic **Blue** will change to the complementary yantra **Orange** as your **Air** nature harmonizes with the Cosmic **Air** Tattva and the impurities of your **Air** tattva dissipate.

> *Becoming absorbed.* Enter into the **full image** and become one with it and feel surrounded by it. Moving inward from the outer **Square** become one with the **Ether** Element, and then move inward to become one with the **Fire** Element, and then further in to the **Bindu** to become one with **All.** Now, moving outward from the **Bindu** point to the **Fire Triangle** and then to the **Ether Egg** and to its outer edge feel the balanced **Ether** and **Fire** elements in your body become harmonized and purified as they are balanced with their **Cosmic Source.**

In particular: feel the **Ether** and **Air** nature of your physical body become free of adverse thoughts of **indecision** and feelings of **restlessness**. Feel your body becoming ideally healthy, strong, and energized. See your body in perfect health, free of any excess weight, free of pain and disfigurement, free of illness, and fully energized. Feel your **mental self "tuned in" to the world around, and your spiritual self enthused with the world of infinite possibilities.**

Step 11. Knowing Elemental Ether compounded with Elemental Air.

Allow yourself to receive any information or messages from you're experiencing of these Elemental Forces. *In particular: receive information involving your* **Physical** *and* **Mental** *and* **Spiritual** *health and strength at* **material, mental** *and* **causal** *levels.* Receive the information without any emotional reaction and know that the knowledge is fully activated within your psyche.

Continue on with the Programs to Conclusion.

DIVINATION GUIDE TO ETHER—SEED OF AIR
Ether—Seed of Air: *the Word—New Beginning,*
or Fresh Re-beginning

"In the Beginning was the Word." No matter what—whether spoken or not and just felt or heard—everything begins with a Word. No matter how small or how large, a Word is a "program" that initiates action that may go on forever unless specifically given instructions to terminate at either a time or a circumstance. Be careful with your words, for you are responsible for the actions that ensue no matter how seemingly small or innocent. Be careful with the words you hear, for your *response* is a re-action for which you are also responsible. Words, language, and thoughtful action distinguish human from animal and lower kingdoms. "In the Beginning IS the Word," for humans are creators in the same way but not degree of the First Speaker, the Creator of all.

In a divination, this signals a "window of opportunity" full of potential for a new start, or one for fresh start-over in relationships soured by previous words. Take advantage of an opportunity to re-write the program. Review and be sure.

CHAPTER FIFTEEN
Case Studies & Cameo Reports
Clairvoyance at its Best

Although research in the controlled lab setting is critical to our understanding of clairvoyance, personal experience provides compelling evidence of the relevance of clairvoyance to daily life. Detailed case studies as well as cameo reports of personal experiences in clairvoyance open a vast window into the diverse manifestations of this phenomenon, often in gripping detail. Included are individual accounts that range from deeply personal concerns to conditions of global significance.

Our analysis of personal reports showed repeatedly that clairvoyance, whether spontaneous or deliberately induced, is consistently purposeful and self-empowering. Clairvoyance can provide a critical key to successful problem-solving and improved quality of life. It can promote happiness, self-confidence, and peace of mind. It can facilitate better decision making and provide workable solutions to complex difficult career situations. It can generate insight related to entangled relationships and complicated social interactions. In emergency life-and-death situations, it can generate decisive and effective action. These are only a few of the self-empowering possibilities of clairvoyance.

Clairvoyant Slip of the Tongue.

Our studies of clairvoyance repeatedly showed that clairvoyance, like other forms of ESP, often originated in the subconscious where it was processed and then transferred to conscious awareness. Strange though it may at first seem, clairvoyance of subconscious origin can occur in a disguised form that may at first appear inconsequential because of its simplicity. In a striking example of that possibility, a college student nearing completion of her B.S. Degree in Business Administration discovered an excellent career opportunity through an apparent *clairvoyant slip of the tongue*. In discussing her career goals with a friend, the 22-year old student mentioned having applied for a position with three companies but had received no offers. In citing the three companies, however, she inadvertently included a fourth company. Though she at first viewed her mention of the fourth company as inconsequential, she nevertheless contacted the company and was informed that a position fitting her credentials had just become available. She promptly applied for the position and was accepted.

Rising rapidly in the company's administrative hierarchy, she presently holds a responsible executive position which she describes as "both challenging and fulfilling". Reflecting upon the experience, she explains, "With perfect timing, clairvoyance spontaneously opened an exciting door to career opportunity and future success. Through a simple clairvoyant slip of the tongue, my subconscious mind spoke. Fortunately, I listened to the message and acted upon it."

In another instance of an apparent but fortuitous clairvoyant slip of the tongue, an unemployed maintenance worker seeking election for an important administrative position in a Northeastern town inadvertently misquoted his campaign slogan, a slip of the tongue that became the turning point is his campaign. Known by his campaign slogan as "The Vagabond Candidate," he misquoted the slogan during a TV interview as "The Victory Candidate." From then, he became known as "The Victory Candidate," a title that apparently generated a powerful self-fulfilling effect that won him election in a landslide.

For both the aspiring student and the self-styled vagabond, an apparent clairvoyant slip of the tongue led to highly positive results. Although it could be argued that precognition could have been involved in both incidents, highly specific clairvoyant insight that helped shape the future seems to have clearly occurred.

Therapeutic Clairvoyance.

Although the therapeutic role of clairvoyance has received very little attention, our case studies and cameo reports found clairvoyance to be among the most powerful therapeutic forces known. It often uncovers the subconscious sources of anxieties, phobias, conflicts, and depression while prescribing effective ways of resolving them. Equipped with that insight, many of the subjects of our studies became empowered to assume greater control of their lives and the forces that affected their success and happiness.

Among the dramatic case examples of therapeutic clairvoyance is that of a college sophomore whose life-long fear of small spaces and darkness generated persistent anxiety that seriously limited her daily life. She required lighting even as she slept, and she avoided all small enclosed places, such as elevators and closets. She was constantly uneasy that she might encounter either darkness or become somehow entrapped in an enclosed space. When attending class, she preferred seating at the perimeter of the group and near an exit if possible. In her efforts to overcome the unrelenting fear, she had undergone extensive counseling, but to no avail.

Finally, by her report, she was attending an evening class session when the lighting suddenly failed. Remaining seated in darkness as her fear rapidly intensified, she saw a small bright orb forming at the distant side of the room. The orb then improved in size to become a bright sphere that slowly approached and then fully enveloped her. Safely enclosed in bright spherical form, she felt her fears of both darkness and small spaces slowly fading and finally vanishing altogether. She knew without doubt that she was at last liberated from the fear of darkness and enclosed places that had constricted her life for years. In reflecting on the experience, she noted, "A sphere of bright light changed my life. It accomplished in an instant what years of therapy had failed to do."

Could the bright sphere have been a clairvoyant creation of the subconscious mind designed to banish the student's persistent fear of both darkness and small spaces? The clairvoyant specialist existing within each of us is a source of insight that not only knows our therapeutic needs; it knows the appropriate techniques that most effectively meet those needs. It is conceivable that the most highly advanced therapeutic specialist is the inner clairvoyant that is constantly poised to empower our lives with enlightenment and power.

Creative Clairvoyance.

Among the multiple functions of clairvoyance is its role in stimulating creativity, including that related to the visual arts. An artist known for her innovative wood carvings reported the regular use of clairvoyance to generate new ideas for her carvings. She begins each of her carvings by first placing her hands upon the wood to be carved and then allowing images of the finished product to emerge. Once a work is in progress, she relies on what she calls "creative clairvoyance" to function as a "mental blueprint" for her carvings. In her words, "Creative clairvoyance is the artist within that identifies the finished carving and then guides the step-by-step process of shaping it. Rather than a controlling influence, it is for me an inspirational companion with a vision of creative possibilities."

In a similar instance of creative clairvoyance, an artist known for both her landscape and seascape paintings reported her use of a quartz crystal as a clairvoyant tool that facilitates the creation of ideas and images for her oils. She recalled a stage in her career when her creative potential became so inactive that she abandoned painting altogether. During that time of "painter's block," as she called it, she was introduced by a friend to the quartz crystal as a meditation device that cleared the mind of clutter and generated a balanced, creative state. It was in that serene state that clear images of distant scenes began to emerge. Given that breakthrough experience, she returned to her studio, and with the quartz crystal worn as a pendant, her artistic creations took on a new dimension of excellence.

As it turned out, the scenes that emerged through simply stroking the quartz crystal were not fantasies but actual realities, mostly of European origin. In her own words, "Through the crystal as a facilitator of clairvoyance, I overcame the barriers that blocked my creativity as an artist. Once activated, clairvoyance provided a clear view of distant scenes that provided the overall designs as well as specific details for my paintings." The remarkable transformation of her work caught the attention of critics who described her paintings as "brilliant creations that set a new standard of artistic excellence."

In his recent book, *Connecting to the Power of Nature,* your co-author (Slate) describes his personal interactions with a certain quartz crystal that became an instrument of power throughout his studies at the University of Alabama. Here's his account of those interactions:

Nothing is by happenstance. A certain quartz crystal, as if by destiny, entered my life when at seventeen I enrolled in the University of Alabama as a freshman. On the day before registration, I anxiously arrived for the first time on campus by bus around midnight. Immediately upon stepping from the bus on the dimly-lit University Avenue, I saw a bright object on the ground directly in front of Denny Chimes, a historic campus landmark. It was a colorless quartz crystal with a highly unusual inclusion in the form of a luminous star. Instantly upon picking it up, I knew with certainty that I was at the right place at the right time! Endowed with two crystals—the Rainbow Crystal from childhood and now this one from out of nowhere—I felt at once doubly empowered with each crystal working in harmony with the other.

The "Star Crystal," as I called it, was to become a valued companion and instrument of power throughout my college years. Because I'd discovered it on campus, I thought of it as my "academic companion." I programmed it time and again for goals involving a variety of research and academic efforts. It was in fact, in my pocked when I appeared before an exigent doctoral committee for the final defense of my doctoral dissertation. While always receptive to programming, the crystal seemed to have a perpetual program of its own—it always went beyond its programmed limits to bring enrichment like a ray of sunlight into my life, regardless of the situation.

Finally, at commencement with the Star Crystal in my pocket, I knew that its mission in my life was accomplished. That night, I returned to Denny Chimes where the special crystal had first entered my life. While sitting on the steps of that tall landmark with a full moon rising above the trees and the crystal in hand, I recalled that night a few years before when, upon stepping from a bus, the crystal shining in the moonlight had caught my eye, as if to welcome my arrival. I remembered having picked it up to experience an incredible connection to it that would continue throughout my college years. I reflected on how the Star Crystal had enriched my life as a student from the start. I recalled how I had interacted with it to accelerate my mastery of a second language, one of the requirements for my doctoral degree. It was there to inspire my research efforts, which ranged from studies of problem-solving in pre-school children to the rejuvenation and longevity secrets of centenarians. Though I still can't explain it, the crystal had been in my pocket when a neatly folded one hundred dollar bill mysteriously appeared in the same pocket just when needed to meet an emergency. It had been in my pocket, along with the Rainbow Crystal, when I barely avoided a head-on collision with a car that crossed over into my lane on the busy University Avenue.

As these and other images flooded my mind, I knew in an instant what I had to do. It was by then around midnight, the same hour the Star Crystal had entered my life. I stroked it one last time and with deeply mixed feelings, placed it on the ground where I'd found it. I walked away but couldn't resist looking back to see it shining in the moonlight more brilliantly than I'd ever seen it before.

Before leaving campus early the next morning, I revisited Denny Chimes but almost as expected, the crystal was nowhere to be found. Could it have already embarked on another mission, perhaps to inspire yet another anxious entering freshman? Given its incredible powers, I thought, "Why Not?" I never saw the crystal again.

Slate, Joe H. (2009), *Connecting to the Power of Nature*. Woodbury, MN, Llewellyn.

When viewed objectively, the evidence is clear: There's but a thin line of demarcation between external facilitators of clairvoyance—whether simply a piece of wood or a quartz crystal—and the host of potentials within each of us. There's likewise but a thin line that separates the multiple capacities of the mind, including precognition, telepathy, and clairvoyance. *Our thoughts, sensations, emotions, and extrasensory powers are designed so as to function as an integrated whole.* Fortunately, we can intervene to activate specific powers and thus enrich our lives. Once you're connected and attuned to the powers within, nothing is beyond your reach.

Extreme Clairvoyance.

In its capacity to connect awareness to external realities, clairvoyance as an overarching extrasensory function can assume a pivotal role in our daily lives. In the absence of clairvoyance, we "see through a glass darkly", unaware of conditions that could either enrich our lives or at another level, exact a heavy toll on our well-being. Even in its most basic, ordinary form, clairvoyance reflects our capacity to experience reality beyond the constricted borders of ordinary thinking. In its most advanced form, clairvoyance lifts consciousness to new peaks of enlightenment and power. It can uncover situations that require our intervention, including in some instances conditions of extreme urgency. The report that follows illustrates that amazing capacity of clairvoyance.

"As a student running late for an early morning class, I was driving much faster than usual when, upon a approaching a sharp curve in the road, I experienced a very clear mental image of a vehicle stalled in my lane just beyond the curve. The vehicle, although out-of-sight, was clearly visible in my mind. I immediately applied my brakes, and as I rounded the curve, I saw the vehicle exactly as seen seconds earlier in my mind. I've never been a strong believer in clairvoyance, but that experience fully convinced me of not only its validity but its critical importance as well."

Automatic Walking.

Believe it or not, but automatic walking, also known as *open space excursion*, is rapidly gaining momentum as an effective on-site search and rescue procedure for locating lost objects, persons, and animals. This approach designed to activate clairvoyance is based on the two-fold premise that:

1. the clairvoyant potential exists to some degree in everyone, and
2. it is receptive to ordinary physical techniques designed to activate it.

The effectiveness of the automatic walking approach seems to be due, at least in part, to its straightforwardness and simplicity. All that's required is a stated objective, a designated area to be searched, and a willingness to engage in unstructured, spontaneous walking with appropriate precautions in place.

Developed at Athens State University, Automatic Walking is an innovative procedure with dynamics similar to automatic writing, except that on-site, active walking is used instead of hand writing to initiate clairvoyance. It is a highly practical approach that can be used by individuals or groups as a physical action technique to activate clairvoyance and generate clairvoyant insight. When used as an on-site search activity, automatic walking typically begins with a wide search of the designated area. Early in the search, however, awareness of a more specific target area typically unfolds. As automatic walking continues, the ability of the individual or group to accurately zero in on the exact target typically increases. As with most paranormal activities, practice in automatic walking improves the effectiveness of this approach.

Our early research of this strategy included an experimental exercise in which students enrolled in Experimental Parapsychology at Athens State University participated in an exercise requiring the location of a portable brass compass concealed somewhere on the grounds of the university. The class of 20 students was instructed to use automatic walking, either independently or as a group, in an effort to locate the compass. As a control measure, the person who hid the compass was not present for the experiment. Following an extensive walk throughout the campus, the students finally gathered collectively at the entrance to a historic campus auditorium. Commanding their attention within minutes was an area to the left entrance where they found the compass hidden behind a large shrub.

It could be argued, of course, that other forms of ESP, especially telepathy, may have enter the exercise, particular near the end where a group consensus was reached. Nevertheless, clairvoyance clearly was an essential component of this solution-oriented activity.

Crime-related Applications of Automatic Walking.

Our case studies of automatic walking revealed a wide range of applications, including not only discovering lost items but also gathering crime related evidence. Among the examples are those of two law enforcement officers who participated in our development of the program. They began using automatic walking as a strategy for gathering forensic evidence, such as locating missing weapons and in one instance a cache of money taken in a bank robbery. In a remarkable instance of automatic walking, they used the procedure to discover a collection of artifacts taken during a museum heist. They began Automatic Walking along a roadside where an unfamiliar vehicle had been seen parked the night of the robbery. Automatic Walking soon led into an open field and eventually to an abandoned shack hidden in a grove of trees and dense undergrowth. Here's their report:

> Upon arriving at the roadside where the vehicle had been spotted, we took a few moments to focus on our objectives, and then began automatically walking, first along the roadside bordering a large open meadow and then into the meadow. Finally our walk led to an abandoned cabin situated beyond the meadow and partially hidden by the greenery. Our search of the cabin uncovered not only the treasured artifacts, but a variety of other stolen items as well. The evidence gathered at the site led to the arrest of an organized criminal group and the recovery of stolen goods stored at several other locations.

Admittedly, more research is needed to determine the effectiveness of Automatic Walking. Nevertheless, the evidence at present is strong and continues to build. Your co-author (Slate) has used the technique personally to locate a wedding ring recently lost on a golf course. Within minutes, automatic walking led to the exact location of the ring.

It is important to note that Automatic Walking, whether practiced by individuals, couples, or groups, requires a clear statement of objectives, and it must be limited to familiar, designated areas with appropriate precautions and safeguards in place.

Clairvoyants Coming Together in Group Practice

Automatic Walking when practiced as a group activity with a clearly designated goal suggests the possibility of a collective form of clairvoyance called *Clairvoyant Coming Together* in which the clairvoyant faculties of a group function to achieve a desired objective. Clairvoyant Coming Together is a research-based strategy that sets the stage for problem solving through clairvoyance and other forms of ESP. It reaches beyond the pre-conceived structures that can inhibit progressive and creative thinking. It is a flexible approach that recognizes the importance of questioning the status quo of strategies that become commonplace but no longer work. It welcomes extrasensory insight as a source of knowledge that may be otherwise unavailable to us. It combines opinions, orientations, and beliefs that generate a synergistic effect with far-ranging implications.

In a research study conducted for the U.S. Army at Athens State University, a group of 20 volunteer students participated in a two-fold effort:

1. to identify basic characteristics of the external human energy system typically called the *human aura* and
2. to develop the technology required for monitoring changes in that system.

The carefully controlled project used electro-photography, first to determine individual difference in the energy system, and then to identify the conditions that influenced the stability of the system. With the accumulation of that information, the project used Clairvoyant Coming Together in which the 20 research subjects participated in a group effort to develop an advanced system for the continuous monitoring of a given individual's energy system.

Throughout the Clairvoyant Coming Together phase of the experiment, the group periodically reviewed their progress, and then used mental imagery as a clairvoyant technique to identify the most effective next step. Although this phase was designed to include both individual and group clairvoyance, the individual efforts of the group soon culminated in a "clairvoyant coming together" of the group in a brainstorming session. The result was the formulation of an advanced energy monitoring system that included ear-tabs and wrist bands for measuring changes and then transmitting that information to a control center where it was analyzed to indicate the effects of those changes in the mental state of the subject. Although implants emerged as among the possibilities for monitoring changes in the energy system, that option was eventually discarded as inappropriate by the group.

The results of this project suggest that group clairvoyance could have wide-ranging implications as a *solution oriented strategy*, even on a global scale. Finding solutions to international problems, from global warming to nuclear proliferation, is all within the scope of this approach when used by leaders of nations to solve international crises. Hopefully, future leaders of diverse backgrounds will come together and combine their independent efforts to find collective, optimal solutions. Such an approach would embrace cultural differences and diverse orientations as essential to effective problem solving and global advancement. The future of the globe could very well rests in our capacity to flex our higher thinking muscles through such non-conventional approaches as Clairvoyant Coming Together.

Automatic Biking.

Intrigued by the concept of automatic walking, students enrolled in Experimental Parapsychology at Athens State University began experimenting with what they called "automatic biking" using either a bicycle or motorcycle. Automatic biking, which can include a combination of walking and biking, is a search approach based on the same concept as automatic walking except that biking is used either independently or with walking, depending on the characteristics of the terrain being searched. In law enforcement applications, automatic biking can be used to investigate a general location followed by automatic walking to investigate a more specific area. In an unusual combination of automatic walking and biking, a student participating in our research used the approach to locate a missing dog companion. Here's his account of the rescue.

> Bogie was a wayfaring dog of mixed breed that showed up at our farm to instantly become a welcomed companion, not only to family members but various farm animals as well. The day after he went missing, I began my "search and rescue mission" by randomly walking to explore a remote forest area beyond the meadow, but without success. Finally, I decided to use automatic bicycling along the roadway in front of our residence. Upon reaching

the road, my bike seemed to automatically turn to the right in the direction of a neighboring church. Upon nearing the church, the bicycle took on what seemed to be a mind of its own as it automatically turned into the church's parking area. At that moment, I actually let go of the handle bars, thus allowing the bicycle to circle to the back of the church where a storage building was situated. There under the steps of the building lay my dog. Having sustained a serious leg injury, possibly from a traffic accident, he had taken refuge in a safe place, hopeful I'm sure that he would be rescued. What was a joyful reunion with Bogie would be followed by his rapid and complete recovery, thanks at least in part to automatic biking.

Although the complex dynamics of automatic walking and biking are yet to be fully explained, it is conceivable that clairvoyant insight can exist in full-blown form in the subconscious where it can be accessed through these techniques. It seems also plausible that automatic techniques could progressively generate clairvoyant insight related to a stated goal. Simply stating your goal in specific, positive terms would thus become the critical first step in generating clairvoyant information. Aside from clearly stated goals, our case studies and cameo reports repeatedly showed visualization to be a critical component of any automatic clairvoyant activity. *The specifically stated goal combined with visualization can effectively activate the clairvoyant potential while providing the essential framework for such strategies as automatic walking and biking.*

As with automatic walking, it is recommended that automatic biking be limited to familiar areas with appropriate precautions in place.

Animal Clairvoyance: Fact or Fiction.

Although our case studies of clairvoyance included no interviews with animals, they did include observations of animal behavior in both the lab and natural settings with strong indications of clairvoyance. It seems only reasonable that clairvoyance among animals could significantly promote survival of the species, particularly in situations involving unseen danger. It requires no quantum leap to further conclude that animals in their natural settings could experience clairvoyance and by their actions, convey important clairvoyant insight to human beings. There are, in fact, certain Biblical accounts suggesting that possibility. For instance, a dove reportedly came forth and perched upon the shoulder of Christ immediately following his baptism by John the Baptist, a clairvoyant representation of approval by a Higher Presence.

In a striking contemporary instance of possible animal clairvoyance, a retired teacher known for her love of animals reported a clairvoyant experience in which a gathering of birds were the messengers of important clairvoyant enlightenment. Because of her love for and "connection with" birds, she had installed on her outside window ledge a bird feeder consisting of an aquarium with the opening facing outward. Watching a variety of birds gathering daily to feed at her window was, in her own words, "both inspiring and relaxing". Playfully interacting, the birds reflected the diversity and beauty of nature. Her daily observation of birds feeding at her window was an excellent stress reliever that connected her to the power of nature.

One day, however, the birds strangely appeared much earlier than usual in the morning, and instead of feeding, simply lingered outside her window. Here's her account of what happened:

> I watched the birds in amazement as they gathered in great number at my window. Some would leave briefly and then return as if to convey an uneasy message. It was then that my phone rang and I received the message that my mother who lived in another state had been seriously injured earlier that morning in an automobile accident. With that disturbing news, I glanced at the window and saw a gathering of birds far greater than any I had ever seen before. Feeling suddenly connected to them, I experienced a powerful sense of tranquility and complete confidence that my mother would fully recover, and she did. The presence of the birds gave comfort and reassurance at a time of great urgency. Beyond that, it connected me to the limitless power of nature. Later reflecting upon the experience, I became convinced that the power of my connection with nature through the gathering of birds at my window reached far beyond my window to promote my mother's rapid recovery. The birds continue to gather at my window, but I now see them in a different light: they are caring friends that offer both comfort and power. They have proved, time and again, to be "a present help in time of need.

In another instance of possible animal clairvoyance, a college sophomore recalled an experience in which his dog companion of mixed breed seemed to have clairvoyantly sensed potential danger, and by his actions attempted to convey that important information to the student. While walking his dog on campus near sunset, the student was surprised when the dog suddenly pulled back on his leash and refused to continue the walk into an area where they had often walked before. Upon prematurely ending the walk and returning to his dorm, the student discovered that a robbery had just occurred in that campus area. Had he continued the walk, the student is convinced that he would have become the victim of that crime. He is further convinced that his dog companion clairvoyantly sensed danger ahead, and by refusing to go forward, attempted to convey awareness of that danger to the student.

Supportive of the possibility of animal clairvoyance in real-life situations are the research findings of animal clairvoyance in the controlled lab setting. In our lab research, for instance, mice were given the task of choosing from five mazes identical in appearance the single maze that led to escape from the controlled situation. On repeated trials, the single escape maze was randomly re-assigned. The study found that certain mice repeatedly performed significantly beyond chance in selecting the maze that led to escape. Further study of the so called "clairvoyant mice" found that their off-spring likewise performed significantly beyond chance when subjected to a similar experimental lab situation.

Although this study of laboratory mice suggests the possibility of hereditary factors related to clairvoyance, it is important to note that human beings who have demonstrated extraordinary clairvoyant skills outside the lab do not always perform well in the controlled lab setting designed to measure those skills. As in the development of other cognitive functions, it is conceivable that genetics as well as environment could function as important influencing factors in the development of clairvoyance. The decisive factor, however, seems to be neither environment nor heredity, but the individual who interacts with those factors. The clairvoyant potential, like intelligence, exists to some degree in everyone. Developing that potential to its fullest, however, requires motivation, practice, and experience. As with intellectual growth, both environment and heredity are relevant to clairvoyance, but the most critical factor in becoming clairvoyantly empowered is personal choice.

Insect Clairvoyance?

Aside from laboratory animals and companion pets, even insects have shown, arguably at least, the possibility of clairvoyance. From the Biblical perspective, insects have demonstrated innate behaviors that are relevant and, in some instances, advanced to those of human beings. Proverbs, for instance, suggests that the sluggard "go to the ants . . . and learn from them."

Following is the account of your co-author (Slate) concerning a personal childhood experience in which a "lowly" wasp with apparent clairvoyant powers came to his rescue. It should be noted that this early experience is only one of many personal experiences in which insects demonstrated various clairvoyant traits.

"As a boy growing up on a farm in Alabama, I developed an early appreciation of animals, including cattle and horses as well as a variety of pet companions. Aside from these, I was intrigued by the many so-called 'lowliest of animals,' to include the secretive lizard, the friendly turtle, and the modest toad frog. I often wondered what life on Earth would be like without these fascinating beings. Even insects commanded my attention and admiration. I was intrigued by the endless diversity of these small but noble creatures.

As a child, I often cared for injured or ailing animals, nurturing and protecting them until they were fully recovered. I also visited regularly the horses' watering trough to free insects trapped in the water, an activity that became a ritual I called 'rescue and release.' Among my most unforgettable rescue and release experience was the freeing of a red wasp that was floating lifeless in the water. Reaching under it, I lifted it gently from the water. Soon, his wings spread and began a slow, trembling movement. Finally, upon regaining his strength, he ascended, but instead of flying hurriedly into the distance, he lingered before me, flying slowly to-and-fro as if to express his gratitude. It was for me a peak moment in which I felt that I had somehow contributed to a better world by having saved this magnificent creature.

"While the experience of freeing the red wasp was alone rewarding, what was to follow a few days later would take the experience to a totally new level. While bicycling along the country road near my home, I noticed a red wasp exactly like the one I had rescued flying close by and directly in front of me. He continued his flight, at times flying from side to side, always with obvious friendliness. Still accompanied by the sociable wasp, I spotted in the distance four familiar bikers known in the community as the neighborhood bully and his gang of three. Having had several previous encounters with them, and knowing that they demanded full right-of-way on the narrow road, I pulled over and waited for them to pass. But instead of passing, the bully and his gang sped aggressively in my direction. As he came nearer, the bully suddenly fell hard from his bike and with his face buried in his hands, screamed with obvious pain, 'I've been stung! I've been stung!' Somewhat reluctantly, the gang of three came to his rescue and helped him to his feet. Still crying out in pain, the bully accompanied by the gang left the scene, slowly pushing their bikes in humiliation along the road. Following the incident, the bully and his gang of three soon disbanded, never again to bully neighboring children.

"Reflecting upon the experience I wondered, 'Could the red wasp I had recently rescued from drowning have joined me at a time of danger on the nearby country road? Could the same wasp that lingered in appreciation after his rescue somehow sense the danger of my situation involving the bully and the gang?' It seemed only reasonable to me at that early age that the same red wasp, which I named Big Red, somehow sensed the danger of the situation and joined me at that urgent time of need for a twofold purpose: to provide protection from the threat of bullying, and more importantly, to end the bullying altogether by permanently dismantling the gang. It could be argued, of course, that the entire incident was merely a chance occurrence, but personal experience is a powerful teacher! I remain convinced to this day that the familiar red wasp, through clairvoyance, sensed the risk of the situation, and of his own volition, took decisive action."

A Master Dowser.

The activation of the clairvoyance potential can be facilitated through the use of a host of appropriate tools. Aside from such familiar tools as the crystal ball, quartz crystal, pendulum, and cards are several more recently developed techniques including the innovative *crumpled paper technique* in which clairvoyance is activated through focusing on the pattern of lines in a wrinkled sheet of paper. Notwithstanding the use of these tools, dowsing with either metal rods or twigs remains among the most popular clairvoyant skills. As with the application of any clairvoyant tool, the dynamics associated with dowsing is complex and often unclear. It's generally believed that dowsing tools are multi-functional in their capacity not only to activate specific inner clairvoyant faculties but to access external sources of information as well.

A highly successful southern artist known for his commitment to environmental protection and protection of endangered species is also recognized as a Master Dowser of the South. His expert dowsing specialties include not only locating subterranean resources such as oil, natural gas, minerals, and water, but also assessing the quantity of the identified resources. For each application, he creates dowsing rods of metal with unique characteristics appropriate for a particular purpose. Included are variations in size and shape of the rods as well as the metal used. Dowsing for gas, he claims, requires smaller gauge rods of copper, whereas dowsing for water requires higher gauge rods of steel. When dowsing for oil, he uses a specially designed pair of steel rods with the ends of the prongs turned slightly downward whereas when dowsing for minerals, he uses rods of a very small gauge with the ends of the prongs turned slightly inward. When the ends of the prongs connect, he claims, the major deposit of the mineral is directly beneath the rods.

In dowsing for water, he uses a pair of steel rods with handles encased in a copper tube. These specially designed rods, he maintains, signal not only the presence of water but its depth and quality as well. The presence of vibrations in the rods, he claims, determines the degree of motion in the water source, with strong vibrations indicating an underground stream in rapid motion. The rods, he further claims, are especially sensitive to contaminated water sources which tend to generate erratic vibrations in the rods. In one highly unusual demonstration of dowsing before a group of college students, he identified a noxious stream that generated such strong "electric-like vibrations" in the rods that he was unable to hold onto them. Upon falling to the ground, the rods continued to visibly vibrate momentarily to the amazement of observing students. Environmental specialists who later conducted test of the stream confirmed the accuracy of the dowsing results.

Among this remarkable dowser's most unique creations is a specially altered pair of brass rods for locating lost personal items and buried treasures, including both coins and paper currency. The unusual pair of rods each has a 90 degree handle of 4 inches and an extended prong of 2 feet. At the end of each prong is a forked extension of 2 inches which, in his opinion, increases the sensitivity of the rods by promoting a clairvoyant interaction.

He attributes successful dowsing to three critical essentials:

The Three Critical Essentials to Successful Dowsing

1. the existence of multiple clairvoyant faculties in everyone,
2. the sensitivity of a particular clairvoyant faculty to specific external tangibles or conditions, and
3. practice and experience.

The tangible devices used in dowsing, from his perspective, are important, not because of any inherent powers in the tangibles, but rather because of their capacity as tools to facilitate the merging of the three critical essentials.

Inter-dimensional Clairvoyance

Clairvoyance can be an inter-dimensional phenomenon that accesses higher dimensions of knowledge and power. Examples include our personal interactions with advanced growth facilitators, protectors, personal guides, and specific higher planes of power. *When we add to these the possibility of traveling out-of-body to literally engage other sources of insight, including our personal archival or Akashic records, the possibilities become endless.* Enrichment, enlightenment, and a forceful infusion of totally new power are among the many rewards of reaching beyond our known tangible realities and engaging the other realms and multiple dimensions that are now available to us.

Conclusion

In this chapter we have explored the empowering nature of clairvoyance through numerous case studies and cameo manifestations of this remarkable phenomenon. We now know that clairvoyance, whether spontaneous or induced, is consistently enlightening and empowering. Best of all, it is now available to everyone.

Sources & Suggested Additional Reading:

Dale, C. *Everyday Clairvoyance*, Llewellyn, 2010.

Hewitt, W. W. *Psychic Development for Beginners*. Llewellyn, 1996.

Katz, D. L. *Extraordinary Psychic: Proven Techniques to Master Your Natural Psychic Abilities*, Llewellyn, 2008.

Katz, D. L. *You Are Psychic*, Llewellyn, 2004.

Slate, J. H. *Connecting to the Power of Nature*, Llewellyn, 2009.

Webster, C. *Clairvoyance*, Public Domain Books, 2006.

ADDENDUM #15 TO CHAPTER 15
Microcosm to Macrocosm & Macrocosm to Microcosm

The Tattvic Connection—
Meditation & Visualization Program #31:
The Feminine Force

The Feminine Force, and Woman as Symbol of Process & Reality

It takes two to Tango, and a Woman and Man together to make a baby—or, does it?

Other than in the Argentine Tango, women do dance alone, often out of spontaneous joy or in sensual pleasure, and in pure self-expression. She often enjoys dancing with other women, sometimes in preference to doing so with a man, and in artistic expression as well as professional entertainment with stars like Madonna and Lady Gaga. Even when she does dance with a man he often is simply a "moving prop" to support her is various positions and movements as in classical ballet and exhibition dancing.

For a man, except for a "date night," his role has nothing sexual about it, or it may be a gender role in a dramatic presentation—a dance story about real life or a fairy tale about imagined life such as the handsome prince awaking Sleeping Beauty with a kiss.

And, Baby makes Three?

As for "making a baby"—despite what the male ego wants to think—his role is really quite secondary even in a genuine and enduring relationship. She is the one who conceives, the one who carries the unborn fetus, the one who gives birth to the baby, and she is the one who immediately nurses and cares for the baby. His role as a "father" is more important to the child than to the woman. And his role as her "husband" is often questionable. Yes, Wife and Husband together are the foundation of an *ideal* family, but even then the actual gender may be less often recognized as fundamental. Also, in the modern world now adapting to a mainly Western economic model and culture, she can do everything and do it alone and often proves it willingly as well as by circumstance. A single mom is truly heroic, and more and more often the contemporary reality, as is the modern highly educated career woman who chooses not to marry.

Unfortunately, regardless of the culture, too often a pregnancy results from the criminal act of rape, or from juvenile enthusiasm and even sexual ignorance. And, in some cultures, there is religious enforcement of "child brides" and continuous pregnancy along with denial of education, legal equality with men, and suppression of her public appearance.

A Woman's Choice

While a woman desiring motherhood may skip marriage and choose to be inseminated by a male friend with no further "father" role, or she may instead choose artificial insemination outside of any relationship with a man.

"Virgin Birth" and Parthenogenesis

"Parthenogenesis" (virgin birth) has been demonstrated when the ovum is "artificially" stimulated to divide and produce an offspring clone that is the exact duplicate of the mother. In addition, natural parthenogenesis does sometimes occur in certain species including the Komodo Dragon, Hammerhead and Blacktip Sharks, and other genera of fish, amphibians, and reptiles, as well as insects.

In recent human history, we have the 1921 case of Geoffrey Russell born to Christabel Russell who claimed that she never had sexual relations with her husband, John Russell, nor any other man. While there are other claims of virgin birth, the Russell case was well known because of various legal actions culminating in a 1924 ruling by the British House of Lords confirming Geoffrey as the inheritor through John Russell of the title, the 4th Baron Ampthill. In other words, the Lords were convinced that Geoffrey was "legitimate," even if mom and dad never had sex together.

In Myth and Religion

Various myths and religions also center about "virgin birth"—Krishna in Hinduism, Mithras in some versions of Iranian religion, Horus in the ancient Egyptian religion, and others. Some stories have the Buddha as virgin born, also Moses in some versions of Judaism, and John the Baptist and Jesus in Christianity. Not all virgin births are of males: just a couple examples—the Greek myths have both Athena and Aphrodite born without human or deific parents.

And, "Mom" is not always needed!

Some versions of the birth of Moses also claim that he had no human parents. And there are other stories and myths of unparented births. Certainly, it would seem such a birth with neither father nor mother to be no more miraculous than one involving a single virgin parent.

The Cosmological Feminine Force

"In the Beginning was the Word." Long before the logical question of *"Which came first—Chicken, or Egg?"* we see gender-free forms of life appearing in the primordial oceanic mother where all life had its origin.

In ancient oral traditions, much older than any recognizable religions and their *Sacred Books*, the "Life Force" was always seen as feminine and named "The Great Mother" or "The Great Goddess." We still refer to "Mother Nature" and see the Earth Element as feminine.

The Great Mother as Archetypal Fact

The *Great Mother"* is an "archetypal" fact who lives in the Universal Unconscious Mind shared by all humanity and—for all we know—perhaps with other life forms as well. In myth and religion, cosmological forces appear as animal deities and sometimes in unrecognizable out-of-this-world "Cthulhuthic" forms. We see evidence of animals dreaming—perhaps they dream of a "Great Mother Cat" or a "Heroic Monster Horse" or of "the Mouse who swallowed New York City."

Shakti, the Goddess of Many Names and Forms

In ancient Tantra (not as religion but as a comprehensive cosmic and personal evolutionary and developmental system), it is the Goddess, Shakti (and all her variations), who is the primary creator and maintainer of the Universe. Her consort, Shiva, is active only on her initiative. She is responsible for all material manifestation, and it is She who is invoked to meet human needs. Physical Life is fundamentally feminine, and all Life descends through Mother and Daughter, generation after generation back to the Beginning, for the male has no womb and cannot reproduce.

Consciousness, Matter, Energy together manifest Life—and *with* Life are in everything, and it is Feminine Force that is their Source. In Humanity (in Reality and in Myth and Symbol) it is Woman as Virgin and Mother who is the source and continuation of Life as we experience it. She is the living creator of Life; she nourishes and sustains Life; and in Her sexuality She expresses Life. Her beauty is part of the process of life as She attracts the male who will then also participate in the process of reproducing the species and of advancing the ever more complex *Never-Ending-Process* to which we all belong.

Man is still relevant

Yes, Man is still relevant, and the Masculine Force is as real as the Feminine—but modern man and woman (until lately) have lost perspective and understanding of their essential cosmic, psychological, social, and even sexual natures. As we grow in our awareness and consciousness, as we advance in psychic empowerment, as we move into this New Age, we will learn anew what it is to be Man & Woman, and learn to make their relationship into a true Cosmic Ritual leading to a better world and their own Super Consciousness attainment. There are books about Tantric Love in the Suggested Reading List at the end of this addendum.

A Woman's Feeling

Perhaps it is because we truly live within *Gaia* (the name adopted by many for our planet as a living home) and hence the fact that all life as we know it is feminine that Woman seems to be more naturally intuitive and psychic. She more commonly turns to her *feelings* than to her rational mind to determine the "Truth" of any situation. Inwardly she, and indeed all of us, connects to the feminine Unconscious and to *Nature's Wisdom.*

The Wise Woman

Mothers *instinctively* know what is best for their children, and women often show intuitive wisdom in matters of healing and nurture. Throughout all cultures, East and West, throughout all the ages until modern suppression, it was the "medicine women" who doctored and cured, the midwives who brought new life into the world and who helped the dying through the gates of death and who wrapped the body for burial, the "wise women" who cured infertility and made potions and spells to bring straying lovers back home, who looked to the sky to forecast the season and weather, and who read the Moon to tell the times for planting and harvesting and when to do what.

And, in truth, the "Man in the Moon" was always a Woman and She is the Goddess who guides through the darkness and teaches the way home. She is *Lady Luna* (see illustration page 601) and many other names and forms for She is universal.

Clairvoyance and Woman's Intuition

A Woman's Intuition, a Woman's Instinct, a Woman's Healing Touch, and a Woman's Love are all part of her natural Psychic Empowerment for She is Shakti, the Feminine Devine, incarnate. She is the Great Goddess, East and West and throughout all Nature-based spiritual traditions.

The "other" Great Mystery

Little explored and barely recognized is the fact of Feminine and Masculine in our "genetic" inheritance that is more than the physical gene code. Looking only at the feminine we see its role at all levels: physical, astral, mental, causal, spiritual, and distinctly in physical and emotional differences in function and expression. Similarly, such "functional" differences continue on into higher realms as well. (When we say "functional" we are saying nothing about abilities, capabilities, or anything else for which we might be attacked as misogynist) Men and Women are equal but different, and how that difference has been transmitted over millions of years remains a mystery.

The Tattvic Meditation & Visualization Program #31:
The Feminine Force

Proceed in your usual relations program, and then visualize the symbol of Lady Luna as given on page 601 (or any other truly feminine deific image of your choice, or one of the Tantric Goddesses of pleasant demure).

Let the feelings associated with this discussion of the primacy of the Feminine Force in your Physical and Emotional manifestation "speak to your Soul," realize that it's only "a Man's World" at the surface level and that your Feminine Force (whether you are Man or Woman) needs stronger expression and that feminine values are needed now to bring balance to the world.

We are out of tune with Nature, our Environment needs care and a return to "greenness" in order to restore a cooperative relationship between Humanity and the Living Planet. In our Body we are part of the physical world and need to recover the natural wisdom of pre-industrial times. We have to become Earth's caretakers before She can resume Her role as our nurturing Great Mother.

This is not an intellectual exercise of steps and procedures. You have to find your own way to move in this new responsibility. It's not a call for marches and sit-ins or violence on the street or even for overt political action. It's a call for *Inner Realization* that can spread from psyche to psyche to change consciousness and restore sense and wisdom.

There's little more to be said here. The next step is yours alone.

Love is the Cause

Sources & Suggested Additional Reading:

Gray, W. G. *Evoking the Primal Goddess: Discovery of the Eternal Feminine Within,* 2002, Llewellyn.

Kraig, D. M. *Modern Sex Magick: Secrets of Erotic Spirituality,* 1998, Llewellyn.

Michaels, M. A., and Johnson, P. *The Essence of Tantric Sexuality,* 2006, Llewellyn.

Michaels, M. A., and Johnson, P. *Tantra for Erotic Empowerment,* 2008, Llewellyn.

Mumford, J. *Ecstasy through Tantra,* 1975, 1977, 1987, Llewellyn.

Neumann, E. *Amor and Psyche: The Psychic Development of the Feminine,* 1971, Princeton.

Neumann, E. *The Fear of the Feminine: And Other Essays on Feminine Psychology,* 1994, Princeton.

Neumann, E. *The Great Mother: An Analysis of the Archetype,* 1972, Princeton.

Sherwood, K. *Sex and Transcendence: Enhance your Relationships through Meditation, Chakra & Energy Work,* 2011, Llewellyn.

Van Lysebeth, A. *Tantra: The Cult of the Feminine,* 1995, Red Wheel/Weiser.

Wolf, N. *Vagina: A New Biography,* 2012, Ecco.

CHAPTER SIXTEEN
Practice Exercises in Clairvoyance

Achieving is more enjoyable than achievement.

Steven Tyrka

Developing Clairvoyance
Commitment and Practice

Developing your clairvoyant potentials requires commitment and practice. Thanks to years of research in the controlled lab setting, structured practice exercises are now available not only to activate clairvoyance but to accelerate your development of this important faculty. Practice exercises in clairvoyance recognize the simple concept that we are here to learn and grow. Through practice, you can master a wide range of clairvoyant skills that can facilitate your growth and empower you with important knowledge unavailable from any other source.

Practice Makes Perfect

Only through research can the *science of clairvoyance* be advanced; but only through practice can the *art of clairvoyance* be mastered. When practiced on a regular basis, exercises in clairvoyance generate a multifunctional effect that is relevant to your total growth and development. Clairvoyant skills, once acquired through practice, will add power, meaning, and success to your daily life.

By regularly practicing clairvoyance, you will discover that practice truly does make perfect. You will also discover, however, that perfection rather than a finished product is a continuous process of growth and self-discovery. Through practice, you can energize that important process and use it to become *far more than you are.*

Here are a few guidelines designed to increase the effectiveness of practice in clairvoyance:

Developmental Guidelines to Increase Clairvoyant Abilities

1. Make a commitment to develop your clairvoyant abilities. Rather than setting high expectations, just think of becoming more clairvoyant through practice.

2. Take small steps rather than giant leaps. Begin with such simple exercises as guessing the time before checking or the amount of change in your purse or pocket. Don't expect too much too soon. Let go of big expectations.

3. Become more attentive to your intuitive impressions. Pay attention to feelings and thoughts that could have clairvoyant significance. Notice things going on around you and allow awareness of unseen situations and happenings to emerge.

4. Stay connected to your subconscious. Think of your subconscious as a source of clairvoyant knowledge and power. Stay attuned and receptive to thoughts and images of clairvoyant significance.

5. Keep it simple. Remind yourself that *complexity seeks simplicity*.

6. Practice daily if only for a few minutes. In developing your clairvoyant potential, there's no substitute for regular practice.

7. Enjoy! Experiencing clairvoyance through practice can add joy and excitement to your daily life.

Laboratory Research in Practical Applications

Practice exercises in clairvoyance are at their best when they apply the findings of laboratory research to practical application. Through structured practice exercises based on research, you can promote the development of your clairvoyant potentials and discover effective ways of using them. You will discover new ways of applying your clairvoyant skills to enrich the quality of your life, to help others, and to promote global progress.

Our early research in the controlled lab setting found several personal characteristics associated with successful clairvoyance. For instance, altruistic persons who are committed to the higher good typically score higher on tests of clairvoyance. Similarly, individuals who experience satisfying personal relationships typically perform better on laboratory exercises in clairvoyance than persons whose relationships were described as unfulfilling or turbulent. Other personal characteristics associated with successful clairvoyance in the lab setting included a positive self-concept, feelings of adequacy and personal worth, and a passionate commitment to solve such global problems as worldwide hunger, abuse of human rights, environmental pollution, and reckless depletion of natural resources.

According to our research participants, clairvoyance contributed to their knowledge of global problems and increased their commitment to solve them. Our studies repeatedly showed that increased awareness of global conditions through clairvoyance is one of the best motivational forces known for bringing forth desired global change.

Resolving global crises and finding workable solutions to global problems such as hunger, disease, endangered species, and environmental pollution are all within the scope of clairvoyance at its best.

A Higher Domain of Power

Can you imagine an inner domain of clairvoyant power that provides a personal, up-to-date register of hidden potentials, external conditions, and unfolding events with important relevance to your life? Believe it or not, such a dynamic domain does exist. It is an essential part of you, and its resources are readily available. Actively interacting with that inner domain, however, requires a clear formulation of your personal goals and a commitment to reach beyond the borders of present awareness. By interacting with that inner domain, you can gain full access to whatever is relevant to you at the moment. Among the many possibilities are solutions to pressing problems, better coping skills, awareness of your undeveloped potentials, and ways of developing them, to list but a few. For conditions involving risk and danger, such as near-accident situations, the inner domain of clairvoyance can provide in an instant the awareness required for prevention or escape. Clairvoyance related to danger often includes a sudden flash of vivid imagery along with, at times, impressions of a protecting presence as later discussed.

Inner Domain Readiness

For college students participating in our research, practice in clairvoyance activated a state of "inner domain readiness" that provided access to inner but often dormant resources, including those related to academic performance. According to them, interacting with that inner domain effectively increased memory, improved problem-solving skills, and generated totally new information on a "need-to-know" basis. A physics major who graduated *summa cum laude* concluded that practice in clairvoyance was a significant contributor to her achievement of that high honor. A pre-law student attributed her admission to law school largely to what she called "clairvoyance at work" during her admissions exam. She is now a distinguished district judge who continues to practice clairvoyance, which she claims adds to the quality and satisfaction of her chosen career. In her own words, "Clairvoyance can stir the subconscious to generate synchronicity in which perception, cognition, memory, and reality purposefully merge. The results are expanded awareness required for quality decision making and problem solving."

The Human Aura: Clairvoyant Power at Hand

Possibly nowhere is the empowering potential of clairvoyance more evident than in the human aura, that energy field enveloping the physical body. But the aura is far more than simply an energy field. It is a unique manifestation of the energy force that characterizes our existence as evolving souls. By interacting with that energy force, you can experience the fundamental nature of your existence—mentally, physically, and spiritually. You can activate your dormant mental faculties, including clairvoyance, and bring forth empowering change in your life and the world.

Because the aura is a manifestation of the very essence of our existence, practice exercises in clairvoyance that utilize the aura are among the most effective known. Our early studies consistently showed that the aura increases in brightness and magnitude with the development of our clairvoyant potentials. Simple practice exercises, including those that use either playing cards or standard ESP cards, tend to clear the aura of discoloration and generate a state of balance throughout the aura system. As clairvoyant skills are mastered through practice, these changes become enduring characteristics of the aura.

Our lab studies repeatedly showed that by simply viewing your own aura or that of another person, you can generate in an instant a focused state of mind that promotes clairvoyance. Through practice in viewing your personal aura, you can access your clairvoyant faculties and focus them on specific objectives. You can use clairvoyance to identify your hidden potentials and find ways of developing them. You can identify conditions that limit your progress and uncover effective ways of overcoming them. You can enrich your personal interactions, build powerful feelings of self worth, and enrich the quality of your daily life, to list but a few of the possibilities. All of these are available to you simply by exercising your aura viewing skills.

Aura Hand-viewing Technique

Among the most effective methods for viewing your own aura as a means of exercising clairvoyance and promoting its development is the Aura Hand-viewing Technique. The technique is based on the premise that the aura enveloping your hand as your body's antennae is the "signature" of the full aura enveloping your body. Consequently, features observed in the aura around your hand are representative of characteristics found throughout your aura system. For instance, brightness in the aura around your hand is characteristic of brightness in the aura around your full body. Similarly, expansiveness in the aura around your hand is representative of expansiveness in the full aura. Here's the 5-step procedure which is conducted in a quiet setting with natural or indirect lighting:

Step 1. With either hand held at arm's length against a neutral background, focus your full attention upon your hand as you hold your fingers in a relaxed, slightly spread position.

Step 2. Following a few moments of focusing upon your hand, slowly expand your peripheral vision above, below, and to each side of your hand.

Step 3. Once your peripheral vision reaches its limits, let your eyes fall slightly out of focus and you will notice a visual phenomenon sometimes called the *peripheral glow effect* enveloping your hand.

Step 4. Focus your full attention upon the glow around your hand and you will notice the slow emergence of the aura. With the aura in view, center your attention upon its distinguishing characteristics, including its colors, patterns, and other unique features.

Step 5. Take plenty of time to center your full attention upon the aura and the clairvoyant insight that typically accompanies this important step. Keep in mind that characteristics of the aura around the hand are likewise characteristic of the full aura. Notice the aura's strengths as well as any feature, such as discoloration or constriction, that suggests the need for corrective intervention. Should the aura begin to fade during viewing, repeat the procedure to bring it back into full view.

Step 6. Conclude aura viewing by turning the palms of your hands upward and visualizing bright beams of radiant energy entering your palms and from there, flowing throughout your body. With your full aura radiating bright energy, visualize your aura's central core situated in your solar plexus fully energized and sending fort radiant energy to permeate every organ, system, and function of your body. Conclude with the affirmation:"I am fully empowered."

As noted in Step 5, it is important during the exercise to note specific aura characteristics and the clairvoyant insights that unfold. Here are a few examples of specific aura characteristics with important clairvoyant implications:

Aura Interpretation Guidelines

- **Fissures** or breaks in the aura are associated with trauma, including that of past-life origin. Victims of abuse or bullying often show fissures in the aura. Sadly, such damage to the aura is often slow to heal. During aura viewing, clairvoyant awareness of the origin of fissures or breaks often becomes clear. With that insight, healing is rapidly accelerated, and in some cases instant, particularly when the condition is associated with past-life trauma. In aura viewing, *clairvoyant awareness is healing power!*

- **Tremors** or turbulence in the aura are often related to uncertainty, indecisiveness, and dissatisfaction, especially in personal relationships. Couples relationships that are enfeebled or on the verge of breaking up are often indicated by tremors in the aura of either partner. Counseling to include such stress management techniques as self-hypnosis, meditation, and progressive relaxation are highly effective in extinguishing tremors or turbulence in the aura.

- **Brightness** in the aura is associated with optimism, satisfying relationships, emotional stability, and mental alertness. **Dullness** or discoloration in the aura is often associated with such conditions as depression, disappointment, and grief. Visualization of relaxing nature scenes accompanied by self-empowering affirmations is usually effective in adding brightness to the aura.

- **Constriction** of the aura is associated with a host of disempowering conditions including anxiety, depression, emotional instability, and social withdrawal. Remarkably, simply turning the palms of your hands upward as you visualize beams of bright energy connecting you to the highest realms of power can instantly restore harmony and balance to the aura system. This technique, called *Cosmic Connection by Design,* is almost always accompanied by clairvoyant insight into the source of the imbalance and how to effectively deal with it.

- **Points of darkness**, also called puncture wounds, in the aura are associated with one-on-one psychic vampirism, a phenomenon in which an energy vampire draws energy from a host victim's aura by tapping into it (See *Psychic Vampires* by Joe H. Slate). Subjects who are recurrent victims of one-on-one psychic vampirism also show severe constriction of the aura due to the loss of aura energy. *The Finger Interlock Technique* developed in our labs is one of the most effective methods known for correcting dysfunctions associated with psychic vampirism. To implement the procedure, simply form two circles by joining the thumb and middle finger of each hand, then bringing the hands together to form interlocking circles. Conclude with the affirmation, "I am fully empowered." Although the procedure requires only seconds to implement, its effects can be profound. Clairvoyant insight into the source of vampirism almost always accompanies the Finger Interlock Technique.

- **Imbalance** or asymmetry in the aura along with discoloration suggests anxiety regarding unresolved conflict as well as important life transitions such as unemployment, personal loss, and physical injury or illness.

- **Points of brightness** observed either within the aura or its surrounding area suggest a guiding presence or protective force. While manifestations of personal guides and protectors are often considered common, their presence as points of brightness in the aura can suggest urgency and the need for clairvoyant insight into their purposes.

Objective Aura Viewing of Another Person

The Aura Hand-viewing Technique can be easily adapted for use in viewing the aura of another person. For that application, attention is focused upon the forehead rather than the hand of the individual who is situated at a comfortable distance for viewing against a neutral background. Following a few moments of focusing upon the individual's forehead, peripheral vision is slowly expanded to its limits. The eyes are then allowed to fall slightly out of focus, whereupon the aura will appear as a glow, first around the individual's head and shoulder region and then around the full body. Attention is then centered on the aura, to include such characteristics as expansiveness, color, pattern, and other distinguishing characteristics. At this stage, clairvoyant impressions related to various aura characteristics typically unfold, often in marked detail.

With practice, awareness of the aura of others becomes a normal, effortless part of our interpersonal interactions. The results include not only clairvoyant insight, but enrichment of social interactions as well.

Aura Self-embracement Technique

Paradoxically, the highly complex aura system seeks simplicity in its various manifestations and applications. Aura Self-embracement is a technique based on the simple premise that actively embracing your physical body following aura self-viewing promotes full embracement of your total being as a person of dignity and incomparable worth. Simply embracing your physical body tends to expand the aura and introduce brightness into it. Further, Aura Self-embracement tends to repair any structural damage to the aura, including fissures and puncture wounds.

Through Aura Self-embracement, important clairvoyant information often emerges in highly detailed form. Examples include clairvoyant insight concerning complex life situations such as entangled relationships, conflicts, and unresolved strivings. Aside from these, Aura Self-embracement can yield highly specific information related to such concerns as the recovery of lost objects, misplaced documents, and lost animals. For instance, a psychology student who had recently lost a fraternity ring during a soccer game used Aura Self-embracement to discover it concealed in grass near a goal post. In a similar instance, a business administration student who had participated in our research used the technique to locate a lost library book. During Aura Self-embracement, she experienced a clear image of the book half hidden in a magazine rack in the reading room at the University's Student Center.

Aside from its clairvoyant applications, Aura Self-embracement as a self-administered technique has been used to increase self-confidence and generate powerful expectations of success. It is among the most effective techniques known for reducing stress, breaking unwanted habits, and managing weight. When regularly practiced, it's an excellent rejuvenation technique that slows aging and promotes quality of life. Our long-term studies showed in some instances that the physical signs of aging were literally reversed through frequent use of Aura Self-embracement. Here's the technique:

Step 1. Begin by viewing your aura using the Aura Hand-viewing Technique. Upon completion of viewing, cross your arms over your chest and rest your hands gently upon your shoulders.

Step 2. With your hands resting upon your shoulders, stroke your shoulders gently as you sense the aura energies in your hands embracing and interacting with the aura enveloping your full body. Note the balancing and attuning effects of that interactive embracement throughout you being.

Step 3. As interactive embracement continues, close your eyes and visualize the aura as a glowing energy force interacting with the highest source of source power. Affirm in your own words your connection and oneness with that source.

Step 4. Let self-embracement and unconditional love emerging from within yourself permeate your total being. As a person of incomparable worth, affirm in your own words your worthiness of total self-embracement and love, the two most powerful forces in the universe. At this critical step, take plenty of time for the interactive power of both forces to reach a level of peak empowerment.

Step 5. Conclude by again viewing the aura around your hand and affirming the empowering effects of full self-embracement and love. Note the clairvoyant insight that typically unfolds during aura viewing at this concluding step.

With practice, the Aura Self-embracement becomes increasingly effective as a personal empowerment technique with a wide range of applications

The Mind/Body Interactive Program

A positive interaction between the mind and body is essential to the development of clairvoyance as a source of both new knowledge and power. Once connected and attuned, the mind and body together generate a positive energy force that is unique in both dynamics and potential. It's through that interactive force that clairvoyance can be activated to provide information available from no other source.

The Mind/Body Interactive Program is a multifunctional approach that is especially useful in providing information required for effective planning and decision-making. Whether used individually or as a group procedure, the program can identify critical factors and ways of integrating them to ensure successful achievement of specified goals. It can identify alternative approaches and accurately predict their consequences. In the business setting, it can facilitate progress through a synergistic integration of theory, causative variables, and promotional ideas into the planning process. Here's the program, which requires approximately 30 minutes in a quiet, comfortable setting.

Step 1. Goal Formulation. Specify your goals and write them down. Goals can range from simply exercising your clairvoyant faculty to targeting clairvoyance upon information required for successful attainment of highly specific goals.

Step 2. Relaxation. Settle back and clear your mind of all active thought. In that passive state, take in a few deep breaths and develop a rhythmic breathing pattern. Relax your body, beginning with the muscles in your forehead and slowly spreading downward throughout your body.

Step 3. Visualization. Visualize a quiet, peaceful scene such as a tranquil lake with a sailboat or clear blue sky with white clouds drifting gently in the breeze. Allow the images to come and go as relaxation spreads deeper and deeper into your body.

Step 4. Solar Plexus Centering. Focus your attention on your solar plexus as your body's center of empowering energy. Allow bright energy from that center to fully permeate your being. Note the serenity that always accompanies solar plexus centering.

Step 5. Clairvoyant Screen. Picture in your mind a blank screen situated before you upon which images of clairvoyant significance can be projected. Note the mental clearing and attuning effects of focusing on the blank screen

Step 6. Spontaneous Clairvoyant Projection. Continue to focus your full attention on the clairvoyant screen as spontaneous images unfold upon it. Note particularly images of color that typically characterize important clairvoyant insight. Mentally affirm your power to determine the clairvoyant significance of the image.

Step 7. Goal-Related Clairvoyant Projection. Spontaneous clairvoyant projection sets the stage of induced projection related to specific goals. To promote goal-related projection, clearly specify your goal and project images related to it upon the screen. The use of symbols at this step can often generate in an instant the clairvoyant images related to your goal. For instance, your projection of a university diploma upon the screen can generate an image of the university that best fits your educational goals. Similarly, your projection of a list of potential employers upon the screen can highlight the employer that best fits your career goals.

Step 8. Conclusion. Allow the clairvoyant screen to slowly fade as you affirm in your own words the empowering effects of this program.

The Mind/Body Interactive Program can be easily revised for use as a group procedure. When used in the group setting, the program is concluded with a group interaction in which the results of the program are discussed.

The Pendulum in Clairvoyant Applications: Pendulumology

The pendulum, a weight at the end of a chain or string, is a simple but highly useful device for gathering clairvoyant information. In its clairvoyant application, movement (or absence of movement) of the pendulum when suspended from the hand can provide highly specific information with its to-and-fro movement signifying a *positive response*, a side-to-side movement signifying a *negative response*, and a circular movement signify a *neutral response* to the question posed. No movement in the pendulum signifies a *no response*. It is important, of course, that no attempt be made to influence the pendulum's response.

Although the pendulum is a popular instrument for gathering clairvoyant information, its dynamics and applications have received but scant attention in the scientific research setting. Our studies of its use, which we called ***pendulumology,*** uncovered abundant evidence of its capacity to respond to very mild energy stimuli originating either from within the individual or group or from some external source. There's considerable evidence that meaningful thought energies of subconscious origin are sufficient to induce movement of the pendulum when suspended over the hand, either of oneself or that of another. The pendulum in that role can effectively convey needed information, including both clairvoyant and precognitive, to conscious awareness.

Aside from its intra-psychic capacity to connect the conscious and subconscious, there is considerable evidence that the pendulum when held in the hand as an extension of physiology can tap into energy sources of information external to the physical body. Those sources can include other persons, other dimensions or planes, and even other objects energized with the capacity to influence the pendulum. For instance, a physical object may retain some of the energies of the individuals and situations associated with it. That concept holds that in the absence of the energy source, the residual energies may remain in or around the object in sufficient intensity to induce movement of the pendulum when brought into proximity with the object, thus facilitating clairvoyance related to the residual energies. Aside from that possibility, the tangible object independent of the application of a pendulum could conceivably activate clairvoyant or other psychic functions, especially when held in the hand, a concept called *psychometry*.

When used as a clairvoyant practice technique, the pendulum in its capacity to gather relevant information has been often applied to gather important information related to both problem solving and decision making. When used in a variety of trouble-shooting situations, the pendulum has demonstrated a high degree of accuracy in diagnosing malfunctions in equipment and in identifying appropriate corrective measures. In our labs at Athens State University, its use as a research tool was instrumental in developing an advanced technology involving the monitoring of the human energy system.

Clairvoyant Sharing

Among our students who practiced the technique both independently and with a partner in the controlled lab setting, clairvoyant performance dramatically improved in a variety of situations. Their successes included marked improvements in such tasks as identifying an object concealed in a box as well as the location of a container of a contaminated liquid situated among other identical containers. Equally as remarkable, their performance on unrelated tasks, such as precognition and telepathy, consistently improved following practice using the pendulum as a clairvoyant tool, a concept we called ***positive transfer of clairvoyant practice.***

Possibly the most challenging application of the pendulum as a clairvoyant tool is in probing the subconscious. In self-hypnosis, this technique can be used to determine one's receptiveness to induction as well as to identify the most productive applications of the trance state. When held over one's own hand, the pendulum can yield important information related to hidden motives, sources of anxiety, and past-life experiences, to mention but a few. Some experts have concluded that its effectiveness as a past-life retrieval technique is equally if not greater than that of past-life regression using hypnosis. Complementing the direct benefits of practice using the pendulum is its usefulness in promoting relaxation and tranquility, benefits that may account for its enduring appeal among behavioral specialists and people-in-general alike.

Crystal Gazing

The crystal ball has for centuries been valued as both an object of beauty and useful alternative for probing the unknown. Through crystal gazing, also called *scrying,* the mental faculties associated with clairvoyance and other forms of extrasensory awareness can be accessed and effectively activated. As a result, *clairvoyant potential* becomes *clairvoyant experience.*

In clairvoyance, the role of the crystal ball is multifunctional. Through gazing, it generates a state of relaxation and focused attention, both of which are essential to productive clairvoyance. It stimulates mental imagery, to include remote viewing of distant realities. Aside from these, it promotes awareness of both the past and future, to include events of important relevance to present life situations. In that role, the crystal ball can be seen as simply a convenient object to convey subconscious awareness to the conscious mind.

The Spherical Screen Technique with Crystal Ball

The Spherical Screen Technique is an exercise designed not only to promote clairvoyant crystal gazing but to facilitate a state of generalized self-empowerment. As a practice exercise, the procedure can be used individually or with groups, with or without an audience. For best results, the crystal ball is situated at a distance of one or two feet from the viewer(s) and at a position that permits slightly downward gazing. Here's the procedure.

Step 1. A practice object, such as an article of jewelry, a flower, or small art object is viewed with special attention given to the object's detailed characteristics such as color, texture, shape, and weight.

Step 2. With your eyes closed form a detailed mental image of the object.

Step 3. Again view the practice object and note any thoughts or feelings related to it.

Step 4. Close your eyes and allow a detailed image of the object to again emerge. Continue to note any thoughts or feelings related to the object.

Step 5. Replace the object with a crystal ball and focus your full attention upon it. Note the feelings, emotions, and thoughts that emerge as focusing continues.

Step 6. Close your eyes and form a mental image of the crystal ball. Focus your full attention on the image and allow clairvoyant impressions to emerge.

Step 7. Again, view the crystal ball as you remain receptive to new images, feelings, and impressions of clairvoyant significance.

As with other practice exercises in clairvoyance, the effectiveness of the Spherical Screen Technique increases with repeated practice of the procedure. With sufficient practice of the full step-by-step Spherical Screen Technique, the procedure can be applied independently of the use of a practice object as detailed in Steps 1 through 4.

Frontalis Muscle Relaxation

Although crystal gazing was designed as primarily a clairvoyant exercise, it is highly valued for its usefulness in relaxation training, meditation, and re-educative psychotherapy. In relaxation training, the technique is particularly effective in inducing frontalis muscle relaxation which is rapidly generalized to other regions of the physiology. That application of crystal gazing suggests important relevance of the technique to biofeedback training and the treatment of such disorders as migraine and tension headaches and hypertension.

Crystal gazing is highly useful in promoting mental imagery conducive to a variety of meditation approaches. The "spherical glow" that often envelops the crystal ball during gazing, especially when peripheral vision is expanded to its limits, can rapidly generate a profound state of focused attention and receptivity. When the eyes are then closed, mental images of clairvoyant as well as precognitive relevance often emerge. Aside from its usefulness in meditation, crystal gazing can be readily adapted for use as an effective hypnotic or self-hypnotic induction procedure.

Re-educative Psychotherapy

In re-educative psychotherapy, crystal gazing can provide the essential physical and mental states required for directing suggestions to the innermost self. Examples of re-educative goal that are particularly receptive to crystal gazing include accelerating learning, improving memory, and increasing creativity. In settings involving age-related cognitive decline, re-educative psychotherapy utilizing crystal gazing has been especially effective as a mental and physical rejuvenation technique when used with such suggestions as, *Time is slowing down; I am at my youthful prime; mentally, physically, and spiritually, I am at my peak of youth and vigor; and living younger, longer, and better is my destiny.*

An important advantage of crystal gazing is its adaptability to groups. As a group technique, it is particularly useful in promoting positive group interactions and increased group cohesiveness. In group therapy, the technique is especially useful with teens and young adults in generating discussion of problem areas, identifying new alternatives and strategies, discovering creative solutions, and gaining personal insight,

In the instructional setting, crystal gazing has shown promise in a variety of learning situations. A marked increase in creativity was noted when crystal gazing was introduced into a college course in creative writing. Similarly, college students enrolled in an oil painting course showed a rapid increase in creative ideas.

Taken together, the evidence is clear: Crystal gazing, when appropriately applied, promotes not only rapid development of the clairvoyant potential existing in everyone, but also enrichment in host of other important areas of human functioning. It adds interest, excitement, and self-empowerment to daily life!

Clairvoyance From Beyond Exercise

Clairvoyance From Beyond goes a step beyond other clairvoyant practice exercises by focusing on the spiritual as an essential component of our existence. It recognizes the potential of the *spiritual* to interact with the mind and body in ways that promote our total growth and wellbeing. From that perspective, clairvoyance and other forms of extrasensory experience along with such phenomena as astral projection, bi-location, synchronicity, and quantum intertwining are seen as spiritually relevant and thus enlightening and potentially empowering.

Interaction with the Non-physical Realm

Clairvoyance From Beyond recognizes the existence of the non-physical realm and our capacity to interact with it as a source of knowledge and power. It embraces the endlessness of our existence and the persistence of our personal identity as evolving souls. It recognizes death as a transition to a higher, more advanced realm of continued growth and self-discovery. It further recognizes death as a transition characterized by a phenomenon called the *preservation of peak growth* in which all previous growth is instantly restored to its peak. Such survival phenomena as spirit guides and the presence of those who have crossed over to the afterlife dimension are thus explained as the persistence of consciousness, intelligence, and identity in discarnate energy form with the capacity for continued growth and interaction, to include communicating with those who are left behind.

The Two Major Premises of Clairvoyance From Beyond

1. The first states simply that energy as a life force is never lost. Though it may undergo transformation, transition, and change, the life force that characterizes our existence is forever. Clairvoyance and other extrasensory phenomena are viewed as meaningful, purposeful manifestations of that life force energy.

2. The second major premise holds that multiple dimensions exist, each with the capacity to interact with the other. Through our awareness and interaction with them, we have access not only to enlightenment but to power in its purest form.

Clairvoyance From Beyond as a practice exercise focuses on our capacity to interface and interact with other reality dimensions. It is a *needs oriented* approach that recognizes the importance of dimensions to interrelate. It focuses on our ability to reach beyond the cumulative knowledge of our present dimension and to access knowledge of a higher level. It embraces the concept of *interdimensional energy infusion* in which we can be energized and empowered through the infusion of energies from higher realms.

The exercise focuses on objectives related to human growth as a dynamic process rather than a fixed state of achievement. It views clairvoyance as a continuous process of personal unfoldment that is receptive to practice and experience. Rather than simply an event, the clairvoyant experience thus becomes an expression of a process of growth. The focus of this procedure is, consequently, not simply the accessing of specific clairvoyant information but rather the promotion of clairvoyant growth. Here's the procedure, which can be practiced either individually or as a group exercise.

Step 1. Settle back into a comfortable, relaxed position and clear your mind of all clutter. Visualize a favorite scene, and let yourself become a part of it.

Step 2. Affirm your intent, either silently or audibly, to interact with other dimensions of knowledge and power. Allow images of other dimensions to clearly form, possibly as expansive planes or other forms enveloped in radiant energy.

Step 3. From among the dimensions observed, select a particular dimension that seems especially relevant to you at the moment. Note its identifying characteristics and your sense of connection to it.

Step 4. Visualize the bright energy enveloping your body reaching outward as if to infinity and interfacing the selected dimension. Note the powerful interaction of energies as you connect to that dimension.

Step 5. Allow plenty of time for the interaction to continue as you sense a powerful infusion of energy throughout your being. Allow impressions and images to progressively unfold. It is at this stage that impressions of a guiding presence often emerge.

Step 6. Conclude by reflecting upon the experience and affirming in your own words its empowering rewards.

Clairvoyance From Beyond is yet another reflection of the concept: *Complexity seeks simplicity.* The complexities of the great beyond are constantly poised to engage our interactions and empower us as needed with new growth energy and knowledge.

Conclusion.

The human quest for knowledge, meaning, and personal empowerment is endless. It is not content with the simple rediscovery of that which is or was known. It insists on probing the illimitable depth, width, and breadth of the cosmos. It knows no limits. It always soars onward and upward.

ADDENDUM #16 TO CHAPTER SIXTEEN
Microcosm to Macrocosm & Macrocosm to Microcosm

The Tattvic Connection—
Meditation & Visualization Program #32:

The Mirror Projection & Analysis Technique
and Program for Shaping the Future

Mind Magic—Shaping the Future & Making it Happen

Can we shape, or actually change, the Future?

Yes, of course. *Everything we do has a future consequence.* We are always *making* the future so it is sensible to believe we can *shape* or *change* the future. The future happens, no matter what, so why not shape it to your desires? *What is it you want to change?* A few examples: Start a diet to lose weight; Start a special training program so you can qualify for a better job; Shop at a new boutique to change your looks; Join a dating club to meet the man or woman of your dreams; etc.

Know the Present, Plan the Future

Mind Magic, or Magick, is not an idle dream or fairy tale—it requires **Knowledge** of the present conditions you want to shape and change; it requires determination of what your want the future to be, i.e. your **Goal**; it requires Understanding of the factors that must be altered, i.e. through **Analysis**; it requires Knowing methods for making the desired change, and setting out a specific **Program** of the necessary Actions; and it requires personal Discipline and a **Schedule** of Actions to take.

It's all either very simple and easy, or very complex and difficult.

Enjoy! That's the Key

It's simple and easy if you enjoy the actions taken toward your goal. For your weight-losing diet, emphasize the foods you actually enjoy, and find ways to mark your progress with rewards. For an exercise program find activities you enjoy doing. Work in a career that makes you happy. Study the subjects that excite you mentally and spiritually. At the same time, make sure that you are not doing these things to fit someone else's ideas, and don't do whatever simply for the money. "Easy Money" opportunities never last, and often backfire to your personal detriment.

Share your accomplishments with people who will celebrate your joy. Keep a weight loss diary and mark each pound lost with a Gold Star. And plan ahead for how you will celebrate your victory: a new wardrobe, a party with special friends, a photograph of the New You, and so forth.

The Role of the Astral; The Power of the Imagination

We gave a very simple example of a Mind Magic program. So, if it's so easy, *why isn't everyone slim, healthy, ideally good looking, radiantly happy, and all that goes with the "Good Life?"*

Constantly throughout this book, and in particular in the series of addenda dealing with the Tattvic Connection, we've made the point that all physical manifestation starts at the Astral Level, and we've also pointed to the power of the Imagination in its most active role of Visualization as the tool for conscious control and application of magical technology.

What is Magic?

Magick—with the "K" added—is the power to bring about change at will. *Easier said than done!* But that's the difference between "magic" and "Magick." Magic (with only a "c") is the descriptive noun for the practice of *illusion,* or a beautiful adjective to describe things that are beautiful or that promise something beautiful. *Today's sunrise over the Gulf of Mexico was magical. This new fabric is magical in the way it drapes and clings to your body. The candlelight provides a magical glow for our dinner together. It was truly a magical night.* Magic (with only a "c") is descriptive of a physical accomplishment. The illusion is real and present, but it's still just an illusion even if it brings happiness and amusement. As already accomplished, it is a "passive" word.

Magick (with a "K") is an "action" word that calls for a lot of carefully planned work in which the roles of Will and Visualization are the key elements of bringing about desired change. But there are other elements too, some of which we've touched on and others we need to develop.

Knowledge, Goal, Analysis, Program, Schedule

1. **Knowledge** begins with understanding of the present moment. No matter your goal, everything has a beginning. That's the meaning of the Earth Element.

    a. *What may be the "hidden" trends and energies involved?* Always precede your action with a Divination. Whether as complex as casting a horoscope for the moment the question is asked (called a "horary" chart), as esoteric as a Tarot or Rune reading, or as simple as a single card draw using your

Tattva Card Deck or asking your Subconscious Mind to select one of the Tattvic Compound images.

b. Another technique to determine the Tattva active at the moment is the following meditation.

The Tattvic Connection Meditation & Visualization Program #32: The Mirror Projection & Analysis Technique and Program for Shaping the Future

i. Deeply relax and then Project (imagine) yourself into your bathroom facing your mirror.

ii. Move very close so your face is practically touching the mirror's surface.

iii. Open your mouth, and exhale sharply to form a mist on the mirror.

iv. Step back and observe the shape of the mist:

> *Oval* signals Ether, indicating Change, and the Importance of Innovations.
>
> *Circle* signals Air, indicating Stormy Emotions, and the Importance of Details.
>
> *Triangle* signals Fire, indicating Extraversion, and the Importance of Self-Expression.
>
> *Crescent* signals Water, indicating Relationships, and the Importance of Cooperation, working together.
>
> *Square* signals Earth, indicating Beginnings, and the Importance of Initiative and Action.

v. Return to normal consciousness to consider the application of this psychic signal to your present situation.

2. The **Goal** is to know and understand where you want to be. To accomplish this mission you have to determine *What is the Primal Element that best relates to your goal?* Here we are concerned only with which one of the five Primal Elements applies. You've been working with them all through these addenda, but here is a quick summary:

Key Future Shaping Primal Elements

Earth—Seed of Earth: The Beginning. All actions related to the "Start"—everything that has to do with "Sowing, Seeding, and Planting," thus: Preliminary Analysis, Step-by-Step Planning, Developing the Infrastructure, Laying the Foundation,

Launching a New Enterprise, etc. Also Earthquakes and Earth Movements, Physical Sciences, Mining and Extraction, Regulation and Management of Natural Resources, etc.

Water—Seed of Water: <u>Communicating and Relating</u>. Selling, Marketing, Publicizing, Networking, Forming Partnerships, Incorporating, Registering, Cooperation and Cooperatives, Contracts and Agreements, Hiring and Firing, Human Resource Management, Job Searching, Friends and Lovers, Stormy Emotions, Affairs, Marriage and Separation, Children and Family, Politics, etc. Aquifers, Water Regulation and Management.

Fire—Seed of Fire: <u>Creativity, Enthusiasm, Inspiration</u>. Promotions, Advertising (not the *communicating* aspect of Marketing or Publicity), Inspired writing, Enthusiastic work of all kind, Passion, Optimism, Extraversion, most Public Events (Celebrations, Conventions, Trade Shows, Conferences), Entertainment. Also Transformation, Transmutation, Illumination, Insight, etc. Fire Prevention, Volcanoes.

Air—Seed of Air: <u>Intelligence, Imagination, Testing</u>. Study of Detail to Forecast Outcome and to Determine Practicality through Accounting, Auditing, Operations Analysis, Systems Management, Prediction (non-psychic), Traffic Management (Air and Ground), Law and Litigation, etc. Also forecasting and reporting Weather Systems, Storms, Tornadoes, Hurricanes, Fog, Smog, Ice, Snow, Forrest Fires, Visibility problems.

Ether—Seed of Ether: <u>Change, Fresh Starts, Restorations, Travel</u>. The Space between things and within which things happen. Changes of Location and Career, Advancement and Promotion, Expansion and Extension, Mergers and Acquisitions, Movement and Transportation, Journeys and Expeditions, Trips and Treks, Tours and Visits, Adventure and Discovery, Invention and Innovation, Alterations and Renovations, Rehabilitation and Reconstruction.

Use both conscious and unconscious awareness to choose the correct Primal Element to best represent your goal.

3. **Analysis** gives us knowledge of the methods to make the desired change. From your Divinations you have determined the Primary Element, along with Earth, needed to include in your Program. With Earth you should determine the fundamental steps that will make up your starting point. Perhaps you need a business plan, along with a list of things to purchase, and so forth. Turning to the compound symbol you will have determined the secondary elements currently

active in your life. Next you found the primary element identified with your goal.

4. We must set forth a **Program** of the necessary actions.

Program for Shaping the Future

a. Look at the geometric yantra for Element Earth as a symbol for the Beginning, and associate it with the *objective* first steps you have identified in your analysis.

b. Look at the geometric yantra chosen through your divination to represent the elements pertinent to your present situation. Let it "speak to you" as to the *subjective* factors you need to recognize as operative although perhaps hidden "behind the scenes."

c. Look at the geometric yantra for the primary element representing the factors in your goal. If you have produced the card, place it against a white background and stare at it until it starts *flashing*. If you don't have a card, visualize the yantra against a while background.

d. Either way, you should have an *after-image*. With eyes closed project this symbol out through your Third Eye into psychic space before you.

e. Enlarge your visualized image of the geometric yantra to form an *Astral Doorway* about 3 feet square.

f. Project yourself through the doorway and visualize a "monitor screen" just beyond the doorway on which you immediately form an image of your goal accomplished. Ideally "put yourself into the picture" if at all possible. In other words, if it is a personal goal, see yourself as slim as you desire, as beautiful as you want, dressed to the perfection you wish, in the job you are applying for, successful in your new career, etc. And *FEEL heartfelt pride at the accomplishment of the goal as fulfilled.*

g. Immediately, withdraw backwards through the door and banish it from your vision, dismiss it from your mind, stand up and do some physical activity without regard to the just completed program.

5. Finally, you must develop a **Schedule** of actions otherwise all your previous work goes to waste. That also means you must have the discipline to adhere to the schedule of actions to fulfill the program. Don't repeat the program so soon or so often that it loses the emotional impact mentioned in (f) above. But do set

a time to repeat again, and again, until you intuitively recognize that it is time to stop. *You can't plant the same seed twice!*

Letting Go

Once you have completed a set of actions, you must let go and let the Future happen. It will happen, regardless, but unless you release your Magick you are preventing your program from manifesting. Life is a Flow, like a Great River, and *Not Letting Go is standing in the midst of a Flood and trying to hold it back with a gesture.* The Great River will flow and your Magickal Gesture will be for naught.

Go with the Flow!

The more you exercise your clairvoyance—whether aided by divinatory tools and practices or direct vision—the more accurate and dependable it will become. Through the first five Tattvic Connection Programs purifying the primal elements your have made your natural psychic power increasingly accurate. Through the next twenty-five Tattvic Connection Programs you have empowered your psychic skills to work with the complexity of real life.

But, like every power and every skill, the more you use it the better it gets. Practice may never make it "perfect" because perfection means completion and human growth, development and evolution is a continuous process that may never be finished.

The Great River of Life Flows Forever.

CHAPTER SEVENTEEN
Clairvoyance & Esotericism

Esotericism & New Age Occultism

"Esotericism" is a somewhat confusing word derived from the ancient Greek. "Esoteric" first appeared in English in Thomas Stanley's 1701 *History of Philosophy* in which he described the mystery school of Pythagoras where the outsiders still in training were in classified the "exoteric" group and the "esoteric" groups were those admitted into the *inner* circle as trained initiates. "Esotericism" was popularized in the 1850' by the French occultist Eliphas Levi and then by the English Theosophist A. P. Sinnett in the 1880s.

Because of the "Bad Rep" the word *Occultism* gained in some circles—especially from those who know nothing about it—many have adopted *Esotericism* as a word without baggage. For all practical usage, they are interchangeable, but in reality there are subtle differences that are rarely explored.

What does it mean?

According to the scholar, Antoine Faire, we can list these characteristics:

The Four Essential Characteristics of Esotericism:

1. The **Theory of Correspondences**—in which all parts of the physical and non-physical worlds are connected in ways that one thing can lead to another, opening paths of knowledge and action.

2. The **Theory of Nature as a Living Entity**—in which there is Life Force or the living presence of deity throughout the natural, non man-made, world. In other words, Nature is alive and is a single entity herself—indeed, the Goddess common to all early religions and mythologies.

3. The **Mediating Elements**—Symbols, Rituals, Angels, and Visions are used to access spiritual knowledge, mostly through the system of correspondences. This is the "secret" language of Myth and Magick that allows a user to "reach into" seeming *chaos* to establish meaning and to manipulate reality.

4. The Experience of **Personal and Spiritual Transmutation** upon accessing true spiritual knowledge. This is the concept of human evolution and self-directed growth that is the core of esotericism.

Inner Sources

As conceived in the works of the Austrian Rudolf Steiner (1865–1925), the emphasis is not on esotericism as "something to be studied objectively" but rather it is "something to be developed," an inner revelation that can be outwardly shared and proven. In other words, it is the science of psychic development and then the psychic empowerment that results as inner revelations become the foundation for outward application and action. Today, we call it the New Science of the Paranormal.

This is the *New Age* that is personal and activist—no longer is the "disciple" to passively grovel at the Master's feet and "do as I say." As Clopper Almon writes in the introduction to the new English edition of Steiner's 1909 classic, *Die Geheimwissenschaft Im Umriss,* "We and the world around us evolve. This evolution is nowhere more marked than in our own consciousness." And he writes that esoteric work itself ". . . is about the majestic, full spiritual being present in each of us, and about the lofty beings above us."

Sources for Esoteric Truths

We might add that there is a general belief that hidden within most world religions is an ancient, rarely acknowledged, but perennial philosophy that corresponds to esotericism. In addition, there is a further belief that even prior to the oldest existing religion there was a secret knowledge of non-human origins taught only to certain worthy disciples who assumed positions of leadership to guide evolving humanity.

Many esoteric traditions claim exclusivity to the "truth." Some of these were the mystery religions of the Roman Empire, others are known as Gnosticism and Hermeticism in the West and there are others in the Middle East, China, and India.

But, and that's a big "BUT," there is already a renewed tendency to claim that esoteric knowledge and practices must be restricted to only "an initiated few" in total contradiction to New Age philosophy—in other words the old view was that humans are only children to be guided by superior authorities like a herd of sheep pulled along by the bishop's crook. In contrast, the ultimate message of the New Age is to welcome growth-motivated and self-responsible humanity as junior partners in a planetary and cosmic hierarchy of evolving and responsible souls.

The Source for Esoteric Power

No "sectarian" Church or Temple, no Occult Lodge or Ashram, no one claiming exclusivity in neither knowledge nor initiatory power (salvation, born-again) is big enough for New Age people. Nor is it any longer possible for a few authorities—no matter their proclaimed (or actual) spiritual level—to guide humanity in the right directions to save the planet from imminent catastrophe that necessitates worldwide action and individual responsibility.

"Salvation" does not come from someone or something external, but only from personal growth and transformation. Even the initiatory ritual dramas performed in Lodges and Ashrams for the benefit of the "candidate" are better performed in the candidate's own imagination with the important roles modeled after the appropriate *archetypal* figures in the Tarot Deck or the deific forces represented in Tantra, Taoism and other sacred systems. Yes, "Power" can pass through the hands of a valid Initiator, but—ultimately—Real Power comes from within, not from the hands of someone else, and your goal should be to train your imagination and understand the archetypal images of the Tarot and mythic powers for Self-Initiation.

Yes, there is value in the group performance of ritual and drama. The organized development and direction of generated power through a group ritual to a specific goal as in Magick can "change the world"; and the expertly choreographed performance of group drama is valid in training the imagination and bringing strength to the visualized imagery involved in self-initiation and personal development. Just do not turn over authority and responsibility to other people. Don't think you can passively lay back and "Let them do it." There's not enough time for that. You are responsible for every action you are actively, or passively, involved in. The time for action is NOW, and "now" is every day.

Alone, and Together, we ascend the Great Pyramid

"Occult" means hidden; "Esoteric" means inner. Esotericism calls for inner growth and development and requires personal determination, self-responsibility and action. "Initiations" are the stepping stones of inner growth into higher levels of consciousness and not the rewards of new robes, strange hats, and secret passwords.

Every step taken in self-directed personal growth is reflected in expanding consciousness and awakening motivation in all humanity. Alone, and together, we climb the Great Pyramid of Consciousness to become more than we are in continuing and accelerating growth. Even as we act alone we benefit all, and then as more act together, we grow faster and more and more become enabled to take self-determined action.

Secrecy, and self-defined Elitism only holds back growth and real progress, and may inhibit the "salvation" of our planetary situation increasingly divided by religious factions and class warfare until recently thought well past.

The Western Tradition

Today, the Western Esoteric Tradition is inclusive of methods for self-directed study and inner development found in the Kabbalah, Personal Alchemy, Magick, Tarot, and Astrology, to which is added such foundational studies as Theosophy & Anthroposophy, Chinese Taoism & Indian Tantra, and the evolving New Science of the Paranormal. In this, we ourselves become scientists, but unlike those scientists of the external physical world, we turn to the internal non-physical world where instead of physical instruments we must develop our own inner organs of perception and action.

To this it should be noted that today, the words *esoteric* and *esotericism* are preferred—at least in many serious circles—to the previously used words *occult* and *occultism* which still carry the adverse onus of being ignorantly designated both as "satanic" by the Catholic Church—a position even adopted among Protestants and in particular among evangelicals—and "mere superstition" by academic communities.

Esotericism is more than the sum of its parts

We could go on and on to describe the esoteric as "bits of this and a lot of that" without really getting to the most meaningful expression of *it's all of the above but with a difference.* There's nothing antique or other-worldly about real esoteric concepts today.

It's from esotericism that we have our present knowledge of the inner dimension of Man, Nature, and the Cosmos. It's the science and technology of the non-physical, and the relationship of the non-physical to the physical: *Macrocosm* to *Microcosm.* It's the knowledge of the subtle bodies and planes: etheric, astral, mental, causal, and spiritual, and of the technologies for our development of the inner potentials: meditation, visualization, and a trained imagination working with the esoteric technologies of self-hypnosis, yoga, tantra, the martial arts, alchemy, Kabbalah, and magick.

Continuing Evolution—Personal & Cosmic

First of all, esotericism is a philosophical attitude towards life best expressed in the concept of continuing evolution and personal inner growth and development. Everything grows, adapts and matures towards an objective that may never be completely fulfilled. It's as if the goal posts are being constantly moved further ahead. In the process some species die out and new ones appear—in some cases aided by human efforts as in the case of agricultural and medicinal products, and—perhaps—in the advancing world of computers and the World Wide Web leading to the development of a *global nervous system and participatory global brain!*

Secondly, evolution has two driving forces—one that is Cosmic and one that is personal. While it might be tempting to call them by paired names such as *inner* and *outer, esoteric* and *exoteric,* or even *human* and *divine,* those words barely touch the meaning and could miss the reality of the moment. The reality is that the "external Comic" cannot be totally separated from the "internal personal." Macrocosm and Microcosm stride together into the future.

A Plan of Self-Development

From the very beginning of what became human life, there has been an *implanted* plan, a program of growth and development that is not absolute but nevertheless is goal-driven, always adapting, always progressing toward one ideal after another that can be summed up as ever increasing awareness, expanding consciousness, and constant development of knowledge and skills.

Gods in the Making

Knowledge of What? "Cosmic Knowledge"—how everything works from the smallest and most personal to the largest and farthest away. We have to know how things work in order to adapt and develop our skills, and through the application of skills grow and play our role in the Cosmic Plan for we are actors in both the personal and the cosmic drama. Esotericism has sometimes expressed this as "humans are Gods in the making."

That expression, taken out of its historic context, is misleading, suggesting enthroned beings in charge of static forces. Instead, think of the Cosmos as a huge and constantly expanding enterprise requiring many managers, sub-managers, supervisors in various levels of action and responsibility. Some departmental managers move up the scale and others are added as growth creates new needs and opportunities. At a higher level there are executive managers responsible for "the forces of nature," and these were the "Gods" of olden times, but they are also active intelligences and not unchanging forces.

Human and non-human Life Streams

Not all these managers are or were human. There are other life-streams with other entities known as angels, archangels, and many other names—all filling roles in the ever expanding, "living" Cosmos.

But the second force is Cosmic in itself—also following a plan that is not absolute but is goal driven. The Cosmos evolves, and everything within it evolves, including humanity and other entities.

"Disturbances in the Cosmos"

The important note here is that there are many forces at work in the Cosmos, many of them cyclical some of which can be seen and measured in astrological terms as well as noted by physicists and astronomers. At vast intervals certain cycles intersect and initiate changes in specific sections of the Cosmos—changes that could be called "disturbances in the Cosmos" (a phrase used on *Star Trek)* for they are accompanied by violence in both the natural world and the super-imposed human world.

We are at one of those intersections now—partly reflected in violent earth changes, extreme weather, and considerable changes in biological reactions. And reflected also in human violence, in increased personal crimes, in accidents brought about by human error and corruption, in military and religious conflicts, and in political and economic turmoil. And, in threats of war.

On a more positive note, we also see changes in philosophical attitudes, and in fundamental science which is rapidly moving from a purely physical understanding of cosmic actions to a metaphysical one. In particular, we see this in Quantum Physics and in the new Longevity Science which—among other things—recognizes aging as a treatable disease. One could say, "If you live long enough, you could live forever."

The Cosmic Shift & Clairvoyance

The most dramatic aspect of this Cosmic Shift is coming at the level of human consciousness bringing expansions in awareness and particularly so at the psychic levels. We see more spontaneous demonstration of psychic skills, but that is insufficient for "Gods in the making." We have to consciously and intentionally develop our innate psychic powers into reliable, everyday, skills that can be programmed and brought into coordinated global action by means of the World Wide Web—not external action, but *inner* actions of meditation, thought forms, and visualizations that shape the external reality.

Yes, this concept simplified as "Gods in the making" will cause considerable reaction among the fundamentalist religions that look only towards a past theology and see esotericism as sinful—but the "push" toward this new evolutionary development is, indeed, "cosmic" in size and strength and quite irreversible. It is happening, and it will accelerate. The 21st century is bringing such vast global changes that *concerted* human actions will be demanded throughout the political and economic spectrum.

The title of this chapter is "Clairvoyance & Esotericism." Clairvoyance is the leading psychic skill of the human person. Yes, we do use aids in focusing it in particular ways—such as Divining Rods and Tarot Cards, and perhaps other aids in helping us reach the higher focus necessary—such as the Crystal Ball for focus or a Meditation

Mask cutting off external interference. What is important are the developing skills and not the aids which are just that—like reading glasses to improve focus.

Not "Toys" but Tools & Aids

A scientific focus on the ways these aids are used might bring about improvements in usage and even in design. Unfortunately, most such aids (the tools and techniques) are thought of as mostly "toys" by both esoterics and researchers. *If something works, we should find out why. And make it work better!*

Most of the innovations in Divining Rods, for example, have been by inspired trial and error by users. Well and good, but perhaps we can do better. Perhaps even the way a Crystal Ball is situated may make a difference, or it may be that a spot of reflected light into the center would be a help? Or the Meditation Mask: users have said that "tightness" is important in order to give the feeling of "turning inward;" most say that the eyes need to be open while others are ambivalent; padding over the ears is desirable but not ear plugs. Leather is preferred by most, but thick rubber is also used. *Have all the potential options been tested?*

We need more research devoted to the mechanics of these aids for Techno-Shamanism has shown that clairvoyance can be developed and extended by them, and no doubt there could be others once we have better understanding of how they function.

A Woman's Affair?

Another question is why clairvoyance is now mostly experienced by women, even though past famous clairvoyants (Nostradamus, Rudolf Steiner, Edgar Cayce, C. W. Leadbeater) were men? During the 19th century and to the present it has become mostly a woman's affair, and judging from advertising on-line and in esoteric publications, increasingly so. But the Witches Cradle dates back to the 1400s and only women were witches until recent times. And from anecdotal reports, women are the primary users of Meditation Masks, possibly because, as some report, it is as much a sensory delight as a sensory deprivation.

We have covered many aspects of Clairvoyance in this book—both historic and technological—and shown the commanding desirability for everyone to consciously develop it and *apply "clear seeing" everyday to worldly matters as well as inner growth.* Many of the aids mentioned above are covered in our earlier book, *The Llewellyn Complete Guide to Psychic Empowerment: Tools & Techniques,* and quite honestly and humbly we urge its presence in your library for reference in your evolutionary work.

Urgency for Clairvoyant Development

We also sense a growing need for urgency in clairvoyant development. If we have learned lessons from our democracy it is that the "common people" need to propel leaders to act in the right way in important matters, and the increasing levels of air and water pollution, the failures in the political structure, and the failure of business organizations and regulatory agencies to always act in an honest and positive manner with their customers, show we are approaching a tipping point where failure can lead to anarchy and terror in the streets.

In other words, we need "we the people" to see clearly for ourselves and to cease depending on political and other *misleading leaders* with their self-serving vision of what's right for their "special interests." Clear seeing (clairvoyance) is everyone's job, and the cosmic and personal evolutionary forces at work at this critical time make it both possible and necessary. *We are responsible for our own destiny*—that's the ultimate principle of esoteric philosophy.

Sources & Suggested Additional Reading:

Slate, J. H. & Weschcke, C. L. *Astral Projection for Psychic Empowerment,* 2012, Llewellyn.

Slate, J. H. & Weschcke, C. L. *The Llewellyn Complete Guide to Psychic Empowerment: Tools & Techniques,* 2011, Llewellyn.

Slate, J. H. & Weschcke, C. L. *Llewellyn's Pocket Guide to Self-Hypnosis,* 2011, Amazon-Kindle.

Slate, J. H. & Weschcke, C. L. *Psychic Empowerment for Everyone,* 2009, Llewellyn.

Slate, J. H. & Weschcke, C. L. *Self-Empowerment and Your Subconscious Mind, 2010, Llewellyn.*

Slate, J. H. & Weschcke, C. L. *Self-Empowerment through Self-Hypnosis,* 2010, Llewellyn.

Steiner, R. *An Outline of Esoteric Science,* 1997, Anthroposophic Press.

ADDENDUM #17 TO CHAPTER SEVENTEEN
Microcosm to Macrocosm & Macrocosm to Microcosm

The Tattvic Connection—
Meditation & Visualization Program #33:
Astral Doorways

The Tattvas as Astral Doorways

In the previous addenda, we described a very simple and basic program of Goal Visualization using the selected element, a yantra as an *Astral Doorway* and then creating an image of the desired goal as accomplished on an imagined computer monitor screen.

Why did we use the image of a computer monitor? Because the Monitor Screen is an effective symbol for all the power of the computer, the full resources of the World Wide Web, and the global communication power of the Internet. It embodies the most powerful scientific and technological achievement Humanity has ever known, and one that has the greatest magnitude for transcending the limitations of "race," nationalities, religious sectarianism, and political empires across the globe we all call home.

Powerful Magical Symbols

Powerful Magickal Symbols are not limited to ancient occult or religious images, no matter how many years old nor how "charged" with psychic energy from those many years of usage in meditation, prayer, or magical invocation. In fact, sometimes that traditional usage can get in the way and distort a contemporary practice. The Monitor Screen—no longer limited to desk top or laptop but appears in smart phones, tablets and e-book readers—is used many hours daily by more people than perhaps any other device to connect the user with deeper information resources than ever before conceivable. Now, in this manner of placing an imagined Tattvic Yantra on the screen, we connect with that Astral/Mental/Causal resource known as the Akashic Records, also known as the Collective Unconscious or Universal Consciousness.

The Immensity of the Astral World

The Astral World is larger than the Physical Plane, and contains vast resources of its own as well as all your memories—*conscious and unconscious*—and all of those of everyone else—past and present. It also contains all the "blueprints" for all that has ever been physically manifested and the memories of all those that have long ago disappeared, and even all the failed plans, all the frustrated dreams and desires, all the images projected by actors, architects, artists, designers, engineers, politicians, preachers, sales and marketing people, scientists, teachers, writers, and all the emotional residue of love, hate, fear, loathing, hopes, passion and lust.

Nothing is forgotten but remains in your subconscious and the Unconscious in this life and in future lives. Memory—consciously remembered or forgotten—is a continuous living foundation, expanding and re-evaluating earlier experiences to change negative energies to positive.

"Emotional—or Astral—Substance"

The Astral World is made of "Emotional Substance" in the same way that the Material World is made of Physical Substance. And there's also Mental Substance and Spiritual Substance, and no doubt other more subtle substances within dimensions far beyond our present vision or comprehension.

What is Astral, or Emotional Substance?

It's the same kind of thing that Physical Substance (Matter), is. It originates in Consciousness and becomes Energy slowly materializing into Matter that can be—under various circumstance—converted back into Energy. There is Physical Matter and Energy, and there is Astral Matter and Energy. We use the word "substance" in reference to this combination of Matter with Energy as a vehicle for Consciousness at each plane or level of the Cosmos (reserving the word *universe* for the whole of physical manifestation—from the dirt beneath our feet to the stars and farthest galaxies above. Just realize that there's more to Ultimate Reality than the eye can behold or even that the mind can imagine. Yet Mind is the instrument with which we perceive all that visibly is and all that we perceive through our subtle senses, our extended awareness, and in our imagination, dreams and visions. The mind is not the brain, although it functions through the brain as well as beyond the brain's limitations.

Time—the 4th Dimension

The Physical Plane has three dimensions, and yet we experience *movement* through the agency of Time, the *4ᵗʰ dimension* which is the interplay of the Astral in the Physical. No plane operates in isolation—*All Play Well Together*—but the world as we know it is primarily the manifestation of the Physical and Astral, the play of Time and Physical Matter. Movement through Space is a function of Time. Without Time, without Movement, we would perceive nothing and would not physically live.

Perception begins with the physical senses, but through Emotion and Feeling we extend our perception and it is through this extended awareness that we experience clairvoyance. By actively entering into the Astral World we begin to see "behind the scenes"—our senses perceive more than mere surface reflections and become aware of emotions associated with objects (things and people). We become aware of those intentions, dreams, hopes, and fantasies leading to physical manifestation. We perceive the energies of things and people in motion through time, and thus become aware of their futures.

Maps, Windows & Doorways

Through the *Miracle of the One Thing,* with our Mind, we perceive that everything is connected, and it is by means of symbols that we can control and direct our awareness to specific areas of the Astral. It is as if particular symbols serve as roadmaps guiding us to specific areas in the astral dimension, or give windows through which to perceive certain activity, or actual doorways to enter into a chosen field of action. With such aids, the astral world becomes navigable and an awesome resource for discovery, information, and our psychic growth and empowerment.

It is by means of our mental image that we are able to relate to the elemental energy matrix of the particular TATTVA. Each image, the geometric **yantra**, opens awareness to embedded consciousness fully embodied in the Divine Forces behind all manifestation. We are able to perceive, and to engage and work with those forces through the host of associations intrinsic to their nature and the human and cosmic history they represent.

Selecting an Astral Doorway

Know what you want to do, and relate it to one of the Five Primal Elements. Review the Element Overview Tables for Earth (page 104), Water (page 131), Fire (page 189), Air (page 214), and Ether (page 272) to re-familiarize yourself with the basic associations. For your convenience, here is a short review list:

Short List of Elemental Associations for the Five Primal Tattvas

Earth: *Prithivi,* Yellow Square becoming a Purple Cube. *Muladhara* Chakra located at the base of the spine. The Physical World, the Feet, the Daughter, the sense of Smell, the assertion: "I Have!" Solidity, stability, support, foundation, beginning, seeding, initiative, possession, ego, the deep unconscious. The Magical Power: to turn dreams into reality. Tarot Court: Page or Princess; Tarot Suit: Coins or Pentacles; Tarot Trump: the World

Water: *Apas,* Silver Crescent becoming a Black "Melon Slice." *Svadhisthana* Chakra, located between genitals and navel. The Lower Astral World, the Womb, the Mother, the sense of Taste, the assertion: "I Feel!" Flexibility, fluidity, relationships, cooperation, fertilizing, germination, irrigating, networking, Feeling, romance, intimacy, analysis. The Magical Power: to Dare. Tarot Court: the Queen; Tarot Suit: Cups; Tarot Trump: The Moon.

Fire: *Tejas,* Red upright Triangle becoming a Green Pyramid. *Manipura* Chakra located at the solar plexus. The Higher Astral World, the Anus, the Father, the sense of Sight, the assertion: "I Can!" Action, ambition, passion, creativity, sprouting, motivating, sex, transformation, transmutation, reason. The Magical Power: Evocation. Tarot Court: the Knight; Tarot Suit: Wands; Tarot Trump: Judgment, the Tower.

Air: *Vayu,* Blue Circle becoming an Orange Globe. *Anahata* Chakra located over the Heart. The Lower Mental World, the Hands, the Son, the sense of Touch, the assertion: "I Love!" Self-control, imagination, harmony, balance, insight. Magical Power: Divination. Tarot Court: the King; Tarot Suit: Swords; Tarot Trump: the Fool.

Ether: *Akasha,* Indigo Oval becoming a Yellow/Orange Egg. *Vishuddha* Chakra located over the Throat. The Higher Mental/Causal World, the Mouth and Vocal Cords, Patriarch or Matriarch, the sense of Hearing, the assertion: "I Speak!" Space, creation, birth, re-birth, clairvoyance, clairaudience, prophesy, fertility, innovation, expansion, intuition. Magical Power: to read the Akashic Records. Tarot Court: All. Tarot Suit: Major Arcana; Tarot Trumps: All.

The Tattvic Connection Meditation & Visualization Program #33
Using the Astral Doorway as a Transformational Program

Step 1. Visualize the selected yantra on a giant monitor screen, enter into meditation as you have been doing in the previous Tattvic Connection Meditation & Visualization Programs and then feel yourself fully identified with the element, aware of the fundamental associations relating to what it is you want to know, understand or become.

Step 2. Visualize and enlarge the selected yantra image to become a doorway on the monitor screen. It may be helpful to see it appear to slightly vibrate and "flash"

into the complementary colors. Let your feelings and instinct be your guide in some of these particulars.

Step 3. When you feel "ready" (Don't push yourself, even wait for another time as these are major steps) see yourself step through the doorway into the chosen Elemental World.

Step 4. Depending on the element selected, feel the particular powers associated with it:

> Earth—Focus on the mental image of the Earth Square to expand and strengthen your ability to turn dream into reality. See your goal in the square and these see yourself in the square as successful.

> Water—The mental image of the Crescent Moon expands your ability to feel your goal as accomplished. See your goal as cupped by the horns of the crescent, and then see yourself in the crescent as successful.

> Fire—The mental image of the Fire Triangle both intensifies and clarifies your desire. See the object of your desire, your goal, in the center of the triangle and see yourself in the triangle as successful in the accomplishment.

> Air—The mental image of the Air Circle itself enhances your ability to concentrate and visualize. See the representation of your goal in the Circle, and then see yourself in the Circle as successful.

> Ether—The mental image of the Ether Oval has the power of the "womb" to manifest your goals. See the representation of your goal in the Oval, and then see yourself in the Oval as successful.

> Continue that focus on the image for five minutes or so.

Step 5. Now, having accomplished your immediate goal as realized through its representation, you will—with more experience (Don't rush it)—more deeply explore the Elemental World of the Tattvic yantra. But, always establishe your objective and maintain the focus on your goal no matter what it is. With experience and observation—just as it would be in the material world, you will be able to add to your road map.

The above program is far less specific than most of the others in this book for the basic reasons that readers should now be able to do what is necessary: to relax, to determine objectives, choose the symbols and know their associations from all the previous work, and act on their own authority with full responsibility for their success (or, lack thereof).

Where to go from here?

Anywhere and everywhere. The Astral World is infinite, and yet it is not some distant world like another planet of a galaxy far, far, away. Astral Substance is part of you just as is Mental Substance, Causal Substance, Spiritual Substance—and Physical Substance. We are a physical body integrated with an astral body, a mental body, a causal body, and so on. We enter more fully into the potential of these through focus often aided by symbols and words and actions.

Every day you can choose to march to a different drummer, and widen your horizons and broaden your experience. That's—ultimately—what *empowerment* is about. Turn off the TV set, stand up from the computer game, skip the ball game, and turn on your mind. Cease being a passive observer and become an active student of the magnificent Cosmos and the most wonderful process we call Life.

Bon Voyage!

CHAPTER EIGHTEEN
Higher Consciousness & Clairvoyance

To Begin at the Beginning!

Everything has a beginning, but there are No Endings —ONLY NEW BEGINNINGS!

Even physical "Death" as we know it is not an Ending but a New Beginning as the Incarnating Spirit moves its focus to the astral level while the vacated physical body eventually becomes many new beginnings of life in other biological forms.

Every seed, once germinated, lives on forever in continuing and multiplying forms. An acorn becomes a tree producing more acorns, and also dropping leaves and limbs that decay and nourish other new beginnings of botanical life. Every Mother's cellular code lives on in her Daughter, and through her in her Granddaughter, and on and on. Generation after generation of human life descends through its feminine half while always evolving through its male partnership and all the experience each lifetime provides.

The Form changes, but Growth is constant

The form changes, but *Growth*, in one way or another, in one dimension or another, is a constant. We can accelerate our growth, but we will never regress.*

> *Even Planet Earth has slowly increased in size through accretion from space (meteorites, space dust and debris, etc.), the emergences of oceans (for which we still have no explanation), layers of decomposed organic matter, and the addition of human constructions and population. The cross section of sediments in the Grand Canyon gives a graphic presentation of this. Today's Earth may be twice the size it was four billion years ago.

Every Action has Consequences

Every action has consequences that never cease and those consequences lead to new beginnings at multiple levels of ever increasing complexity. What was a Beginning in the long, long ago past has led to many new beginnings in many forms, in many levels, spread out into many dimensions of increasingly complex realities throughout many universes within an ever expanding cosmos whose limits are beyond comprehension.

When you begin a new program—of any sort—in personal development, there will be consequences—even if you interrupt your efforts for a time. The "Great Work,"* once begun, continues in the background—bringing you opportunities, contacts with helpful people and spirit entities, even seemingly chance encounters with books, articles, and happenings. It's as if the Universe is saying, *Welcome, "Pilgrim," welcome to the "Path."*

> *"Great Work" is a term given to the work of personal growth and evolution, including anything that contributes to self-understanding and self-improvement. It is commonly in reference to as initiatory progress in Western Magick but is in no way limited to it. "External" initiations can, at best, only trigger "internal" growth spurts if you are ready. No one can give you what you haven't earned!

It may sound a bit too "New Agey," but you will realize its truth, sooner or later. It has been a long journey from our first Beginning to wherever we are now, but now the pace is accelerating. Look at worldly and personal events with that perspective in mind and you will see things with a new understanding for what is happening

In the Beginning: Evolving Consciousness

In the Beginning, there was only Consciousness, undivided and without form. There was no Cosmos, no material universes, no bodies, no feelings, no minds, no souls.

In the Beginning, Consciousness manifested Energy and Matter.

In the Beginning, Consciousness, Energy and Matter—the three as one—manifested the Cosmos.

Then, Consciousness manifested the *WORD* to "program" the Cosmos *to* evolve increasingly conscious forms. Thus:

After a time, consciousness created Spirit.
After a time, consciousness created Form.
After a time, consciousness created Souls.
Then, Forms became vehicles for Evolving Consciousness.

Spirit Forms became vehicles of Evolving Universes.
Spirit Forms became vehicles of Evolving Powers.
Spirit Forms became vehicles of Evolving Souls.
Then, Spirit Forms became vehicles of Evolving Matter/Energy.

Evolving Universes manifest Galaxies, Solar Systems and Planets.

Evolving Powers manifest Spirit Powers, Forces and Forms.

Evolving Souls manifest Incarnating Persons, their Bodies and Developmental Processes.

Then, Evolving Consciousness in Matter/Energy begins the Evolutionary World of Action and Experience we know as Reality today.

When did all this happen? In the Beginning, of course! There is no meaningful answer from Science or Religion or Myth. According to Eastern lore, our current universe is only one among many—like the breathing out, and the breathing in, of a Great but unknowable Being.

The World of Action & Experience

The Forms and Forces of Evolving Matter/Energy create a series of Planes ("Levels of Manifestation")—commonly named Divine, Spiritual, Causal, Mental, Astral, Etheric, and Physical. As Evolving Souls manifesting through life-long *Spirit Forms*, we incarnate in a series of bodies composed of the same substance as the lower five planes and hence named similarly—Causal, Mental, Astral, Etheric, and Physical. These, together—Planes and Bodies—are the World of Action and Reaction that we know as our World of Experience—it is our field of dreams, our theatre of desire, our school of learning, our base for action. We are Consciousness, and we are also Agents of Consciousness. We are Co-Creators and (far, far from now)—*Gods in the Becoming*—manifesting Consciousness in increasing diverse forms throughout our World of Experience while at the same time focusing on our own developmental path.

The Planes and Bodies, including the Physical, manifest through "sub-planes" and "sub-bodies" of the five primary levels. Every primary level (Planes and Bodies) functions through specific and unique Substance and Laws. However, it is at the seven *sub* levels of each that Action and Reaction happens, and it is in these sub-levels that *conscious intervention is real.* It is at these sub-levels that <u>intentional</u> acts can bring about progressive change and development. And, as the Evolutionary program pushes us forward from being *passive* "victims" towards becoming *active* agents, an understanding of these "leverage" points in the cosmic structure is vital.

Despite their importance, we must not make the mistake of thinking of these as planes and sub-planes as definitive layers of substance, laws, and of consciousness. There are no rigid boundaries. As a clairvoyant, you will not see a schematic map of these levels and sub-levels unless you create a "thought form map" to conveniently do so—and that is really unnecessary and probably limiting. More of this will be discussed in appropriate chapters.

Evolution, the Great Plan & the Great Work

Evolution is a "program" manifesting the *Great Plan** of which we have, as yet, only limited perception. Nevertheless, within its delineations we perform what we know as the *Great Work*—advancing in focus and mastery of the bodies composing our incarnating Spirit Form as an *Agency* for our Evolving Soul.

> *A phrase used in the writings of Alice Bailey, also called the "Divine Plan" by Geoffrey Baborka, and largely based on the "Secret Doctrine" by H. P. Blavatsky. The concept is of a "non-religious" evolutionary plan of the universe and all within. It is not the same as purely sectarian religious statements of "God's Plan for Man" or "Christ's Plan for Mankind." It is a Consciousness driven plan of Action and Reaction from The Beginning through every New Beginning leading toward the "perfection" of human-kind.

We will be exploring Evolution, the Great Plan and the Great Work as they relate to Higher Conscious and Clairvoyance in greater detail, but—for now—just remember that: *All is Consciousness* and *Everything is Evolving Consciousness.*

What is Consciousness?

Conscious is not the "Ultimate Source"—whether that is called God, Goddess, Creator, Source, Ultimate Being, *Ain,* or nothing at all. Consciousness was/is the First Manifestation; Matter/Energy was/is the Second & Third Manifestation bound together and hence interchangeable one with the other. Reference to the traditional Kabbalistic Tree of Life diagram shown on the next page should prove useful as a background for your further study. Just remember, however, that the same Tree of Life is repeated four times for each World of Manifestation. ***Can Consciousness know itself? Can Consciousness define itself?***

French philosopher Rene Descartes (1596–1650), the father of analytical geometry, famously said: "I think, therefore I am."*

> *Descartes died from an arsenic-laced communion wafer given to him by a Catholic priest who feared Descartes' radical theological ideas which included the belief that "truths" could be known philosophically. In 1663, his works were placed on the "Index of Prohibited Books" The Index (finally abolished in 1966) was intended to protect the Catholic faithful from reading books containing theological "errors" which included most scientific works until 1835. It also prohibited the reading of translations of the Bible into the "Common tongues." Astronomer Giordano Bruno was burned alive at the stake in 1600 for refusing to recant his scientific conclusion that the Sun was a star among many stars.)

I think, therefore I am! I am that I am!

Descartes was an intellectual *man,* a mathematician, a philosopher, a theologian, a scientist. Defining himself through thinking was natural to him. But, an emotional *woman,* an actress perhaps, could as truthfully say: *I feel, therefore I am.* A non-professional, ordinary working person might just as truthfully speak: *I am, therefore I am!*

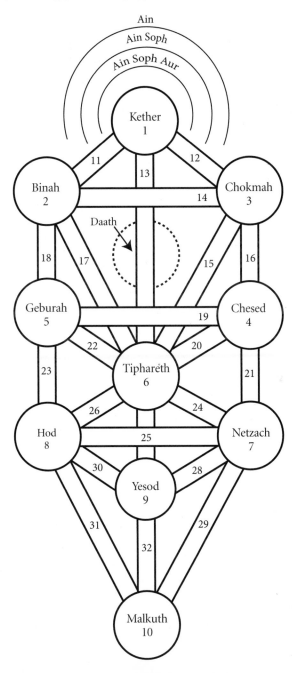

The Kabbalistic Tree of Life

I Am that I Am was God's response to Moses' question as to God's name in Exodus 3:14. It is pronounced *Ehyeh asher ehyeh* and is one of the Seven Names of God recognized in the Jewish tradition in reference to the "Supreme Being."

"I AM" is the common thread throughout this mini-discourse, and it is the defining expression of person-hood. It is the individual who thinks, feels, and is, and it is the acts, and reactions of the individual that defines a person's life and role in evolving consciousness. The individual is not a crowd, group, or community; the individual must necessarily think, feel, and act responsibly himself and not be a mere "cog" in someone else's machine. *Think, and therefore be. Let Feeling become expressed through Thought. Let Personal Existence become expressed through Thought. Through Thinking the individual person can come to judge his potential actions in terms of rightness, and then act responsibly.*

Consciousness is more than thinking and feeling, and encompasses all that we know as a person. Consciousness is also all that is the world—visible and invisible—around us. However, we are conditioned not to think of the physical body as conscious, or of physical things as having consciousness. Yet, were it not for consciousness, nothing would exist. We are both consciousness and manifestations of consciousness.

Personal Consciousness is divided

But, as the person of mind, emotion, and body each of us is, we *think* and *understand* better when we divide our personal consciousness in various ways. The two primary ways—which are complimentary and not contradictory—can be designated as **Exoteric and Esoteric.***

> *We have to understand that our terminology—no matter the language—is never fully definitive in the manner of mathematics. Modern language is abused and commercially distorted. Esoteric, for example, has been used by booksellers as a synonym among clients for expensive and rare erotica. It is also used as branded cosmetics, soaps, foods, fashions, shoes, jewelry, and more.
>
> Esoteric is the preferred alternative to occult, a word that properly means "hidden" as when the Moon <u>occults</u> the Sun—meaning that one body passes in front of the other body in an eclipse. Words once strictly esoteric or magickal in usage are now used in product names and advertising for everything from cosmetics to automobiles, software programs to songs and music, often giving distorted impressions about the subjects themselves.

Exoteric will be used to refer to the "outer world" usage to mean objective, material, familiar, non-spiritual, physical, etc., but also psychologically and even spiritually "correct" in the contemporary *political* sense.

Exoterically, we do divide the personal consciousness into the Conscious Mind and the Subconscious Mind. We use the word "Soul" to mean what it is commonly believed—something that we have that will remain after physical death and take our essence to heaven when we die.

Thus, from the exoteric perspective we are a physical body in which physiological processes are managed by the autonomic nervous system, in which mind is a function of the brain, desire and feelings are functions of hormones, and soul is a comforting illusion and part of a balanced social life that includes weekly church attendance.

Exoterically, consciousness is largely synonymous with mind as in an awake brain.

Esoteric will be used in relation to an "inner world" usage to mean subjective, non-material, spiritual, non-physical, and as an alternative to "occult." Esoterically we continue to divide personal consciousness into the Conscious Mind and Subconscious Mind (aka Unconscious), but also add a Super Conscious Mind and extensively relate to the Collective Unconscious (aka Great Unconscious) and the Universal Consciousness. We treat the Conscious Mind as a function of the Mental Body, Feelings as a function of the Astral Body, the Autonomic Nervous System as a function of both the Physical Body and its Etheric Double, and the Soul as the real and immortal home of the incarnating forms through which the Personal Consciousness acts, experiences, learns, and grows.

In every case we will attempt to avoid the generally confusing use of Sanskrit, Hebrew, and other non-English terms except in explanatory parenthesis and footnotes, and for those terms that have become commonly used in English—such as *Prana, Kundalini, Chakras, Karma.*

What is the "Great Evolutionary Plan"?

While the kind of "evolution" we are writing about includes the Darwinian concept of natural selection (through trial & error) within a species over vast stretches of time, it relates to three further concepts:

1. An evolutionary force that pervades all there is, and which "pulls" the process forward at an accelerating pace possibly related to the 2,000 year Zodiacal Ages (currently we are just entering the Aquarian Age).

2. A human evolution brought about by the application of specific "spiritual" practices that awaken and develop faculties dormant in the average person. But, that awakening and development in the single practitioner has some "preparatory"

effects that facilitates the way for others to more easily and quickly follow the same path.

3. Evolution is the continuing result of development and growth based on the programmed process of actions directed to the realization of established objectives which may or may not be fully known to the "agents of consciousness." All humans and all spirit powers are agents of consciousness, knowingly or unknowingly.

In some sense (but not that so proclaimed) the Christian Fundamentalist's argument for "Intelligent Design" has it correct but not to the exclusion of Darwinian Natural Selection which is a process within the Great Evolutionary Plan. And the Fundamentalist as well as the Catholic view of human origin is not evolutionary at all in regard to the Human Form. Instead it sees human history as very short-lived and ending apocalyptically in a near future time (always failing to occur on the "due dates" because of false measurements).

What is "Higher Consciousness"?

Going on-line to find the latest perception, *Wiktionary* defines it as "a supposed mode of cognition beyond human self-awareness." The site also references to Hegel's concept of "historical progress in the evolution of the human mind," and the "concept of mystical transcendence of human consciousness, especially in Hinduism-inspired New Age philosophy."

Wikipedia lists many alternative names and their sources. Among them:

Alternative Names for Higher Consciousness

Super Consciousness (Yoga)

Objective Consciousness (Gurdjieff)

Buddhic Consciousness (Theosophy)

Cosmic Consciousness (Bucke, Sufism, and others)

God-Consciousness (Hinduism, and others)

Christ Consciousness (New Thought)

All express the concept that a human being can grow and reach a higher level of consciousness through evolutionary development enabling a person to know "What is Real" with greater clarity. None make the claim of theistic religions that an "Ultimate

Truth" was known by the Prophets in past times and is known today by specially initiated humans (loyal to the "faith") who converse directly with God at will.

In contrast, the Esoteric view is that in the Far, Far Past, when the "veils" of time and dimension were thinner, Great Seers incarnating from earlier ages, had awakened psychic faculties enabling them to achieve visions extending into the far past and far future while at the same gaining understanding of the processes involved and the goals to be accomplished. While these visions were recorded in the Sacred Traditions and Writings of many cultures, most of it was destroyed by monotheistic missionaries leaving those writings in India and China as the most complete collections to which we have access today. Yet, even those early writings were sometimes purged and distorted as invaders continually replaced Old Religion with New Religion supporting the new political realities. It is, perhaps, in the scholarly study of surviving remnants of oral traditions and myths that we come close to these cosmic visions.

Such visionary capabilities—*clairvoyance*—has not been lost to present day humanity, but has slipped mostly into dormancy. Methods of Psychic Development do awaken particular of these dormant faculties but, perhaps, it is best descriptively described in yoga as through the activation of the *Kundalini Fire* and its more complete Lighting of the Crown Chakra that we move into Higher Consciousness.

Higher Consciousness is quite different than half-awake ordinary consciousness.

Most People are Half-Asleep

Quoting from the Wikipedia article:

The concept of higher consciousness rests on the belief that the average, ordinary human being is only partially conscious due to the character of the untrained mind and the influence of 'lower' impulses and preoccupations. As a result, most humans are considered to be asleep (to reality) even as they go about their daily business. Gurdjieff called this ordinary condition of humanity 'waking sleep,' an idea gleaned in part from ancient spiritual teachings such as those of the Buddha. In each person lie potentialities that remain inchoate as a result of the individual being caught up in mechanical, <u>neurotic</u> modes of behavior where energy for personal spiritual development is not used correctly, but squandered in unskillful ways. As a result of the phenomenon of projection, the cause of such a person's suffering is often seen to lie in outer circumstances or other individuals. One prerequisite for the development of consciousness is the understanding that suffering and alienation are one's own responsibility and dependent on the mind's acquiescence (through ignorance, for example).

Most readers will refuse to acknowledge the idea of being "only partially conscious" and being "half-asleep as they go about their daily business," but instead of resisting this observation think what it is really saying: *Are you really <u>conscious</u> when watching evening or daily TV? When watching Saturday afternoon Football? When listening to Rock Music?* If you are honest with yourself, you realize that you've fallen into a kind of trance, as happens when driving and you fall into "highway hypnosis." Compare that trance consciousness to times when you are fully alert: When applying for an important new job. When caring for your very sick child. And, *sometimes,* when you are making love. (See later reference, page 662, to *Modern Sex Magick* as a short-cut.)

Sometimes you do certain things *mechanically* or *by rote* rather well—so well in fact that you can occupy half your mind with day dreams and fantasies. Even when you think you are fully engaged as when cheering at a football game you are really involved with the crowd consciousness and are yourself only half a person. **Without INTENTIONAL *FOCUS, you are not fully awake.***

With focus and attention, there is awareness and perception, and awakened consciousness. It is these that lead toward Higher Consciousness with greater awareness of reality. You learn to see <u>*behind*</u> *the scene* that entertainers and politicians want you to believe in. *You Wake Up!* Awake you pull aside the curtain and see the Wizard of Oz for the charlatan he really is. Awake, the sharp sales person cannot sell you a dream you cannot afford. Awake, you see the lie in the religionist's promise of heavenly rewards if you pay real money *now* to the new Mega Church. Awake, you see the phony politicians' statements as lies and deceit, and the method of corruption that has become the modern way of life. Awake, you begin to move beyond the adolescent thinking and tribal behavior of most of modern society occupied with watching and playing games, filled with violence and repression, guided by dictatorial father figures.

Awake, you can restore honesty and ethics to our way of life. Awake, you live life more fully, you fulfill your ambitions and become more than you are. Awake, your "dreams" become founded on attainable reality. Awake, Spirituality becomes a personal path of growth, realization, empowerment, and transcendence.

Ordinary Consciousness

We live most of our life through three states of consciousness: *waking, dreaming* and *sleeping.* In the waking state of consciousness—where we think we are fully conscious, we experience the world through the five familiar physical senses. But we are constantly deluged with powerful sensory stimulations that "command" our responses—in buying the latest and best of every kind of consumer goods, in cheering the latest sports heroes, in adoring the latest Hollywood Stars, and the most beautiful or handsome fashion models, in watching and following the latest TV dramas, in wanting bigger and better houses, faster and more powerful cars, fancier and more featured appliances, and dressing in the latest and most sexy fashions.

At every step we are reminded that the health of our economy is dependent upon consumer spending and now even financial "products" are marketed in "store fronts" where false promises are sold as the "flavor of the day" by professional "consultants" taught that *greed* is the highest ethic.

Giving so much importance to physical objects and consumer goods leads to greed; giving so much importance to the physical senses and emotional sensation leads to constant desire and lust for material pleasures; and directing so much "packaged" stimulus to the mind and imagination leads to fantasy and even delusion.

Because of the constant deluge of sensation and desire, and the impact of media communications, we develop expectations for events to happen in certain ways. As a result, we construct mental images that actually impede us from perceiving things as they really are. Our "reality" becomes distorted and the concepts in our mind prevent us from experiencing the infinite consciousness that is a part of us.

It is not that the physical senses or mental functions are bad, but that *passivity* of consciousness is. We must learn to discriminate between things and become *actively* aware of what is really happening at all times inwardly and outwardly. Then we begin to see the world clearly. Clairvoyance means to "see clearly." This is one step towards the higher state of consciousness.

Clairvoyance at the higher level is not just a psychic skill but a culmination of a developmental process involving the Whole Person. It's not merely the awakening of a dormant psychic power but the purposeful evolution of innate clairvoyant power brought about by a deliberate and personal program of "spiritual"* practice.

> *Once again we are forced to use the ambiguous word (spiritual) for something that is not necessarily spiritual at all! Spirit, Spiritual, Spirituality, and even Spiritualism and Spiritism all lack specific reference. In this instance it is used to signify a practice whose goal relates to something vaguely identified as not physical and not materialistic. In other words, "spirit" and "spiritual" are mostly used to signify a <u>not-this</u> and a <u>not-that</u> in relation to not only the material world but to things common to it—goals of "money, sex, and power" as more than one famous occult teacher described it in personal conversation.

> But the problem is compounded because of past writers' usage of the terms in the vernacular of the day and culture. The usage by a Victorian era high caste Indian writer as then understood by an English academic and re-interpreted by a 20th century yoga writer and then by another writer in the 21st

century influenced by a Christian religious orientation can leave the current reader confused if he anticipates a definitive usage and unknowingly finds none.

Without such higher-level clarity, the individual's perception of "reality" at any moment is influenced by his unconscious conditioning from the external world as well as internal factors including karmic reactions. Each individual has his own personal "filtering" and sources of illusion based on unique past experiences. One goal of spiritual practice (such as that given in the Tattvic Connection Meditation & Visualization Programs presented in the chapter addenda to this book) is clarification and transformation of such conditioning so that reality is finally seen as it is rather than as distorted images.

As Dr. Slate points out in Chapter Eleven of this book:

Even in its most basic, ordinary form, clairvoyance reflects our capacity to experience reality beyond the constricted borders of ordinary thinking. In its most advanced form, clairvoyance lifts consciousness to new peaks of enlightenment and power. It can uncover situations that require our intervention, including in some instances conditions of extreme urgency.

Spiritual approaches to consciousness

"Stress is a Killer" in more ways than causal to heart disease. Stress is a barrier to clear perception and a barrier to the release of false perceptions. Stress keeps Mind and Emotions in a perpetual swirl of old ideas and feelings that keep fresh ones out.

Meditation helps in two ways—it prevents stress from entering the system and simultaneously releases accumulated stress. When meditation practices become part of daily life, the straight jacket of rigid thinking is released and a higher state of consciousness that some call "cosmic consciousness" opens before us.

Cosmic consciousness unites the personal with the whole cosmos, and a greater love flows between us to overcome the opposing forces and the disturbances in life. Negative feelings and thoughts melt away into nothingness.

With higher consciousness we learn to exercise control over Mind and Will, and with clarity of perception we gain Intellectual and Moral* Enlightenment.

*Not to be confused with religious codes and beliefs that too often have been interpreted and re-interpreted to justify the authority of church hierarchies, and—in the case of theocracies—of the church/state leader. In past and present this has led to outright abuse: sexual, financial, and political. Millions of people have been subjected to torture and sent to their deaths in the name of Allah, God, Christ, Jehovah, Tohil, Ogoun, Macha, Guan Yu, Woden, Sekhmet, Ares, Durga, Hachiman, Thor, Mars, and thousands of other names for the Creator, all under the orders of the "interpreter of the faith" who denies the right of divine contact to those sent to war but promises heavenly rewards for their sacrificial death.

Why the need to develop Higher Consciousness?

This question raises several issues.

The first is that most people don't really believe that they are not a "finished product." It's one thing to talk abstractly about spiritual growth but another thing to say that without genuine and particular development you cannot have the capacity for higher clairvoyance. When we discuss something like "self-improvement" it is relatively easy to acknowledge that learning another language might help your career, or that losing weight could help both your appearance and your health, but to say—even to a practicing psychic reader—that you do not now have the capacity for higher clairvoyance is practically a *violation* of your self-hood!

The second thing is to personally understand and accept that there really are levels of consciousness, and that at present you cannot experience what we are calling "higher consciousness." It almost has the feeling of some kind of *discrimination*.

And a third difficulty—one already mentioned in passing—is that there are levels not only of clairvoyance but of most other psychic powers! Even if you are an accomplished Astrologer or Tarot Reader, it is unlikely that you are operating from this higher level of consciousness, or that you are looking at your horoscopes or layouts from the esoteric perspective. And, by that, we are not just referring to what is sometimes called "Esoteric Astrology" (dealing mostly with past lives) but of the Astral and Mental plane dimensions of the person and of the level for action. "Karma" is perhaps the initial concern of an esoteric reading but the reality is that everything that manifests in the physical world that is the focus of your present consciousness originates in the Causal, Mental and Astral planes and the ability to "see clearly" at the astral and mental levels provides true precognition.*

> *Nevertheless, the future is not "fixed." Actions, based on knowledge and understanding of the "shadows cast ahead by forthcoming events," can bring about positive changes. But, such actions may have to come from many, many people. The act of one single person is unlikely to prevent an asteroid impact!

Your Assignment: The Next Step

No one is going to touch you on the forehead and magically initiate you into a higher level of consciousness. It happens in stories, but they are the same kind of stories where the Prince, after penetrating a maze of brambles and climbing the castle wall, awakens the Sleeping Princess with a kiss. It is you who must penetrate the maze and climb the wall and awaken your own self to its higher glory.

It's an alchemical transformation of the "lead" of the ordinary self-consciousness, your conscious mind, into the "gold" of higher consciousness and the awakening of your Higher Self also known as your "Guardian Angel." The Higher Self is real, but its attainment is the goal of the Great Work of personal growth and transformation.

"If you accept this assignment" was the opening statement in a long-running television series called *Mission Impossible,* and that's the same kind of choice you have to make. To attain higher consciousness through direct efforts may indeed seem like a *Mission Impossible*—but it's not: others have prepared the way and their footsteps have worn not only one Path, but many. It is only the religionist with his own agenda that will say "there is only one true path, and it's <u>my way or the highway!</u>"*

> *The World Religions contain great wisdom and many powerful "mystical" practices. But sometimes particular religious leaders step into secular territory and try to impose their "one way" for all. Politics, Economics, Law, Education, Women's Health, etc., do not mix well with sectarian Religion.

Every mission is a new beginning and it is you who must take the Next Step in following the many first steps taken by those who pioneered these many paths from which you may choose.

The "Triumph of Will"

As in most aspects of human progress, self-development is itself necessary. Without the non-sectarian Universal Education that is part of modern life, both the individual and all of society would suffer. Without the scientific progress in Nutrition and Health Care, the average life span would still end in the third decade and very few would have the opportunities of growth and development that today's longer-lived people have. Without the benefit of communications (including book publishing!), access to Knowledge by personal choice would be denied and leave society under the dictatorial control (and censorship) of the elite few.

In previous chapters, we have already explored the necessity for self-development of "Body, Mind & Spirit" (the Physical/Etheric, Astral & Mental Bodies) and outlined the role of the chakra system as a doorway to evolving consciousness where each Chakra corresponds to specific aspects of consciousness and has its own characteristics and functions.

But, without personal effort, self-discipline, and direction, the higher consciousness and higher level of clairvoyance you desire is not possible. It is through a "Triumph of Will" that we raise the focus of consciousness from the lower chakras to the higher. We will outline a program of progressive meditation in which your objective is to awaken the *Kundalini Fire* (the sleeping princess) in the base chakra and raise her to fully enlighten the crown chakra.

The Crown Chakra

There is a lot of yogic literature on this chakra; *Sahasrara* is the Sanskrit name, and it is often referred to as the "thousand-petaled lotus." Some writers say that all the other chakras emanate from this—from top down. Others state the reverse—from bottom to top. The real point to remember that all the chakras are connected by three channels, and that the Kundalini energy in the bottom chakra can be raised to the top chakra through programs of meditation and visualization, thus accelerating the evolutionary process.

There are three "benefits" from this awakening of the crown chakra that interest us in our discussion of Clairvoyance:

The Three Benefits from Awakening the Crown Chakra

1. It brings detachment from illusion, opening the way to the higher consciousness realization.

2. When *Kundalini*—called the "energy of consciousness"—is raised to the crown chakra, union with the Divine is experienced. This is called *Samadhi* in Sanskrit.

3. Meditation on the crown chakra activates all the occult powers (*Siddhis* in Sanskrit) previously nascent in most people. More importantly, these are the fully developed occult (or psychic) powers.*

> *Full development is only possible at this level. Most psychic powers are related to base chakra, the solar plexus chakra, and some of the more highly developed to the brow chakra, but it is only here in "the Seventh Heaven," as poetically described, that we have their full, Divine, expression.

Things may be more complex than just a single "crowning achievement." Some writers assert that there are several chakras related to the crown. On the forehead above the brow chakra, *Ajna,* and closely associated with it, there is the *Manas* chakra. Above *Manas* there is the *Bindu Visarga* chakra at the back of the head, then there is *Mahanada* and *Nirvana* chakras on the crown, and *Guru* and *Sahasrara chakras* actually located above the crown.

In addition, within the crown chakra are various subtle points activated through particular symbols during meditation that bring higher levels of consciousness and self-integration with higher levels of Divinity.

Illumination starts when *Kundalini Fire* "ignites" or "turns on" subtle connection in the physical brain with corresponding levels or aspects in Sahasrara. While the physical brain is not the source of human consciousness, it is a facilitator and instrument for its expression. "Turning on" these subtle switches and connections does facilitate the physical expression and manifestations of the higher psychic powers.

Further studies of the Chakra System are beyond the scope of this book but we recommend the suggested reading resources listed at the end of this chapter. In addition, Wisdom and Illumination are not geographically limited to India. Tibet, China, Egypt, the Jewish people, and "the West," and other ancient and modern cultures have all added to the collective knowledge of super-consciousness and methods of attainment. The Western Kabbalah, in particular, is a rich system for understanding of the inner and outer worlds and of meditational techniques for attaining higher consciousness and the opening level of psychic powers.

A Crowning Meditation

There are many Techniques and procedural programs to raise *Kundalini* through the chakras, but what we want to emphasize is the value for you to experiment and discover those that are best for you.

I assure you that many readers and teachers will raise their hands in horror at this idea of unguided work with the *Kundalini* "Fire"—it is named that for good reason that it is a very powerful force—and insist that you must follow *their* specific program, which often includes sexual chastity, vegetarianism, abstinence from alcohol, coffee, and other "drugs," and the use of mantras and yantras in meditation, or—in a Western mode—carefully choreographed guided meditations called "Path Workings" in the Kabbalistic system. And one last "horror upon horror," there are "short-cut" methods (especially for women) practiced in both Eastern Tantra and modern Western Sex Magick.

These people are all right! But their programs are "systems" for whole person development while in this book we are primarily focused on Clairvoyance in Psychic Empowerment. And, yes, we *can* have specialized development of psychic powers outside of whole person development. At the same time we have to emphasize that each will contribute to the whole. Every stop takes us onward and upward.

We urge you to study any or all of these systems, but let's focus here on building on what we have learned so far.

We have learned basic details of all seven of the major chakras, and we have explored some of the ways in which knowledge of those details can be used in meditation to awaken the psychic powers within.

Here is a simple "beginner's" meditation to bring about higher clairvoyance through what is correctly called "the Crown." Fully developed, it will be our crowning achievement, a "crown of glory." But everything is up to you. It's what you study and practice that is real, and the reality is here and now—not a lifetime of austerity, fasting, prayer, and subjugation to a teacher or adoration of a distant deity—all of which are valid but not the choice of Westerners who live many lives in one.

Go back to Chapter Five on Chakras and Clairvoyance, and re-read the chapters on *Muladhara,* the base chakra and its symbolism; and likewise on *Svadhisthana,* the sacral chakra, *Manipura,* the solar plexus chakra, *Anahata,* the heart chakra, *Vishuddha,* the throat chakra, *Ajna,* the brow chakra, and Sahasrara, the crown chakra. Then re-read the section on the Chakra Images, Names & Location—making notes if necessary so that it will all recall and be readily available during meditation.

Review the three levels of meditation, seeing the Tattwa Yantra for each and hearing the Bija Mantras.

Now, here is the challenge: We're going to add a fourth level, and then along with the original three, condense the four separate meditations into four stages of a single meditation.

Awakening the Crown Chakra Program

Always start in your Astral Room.

1. See, feel, and raise Kundalini up to the Solar Plexus Chakra in a single long inhalation. As you do, see the three Tattwa Yantras successively flash by and hear the three Bija Mantras, one after the other.

2. Hold your breath for a comfortable length of time, while holding the image and feeling of Kundalini in the Solar Plexus Chakra.

3. Continue holding the image and feeling of Kundalini in the Solar Plexus Chakra while slowing exhaling.

4. On a long inhalation, see, feel, and raise Kundalini up from the Solar Plexus Chakra through *Anahata, the Heart Chakra,* to the Throat Chakra. See the two Tattwa Yantras flash by and hear the two Bija Mantras, one after the other.

5. Hold your breath for a comfortable length of time, while holding the image and feeling of Kundalini in the Throat Chakra.

6. Continue holding the image and feeling of Kundalini in the Throat Chakra while slowing exhaling.

7. On a long inhalation, see, feel, and raise Kundalini up to the Brow Chakra. See the Winged Globe image and hear the Bija Mantra.

8. Hold the breath for a comfortable length of time, while holding the image and feeling of Kundalini in the Brow Chakra.

9. Continue holding the image and feeling of Kundalini in the Brow Chakra while slowing exhaling.

10. On a long inhalation, see, feel, and raise Kundalini up to the Crown Chakra. See the Rose image. Hear only Silence.

11. Continue holding the image and feeling of Kundalini in the Crown Chakra while slowing exhaling.

12. And continue holding the image and feeling of Kundalini in the Crown Chakra as you resume a normal breathing pattern.

13. See and feel Kundalini as a "pressure pervading the physical brain and the Crown Chakra. Feel it as nourishing warmth, and continue doing so for approximately ten minutes.

14. Slowly relax and let the image and feeling dissipate.

15. Repeat daily, slowing extending the meditation/visualization *comfortably* to as long as approximately 30 minutes.

16. When you feel "ready," you can proceed in several directions:

    a. Filling the brain and Crown Chakra with pure White Light.

    b. Opening your clairvoyant vision to seeing things as set forth in your goals.

    c. Drawing your astral self up from the physical toes to the crown of your head, and project it outward as an image of your body or as simple globe, or just as an awareness of self. All of these are valid.

    d. Extending your clairvoyant vision in other psychic operations: dowsing, aura reading, crystal ball reading, tea leaf reading, etc. While these tools would seem unnecessary to this higher form of clairvoyance, they function as a means of focus, which is necessary no matter what convenient tool or technique we use with our clairvoyance.

17. Always "close down" when finished. It can be as simple as closing the door to your astral room—but do feel the closure. Consciously return to "normal," and record every step and realization in your journal.

Onward and Upward!

This brings this chapter to its close, but we have lots more to cover in the remaining chapters. And, once again, we want to state that in all our writings we are not "teaching you what to do" in a *how-to* format, but giving you the knowledge and means to self-empowerment as well as psychic empowerment.

That's what the "New Age" really means. It's not Eastern or Western ideas and practices; it's not a collection of sweet phrases and joining with like-minded people; and it's not any kind of "collective" effort to save the world. This New Age is happening. It is happening as a spark of Higher Consciousness touching everyone, but manifesting in many challenging ways. Each of us has a role to play, whether we know it or not, and whether or not it appears to fit into any ideal belief system.

To the extent that you, individually, have a more clear vision of what's happening in your inner world or outer world, you may be able to act from the perspective of a "higher" vision, but—remember—ALL IS CONSCIOUSNESS and it is within Consciousness that we truly grow, change, and transform.

Yes, we can act with others through shared consciousness to multiply the application of psychic power, whether in shared rituals or timed meditation and prayer practices, but it is important that the individual act independently and not turn over "leadership" to someone else. Yours is the Power, and the Glory; without individual action and conviction, your *intentional* action upon specific leverage points in the astral plane will be mitigated.

Sources & Suggested Additional Reading:

Dale, C. *The Complete Book of Chakra Healing: Activate the Transformative Power of Your Energy Centers,* 1996 and 2009, Llewellyn.

Dale, C. *Kundalini: Divine Energy, Divine Life,* 2011, Llewellyn.

Dale, C. *The Subtle Body: An Encyclopedia of Your Energetic Anatomy,* 2009, Sounds True.

Denning, M., and Phillips, O. *The Foundations of High Magick: The Foundation of All Magick Is Found in the Nature and Structure of the Psyche Itself and Its Language of Symbolism,*1974, 1975, and 1991, Llewellyn.

Denning, M., and Phillips, O. *The Sword & The Serpent: The Two-Fold Qabalistic Universe,* 1975, 1988, and 2005, Llewellyn.

Hodson, G. *Clairvoyance and the Serpent Fire,* nd, Theosophical Pub. House, London.

Judith, A. *Wheels of Life: A User's Guide to the Chakra System,* 1987, Llewellyn.

Kanga, D. D. *Where Theosophy and Science Meet, 2 vols.,* 1949, 1951, Adyar Library Assn., Adyar.

Kraig, D. M. *Modern Sex Magick: Secrets of Erotic Spirituality,* 1998, Llewellyn.

Mumford, J. *A Chakra & Kundalini Workbook: Psycho-Spiritual Techniques for Health, Rejuvenation, Psychic Powers & Spiritual Realization,* 1997, Llewellyn.

Mumford, J. *Ecstasy Through Tantra,* 1975, 1977, and 1987, Llewellyn.

Ponce, C. *Kabbalah: —An Introduction and Illumination for the World Today,* 1973, Quest.

Regardie, I. with Cicero, C. & Cicero, S. T. *A Garden of Pomegranates: Skrying on the Tree of Life,* 1970 and 1999, Llewellyn.

Regardie, I. with Cicero, C. & Cicero, S. T. *The Middle Pillar: The Balance Between Mind and Magic,* 1970 and 1998, Llewellyn.

Slate, J. H. & Weschcke, C. L. *Astral Projection for Psychic Empowerment: The Out-of-Body Experience, Astral Powers, and their Practical Application,* 2012, Llewellyn. Note, this book has an extensive chapter on Astral Love, Sex & Magick pertinent to the previous discussion of modern Western Sex Magick as a "short-Cut" toward the attainment of higher psychic powers.

CHAPTER NINETEEN
Clairvoyance—for Psychic Empowerment & Self Empowerment

Clairvoyance <u>FOR</u> Psychic Empowerment

The title of this book includes that particular word "for" indicating that we are not writing only *about* Clairvoyance by itself but rather clairvoyance and its particular function <u>for</u> the *Empowerment* of your Psyche.

Most readers consider Clairvoyance just as a psychic or paranormal ability, or perhaps as merely an extension of some other normal faculty—like putting on magnifying glasses to improve your reading comfort, and adding a hearing aid. Others consider it a "skill" by itself that can be learned like playing the piano or learning to type on a keyboard.

What is the "Psyche"?

Yes, using a keyboard is a means to open a new world of communications and applications facilitated by the personal computer, but it does not in itself *transform* or *empower* the psyche.

But what, really, is the *Psyche?* We use words as if saying them actually means something; we go to the dictionary and have words telling us something about the word we are looking up. So, a "thing" is a "thing." Just because we can now describe some "thing" with more words, do we now really know what we are talking about?

A "toe" is an appendage of a foot, which is the bottom extremity of a leg. *Words.* Drop a brick on to your bare toe and you localize (and loudly verbalize!) your experience of a hurt toe. Put on an ill-fitting high-heel shoe that squeezes your toe as you walk, and you have another experience of a hurting toe. Take off your shoe and let your lover massage and then "kiss the pain away" and you have another experience of *toeness* that builds meaning into your experiential word definition of "toe."

You can get a book on anatomy, and learn more about toes. You can study about injuries and diseases of toes, and you build still more meaning and knowledge of "toe." You can look at toes in real life and in art; you can find poetic descriptions of toes and of a lover's feeling about the toes of his beloved. Go ahead, and learn so much that you can win the Nobel Prize for your expertise on toes.

But, the psyche is not a "living thing" in the same way a toe is, nor is it just a "thing" like your kitchen stove. With either of these things, we can add to our understanding of the physical thing by including our emotional experience and even mental knowledge. It's hard to even call the psyche a "thing," and yet that is the tendency when we try to describe it objectively with words. *Your* psyche is subjective to you as someone else—even a psychiatrist—tries to objectify it.

We use words to form a kind of "matrix" to encompass our living experiences and our continuing attempt to understand it in relation to the whole of our reality.

Carl Jung wrote: "By psyche, I understand the totality of all psychic processes, conscious as well as unconscious." In other words, the Psyche is inclusive of Subconscious, Conscious, and Superconscious Minds, without limitations of physicality (brain processes) and hence integrates all the personal functions of physical/etheric, astral, and mental bodies including all those energies and experiences that we refer to as "psychic."

The Psyche is not "physical" but is inclusive of all emotional and mental processes seeming to result from brain, spinal, nerve, and hormonal activities, and it is not "spiritual" in the sense of what we mean as a person's unique "Immortal Soul" that obtains growth and experience through the individuating unit that incarnates in a physical body.

What is "Personality"?

The easiest answer is to say that your personality is all that your psyche is, minus everything psychic. We can refer to someone as "a psychic" or as having "psychic abilities," but that is merely an attempt to objectively describe you from the "outside." It is how others see you, but it can't be complete because you may be seen differently by each of many people. It is also how you project yourself to others, but again you project many different "masks" in relationships to other people and in differing circumstances.

There is only one "true" you, and that is your persona. You can also think of the Soul as a kind of "ultimate" you standing behind the incarnating persona—but the Soul is <u>not</u> you as the actor and experiencer of your current life.

The persona is the actor seeking experience in this life. It is the person who develops psychic abilities and grows and experiences through all the senses, physical as well as those extended by psychic development.

As we have evolved, we move inwardly to become more whole, to become more of the persona and an active actor in contrast to the personality as a passive reactor. The more extensive our psychic development, the greater our psychic empowerment and ability to be an active actor responsible for our own self-development, and self-empowerment.

Clairvoyance & Astral Projection—Separately and Together

Clairvoyance and Astral Projection, separately and considered together, are the most important and dynamic of psychic powers. It can easily be said that all other forms of divination and "psychic reading" are just aspects in degree and style of Clairvoyance. And, that what we call "astral projection" is a phenomenon of the extended consciousness that is, in fact, clairvoyance. Almost equally, we can define clairvoyance as a focused extension of consciousness by reaching out with the astral body or even of just an etheric or an astral hand to touch and see that which we want to know.

It's important to realize that we cannot make absolute definitions with rigid boundaries when working with non-physical matters. Even within the physical world, we have to be careful as we work at different levels of matter and energy. As we are learning in Quantum Physics, the act of observation itself changes the parameters of the observed. The smaller the particle and the more subtle the matter, the more sensitive and responsive to observation, intention, and other willful influence it is.

The Weird Astral World

In the case of the astral world, the situation is even more "weird." The astral world is the *emotional* world, and the "reality" we experience is influenced by feelings and is responsive to the imagination. In other worlds, astral sight is easily distorted by "passive" imagination which in turn is distorted by such emotions as hopes, desires, fears, and even by love.

It is vital to understand the nature of the astral world because strong emotions and resulting images "project" downward to—in varying degrees—shape physical reality and your life experience. Fears can create monsters, and collective fears can bring those monsters "out of the closet" to manifest in the "real" (physical) world in the form of hate, discrimination, massive abuse as with the KKK in America and Auschwitz in Germany.

At the same time as we too often see, Love can lead to stupid behavior as in teen pregnancies, Love can be a powerful force in changing and shaping physical reality, reinforcing growth and development in another person.

The Superstitions about "Higher" Worlds

This is the reverse of the common belief (really, a *superstition*) that the "higher" into the subtle, non-physical, "heaven worlds," we go the more direct and "pure" our insight. That would be true, if the "level" of our awareness (or "intelligence") was as high, or higher, than the level of non-physical substance being observed. It doesn't always work that way. A two-year old child can sit at the piano and plink out some noise, but it will not sound like Chopin or Mozart. A four-year-old can draw a stick-figure and call it "Mommy" but it will not be a great portrait of a beautiful and loving woman. Even a trained mathematician will be inadequate at solving Fermat's Last Theorem.

"Purity" and "Discipline" of the physical body may lead to greater sensual sensitivity, but probably not to accurate insight and understanding at super-sensual levels.

Knowledge Builds on Knowledge

"Knowledge builds on Knowledge." Even in the normal, everyday, physical world, we—to varying degrees—see what we expect to see (or, sometimes, what we want to see). The more inclusive and the more specific the details, the more this is true. You may see the color purple, but the artist will see varying shades between magenta and violet compounded from red and blue and sometimes with additions of yellow and green. You may see dark clouds, but the meteorologist knows that all clouds are actually white, appearing darker depending on their thickness, and their water content, and then interprets more through their shape, temperature, motion, and the surrounding wind and even the direction of the wind.

It's all in the Details

It's not that "the Devil is in the details," but it is in the accuracy with which we perceive the details, and then our ability to interpret those details through the extent of our knowledge and experience that influences the accuracy of our weather forecast. With that foundation of knowledge, we may further refine our forecast with clairvoyance.

Clairvoyance, by itself, is an empty vision, a sound without meaning. But clairvoyance, when applied to a goal is not limited to a single vision of the single moment of time, but can expand to incorporate the *process* of Past into the Present and project into the Future. It becomes a vision filled with life, and sound colored with meaning.

As it was important to visualize your object with as much knowledge of the details as possible, now with the clairvoyant vision you must let the vision itself fill in the details and not allow your emotions to project unreal details into the vision. It's those projected "unreal" details that can turn a mere dream monster in the closet into a real monster out of the closet. Never let fear and illusion enter your closet!

While "sensitivity" raises our vibratory perceptions into the astral, and even the mental realms, we have to move beyond passive receptivity to actively create a kind of visualized prototype in our imagination based on "Big Picture Knowledge" defined by our awareness of the details and given direction by the specificity of our question, i.e. our "goal" in asking the question.

The Active Imagination & Visualization

We have to control our passive vision by the active approach of *visualization* based on knowledge.

As pointed out earlier in Chapter Six:

- We start with the recognition that to imagine is to create. The imagination (image-plus-action) is our faculty that puts an image into action. Visualization is the recognition that to act upon an image is to turn it into reality.

- Visualization is more than "seeing things in your mind" even though it does work through Visual Imagery. Properly trained, Visualization brings together all the developed Psychic Senses to focus on a specific objective, goal, program, and/or process, and then adds emotion (energy-in-motion) to attract the necessary substance to move towards manifestation and intellectual understanding.

- Visualization is powerful, and it is for that reason that the visualized image must be specific in detail so that you actually get "what you wished for" and not something that may be surprising in unfortunate ways.

Using our Psychic Power Tools

From Tea Leaf Reading to Tarot Reading, and from Crystal Ball Gazing to extending Divining Rod and the swinging Pendulum we are employing particular and in some cases very sophisticated aids to the clairvoyant function. The I Ching, Tarot and Runes, for example, employ rigorous languages of symbols that themselves extend through a vast system of correspondences to connect like things to like ideas just like e-mail addresses and websites do.

These symbols (the language of correspondences) are like little boxes that *attract* meaning from the environment to which they are applied. In algebra, we employ empty boxes which we fill with meaning; those algebraic boxes are, in turn, bound by mathematical rules to produce answers. The same is true of our symbol language employed in the Tarot or Runes.

The Divining Rod is an aid magnifying and measuring particular earth currents, connecting with them by etheric means, and relating them to *known properties* via the subconscious mind. Essentially, it is an extension of the etheric double to bridge

between the subconscious mind and the delineated portion of the planet with a particular criterion (knowledge) in mind.

The Pendulum is similar, but even more of a "two-way street"

Again, referring back to Chapter Six:

- *Visualization used in conjunction with your imagination is an important technique. Your ability to effectively visualize turns your imagination into a **psychic
power tool** for use in psychic work, active meditation, astral travel, remote viewing,
the development of clairvoyance, activating archetypal powers, the assumption of
god forms, entering mythic worlds, Qabalistic path working, symbol "doorways" to
access specific areas of the astral world, as well as in all forms of magical application,
and much more. In each of these applications, visualization is a process of moving
psychic energies along particular symbolic pathways. This includes techniques previous discussed involving the Chakra System and used to actually stimulate neural
pathways in the physical body and brain.*

- *Effective visualization is the key to empowering your imagination to "make real the
unreal."*

Warning! Be wary of making "the Unreal the Real"

The danger comes when the untrained imagination makes "the unreal the real." It
may only be your own personal reality or become the "reality" of a small group, but
it can lead to injury, illusion, hysteria, and terrible criminal acts when small vision is
directed towards large scale affairs. That's why we say "a little knowledge can be dangerous" because it deals only with parts rather than the whole. It's like connecting a
broken wire without turning off the main circuit because your knowledge of electrical
power and wiring didn't extend far enough.

A little knowledge is often sufficient, or at least not harmful, when the application
is personal and limited. This is the case with most clairvoyant work, especially when
used with the various tools we call "aids." "Readings" for self, relatives, and clients can
be quite accurate and insightful. However, when readings are applied to the "Big Picture," they usually reflect the personal bias and lack of reference characteristic to one
not broadly educated in such mundane sciences as economics, commercial or criminal law, international affairs, meteorology, etc., as may be the subject of forecast or
interpretation when the reading relates to stock market prediction, world economic
affairs, natural resources, foreign policy trends, etc.

Reach Out and Touch Someone

When a reading is personal, the reader not only reaches out psychically and "touches" the client but awakens her or his own knowledge and experience in the subject area of the reading. In doing so, there is a response from the subconscious mind of both reader and client and sometimes further out toward yet another person when the question—as is most common—involves the client's relationship. Knowledge builds on knowledge and even uncovers buried or "secret" knowledge following the known connections.

Knowledge is built upon knowledge, and clairvoyance is an extension of perception and not a substitute for it. That's why *we must never stop learning*, and that applies in particular to those involved with Paranormal Science because our vision is directed forward, towards the unknown. As we reach forward, we are extending awareness, expanding consciousness and actually constructing our superconscious mind.

Clairvoyance is more than an extension of physical details

This is an important point. While knowledge of the physical details builds accuracy in the matrix that is your visionary goal, clairvoyant vision is not of the physical dimension but of the astral and then into the mental. Each plane or world is composed of its own "substance" and "regulated" in accordance with its own rules. The connection between the worlds passes downward, and not upward so that the astral is formative to the physical and not vice-versa. The astral adds a dimension to the visualized object, and the mental adds another. Combined with the downward connection, from higher to lower, clairvoyance adds reality to our perception which becomes better described in symbolic language than with words.

In developing our innate psychic powers and growing our psychic skills, we are *becoming more!* We are become more *whole*, fulfilling the potential that has always been our gift and promise.

Psychic Empowerment is both a Process and a Promise

The "process" of clairvoyance is to find and follow lines of connectedness that will enrich our knowledge and understanding of the things so connected, and then to extend our consciousness to the targeted thing to unite with it and explore it from within.

The "promise" of clairvoyance is that it is the next step in human evolution. When we speak of "psychic empowerment," we are really talking about the culminating mastery of clairvoyance which involves the complete integration of all the lower levels of the Whole Person—the Astral, Mental, and Causal levels that use the Physical/Etheric Body as a temporary vehicle during incarnation.

In developing our psychic powers (referring to any or all of those tools and techniques we call "psychic")—probably over several life times of accelerating growth—we are completing construction of our "super consciousness," the third level of our triune persona.

As emphasized several times throughout this book and in all our writing, humans are not finished products but works-in-progress. It's something that most people don't want to hear and far less think about. Mostly we act like kids who as soon as they are sexually mature (if we ever are!) think they are fully qualified adults and consider school a waste of time, or at least just a means to an end (lots of parties and sex, marriage and sex, a high-paying job, exciting vacations and sex, and more parties and sex).

Evolution is inexorable, but Empowerment is not!

There comes a time when a decision must be made. The question comes down to whether humanity is abandoned to work out its own failure to grow and develop, or will enough people push forward in pursuit of personal growth and self-development.

The drive of evolution is inexorable, but life as we know it can end. The skies can go gray with pollution and plant life can die followed by dying animal life. The Earth can tremble, quake, and shatter; the ice can melt and drown cities and human life; the weather can become more and more extreme with alternations of heat and cold, floods and drought, and winds can increase in severity and blow everything away.

Humanity has a choice: we can let it happen as we squabble and blame one another, and appeal to a higher power to save the faithful and punish the "others." We can resort to nuclear war between the faiths in the belief that "our God" will prevail and return humanity to a promised paradise. We can hope for salvation from wise and benevolent beings arriving in saucer-shaped space ships.

Or Humanity can embrace a global civilization, and bring rational empowerment based on Knowledge to solve problems and set out on a renewed path of secular education, science freed of sectarian restraints, and politics uncorrupted by greed and unfed by special interests. The challenge is enormous because the scale has to be global, free of nationalist and religious bigotry. Vision must be brought to higher levels through personal psychic development and transformative self empowerment.

Humanity has to grow beyond itself

The answers are not in politics or institutions. The call is not for mass action and painful revolution. Only individuals can grow and become transformed. Organizations are tools for individuals who grow and become more than they are and act together to bypass the collectivist institutions dominated by power-greedy leaders.

We are not "finished products" but are works "in progress." But time is running out. Each of us must make the decision: To Grow, or not to Grow. Each of us must determine his own course of action for his and her psychic development and self self-empowerment.

Our World is on the edge where we can finely act together through the vast connections of our global nervous system we call the "World Wide Web," the Internet connecting us together individually and through communities, accessing Knowledge and Know How, directly communicating with one another to discuss and inspire intelligent decisions and non-violent actions.

As individuals communicating with one another we can demonstrate alternatives to decadent institutions and their greedy leaders, we can show the benefits of freedom from political and religious domination, the glory of human rights regardless of gender, age, race or other categorizations used to limit people. We can show the benefits of real education, real science, and real personal empowerment.

The responsibility for such a future is yours and yours alone. Each of us, individually, must choose growth and develop a course of development using the tools and techniques provided here and in other books. A Future of Peace, Prosperity, and Progress is beckoning and asking you to move forward, asking each of us to move forward one step at a time at a faster and faster pace.

No, the Future is not Pre-determined

The stark choices described above are only one vision. It is just one person's clairvoyance, and one that is inclusive of an extensive background of knowledge, and of demonstrated accuracy. But its two visions in which human choices can make differences.

And, being visions of the *future,* and being visions of a *Very Big Picture,* there are many, many variables—even including some that are extra-terrestrial and some that are sub-nuclear, and others biological and cellular—any of which could tip the scales one direction or another or add new dimensions of the equations.

The Future is not pre-determined, but is still determinable, and the most important consideration is what decisions you can make to grow and become more than you are. Expanding your personal vision through your developing clairvoyance expands your options and the possibilities for all of us.

Dominant species on this planet have died before, and there is nothing external to prevent it happening again. But, *internally*—the decisions and actions you can take based on extended vision and expanded wisdom—are another matter. Your choice to grow and to become more can empower all of humanity to not only survive but to all grow into new life and being.

CHAPTER TWENTY
The New Science of the PARANORMAL

The intention of this chapter is to outline research areas and specific projects for volunteers, students, practitioners, and scientists to carry out for developmental study through the International Parapsychology Research Institute and Foundation (PRIF) and publications under the new category of "The New Science of the Paranormal." Further details will be found in Appendix C.

Parapsychology—at a "Dead End"?

No, not exactly. But it's *stuck!* It's stuck in an outdated concept of a clockwork Newtonian physical universe while Paranormal Science has moved on to a consciousness-filled universe inclusive of Quantum Theory and non-physical realities as well as physical realities of matter and energy.

In a way, parapsychology hasn't been much alive since it stopped dealing with dead people in the midst of 19th century Spiritualism and stopped being called "Psychical Research."

Early 20th century parapsychology did serve to prove "there's something there" using statistical methods, but couldn't develop models that had a place for phenomena outside the closed environment of the laboratory and the closed thinking centered in a purely physical universe. Scientists, and others, preferred to say that anything outside of "normal" was nothing but superstitious nonsense and *dangerous thinking!*

From the Dark Ages to Enlightenment and the Age of Reason

A long segment of Western History—from the 5th to 15th centuries—has been called "the Dark Ages" as repressive Christian theology aggressively punished scientific thinking that deviated from approved Catholic doctrine and Bible-based theology, and declared all non-Christian practices to be "evil Witchcraft" and the work of "Satan." Vast libraries of hand-copied books were burned, and thinkers refusing to recant their beliefs were likewise burned to death.

The American Revolution & the Bill of Rights

Once the yoke of the Church was broken, the darkness was replaced by the Enlightenment and the Age of Reason in Europe. And then the American Revolution and the Bill of Rights in 1791 firmly established the freedom from imposed religion with the separation of Church and State, the freedom of speech and press, the right of assembly, the rights to privacy and personal security and ownership of property.

The Reading Revolution & Universal Education

And the 18th century birth of the "reading revolution" as book publishing became more widespread and books became affordable, facilitated the concepts of free public and universal education in the United States along with the birth of public universities. These are concepts that slowly spread across the world in a revolution that is still continuing despite challenges from repressive religionists using terrorism as a weapon of choice.

The "real" New Age

Why is this so important? Because the Age of Reason was the "preface" to the "real" NEW AGE that we live in now. The New Age didn't begin in the Haight-Ashbury area of San Francisco during the drug-hazed 1960s but with the age of rational thinking, the advent of universal education, and the spread of knowledge with the advent of cheap books and the freedom to talk about them and explore new ideas.

The New Age (also called "the Age of Aquarius") is in its infancy and will last through two millennia. It is hard to imagine what life was like in the Dark Ages before the Enlightenment, and perhaps even more difficult to imagine what life will be like in the coming years of advancing knowledge and scientific achievement—but the obvious import is that Humanity is no longer enslaved by antique theologies and a repressive culture. Our minds are free to grow, and are inspired by advancing knowledge to acquire more knowledge and use it to build a better world dominated by rational thought and expanding dimensions of consciousness.

"Knowledge Builds on Knowledge"

Knowledge Builds on Knowledge in a constant process of review, renewal, and discovery—free of restraint, restriction, and isolation.

Knowledge does not grow in ivy-covered towers separated from the surrounding culture, but is itself inspired and renewed by the challenges of day-to-day life founded in and integral with the Natural World which is not *given* to us to use and abuse. All Life is a partnership, and all things are inter-connected within a "web" of consciousness.

The Intellectual Abuse and Misuse of Language

The misuse of language and the *imperial* practice of proclaiming that a word means more than its specific definition lead to imprecision and conflict. Both Religion and Science are guilty of these practices but our general and commercial communities are even more guilty of gross language abuse.

The Origins of Mythology & Religion

Mythology is a story attempting to explain the origins and nature of the world and of humanity as experienced within a defined geographic environment. Each myth is spiritually inspired, usually aided by shamanic techniques, and characterized by features of the local environment and the history and lore of humanity's presence there. Almost always, the subsequent religion incorporates an established local mythology, or the religion may be entirely based on a single or coordinated mythology.

Most modern religion is a specific set of principles and practices *believed* to be mostly derived from the teachings of a single person whose life has been mythologized by his (almost always a male) followers, and then dogmatized into a theology protected and administered by an institution, and codified into administrative and criminal law.

Creators of both Myth and Religion claim a Divine beginning of some sort, and in the process of doing so deny that same opportunity to any other persons. In the case of Myth, the "Teacher of Humanity" is a central, non-human, deity. In the case of Religion, the "Teacher" is always humanized in some way and usually proclaimed to have a verifiable history, albeit a largely mythologized one derived from multiple sources.

"Truth," and Fiction

Just because the proclaimed origin may not be historically verifiable does not necessarily deny value and meaning to the particular religion for its adherents. Problems arise when the Institutional Hierarchy or a single leader assumes the function of a theocratic dictator and claims the soul authority to interpret the ancient beliefs in relation to contemporary challenges. In some cases, both historic and contemporary, the religion's dictator commands punishment for those who do not sufficiently adhere to his dictates—including even people who are not members of the "faith."*

> *Note: All political dictators surround themselves with religious accoutrements. Lenin, Hitler, Stalin, Peron, Mao, Castro, Gaddafi, etc. created state religions with symbols, music, chants, uniforms, and added "authorized" biographies that at the minimum hinted at Divine authority of some sort.

All religions, and all mythology, contain valid lessons for any student. They are the stories of humanity's search for understanding and purpose, and even when those stories are taken out of their historic context and localized geography they find place in our Unconscious core and can be automatically filtered and recalled to speak to our own personal story and needs. But we have to be intellectually free to do so and not live in fear of the dictator and his enforcers.

In addition, the study of their history provide valuable lessons in psychology. Working in the opposite direction, Hitler intensely studied American advertising techniques to develop his methodology of "religious" governance.

Religion vs. Spirituality, and "Institutional Science" vs. the Scientific Method

Being "religious" is not the same things as being "spiritual." Spirituality is a state of higher consciousness in which there is a broad vision of the presence of Divinity throughout the natural world of which humanity is a part, and of the living philosophy that the Divine Presence generates.

Being "religious" requires adherence to fixed theology established in a past time and administered by an institutional hierarchy. The presence of the Divine within an ordinary person is deemed heresy. Morality is doctrinal and intended to preserve the authority of the institution and its administrators.

The "scientific method" is an unbiased perception of phenomenon and an exploration of meaning through experimental testing of theory based on observation—without limitation (other than ethical) placed on the means and methods of observation or testing methods.

That which we are calling "institutional science" is as rigid and protective of the past as is any religious institution. It is extremely reluctant to challenge previous "doctrine" and part of the problem originates in the academic community where it is sometimes heretical not to give precedence to past research and publication even when new data contradicts that earlier work.

The Denial of non-Physical Reality

But an even greater problem lies in the common denial of any reality beyond the *physical* dimension. In other words, there is no "scientific" recognition of consciousness beyond the functions of the physical brain and of perceptions beyond the limits of the five physical senses. There is a *pre-emptive* denial of anything resembling a "sixth sense," of intuition, and a rejection of all matters "psychic."

It isn't easy to buck established doctrine, but we have to outline a "metaphysical leap" to guide people—not just scientists—into new thinking and openness to cosmic worlds and consciousness worlds beyond their strictly materialist viewpoint. Napoleon Hill (*Think and Grow Rich*) wrote: "What the mind can conceive and believe, the mind can achieve." But there's and even older adage that says: "What the Mind conceives to be real becomes real."

"What the Mind Conceives to be Real, Becomes Real"

To full grasp this we have to again affirm that m*ind is not a function of the physical brain, but that mind functions through the brain.* What we know as mind starts in a dimension above that of the physical brain called the "mental plane," taking its function and purpose from the causal plane and the Soul.

What the mind conceives takes shape and substance from the mental place, and then—gathering more shape and substance—filters downward through the levels of the astral to establish a kind of formative matrix in the etheric plane to begin the process of manifestation on the physical plane.

From Higher to Lower, and from Lower to Higher!

Establish that concept of "Higher to Lower" firmly in your own mind, and then accept the realization that there are other and greater minds likewise at work in these higher dimensions with shared purpose. As we participate in the "Great Plan," more consciously, our lives take on deeper meaning and our Vision expands to more completely comprehend the Reality that is.

That is the highest Clairvoyance we can achieve, but there are many levels beneath that Grand Vision, and each serves as a stepping stone in our personal psychic development. In our development, we reverse the process, and reach toward the Higher from the Lower, and with each step upward we gain understanding and likewise *find answers to our questions!*

The Key to Divination, and the Key to Magick

"From Lower to Higher" is the key to successful divination, and "From Higher to Lower" is the key to successful magick, and the great secret behind effective prayer.

What do we learn from this historic transition from Intellectual Darkness to that of Spreading Enlightenment?

Among other things, we are still in a battle to protect the freedom of education from the threat of religious domination, from the encroachment of so-called "Biblical Theocracy" (or that of any other "Book") on scientific research and the applications of its discoveries, and the abuse of corrupted science by bureaucracies protecting tainted pharmaceuticals and noxious pollution of air, water, and food.

Money Talks, and there is money to be made and/or protected through scientific dishonesty that is handsomely rewarded.

The Birth of Psychical Research and Parapsychology

The term "parapsychology," was coined in 1889 by philosopher Max Dessoir and adopted in the 1930s by J. B. Rhine to replace "psychical research" as used by the British *Society for Psychical Research* founded in London in 1882 for the *critical* investigation of paranormal phenomena inclusive of telepathy, hypnotism, apparitions and haunting, and—of course—the physical phenomena associated with Spiritualism such as the movement of objects and materialization. One of their first efforts was a study of *hallucinations in sane people*—which pretty well summarizes the attitude of science toward the paranormal even today.

Much of the early Psychical Research was devoted to the search for trickery and fraud in the spiritualist phenomena associated with the séance and with mediumship itself. Researchers looked for possible mechanical methods to produce phenomena resembling the "illusions" of magical trickery such these listed in Wikipedia:

Magical Illusions:

- **Escape**: The magician (an assistant may participate, but the magician himself is by far the most common) is placed in a restraining device (i.e. <u>handcuffs</u> or a <u>straitjacket</u>) or a death trap, and escapes to safety. Examples include being put in a straitjacket and into an overflowing tank of water, and being tied up and placed in a car being sent through a car crusher.

- **Penetration**: The magician makes a solid object pass through another—a set of steel rings link and unlink, a candle penetrates an arm, swords pass through an assistant in a basket, a saltshaker penetrates the table-top, a man walks through a mirror. Sometimes referred to as "solid-through-solid."

- **Production**: The magician produces something from nothing—a rabbit from an empty hat, a fan of cards from thin air, a shower of coins from an empty bucket, a <u>dove from a pan</u>, or the magician him- or herself, appearing in a puff of smoke on an empty stage—all of these effects are *productions*.

- **Restoration**: The magician destroys an object, then restores it back to its original state—a rope is cut, a newspaper is torn, a <u>woman is sawn in half</u>, a borrowed watch is smashed to pieces—then they are all restored to their original state.

- **Transformation**: The magician transforms something from one state into another—a silk handkerchief changes color, a lady turns into a <u>tiger</u>, an indifferent card changes to the spectator's chosen card. A transformation can be seen as a combination of a vanish and a production.

- **Vanish**: The magician makes something disappear—a coin, a cage of doves, milk from a newspaper, an assistant from a cabinet, or even the <u>Statue of Liberty</u>. A vanish, being the reverse of a production, may use a similar technique, in reverse.

Magical Illusions Resembling Séance Phenomena:

- **Levitation**: The magician defies gravity, either by making something float in the air, or with the aid of another object (suspension)—a silver ball floats around a cloth, an assistant floats in mid-air, another is suspended from a broom, a scarf dances in a sealed bottle, the magician hovers a few inches off the floor. There are many popular ways to create this illusion, including <u>Asrah levitation</u>, <u>Balducci levitation</u>, <u>Looy's Sooperman</u>, and <u>King levitation</u>. Much more spectacular is the apparent free flight <u>flying illusion</u> that is often performed by <u>David Copperfield</u> and more recently by <u>Peter Marvey</u> (who may or may not be using a technique similar to that of David Copperfield). <u>Harry Blackstone's</u> floating light bulb, in which the light bulb floats over the heads of the public, is also spectacular.

- **Prediction**: The magician predicts the choice of a spectator, or the outcome of an event under seemingly impossible circumstances—a newspaper headline is predicted, the total amount of loose change in the spectator's pocket, a picture drawn on a slate.

- **Teleportation**: The magician causes something to move from one place to another—a borrowed ring is found inside a ball of wool, a canary inside a light bulb, an assistant from a cabinet to the back of the theatre. When two objects exchange places, it is called a transposition: a simultaneous, double teleportation.

The Parapsychological Association was founded by J. B. Rhine in 1957. Under the leadership of anthropologist Margaret Mead, the Parapsychological Association became affiliated with the American Association for the Advancement of Science in 1969—

essentially recognizing the study of the paranormal as a science. However, the emphasis remains on parapsychology—sometimes also called psychotronics—as a physical science.

And, it must be noted that many consider parapsychology to be a *pseudoscience,* undeserving of scientific respect and funding.

Recognized Areas of Paranormal Research

The most recognized areas of paranormal phenomena today include:

- **Telepathy**: Transfer of information on thoughts or feelings between individuals by means other than the five classical senses.

- **Precognition**: Perception of information about future places or events before they occur.

- **Clairvoyance**: Obtaining information about places or events at remote locations, by means unknown to current science.

- **Psychokinesis**: The ability of the mind to influence matter, time, space, or energy by means unknown to current science.

- **Near-death experiences**: An experience reported by a person who nearly died, or who experienced clinical death and then revived.

- **Reincarnation**: The rebirth of a soul or other non-physical aspect of human consciousness in a new physical body after death.

- **Apparitional experiences**: Phenomena often attributed to ghosts and encountered in places a deceased individual is thought to have frequented, or in association with the person's former belongings.

The definitions for the terms above may not reflect their mainstream usage, nor the opinions of all parapsychologists and their critics.

According to the Parapsychological Association, parapsychologists do not study all paranormal phenomena, nor are they concerned with astrology, UFOs, Bigfoot, paganism, vampires, alchemy, or witchcraft (*Wikipedia, February 2012*).

Illusionary Magic has a long history of use both in entertainment and in fraud—some of which was involved in providing "proofs" of religious power through the millennia.

The resemblance to illusionary phenomena does not detract from genuine Spiritualist phenomena. However, such phenomena are less common today, except for those involved with the production of *ectoplasm* from the medium's entranced body. People (the "audience") enjoy the entertainment of magical illusion but are far less impressed with such phenomena as proof of psychic, religious, or spiritual power than were less sophisticated people in previous times right up to the 20ᵗʰ century.

Now such phenomenon is perceived and investigated within the "equation" of whatever psychic power or healing technique is being used.

New, and Broadened, Horizons of Research

In other words, we no longer accept things by "faith" but look for logical consistency between theory and phenomena. The phenomena of the Divining Rod, for example, is consistent within the framework of geo-magnetic science and knowledge of the association between the vibratory rates of particular materials and that of the sample attached to the rod or the mental statement held in the diviner's mind.

We seek understanding and then practical application. Our horizons are far different today than previously, and our *New Science of the Paranormal* must be inclusive of the new sciences of Quantum Physics, Cellular Biology, Archetypal and Analytical Psychology, and new understandings of older practices like Lunar Agriculture, Magnetic Healing, Palmistry, Homeopathic and other non-Allopathic Medicine practices, etc., and alternative views of the Universe through Astrology, the Kabbalah, Indian Tantra and Taoism, and such tools of insight as the Tarot, I Ching, Runes, and more. These must be combined with broad education in mythology, comparative religion, world history, geography, logic, ethics, mathematics, economics, the physical and life sciences and exposure to literature, the arts, and to paranormal science and phenomenon.

There is nothing "Normal" about the Paranormal

We have to accept that *there is nothing "normal" about the paranormal.* It has been defined as "outside the range of normal experience and scientific verification." A new word has been coined, "Paraphysics," but we have to understand that there is nothing physical or parallel to physics about paranormal phenomena. We can't explain or understand non-physical phenomena in terms of the physical, except—perhaps—at the Quantum level.

At the same time, instead of trying to understand consciousness as phenomena of the physical brain we must accept consciousness as originating and having its "being" outside of the brain even though it can function through the brain and uses our physical senses and all the attributes of the physical body.

Our Multi-Dimensional Universe

While there is no "flatland" of two dimensions outside of mathematics, there are worlds of more than just the three dimensions of our known physical universe, and we are capable of understanding four and five dimensions (and more), and functioning with such multi-dimensional universes even though we cannot as yet fully understand the applicable laws or control the related phenomena.

Through psychic abilities, we move into these other dimensional realities, and it is the goal of our psychic development and eventual "empowerment" to become fully conscious within such "higher" worlds.

Do not accept intellectual barriers!

Just as we can intellectually understand a two-dimensional "flatland," we can also intellectually move beyond the present limits of three-dimensional thinking. We start by expanding our horizons and integrating our knowledge outside of mental "silos" no matter how "established" they are in academic and scientific circles.

The real world is beyond intellectual limits just as there are realities beyond the "normal" reach of most physical senses.

No science operates in isolation

Archaeology that ignores the facts of geology is a lie; Medicine that ignores the mind is ignorant; Environmental Science that is blind to the melting icecap is a fraud as criminal as the greed-motivated financial mismanagement of the early 21st century.

Science is a method, not a thing or a single subject. Each "science" is a sub-division within the whole of knowledge about the cosmos we live in. Such divisions are a con-venience for limited thinking—but *thinking need not be limited!* We can stretch, we can expand our awareness, and we can reach higher levels of consciousness.

When there is need, human consciousness responds with growth. And today there is need. When we speak of "raising consciousness," we are not talking about some-thing mystical and fuzzy. When the mind is opened to new realities, it starts to grow to meet those new opportunities just as it has since the advent of universal education and the wide availability of books. But, then new growth was inhibited by false restrictions of belief and competing "entertainment"—addictions to spectator sports, all night television, the chase after wealth beyond practical benefit, bigger house and faster car consumerism, the gluttony of chemically enhanced foods, drugs, and around and around the merry-go-round goes.

We are here to grow, but the choice is yours while at the same time your obligation is to all of us.

The Interconnected Global Society

In a totally interconnected Global Society, the effects of Greed, Corruption, Ignorance, Arrogance, Abuse of Power—even at the smallest local level—is absolutely dangerous to all of us and must be seen as intolerable evil. *This simply means that they must be prevented rather than treated.*

We mention this imperative need to broaden our horizons because it applies to everything we do—not just to our *New Science of the Paranormal*. We *are* in the New Age—one that is raising consciousness and expanding awareness in a new focused evolutionary drive that *commands participation in global citizenship*. But it is also through our practice of the New Science, through our development of Clairvoyance and other psychic powers that we grow into *more than we are* and attain the greater capacity and wholeness needed to meet these new challenges with personal responsibility.

Science & the Psyche

The human psyche is not a "thing" to be examined *objectively* under a microscope. While certain *paranormal* phenomena associated with the psyche can be—at least partially—studied and measured objectively with physical senses and instruments, their origin is not physical even though occasional physiological changes can be noted.

Mind, psyche, soul, and emotion are not products of the brain even when we can see physiological effects from their functioning. The obverse: stimulating the brain with an electric probe will not produce an Albert Einstein genius, nor the poetry of Rumi, or the visionary art of William Blake—nor turn you into a clairvoyant.

The Psyche operates through other dimensions than just the physical, and that are better explored subjectively rather than dissected and measured objectively with physical instruments.

Nevertheless, our New Science of the Paranormal cannot ignore the physical world for the simple and obvious reason that we are both physical and non-physical living beings.

Two Approaches: Cosmic & Personal

Our science is necessarily both objective and subjective because we are dual beings. We seek to understand the world we live in, and the human person-in-the-world and outside-of-the-world. We live in a cosmos that is both visible and invisible, with phenomena that is both exterior and interior to our Being. Our studies are of both physics and "psyche-ology," founded in matter, energy, *and* consciousness.

And, above all, we seek to know what it is all for—what is the purpose of existence and the meaning of our lives. We see change and growth, both cosmically and personally that we ultimately define as "evolution" and finally as growth of the psyche currently manifesting in psychic growth and development leading to psychic and self-empowerment.

Words! Just words, but words laden with tension and promise. Scary words that challenge all we know, all that we've been told in school and myth, and yet we instinctively know they must become *part* of our life work. We place emphasis on that word "part" because our life work is inclusive, not exclusive, of things we consider normal to our daily life. No one benefits from the hermit in the cave no matter how deep his meditations. He's a "drop out" of the most selfish kind. We are each part of All Life and of Universal Consciousness. Your growth is my growth, and mine is yours, and together we fulfill the call to grow and to become more.

The New Science of the Paranormal is not just for scientists, but for all of us. We can all participate in research projects even as we are also students and users of the techniques and their applications for psychic development and empowerment. It's all about growth, and growing is an on-going process of life.

We are "growing" as part of the continuing evolutionary process, but more growth comes with deliberate participation and conscious development that induces an acceleration of personal growth. That's what "Clairvoyance <u>for</u> Psychic Empowerment" is about, and what is called for in *The New Science of the Paranormal*. It is your own science, and your own growth program. You become the donor as well as the beneficiary in this, the Great Work of Self Empowerment.

Clairvoyance is the primary Psychic Skill

In Chapter Seventeen, "Clairvoyance & Esotericism," we wrote that clairvoyance is the leading psychic skill of the human person in which we often do use aids in focusing it in particular ways—such as divining rods and Tarot cards, and perhaps other aids in helping us reach the higher focus necessary, like the crystal ball for focus or a meditation mask cutting off external interference. What is important are the developing skills and not the aids which are just that—like reading glasses to aid physical sight and improve visual focus.

Not "Toys" but Tools & Aids

A truly "scientific" focus on the ways these aids are used might bring about improvements in usage and even in design. Unfortunately, most such aids (the tools and techniques) are thought of as mostly "toys" by both esotericists and researchers. In contrast, our view is that *"if something works, we should find out why. And make it work better!"*

Most of the innovations in divining rods, for example, have been *inspired* through trial and error by users. Well and good, but perhaps we can do better by studying the individual parts and how they, individually, function. Perhaps even the way a crystal ball is situated may make an important difference. Or it may be that a spot of reflected light of varying colors into its center would produce new results? Or the meditation mask: users have said that "tightness" is important in order to give the feeling of "turning inward;" most say that the eyes need to be open while others are ambivalent; padding over the ears is desirable but not ear plugs. Leather is preferred by most, but thick rubber is also used. *Have all the potential options been tested?*

We need more research devoted to the mechanics of these aids for Techno-Shamanism (Chapter Eight) has shown that clairvoyance can be developed and extended by them, and no doubt there could be others once we have better understanding of how they function. That's the method of science applied in the development of technologies, and adapting them in new applications.

Yes, parapsychology has studied and statistically demonstrated that certain aspects of clairvoyance do apparently work—that is to say there is a slight positive edge to long runs of predicting what cards have been turned over, or that will be turned over. But largely neglected by the scientific community is the study of *traditional* methods for inducing clairvoyant vision. It's no better than listening to a child plinking on the piano and occasionally producing a short series of harmonious notes, and ignoring entirely the methods by which an accomplished musician has mastered the art. And how about testing clairvoyance in forecasting "Big Picture" phenomena—such as timing and details involved in the recent Mars landing? Such "Big Picture" questions off more excitement, hence more energy, than the repetitive cycling of familiar cards.

Music comes from a higher dimension, one beyond the limits of a three-dimensional reality even though it is reproduced within our familiar physical world. Instead of random plinking, perhaps the child could be asked to tell a familiar story with music. Such a challenge may seem outlandish and perhaps difficult to "measure," but it moves the question upward and that could trigger results from beyond the three-dimensional reality. Isn't that what we want? Isn't Psychic Empowerment one step beyond the outer limits of the familiar world? Let's push our science upward as well as forward. Boredom in scientific study rarely induces excitement, and excitement itself induces growth and progress.

Obviously this failure is even more true when it comes to studying traditional methods (especially those relating to "primitive" methods of shamanic practice) for astral projection, the applications of the out-of-body experiences in clairvoyance, in the diagnosis of health problems and the applications of energy healing, in the methods of magick and the charging of a talisman with specific intentional energies, in the practices of palmistry and astrology, and in the relevance of the Kabbalah to understanding the world, the psychological program intrinsic to the Tarot, and the ways of divinatory practices.

We should learn the *mechanics* of these methods, both at the physical level and—aided by clairvoyance—the non-physical, for better understanding and improvement of their methodology.

A Call for Personal & Organizational Research.

As we enter a new age of advanced computer-based technology and the World Wide Web, new techniques and applications of psychic empowerment should be the goal of *The New Science of the Paranormal.*

The fundamental teaching of Esotericism is that "Higher" creates the basis for the manifestation of the "Lower." Just as an architect's blue print projects the structure for the house that is to be built, so is a "matrix" *downloaded* from higher dimensions, creating form and substance as it moves from spirit to mental, and downward through astral to etheric and physical.

The traditional techniques of divination reverse the flow and use the tools, technologies, and languages of the Lower to communicate with the Higher. We direct our questions upward, and prepare the way for the answers to flow downward to influence our tools.

The traditional techniques of magick reach upward to establish a matrix for the energies summoned to flow downward into manifestation at the etheric and physical levels.

With the Tarot, we project a particular psychological formula and a symbolic language upward that then responds to our questions making use of the same tools in a downward flow.

With meditation mask we reduce sensory "static" to clear a channel for the psyche to move higher and then to return to the lower with answers to our questions.

With palmistry we use the body's own reflective language (the downward flow of manifestation) to tell us truths about the psyche that we project upward.

All of these, and more (see, for example, those described in *The Llewellyn Complete Book of Psychic Empowerment)* can be broken down into function details, and each detail examined and tested for efficacy in order to gain understanding of the process in its entirety, and then each detail and be replaced with a variation to explore for more understanding and to bring about improvements.

Sources & Suggesting Additional Reading:

Slate, J. H. & Weschcke, C. L. *The Llewellyn Complete Book of Psychic Empowerment: A Compendium of Tools & Techniques for Growth & Transformation*, 2011, Llewellyn.

APPENDIX A
The New Power of How-To

Throughout this book, in nearly every chapter or addendum, we have included specially written programs and procedures, mostly in the form of step-by-step meditation guides that involve the total persona—subconscious and conscious minds.

In recent years, many writers have neglected the "how-to" concept in favor of personal biographies of "this is what I do" and presume that the readers isn't interested in "doing it" too. In other words, "what I do" books are rather like personal adventure stories filled with references to their clients' experiences and to their own lives living with their special psychic talents. Many of these books enjoy great success and obviously reach a market of readers rather than doers. Their great values are as living *proof* of the value of clairvoyance in helping people in their daily lives.

For those who want to DO

This book was written for those who want to become clairvoyant themselves and who understand the transformative nature of doing so. It is your authors' conviction that becoming clairvoyant is a desirable "Next Step" in human and—more importantly—personal evolution.

Why is "personal evolution" so important? Even though the "matrix" (rather like an astral-mental blueprint) of expanding consciousness lies within every person's subconsciousness, its activation depends upon individuals developing their natural psychic power into a "skill" and then applying it in their daily life. It is the "becoming more than you are" phrase that we repeat so often like a veritable *mantra.*

These programs and procedures are presented in four major variations:

1. Preparatory Exercises, including physical relaxation, that are necessary for any meditation, self-hypnosis, or personal affirmations to penetrate past our normally busy conscious mind to reach the subconscious where transformation activity takes place.

2. Objective Guided Empowerment Meditations that take you step-by-step through particular and often specific mental programs and procedures involving both conscious and subconscious minds mostly focused on a specific goal or objective.

3. Subjective Guided Self-Transformative Visualization Meditations that take you step-by-step through a very specific astral process focused on a single major aspect of the psyche in a purification and balancing process facilitating the removal of emotional and psychic "garbage" for a clear vision in clairvoyance and a healthier personality.

4. Focused step-by-step Meditation for specific Divinatory or Magickal purposes.

All of these are conveniently listed by content sequence in the Table of Programs & Procedures you will find on pages XLVII to LI, and in the Index alphabetically by the objective of the program.

You as Agent of the Evolutionary Process

This is really important to understand, and then to accept as your personal responsibility. It is the action of individuals, and intentional and positive nature of their actions, that brings change and development to the whole of humanity, and perhaps even beyond to Spirit of Earth, *Gaia*, Herself. Everything is connected, but intentional actions carry vast transformative power beyond the immediate personal environment.

Putting it another way, your success in all you do can benefit everyone of us. And more so when you can yourself see the broader picture as your contribution to the betterment of the World about you.

There is every value to repeating many of these programs and procedures often in your progressive work and acceptance of their value in your growth and development, and Psychic Empowerment.

APPENDIX B

Companion Guide Audio CD for the
Development & Activation of Clairvoyance

Vibratory Astral Projection & Clairvoyance

In Chapter Eleven we provided an introductory program relating to the essential vibratory nature of all physical and subtle energies within the several bodies making up your total psyche—and the universe and cosmos within which we all live and function.

Of course, we rarely can perceive the vibratory nature of the world within and without but there are times when we feel the "vibes" of another person either in sympathy or antagonistic to our own.

In addition, spontaneously in pre-sleep experiences or during stages of meditation and other alterations of consciousness, we often do directly experience vibrations as waves during which the etheric and astral bodies move within and sometimes move outward from the physical body.

This phenomenon can itself be consciously directed to induce the out-of-body experience, i.e. projection of the astral body. But projection is not the only object of experiencing consciousness at the astral level. Here we want to recognize the "higher and larger" view that the astral offers, and it is at the astral and mental levels that clairvoyance functions most accurately and penetratingly to both see "behind the scenes" and to foresee the future through "the shadows cast ahead by coming events."

We can experience this expanded view of the world about purely from the physical body when we climb to higher altitudes on a mountain or by airplane. The horizon moves farther and farther away as we move higher and higher—but the details of our view are diminished by the limits of physical reality. Not so in the case of the higher realities of astral and mental perceptions which can focus at will on distant objects and events and magnify the view as with a telescope. Or, magnify the view of things up close as with a microscope—*only to a greater degree than can be experienced with a physical instrument.*

In a sense, we can "ride" the vibratory wave to the level desired.

Your Companion Guide Audio CD

Dr. Slate has developed and recorded the script for the "Vibratory Astral Projection & Clairvoyance" to facilitate your own experience—*and further personal development*—of this powerful psychic technology.

Note that phrase: "and further personal development," because that is not something that can be done <u>for</u> you but only <u>by</u> you. You have to build your own astral "muscles" and you have to learn how to direct and apply this ability yourself.

It's all part of your own continuing "Journey of a Lifetime." You can share the results of your experiences and visions with others (see Appendix D), but the journey itself is personal and yours alone. Nevertheless, your experiences become part of the Collective Unconscious that adds to the resources of the Akashic Records accessible by any of us developing the ability of higher vision. Then your ventures becomes part of the Human Adventure adding depth and breadth <u>to</u> the substance of all Humanity.

For this Journey of a Lifetime, we wish you

Bon Voyage!

APPENDIX C
You, a Scientist?

Yes! You can and should be a Scientist!

Being a scientist isn't really a matter of academic degrees and highly specialized and advanced academic training and experience. Anyone can practice the "scientific method" in ordinary daily life. And, really, you should. As a clairvoyant seeking "clear seeing," the scientific method lays a clear foundation for the physical senses upon which clairvoyance is an extension.

If your front yard is cluttered with abandoned cars, old tires, ancient swing sets and accumulated refuse mixed in with overgrown bushes and dead trees, you may have a hard time even seeing across the street. Physical vision has its limitations, and these do affect your higher perceptions as well—in a different way. Thus the first step is always to clear the field of obstruction or factors that skew your vision.

Clear thinking starts with clear observations. Clear seeing also starts with clear observations.

What is the Scientific Method?

There's the key. The Scientific Method is a basically simple way of looking at things. It is a *disciplined* attitude in which you start by freeing yourself of emotional bias and maintain an objective and rational approach, free of pre-judgment. The method simply requires that experiment and observation takes precedence over belief in determining the nature of reality, while real life experience readily questions past proclamations and calls for new and further testing because life is on-going and new experiences expand the field of observation.

The "scientific method" is an unbiased perception of phenomenon and an exploration of meaning through experimental testing of theory based on observation—without limitation (other than ethical considerations) placed on the means and methods of observation or testing methods. The benefit of the scientific method is: *Better understanding leads to increased reliability and enhanced benefits.*

New Research Opportunities

Today, the New Science of the Paranormal recognizes many area of research. As outlined in Chapter Twenty, we have these most recognized areas of paranormal phenomena for research:

- **Telepathy**: Transfer of information on thoughts or feelings between individuals by means other than the five classical senses.

- **Precognition**: Perception of information about future places or events before they occur.

- **Clairvoyance**: Obtaining information about places or events at remote locations, by means unknown to current science.

- **Psychokinesis**: The ability of the mind to influence matter, time, space, or energy by means unknown to current science.

- **Near-death experiences**: An experience reported by a person who nearly died, or who experienced clinical death and then revived.

- **Reincarnation**: The rebirth of a soul or other non-physical aspect of human consciousness in a new physical body after death.

- **Apparitional experiences**: Phenomena often attributed to ghosts and encountered in places a deceased individual is thought to have frequented, or in association with the person's former belongings.

The definitions for the terms above may not reflect their <u>mainstream</u> usage, nor the opinions of all parapsychologists and their critics.

According to the Parapsychological Association, parapsychologists do not study all paranormal phenomena, nor are they concerned with astrology, UFOs, Bigfoot, paganism, vampires, alchemy, or witchcraft.*

The following is a starter list of possible specific research projects that invite involvement of individual practitioners, students, and academics. Each can be refined as to specific segment and feature being investigated. For some broad subjects there will be many specific segments and features, and each investigation could presumably lead to others. If, as in the case of Astrology and Numerology, there are both popular-entertainment and serious-scientific levels, it is the latter—unless otherwise specified and justified—that is to be investigated.

Certainly there are many more possible subjects that can be drawn from a wide range of cultures if given due respect without bias. The point is that we can learn from all, and what we learn may be widely applied. Whether called Magick, Ritual, Religion,

Spirituality, etc., every system includes functions of vision, divination, and non-physical energy exchanges leading to paranormal phenomenon, psychic empowerment, self-improvement and transformation and empowerment whether also called Powers of Attraction, Laws of Success, or other more fashionable names.

Alchemy (see also Personal Alchemy, below)

Astral Body

Astral Projection

Astrology

Aura Reading

Cartomancy (divination with playing cards)

Casual Body

Ceremonial Magick

Chakra System

Chanting (techno-shamanic function)

Clairaudience

Clairsentience

Clairvoyance (inclusive of clairaudience, clairsentience, etc.—all the clairs.)

Crumpled Paper

Crystal Ball

Dervish Dancing

Divination—in general and including minor techniques like Bibliomancy, Face-Reading, Head-Reading, Body Posture, Eye-reading, etc.

Divining Rod

Dream Interpretation

Ecstatic Dancing (techno-shamanic function)

Energy Healing

ESP

Etheric Body

Etheric Projection

Evocation

Evolution, human, natural world, and cosmic

Geomancy

Guided Meditation

Hands on and Touch Healing

Handwriting Analysis

Hawaiian Magic

Herbal Magic

Hypnosis & Self-Hypnosis

I Ching

Incense & Oils

Invocation of Deity and Deific Forces

Japanese Rope Binding (techno-shamanic function)

Kabbalah

Kabbalistic Path-Working

Lucid Dreaming

Magick

Martial Arts and the energies involved, the philosophy behind it.

Meditation

Meditation Mask (techno-shamanic function)

Mediumship

Mental Body

Mental Projection

Mysticism

Palmistry

Path-Working

Pendulum

Personal Alchemy

Prayer, Science of

Precognition

Psychokinesis

Remembering Past Lives

Remote Viewing—resolving Clairvoyance or Astral Projection, or both?

Rising on the Planes

Rune Casting

Sand Reading

Self-Hypnosis—going beyond the association with hetero-hypnosis to its full development similar to advanced meditation.

Self-Talk

Sensory Deprivation—Meditation Mask, Tanks, Witches Cradle

Sex Magick—as distinct from Tantra

Shamanic Bondage (techno-shamanic function)

Shamanism (see also Techo-Shamanism, below)

Sigils

Spell-working

Spirit Communication—Mediumship, and Spiritualist Phenomena

Subtle Bodies—analysis of

Subtle Energies—meridians, etc.

Table Tipping—Ouija

Tantra, including Tantric occultism of which sexual Tantra is only a technique for self-development, as is Yoga

Taoist Practices

Tarot

Tea Leaf Reading

Techno-Shamanism

Telepathy

Thought Forms

Throat Singing

Traveling in Spirit

Tree of Life

Vibrations, Raising of

Visualization

Voudoun

Witches Cradle (techno-shamanic function)

Yoga—each of the major branches from Hatha through Raja

Zen Meditation

Recommended practice for New Paranormal Science Research Programs:

While the above list is not exhaustive, it is representative of the major techniques of psychic interest and practice. It is recommended that each project should be studied in a sequence of:

A. Name of the Subject, Name and Contact Address of the Volunteer investigator, Name of the Research Foundation Reporter and Contact Address, Dates of start and finish, Date submitted to Editor.

B. A broad statement and definition of the subject itself.

C. The specific statement and definition of what narrow segment of the broad subject is being investigated.

D. A specific description of the single feature being investigated, along with any appropriate standards of measurement (in metric scale) to be used, definitions of terminology used if specific to the subject matter, a list of the factors to be measured and analyzed, a list of pertinent questions to be answered.

E. Mythological origins.

F. Applicable folklore.

G. Factual history.

H. The "apparent" philosophy, science, and psychology involved. In other words, what both traditional and contemporary users believe and claim to experience in its usage.

I. A detailed analysis of the physical structure of the tool or the resources employed, or of the psychic or psychological technology used.

J. Reports, both factual and anecdotal, of its successful employment.

K. Conclusions in relation to the science behind the tool, the psychology, the technique, and even the physiology where applicable.

L. Recommendations for improvements and new applications, as well as adaptation's for computer and Web usage.

What you can do

The suggested subjects and the recommended practices are by no means rigid, nor are they the only things you can do. We encourage contact with PRIF the International Parapsychology Research Institute and Foundation, but we also encourage article writing for the various media (including the Llewellyn Journal), participation in various conferences, and exchange with other interested people.

The nature of research itself invites sharing in experiment and observation, and it only at later stages when new theories have been developed that following such guidelines for reports is desirable and often necessary.

The key element is for you to observe, experiment, practice, test, observe and test more, study and develop rational theories that can be shared with a broader community for mutual learning and benefit.

Alone, and Together, we gain knowledge and advance in our journey, in our great adventure, along the path, and for the good of all.

GLOSSARY
A Veritable "GALAXY" of Words & Meanings and Suggested Additional Reading

This is a Glossary of words primarily pertinent to this book. It is not a comprehensive dictionary or encyclopedia, although most of these words—usually with expanded definition and reference—will be found on-line in the Llewellyn Encyclopedia at: www .llewellynencyclopedia.com.

In addition, there are many words mentioned but not actively discussed that can be found in the various lists in the Table of Charts, Lists & Tables on page XLI.

Note that some Glossary entries are expanded beyond definition to serve as helpful aids to the reader. *It is worthwhile to read the Glossary as a supplement to the text.*

Adepts: Some believe advanced beings from super-physical levels of consciousness—superhuman or beyond human—have previously communicated at least partial *factual* information about the inner and greater realities of the Cosmos and the potentials for advancing human development. Perhaps their work continues "behind the scenes" and is real and effective. Personally, I don't believe there is any contemporary direct communication between human and superhuman beings. We now have plenty of "esoteric" knowledge available and every opportunity to grow and advance without supernatural intervention at this time—and *that's what we are supposed to do! Grow Up!*

Afterlife: <u>Where</u> does <u>What</u> *go after death of the physical body?* Many different answers to those two questions are offered depending on different belief systems. We take a non-religious perspective in which the etheric double, along with the astral, mental and causal vehicles, separates from the physical body to slowly decay over a few days. After that, consciousness awakens in the astral vehicle and experiences the astral world.

Ajna: The *Brow* Chakra, *Eye of Horus, Third Eye.* This chakra is located between the eyes above the brow line, physically manifesting through the nasocilicary plexus and anatomically indicted by the pituitary gland. In terms of psycho-physiology, the pineal gland relates to balancing our higher and lower selves and to inner guidance.

Physically it relates to our sense of awareness and our visual consciousness, and emotionally to intuitive clarity. The associated psychic powers are clairvoyance, telepathy, telekinesis, precognition, remote viewing, and aura reading. It is symbolized by an indigo-colored lotus with two petals, represented graphically in a white-winged globe. Each petal or wing itself consists of 48 spokes for a total of 96. One wing is rose colored and the other is yellow. The two wings represent Sun and Moon, mind and body, *Ida* and *Pingala.* The seed mantra is *AuM.* The element is *Manas* ("mind-stuff"), the energy of consciousness.

With its activation, perception of duality ceases. *Sushumna,* along with *Ida* and *Pingala,* rises up from *Muladhara* chakra to curve over the Crown of the head and then down to terminate in *Ajna,* while *Ida* and *Pingala* continue down to the two nostrils.

Ajna (Brow) *Chakra (Correspondences*		
Alchemical Planet: Moon	Alchemical Element: Silver	Tattva: Manas (Mind)
Animal: Owl	Basic Drive: transcendence	Tattva Color: Half, rose with yellow; Half, with purplish blue
Body Function: sight, consciousness	Gemstone: Quartz, Lapis lazuli	Tattva form: Winged globe
Gland: Pituitary	Goddess-form, Egyptian: Isis	Tattva Sense: Mind
God-form, Greek: Apollo	Incense: Saffron, mugwort	God-form, Hindu: Shiva-Shakti1
Location: Brow	Order of chakra unfoldment: 6th	Goddess-form, Hindu: Hakini [2]
Part of Body: Eyes	Sense: Mind, awareness	Yogic Planet: Moon
Psychic Power: clairvoyance, pre-cognition, remote viewing, aura reading	Seed Syllable/Number: AuM (0)	Chakra Color: Indigo
Psychological Attribute: Logical thinking	Sense: Awareness	Element: Light, Mind
Spinal Joint: 32nd	Tree of Life Sephirah: Chokmah & Binah	Spinal Location: 1st Cervical
Tarot Key: II, High Priestess		
[1] Male & female in union		
[2] Insight		
Source: Slate, J. & Weschcke, C.: *Psychic Empowerment: Tools & Techniques,* 2011, Llewellyn		

Akasha: The primal tattvic element of ether perceived as space and represented by a indigo oval ("Egg") to convey the basic drive for creativity, the psychological attribute of communication, the sense of hearing and the magical tool of the voice.

Akashic Records: A non-physical universal memory bank in which everything is recorded.

Alpha: Brain waves vibrating at 8 to 13 per second associated with states of relaxation, creativity, and psychic perception.

Altered States of Consciousness (ASC): States other than ordinary waking consciousness include dreaming, day dreaming, hypnagogic (half-asleep) and hypnopompic (half-awake) states, and conscious self-programming; types and levels of trance induced by sleep deprivation, chanting, fasting; ecstatic states induced by extra-sensory stimulation, drumming, extended sex and dancing; shamanic states induced by hallucinogenic herbs, sensory deprivation and isolation, restraints, pain, flagellation; meditative and hypnotic states; Out-of-Body Experiences, etc. Some of these are "exclusive" and not remembered during waking consciousness, while others are "inclusive" and readily remembered.

Anahata (AKA "Heart"): This chakra is located in the upper thoracic area over the heart, and physically manifests through the cardio-pulmonary plexus and the thymus gland at the "heart" of the immune system and the site of T-cell maturation. It relates to compassion, tenderness, unconditional love, and personal well-being. Physically it rules circulation, emotionally our unconditioned love both for others and for self, mentally our passionate interests, and spiritually our devotion. It relates to the sense of touch. The element is Air. The associated psychic power is hands-on-healing. *It carries consciousness to the next life.*

It is symbolized by a *yantra* consisting of a hexagram of two interlaced triangles representing the union of female and male, within a lotus of twelve green spokes or petals, and its tattva is represented geometrically in a blue hexagram (or a circle). This yantra—more than a symbol of man and woman united—is a powerful meditation device for uniting lower with higher, anima with animus, microcosm with macrocosm, and human with Divine. It is the heart of Man and the heart of the Divine manifest in Man. The audible seed mantra is *YuNG* followed by mental echo of *YuM*.

Angels: Astral "helpers" and "shapers" responsible for various manifestations of life in the physical world—human, animal, plant and mineral kingdoms—and also as personal "guardian angels." The seven Archangels have an archetypal function.

Anima: The Woman in every man. In Jung's psychology, it is the mythic ideal of the feminine that a man projects on to women. It manifests in fantasy, romance, sexual behavior, the estrogen hormone, and in feminine energy. *See Animus.*

Anima Mundi: The "Soul of the World" The World Mind or Global Consciousness, divided into *spiritus mundi* or world vital force, and *corpus mundi* or the world physical body. Also the Divine Essence that permeates everything as Astral Light, Prana, Animal Magnetism, Spirit.

Animal Communication: Commonly a form of mental telepathy transferring information between animal and human, generally by uncharacteristic behavior.

Animal Magnetism: The etheric or life energy present in all animal life. It can be concentrated, stored, transferred, and projected by magical practices.

Animus: The Man in every woman. In Jung's psychology, it is mythic ideal of the masculine that a woman projects on to men. It manifests in fantasy, romance, sexual response, the testosterone hormone, and in masculine energy. *See Anima.*

Apas: The primal tattvic element of water perceived as liquid and represented by a silver crescent to convey the basic drive for pleasure, the psychological attribute of flexibility, the sense of taste and the magical tool of the chalice.

Apparition: A psychic projection of one's image often connected with a personal crisis or intense interest in the other person hat. Unlike Astral Projection, this projection is mostly spontaneous and does not involve the projector entering into a trance state. Sometimes it is coincidental with the person's death.

Aquarian Age: The zodiacal age approximately 2,150 years long following the Piscean Age. The 'spirit' of these Ages is characterized by those described by the astrological sign. The Piscean Age, symbolized by fishes swimming in opposite directions (mind vs. feeling), was identified with emotionally imposed authoritarian religions. In contrast, Aquarius is symbolized by the image of Man, and characterized by intellect rather than emotion, self-responsibility rather than the 'shepherd's crook of theocratic dictatorship. It is the "New Age" that Carl Jung believed to begin in 1940. Others date it between 2012 and 2374.

The Aquarian Age calls for Knowledge applied to both practical and spiritual needs, with schools becoming places of meaningful learning & self-development. The New Age of the Mind and Spirit is the new frontier during which our scientific and technological thrust is directed to the common benefit and to opening the inner doors of consciousness.

The Piscean originated world crises require that we make esoteric science a living knowledge for all, not a static faith. There can be no inner secrets that only initiates know, for human needs are universal. We must provide opportunities for people to come together in learning esoteric systems of psychic and spiritual growth, in research and sharing of discovery, participating in a revival of the wisdom of Nature and Heart, and learning that Man and Woman can liberate each other. We are balanced upon a precipice from which we can fall or ascend. The Age thrusts upon us the opportunity for a tremendous leap forward in planetary evolution.

Archetypes: A universal image and energy matrix, mostly the same everywhere but with minor variation across long established cultures as expressed in dominant religions and personal variants. The Archetypes have been experienced as the 'gods' of major mythologies, each charged with particular responsibilities in the natural world. They are found in the major arcana of the Tarot, may be seen and experienced through Kabbalistic path-working and shamanic trances, and are often met in dreams and projected on to real life figures in times of crisis. One of the goals in programs of self-knowledge is to gain understanding of our particular interaction with them, and possibly change those interactions from a childish to a more mature level.

As Above, So Below: The concept that the Lower Plane is controlled by the Higher Plane, but also that actions on the Lower Plane are replicated—in some fashion—on the Upper Plane. See *Emerald Tablet.*

As in the Macrocosm so it is in Man the Microcosm: As a person *awakens* the Energy Forms within the "Inner World Matrix" he harmonizes with the natural order of the "Outer World Matrix" for health, psychic awareness, and self-empowerment. Each of us is in process of becoming more than we are. The life purpose of each person is to grow in our wholeness, developing innate powers into actual skills, uniting the Lower Self with the Upper Self.

Association: Coincidence between thought and event, generally related to personal experience. It is often used in dream interpretation.

Astral Aura: In aura seeing, each higher vehicle's aura extends further beyond the skin of the physical body in this sequence: physical body, etheric double, astral, mental and causal vehicles. Each body or vehicle is inclusive of the one "beneath" it in the familiar scheme of levels of consciousness.

Astral Awareness: The essential goal of astral projection is to extend awareness beyond the limitations of the physical brain to become fully conscious on the astral plane.

Astral Body, aka Astral Vehicle: Also called the Desire or Emotional Body or "Envelope." The third *vehicle* "upward" in the general scheme of levels of consciousness. It is the extra-biological part of our being as a conscious, intelligent, and indestructible entity. In the process of incarnation, the astral vehicle is composed of planetary energies in their aspects to one another to form a matrix guiding the structure for the physical body and defining karmic factors.

It is the Lower Self of emotion, imagination, thought, and memory—all the functions of the mind in response to sensory perception and emotional reaction. It is the field of dreams, of the subconscious mind, and the vehicle for most psychic activities. Yet, a distinction must be made: The Physical Body is the field of ordinary conscious mind and the Astral is that of the sub-conscious mind, and a doorway to the collective unconscious.

Astral Doorways: Certain objects may be used to induce alternative states of consciousness and bring access to specific areas of the sub-conscious mind and astral plane. Among these are fascination devices that focus awareness and induce trance: crystal balls, magick mirrors, swinging pendulums, pools of ink, etc.—allowing the user to receive impressions. In addition, meditation upon particular symbols such the Tattvas and Yantras, certain decks of Tarot Cards, Rune Symbols, the I Ching Hexagrams, Hebrew and Sanskrit letters, Egyptian Hieroglyphs, Planetary and Magickal Sigils, and certain "pure" deific images can be visualized as "doorways" through which to project consciousness or the Astral Vehicle to access subjective states of consciousness and explore specific "areas" of the astral dimension.

Suggested Reading—Tyson, D.: *Soul Flight, Astral Projection & the Magical Universe*, 2007, Llewellyn.

Astral Light: The lowest principle of Akasha; the 'substance' of the Astral Plane that responds to emotion and holds impressions of thought and feeling to form memory.

Suggested Reading—Regardie, I. and Ciceros, C. & T.: *The Tree of Life—An Illustrated Study of Magic*, 2000, Llewellyn.

Astral Matrix: The astral body is a non-physical replica of and model for the physical body that can be used as an organizing matrix perceived to be ideally healthy. Upon re-engagement with the physical body, health images can be transferred for healing and rejuvenation.

Suggested Reading—Slate, J. H. and Weschcke, C. L. *Astral Projection for Psychic Empowerment*, 2012, Llewellyn.

Astral Plane/World: The level immediately "above" the Physical and the dimension of Time—the 4th dimension—that brings *movement* to the material world. It is the astral world and the astral/emotional vehicle working through the physical/etheric complex that are fundamental to paranormal phenomena and powers—especially clairvoyance.

The astral world has its own landscape, generally replicating the physical world, but is far more extensive, reaching wherever consciousness has gone. It has its own inhabitants, including the astral bodies of physical world inhabitants forms that have never incarnated into physical bodies, temporary inhabitants created by human imagination, emotion and fantasy. It is also possible certain paranormal entities such as UFOs, Aliens, the Loch Ness and other 'monsters' that slip in and out of the physical world have their origin in the astral, and that mythical beings like dragons also exist in the lower astral close enough to the physical that they sometimes appear to physical world inhabitants.

In this New Age, we will experience the same drive that led us to explore and adapt to the far reaches of the physical world extended to these additional worlds that make up the vaster cosmos that is both physical and non-physical. The astral plane is in many ways *our new frontier,* and as we focus more and more in this added dimension we hope that we will at the same time bring peace and true prosperity and full realization of the beneficial opportunities in the physical plane that is the *foundation* for our evolutionary journey.

Astral Projection: A phenomenon in which the astral body disengages from the biological body and deliberately projected beyond the physical body's environment to consciously experience distant realities. In most situations, we are interested in using the astral to explore the non-physical universe and to influence physical actions. Still anchored in the physical body, we make use of various OBE procedures to do these things. In most cases, it is vital to set specific goals, and it is through such work that we do gain skills, train our astral "muscles," and grow in consciousness. Among Spiritualists, this is referred to as "spirit leaving the body." *See Out-of-Body experiences (OBEs).*

Suggested Reading—Slate, J. H. and Weschcke, C. L. *Astral Projection for Psychic Empowerment,* 2012, Llewellyn.

Astral Room: A space that is, or can be temporarily isolated and designated as "Do Not Disturb" while in use. In addition to the physical space, through visualization you create a temporary (that is actually large and longer lasting than you think) astral room. You should do your meditation, magickal, and other astral/psychic work in this space and always think of it as your "Astral Room." (You may prefer to call it your *temple* but that word has associations that "clutter" your specific astral work space.)

Astrology: The most scientific system for determining the value and meaning of "the moment" by measuring celestial positions of the Sun, Moon, Planets, and sometimes of fixed stars and asteroids, and the advent of comets in relation to exact birth times and locations" on Earth. The resultant pattern is the horoscope, and interpreted through meanings based on thousands of years of observation and logical associations. The time and place of birth sets the "plan" and meaning for the life of a person, event, corporate or other legal entity, while changes to the celestial positions (transits) in relation to the birth horoscope will forecast coming events.

Audgita: The silent or mental chanting of a mantra as an attention-fixing, cognitive device "silencing" disturbances.

Aura: An egg-shaped sphere of energy extending two to three feet beyond the physical body and viewed by clairvoyants in colorful layers that may be 'read' and interpreted. It includes layers outward from the physical: the Etheric, Astral, Mental, and Spiritual bodies. The aura is also known as the "magical mirror of the universe" in which our inner activities of thought and feeling are perceived in colors that can be analyzed in relation to health, ethics and spiritual development. It is also the matrix of planetary forces that shapes and sustains the physical body and the lower personality. The aura can be shaped and its surface made to reflect psychic attacks back to their origin.

> Suggested Reading—Andrews, T.: *How to See and Read the Aura*, 2002, Llewellyn.
> Slate, J. H.: *Aura Energy for Health, Healing & Balance*, 1999, Llewellyn.
> Webster, R.: *Aura Reading for Beginners, Develop Your Psychic Awareness for Health & Success*, 2002, Llewellyn.

Automatic Writing: A valuable strategy for psychic development in which a person, sometimes in trance, writes or even keyboards messages generally believed to originate with spiritual beings, or with aspects of the subconscious mind.

> Suggested Reading—Wiseman, S.: *Writing the Divine: How to Use Channeling for Soul Growth & Healing*, 2009, Llewellyn.

Base Chakra: *Muladhara*, base of spine, color red, associated planet Saturn, Sephirah Malkuth, associated Tattwa *Prithivi,* symbol of the element of Earth.

Become more than You are: A phrase coined by Carl Llewellyn Weschcke to express the concept of self-directed evolution in which we all are seen as a 'work-in-progress' toward fulfilling the potential of the Whole Person already existent as a 'matrix' of consciousness into which we are evolving. It is the goal of everyone who accepts the *opportunity* and *responsibility* of accelerated development and Self-Empowerment.

Belief System: The complex of 'feelings' that defines the way we perceive reality. Belief is also described as "Faith" that filters our perception of reality as defined by religious institutions. Also see *Feelings* and *Operating System*.

Suggested Reading—Braden, L.: *The Spontaneous Healing of Belief, Shattering the Paradigm of False Limits*, 2009, Hay House.

Big Picture: It is through awareness and understanding of the "Big Picture" that the details of the "small picture" gain meaning and can be constructively manipulated. Clairvoyance enables seeing "behind the scenes" to comprehend both big and small.

Bija (*Sanskrit* "Seed"): The root sound of a chakra intoned as a mantra to release its potential. *Bija* sounds of the first five chakras are *Lng, Vng, Rng, Yng*, and *Hng*.

Bladon, Lee: See *The Science of Spirituality*, 2007, www.esotericsciences.org.

Body of Light: Sometimes used as an alternative for the Astral Body, but more correctly as an image created ritually out of the astral light through the power of imagination and used by a magician as a vehicle for conscious perception and action.

Suggested Reading—Ashcroft-Nowicki, D., and Brennan, H.: *Magical Use of Thought-Forms: A Proven System of Mental & Spiritual Empowerment*, 2001, Llewellyn.

Slate, J. H. and Weschcke, C. L. *Astral Projection for Psychic Empowerment*, 2012, Llewellyn.

Brain Waves: The brain generates weak electrical impulses representative of its particular activities. As recorded by the electro-encephalograph (EEG), they fall into particular levels assigned Greek letters. *Beta*, at 14 to 28 cycles per second, is our normal waking state including focused attention, concentration, thinking, etc. *Alpha*, 8 to 13 cycles, is the next level down characteristic of relaxation, alert receptivity, meditation and access to the subconscious mind. It is at 8 cycles per second, the border between alpha and theta, that trance occurs. *Theta*, 4 to 7, is lower yet and occurs just before hypnopompic or after hypnagogic sleep and is characteristic of light sleep, deep meditation, dreaming, vivid imagery, and high levels of inner awareness. *Delta*, 1 to 3, is characteristic of deep dreamless sleep. 0 to 0.5 is the state of death or unconsciousness.

Brow Chakra: *Ajna*, the 'third eye' chakra. The sixth psychic center, located at the brow, color indigo, associated planet Moon, associated Sephiroth Chokmah and Binah. The "Third Eye" is the primary means for clairvoyance and other psychic faculties.

Causal Body/Vehicle: The incarnating self most identified as the "Soul."

Causal Plane/Level/World: The upper level of the Mental Plane that acts as a primary source for energies eventually manifesting through the lower levels to "incarnate" or physically manifest.

Causal Substance: For each subtle level there is specific "substance" as well as "laws." The Causal shares the third level with the Mental Plane, but the two share the characteristic of five dimensions in contrast to the familiar three of the Physical and Etheric Planes of the first and lowest level.

Ceremonial Magick: The object of ceremonies in magick is to stimulate the senses, to power-up the emotions, and to firmly conceptualize the purpose of the operation: to create a transcending experience uniting Personality with Divine Self. To this end, rituals, symbols, clothing, colors, incenses, sound, dramatic invocations and sacraments are selected in accordance with established 'correspondences' of one thing to another to transport the magician towards a mystical reality.

Chakras (*Sanskrit* "Wheel, Vortex or Whirlpool"): Psychic centers located in the aura functioning through the etheric body that exchange particular energies between the physical body and higher sources of energy associated with the planets, the Solar System, and the cosmos. They are interfaces between Mind and Body.

There are seven traditional "master" chakras and dozens of minor ones located in such places as the palms of the hands, soles of the feet, joints of arms and legs, and just about any place traditionally adorned with jewelry. While we are listing some correspondences to planets, colors and the Kabbalistic sephiroth, there is considerable debate about these and the correlations cannot be specific because the chakras and the sephiroth involve two different systems. Likewise, although not listed, there are differences between both these systems and those of Oriental martial arts and healing systems.

The following chart is a simplification of the primary chakra system.

No.	Common Name	Sanskrit Name	Location [2]	Color [1]	Spokes or Petals	Associated Gland [6]
1	Base	*Muladhara*	Base of Spine[5]	Red	4	Ovaries, Testicles
2	Sacral	*Svadhisthana*	Over Spleen	Orange	6	Pancreas
3	Solar Plexus	*Manipura*	Over Navel	Yellow	10	Adrenals
4	Heart	*Anahata*	Over Heart	Green	12	Thymus
5	Throat	*Vishuddha*	Throat	Blue	16	Thyroid

| 6 | Brow | *Ajna* | Brow | Indigo | 96 [3] | Pituitary |
| 7 | Crown | *Sahasrara* | Top of Head | Violet | 960 + 12 [4] | Pineal |

[1] These are the most commonly assigned colors, but authorities differ.

[2] These are the most commonly assigned locations, but authorities differ. Instead of the Solar Plexus, Theosophists identify it with the Spleen, others with the navel.

[3] Commonly, this is given as two, but it is really two "wings" of 48 each.

[4] Most commonly, it is identified as a thousand petaled lotus. The crown chakra has 960 spokes plus another 12 in its center which is gleaming white with gold at its core.

[5] Between anus and perineum.

[6] Again, there are disagreements among authorities. Remember that there is no direct physical connection between the etheric chakras and the physical body.

Source: Slate, J. and Weschcke, C.: *Llewellyn Complete Book of Psychic Empowerment: Tools & Techniques, 2011, Llewellyn.*

Suggested Reading—Judith: *Wheels of Life, A User's Guide to the Chakra System* Mumford—*Chakra & Kundalini Workbook: Psycho-spiritual Techniques for Health, Rejuvenation, Psychic Powers & Spiritual Rejuvenation*

Channeling: Receiving information from a discarnate entity or higher spiritual being. It may also refer to communication with an aspect of one's own subconsciousness. It is similar to, but not necessarily identical, spirit communication of mediumship. In both, however, one person serves as bridge between a spirit or non-physical intelligence and people of ordinary consciousness. In spirit communication, the medium is often unaware of the communication; in channeling, the channeler is often aware and sometimes a participant.

Channeling the Sub-Conscious: Similar to "channeling" and "mediumship" in technique, our intention is to open the Conscious Mind to the Sub-Conscious and experience the unity of consciousness. As with the ocean everywhere on planet earth with its layers, currents, variations in temperature, etc., we will often contend with barriers preventing the free flow of information from one level to another.

Through mental disciplines we must do the same thing done with wireless communications technology: establish a channel of our own that is "interference free." We calm the mind through relaxation and meditation, breath control, ritual and routine. We isolate our channel from the noise of others and direct it toward known sources. In studying both channeling and mediumship we benefit from the cumulative experience of many thousands of practitioners recorded in studies, journals, folk lore, and expositions of theory, practice, and application. With either approach we must develop means of conscious control.

No matter which approach we adopt, it is what the practitioner does that 'powers up' the actual process with defined intention to establish the *channel* and then to clear if of all interference. The 'channel' may be one of the familiar divinatory tools, or visualized tools only using the mentally created channel. It is the practitioner's intention that matters. The conscious mind can create the channel as an act of creative imagination in which a gate, door, natural stream, road of light, tunnel, etc., can serve as an "information highway," or it can just feel the intention itself, or your own journal will itself serve as a channel (as in dream processing and in automatic writing). Find what has the strongest appeal to you, one that satisfies your sense of drama or propriety.

Clearing the channel of interference is commonly accomplished by keeping the whole operation secret, or revealed only to a group of supporters so that no expression of amusement, criticism, contrary images, or doubts interferes with your own sense of correctness. The choice of either direct experience or of a divinatory or communication tool will, to some degree, shape the remaining elements of composition, transmittal, receiving and interpretation.

Circle: A temporary boundary within which a séance or magical operation may take place. The theory is that it becomes a kind of psychic container for the energies used in the operation and a barrier to unwanted energies from outside. Spiritualist mediums work in a circle with participants—mostly regulars—to energize contact spirits of the deceased.

Clairvoyance: Clairvoyance is the *direct perception of realities hidden* to normal perception by the limitations of physical senses. It is possibly the most intricate and advanced form of ESP, demonstrating the wondrous capacity of the human mind to expand its own field of awareness to encompass limitless realities Clairvoyance isn't just about "secret" alternative knowledge, but is a means to *expanded knowledge through expanded awareness.* To understand this requires an understanding that you, and every person, are more than you think you are and psychic development and empowerment is about *becoming more than you are.* It's about expanding your "objective consciousness" in union with the subjective.

We have to learn the art and practice of clairvoyance just as we do any other human skill, and there's a science to that. We believe its development should be encouraged as a matter of growth and movement into wholeness. We believe psychic empowerment should be your goal because you should be an empowered person. There will be many practical benefits to your developed clairvoyance as well—extending your inter-dimensional perceptions of reality means that you see more and are better able to judge the meaning and value of your inter-actions with the complex world in which you live. It gives you a greater foundation for the decisions you must make in life. You will gain deeper insights into your own physical and emotional reactions to both external events and internal issues.

"Clear Seeing:" Clairvoyance simply means "clear seeing," the implication being the particular *psychic vision* involved reveals the hidden nature of an object, event, or person.

When we look at any object with our physical eyes we are limited to its three ordinary physical dimensions. We are not only unaware of the sub-atomic aspects functioning in the object, but many of us are not truly observant of the finer details of color, shape, odor, taste, and feel, and of **the *resident consciousness* fundamental to the object itself.** There is consciousness even in a brick, and more so in a blade of grass, a swimming fish, etc. And, where there is consciousness, there is *life. The universe is alive at all levels and in every dimension.*

On the physical level, we perceive with our physical senses. As we focus consciousness at higher levels, we don't perceive with "sense organs" but through awareness of the substance and changing vibrations emitted from the object of our attention. The higher we ascend in awareness, the greater our vision. At the astral level, we are aware of a fourth dimension, and at the mental level we perceive five dimensions.

Collective Unconscious: A kind of group mind inherited from all our ancestors and includes all the memories and knowledge acquired by humans. It is believed to exist on the higher astral and lower mental planes and to be accessible by the super consciousness through the personal subconscious mind in deep trance states induced through hypnosis, self-hypnosis, meditation and guided meditation. The ability to call up infinite information and integrate it into your present life needs is of enormous benefit—similar to but beyond the capacity of any present-day Internet Search Engine.

The contents of the collective unconscious progress from individual memories to universal memories as the person grows in spiritual development and integration of the whole being. There is some suggestion that this progression also moves from individual memories through various groups or small collectives—family, tribe, race, and nation—so the character of each level up to union with consciousness with all humanity. This would seem to account for some of the variations of the universal archetypes each person encounters in life. Also see *Akashic Records*

Suggested Reading—Dale, C.: *The Subtle Body: An Encyclopedia of Your Energetic Anatomy*, 2009, Sounds True, Inc.

Complementary (Flashing) **Colors:** Each primary color has an opposite on the color wheel, and when vision is focused on the one color, it will start to flash the opposite color, its complementary color. As used in this book, the complementary colors are:

Bright Yellow	Bright Purple
Bright Purple	Bright Yellow
Bright Blue	Bright Orange
Bright Orange	Bright Blue
Bright Red	Bright Green
Bright Green	Bright Red
Bright Indigo	Bright Yellow/Orange
Bright Yellow/Orange	Bright Indigo
Metallic Silver	Black
Black	White, or Silver
White	Black

Conscious Awareness: We have many examples and levels of *unconscious awareness* (many of them psychic in nature), and we are increasingly experiencing an expansion in conscious awareness of the depth and breadth of the world around us, and discovering now available techniques to extend awareness of our own depth of being to that of the Greater Cosmos in which we live and have our being resulting from an influx of new energies and matrices that is the *New Age*.

Conscious Mind: This is the 'middle' consciousness, the 'ordinary' consciousness, the 'objective' consciousness with which we exercise control and direction over our 'awake' lives. With your Conscious Mind you can take charge of the great resource of the Sub-Conscious Mind. Information is constantly coming in, and much of it is automatically diverted to the Sub-Conscious Mind. The Sub-Conscious Mind is more that a passive collection of memories, it is also your personal connection to the Universal Consciousness within which are all the potentials you will ever need.

All that is the Conscious-Mind—with its magnificent potentials for rational thinking, for creative development, for abstract analysis, for organization, for the use of imagination, for planning, and all those skills that make it possible for the human being to manage the resources of the natural world—rise out of the Sub-Conscious Mind. The job of the Conscious Mind is to manage the Sub-Consciousness and develop its innate powers into skills that we can then consciously deploy with awareness and intention to work with the Great Plan of evolving life. It is to make Conscious the Unconscious through careful management of its resources.

When you take deliberate conscious charge of the subconscious, your life takes on a new dimension of meaning and power. Rather than merely reactive, your probe of the subconscious is an "inward leap of power" that clarifies the nature of your existence and reaffirms your destiny. It's a leap of progress that not only accelerates your growth, but guides you toward greater happiness and fulfillment as well.

As we became more aware of ourselves as individuals and operated more in the Conscious Mind, developing personal memory, rationality and new ways of thinking, we perceived ourselves *in relationship to the natural world* rather than as <u>part</u> of it. We learned to store knowledge in our memory rather than having subjective 'feeling' access to it. Rather than relating internally to the rhythms of Sun, Moon, and Planets, we saw them externally and developed sciences of astronomy, astrology, and agriculture. And we became aware of linear time.

Nature can show the ways to knowledge and understanding of her secret powers when you learn to see and listen. The Sun, the Moon, and the Planets, too, have powers to share with Man in his wholeness. As Manager, it is the job of the Conscious Mind to know, understand, and direct all these resources. It's the most exciting, most gratifying, most rewarding and grandest job you will ever have, and it's one that is yours forever! You can't be fired, nor can you abdicate. It's your forever job.

Consciousness: Everything that is, out of which Energy and Matter emerge and Life evolves. Consciousness is the beginning of all things and part of the trinity of Consciousness, Energy and Matter. We can't really define consciousness because we are nothing but consciousness and consciousness cannot really define itself. "I AM THAT I AM."

Consciousness is not a 'thing' nor is it a function of a 'thing' called the brain. Killing the brain doesn't kill consciousness but it limits its expression in the familiar physical world. Consciousness is expressed through the brain, but it exists outside the brain

There are three levels of consciousness:

I for Instinct, a function of the lower subconscious

I for Intelligence, a function of the ordinary consciousness

I for Intuition, a function of the super-consciousness

The ancients were far more sophisticated in their understanding of "consciousness" than we give them credit for. Moderns tend to judge everything from the background of technology and material sciences, believing that the lack of advanced scientific instrumentation means a lack of understanding about "how things really work."

In more than one sense, today's science is still catching up with the "Ancient Wisdom" which expressed understanding of the universe through myth and symbol. The single greatest difference is that the "old" wisdom was the *property* of the few and today we extend our knowledge to nearly any and every one. Modern education seeks to give everyone a basic knowledge of physical science, although there is a serious gap when it comes to "spiritual science."

One great difficulty arises because spirituality is thought to be the province of religion, and the institutions of religion limit themselves and their adherents to rigid theological interpretations of scriptures written down long ago within specific cultural environments vastly different than today. The truth is that spirituality is not religion but involves study of the higher levels of the psyche and an understanding of their role in the growth of the Whole Person and their beneficial applications to personal life and cosmic relationship.

Control: The spirit who acts as a kind of manager through which other spirits communicate to or through the medium during a séance.

Correspondences: The Kabbalah, using the symbolic organizational system of the Tree of Life and numerological associations provided through the Hebrew language, Astrology, and Natural Science, identifies a wide range of *correspondences* between subjects, planets, herbs, plants, metals, crystals, colors, animals, angels, deities, etc., that allow substitutions of one thing for another, or that augment understanding about one thing by knowledge of another of corresponding value.

Suggested Reading—Whitcomb, B.: *The Magician's Companion*, 2002, Llewellyn. Hulse, D.: *Western Mysteries*, 2002, Llewellyn.

Cosmic Consciousness: A phrase coined by Richard Bucke to describe his own experience of unity with the universal consciousness of the cosmos. Bucke believed this to be the goal of human evolution.

Suggested Reading—Bucke, R.: *Cosmic Consciousness*, 2007, Penguin.

Cosmic Involution: The downward process from Creation to the completion of "Reality." See Figure #1.

Cosmic Wide Web (CWW): Modeled after the World Wide Web (WWW) of the Internet, the CWW recognizes existence of the Akashic Records imagined as "infinite-sized and capable data banks and servers, accurately accessed through a speed-of-light fast astral search engine using an imaginary keyboard and large monitor to call up and see those records we desire." It is developed clairvoyance as a controlled combination of extended awareness and focused attention on a specific thing and specified connections so that your resulting knowledge is meaningful and practical. It takes you beyond the *free-for-all* electronic dimensions of the World Wide Web into the defined and *narrowly-specific* but multi-dimensional "**Cosmic Wide Web.**"

Cosmos: The Great Reality inclusive of all that is. Whether it is inclusive or exclusive of the Creator is beyond our capacity to know.

Crowd Psychosis: Crowd Psychosis is an unconscious group response to powerful symbols (and music, words, rituals) that often excite strong emotional reactions that lack the control of the conscious mind and may lead to totally irrational, "out of (self-) control" behavior often manipulated with that intent by religious and political leaders. Such reactions often lead to riots, mass hysteria, violence, criminal anti-social acts, and even to war as ably described back in Charles Mackay's 1841 classic "Extraordinary Mass Delusion and the Madness of the Crowd."

The "cure" starts with mental dominance of emotional reaction. Emotional energy is a powerful magical force that can be controlled and directed for positive benefit through self-awareness, self-discipline, and magical direction through ritual and meditation (or prayer).

Crown Chakra, also called Sahasrara (which see): The chakra located at the crown above the head, color violet, associated planet none, associated Sephirah Kether.

Crystal Ball: *A very effective instrument for developing the clairvoyance.* A round ball of quartz crystal or glass used as focal point in skrying. Gazing at the ball, one enters into a trance-like state where dream-like scenes and symbols are seen and interpreted. A similar aid is the Magic Mirror. **Crystal Gazing** typically uses a crystal ball to engage and liberate the mind's psychic powers while promoting a state of general self-empowerment. Crystal gazing opens channels between conscious and subconscious minds and permits the free expression of multiple inner faculties.

Suggested Reading—Andrews, T: *Crystal Balls & Crystal Bowls*, 2002, Llewellyn.
Cunningham, S.: *Divination for Beginners*, 2003, Llewellyn.
Slate, J. H. and Weschcke, C. L.: *Psychic Empowerment: Tools & Techniques*, 2011, Llewellyn.

Demystifying the Paranormal: A goal of our research is to take the mystery out of the paranormal without loss of respect for the early pioneers and for the varieties of the subjects involved. Even where "scientific" understanding is still lacking, experiential evidence has its place.

The evolving body of evidence for psychic phenomena demands a careful re-examination of our thinking and a restructuring of traditional views about life and experience. That the mind is capable of experiencing realities beyond the known limits of sensory perception challenges conventional systems and raises new questions about the nature of reality and human existence itself.

Our challenge is to demystify the paranormal to explain its nature and unleash its empowering potentials. The psychic experience, whether voluntary or involuntary, is always empowerment driven. Discovering its capacity for empowerment requires attention to the psychic event and understanding its significance.

Desire: "Desire" is an alternate name for the Astral Plane (or Level) and likewise for the Astral (or Emotional) Body or Vehicle. But "Desire" is also one of the most fundamental of human emotions and is the qualifying adjective associated with such basis drives as Sex, Food, Money, Security, Comfort, Romance, etc. While older esoteric teachers taught that desire should be repressed (especially in connection with sex), such repression is both unhealthy and undesirable in terms of the Wholeness of the human person. Desire is neither good nor bad, but it is motivation and liberates and directs the energy of Life. Self Control and "Balance" keep desire in perspective.

Development: While many people are born with some degree of clairvoyant or other psychic talent, all innate talents need development just as an athlete needs to develop particular muscles and styles of movement. Even a "born" artist or musician must develop talent into trained skills and gain knowledge, understanding, and become ethically sensitive to their application. Clairvoyance is no different. Psychic development is an expansion of consciousness and an extension of awareness, and is the *next step* in the evolutionary ladder for individual and for all humanity.

Developmental Circle or Class: Mostly for people desiring to develop or enhance their mediumistic and psychic abilities. Usually the teacher is a medium.

Direct Voice: When a medium allows a spirit to directly speak through her/him, it appears to be the voice of the deceased. Sometimes during a Spiritualist Séance, a voice will be heard that does not directly emanate from a participant's larynx, but rather from an "artificial" larynx formed out of ectoplasm ejected from a medium's body. Often, the voice is very faint, and is magnified by a very lightweight aluminum "trumpet" that levitates and floats around the séance room.

Divination: Prophesy and information by psychic methodologies.

- By reading naturally produced signs ranging from the shape of clouds to the positions of planets (astrology).

- By reading artificially produced signs ranging from tea leaves to the throwing of dice or dominoes.
- By reading symbols such as the Tarot cards or the I Ching hexagrams.
- By reading visions as seen in Dreams or in Trance.

In each situation, something experienced is interpreted usually by means of long-established rules justified by many years of observation across many cultures. In most cases, these interpretations are supplemented by psychic impressions or intuition naturally arising in either conscious or sub-conscious trance states.

Divination should not be undertaken for amusement but because of true need for an answer or experience. Ask the question when it becomes so *imperative* that it will reverberate in your mind and cause an equal reverberation in the cosmos leading to the answer given in the form of a traditional set of rules to be interpreted. Make the question concise and clearly worded with no ambiguity and confined to earthy, practical matters, unconcerned with issues of morality or judgment. The simpler the question, the more precise the answer; the more serious the question, the more accurate the answer. The best question can be simply answered with a "yes" or a "no."

How Divination Works. In some sense, avoiding technical details, the future already exists as trends; but it is also important to know that your future is *not* fixed. Changes in your current situation can make changes in your future situation. At the same time, in terms of the bigger universe of which each of is a minute part, small changes rarely impact on the future.

In *your* future there are points of leverage that, if discovered and manipulated with willed intention, can make a difference. *But, that's magic, another subject altogether.*

However, most readings are not concerned with changing the future but with answering questions about the present and near future. Read the following few paragraphs carefully:

Each person is surrounded by a field of energy called the "aura." Your own aura permeates your entire body and represents your feeling, your mind, and your spirit. It's all about you.

Every cell in your body contains all the information about you—not only the present but the past and the probable future. Not only that, but every cell also contains a hologram of the universe; that is, all knowledge is resident within each one of us, and it is ours to retrieve if we know how.

Your aura further permeates your immediate surroundings—out to about three feet—and especially things you touch. Some substances more easily absorb the auric influence than others, and wet tea leaves are especially sensitive to this influence, serving as an ideal medium for *our reading. The minute particles, actually right down to the <u>sub-atom-</u><u>ic level</u>, of the tea leaves or other materials being used are responsive to your energy field—including the questions and concerns you have at the moment of the reading. The more often you practice this psychic talent, the more able will your aura project the image-forming energy to the sensitive media.*

It is important to realize that all divinatory systems connect the Conscious Mind to the Sub-Conscious and thence to the Universal Consciousness. Successful divination and, hence, our personal "psychic empowerment" depends on our abilities to consciously *channel* our questions to these *lower* realms and to take the answers into our *awakened consciousness* for their analysis and application.

Divination, in contrast to "fortune telling" is not a *passive* mere acceptance of answers from the tea leaves or the cards or other objects that are converted into "tools," but uses those tools in *inter-active* communication between the Unconscious and the Conscious Mind. The "language" of that communication—ultimately—is symbolism but the symbols themselves are not static but instead constantly evolve in response to "the times" and your personal experiences.

The challenge for the diviner is to use symbols as a frame or vehicle in asking questions, and then to newly interpret those symbols conveying the answers.

Suggested Reading—Cunningham, S.: *Divination for Beginners*, 2003, Llewellyn.

Slate, J. H. and Weschcke, C. L.: *Psychic Empowerment: Tools & Techniques*, 2011, Llewellyn.

Divine Plan: Most esoterics believe that there is a Divine Plan, or Great Plan, guiding the evolution of Humanity, and indeed of all life, all consciousness, and the Universe itself. *Is the Plan knowable by mere mortals?* Perhaps not, but some believe there are "Masters," "Inner Plane Adepts," or other "Great Ones" who do, at least partially, know it, and who themselves work under its guidance at high spiritual levels.

Do these Masters ever appear on Earth? In physical form? Some say yes. And even that they have incarnated in such men as the Buddha, Christ, and others in order to bring about certain transitions in Humanity, in Consciousness, perhaps even in the genetic structure of coming generations.

Can more be said? Is there really an Inner Plane Hierarchy guiding the affairs of men? An "inner government?" The answer given, at least generally, is that we have to work things out for ourselves. That's how we grow, and that is the purpose of our existence. Each of us must become self-dependent and self-responsible. We may be the children of God, or of the Goddess, but children must grow up and act as adults.

Dowsing: *Actually, one of the most important forms of clairvoyance, and of training the physical, etheric and astral faculties.* Psychic empathy with the natural world enables the practitioner to locate specific resources. The use of a forked stick or bent steel clothes hanger or other metallic imitation of the forked stick in order to sense the presence of water or other resource or lost object. The instrument moves in the dowser's hands when he walks over the searched for substance believed to radiate a perceptive energy. Some dowsers work with a pendulum and a large-scale map and obtain equally valid results. The practice of dowsing provides valuable development of psychic sensitivities and subconscious awareness and communication, the essence of clairvoyance itself.

Many operators using pendulums and dowsing rods use "specimen samples" held in one hand or incorporated into compartments on the instrument. The sample is of the material objective to the outer physical dowsing work—water, oil, gold, nickel, etc.—and functions as a *focus* for the inner psychic, part of the operation. Other operators simply keep the objective in mind during the mechanical process with either pendulum or dowsing rod.

Dowsing, combined with pendulum working, has become a useful technique in forensic work and in health diagnosis. See also "Pendulum."

Suggested Reading—Slate, J. H. and Weschcke, C. L.: *Psychic Empowerment: Tools & Techniques,* 2011, Llewellyn.

Webster, R.: *Dowsing for Beginners,* 1996, Llewellyn.

Dream Clairvoyance: The clairvoyant dream will often provide clues concerning its significance. The immediate awakening upon conclusion of the dream is one such clue, as are vivid physical sensations and the often urgent nature of the dream. The clairvoyant dream can generate a strong motivational state to either act upon the dream or to investigate its psychic significance.

Dream Interpretation: While often associated with the use of a "dream dictionary," it really involves methods of allowing the dream "to speak" to the dreamer. An important factor in Self-Empowerment is the more complete utilization of lines of communication between levels of consciousness. While commercial "dream dictionaries" may have limited application, one that you compile yourself may be immensely helpful. Through the regular use of a Dream Journal, you become familiar with your own symbol meanings and can explore each further for more insight. When you actually pay attention to your dreams, they pay attention to you and can deliver information and guidance of immediate application.

Suggested Reading—Gongloff, R.: *Dream Exploration,* 2006, Llewellyn.

Gonzalez-Wippler, M.: *Dreams and What They Mean to You,* 2002, Llewellyn.

Dreaming True: Programmed dreaming where a question or an intention is formulated before sleep, and left to the subconscious mind to respond with an answer or an action. It can also be effectively programmed with self-hypnosis.

Earth (Elemental)—see also Prithivi: The primal element that is the foundation and starting point for all physical beginnings. In Tantra, Earth is the Goddess and many Goddesses, and through Love and Worship of Goddesses we enter into the forms and energies that they embody and symbolize. Worship is another name for a unique meditative invocation entering into "oneness" with the nature of her form. As the Earth Goddess, she is Shakti, companion of Shiva the Sky God. Feminine and Masculine, Yin and Yang, Negative and Positive, Magnetic and Electric—all that exists comes from their union—a union of equals in which opposites are always in constant blending. Earth is alive—and that includes the entire electro-magnetic system that reaches out from the planet's core to the Moon and beyond. The Solar System is alive, and with it vast fields of energy connect from all planets and other solar bodies to Moon and Earth, and the inhabitants of Earth. We are part of the Whole, and the Whole is within us.

Ectoplasm: An "exteriorized substance" unique to Spiritualist terminology, although sometimes also associated with religious, magical and yogic practitioners under other names. It is described as a "cloudy substance stream(ing) out of mediums … usually from the mouth or nose, and frequently from the solar plexus, but can emanate from any orifice." (Owens, E.: *How to Communicate with Spirits,* 2001, Llewellyn.)

Ectoplasm is used by a spirit to give itself visibility. It is also used to give shape and visible appearance to a thought form in various magical and religious practices.

Elementals:

1. Non-human nature spirits associated with the state, quality, and character of the five elements or Tattwas.

    Air (gaseous; mediating, embracing and pervasive; intellect): Sylphs

    Earth (solid; stable and enduring; sensation): Gnomes

    Fire (energy; active, energizing and transforming; will): Salamanders

    Spirit, Ether (underlying; universal and originating; awareness):

    Water (fluid; receptive and responsive; feeling): Undines

2. A thought form charged with energy and intention by a magician to carry out a particular operation, such as a household guardian.

3. Beings that carry the elemental forces of this world and possibly for the whole Universe.

4. Elemental Spirits, or Forces, that are the Guardians of the Four Directions of the Magickal Circle, thus transforming the Circle into a miniature of the Universe.

5. Beings that function as agents-in-charge of the various manifestations of each of the "Kingdoms" of Animals, Plants, and Minerals.

Emerald Tablet: A famous esoteric aphorism revealing the transmutation of primordial matter into the world of forms. It purportedly was written by the mythical figure, *Hermes Trismegistos* (Thrice Greatest Hermes) and transcribed onto a fabulous emerald secreted within the Great Pyramid.

> *Truly, without Deceit, certainly and absolutely—*
>
> *That which is Below corresponds to that which is Above, and that which is Above corresponds to that which is Below, in the accomplishment of the Miracle of One Thing. And just as all things have come from One, through the Mediation of One, so all things follow from this One Thing in the same way.*
>
> *Its Father is the Sun. Its Mother is the Moon. The Wind has carried it in his Belly. Its Nourishment is the Earth. It is the Father of every completed Thing in the whole World. Its Strength is intact if it is turned towards the Earth. Separate the Earth by Fire: the fine from the gross, gently, and with great skill.*
>
> *It rises from Earth to Heaven, and then it descends again to the Earth, and receives Power from Above and from Below. Thus you will have the Glory of the whole World. All Obscurity will be clear to you. This is the strong Power of all Power because it overcomes everything fine and penetrates everything solid.*
>
> *In this way was the World created. From this there will be amazing Applications, because this is the Pattern. Therefore am I called Thrice Greatest Hermes, having the three parts of the Wisdom of the whole World.*
>
> *Herein have I completely explained the Operation of the Sun.*

There are many alternative translations mostly by Western alchemists appearing in Europe from 650 AD on. It was also the subject of a series of dreams and visions by C. G. Jung as recorded in his "Seven Sermons to the Dead" published in 1916. Aldous Huxley in his "Perennial Philosophy" referred to its message that there exists an archetypal level of mind that determines physical reality that we can access through direct knowledge of the Divine core in every person.

Emotion: "E-Motion, EM or Energy-in-Motion." Emotion is a dynamic and powerful response to something perceived that connects to universal human experience and archetypes. Emotion is the energy 'powering' most intentional psychic and magical operations, the energy responsible for many types of psychic phenomena, possibly including hauntings, poltergeists, rapping, etc., where there is potential for the emotion to have been 'recorded' in the woodwork of the building. Emotion is found in Netzach as part of Ruach, the Conscious Self. The substance (matter) of the astral plane, of its energies and "operating system" is Emotion.

Emotional (Astral) Body/Vehicle: An alternate name for Astral Body (which see) or vehicle, used by many modern esoteric writers like Henry T. Laurency and Lee Bladon because they consider the substance of the astral (emotional) plane or world to be best defined as *emotional* as is the consciousness of that body and level. The strength and the challenges are emotional.

   The emotional body is the primary vehicle for consciousness between incarnations, first dissolving at the three lowest sub-planes to cut contact with the physical world. The three highest sub-planes provide the substance fulfilling personal and religious fantasies without veracity from the Mental and Causal levels.

   Suggested Reading—Laurency, Henry T.: *The Philosophers Stone*, 1985, np.

Emotional (Astral) Plane/World: An alternate name for Astral Plane (which see) or World, because its nature and substance seems best defined as *emotional*, i.e. "matter in motion" and responsive to human feelings and emotions.

Emotional Matter: The substance (matter) of the astral plane, of its energies and "operating system" is defined as E-Motion. Whenever and however we experience feeling, love, desire, affection, ambition, gratitude, etc., our astral body and the astral world are the field of action. Emotion is the energy 'powering' most intentional psychic and magical operations, and the energy responsible for many types of psychic phenomena, possibly including hauntings, poltergeists, rapping, etc.

Emotional and Psychic Garbage: Throughout this life time (and continuing from previous lives) we accumulate unresolved fears, reactions, hates, loves, desires, etc., along with unconscious psychic attachments. Mostly these reside in your subconscious mind, but they still influence your thinking and feeling, and color your physical and astral perceptions. Through the Tattvic Connection Meditation and Visualization Programs we purify ourselves of the "garbage" by balancing the personal against the cosmic tattvas. This provides for clarity and accuracy of clairvoyant visions, and relieves us of confusion and frustration from meaningless retained memories.

Empowering Imagery: Empowering imagery is second only to self-dialogue as an empowerment essential in activating the therapeutic powers of the subconscious. Once you've formulated your goals in positive terms, relevant imagery gives them the substance required for full embracement by the subconscious.

Goal-related imagery can be seen as a present manifestation of a future reality. For instance, if your goal is rejuvenation, imagery of your body at its youthful prime actually activates the subconscious processes related to rejuvenation. By visualizing yourself at your youthful prime while affirming, "I am now empowered with the energies of youth and vitality," you can take charge of the aging process and not only slow aging, you can actually reverse its effects. Living younger, healthier, and happier becomes your destiny.

Empowering Symbolism: The use of symbols related to your stated goals can efficiently activate at a moment's notice the subconscious faculties related to even highly complex goals. For instance, if your goal is financial success, simply visualizing a gold coin can increase your motivation and facilitate optimal decision making related to your financial success. Should you decide to do so, you can take that effect a step further by carrying on your person a gold coin and periodically stroking it.

Ether: Identical with Tantric *Akasha* and the fifth element in Western Magic, Spirit which is believed to originate the other four: Earth, Water, Fire and Air. Also called Astral Light, Ch'i, Odic Force, Orgone, Prana, Vril, the Force. It can be concentrated and directed by will, and intensified by breath.

Etheric Aura: The Etheric Aura is also called the "Health Aura" because it reflects the physical body's energy complex, and provides the perceiver with the means to determine the health status and even—for an experienced reader with medical training—a means for diagnosis and perception of progress or lack of progress in treatment of diseases. For any medical practitioner, the ability to see *inside* the health factors revealed by the aura is of immense value and especially relevant in the case of energy work such as acupuncture, Reiki, chakra balancing, Rolfing, massage, etc. where seeing the immediate effect of the therapy could be extremely helpful.

Etheric Double: The second, or energy body that is closest to the physical body. As with all the subtle bodies, it has two layers:

The first, sometimes called the "Etheric Double," is fully coincident with the physical body in health and extends about an inch beyond physical skin. It is the psycho-physical circuitry of the human body (the chakras, nadis, and meridians) through which the life-force flows under direction of the astral matrix. To clairvoyant vision, it is the health aura and appears as very fine needles of radiation—standing straight up in health and lying down in illness.

The second layer, along with the astral and mental bodies, forms the egg-shaped aura surrounding the human body. It is an interface between the individual and dynamic planetary energies and cosmic forces that sustain life.

Etheric/Physical Matter exists in seven orders of density:

Atomic	]	
Sub-Atomic	]	
Super-Etheric	]	Etheric Double
Etheric	]	
Gaseous	]	
Liquid	]	Physical Body
Solid	]	

Particles of these densities compose the physical body, but it is itself divided in the "dense" physical body and the Etheric Body (or "Double.)"

Etheric Plane: The Energy Plane between the Physical and Astral planes. Its energies are in constant movement, like tides and currents, ruled by the Moon, Sun, and Planets and moving in cycles. In theory and practice, the etheric is considered to be the upper "layers" of the physical plane and consists of substance and energy not perceptible to the "hard" physical senses. However, its substance and energy permeates the physical plane and the physical body to provide the life force—mostly "regulated" by the Moon and Planets—that enlivens all physical life.

Etheric Projection: A portion of the etheric body, sometimes along with other etheric material for added substance, can be formed as a vehicle for the operator's consciousness and projected to other physical locations in order to perceive physical information about physical events. It is also possible to use the etheric body to affect physical events, as in healing. Being of near physical substance and energy, it is sensitive to certain physical materials, like iron and silver. It can be injured, and such injuries will repercuss back to the physical body. The etheric body can also be shaped to resemble other entities, and is a factor both in the lore of were-wolves and were-leopards.

Etheric Substance: Etheric Substance is composed of the three higher molecular kinds of physical matter and is the substance of the Etheric Double or Energy aspect of the physical/etheric body.

Etheric Template: In the incarnation process, the "information" needed for the whole physical body and associated subtle bodies is brought down from the Causal level, through the Mental and Astral levels to form an actual "template" at the Etheric level to guide the formation of the embryo and its birth in relation to the pre-determined birth horoscope. It is this Template that provides the blueprint for the physical life.

Evolution: Unlike the Darwinian concept focused primarily on the physical form, esotericism extends that concept of evolutionary change to every aspect of life and consciousness including the Soul, and sees a constant movement of growth and development throughout the Cosmos, both visible and invisible. Evolution is not a thing of the past but continues, both in physical response to the environment but also in fulfillment of a primal program set forth at the "Beginning."

For the human being, the evolutionary process is primarily in the fulfillment of the potentials of the Personal Consciousness, in particular in the fulfillment of the Whole Person and the growth and development of the Super-Conscious Mind. Many in the esoteric community believe that the beginning of the New Age in the 1960's coincident with the influx of Aquarian Age energies brought an expansion and actual change in consciousness that is having an increasing effect on personal and social development.

Dennis Bushnell, NASA's chief research scientist at their Langley Center has written: "Humans are now responsible for the evolution of nearly everything, including themselves. . . . The ultimate impacts of all this upon human society will be massive and could 'tip' in several directions" (speech at World Futurist Society's Annual Conference July 8, 2010).

In the personal area, this is having an immediate effect in the development of innate unconscious psychic powers into conscious psychic skills. In the social area it could translate into world government and global economy, law, and universal human rights.

Suggested Reading—Hodson, F.: *The Kingdom of the Gods,* 1953, Theosophical Pub. House, Madras India.

Expectancy Effect: The effect of expectation on the future can facilitate such fulfillment at the personal level.

ExtraSensory Perception (ESP): Perception not limited by the physical senses. The "bridge" between Consciousness and Perception is *Awareness*. We perceive things specifically, but our awareness extends beyond the thing itself, whether it's physical or non-physical. Around the "thing," there is a field of energy that is not defined by its simple borders but may fluctuate as the thing itself is subjected to contacts with other energy fields.

Clairvoyance can dramatically expand our world of awareness and perception of spatially distant realities, uncover critical sources of new knowledge and power. Pre-cognition can provide advanced awareness allowing us to prepare for future events and, sometimes, to influence or prevent them altogether. While some future events seem to be unalterable destinies, others may be probabilities subject to our inter-vention. Through precognition we are empowered to eliminate negative probabili-ties while accentuating the positive. Given precognitive knowledge, we can generate a powerful expectancy of success that literally transforms probabilities into realities. We *can* literally create the future of our choice.

Dr. Joe H. Slate, working at Athens (Alabama) State University, described an emerging body of evidence that ESP, rather than an unexplained extension of sensory perception, is a fine-tuned manifestation of the non-biological or spiritual nature of our being, and includes interactions with spirit realm.

Extended Awareness: Clairvoyance is essentially a function of extended awareness and *focused* attention. Without focus, your psychically open and extended aware-ness could result in total sensory bombardment like being in the middle of a rock concert with multiple flashing lights and massive discordant music while under the influence of hallucinatory drugs. You could be permanently damaged by such over-stimulation. Focus is a necessary function for personal health and well-being. Such focus is dependent on self-discipline.

Eye Blink Procedure: A procedure that incorporates eye blinks to induce both remote viewing and astral projection.

Suggested Reading—Slate, J. H.: *Beyond Reincarnation*, 2005, Llewellyn.

Slate, J. H. and Weschcke, C. L.: *Doors to Past Lives & Future Lives*, 2011, Llewellyn.

Fascination devices: Crystal balls (often made of glass), crystals, cut glass, mirrors, magick mirrors (black glass), swinging pendants, crystal bowls, painted eyes, icons and images painted in flashing colors (complimentary colors placed together), spinning disks, and other devices that focus the attention but tire the vision. Some-times a small focal object is placed above the eye level forcing one to soon close the eyes. Combined with either a hetero or an internal dialogue, their use can be very effective in hypnotic induction.

Suggested Reading—Andrews, T.: *Crystal Balls & Crystal Bowls*, 2002, Llewellyn.

Cunningham, S.: *Divination for Beginners*, 2003, Llewellyn.

Field: "The First Thing" is the field of manifestation. It is Consciousness from which first Energy and then Matter arose as Energy/Matter packets manifesting as Waves or Particles. The Field is the Source for all that follows and can be accessed through deliberate thought and responds to emotion expressed with intention. Through the Field we can change 'reality,' hence it is the field of magic, phenomena, and of miraculous things that matter.

Suggested Reading—McTaggart, L.: *The Field, the Quest for the Secret Force of the Universe*, 2008, Harper.

McTaggart, L.: *The Intention Experiment*, 2008, Free Press.

Field of Awareness: A definable field of various energies that surround any physical object or person, and even around the location of an event. Such a field contains "information" that may provide an "address" attracting clairvoyant search and data that may be read by the clairvoyant either when present or sometimes from a distance. This field also connects with other objects and persons through association. A photograph may thus connect with the location of a missing person.

Fire (*Tejas*): The subtle element that enables change and transformation, enabling us to live in cold places and to move where we want—even to travel beneath the sea and to the stars someday.

Force, The: The primal Energy in the Field. As the Force, Prana, Chi, Orgone, etc., it is everywhere and is the Power that gives us Life.

Forces: Physics recognizes four primary forces: Gravity, Electro-magnetism, and the Strong and Weak Nuclear Forces. In occult theory, East and West, and in classical natural philosophy, these are the four primal elements: Earth, Fire, Air and Water. In magickal practices, the four elements are used as "forces" and often imbued with consciousness as when they are identified with particular archangels. *Might these really be the same as the four forces of physics?* In occult theory, Spirit is the fifth element from which the other four are derived. *If, as some speculate, Consciousness is the primary force, then are Spirit and Consciousness one and the same?* If Consciousness is the primary force from which the others are derived, is *this primary consciousness or Spirit the same as the Creator, we otherwise call God?*

Fourth Dimension: While Time is called the fourth dimension in Relativity Physics it is also a non-spatial addition to the physical three dimensions of space found on the astral plane enabling a clairvoyant to see all three dimensions of an object at once.

Global Culture: With the emergence of worldwide communication, connection, and everyday awareness in finance, industry, trade, and even in entertainment, fashion and commercial integration, we are experiencing an internationalization of education, human rights, and even legalization extending beyond national boundaries. More important, we witness international efforts to meet such planet-wide challenges as global warming, piracy in international waters, the illegal drug trade, and nationalist threats to world peace, health, and prosperity.

Goals: In the absence of consciously determined goals, paranormal phenomena is spontaneous and haphazard. When goals are determined, paranormal energies and skills have direction and produce desired results.

Golden Dawn, Hermetic Order: Founded in England in 1888, this magical order provided the impetus and source for magical study and practice within the Western Esoteric Tradition.

Israel Regardie's *The Golden Dawn* is an encyclopedic resource for the rituals and knowledge lectures of the GD, while his *The Tree of Life, The Middle Pillar* and *A Garden of Pomegranates* provide in-depth exposition of the GD's magical system.

See also:

Christopher: *Kabbalah, Magic and the Great Work of Self-Transformation*—based on the Order of the Golden Dawn, a step-by-step program toward spiritual attainment.

Cicero: *Essential Golden Dawn, an Introduction to High Magic*—explores the origins of Hermeticism and the Western Esoteric Tradition, the Laws of magic and magical philosophy, and different areas of magical knowledge.

Cicero: *Self-Initiation into the Golden Dawn Tradition*—Become a practicing Golden Dawn magician with essential knowledge of Qabalah, Astrology, Tarot, Geomancy, and Spiritual Alchemy.

Denning and Phillips: *Sword & Serpent, the Two-fold Qabalistic Universe*—the philosophy of ceremonial magic and its relationship to the Qabalah.

Great Plan, the: See *Divine Plan*.

Great Secret, the: The "Higher" always controls the "Lower." What is *magically* created on the higher planes—Causal, Mental, and Astral—will precipitate action on the next lower plane, and if so "instructed" through ritual and intention will manifest as physical reality.

Suggested Reading—Slate, J. H. and Weschcke, C. L.: *Astral Projection for Psychic Empowerment*, 2012, Llewellyn.

Great: The path of self-directed spiritual growth and development. This is the object of your incarnation and the meaning of your life. The Great Work is the program of growth to become all that you can be, the realization that you are a 'god in the making.' Within your being there is the seed of Divinity, and your job is to grow that into the Whole Person that is a 'Son of God'. It is a process that has continued from 'the Beginning' and may have no ending but it is your purpose in life. It is that which gives meaning to your being.

In this new age, you are both teacher and student and you must accept responsibility for your own destiny. *Time is of the essence!* Older methods give way to new ones because the entire process of growth and self-development has to be accelerated. Humanity has created a *time bomb* that's ticking away, and only our own higher consciousness can save us from self-destruction. But—have faith and do the Great Work for it is all part of a Great Plan.

The Great Work is not denial and restriction but fulfillment. There's not just one narrow Path, but many paths—one for each of us.

Suggested Reading—Denning and Phillips: *Foundations of High Magick*, n.d., Llewellyn.

Group Mind: The collective consciousness of a group or team of people working together on projects or studies. It may be a spontaneous function of a group of like-minded people or deliberately created by a magical group or a functional organization such as a business corporation or working partnership. It was part of the teachings of Napoleon Hill, author of "Think and Grow Rich."

Group Soul: The collective consciousness of a community, herd, nation, ethnic group, or nation, reflecting and then reinforcing distinctive behavior, thoughts, and culture.

Guardian Angel: Often identified as one's *Higher Self* and sometimes as an *Angelic Being* assigned to each person at birth, or incarnation. It is not necessarily the same as the *Holy Guardian Angel* described in certain High Magick operations.

Guide: The name we apply to certain intelligences encountered through clairvoyance and astral projection, and sometimes in dreams, and that appear to exists on the Inner Planes with no or rare physical manifestation. Some are referred to as *Psychic* or *Spirit* Guides and may or may not be identical with *Angels*. See also "Guardian Angel."

Heart Chakra: *Anahata,* heart, color green, associated planet Sun or Venus, sephirah Tiphareth, associated Tattva *Vayu*, symbol of the element of air.

Higher Self: The third aspect of personal consciousness, also known as the Super-Conscious Mind. As the Middle Self, or Conscious Mind, takes conscious control of the Lower Self, or Sub-Conscious Mind, the Higher Self becomes more directly involved in functioning of the Personal Consciousness. Even though also known as the Holy Guardian Angel, there is value in using a more easily comprehended psychological term. Words are words and there are often many names for the same thing. But each gives a particular shape or color or tone to the thing named to expand our understanding comprehension when we are relating to larger concepts.

Hypnagogic and **Hypnopompic:** These are the states between being awake and falling asleep and being asleep and waking up. Also called the 'Borderland Consciousness.' It is the state of consciousness when we are most receptive to images, symbols, impressions, sounds, ideas and feelings. It is also a state very receptive to Intuition.

I Ching aka **Yi King:** The casting of sticks or coins to establish 64 Hexagrams each consisting of six solid or broken lines. The I Ching is the oldest and most universal system of Chinese divination originating at the very foundation of Taoism, with something of their basic meanings.

***Ida** (Sanskrit):* One of the three major *nadis* (psychic nerves). Ida runs up the left side of the spinal column (the Middle Pillar) carrying feminine, intuitive, cooling energy, exiting in the left nostril and triggers right brain hemisphere functions.

Images: It is through symbols, images, and icons that we open the doors of our inner perception. The great secrets of magicians, shamans, and modern scientists are in the associations they attach to such icons, and in the power of certain signs and formulae to function as circuits and pathways—not in the brain but in consciousness.

Imagination: The ability to form and visualize images and ideas in the mind, especially of things never seen or experienced directly. It is an amazing and powerful part of our consciousness empowering the actual ability to create through the making of images, and by making their movement real. Some of that reality comes in the process of charging those images with energy, but more comes by the acceptance of their reality on the astral plane. As images are charged in the astral world, they can be drawn into the physical world, or to have an effect on the physical plane.

Inner Clairvoyance: When focused outward, clairvoyance can reveal important physical realities not otherwise available to conscious awareness. When focused inward, it can reveal important non-physical realities that are also hidden from conscious awareness. It can discover growth blockages and reveal ways of dissolving them. It can target subconscious conflicts and repressions and alleviate the anxiety generated by them. Inner-clairvoyance is, in fact, among the self's most powerful therapeutic techniques. Inner-clairvoyance can access the vast subconscious storehouse of past experience, including that of distant past-life origin. Given past-life enlightenment through inner-clairvoyance, you can awaken past-life memories and energize them with empowerment possibilities.

Inner World Matrix: We live in an "outer world matrix" (which see) and within an "inner world matrix," each an organizing template complete in itself. The two are interconnected through the personal subconscious and the universal mind. As elements (tattvas) are "awakened" within the personal inner world matrix of the individual, those connections enable consciously directed exchanges to occur between inner and outer world.

Integration: Integration is more than a bringing together. As the uniting of parts into a new whole it describes the goal of psychological development in Jungian Psychology culminating in the person actually becoming the Higher Self rather than the personality.

It is a difficult concept because it is a change of identity from the "I" of the personality into a new "I" that incorporates the transformed elements of the old personality into a new Whole Person centered on the Higher Self. "Who am I?" requires a new answer.

Intention: Acting with a goal in mind. However, "Intention" has become a key word in applied Quantum Theory where it is demonstrated that directed thought and image can effect changes in the Universal Field at the foundation of physical reality.

Intentional Perception starts with "visualization": the formation of unambiguous specific images (often of symbols functioning as *keys* to particular information) in the imagination. Even though the "directive" for training and development comes from the mind, "the *theater*" for the faculty of imagination is primarily an astral function. Every image you see—even though it may be entirely generated with physical sight—has an astral replica in the imagination.

Interactive PK Effect: The influences of mind over matter and motion are evident in a variety of sports related situations in which the mental state of athletes and spectators alike appear to influence outcomes in competitive events. Evidence indicates that a highly positive mental state with strong expectations of success asserts a powerful influence in any performance situation. In team sports, the positive energies of the team can generate a force that increases its physical capacities and sharpens its skills. Complementing that effect is the influence of supportive spectators whose energies can tilt the balance and determine which team wins. The "pull" of the audience generates a powerful PK interaction that literally increases the team's performance powers.

Intuition: A somewhat vague term for a non-verbal "feeling" message from the Higher Self sometimes experienced as a blinding flash of insight answering a question or solving a problem. "Our central nervous system automatically responds to events that have not yet happened and of which we are unaware in the present." (Research by Dean Radin of the Institute of Noetic Sciences, quoted in Larry Dossey's *The Power of Premonitions.*)

Invocation: Invocation and Evocation are often, mistakenly, used interchangeably and with little appreciation of their vast difference. Invocation precisely means to actually bring a spirit or divine presence <u>into</u> the psyche and even the body of the magician.

Evocation, in contrast, calls a spirit or other entity into the presence, not the being, of the magician and usually into a magical triangle placed outside the magic circle of the magician. Invocation requires psychological and spiritual strength as well as proper preparation. It's not just that there are dangers but that the opportunities are so great.

Japa (*Sanskrit*): Constant repetition (silently or audibly) of an affirmative mantra to *drive* it deeply into the subconscious mind.

Journal: As a student (and you are always a student so long as you want to grow and develop particular abilities no matter what they are or the subject is), you *must* write things down. The process of journaling is also the process of "objectifying" to bring all the elements of your consciousness together to focus on the matter at hand. Make notes of your studies, the books you read, the classes and lectures you attend, the lessons learned, the opinions and questions you have. Record your goals and your feelings about them; record the questions you ask and the answers you receive; record your "experiments" and practice sessions and what you learn; if you become a "professional" teacher or consultant serving others, record every session and what was accomplished.

Karma: In general, the force generated by a person's actions, usually associated with past lives. **Karma Yoga** is the Yoga of detachment by consciously cutting the emotional and energetic tie between action and reaction. No reaction, no pain, no karma.

Knowledge: All knowledge starts with observation, begins as theory, followed by questions and speculations, then explanations that are tested with experiment and the results lead to new theories, new observations, new tests, etc., so ultimately all knowledge is and remains theory until proven otherwise. Even "statements of fact" are theoretical interpretations of massive evidence that could be overturned with new discoveries. It is this process that allows and encourages new knowledge and stimulates new growth and personal development in contrast to authoritarian denials and resistance to change as in Religion, Law, Ideology, and—unfortunately—sometimes in Academia.

Kundalini: The transforming Life Force rising from the base of the spine, the *Muladhara* chakra, and animating the body, our sexuality, the etheric body, and passing through the chakras to join with its opposite force descending through *Sahasrara* chakra to open our higher consciousness. It exists on all planes in seven degrees of force, and is the driving force of evolution and individual development. Bringing astral experiences into conscious (physical brain) awareness requires some arousal of Kundalini and its movement through other chakras whether deliberately or spontaneously.

> Suggested Reading—Mumford: *A Chakra & Kundalini Workbook,* 1997, Llewellyn Paulson, G.: *Kundalini and the Chakras, Evolution in this Lifetime,* 2002, Llewellyn.

Laurency, Henry: See *The Knowledge of Reality,* 1979, Henry T. Laurency Publishing Foundation, www.laurency.com.

Left Brain: Western Culture is primarily Left Brain dominant as the result of our educational and cultural specializations that are both cause and effect. *Right*-handedness relates to the Left Brain and this simple fact has had enormous ramifications in cultural and technological development.

Leitmotiv (German): The guiding motivation of an Age.

Linga (Sanskrit) "Male Sex Organ, the Penis:" (See also **Shiva Lingam**) While represented by the erect penis as an object of religious veneration, the reality is as a symbol of Male Positive Sexual Force operative at the Etheric (and above) level.

Lower Astral: The lower sub-planes of the Astral Plane with vibrations close to the physical level. It is the realm of ghosts, hauntings, and poltergeist phenomena.

Lower Self: Basically, the conscious mind and the subconscious mind, together, are the Lower Self. From another perspective, they are the Physical, Etheric, Astral, Mental and Causal Vehicles functioning together at the physical and astral levels.

Magic: The power to change things in conformity with will or desire. It is a function of focused consciousness accompanied by emotional force intending change by reaching down into the Universal Field where everything exists as potential until affected by the operation of intention also known as magic. This means that magic is happening all the time, but as magicians we have the opportunity and responsibility as co-creators to direct change in accordance with 'The Great Plan,' meaning no more and no less than whatever the underlying purpose of creation is.

As "low (or practical) magic" it is the intentional ritual action supported by various physical correspondences with particular herbs, astrological factors, symbols, etc. lending strength to the visualized accomplishment through psychic powers to make things happen as a materialization of desire. As "High Magick" it is the intentional ceremonial action supported by particular philosophical correspondences to bring about self-development, including increased psychic skills, and the realization of the Whole Person. Which is what the Great Plan is all about.

"Magic, it is said, is the process of producing visible, physical results determined by the trained will-thought of the magician who has found the way to communicate with the appropriate angelic Intelligences and win their collaboration. Magic has therefore been described as the power to address the Gods in their own tongues," *The Kingdom of the Gods,* by Geoffrey Hodson, Theosophical Pub. House, Madras, 67.

Magical Mirror of the Universe: The Hermetic Order of the Golden Dawn described the *aura* "as an etheric structure filled with astral energies" and serving as the "magical mirror of the universe" in which all objects of perception and all inner activities of thought and feeling are reflected. In his most comprehensive book, *Aura Energy for Health, Healing & Balance,* Dr. Slate outlined the multiple roles of the aura system:

- It is a highly complex system that generates energy and sustains us mentally, physically, and spiritually.
- It is a sensitive yet dynamic force that encodes the totality of our individuality and connects us to the cosmic origins of our existence.
- It is an evolving chronicle of our past, present, and future.
- It is an interactive link between our innermost self and the external environment, including the aura systems of others.
- It is a repository of abundant resources with potential to enrich our lives.
- It is an interactive phenomenon receptive to our intervention and empowerment efforts.
- At any given moment, it is a weathervane of our personal development.
- The more we learn about the aura, the better we understand ourselves.

In summary, the aura is your own personal mirror, not only of health but of character, emotional strength, mentality, and spirituality. The aura can be strengthened, massaged, healed, enlarged, shaped, and charged with specific energies and energy forms for direct interaction with other entities.

Maithuna (*Sanskrit*) *"Sexually Paired Couple, Male & Female."*

Manas: (*Sanskrit*): The Higher Mind or thinking function. The action of mind which produces or modifies the manifestation of objects. The incarnating ego.

Manipura (*the Solar Plexus*): This chakra is located in the lumbar area above the navel, and physically manifests through the adrenals, and the solar plexus. It relates to the conversion of food into energy, the expression of personal power, the formation of personal opinions, and the transformation of simple into complex emotional expression. Physically it rules our digestion, emotionally our expansiveness, mentally our personal power, and spiritually growth. It relates to the sense of sight. The element is Fire.

The associated psychic powers are clairsentience, empathy, premonitions and prophetic dreaming. This is the center of the salamander (fire-walker) whose inner life is sustained by the primal heat element. The fire-walkers of North India walking across beds of glowing embers and the Pacific islanders walking upon white-hot stones employ the Manipura chakra. Other so-called "fire-eaters" unknowingly use Manipura chakra together with Anahata chakra to perform their feats, including dipping the hands into boiling water, boiling oil, molten, and molten steel. Simultaneous mastery of earth, water, and fire with subsequent immunity to pain and searing of flesh by heat is accomplished through manipulating the forces inherent in the first three chakras and culminating in Manipura, the Solar Plexus chakra.

Manipura is symbolized by yellow inverse triangle within a lotus with ten spokes, and its tattva is represented geometrically in a red inverse triangle. The audible seed mantra is *RuNG* followed by mental echo of *RuM*. Like Muladhara, it contains a feminine energy.

Manipura Chakra Correspondences		
Alchemical Planet: Jupiter, Sun	Alchemical Element: Tin	Tattva: Tejas (Fire)
Animal: Ram	Basic Drive: Pleasure	Tattva color: Blue
Body Function: Digestion	Chakra Color: Yellow	Tattva form: Crescent
Element: Fire	Gemstone: Amber, topaz	Tattvic Sense: Taste
Gland: Adrenals	Goddess-form, Egyptian: Tefnut	God-form, Hindu: Braddha-Rudra

God-form, Greek: Apollo, Athena	Incense: Carnation, cinnamon	Goddess-form, Hindu: Lakini[1]
Location: Over navel	Order of chakra unfoldment: 4th	Yogic Planet: Sun
Part of Body: Solar Plexus, Navel	Psychological attribute: Power, passion, energy	Psychic Power: empathy, psychic diagnosis Sense: Sight
Spinal Joint: 7th	Bija Mantra: RuNG, RuM (4)	Spinal Location: 1st Lumbar
Tarot Key: XVI, Tower	Tree of Life Sephiroth: Hod, Netzach	Tarot Suit: Wands
Yantra (internal) Green inverse triangle		
[1]Authority		
Source: Slate, J. and Weschcke, C. L.: *Psychic Empowerment—Tools & Techniques*, 2011, Llewellyn		

Mantra: A word or phrase, usually in Sanskrit, Hebrew or Latin, repeated or chanted repeatedly as a way to still the mind in meditation, and/or to instill a particular feeling or to invoke a special state of consciousness. Mantras are usually associated with particular images or *yantra,* which may be visualized during meditation and chanting for increased effect. Some of the mantras are 'God Names' and the associated images are of the deities.

Mantra Meditation: is by far the best known form of meditation in which you repeat words, phrases, and short prayers in a rhythmic fashion, often involving the use of associated images visualized during meditation and chanting. Each mantra while having similar physical and mental effects will produce different emotional feelings and induce unique spiritual effects identified with the particular tradition and the words or names used. Phrases containing "God Names" are especially powerful, as you would expect. Every tradition includes such mantras that may be used in the same way but with effects that do reach into the spiritual dimension.

Marmasthanani (Sanskrit): The sixteen vital body areas that are concentrated upon in certain exercises of Raja and Hatha Yoga. The location varies in different traditions.

Materialization: The presence of a spirit perceived either objectively to physical sight or subjectively to non-physical sight through imagination and visualization. Also, the actual "participation" of a spirit or non-physical visualization into material objects that may or may not have endurance. This includes objects teleported from one physical location to another and is also associated with poltergeist-like activity when stones appear in mid-air to fall on a house. There are also materializations of human forms or just of limbs and hands sometimes occur in séances, and wax impressions have been made of them.

Matrix: The background framework for all and any manifestation; a "structural pattern" located in a higher dimension (plane) around which substance and energy conduits are formed in each subsequent lower dimension. It is a union of Consciousness in the Universal Field of primary energy/matter potentials.

We live in two worlds: The universal matrix is the pattern for evolving universe and all within it. The individual matrix is the pattern of energy/matter guiding the development and function of each life form. It is mostly a function of Mental, Astral, and Etheric levels of consciousness guided by an intention expressed at the Soul level. It functions as the Etheric Body.

Suggested Reading—Bradden: *The Divine Matrix*, 2007, Hay House.

Meditation: (1) An emptying of the mind of all thoughts and 'chatter' often by concentration only on the slow inhalation and exhalation of breath and is characterized by slow alpha and theta waves. It induces relaxation and a 'clean slate' preparatory for receiving psychic impressions. (2) A careful thinking about a particular subject in a manner that brings access to physical memories as well as astral and mental level associations of knowledge about that subject. (3) A state of consciousness characterized by relaxed alertness reducing sensory impressions with increased receptivity to inner plane communications.

Meditation can be further classified into three types according to their orientation which in turn can be distinguished from each other by brainwave patterns.

Concentration is focused attention on a selected object, thought, image, sound, repetitive prayer, chant, mantra etc., while minimizing distractions and constantly bringing the mind back to concentrate on the chosen object.

Mindfulness requires a non-reactive monitoring of present experience: perception, thought, feelings, etc. The meditator focuses awareness on an object *or* process—such as breath, sound, visualized image a mantra, koan, or on a physical or mental exercise—while maintaining an "open" focus that may lead to insight or enlightenment. The meditator must passively observe without reaction.

Transcendent Mindfulness requires that the meditator is open to experiencing a *shift* in consciousness and even changes in the physical/etheric body, all the while focusing on a thought, image, or object to the point of identifying with it.

Meditation (concentration) as a focus on a single thought is really a willed act of attention, the act of the active, disciplined conscious mind that does not passively react to every passing thought and perception (as is all too common in today's enter-tainment-dominated culture). To escape that, you must learn to pay attention, totally oblivious to external activity and internal fantasy.

Meditation that focuses attention on an idea or subject is one of the finest meth-ods of study and research in such subjects as astrology and Tarot, and as adjuncts to such practices as dowsing, any type of research, and forms of self-analysis and even medical diagnosis. Such focus can secure information or answer a question, or focus on single symbols (such as a tattva) or on a symbolic complex such as imagined move-ment ("path-working") on the Kabbalistic Tree of Life. Included in this approach is meditation on such divinatory symbols as Runes, I Ching hexagrams, and even defined "signs" such as use in tea leaf reading, handwriting analysis, palmistry, etc.

Meditation, hypnosis, and self-hypnosis are all associated with special mental states which facilitate positive personality changes and connect with higher dimen-sions of the psyche. In addition, those particular mind disciplines being used to achieve particular therapeutic results are receiving increasing professional and sci-entific attention. In one form of meditation using visualization, such as Chinese Qi Gong, the practitioner concentrates on flows of energy (Qi) in the body, starting in the abdomen and then circulating through the body, until dispersed.

Meditation can be practiced while seated or standing in particular positions (called *asanas* in yoga), but once you have broken habitual mental patterns that pro-duce stress, you can be meditating while walking or doing simple repetitive tasks.

Medium, Spiritual: In Spiritualist work, a person who is able to consciously com-municate with spirits or other non-physical entities, guides, messengers, teachers, etc., or to enter into trance and speak or write messages from those on the "other side." **Mediumship** is the study and development of the skill necessary to function as a spiritual medium facilitating communication between the worlds of spirit and the living

Suggesting Reading—Van den Eynden, R.: *So You Want to Be a Medium? A Down-to-Earth Guide*, 2006, Llewellyn.

Mental Body/Vehicle: The fourth body. The mental body "thinks" in abstract rather than emotional form. The lower mental body unites with the astral and etheric bodies as the personality for current incarnation. The higher mental body is home to the Soul between incarnations.

Mental Imagery: The ability to visualize specific images is an acquired cognitive skill. Mental images are the language of the subconscious mind. Combining imagery with self-talk, you can successfully interact with your subconscious resources and even expand them. You can awaken your dormant resources and exercise them in ways that enrich your life with new potentials for growth and success. You can energize your biological systems and even influence brain activity to rejuvenate and recreate yourself. You can increase the length and quality of your life by protecting and fortifying your innermost energy system.

With the powers of your subconscious mind at your command through a combination of self-talk and imagery, literally nothing is impossible for you.

Mental Plane/World: The third plane up from the physical/etheric between the Astral and the Spiritual Planes. It is the plane of abstract consciousness, where we find meaning, patterns, the laws of nature and mathematics, number and form. It is the plane where all thought is shared. It is the upper home for the Akashic records shared with the astral.

Mental Projection: Projection of the mental vehicle. (It should be clarified that all projections involve more than just the etheric, or just the astral, or just the mental vehicle but rather are inclusive with each having one substance and level of consciousness that is predominant.)

Mental Telepathy: Mind to mind communication by non-physical means. Usually, an image of the intended receiver is held in mind while a simple message, such as "Call me," is projected. Once the message is sent, it is important to "let go" of it rather than doing constant repetition.

Message: Information, advice, warning, etc., communicated through a medium or channeler to a person or persons in a Spiritualist setting, or in a dream or unexpected direct voice. In the latter, it is often a warning that acted upon avoids an accident or other imminent disastrous event. And like symbols in dreams, our Higher Self may alert us to some needed idea by awakening our interest to something happening in our environment.

While not exactly the same thing, it is fascinating to let things "speak" to you in divination. Rather than following other people's interpretations, let the cards, crystals, shells, bones, stones, coins, sticks, or whatever speak through your touch and gaze. Let yourself slide into a mild trance, and "let your fingers do the talking" as they manipulate the chosen objects.

Don't impose a *left brain* rigidity of rules on what is essentially a *right brain* work of creative response. Patterns found in a tea cup may seem to say things, but the wisdom is in yourself and not the bottom of the cup.

Mind Magic: Mental level consciousness to control and shape astral energies and substance to project future happenings at the physical level. A very difficult proposition for other than the immediate personal environment—and yet we try it all the time in simple tasks such as making architectural drawings, business plans, a woman "putting on her face" in the morning, dressing for "effect," planning for a child's future, etc.

Moon (as symbol of Elemental Water): The Moon is a power in itself, causing tides in all fluids around and within all life. And, it is a living symbol for that power when used in meditation and magick to influence both actual fluids in the personal microcosm and in psychic and astral activities. As a symbol appearing in dreams and in divination it has numerous well-cataloged meanings. As the astronomical partner to Earth, the measurements of its phases and signs provides a means to factor its influence in planting and harvesting, in health and healing, in fishing and in water management, in practical decisions relating to fluid energies and emotions including most "What to do When" choices, questions relating to Romance, Fashion, Love & Sex, matters about home and sustainable life styles, and more.

See Llewellyn's annual *Moon Sign Book* for daily guidance.

Muladhara (*Sanskrit*) "Base or Root": This chakra is located at the base of the spine about half-way between the anus and sex organs, and physically manifests through the pelvic plexus, the gonads (testicles and ovaries), and the muscle that controls male ejaculation and vaginal movement. It relates to the basic instincts of security, survival, and basic human potentiality. Physically it rules our sexuality, emotionally our sensuality, mentally our stability, and spiritually our sense of security. It relates to the sense of smell. The element is Earth. It is symbolized as a red square with 4 red spokes (petals), and its Tattva is represented geometrically in a yellow square. The audible seed mantra is *LuNG* followed by silent mental echo of *LuM*

The associated psychic powers are pain control, psychometry, dowsing and telekinesis. Opening of Muladhara gives power over all the earth elements and metals, and the physical body. Pain control becomes a reality as demonstrated by walking on hot coals, lying on a bed of nails, insertion of pins through the tongue, etc.

It is the seat of Kundalini. From this chakra three channels—*Ida, Pingala,* and *Sushumna*—emerge, separate, and spiral upward to Sahasrara chakra.

Muladhara (Base) Chakra Correspondences		
Alchemical Planet: Saturn	Alchemical Element: Lead	Tattva: Prithivi (Earth)
Animal: Bull, elephant, ox	Basic Drive: Security	Tattva color: Yellow
Body Function: Elimination	Chakra Color: Red	Tattva form: Square
Element: Earth	Gemstone: Ruby, garnet, lodestone Tattva Sense: Smell	Gland: Adrenals
God-form, Greek: Gaia, Demeter	God-form, Egyptian: Geb	God-form, Hindu: Bala Brahma [1]
Goddess-form, Hindu: Dakini [2]	Incense: Cedar	Location: Base of spine
Psychic Power: pain control, psychometry, dowsing, telekinesis	Order of chakra unfoldment: 1st	Yogic Planet: Saturn
Part of Body: Between anus & genitals	Psychological attribute: Solidarity	Bija Mantra: LuNG, LuM (3)
Spinal Joint: 1st, 2nd, 3rd	Spinal Location: 4th Sacral	Sense: Smell
Tarot Key: XXI, World	Tree of Life Sephiroth: Malkuth	Yantra (internal) Blue Square
Tarot Suit: Pentacles		
[1] Child-God		
[2] Security		
Source: Slate, J. and Weschcke, C. L.: *Psychic Empowerment: Tools & Techniques,* 2011, Llewellyn		

Mumford, Dr. Jonn: An Australian chiropractor, yoga teacher, and author of pioneering books on Tantra. He is the inspiration behind many of the Tattvic practices in this book. Among his books, all highly recommended, are *Ecstasy Through Tantra, A Chakra & Kundalini Workbook, Magical Tattwas,* and others. He and Carl Llewellyn Weschcke jointly created the Tattwa Card deck included in the Magical Tattwa Kit. He teaches a very extensive on-line course on Kriya Yoga and Tantra.

Dr. Mumford may be contacted at the following sites:

Dr. Jonn Mumford

(Swami Anandakapila Saraswati) Consultations: Distance Learning Programs http://www.jonnmumfordconsult.com/

Swami Anandakapila's OM Kara Kriya ® Graduate Teachers http://anandakapila-graduateteachers.weebly.com

Nadi (*Sanskrit*) "Motion:" An astral nerve *tube* involving the polarization and depolarization waves of activity in the nervous system. Yoga teaches that 72,000 such nadis exist in the psychic counterpart of the gross body.

New Age, The: What we call "New Age" didn't just happen at a particular time, nor is it specifically identical with "The Age of Aquarius," but there are common elements that make the terms more or less interchangeable. The New Age corresponds to an influx of physical and subtle energies, an expansion of consciousness, and an explosion of interest in certain subject matters, including alternative healing, mind-body medicine, psychic practices, growth practices, yoga, etc. alongside of new interests and renewed studies in Kabbalah, Magick, Paganism, Wicca, Gnosticism, Hinduism, Tantra, Taoism, and more. While "metaphysics" is an alternative used more and more often in the book trade, it doesn't carry the same connotation of "newness" that is fundamental to the real changes and expansions of awareness and consciousness that have been on-going and accelerating since the mid-nineteenth century.

New Consciousness: In just the last few decades, there has been a whole new perception of the sub-conscious mind as a resource for knowledge and power, and a realization that "consciousness" itself is bigger, older, and more fundamental than previously perceived.

Consciousness is even more elemental than Energy and Matter and extends throughout Time and Space. Modern science, and in particular quantum physics and what we now dare to call 'new age psychology' along with paranormal studies, have restored balance to our cosmology. We see Life and Consciousness as universal and limitless.

The divisions between the conscious mind and the sub-conscious mind are becoming less substantial and are merging toward Wholeness, with the conscious mind functioning more like a Managing Director and the sub-conscious as a Director of Resources with the relationship of conscious to sub-conscious becoming more of interactive teamwork than previously.

We are evolving into a new relationship between different levels of personal and extended consciousness with the conscious mind as manager able to call upon the resources of the extended range of consciousness to tap into memories, knowledge and perceptions. The new relationship is a two-way communication with the conscious mind calling up specified content from the sub-conscious, the collective unconscious, and the greater universal consciousness using nearly forgotten psychic powers to expand awareness beyond the limitations of the physical senses.

Evolution for humanity is continuing and accelerating, driven by purpose and meaning, and not just chance and Darwinian natural selection. Evolution is not founded in biology but in consciousness, and continues to build upon a long-ago 'programming' for which no end is in sight.

New Person: Recognition of the evolving person subsequent to the "Next Step" (which see). This *new person* has a mind "outside the brain," emotions beyond hormones, a body inclusive of subtle energies, and levels of being and consciousness that extend from the cellular to the spiritual and even "divine." As a "being of consciousness" (rather than just a body with a brain), we have divided the human psyche into subconscious, conscious, and superconscious minds along with soul and spirit, and all somehow connected to a "Collective Unconscious" and a "Universal Consciousness" shared with all other beings across time and space.

The "New Person" is an evolving reality, unlike the ideal "New Man" conceived by Nietzsche as a yet to-be-born superman, or the utopian New Man visioned by Thomas Paine and Robert Owen, or the "Superior Man" of Fascisms and Communism whose programs would be to enforce change on society to fit their political model. Evolution is an *internal* process of growth in fulfillment of the spiritual matrix that has existed from the "Beginning" and will continue to the Never End.

New Science of the Paranormal: The scientific study of the paranormal includes psychic skills *and* phenomena, and sees the people involved in real life applications. Replacing, or expanding upon the old science of parapsychology, this new science has grown out of the advanced and humanistic research led by Dr. Joe H. Slate at Athens (Alabama) State University and furthered under the influence of the Parapsychology Research Institute & Foundation (PRIF). Aside from laboratory-based research programs, reports of paranormal experiences outside the lab were given equal respects and scientific analysis. Common, everyday paranormal experiences are given equal recognition as "real" and have resulted in new developmental methods and new applications of psychic skills and tools.

Many of these technologies make use of self-hypnosis, thus enabling an individual to have full control of the development and the application of paranormal skills in everyday life.

"Next Step:" Advancement, growth, development, expansion all comes about when we are willing to take the "next step" out of self-imposed and societal limitations. Whether we are concerned with astral projection, aura reading, psychic development, or advancements in career, education, innovations in science and technology, we have to jump over the fence, get out of the rut, breakthrough the walls. Evolution results

from the series of next steps that societies and individuals have taken and will take—
for evolution is not just the past but even more the future. Without growth, without
evolution, we are passé, in fact doomed like dinosaurs. *What does this have to do with
you?* It is you, the individual, who is the vehicle of evolution. Unless you take the next
step in your own life, growing in consciousness and psychic powers, you fail to lend
your strength to our better future.

Psychic powers are not incidental to our evolutionary advancement; rather they
are essential to the process. Undertaking their conscious development accelerates personal growth at a most critical time in world history.

Clairvoyance and Astral Projection are vital contribution to this acceleration and
to our ability to meet the challenges of this moment. Astral experiences *ignite* psychic
development and the expansion of consciousness that is clairvoyance and necessary
for new knowledge and understanding of the cosmic adventure that is our origin and
our destiny. The experience of expanding consciousness is the "next step" necessary
to move forward, to make the transition into the real New Age that is reality for those
willing to commit themselves *to becoming more than they are.*

Old Religion, The: The name sometimes given to the worship of the Great Mother,
the Goddess of all life. While this "Nature Religion" is far older than even "pre-
Christianity," it continued into modern times in Shamanic practices and European
Witchcraft, and is used as an alternate to Wicca. As the Old Religion it has many
fundamental similarities to *ancient* Tantra.

Operating System: Inside every computer there is a software package providing the
instructions for the hardware to carry out the work requested by application software packages like Microsoft Word and Excel. The operating system is the interface
between the computer hardware and the world, while the application packages are
like the skills and training we learn by study and experience. Like every other computer the human brain requires an operating system that interfaces with the world
and filters our perceptions to correspond to what we are conditioned to expect
through parental guidance, our life experiences, education, training, and interaction with authority figures, social expectations, and to an undetermined extent by
our genetic heritage and past-life memories. This operating system also conditions
and directs the way we respond to external stimuli. Much of this operating system functions in the subconscious mind. Like computers, the operating system can
be modified, updated, changed and even replaced. Self-understanding is learning
about our operating system; self-improvement is about modifying and changing

our operating system; self-transformation is about updating and largely replacing our operating system.

Ophiel: The pseudonym of Edward C. Peach, a brilliant but little recognized pioneering American occult writer. More than a scholar, he researched subjects personally and in depth, originating and proving techniques of Astral Projection, Creative Visualization, Clairvoyance, Divination, "Caballa" Magic, and more.

Ouija™ Board: A simple board with the alphabet and numbers printed on it along with 'yes' and 'no,' and sliding planchette "pointing device" used to communicate with spirits. The users, usually two people of opposite gender, rest fingers on the device which slides quickly to the variously letters to spell out answers to questions. While commonly used as entertainment, the proper use would be to enter into a light trance and let the planchette spell out messages.

Outer World Matrix: We live in an "outer world matrix" and within an "inner world matrix,"each a complete organizing template complete in itself but the two are also interconnected through the personal subconscious and the universal mind. As elements (tattvas) are "awakened" within the personal inner world matrix of the individual, those connections enable consciously directed exchanges to occur between inner and outer world.

Parapsychology: Dr. Joe H. Slate (*Psychic Phenomena,* 1988, McFarland, Jefferson, NC) writes "Parapsychology is the study of extrasensory perception (ESP), psychokinesis (PK), and related topics. As a science, it pushes back the borders of human experience and offers new ways to understand ourselves and the universe. Contemporary parapsychology focuses on two major goals: first, to engage scientific research to discover new knowledge, and second, to liberate and optimize the development of human potential. Both goals are based on the premise that undiscovered knowledge and underdeveloped human potential do exist in forms which can be reached through the application of parapsychological concepts and techniques.

"Through its emphasis on mental faculties and phenomena beyond recognizable physical explanations and causes, parapsychology reveals new possibilities for acquiring knowledge and for explaining higher mental processes. The challenge facing parapsychology . . . is the discovery and understanding of the complex parapsychological processes underlying human behavior, the mastery of the techniques of personal unfoldment, and the productive application of parapsychological skills. Because parapsychological concepts and techniques are not limited by the boundaries of physical perception and experience, they suggest new and more efficient ways to increase awareness and expand the human capacity for new knowledge and understanding."

Parapsychology challenges conventional thinking about life and death, the known and unknown, human potential and personal achievement, the nature of mind and body, known reality and perceived reality, and the meaning of our existence. All these age-old questions have been asked before with many different answers depending on conflicting ancient religious teachings.

In place of religious answers Parapsychology explores paranormal phenomena—including direct revelation by psychic technologies. Despite its apparent newness, Parapsychology explores the unknown through two age-old approaches:(1) the use of particular physical objects, some with associated symbols, and (2) particular mental disciplines. The first includes such objects as gazing crystals, dowsing rods, pendulums, tea leaves, as well as Runes, the I Ching, Tarot, Geomancy, etc.—all involving some form of physical contact and manipulation with degrees of mental focus and extended awareness. The second includes the use of hypnosis (more often self-hypnosis), active and passive forms of meditation, dream analysis, and the out-of-body state. In both approaches, the goal is two-fold: To gain particular information, often in response to precise questions; and to grow in psychic skills and the fulfillment of innate potentials, and thus to "become more than we are."

Modern parapsychology places an increased emphasis on practical applications by means of information not otherwise available through sensory channels. Examples include precognition, telepathy, clairvoyance, dowsing, remote viewing, reading the aura, past-life regression, spirit communication, and meditation

Parapsychology Research Institute & Foundation (PRIF): Established at Athens State University in 1970 by Joe H. Slate, Ph.D., Psychology Research Foundation), this foundation is committed to the study of parapsychology and related topics. It has conducted extensive research and established student scholarships in perpetuity at Athens State University and the University of Alabama. The president of the foundation is District Judge Sam Masdon of Montgomery AL. For more information, contact Joe H. Slate, Ph.D. at joehslate@aol.com.

Path-working: Procedures involving "moving meditation," often in guided programs, most often derived from the Qabalistic Tree of Life and providing psychic journeys along particular paths connecting two stations (Sephiroth) containing vast astral resources. The path-working experience are condensations of universal experience and knowledge that awaken actual memories that are both personal and universal, and that access all that may be knowable.

Persona: The **persona** is the "mask" or appearance one presents to the world. It may appear in dreams under various guises (see Carl Jung and his psychology).

Personal Consciousness: Your Personal Consciousness that was once part of the Universal Consciousness remains forever connected to it. And thus it can be said to be created in the image of God. The image is a matrix called 'the anatomy of the Body of God' by Carl Llewellyn Weschcke. It can be visualized as the Great Pyramid with levels for the *Lower, Middle* and *Higher* Consciousness, i.e. Sub-Conscious Mind, Conscious Mind and Super-Conscious Mind. This 'matrix' is to be filled in by experience.

See Slate, J. H. and Weschcke, C. L.: *Self-Empowerment and Your Subconscious Mind,* 2010, Llewellyn.

Personality: The immediate vehicle of personal consciousness we believe to be ourselves. It is a temporary complex drawn from the etheric, astral, and mental bodies containing current life memories, the current operating system. It is the relatively enduring complex of attitudes, interests, behavioral patterns, emotional responses, social roles, and other individual traits.

The Personality is only one chapter in the full biography of the evolving Soul. And each chapter is analyzed and abstracted to secure the essential lessons and experiences of the entire lifetime, while the memories of that lifetime flow into the Subconscious Mind and become part of the Universal Consciousness providing a complete history of the Soul's many lifetimes. In between lives, the Soul absorbs lessons from the many successive personalities and thus evolves. From his now greater perspective, the Soul outlines a new chapter and sends part of his essence into incarnation to gain new experiences that will become new lessons for the evolving Soul. It is somewhat as if a mature adult could have planned the years of his childhood to get the right experiences and education for the professional life he has chosen.

Physical/Etheric Body/Vehicle: When awake, the physical and etheric bodies are inseparable, although an adept is able to project parts of the etheric body in magical operations. Asleep, it is possible to partially separate the etheric body from the physical for travel on the physical plane. It is this physical vehicle that is the means to the experiencing of life's lessons.

Physical Phenomena: "Physical" phenomena associated with a séance, such as: movement or levitation of a trumpet, planchette, table or other physical object, the materialization of a spirit most often out of ectoplasm, voices and sounds sometimes emanating from a person or object and other times without apparent source, and other physical manifestations usually in relation to Spiritualist activity.

Physical Plane: The material plane of matter and energy as objective reality, and the end product of creation.

Physical Universe: The physical universe is our "home plane" during physical life, and is that which we perceive and know best as the foundation for our manifest being. While the physical universe contains matter both visible and the invisible which extends beyond the physical plane into the non-physical planes generally known as Etheric, Astral, Mental, Causal, and Spiritual. Each person is more than his/her physical body as our consciousness extends into the non-physical and uses bodies of etheric, astral, mental and causal substance.

Pingala *(Sanskrit)*: One of the three major psychic nerves or nadis. Pingala is visualized as running up the right side of the spinal column conveying masculine, healing, rational energy. It exits in the right nostril and is a trigger for left-hemisphere functions.

Plane: The old word, still in common use, for the various *worlds* and *levels* of reality and consciousness. While there is debate on their total number and classification, the most common is that of the five planes plus a collective designation under Spiritual:

> **Physical** (sometimes with the lower part of the etheric attached)
> **Etheric** (sometimes considered as two layers, one always attached to the physical and the other always to the astral)
> **Astral** (commonly divided into Lower and Higher)
> **Mental** (commonly divided into Lower and Higher)
> **Causal** (the Highest level of the Mental)
> **Spiritual** (sometimes considered as consisting of two or more additional planes)

Postures, and Movements, East and West: "Postures" generally refer to Eastern yogic postures (asana) along with controlled breathing, and our familiar Western postures of standing and sitting. In addition, postures involve intentional movement, even if just sitting with grace, and awareness of energy flow. There are, of course, other postures: those of the martial arts in China and Japan, belly and dervish dances in the Middle East, Hula from Hawaii, and much more. Any movement and posture that involves energy probably had an associated shamanic or sacred tradition. Every posture, movement, and gesture involves muscles and nerves, electrical currents and chemicals, energy flows and hormones, along with emotional and spiritual responses, and changes in the aura. Every movement of the physical body triggers a complex of responses, but some are very specific in what they do. The important point is to understand that there is a psychic and magickal side of all these positions, postures, movements, signs and gestures.

The Western Esoteric Tradition has adopted the Egyptian God postures as seen in paintings on tomb and temple walls. Whether standing, moving, or seated, these show positions of dignity and energy restraint. You can sense power that would be released in a simple gesture. When you assume any of the magical positions and make the movements, you should learn to be sensitive to the energy flow, and with that learn to adjust your stance and movements until the energy flow feels just right. It will help to allow yourself to "imagine" seeing those energies from outside your body, seeing them just as if viewing a schematic diagram of channels and centers.

The best analogy I can offer is to consider actual Martial Arts postures and movements. You know that these movements—no matter the particular style—generate and deliver amazing power. And when you study any of the martial arts you will often find illustrations showing the many subtle body energy channels, meridians and psychic centers involved.

Now, think of your own body. A simple smile causes your body and emotions to respond to that simple 'posture.' "When you smile, the whole world smiles with you" is more than a pretty phrase because that gesture is infectious and brings smiles to other people as well. But, *what happened to you when you smiled?* You felt better! The small act triggered not only an emotional response but through the nerves and muscles involved switched on many electrical and chemical transfers in your body. And then projected energy into your aura and broadcast it to these other people who "smiled with you."

Prana (Chi, the Force, the Power): The universal life-force flowing throughout the universe, and locally emanating from the sun as vitality absorbed from the air we breathe and the food we eat. It can be visualized as flowing into the body as you inhale, and then distributed throughout the body as you exhale.

Prana is also considered as one of the "seven elements:" Prana, Manas (mind), Ether, Fire, Air, Water and Earth, corresponding to seven regions of the universe. In Hebrew Kabbalism, Nephesh (the Psyche) is Prana combined with Kama (Love), together making the vital spark that is the "breath of life." Prana is comparable to Chi (Chinese), Ki (Japanese), vitality globules (Theosophical), Nous (Rosicrucian), Orgone (Wilhelm Reich), animal magnetism (Mesmer), Quintessence (alchemical), and Mana (Hawaiian priests).

Pranayama (*Sanskrit*) "breath control:" The control of life force (prana) through the regulation of the respiratory process, coupled with visualization. "Pra" means "first or before," and "ana" means "breath"—literally, the first essence underlying the breath. Also see **Prana**.

Precognition: The psychic awareness of the future, including events, trends, and conditions. Like other psychic faculties, the ability to perceive the future independently of presently known predictive circumstances exists to some degree in everyone. Some believe that events yet to occur already exist in a fixed, unalterable form. Another view assumes that the future exists only in varying degrees of probabilities, ever dependent on past and present realities including human intervention.

Each view related to the fixedness of the future assumes the existence of time as an energy dimension within a continuum of the past, present, and future. From that perspective, personal consciousness, likewise an energy phenomenon is endowed with the capacity to interact with that dimension to generate a *mind/future interaction* that not only perceives the future but influences it as well. In today's complex world, the precognitive challenge thus becomes twofold: to develop our precognitive powers to their peaks and use them to bring forth desired change.

By developing our capacity to interact with the time continuum, we become empowered to access the future through precognition, *and* to dip into the past through retrocognition. While the past exists in unalterable form, increased knowledge of that dimension can alter our perceptions of the present and empower us to more effectively shape the future.

Dr. Joe Slate writes: "For instance, personal growth blockages including phobias and conflicts of past-life origin can be resolved, often instantly, through the retrocognitive retrieval of relevant past-life experiences. On a broader scale, awareness of the sources of global problems ranging from disease to environmental pollution can be essential to the correction of causative conditions. Once you're attuned to the continuum of time, your retrocognitive and precognitive potentials will become activated to work hand-in-hand to empower you as never before to increase the quality of your life while contributing to a better world." (Slate, J. and Weschcke, C. L.: *Psychic Empowerment: Tools & Techniques,* 2011, Llewellyn.)

Accepting this interdependent view of time opens considerable speculation regarding *interdimensional interaction* through our psychic faculties such as *telepathy* with its capacity to send and receive thought messages with relevance to future happenings. An even more challenging possibility is the capacity to actually influence distant causative happenings through *psychokinesis* (PK).

Precognition, as an enriched extension of sensory perception, is an expression of our innate ability to perceive the future psychically. In its voluntarily induced form, precognitive awareness is activated deliberately through certain procedures and techniques, some of which were developed in the controlled laboratory setting at Athens State University under the auspices of the International Parapsychology Research Foundation. (See Slate, J. H. and Weschcke, C. L.: *The Llewellyn Complete Book of Psychic Empowerment*, 2011, Llewellyn for details.)

Pre-Sleep Intervention: A self-hypnosis program based on the premise that consciousness and subconsciousness, rather than simply categories or content areas, are complex mental processes that exist on a continuum which is receptive to our intervention.

Through pre-sleep intervention, you can tap into that continuum in ways that influence those processes. As a result, you access dormant potentials and activate them to achieve your personal goals. Beyond that, you can actually generate totally new potentials by taking command of the resources within. By perceiving consciousness and subconsciousness as a continuum, we are activating the 'Whole Person' rather than seeing division and separation. In the program, the most important step is before the beginning—that you really know what your goals are. Only work with one at a time but know that it is a vitally important goal and truly <u>feel</u> its importance and value. Be willing to say to yourself that you are wholeheartedly <u>praying</u> for its realization.

Prithivi (*Sanskrit*): The primal tattvic element of earth perceived as solid represented by a yellow square or cube to convey the basic drive for security. It is the Tattwa of Muladhara Chakra with cohesion and solidarity as principle characteristics, the sense of smell and the magical tool, the pentacle.

Probable Future: Based on better understanding of the Quantum world, the future is not seen as either fixed or unknowable, but in terms of probabilities that can be changed either by unexpected events or deliberate human action.

Process: It is important to understand all the practices of growth, development, magick, and especially those involving self-transformation, as parts of a process and not merely as single and isolated actions. Dream Recall has value in itself, but here it is presented as part of the process leading to psychological integration.

Progressive Tension & Release: A very precise system of physical body relaxation during which specific muscle groups are tensed and then released, progressing from toe to scalp. It is often, and perhaps best (at least initially) carried out as a guided procedure, either as meditation or hypnosis. Relaxation of the body is an essential pre-cursor to meditation but also a valuable discipline in health and healing. Physical relaxation also releases emotions that are the source of tension and stress that are real "killers" of physical health, and also inhibitors of clear thinking and pure feeling.

Projection of a Familiar: This is a variation of etheric projection in which a Thought Form of an animal or person is created from etheric and astral substance under direction of mind either with a single duty "charge," or a longer term duty charge. It is sometimes called "indirect psychic spying" in contrast to Remote Viewing.

Psyche: That function of the Personal Consciousness that <u>expresses</u> the feeling of selfhood. Jung wrote: "By psyche, I understand the totality of all psychic processes, conscious as well as unconscious."

Psychic Development Exercises: We can easily stimulate our psychic growth by exercising our ESP potentials through simple practice exercises, including the use of a deck of playing cards. Begin by shuffling the cards, and then with the cards turned downward, draw a card at random from the deck and use your clairvoyance skills to identify it. Check the card to determine the accuracy of your response. Do it again several times. To exercise your precognitive skills, before drawing the card predict which card you will draw from the deck. Draw the card and check it to determine your accuracy. To practice your telepathic skills, have another person draw a card from the deck and attempt to telepathically send its identity. Check the accuracy of your responses. Repeat each of these exercises several times and record the accuracy of your response after each trial. You will probably note that the accuracy of your responses increases with practice.

Psychic Empowerment: Psychic empowerment, rather than a theoretical possibility, is a measurable though complex process of personal evolvement. By following a specific plan or program, sometimes involving self-hypnosis and meditation, and using the traditional and newer tools and techniques you can accelerate that process by accessing your dormant inner potentials and activate them to enrich the quality of your life. Beyond that, you can become the master builder of an endless *tower of power* to the great beyond, a tower that connects you to the far reaches of the cosmos and the entire powers underlying it. Built of the finest materials—those found in your own being— the tower of power can become your empowerment connection to the boundless resources of the great beyond. It's a tower that brings you into balance and constant attunement to the universe. With empowerment, the psychic or spiritual bodies can be integrated into the Whole Person.

Suggested Reading—Slate, J. H. and Weschcke, C. L.: *Psychic Empowerment for Everyone*, 2009, Llewellyn.

Psychic Power Tool: It is your ability to effectively visualize that turns your imagination into a "psychic power tool" for use in psychic work, active meditation, astral travel, remote viewing, the development of clairvoyance, activating archetypal powers, the assumption of god forms, entering mythic worlds, Qabalistic path working, symbolic "doorways" to access specific areas of the astral world, as well as in all forms of magical application, and much more. In each of these applications, visualization is a process of moving psychic energies along particular symbolic pathways. This includes techniques involving the Chakra System and is used to actually stimulate neural pathways in the physical body and brain. Visualizations of persons, living or deceased can be used to make communications more accurate and more powerful. The visualization of a Spirit Entity or a God-Form can be employed in Evocation or Invocation, and in "conversation" with such beings to access Knowledge or specific Powers. Effective visualization is the key to empowering your imagination to "make real the unreal."

Psychic Shield: An easily visualized formation of White Light surrounding you in an egg shape reaching just beyond the distance measured by your outstretched arms. This field is as transparent as the clearest glass. Know that the outer surface of this field is a psychic shield protecting you from external influences while containing your own healthy aura and energy. You can form this shield at any time you feel the need for protection against psychic influences, emotional energies directed against you, and to protect you from your own unwanted responses to advertising and sales pitches, political or religious proselytizing, and unethical and sham charitable requests.

Purification: We need to "purify" our subtle organs and functions to assure accuracy and clarity of clairvoyance and other psychic activities. Clairvoyance primarily functions at the astral level of consciousness, and both the astral world and the astral vehicle are composed of astral/<u>emotional</u> substance carrying subconscious childhood and previous life memories of fears, illusions, traumas, etc. This "emotional garbage" distorts the astral senses and hence our clairvoyance visions and their interpretation. Through the Tattvic Meditation & Visualization Programs we connect the personal primal tattvas with their cosmic source, and thus restore their essential functioning.

Quantum Theory: The new science of Quantum Theory tells us that the beginning <u>is</u> (not just *was* but still *is)* the Universal Field of Possibilities that manifests first as

Energy/Matter under the guidance of packets of information/instruction. Thus we can see an analogy with a computer with its Operating Program & its Application Programs.

Reality: The personal world as seen through our belief system. While it mostly coincides with that of other people, self-analysis will show deviations and distortions reflecting the 'feelings' of the person.

Responsible Student: Books are no longer just "about" subjects, or "how to" manuals, but the new books even go beyond "theory and practice" to fully *develop* the theoretical foundations of a subject, explain the whys and the benefits of practice and application, often include case studies and examples, provide specific self-applied techniques for personal use, and sometimes even self-administered tests and questionnaires to affirm your understanding and knowledge.

It's not only such new books but the entire "responsible student" concept has carried over into self-study courses, on-line universities, down-loadable lessons, and has changed the style for author and conference lectures. Teachers are no longer reigning authority figures or unquestioned gurus but helpers taking their lead from students. As a result, more university classes provide for students to participate in research and experimentation on a co-equal basis with teachers for true "hands-on" study. In other words, everyone participates and everyone grows.

Responsibility, Personal: Every adult person, unless mentally or emotionally handicapped, must be self-responsible. That doesn't mean not seeking help or advice in specific matters and times of need but otherwise we must move beyond dependence whether on teacher, preacher, doctor, government, or employer. Adult relationships should be partnerships.

As with any clairvoyant experience, whether apparently sourced from the Spirit Realm or even perceived as coming from one's Higher Self, Guardian Angel, or some Inner Plane Adept, or Messenger of Deity, or as an interpretation of a Symbol, it is important to engage with the Conscious Mind to bring the message into context of the physical world and your personal environment.

You have the ultimate responsibility for rational and practical application of all other-dimensional guidance in relation to physical plane matters. Be particularly wary of all guidance regarding money, property, relationships, etc., especially those that may benefit another person, religious organization, spiritual leader, or other promising extraordinary benefits or "other-worldly" return on your investments. Remember the challenges of growing from childhood, through the hormonal teen years, into the early years of adult life, and then into the more mature years, and then understand that you are entering into expanded and unfamiliar areas of consciousness and awareness. It is somewhat similar to moving to a foreign culture where it sometimes is easy to misinterpret the language and culture. We have to grow into familiarity with these new worlds and "put away childish things" to accept the new responsibilities that go with vast new opportunities.

Right Brain: Right Brained people tend to more naturally psychic and to more easily develop their paranormal abilities. If we want to increase our paranormal sensitivities we can deliberately adopt one or more Right Brain characteristic activities. You could, for example, set out to learn Hebrew or even just to chant Hebrew phrases and mantras, read more fantasy literature, find ways to "enjoy the moment," and even practice doing things with your left hand. Note, of course, that some of the specific examples are just that, examples—there are other Right Brain languages than Hebrew, and other Left Brain languages than English.

Root Chakra: also called Muladhara located at the base of spine, color red, associated planet Saturn, associated with the Sephirah Malkuth. It is home to Kundalini, and sexual energy.

Sacral Chakra, also called **Svadhisthana** (which see): The sacral chakra located at the genital area, color orange, associated planet Jupiter or Moon, associated sephirah Yesod associated Tattva *Apas,* symbol of the element of Water.

Sahasrara (AKA the *Thousand Petaled Lotus* and the *Crown* Chakra): This chakra is located at and then just above the crown of the head. It manifests through the pineal gland, which produces melatonin—the hormone regulating sleep. Physically, it relates to the basis of consciousness—physically with meditation, emotionally with "beingness," mentally with universal consciousness. The female Kundalini *Shakti* energy rises from Muladhara to the crown to unite with the male *Shiva* energy to produce *Samadhi.* It relates to our sense of the Divine Connection. The associated psychic powers are astral projection and prophecy.

It is symbolized by a violet lotus with 1,000 multi-colored spokes (actually 12 in the center and then 960 around the center for a total of 972), and represented graphically by an image of a red rose. There is no seed mantra. The element is "Thought."

Sahasrara (Crown) Chakra Correspondences		
Alchemical Planet: Mercury, Uranus	Alchemical Element: Mercury	Tattva: Bindu (a dot)
Animal: None	Basic Drive: union	Tattva Color: Clear
Body Function: Super-consciousness	Chakra Color: Violet	Tattva form: rose seen from above
Element: Thought	Gemstone: Diamond	Tattva Sense: Higher Self
Gland: Pineal	God-form, Egyptian: Nut	God-form, Hindu: Brahma Vishnu[1]
God-form, Greek: Zeus	Incense: Lotus, gotu kola	Goddess-form, Hindu: Maha Shakti [2]
Location: Crown of Head	Order of chakra unfoldment: 7th	Yogic Planet: Mercury, Uranus
Part of Body: cerebral cortex, central nervous system Psychological state: Bliss Seed Syllable/Number: H(0)		
Psychic Power: astral projection, prophecy	Sense: the Divine Connection	Spinal Joint: 33rd
Tarot Key: I, Magician	Spinal Location: none	Tree of Life Sephiroth: Kether
[1] Inner teacher		
[2] Union		
Suggested Reading—Dale, C.: *The Subtle Body: An Encyclopedia of Your Energetic Anatomy*		
Source: Slate, J. H. and Weschcke, C. L.: *Psychic Empowerment: Tools & Techniques,* 2011, Llewellyn		

Samadhi (*Sanskrit*) "With God:" The merging of the individual consciousness with universal consciousness; the ultimate personal realization of the "Collective Unconscious." Samadhi is goal of all Yoga.

Sāmkhya (*Sanskrit*): Sāmkhya is one of the six orthodox systems of Hindu philosophy and is one of the primary influences on Tantra, itself the source for Yoga, the concepts of the Chakras and Tattvas, and of dynamic meditation practices. S mkhya is a dualistic philosophy that denies the existence of an external Deity (or any other external influence) because—ultimately—there is no distinction between individual and universal Consciousness. Rather, it perceives the universe as consisting of two realities:

Purusha (consciousness: the transcendental Self) and *Prakriti* (phenomena: the first cause of the manifest universe). *Prakriti* divides into sensor (person) and sensed (environment) realms, while *Purusha* separates into countless individual units of consciousness (souls) which fuse into the mind and body of the sensor. The person (sensor) consists of 13 *karanas* (instruments), firstly the three inner: intelligence (*buddhi*), ego (*ahamkaara*), and mind (*mana*) and then the ten outer: the five sense organs and the five organs of action (*karma*).

Prakriti, as the "First Cause" for whatever is physical, both mind and matter/energy or unconscious force itself divided into *sattva* (feeling), *rajas* (activity), and *tamas* (inertia). All physical events are manifestations of the evolution of *Prakriti,* or primal nature (from which all physical bodies are derived). Each sentient being is a fusion of *Purusha* and *Prakriti,* whose soul is limitless and unrestricted by its physical body. *Samsāra,* or bondage, arises when the *Self* does not have the discriminate knowledge and so is misled as to its own identity, confusing itself with the Ego, which is actually an attribute of *Prakriti.* The spirit is liberated when the discriminate knowledge of the difference between conscious Purusa and unconscious Prakriti is realized. *(Some of this entry is paraphrased from Wikipedia., which is gratefully acknowledged and one of the most valuable resources of the Information Age)*

Scientific Age: Generally recognized as beginning in the 14th century with the beginning of the scientific revolution that separated the physical from the non-physical in arriving at an understanding of the physical world. The non-physical was then mostly relegated to the "Spiritual World" dominated by the Catholic Church and a few daring Occultists.

Scientific Verification of Clairvoyance: There is a particular need to verify Psychic Perceptions since they appear to originate with higher "spiritual" sources and hence the presumption that they *must be true and reliable.* That's not always the case, but there is an additional benefit to using scientific methods of verification in the resultant identification and understanding of variables associated with successful clairvoyance and thus extending applications to practical matters of daily life. It's the same benefit of the scientific method wherever applied: *Better understanding leads to increased reliability and enhanced abilities.*

Séance: The event of a Spiritualist meeting in which a medium serving as an intermediary in communication between the world of spirits and living people. It usually takes place in a private room with a circle of a half-dozen or so participants to give energy support, although some mediums will function in large group and "work the crowd" to provide messages for most of those attending.

Search Engine-like Functions: Many things are *causally* related to Natural Forces which then function as "rulers" of those groups. In the past, those forces and their rulerships were personalized as Gods, Goddesses, and their ministering agents, and these were identified by names and images. In the course of time, Symbols have come to replace those deities while connecting more universally—beyond cultural limita-tions—to these forces and their rulerships of related things. Symbols now provide the means to invoke the forces and to *divine (seek)* answers *to* specific questions through "correspondences" with things related by rulership. As a result, *symbols can function like a search engine listing.* More specific addresses connect to smaller and more specialized groups, while a master address connects to the rulership. And symbols themselves become part of the system of correspondences. By means of symbols related by a system of organized correspondences on the Kabbalistic Tree of Life, we have a means—similar to mathematics—of relating parts (correctly) to the whole.

"Self": We distinguish between a little self (small 's') and a big Self (large 'S'). The small self is that of the personality, the person we think we are, and in fact are until we identify with the big Self that is also the 'Higher Self,' the permanent Self exist-ing between incarnations.

Self-Awareness: Awareness of Self, enabling the person to focus attention at will.

Self-Empowerment: The goal of all growth, all therapies, all methods of psychic and other personal development is empowerment of the Self. Each person is an agent of and for evolution, and it is through personal growth that the evolutionary message is carried forward. We are not "finished products;" quite the contrary. The road before us is long and the forthcoming journey glorious.

Self-Hypnosis: The self-induction of hypnotic trance and the <u>catalytic power</u> of direct self-programming through simple but carefully developed affirmations mostly expressed as already accomplished "I AM" conditions, such as "I AM slim." "Self-hypnosis can be best defined as a self-induced state of altered consciousness that gives direct access to the vast reserve of resources and underdeveloped potential existing in everyone. It's a strategy based on the premise that you alone are your best personal hypnotist and growth specialist." (from Slate and Weschcke: *Psychic Self-Empowerment for Everyone*)

Suggested Reading—Park: *Get Out of Your Way, Unlocking the Power of Your Mind to Get What You Want.* Includes audio CD of self-hypnosis programs.

Slate, J. H. & Weschcke, C. L.: *Self-Empowerment through Self-Hypnosis*, 2010, Llewellyn.

Serial Insight: Clairvoyant dreams, like precognitive dreams, often occur in a series to guide the dreamer, often symbolically, and monitors the dreamer's progress. Serial dreams usually have a central theme and a succession of related events. Transitional life situations and personal crises tend to precipitate the serial clairvoyant dream. Its goal is empowerment through personal insight. Once recognized and understood, such dreams can provide important therapeutic support and guide the growth or recovery process.

Shadow: In Jung's psychology, the Shadow is a somewhat independent splinter personality representing those elements which have been deliberately or unconsciously repressed and denied expression in your life, or that are dormant and unrecognized. It is the Nephesh located in Yesod, the Lower Self or lower subconscious with primal instincts and drives, most which have been unconsciously banished in the drive for conformity and approval by the authorities in one's life.

With repressed elements there is a lot of emotional energy locked up. It's like prisoners in jail—human energy denied freedom. Sooner or later we need to confront these repressions and release those of childhood trauma, understand those repressed in the name of conformity and rationalize those that represent sensible behavior and customs and get rid of the rest, while coming to terms with any that remain.

Shakti (Sanskrit) "Sacred Force:" The feminine form of Divine energy responsible for the Creation of the Universe, and continuing to express the "Motherhood of God" in contrast to "God the Father." It takes the forms of Spirituality & Compassion vs. Materialism & Passion. It is the active *fertilizing* manifestation of the Feminine creative energy. She is 'The Great Divine Mother' in Hinduism, and the active agent of all *change.* She is Kundalini Shakti, the mysterious psycho spiritual force of *liberation.* In Shaktism, Shakti is worshiped as the Supreme Being. In Shivaism, She embodies the active feminine energy called Prakriti, Vishnu's female counterpart. She is also seen as the female half of Shiva.

Shamanic Practices & Techniques: The projection of conscious awareness into the astral world accomplished through trance induction by deliberate repression or excessive stimulation of the physical senses through various techniques of sensory overload, extended sex, ecstatic or exhaustive dancing, drumming; methods of physical stress including fasting, flagellation, sexual or physical exhaustion, and the use of hallucinogenic and psychoactive substances; methods of sensory deprivation including fasting, sleep deprivation, prolonged bondage, isolation, sexual or physical exhaustion, etc., all leading to altered consciousness including—in particular—the Out-of-Body Experience of expanded awareness from beyond the physical world. The shaman is often in contact with "spirit guides" to facilitate his special "assignments."

Suggesting Reading—Walsh, Roger: *The World of Shamanism*, 2007, Llewellyn.

Shiva Lingam *(Sanskrit)* "Phallus of the God Shiva:" (Also see **Lingam**) It is a central object of veneration in a Hindu Temple, even as the focus of "adoration" by female worshippers in a magical invoking of the God Force to achieve pregnancy. Note, however, there is no suggestion here that the child will be other than human. A particular note should be made the Lingam is represented as *rising* out of a *Yonic* base. Thus, the Lingam (male sex organ) does not *penetrate* the Yoni (the Female sex organ) but *emerges* from the Yoni as from a *matrix*. Thus, the Yoni gives birth to the Lingam as the Great Goddess is mother to all life.

Siddhis *(Sanskrit)*: from "sidh" meaning "to succeed, accomplish:" Siddhis are the potential "psychic" powers that are experienced and thus developed along the path of Yoga and other techniques of Psychic Empowerment. They are the undeveloped abilities of ESP which most people are unaware of possessing.

Single Reality: Following the Scientific Revolution, visible phenomena was perceived as *real* and anything invisible was *not real*. With the advents of Spiritualism in the 19th century and scientific investigation of psychic phenomena, and the increasing popularity of Esoteric subjects in the 20th, followed by the discoveries of Quantum Physics in the 21st century, we are now experiencing a restoration of the Physical and the "Super-physical" into a single reality as was the essence of belief systems prior to present era as demarked by our current calendar at 0000 AD. The "Old Religions" of East and West, the practices of the ancient Greeks, Egyptians, Hebrews, Gnostics, Tantrics and Taoists (and others) all saw a single and comprehensive *Living* Cosmos in which "Man" had an integral part. All is One, Everything is connected, and Divinity is within and without and beyond all division.

Solar Plexus Chakra: Also known as **Manipura**—*Sanskrit* (which see)

>   Source: Slate, J. H. and Weschcke, C. L.: *Psychic Empowerment: Tools & Techniques*, 2011, Llewellyn.

Soul: The soul is not your personality, but the eternal part of the human being, attributed to Chesed, Geburah, Tiphareth, Netzach, Hod and Yesod on the Tree of Life. The personality is a transient manifestation of soul during a life time. The soul is the absolute ultimate and immortal essence of who you are, have been, and will be.

Soul's Vehicles:

<u>Causal Body</u> (Higher Mental)—	To evolve with—	Ideals & Abstract Thought.
<u>Mental Body</u> (Lower Mental)—	To think with—	Ideas & Concrete Thoughts
<u>Astral Body</u> (Upper & Lower)—	To feel with—	Emotions & Desires
<u>Physical Body</u> (incl. Etheric Body)—	to act with—	Sensorial Reactions & Actions

Personality, the Lower Self—	Lower Manas, Concrete Mind	Mental Body
Astral, Desire Nature		Astral Body
Physical, Functioning Body		
Physical/Etheric Body		
Body Consciousness—	Autonomic nervous system	

Source: Jinarajadasa: *First Principles of Theosophy*, 1861

Spirit: See also "Ether" and "Akasha." This word has multiple meanings.

    a. The Spiritual Body, or Soul.

    b. The entity surviving physical death—believed to temporarily function on the Astral Plane. The fifth element from which the lower four—Fire, Air, Water, and Earth are derived.

    c. Entities from other dimensions or planets channeling to humans.

    d. A non-physical entity functioning on the Astral or other planes.

    e. The 'collective' of etheric, astral, mental and spirit bodies other than the physical.

    f. God, or an aspect of Deity.

    g. A collective term for non-individual spiritual power and intelligence, probably an aspect of the Collective Unconscious or Universal Consciousness

    h. Non-human inhabitants of the astral plane.

    i. The inner reality of something—as in "the spirit of the times."

    j. The Alchemical element symbolized by an 8-spoked Wheel is the higher level of reality of Eight Dimensions from which other elements and levels flow.

    k. Symbolized by the "Egg," it is the Great Mother Goddess, the source of all physical manifestation.

    l. The "interdimensional" function through which all things and entities seem to appear and disappear with a change in their nature.

    m. Spirit is also the "Space" between things and around things. In a broad sense, it is the old, pre-Einstein Ether of empty space.

    n. The 'Holy Spirit' which may be the Primal Consciousness or Matrix that can be activated by prayer or other affirmative thoughts.

    o. That part of the Human Being attributed to Kether, Chokmah and Binah.

Spirit Body/Vehicle: In the hierarchy of subtle bodies, Spirit is higher than Mental, Astral, Etheric, and Physical. There is lack of specific definition, but it could be that the Spirit Body is first in the process of the descent of the Soul into physical incarnation. In this scheme, the Soul creates the Spirit Body which then serves as a kind of matrix for the Mental Body formed of mental 'substance,' then the Astral Body of astral substance, etc.

Spirit Communication: Contact with "spirits" of the deceased or other entities most often through a person acting as a "Medium" or "Channel" under the direction or "Control" of a Spirit Guide.

Spirit Guide: An entity manifesting on the astral or mental plane exhibiting high intelligence and wisdom with a personal interest in the welfare of the individual experiencing the more or less constant presence of the Guide.

Suggested Reading—Andrews, T.: *How to Meet and Work with Spirit Guides*, 2006, Llewellyn.

Webster, R.: *Spirit Guides & Angel Guardians*, 2002, Llewellyn.

Spirit World: The non-physical world. The subconscious is, in fact, in continuous interaction with the higher realms of power to meet your empowerment needs, including protection in time of danger, comfort in times of grief, and hope in times of despair. Through your connection to the spirit realm, you will experience the full beauty and power of your existence—past, present, and future—as an evolving soul.

States of Matter ↔ States of Consciousness: *Everything is connected.* Universal Mind, including our individual minds, is the energetic connection that enables you, with your mind, to access and work with these fundamental energies and forces behind all material manifestation.

The tattvas are present—unconsciously—in your body and mind just as they are present throughout the Cosmos. In essence, we live in two worlds simultaneously— the outer world and a true inner world of personal consciousness that functions as a "matrix" for *your world of body, mind, and immediate environment*. We live in the outer world matrix and within the inner world matrix—and the two can get "out of synch" with one another at fundamental energy levels. This disharmony can start us on paths to ill-health and even social conflict. But when you consciously *awaken* the "Tattva Connection" through meditation and visualization practices you can restore natural harmony between the inner and outer worlds.

Sub-atomic Field: Also called simply 'the Field' in which primal/universal energy and matter appear as waves and then as particles when observed. It is the foundation for the study of Quantum Physics (also called Quantum Mechanics and Quantum Theory). Packets of energy/matter are called Quanta.

Subconscious Mind: That part of the mind below the threshold of consciousness. Normally, unavailable to the conscious mind, it can be accessed through hypnosis and self-hypnosis, meditation, automatic writing, etc. It is never asleep and always aware. It is *Nephesh* on the Tree of Life. "The subconscious is not only a content domain but a dynamic constellation of processes and powers. It recognizes that the wealth of our subconscious resources is complementary to consciousness rather than counteractive. It's a powerful component of who we are and how we function" (from Slate and Weschcke: *Psychic Self-Empowerment for Everyone*, 2009, Llewellyn).

The Sub-Conscious Mind has no ethics or morals; it is your Conscious Mind that must make choices and impose order on chaos, develop distinct channels to reliable resources, and otherwise understand and learn that your Sub-Conscious Mind is your key to the infinite resources of the Universe. Helping you to build the relationship between the Sub-Conscious Mind and the Conscious Mind is the purpose of *Self-Empowerment & Your Sub-Conscious Mind,* by Weschcke and Slate, 2010, Llewellyn.

Super Conscious Mind: The Super Conscious Mind is the *higher* level of personal consciousness with access to the universal of Collective Unconscious. Your subconscious mind is mostly conditioned by the past, and your conscious mind by the present. You are born with a basic purpose, with some specific learning goals for this life. The Super Conscious Mind is your doorway to and from the future, and the source of your inspiration, ideals, ethical behavior and heroic action, and the very essence that is "the Light of Men" as it was in the beginning and as it is now and as it will always be . . . .

Sushumna (*Sanskrit*): The major central *nadi* corresponding to the spinal cord, the channel through which *Kundalini* (spiritual fire) ascends to unite in *Sahasrara,* the Crown Chakra.

Svadhisthana (AKA *Sacral*): This Chakra is located in the sacrum over the spleen and below the navel, and physically manifests through the pancreas, kidneys, and the hypogastric plexus. Like Muladhara, it relates to the gonads, the production of sex hormones, and the female reproductive cycle. It relates to relationships, basic emotional needs, and sensual pleasure. Physically it rules our reproduction, emotionally our joy, mentally our creativity, and spiritually our enthusiasm. It relates to the sense of taste. The element is Water.

The associated psychic powers are empathy and psychic diagnosis. It is the fluid control point for the entire body system, including blood flow. Vasoconstriction and vaso-dilation of the arterioles are controllable at will. Stigmata, the percolation of blood through the skin, can also be demonstrated. It is symbolized by a crescent moon within a white lotus with six orange spokes, and its Tattva is represented geometrically in a silver crescent. The audible seed mantra is *VuNG* followed by mental echo of *VuM*.

Svadhisthana (Sacral) Chakra Correspondences		
Alchemical Planet: Mars, Pluto	Alchemical Element: Iron	Tattva: Apas (water)
Animal: Crocodile	Basic Drive: Pleasure	Tattva color: White
Body Function: Sexuality, Pleasure	Chakra Color: Orange	Tattva form: Crescent
Element: Water	Gemstone: Coral	Tattvic Sense: Taste
Gland: Pancreas	Goddess-form, Egyptian: Tefnut	God-form, Hindu: Vishnu[1]
God-form, Greek: Pan, Diana	Incense: orris, gardenia, damiana Goddess-form, Hindu: Rakini [2]	Location: Over the spleen
Part of Body: genitals, kidney, bladder, circulatory system	Order of chakra unfoldment: 3rd	Yogic Planet: Sun
Psychological attribute: Flexibility, equanimity	Psychic Power: empathy, psychic diagnosis Sense: Taste	Spinal Joint: 7th
Spinal Location: 1st Lumbar	Bija Mantra: VuNG, VuM (4)	Tarot Key: XIX, Sun
Tarot Suite: Cups	Tree of Life Sephiroth: Yesod	Yantra (internal) Black Crescent
[1] Preserver		
[2] Sexuality		
Source: Slate, J. H.and Weschcke, C. L.: *Psychic Empowerment: Tools & Techniques,* 2011, Llewellyn		
Suggested Reading—Dale: *The Subtle Body: An Encyclopedia of Your Energetic Anatomy*		

Symbol: A true symbol contains *power* because of its shape, form, color, and its name which connects it to an established and constantly updating "system of correspondences" retrieved from the 'information storage' function of the subconscious mind. The tattvic symbols, in turn, are "the primary building blocks from which all magical symbols, sigils, talismans, ciphers and designs are composed." As Dr. Mumford wrote: "The Tattwa 'triggers' the psychic layers of our mind through the compressed power of its geometrical shape, the primal colors vibrating forth, and the implied numerical concepts in each shape."

When we *consciously* evoke the power of a symbol, it triggers the psychic layers of our mind through its compressed power and brings forth the needed knowledge and energies to accomplish the set task. In this case, it is the awakening of the inner tattvic matrix so that the clairvoyant can more accurately "read" the external situation required by the task set forth.

Tantra Tradition: It is not any of the more modern "religions" or yogic or sexual practices sometimes called "neo-Tantra," but a *system* of psychological, psychic, and physical practices including specific sexual techniques based upon and incorporating knowledge of both human subtle anatomies and their cosmological connections.

Tantra is the source for much esoteric knowledge of the complex nature of cosmic reality beyond physical universe, and inclusive of our physical & subtle bodies and the energetic system of chakras, nadis, tattvas, mantras, yantras, breath-regulation, kundalini, and all that is developmentally important to the fulfillment of our Divine purpose.

Unlike many Eastern and Western spiritual systems, Tantra is "world embracing" rather than "world denying," and sees the world as *real* and not an illusion and the whole of reality as the <u>self</u>-expression of a single Creator Consciousness in which there is no division of spiritual versus mundane. Tantric practices are intended to bring about an inner realization that "Nothing exists that is not Divine," and their goal is freedom from ignorance. We live in a holistic universe and need to live holistically with awareness of the spiritual as part of our reality. We are born into the material world to grow and develop the whole person we are intended to be. Tantric principles should be incorporated into every aspect of daily life as a continuing spiritual growth practice.

Tantric sexual practices, perceived as the union of male and female and the re-union of god and goddess, Shiva and Shakti, are a means into an intense and expanded (ecstatic) state of awareness, freed of mind-created material boundaries to reaffirm our identity with the Divine Source found within each person.

Tantra is a complete system of esoteric knowledge and practice that in its ancient purity is a personal resource for every person seeking understanding and development. It is the most radical form of spirituality, and the ideal <u>personal</u> "religion" of the modern world that has had a profound influence on Western Occult Philosophy and practice, and on the development of today's Neo-Paganism. It is this Tantra that is the source of our knowledge of the tattvas.

Tattvas: The Sanskrit word, tattva, is translated approximately as "the true nature of reality." We experience them primarily as the five primal elements that are the fundamental *Energy Forms* behind the manifestation of all Matter composing the entire Physical Universe. Einstein's famous equation: $E=mc^2$, where "E" stands for Energy and "m" stands for Matter, demonstrates that every *substance* is made up of these five fundamental elemental energies.

Tattvas, Pure & Compound: The tattvas are not manifest in the physical world in their full purity, but always in combinations. We refer to these combinations as one containing the "seed" either of itself or another tattva—thus there are 25 combinations of the basic five.

Tattvic Connection, The: A meditation and visualization program that awakens the unconscious tattvic elements within the "Inner World Matrix" and establishes a natural harmonization with those elements in the "Outer World Matrix" to accomplish the *Miracle of the One Thing* wherein "through unity there is power." It is through such unity that the clairvoyant vision becomes free of personal emotional bias and hence clear and accurate.

Tattwa Cards: A set of 25 cards providing geometric yantras of the five primal tattvas and their twenty compounding used in divination described in *Magical Tattwas* by Jonn Mumford. Many subsequent decks based on this original concept have since been published.

Techno-Shamanism: Generally the modern use of aids and devices to induce higher states of consciousness beyond ecstasy by means of sensory overload or sensory deprivation. Many of these are found in the sexual experimenter's tool chest.

Tejas: The primal tattvic element of fire perceived as plasma and represented by a red triangle to convey the basic drive for power, the psychological attribute of passion, the sense of sight and the magical tool, the wand.

Third Eye: A colloquial reference to the *Ajna,* the "brow chakra" believed to be the main etheric source of psychic powers.

Thought Form: 1) An astral image created by concentrated thought intended to accomplish a specified objective. When reinforced with emotion and charged with etheric energy, it will become physically manifest. 2) A spontaneous image created in the imagination that is charged with emotional energy. Either is perceived by a clairvoyant and is felt by ordinary people with some degree of psychic sensitivity. A carefully constructed mental image that is charged with emotional energy can become a manipulative tool used in product marketing, political action, and religious domination.

Suggested Reading—Ashcroft-Nowicki and Brennan: *Magical Use of Thought Forms*, 2001, Llewellyn.

Throat Chakra, also called *Vishuddha*: The chakra located at the throat, color blue, associated planet Mercury, associated Sephirah Daath, associated Tattva *Akasha*, symbol of the element of Spirit.

Trance: A state of consciousness in which awareness is concentrated, focused and turned inward to the subconscious mind either unconsciously through repetitive stimuli or consciously induced in hypnosis, meditation, or religious or shamanic practice. During a trance state, carefully designed programs of suggestion and affirmation can lead to dramatic changes in conscious behavior and perceptions.

Tratak: A particular Tantric meditation and Visualization process to *internalize* a duplicate image of an external object so that it will perceptively *float* in the space in front of your brow chakra (between your eyes where the brow ridge starts) either with the eyes closed or open looking at a blank while wall or piece of white paper.

The "secret" is to stare fixedly at a brightly lit object or image for as long as possible until your eyes actually feel that they are burning. In the case of the properly colored tattva yantras, stare at the *center* of the image and the colors will start to "flash" around the edges and the image will turn three-dimensional almost float off the card. Then, close your eyes and you will see an after image in complementary colors floating before your Third Eye. Initially, you may have better results by staring at a white space instead of closing your eyes, but, if so, use that as a starting point and do learn to see with your closed eyes. The psychic factor is strongly enhanced by this technique which can be used with almost any magical or spiritual symbol or object.

Trumpet: A cone-shaped instrument made of very light-weight aluminum used in connection with the physical phenomena of a séance. See "Direct Voice."

Trust, but verify: Phrase famously used by American President Ronald Reagan during the Cold War with the Soviet Union. The same principle needs to be applied in Clairvoyant and other Psychic Perception—just as with any information resources. There is a particular hazard with Psychic Perception, since it appears to originate with higher "spiritual."

Universal Consciousness: "In the Beginning is the Word." But before the manifestation of the physical cosmos there was the emanation of Consciousness and the Great Plan that first guided the formation of Spirit and then of Space/Time and Energy/Matter leading into the Big Bang of physical creation. With physical creation we have Universal Consciousness (or the Unconscious, or the Great Unconscious) functioning in the background of all there is, and permeating every life, visible and invisible, and everything, visible and invisible.

Universal Mind: *Everything is connected.* Universal Mind, including our individual minds, is the energetic connection that enables you, with your mind, to access and work with these fundamental energies and forces behind all material manifestation.

Vayu: The primal tattvic element of Air perceived as gaseous and represented by a blue hexagram (or, sometimes, a circle) to convey the basic drive for love, the psychological attribute of compassion, the sense of touch, and the magical tool, the sword.

Vehicle: A newer esoteric term for the word "body" in reference to the vehicle of consciousness. Thus: the Astral *Vehicle,* the Mental *Vehicle,* the Spiritual *Vehicle,* etc.

Vibrations: The *motion* of physical atoms within all matter. It further recognizes that in our sharing of consciousness with all things, we can be aware of that motion. More importantly, however, the nature of matter and of consciousness changes as the *rate* of vibration changes. As we consciously raise our own vibrations we perceive the matter at different levels, or "planes."

Vishuddha (Sanskrit) *"With purity"*: The fifth chakra, primarily known as the **Throat Chakra.** This chakra is located in the cervical (neck) area, and physically manifests through the thyroid and parathyroid glands, the pharyngeal plexus and the vocal cords. The thyroid hormones are responsible for growth and maturation. Physically it rules our communications, emotionally our independence, mentally our fluent thought, and spiritually our sense of security. It relates to the sense of hearing.

The associated psychic powers are channeling, clairaudience, and telepathy. It plays a role in Dream Yoga and Lucid Dreaming. It is symbolized by a silver crescent within a lotus with sixteen blue spokes, and its tattva is represented geometrically by a black upright oval. The audible seed mantra is *HuNG* followed by mental echo of *HuM.*

Vishuddha is considered a main alchemical transmutation point in Kriya Yoga. It is said to secret a fluid of immortality ("Amrit," meaning "against death") which is burned by the Solar Plexus (*Manipura)* chakra. When this process is reversed, decay is slowed.

Vishuddha (Throat) Chakra Correspondences		
Alchemical Planet: Venus, Jupiter	Alchemical Element: Copper	Tattva: Akasha (Ether, Spirit)
Animal: Bull, Lion, Elephant	Basic Drive: Creativity	Tattva Color: Blue-Violet
Body Function: Speech	Chakra Color: Bright Blue	Tattva form: Oval
Element: Spirit (aethyr)	Gemstone: Turquoise	Tattva Sense: Hearing

Gland: Thyroid, Parathyroids	God-form, Egyptian: Seshat	God-form, Hindu: Pancha-Vaktra[1]	
God-form, Greek: Hermes	Incense: Frankincense	Goddess-form, Hindu: Shakini [2]	
Location: Throat	Order of chakra unfoldment: 5th	Yogic Planet: Venus	
Part of Body: neck, shoulders, arms, hands[1]	Psychological Attributes: Communication, Empathy[2]		
Psychic Power: channeling, clairaudience, telepathy	Bija Mantra: HuNG HuM		
Spinal Joint: 31st	Spinal Location: 3rd Cervical	Sense: Hearing	
Tarot Key: III, Empress	Tree of Life Sephirah: Chesed & Geburah		
Goddess-form, Celtic: Brigit	Yantra (internal) white oval		
[1] 5-faced Shiva			
[2] Knowledge			
Source: Slate, J. and Weschcke, C.: *Psychic Empowerment: Tools & Techniques,* 2011, Llewellyn			
Suggested Reading—Dale: *The Subtle Body: An Encyclopedia of Your Energetic Anatomy*			

Visualization: The process of turning an imagined image or picture into an energy-charged astral "matrix" used in magickal operations, meditation, hypnosis, and prayer to in some degree modify current material reality.

Water: (Elemental) also see *Apas*: Water is one of the five primal elements.

Western Magick: Largely founded on the Kabbalah and today includes Tarot and Ritual Magick. At the same time, there are different traditions as to the understanding of various correspondences and symbols. At the practical levels, one system is not necessarily enriched by another. Learn the basic correspondences and symbols of the system you practice.

Suggested Reading—Hulse, D.: *The Western Mysteries*—Catalogs and distills—in hundreds of tables of secret symbolism—the true alphabet of magic of every Western magical tradition.

Regardie and Cicero:s *The Tree of Life: An Illustrated Study in Magic*—Combining Ancient Wisdom with modern magical practice, developing the principles of magic that cut across boundaries of time, religion and culture.

Skinner: *The Complete Magician's Tables*—The most complete collection of magician's tables available, documenting thousands of magical links, pagan pantheons,

Kabbalah, Astrology, Tarot, I Ching, Angels, Demons, Herbs, Perfumes, and more, and how it's all connected together.

Skinner and Rankine: *The Veritable Key of Solomon*—Never before published material and based on one of the best-known Grimoires of the Western world, this is a complete and workable system of high magic. Over 160 illustrations.

Tyson: *Ritual Magic: What It Is & How to Do It*—What magic can do for you, and what it can't, the differences among various magical paths, and instructions for two rituals.

Whitcomb: *The Magician's Companion: A Practical and Encyclopedic Guide to Magical and Religious Symbolism*—The theory and practice of magic and ritual with over 35 magical models, and tables and data on Runes, the Tree of Life, Yoga, Enochian Magic, the I Ching, Symbology, Magical Alphabets, the Chakras, Planetary Spirits, Hindu Tattwas, the Wheel of the Year, Eight Psychic Channels, Geomancy, the Tarot, Astral Travel, the Body of Light, Magical Squares and Sigils, Descriptions of Major Deities, and much more.

White Light: Both experienced and visualized, the White Light is believed to be a function of a higher spiritual power. When visualized as surrounding a person, it is a means of protection from harm, particularly as originating from non-physical worlds.

Whole Brain: While recognizing the reality of the Right Brain/Left Brain Split, we are whole-brained people and can benefit by overcoming or lessening that split by deliberately practicing functions commonly indented as opposite to our primary identity.

Whole Person: In addition to the physical/etheric composite, the entire spirit manifested "whole-person" is made up of the astral, mental, and causal vehicles. The chakras repeat in some manner through all levels, including the physical where they relate to the nerve complexes mainly located from the bottom to the top of the spinal column, culminating with the brain. Each etheric chakra is a *channel* between the physical nerve plexi and the astral chakras.

Worship: Generally associated with religious practice but better understood as two forms of meditation or magick:

1. The *external* in which a person prays to a deity or other spiritual identity most often represented with an physical image and a name. It often includes rote, mantra-like repetitions of passages from scripture. It can take the form of extreme "groveling" before a statute, emotional pleading for particular benefits and promises of behavioral changes, or less extreme postures of kneeling in

prayer. It is comparable to a magical *evocation* in which the called upon entity is kept outside the circle, hence outside the psyche.

2. The *internal* in which a person seeks to actually identify with the spiritual entity or force or principle by bringing its image *within* the psyche, even perceived as bringing within the physical body. Magically, it is comparable to *invocation.*

In either operation, the practice can be relatively simple or become extremely complex. And there are variations that appear to mix the two forms—as in the "assumption of a god-form" in which the person places himself within the image rather than bringing the image within himself. And with either form the practice can be intensified with shamanic techniques of ecstatic energy charging of the image or of the practitioner.

Yantra: A Sanskrit word meaning "instrument" or "machine" as represented and embodied in a graphic symbol or geometric figure that can, when used as a focal point in meditation, visualization or as a charged magical talisman, itself initiate a process of invoking elemental forces. As derived from the Tantric tradition, such figures are used to balance the mind or focus it on magical, psychic, or spiritual actions. The act of wearing, drawing, tracing, or concentrating on a yantra evokes spiritual or <u>talismanic</u> or <u>magical</u> benefits.

Dr. Jonn Mumford describes the function of the tattva yantras as "information storage and retrieval devices of amazing potency. They are the primary building blocks from which all magical symbols, sigils, talismans, ciphers and designs are composed." "The tattwa 'triggers' the psychic layers of our mind through the compressed power of its geometrical shape, the primal colors vibrating forth, and the implied numerical concepts in each shape."

Though mostly rendered in two dimensional art forms, yantra are then visualized in multi-dimensional images and may be presented in three dimensional objects. In meditation and trance, the visualized image generates the yantra in the <u>subtle bodies</u>. Because a yantra is composed of archetypal forms common to all existing phenomena, the process of drawing or otherwise representing the form actually reaches down into the genetic structure to make it an energetic reality. The drawing act activates the right brain.

In its most extreme form, a yantra becomes the "body" of a particular deity.

Yoni: *(Sanskrit)* "Lap, vulva."

You are more than you think you are: Every person has immense undeveloped potential. The familiar phrase that we use only 10 percent of the brain's capacity is itself a minimal recognition of the reality of not only our cranial potential but of the non-physical aspects of personal consciousness and its connections with universal consciousness. Your goal must be to ***become more than you are!*** That's the purpose and function of this book.

Sources and Suggested Reading:

Dale, C. *The Subtle Body: An Encyclopedia of Your Energetic Anatomy,* 2009, Sounds True.

Judith, A. *Wheels of Life: A User's Guide to the Chakra System*, 1987, Llewellyn.

Khanna, M. *Yantra: The Tantric Symbol of Cosmic Unity*, 1979, Thames & Hudson.

Owens, E. *How to Communicate with Spirits*, 2001, Llewellyn.

Owens, E. *Spiritualism & Clairvoyance for Beginners: Simple Techniques to Develop Your Psychic Abilities*, 2005, Llewellyn.

Saraswati, Swami S. *Kundalini Tantra,* 1985, Bihar School of Yoga.

Saraswati, P. S. *Tantra of Kundalini Yoga,* 1973, Bihar School of Yoga.

Tigunait, P. R. *Tantra Unveiled: Seducing the Forces of Matter & Spirit,* 1999 & 2007, Himalayan Institute.

For further studies in Tantra Yoga:

Consultations: Distance Learning Programs http://www.jonnmumfordconsult.com/

Index

A

Adepts, lviii, 16, 701, 720

Affirmation, 91, 110, 136, 194, 220, 239, 245, 246, 278, 291, 389–391, 399, 506, 542, 611, 612, 769

Afterlife, 38, 233, 620, 701

Air/Air—Activation: Tattvic Connection—Program, 218

Air/Air: Tattvic Connection—Program, 512

Air/Earth: Tattvic Connection—Program, 517

Air/Ether: Tattvic Connection—Program, 532

Air/Fire: Tattvic Connection—Program, 527

Air/Water: Tattvic Connection—Program, 522

Air, the element, 172

Ajna, 106, 156, 169, 172–179, 262, 270, 342, 557, 657, 659, 701, 702, 709, 710, 768

Akasha, 85, 100, 128, 161, 187, 213, 270–272, 275, 276, 280, 281, 342, 417, 419, 455, 457, 496, 498, 531, 533, 561, 563, 565, 567, 570, 572, 575, 577, 580, 582, 640, 703, 706, 725, 763, 769, 771

Akashic Records, 7, 85, 257, 271, 274, 426, 429, 599, 637, 640, 692, 703, 713, 716, 741

Alchemical Rose, 180

"All is Consciousness," 646, 661

All Knowledge begins with theory and is fulfilled through practice," 65

"Alone and Together, we climb the Great Pyramid of Consciousness to become more than we are," 631

Alpha, 703, 709, 739

Altered Personality, 214

Altered States of Consciousness, 26, 214, 297, 308, 309, 703

Anahata, 101, 153, 154, 159, 161, 162, 165, 167–169, 172, 173, 180, 214, 222, 270, 342, 415, 453, 493, 514, 518, 523, 528, 533, 547, 554, 555, 582, 640, 659, 703, 710, 732, 737

"An Eastern Gift to Western Esotericism," 43

Anandakapila Sarawati, Swami, 108

Angels, 10, 149, 230, 253, 257, 271, 296, 429, 629, 633, 703, 716, 732, 772

Animal Clairvoyance, 36, 125, 594–596

Animal Communication, 27, 704

Apas, 100, 127, 128, 131, 134, 138, 139, 187, 213, 270, 342, 352, 356, 396, 438, 440, 442, 444, 446, 448, 451, 453, 455, 457, 486, 488, 521, 523, 570, 572, 640, 704, 757, 766, 771

Aquarian Age (Aquarius, the Age of), liv, 25, 80, 85, 101

Aquarius, the Zodiacal Sign, lviii, 5, 212, 216

As Above, So Below, 46, 186, 705

To Write to the Authors

If you wish to contact the author or would like more information about this book, please write to the author in care of Llewellyn Worldwide Ltd. and we will forward your request. Both the author and the publisher appreciate hearing from you and learning of your enjoyment of this book and how it has helped you. Llewellyn Worldwide Ltd. cannot guarantee that every letter written to the author can be answered, but all will be forwarded. Please write to:

Carl Llewellyn Weschcke & Joe H. Slate, Ph.D.
c/o Llewellyn Worldwide
2143 Wooddale Drive
Woodbury, MN 55125-2989
Please enclose a self-addressed stamped envelope for reply,
or $1.00 to cover costs. If outside the U.S.A., enclose
an international postal reply coupon.

Many of Llewellyn's authors have websites with additional information and resources. For more information, please visit our website at:

http://www.llewellyn.com

A PERSONAL EMPOWERMENT AUDIO PROGRAM

VIBRATORY ASTRAL PROJECTION
& CLAIRVOYANCE

YOUR NEXT STEPS IN
EVOLUTIONARY CONSCIOUSENESS
& PSYCHIC EMPOWERMENT

An audio CD companion to the book,
CLAIRVOYANCE FOR PSYCHIC EMPOWERMENT

CARL LLEWELLYN WESCHCKE
JOE H. SLATE, PHD

Audio script & program by Dr. Joe H. Slate,
instruction & explanatory booklet by Carl Llewellyn Weschcke

Vibratory Astral Projection & Clairvoyance CD Companion
Your Next Steps in Evolutionary Consciousness & Psychic Empowerment
Carl Llewellyn Weschcke & Joe H. Slate, PhD

The out-of-body experience (OBE) and extrasensory perception (ESP) are not merely interesting and beneficial phenomena. They are crucial steps in our evolution toward personal empowerment, growth, and higher consciousness. This specially developed audio CD and companion to *Clairvoyance for Psychic Empowerment* will guide you safely though a process known as vibratory astral projection. Music designed to facilitate deep relaxation, along with vocal guidance from Dr. Joe H. Slate, will help you embark on a life-changing journey to the astral realm—and higher dimensions of mind and spirit.

978-0-7387-3913-7, 22 pp., 5¼ x 7½ $17.99

To order, call 1-877-NEW-WRLD
Prices subject to change without notice
Order at Llewellyn.com 24 hours a day, 7 days a week!

THE
LLEWELLYN
COMPLETE BOOK
OF
PSYCHIC
EMPOWERMENT

A Compendium of
Tools & Techniques for
Growth & Transformation

CARL LLEWELLYN WESCHCKE
JOE H. SLATE, PH.D.

The Llewellyn Complete Book of Psychic Empowerment
A Compendium of Tools & Techniques for Growth & Transformation
Carl Llewellyn Weschcke & Joe H. Slate, PhD

Embark on the journey of a lifetime—master the psychic tools and techniques required to develop your highest potential and enjoy success beyond your wildest dreams.

Written by Carl Llewellyn Weschcke and Joe H. Slate, PhD, this is the most comprehensive guide to psychic development available anywhere. It's a do-it-yourself journey that organizes the concepts of psychic empowerment into a cohesive plan that progresses from positive self-affirmations to powerful step-by-step psychic development techniques. Whether a simple affirmation or an empowering exercise, each technique strengthens the divine spark of greatness existing in everyone—and leads to better health, happier relationships, greater financial success, and enhanced spiritual growth.

This is the ultimate reference for people already on their own path of psychic empowerment and for those wanting to instruct and train others. Filled with charts, graphs, knowledge, and explicit instructions, this book is vital for you as you develop. Whether you're involved in an Eastern or Western path, this is the book you must have and use!

978-0-7387-2709-7, 744 pp., 7 x 10   **$29.95**